Lecture Notes in Computer Science   11903

Founding Editors

Gerhard Goos
Karlsruhe Institute of Technology, Karlsruhe, Germany
Juris Hartmanis
Cornell University, Ithaca, NY, USA

Editorial Board Members

Elisa Bertino
Purdue University, West Lafayette, IN, USA
Wen Gao
Peking University, Beijing, China
Bernhard Steffen
TU Dortmund University, Dortmund, Germany
Gerhard Woeginger
RWTH Aachen, Aachen, Germany
Moti Yung
Columbia University, New York, NY, USA

More information about this series at http://www.springer.com/series/7412

Yao Zhao · Nick Barnes ·
Baoquan Chen · Rüdiger Westermann ·
Xiangwei Kong · Chunyu Lin (Eds.)

Image
and Graphics

10th International Conference, ICIG 2019
Beijing, China, August 23–25, 2019
Proceedings, Part III

 Springer

Editors
Yao Zhao
Beijing Jiaotong University
Beijing, China

Nick Barnes
The Australian National University
Canberra, Australia

Baoquan Chen
Peking University
Beijing, China

Rüdiger Westermann
The Technical University of Munich
Munich, Bayern, Germany

Xiangwei Kong ⓘ
Zhejiang University
Hangzhou, China

Chunyu Lin ⓘ
Beijing Jiaotong University
Beijing, China

ISSN 0302-9743   ISSN 1611-3349 (electronic)
Lecture Notes in Computer Science
ISBN 978-3-030-34112-1   ISBN 978-3-030-34113-8 (eBook)
https://doi.org/10.1007/978-3-030-34113-8

LNCS Sublibrary: SL6 – Image Processing, Computer Vision, Pattern Recognition, and Graphics

This Springer imprint is published by the registered company Springer Nature Switzerland AG
The registered company address is: Gewerbestrasse 11, 6330 Cham, Switzerland

Preface

We would like to present the proceedings of the 10th International Conference on Image and Graphics (ICIG 2019), held in Beijing, China, during August 23–25, 2019.

The China Society of Image and Graphics (CSIG) has hosted this series of ICIG conferences since 2000. ICIG is a biennial conference organized by the CSIG, focusing on innovative technologies of image, video, and graphics in processing and fostering innovation, entrepreneurship, and networking. This time, the conference was organized by Tsinghua University, Peking University, and Institute of Automation, CAS. Details about the past nine conferences, as well as the current one, are as follows:

Conference	Place	Date	Submitted	Proceeding
First (ICIG 2000)	Tianjin, China	August 16–18	220	156
Second (ICIG 2002)	Hefei, China	August 15–18	280	166
Third (ICIG 2004)	Hong Kong, China	December 17–19	460	140
4th (ICIG 2007)	Chengdu, China	August 22–24	525	184
5th (ICIG 2009)	Xi'an, China	September 20–23	362	179
6th (ICIG 2011)	Hefei, China	August 12–15	329	183
7th (ICIG 2013)	Qingdao, China	July 26–28	346	181
8th (ICIG 2015)	Tianjin, China	August 13–16	345	170
9th (ICIG 2017)	Shanghai, China	September 13–15	370	172
10th (ICIG 2019)	Beijing, China	August 23–25	384	183

This time, the proceedings are published by Springer in the LNCS series. At ICIG 2019, 384 submissions were received, and 183 papers were accepted. To ease in the search of a required paper in these proceedings, the 161 regular papers have been arranged into different sections. Another 22 papers forming a special topic are included at the end.

Our sincere thanks to all the contributors, who came from around the world to present their advanced work at this event. Special thanks go to the members of the Technical Program Committee, who carefully reviewed every single submission and made their valuable comments for improving the accepted papers. The proceedings could not have been produced without the invaluable efforts of the publication chairs, the web chairs, and a number of active members of CSIG.

September 2019

Yao Zhao
Nick Barnes
Baoquan Chen
Rüdiger Westermann
Xiangwei Kong
Chunyu Lin

Organization

Organizing Committee

General Chairs

Tieniu Tan	Institute of Automation, CAS, China
Oliver Deussen	University of Konstanz, Germany
Rama Chellappa	University of Maryland, USA

Technical Program Chairs

Yao Zhao	Beijing Jiaotong University, China
Nick Barnes	ANU, Australia
Baoquan Chen	Peking University, China
Ruediger Westermann	TUM, Germany

Organizing Committee Chairs

Huimin Ma	Tsinghua University, China
Yuxin Peng	Peking University, China
Zhaoxiang Zhang	Institute of Automation, CAS, China
Ruigang Yang	Baidu, China

Sponsorship Chairs

Yue Liu	Beijing Institute of Technology, China
Qi Tian	University of Texas at San Antonio, USA

Finance Chairs

Zhenwei Shi	Beihang University, China
Jing Dong	Institute of Automation, CAS, China

Special Session Chairs

Jian Cheng	Institute of Automation, CAS, China
Gene Cheung	York University, Canada

Award Chairs

Yirong Wu	Institute of Electrics, CAS, China
Zixiang Xiong	Texas A&M University, USA
Yuxin Peng	Peking University, China

Publicity Chairs

Moncef Gabbouj   TUT, Finland
Mingming Cheng   Nankai University, China

Exhibits Chairs

Rui Li   Google, China
Jiang Liu   Meituan, China

Publication Chairs

Xiangwei Kong   Zhejiang University, China
Chunyu Lin   Beijing Jiaotong University, China

Oversea Liaison

Yo-Sung Ho   GIST, South Korea
Alan Hanjalic   Delft University of Technology, The Netherlands

Local Chairs

Xucheng Yin   USTB, China
Kun Xu   Tsinghua University, China

Tutorial Chairs

Weishi Zheng   Sun Yat-sen University, China
Chen Change Loy   NTU, Singapore

Workshop Chairs

Jiashi Feng   National University of Singapore, Singapore
Si Liu   Beihang University, China

Symposium Chair

Jinfeng Yang   Civil Aviation University of China, China

Website Chair

Bo Yan   Fudan University, China

Contents – Part III

Security

Surveillance and Remote Sensing

Virtual Reality

Feature Learning for Cross-Domain Problems

Advanced Signal Processing Methods in Spectral Imaging

Compression, Transmission, Retrieval

Measurement-Domain Spiral Predictive Coding for Block-Based Image Compressive Sensing

Wei Tian and Hao Liu[(✉)]

College of Information Science and Technology, Donghua University,
Shanghai 201620, China
liuhao@dhu.edu.cn

Abstract. To improve the rate-distortion performance of block-based image compressive sensing and reduce the influence of image edges, this paper proposes a measurement-domain spiral predictive coding method, which can make full use of the intrinsic spatial relationship of natural images. For the measurements of each compressive-sensing block, the optimal measurement prediction is selected from a set of measurement prediction candidates that are generated by eight possible directional prediction modes. Then, the resulting residual is processed by scalar quantization. The block prediction starts from the center of an image and spreads around in spiral scanning, where each block can select the optimal measurement prediction from the measurement prediction candidates as many as possible. The experimental results show that the proposed method can achieve the best rate-distortion performance as compared with the existing methods, while the complexity is basically similar.

Keywords: Spiral predictive coding · Measurement prediction · Scalar quantization · Rate-distortion

1 Introduction

In recent years, there has been significant interest in the paradigm of compressive sensing (CS) [1, 2], which is an emerging technique for sparse or compressible signals. A small amount of measurement data can be obtained by using linear random projecting, and then the signal can be reconstructed with high probability by the non-linear optimization. To achieve the perfect reconstruction, some block-based compressive sensing (BCS) methods have been proposed [3–7], which usually utilize the BCS smoothed projected Landweber (BCS-SPL) algorithm to reconstruct an original image [8].

Many literatures assume that the measurement process is effectuated within the sensing device, wherein lower-dimensional measurements are obtained with respect to high-dimensional data. Accordingly, the measurement process can be regarded as conducting data acquisition and data compression simultaneously. However, the measurement process does not bring a real compression in the strict information theoretic sense, because it cannot produce a bitstream from the sensing device directly, which only can be seen as a technology of dimensionality reduction in essence [9].

Y. Zhao et al. (Eds.): ICIG 2019, LNCS 11903, pp. 3–12, 2019.
https://doi.org/10.1007/978-3-030-34113-8_1

The real compressive sensing is the process that produces an ultimate compressed bitstream from the input data, which needs to be cooperated with quantization and entropy coding modules. Without effective quantization process, the image compressive sensing is found inefficient in rate-distortion performance [10]. As a result, much attention has been devoted to the improvement of rate-distortion performance of quantized compressive sensing [11–13], which appears very complicated and is not applicable to the BCS framework. Therefore, one straightforward solution is to simply apply the scalar quantization (SQ) to the measurements acquired by the sensing device.

Inspired by the success of the block-based hybrid video coding, the intra prediction coding technology can be also used in the BCS measurement process. Mun and Fowler [14] proposed the block-based quantized compressive sensing of natural images with differential pulse-code modulation (DPCM), coupled with uniform scalar quantization, where the previous reconstructed measurement is taken as the candidate of the current measurement and subtracted from the current measurement. Instead of applying quantization directly to each block of BCS measurements, the resulting residual is then scalar-quantized. The simple DPCM-plus-SQ method provides surprisingly competitive rate-distortion performance. However, it is not efficient enough to leverage previous measurement as the prediction of the current measurement, because the non-stationarity of natural images is ignored. Zhang et al. [15] extended the DPCM-based BCS measurement coding and proposed the spatially directional predictive coding (SDPC), where the intrinsic spatial correlation between neighboring measurements of natural images are further explored. For each compressive sensing block, the optimal measurement prediction is selected from a set of multiple measurement prediction candidates, which are generated by four directional prediction modes. Unlike SDPC, Li et al. [16] introduced a median filter predictive quantization (MFPQ) method and took the median of several reconstructed adjacent blocks around the current measurement as the optimal measurement prediction of the current measurement. Although the R-D performance is slightly lower than that of SDPC, the computational complexity of MFPQ is also lower than that of SDPC, and better error resilience is achieved. Compared with DPCM, the SDPC method obtains accurate measurement prediction with better rate-distortion performance, but it also increases computational complexity. Another problem is that Refs. [15, 16] are affected by image edge. For the measurements of image edge, only the measurements from their vertical direction, that is, the previous measurement is effectively utilized. What's more, the existing methods only consider the measurement-domain prediction of maximum four directional modes, not all possible directional modes. In theory, there are eight directional modes in the current measurement. Zhou et al. [17] further proposed an angular measurement intra prediction with compressive sensing, and designed more structural rows in random measurement matrix for embedding more accurate adjacent boundary information, but it requires far large computation due to its pixel-based operation.

To overcome the shortcomings of the aforementioned methods, this paper proposes a measurement-domain spiral predictive coding (SPC) method. The proposed SPC-plus-SQ method starts from the central block of an image and continues to predict the next block in spiral scanning order. For each current measurement, the optimal measurement prediction is selected from a set of multiple measurement prediction candidates generated by at most eight direction prediction modes, which is more accurate than the aforementioned methods. The proposed SPC-plus-SQ method is not affected by image edge simultaneously. This process is shown in Fig. 1, and the experimental results will verify that the proposed method can achieve the best rate-distortion performance as compared with the SQ alone, DPCM-plus-SQ, SDPC-plus-SQ and MFPQ-plus-SQ methods. In addition, its computational complexity is also almost similar with the SDPC-plus-SQ method.

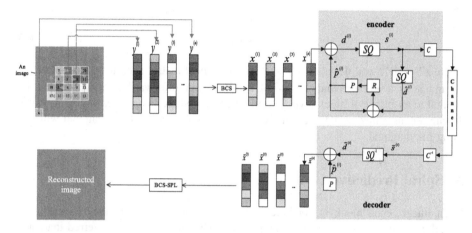

Fig. 1. Architecture of SPC-plus-SQ for block-based compressive sensing (BCS). SQ is uniform scalar quantizer; SQ^{-1} is inverse uniform scalar quantizer; P is the proposed spiral directional predictive coding module; C is an entropy encoder; BCS-SPL is an image reconstruction module.

This paper is organized as follows. Section 2 briefly reviews the BCS framework. The details of proposed method are given in Sect. 3. Experimental results are shown in Sect. 4, and conclusions are drawn in Sect. 5.

2 The BCS Framework

For real signal $y \in \Re^N$, if it is k-sparse in orthogonal transformation domain Ψ, then

$$y = \Psi\theta \tag{1}$$

where θ is a sparse coefficient vector, and real signal y is sparse under the domain Ψ. The measurement matrix $\Phi = \left[\varphi_1^T, \varphi_2^T, \ldots \varphi_i^T, \ldots, \varphi_M^T\right]$ is used to measure the signal y and the measurement vector $x \in \Re^M$ is obtained, where $\varphi_i^T \in \Re^N$ is the row vector, $k < M \ll N$. Then, the measurement equation can be expressed as

$$x = \Phi y \tag{2}$$

where the signal x can be reconstructed accurately by the non-linear optimization calculation.

In order to avoid the large storage cost of measurement matrix and the rapid increase of sampling/recovery complexity as the size of sensing signal increases in compressive imaging, a BCS framework of 2D image was proposed, wherein the sampling of an image is driven by random matrices applied on a block-by-block basis. That is, an image y is firstly divided into n non-overlapped blocks of size $B \times B$ with each block denoted by $y^{(i)} \in \Re^{B^2}, i = 1, 2, \ldots, n$ in vector representation along the vertical or horizontal scan order. Then, its corresponding measurement $x^{(i)}$ is obtained by

$$x^{(i)} = \Phi_B \, y^{(i)} \tag{3}$$

where $x^{(i)} \in \Re^{M_B}$ and Φ_B is an $M_B \times B^2$ measurement matrix such that the subrate for the image as a whole remains $S = M_B/B^2$. It is straightforward to conclude that Φ_B applied to an image at block level is equivalent to a whole image measurement matrix Φ with a constrained structure, namely, Φ can be written as a block diagonal with Φ_B along the diagonal.

3 Spiral Predictive Coding

In an image, each block is not independent with each other, and they have certain spatial correlation with the surrounding blocks. Therefore, it can be inferred that each BCS measurement has some spatial correlation with the measurements around it. Further, Because of the non-stationarity of natural image, correlation coefficients of a measurement are different with its adjacent measurements in different directions. The optimal measurement prediction should be selected from the adjacent reconstructed measurements set for the current measurement. Actually, if the current measurement has more measurement prediction candidates to be chosen, the optimal measurement prediction is closer to the current measurement. This is basic idea of spiral prediction coding for BCS. The details are as given below.

As shown in Fig. 1, an input natural image y is first divided into n non-overlapping blocks, and the block size is $B \times B$, and each block is denoted by $y^{(i)} \in \Re^{B^2}, i = 1, 2, \ldots, n$ in vector. The proposed method is that the first block begins in the center of the image, which is denoted by $y^{(n/2)}$ and is sampled by the BCS measurement matrix in spiral scanning order. Then, all BCS measurements are acquired by Eq. (3). Next, for measurements which have just been acquired by BCS measurement matrix, each measurement is denoted by $x^{(i)} \in \Re^{M_B}, i = 1, 2, \ldots, n$ in vector. The proposed method fully considers all eight directional prediction modes from its neighboring BCS measurement which have already been reconstructed, namely, up, up-right, up-left, right, left, down, down-right, and down-right. More specially, let $\tilde{x}_A^{(i)}$, $\tilde{x}_B^{(i)}$, $\tilde{x}_C^{(i)} \tilde{x}_D^{(i)}$, $\tilde{x}_E^{(i)}$, $\tilde{x}_F^{(i)}$, $\tilde{x}_G^{(i)}$, and $\tilde{x}_H^{(i)}$ denote the up, up-right, up-left, right, left, down, down-right, and down-right of measurements with regard to $x^{(i)}$ respectively, as illustrated in Fig. 2.

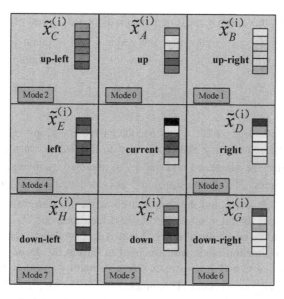

Fig. 2. The proposed eight directional predictive modes and eight corresponding predicted measurement blocks with respect to current measurement block $x^{(i)}$ from its neighboring measurement blocks.

It is worth noting that the deficiency of the SDPC-plus-SQ method is that there are fewer spatial direction measurement predictions for the blocks of image edge, usually only the previous measurement prediction. The proposed method starts from the center block and proceeds in the spiral scanning order. Even in the edge blocks of the image, there are more spatial direction measurement predictions to be chosen. Furthermore, the proposed method takes into all-direction measurement predictions around current measurement as the measurement prediction candidates set. Therefore, the proposed method may perform better than the existing methods.

Here defines a set of measurement prediction candidates as follow:

$$R = \left\{ \tilde{x}_A^{(i)}, \tilde{x}_B^{(i)}, \tilde{x}_C^{(i)} \tilde{x}_D^{(i)}, \tilde{x}_E^{(i)}, \tilde{x}_F^{(i)}, \tilde{x}_G^{(i)}, \tilde{x}_H^{(i)} \right\} \tag{4}$$

where R is a collection of above eight directional prediction modes. The measurement prediction candidates in the sets are reconstructed measurements of previously non-overlapped blocks. For the current measurement, the optimal measurement prediction denoted by $\hat{x}_P^{(i)}$, is determined by minimizing the residual between the current measurement $x^{(i)}$ and the measurement prediction candidates in the sets.

$$\hat{x}_P^{(i)} = \arg\min_{x \in R} \left\| x - x^{(i)} \right\|_{\ell_1} \tag{5}$$

Here, $\|*\|_{\ell_1}$ is ℓ_1 norm which adds all the absolute values of the entries in a vector.

After obtaining the optimal measurement prediction $\hat{x}_P^{(i)}$, the residual can be calculated by $d^{(i)} = x^{(i)} - \hat{x}_P^{(i)}$. Following, the residual $d^{(i)}$ is quantized by a uniform scalar quantization with quantization step q to obtain the quantization index $s^{(i)}$.

$$s^{(i)} = \mathcal{Q}\left[d^{(i)}\right] \tag{6}$$

Then, the quantization index $s^{(i)}$ is encoded by the entropy encoder to further reduce its statistical redundancy and transmitted to the decoder at the receiver. Continue to the encoder, the quantized residual $d^{(i)}$ is obtained by inverse quantization of the quantization index $s^{(i)}$, then residual $d^{(i)}$ is added to the optimal measurement prediction $\hat{x}_P^{(i)}$ just obtained, and the sum is used as the measurement prediction candidate of the adjacent direction mode for the next measurement.

The bitstream to be transmitted in Fig. 1 consists of two parts: the standard bits of the best prediction direction mode which is used to inform the decoder of the selected measurements prediction and the bitstream data obtained by encoding the quantization index $s^{(i)}$ with the entropy encoder. This process is applied for all BCS measurements to achieve the final bitstream.

At the decoder side, contrary to the above encoding process, by the de-quantization on the quantization index from the bitstream, the quantized residuals $\tilde{d}^{(i)}$ can be obtained, which is then added by the prediction $\hat{x}_P^{(i)}$, producing the CS measurements $\tilde{x}^{(i)} = \hat{x}_P^{(i)} + \tilde{d}^{(i)}$. At last, all groups of reconstructed measurements $\tilde{x}$ are obtained sequentially, which are then utilized for the natural image reconstruction by using the BCS-SPL reconstruction algorithm.

In order to demonstrate the superiority of the proposed method, a correlation coefficient ρ is used for quantitative comparison with DPCM, SDPC, and MFPQ.

$$\rho\left(X^{(i)}, X^{(j)}\right) = \frac{X^{(i)^T} X^{(j)}}{\|X^{(i)}\| \|X^{(j)}\|} \tag{7}$$

The correlation coefficients can measure and compare the measurement vectors of current measurements and their optimal measurement predictions. For each current measurement, the MFPQ method computes the median value of components in measurement vectors of neighboring measurements as the optimal measurement prediction, the DPCM method uses directly previous measurement as the optimal measurement prediction, and the SDPC method selects the optimal measurement prediction from four directional modes by using the least square error criterion. The proposed method is similar to the SDPC method, selecting the optimal measurement prediction from eight directional modes, but the proposed method is not affected by image edges because of the spiral scanning order. In theory, the proposed method can get the most accurate measurement prediction in these methods due to more measurement prediction candidates to be chosen. It can be verified by Table 1 which presents the average correlation coefficients of DPCM, SDPC, MFPQ and SPC. The correlation coefficients are calculated by Eq. (7) over all 16×16 blocks for three 512×512 test images with different sampling rates. There is no doubt that the maximum average correlation coefficients are obtained by the proposed method in all methods.

Table 1. Average correlation coefficients for various methods in measurement domain

Image	Lenna	Peppers	Cameraman	Avg.
subrate	0.10			
DPCM	0.961	0.9396	0.9102	0.9369
SDPC	0.971	0.9616	0.9138	0.9488
MFPQ	0.9653	0.9495	0.9133	0.9427
SPC	0.9755	0.9641	0.9299	0.9565
subrate	0.25			
DPCM	0.9576	0.9338	0.8962	0.9292
SDPC	0.9674	0.9558	0.9027	0.9420
MFPQ	0.9608	0.9425	0.9031	0.9355
SPC	0.9727	0.9605	0.9240	0.9524
subrate	0.35			
DPCM	0.963	0.9401	0.9001	0.9344
SDPC	0.9713	0.9608	0.9027	0.9449
MFPQ	0.9666	0.9408	0.9031	0.9368
SPC	0.9756	0.9641	0.9240	0.9546
subrate	0.5			
DPCM	0.9633	0.9432	0.9118	0.9343
SDPC	0.9731	0.9621	0.9157	0.9503
MFPQ	0.9688	0.9526	0.9131	0.9448
SPC	0.9768	0.9656	0.9309	0.9578

It is worth noting that, as shown in the Table 2, although the proposed method achieves the maximum correlation coefficient among these prediction methods, the computational complexity is even slightly lower than that of SDPC. The computational complexity of MFPQ and DPCM is lower than the proposed method, but their average correlation coefficient is much lower, which will affect the quality of image reconstruction.

Table 2. Computational complexity of different prediction methods for each block (M denotes the length of measurement vector of each block)

Methods	Multiplications	Additions	Comparisons
DPCM	0	0	0
MFPQ	0	0	$6M$
SDPC	9M-4	M	3
SPC	0	$4\,M$	4

4 Experimental Results

The experimental results are provided to verify the performance of the proposed method. The rate-distortion efficiency of the proposed SPC-plus-SQ method is examined by comparing it to SDPC-plus-SQ, DPCM-plus-SQ, MFPQ-plus-SQ and SQ alone applied to BCS measurements. The BCS-SPL algorithm is always exploited to reconstruct the decoded measurements by the above five prediction methods.

In the implementations, two grayscale test images are 512×512 pixels, the block size for BCS is typically set to be 16×16 and the measurement matrix Φ_B is an orthogonal random Gaussian matrix. Image quality is evaluated by means of the rate-distortion performance in terms of peak signal-to-noise ratio (PSNR) in dB at different bitrates in bits per pixel (bpp). The actual bitrate is estimated by the entropy of the quantizer indices, which would be actually produced by a real entropy coder. The setup of the combination of step-size and subrate is the same as that in Refs. [14–16].

Tables 3 and 4 respectively give the PSNR results of two images (namely *Lenna* and *Peppers*) at various bitrates (from 0.6 bpp to 1.6 bpp) under the BCS-SPL algorithm, coupled with five prediction & coding techniques, namely, SQ alone, DPCM-plus-SQ, SDPC-plus-SQ, MFPQ-plus-SQ and SPC-plus-SQ. One easily observes that, the proposed method obtains the best PSNR performance among five methods, and it improves 0.18 dB gain in the first test image and 0.12 dB gain in the second test image on average PSNR as compared to SDPC-plus-SQ relatively, which can demonstrate the superiority of the proposed SPC.

Table 3. PSNR (dB) comparison for five methods on the image *Lenna*

Bitrate (bpp)	SQ alone	DPCM-plus-SQ	MFPQ-plus-SQ	SDPC-plus-SQ	SPC-plus-SQ	Gains
0.6	28.24	30.54	30.27	30.93	31.03	0.10
0.7	28.84	31.02	30.80	31.48	31.65	0.17
0.8	29.54	31.56	31.28	32.04	32.16	0.12
0.9	29.95	32.02	31.77	32.42	32.55	0.13
1.0	30.33	32.41	32.16	32.67	32.86	0.19
1.1	30.65	32.69	32.50	33.20	33.49	0.29
1.2	31.05	33.15	32.72	33.63	33.77	0.14
1.3	31.36	33.57	33.21	33.94	34.14	0.20
1.4	31.67	33.88	33.60	34.64	34.64	0.28
1.5	31.88	34.23	33.80	34.77	34.97	0.20
1.6	32.15	34.64	34.50	34.99	35.14	0.15

Table 4. PSNR (dB) comparison for five methods on the image *Peppers*

Bitrate (bpp)	SQ alone	DPCM-plus-SQ	MFPQ-plus-SQ	SDPC-plus-SQ	SPC-plus-SQ	Gains
0.6	28.70	30.35	30.45	30.86	30.96	0.10
0.7	29.45	30.92	30.99	31.51	31.59	0.08
0.8	29.88	31.36	31.45	31.95	32.06	0.09
0.9	30.28	31.76	31.85	32.35	32.47	0.12
1.0	32.15	32.16	32.23	32.73	32.84	0.11
1.1	31.11	32.54	32.59	33.01	33.14	0.13
1.2	31.38	33.85	32.87	33.37	33.58	0.21
1.3	31.63	33.05	33.13	33.70	33.80	0.10
1.4	31.87	33.68	33.46	34.02	34.18	0.16
1.5	32.15	33.69	33.74	34.31	34.42	0.11
1.6	32.49	33.95	34.20	34.57	34.69	0.12

5 Conclusion

A new measurement-domain spiral predictive coding is proposed, which can make full use of the intrinsic spatial relationship of natural images and is not affected by image edges. The direction prediction block in the proposed method starts from the center of an image and spreads around in spiral scanning, where each measurement-domain block can select the optimal measurement prediction from the candidates set as many as possible. The experimental results show that the proposed SPC-plus-SQ method can achieve the best rate-distortion performance as compared with the existing methods.

Acknowledgement. This work was supported by the Natural Science Foundation of Shanghai under Grant 18ZR1400300.

References

1. Trevisi, M., Akbari, A., Trocan, M., Rodrmíguez-Vázquez, Á., Carmona-Galán, R.: Compressive imaging using RIP-compliant CMOS imager architecture and Landweber reconstruction. IEEE Trans. Circuits Syst. Video Technol. (2019). https://doi.org/10.1109/TCSVT.2019.2892178
2. Candes, E.J., Romberg, J., Tao, T.: Robust uncertainty principles: exact signal reconstruction from highly incomplete frequency information. IEEE Trans. Inf. Theory **52**(2), 489–509 (2006)
3. Kulkarni, K., Lohit, S., Turaga, P., Kerviche, R., Ashok, A.: ReconNet: non-iterative reconstruction of images from compressively sensed random measurements. In: IEEE Conference on Computer Vision and Pattern Recognition (CVPR), Las Vegas, pp. 449–458 (2016)
4. Amit, S.U., Deepthi, P.: Rate-distortion analysis of structured sensing matrices for block compressive sensing of images. Sig. Process. Image Commun. **65**, 115–127 (2018)

5. Liu, Y., Yuan, X., Suo, J.L., Brady, D., Dai, Q.H.: Rank minimization for snapshot compressive imaging. IEEE Trans. Pattern Anal. Mach. Intell. (2018). https://doi.org/10.1109/TPAMI.2018.2873587

6. Xie, X.M., Wang, C., Du, J., Shi, G.M.: Full image recover for block-based compressive sensing. In: International Conference on Multimedia & Expo, San Diego, pp. 1–6 (2018)

7. Liu, X.M., Zhai, D.M., Zhou, J.T., Zhang, X.F., Zhao, D.B., Gao, W.: Compressive sampling-based image coding for resource-deficient visual communication. IEEE Trans. Image Process. 25(6), 2844–2855 (2016)

8. Fowler, J.E., Mun, S., Tramel, E.W.: Block-based compressed sensing of images and video. Found. Trends Sig. Process. 4(4), 297–416 (2012)

9. Chen, Z., et al.: Compressive sensing multi-layer residual coefficients for image coding. IEEE Trans. Circ. Syst. Video Technol. (2019). https://doi.org/10.1109/TCSVT.2019.2898908

10. Jacques, L., Hammond, D.K., Fadili, J.M.: Dequantizing compressed sensing: when oversampling and non-Gaussian constraints combine. IEEE Trans. Inf. Theory 57(1), 559–571 (2011)

11. Sun, J.Z., Goyal, V.K.: Optimal quantization of random measurements in compressed sensing. In: IEEE International Symposium on Information Theory, Seoul, pp. 6–10 (2009)

12. Wang, L.J., Wu, X.L., Shi, G.M.: Binned progressive quantization for compressive sensing. IEEE Trans. Image Process. 21(6), 2980–2990 (2012)

13. Ahn, J.H., Jiang, H.: Architecture and noise analysis for block-based compressive imaging. In: International Conference on Image Processing, Athens, pp. 31–35 (2018)

14. Mun, S., Fowler, J.E.: DPCM for quantized block-based compressed sensing of images. In: 20th European Signal Processing Conference, Bucharest, pp. 1424–1428 (2012)

15. Zhang, J., Zhao, D.B., Jiang, F.: Spatially directional predictive coding for block-based compressive sensing of natural images. In: IEEE International Conference on Image Processing, Melbourne, pp. 1021–1025 (2014)

16. Li, R., Liu, H.B., He, W.: Space-time quantization and motion-aligned reconstruction for block-based compressive video sensing. KSII Trans. Internet Inf. Syst. 10(1), 321–340 (2017)

17. Zhou, J.B., Zhou, J.J., Guo, L.: Angular intra prediction based measurement coding algorithm for compressively sensed image. In: IEEE International Conference on Multimedia & Expo, San Diego, pp. 1–6 (2018)

Semantic Map Based Image Compression via Conditional Generative Adversarial Network

Zhensong Wei, Zeyi Liao, Huihui Bai$^{(\boxtimes)}$, and Yao Zhao

Institute of Information Science, Beijing Jiaotong University, Beijing 100044, China
{zhswei,zyliao,hhbai,yzhao}@bjtu.edu.cn

Abstract. Recently, deep learning methods have been applied for image compression and achieved promising results. For lossy image compression at low bit rate, the traditional compression algorithms usually introduce undesired compression artifacts, such as blocking and blurry effects. In this paper, we propose a novel semantic map based image compression framework (SMIC), restoring visually pleasing images at significantly low bit rate. At the encoder, a semantic segmentation network (SS-Net) is designed to generate a semantic map, which is encoded as the first part of the bit stream. Furthermore, a sampled image of the input image is compressed as the second part of bit stream. Then, at the decoder, in order to reconstruct high perceptual quality images, we design an image reconstruction network (Rec-Net) conditioned on the sampled image and corresponding semantic map. Experimental results demonstrate that the proposed framework can reconstruct more perceptually pleasing images at low bit rate.

Keywords: Image compression · Semantic map · Generative adversarial network

1 Introduction

Over the past few years, there has been an active interest in making a prediction at every pixel in whole-image, named pixel-wise semantic segmentation. In a semantic segmentation map, each pixel is labeled with the class of its enclosing object or region. Semantic segmentation has a wide array of applications ranging from scene understanding, autonomous driving to inferring support-relationships among objects in images. Recently, some of the approaches based on deep learning (DL) particularly are designed for semantic segmentation, obtaining the promising results by learning the mapping from low resolution features to categories of the input image [1–3]. Recent advancements in generative models also show promise for the task of semantic segmentation [4–6]. In addition, it is further shown that generative models can synthesize a high-quality image using only a semantic map as input [7].

© Springer Nature Switzerland AG 2019
Y. Zhao et al. (Eds.): ICIG 2019, LNCS 11903, pp. 13–22, 2019.
https://doi.org/10.1007/978-3-030-34113-8_2

Image compression has been a fundamental and significant research topic in the field of image processing for several decades, which refers to the task of representing images using as little storage as possible. For the task of image compression, there are two main categories, named lossless compression and lossy compression. In lossless image compression, that is, an original image should be completely recovered with limited compression rate, while in lossy image compression, a greater reduction in storage can be achieved by allowing some reconstruction distortion. The traditional image compression algorithms, such as JPEG and JPEG2000, rely on handcrafted codec blocks. They usually consist of three parts: transform, quantization and entropy code. At the very low bit rate, the compressed image may incur serious blocking and blurring artifacts with quantization operation, leading to poor perceptual quality. These compression artifacts not only affect the expression of information in the image but also impact on the accuracy of high-level computer vision tasks.

Recently, DL-based approaches have the potential to improve the performance of image compression. Several methods have been proposed using different networks, achieving promising image compression results [8–10]. In [8], the authors proposed a framework for end-to-end optimization of an image compression model based on nonlinear transform. The work of [9] used learned context models for improved coding performance on their trained models when using adaptive arithmetic coding. In [10], the researchers proposed an end-to-end trainable model for image compression based on variational autoencoder, and the model incorporated a hyperprior to capture spatial dependencies in the latent representation. Furthermore, the main idea of GAN has enabled a significant process in photo-realistic image generation, which is particularly relevant to the real world and has visually pleasing results. In [11], they trained the synthesis transform as a generative model for generative compression, and demonstrated the potential of generative compression for orders-of-magnitude improvement in image compression.

In this paper, we propose a novel semantic map based image compression framework (SMIC), focusing on the low bit rate, as shown in Fig. 1. The compression framework consists of two parts: encoder and decoder modules. The semantic map contains the category information and location information of the original image, which is important for understanding the content of the image. In addition, a semantic map can be compressed to very low bit rate, requiring little storage space. In the encoder module, firstly, we propose a semantic segmentation network (SS-Net) for extracting semantic maps from the given input images. The extracted semantic maps are encoded as the first part of the bit stream. Then, the input images are down-sampled to obtain low-resolution images, which are losslessly encoded into the second part of the bit stream. Two parts of the bit stream are transmitted to the decoder through the channel. For the decoder module, the two parts of the bit stream are respectively decoded to the semantic maps and the low-resolution images by the corresponding decoder. The decoded low-resolution images are up-sampled to obtain the original resolution, which together with the decoded semantic maps for reconstructing the original image.

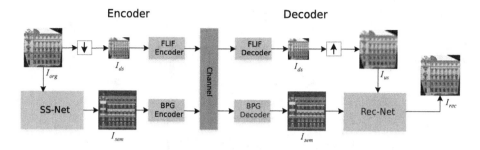

Fig. 1. The overall framework of our proposed SMIC.

Finally, we propose an image reconstruction network (Rec-Net) to obtain high-quality results by the decoded semantic maps and up-sampled images. We validate the proposed approach and compare our performance against the traditional compression algorithms including JPEG and JPEG2000. Experimental results show that our proposed image compression framework can yield visually more appealing results at low bit rate.

The remainder of this paper is organized as follows. Section 2 introduces the proposed SMIC in detail. The experimental results are demonstrated in Sect. 3. The conclusion of this paper is presented in Sect. 4.

2   Proposed Method

2.1   Encoder Framework

The overall image compression framework is shown in Fig. 1, which includes two parts: encoder and decoder. In order to extract the semantic maps, we propose a semantic segmentation network (SS-Net) based on conditional generative adversarial network, as shown in Fig. 2. The input image is first down-sampled to obtain a low-resolution image I_{ds}, which is losslessly encoded using the FLIF codec [12], which is state-of-the-art in lossless image codec. Then, the semantic map of the input image is extracted by our proposed SS-Net, which is encoded by a lossy BPG codec [13]. The BPG codec is based on the H.265/HEVC standard technology, which is a state-of-the-art lossy image codec. Two parts of the bit stream are transmitted to the decoder through the channel.

Our SS-Net model is based on the architecture of conditional GAN [14] and consists of two networks: generator and discriminator, which are alternately trained to compete with each other. The task of the generator of SS-Net is to extract features from the input image to generate a corresponding semantic map. The task of the discriminator is to determine whether the input image is from real or fake semantic map. By training the generator and discriminator alternately, we can improve the performance of the generator, generating an indistinguishable semantic map. For the SS-Net, the architecture of the generator is illustrated in Fig. 2(a), which consists of three parts: the encoder, the residual

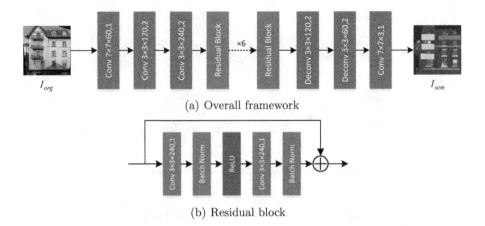

(a) Overall framework

(b) Residual block

Fig. 2. The generator of our proposed SS-Net.

blocks and the decoder. In the encoder part, there is a 7×7 convolution layer which outputs a 60-channeled feature map. And then two 3×3 convolution layers are performed to extract high-dimensional features. In the residual blocks part, we use 6 residual blocks, which are designed to learn the mapping from the encoded features to corresponding semantic information. The residual block is shown in Fig. 2(b). Each residual block make small changes to the input feature map to make it better, and the last residual block can generate good enough feature maps. Finally, the decoder part consists of two 3×3 convolution layers and a 7×7 convolution layer. The 3×3 convolution layers are performed to up-sample the feature maps to ensure that the output size is the same with the input. Then, the feature maps pass through a 7×7 convolution layer, and finally output a semantic map.

The architecture of discriminator D_1 is illustrated in Table 1. For the discriminator D_1, two pairs of image are required as input. The input image is concatenated with the ground truth semantic map as the input of 'real' discriminator. Meanwhile, the input image is concatenated with the generated semantic map as the input of 'fake' discriminator. The concatenated results are fed through 5 convolution layers, producing a feature map that each pixel represents a classification result of the image patch. Finally, the discriminator tries to determine if each image patch is 'real' or 'fake'. Such a discriminator can run faster because it focuses on the image patches but not the entire image.

2.2 Decoder Framework

Here, we introduce the decoder module of our image compression framework, the decoder framework is shown in the right part of Fig. 1, which includes a deep learning based network Rec-Net. At the decoder, the semantic map and low-resolution image are decoded by the corresponding codec respectively. The low-resolution image is first up-sampled, together with the semantic map as

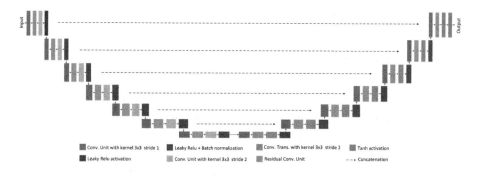

Fig. 3. The generator of our proposed Rec-Net.

the input of Rec-Net. Although GAN-based network can synthesize an appealing image using only a semantic map, which is quite different from the original image in details. In order to reduce the difference between the synthesized image and the original image, we propose an image reconstruction network (Rec-Net) conditioned on the up-sampled image and corresponding semantic map. By adding the up-sampled image, the Rec-Net can be easy to generate a high-quality image, which is indistinguishable from the original image. By training to learn the difference between the reconstructed image and original image, our model can reconstruct a high perceptual quality image.

Our Rec-Net is also based on conditional GAN architecture and consists of a generator and a discriminator. The generator of Rec-Net is based on the architecture of basic U-Net [15], as shown in Fig. 3. We select the architecture of U-Net as our generator due to its simplicity and effectiveness for many image tasks. Basically, U-Net is fully convolution network, which includes a series of down-sampling layers followed by a series of up-sampling layers. The feature maps are cropped and copied from down-sampling layers to up-sampling layers. To keep the spatial size of the output same with the input, we modify the padding scheme in our Rec-Net. We also remove the cropping and copying unit from the basic U-Net model and use concatenation operation. We add a residual block in each layer of the generator of Rec-Net to learn the semantic information and low-frequency information, yielding an improved architecture that results in better performance. The residual block is shown in Fig. 2(b). As shown in Fig. 3, the network consists of two main parts: the encoding and decoding units. The convolution layers with kernel size 3×3, stride 1 are designed to extract more feature information in each unit. By the adversarial training, the residual block can learn the feature mapping relations from the input to the original image. The convolution operations are performed followed by Relu activation and Batch Normalization (BN) in both parts of the network, except that the first and the last one. We use the skip connections to concatenate feature maps from the encoding unit to the decoding unit. The skip connection has a benefit that gradients can flow from the higher layers to the lower layers, which can improve the performance of the generator and make the training process easier.

Table 1. The discriminator architecture.

Layer	D_1	D_2
Conv 1	$4 \times 4 \times 64$, s $= 2$, relu	$4 \times 4 \times 64$, s $= 2$, relu
Conv 2	$4 \times 4 \times 128$, s $= 2$, relu	$4 \times 4 \times 128$, s $= 2$, relu
Conv 3	$4 \times 4 \times 256$, s $= 2$, relu	$4 \times 4 \times 256$, s $= 2$, relu
Conv 4	$4 \times 4 \times 256$, s $= 1$, relu	$4 \times 4 \times 512$, s $= 2$, relu
Conv 5	$4 \times 4 \times 1$, s $= 1$, sigmoid	$4 \times 4 \times 512$, s $= 2$, relu
Conv 6	–	$4 \times 4 \times 512$, s $= 1$, relu
Conv 7	–	$4 \times 4 \times 1$, s $= 1$, sigmoid

For the discriminator D_2, we use an architecture similar to the discriminator D_1, adding two convolution layers, as shown in Table 1. Two pairs of image include the input and the original image, the input and the reconstructed image. The concatenated results are fed through 7 convolution layers, producing a feature map that each pixel represents a classification result of the image patch. Finally, the discriminator tries to determine if each small image patch is real or fake, allowing the generator to reconstruct an image with better details.

2.3   Loss Function

The loss function for our generator consists of the L_1 loss, the adversarial loss and the perpetual loss. For the task of image reconstruction, the generator can reconstruct the image closer to the original image in pixel-wise. The L_1 loss function can be formulated as:

$$L_1 = \lambda \frac{1}{N} \sum_{i=1}^{N} \| I_{GT} - I_{out} \|_1 \tag{1}$$

where I_{GT} represents the ground truth image, I_{out} is the output image by our generator and N is the total number of image elements.

For the adversarial loss, we use the regular loss form in [16]. The adversarial loss can encourage the generator to generate a high-quality image with more photo-realistic details. The conditional GAN trains the generator G and the discriminator D by alternatively minimizing L_{adv}^G and maximizing L_{adv}^D, which are defined as follows:

$$L_{adv}^G = E[\ log(1 - D(G(I_{in}), I_{in}))] \tag{2}$$

$$L_{adv}^D = E[log D(I_{GT}, I_{in})] + E[\ log(1 - D(G(I_{in}), I_{in}))] \tag{3}$$

where I_{GT} and I_{in} denote the ground truth image and the input image of the generator, respectively. We minimize $-log(D(G(I_{in}), I_{in}))$ instead of $log(1 - (D(G(I_{in}), I_{in})))$ for the generator, which can have a better gradient behavior.

For the semantic segmentation network SS-Net, the final loss for the generator can be represented as:

$$L_{SS-Net} = L_{adv}^{G} + L_1 \tag{4}$$

In order to improve the perceptual quality of the reconstructed image, our also use a perpetual feature-matching loss based on the VGG networks [17], named VGG loss. The VGG loss is based on the ReLU activation layers of the pre-trained 19 layers VGG network, which can be defined as:

$$L_{VGG/i,j} = \lambda \frac{1}{W_{i,j}H_{i,j}} \sum_{x=1}^{W_{i,j}} \sum_{y=1}^{H_{i,j}} \| F^{(i,j)}(I_{GT})_{x,y} - F^{(i,j)}(I_{rec})_{x,y} \|_2 \tag{5}$$

where I_{GT} and I_{rec} represents the ground truth image and the reconstructed image. $F^{(i,j)}$ denotes the feature map obtained by the j-th convolution before the i-th max-pooling layer in the VGG network. $W_{i,j}$ and $H_{i,j}$ represent the dimensions of the feature maps in the VGG network.

For the image reconstruction network Rec-Net, the final generator loss can be formulated as:

$$L_{Rec-Net} = L_{adv}^{G} + L_1 + L_{VGG} \tag{6}$$

3   Experimental Results

3.1   Implementation Details

Our model is trained in a supervised fashion on pairs of images and semantic maps. In this paper, we use the CMP Facades dataset [18], which consists of just 400 images for training. We use the validation set for testing, which consists of 100 images. We sample the original images to 256×256 resolution and scale the range of the images to $[-1, 1]$ for our experiments. We encode the downsampling images using BPG codec with different sampling factors. We use the VGG loss $L_{VGG/5,4}$, which is defined on feature maps of higher level features from deeper VGG network layers, yielding better texture details. We consider the weight $\lambda = 100$ for L_1 and L_{VGG}. For the architecture of Rec-Net and two discriminators, all Relus are leaky with slope 0.2. In our experiment, we use the Adam [19] optimizer with a mini-batch size 1 and a momentum parameter 0.9 for training. The learning rate is fixed at 0.0002. We train the SS-Net and Rec-Net model for 200 epochs.

3.2   Perceptual Results

In this work, the ultimate goal of our work is not to achieve the best objective evaluation results, but instead to generate a restoration image with high perceptual quality. The traditional metrics used to evaluate the reconstructed image are PSNR and SSIM, both of which have been found to correlate poorly with human assessment of visual quality. At the extreme low bit rate, it becomes impossible to preserve the full image content. Because the PSNR and SSIM favor exact preservation of local structure (high-entropy), they are meaningless to evaluate the reconstructed images. We use a recently developed image quality assessment metric employing deep feature for measuring the perceptual quality, termed LPIPS [20], which tries to measure the perceptual similarity between two images. In Fig. 4, the perceptual results of our experiments are shown, compared with JPEG, JPEG2000 at low bit rate. Our results achieves better perceptual similarity scores than JPEG and JPEG2000.

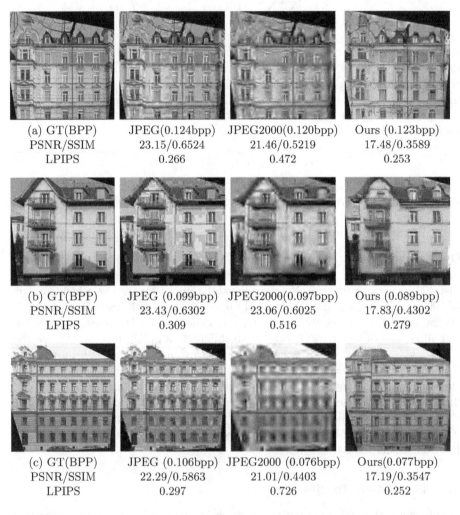

	(a) GT(BPP)	JPEG(0.124bpp)	JPEG2000(0.120bpp)	Ours (0.123bpp)
PSNR/SSIM		23.15/0.6524	21.46/0.5219	17.48/0.3589
LPIPS		0.266	0.472	0.253

	(b) GT(BPP)	JPEG (0.099bpp)	JPEG2000(0.097bpp)	Ours (0.089bpp)
PSNR/SSIM		23.43/0.6302	23.06/0.6025	17.83/0.4302
LPIPS		0.309	0.516	0.279

	(c) GT(BPP)	JPEG (0.106bpp)	JPEG2000 (0.076bpp)	Ours(0.077bpp)
PSNR/SSIM		22.29/0.5863	21.01/0.4403	17.19/0.3547
LPIPS		0.297	0.726	0.252

Fig. 4. Subjective comparison on several images compressed by JPEG, JPEG2000 and our method. Corresponding BPP (bits/pixel/channel), PSNR(dB), SSIM and LPIPS score (lower score is better) are shown in bottom.

As shown in Fig. 4(a), it can be found that there are some blocking artifacts and color distortion in JPEG images compressed at low bitrate. And there are some blurring artifacts in JPEG2000 images, which can not exhibit a good subjective quality. However, our method can produce very good details in reconstructed images and keep the edges sharper, which make the whole image perceptually pleasing.

As the bit rate decreases, we can see that the JPEG image has more serious blocking artifacts and color distortion, and it also has serious blurring artifacts for image reconstructed by JPEG2000. Due to the limitation of bitrate, the traditional methods can recover some the low-frequency information, but the recovery of high-frequency information is very difficult, which leads to the serious degradation of recovered image quality. As shown in Fig. 4(b), it can be observed that the other methods recover results with noticeable color distortion and artifacts such as blocking and blurring artifacts at low bitrate. Compared to other methods, our method effectively suppresses such artifacts and distortion through the semantic information and the robust perceptual loss function, generating an image with high perceptual quality.

When the bitrate is about 0.07bpp, our approach can still restore an image with high perceptual quality than the comparison methods. As shown in Fig. 4(c), we can see that the performance of JPEG and JPEG2000 has serious distortion, whereas our method can recover high-quality images with much cleaner and sharper details. In contrast, our method does a good performance in the perceptual results, reconstructing much more visually pleasant high-quality images.

4 Conclusion

In this paper, we propose a novel semantic map based image compression framework (SMIC) for image compression at low bit rate. Firstly, we propose a semantic segmentation network (SS-Net) to extract the semantic map from the input image. The semantic map and the down-sampled image of the input image are encoded into the bit stream respectively. Then we propose an image reconstruction network (Rec-Net) conditioned on the decoded semantic map and the upsampled image of the input image, yielding more perceptually pleasing image at low bit rate. Contrast to the traditional compression codecs, our method can achieve good performance in perceptual quality. According to experimental results, our proposed method can reconstruct many perceptual details and generate sharp edges comparing with traditional methods.

Acknowledgment. This work was supported by Fundamental Research Funds for the Central Universities (2019JBZ102).

References

1. Badrinarayanan, V., Kendall, A., Cipolla, R.: SegNet: a deep convolutional encoder-decoder architecture for image segmentation. IEEE TPAMI **39**(12), 2481–2495 (2017)

2. Zhou, Q., Zheng, B., Zhu, W., Latecki, L.J.: Multi-scale context for scene labeling via flexible segmentation graph. Pattern Recogn. **59**, 312–324 (2016)
3. Chen, L.-C., Papandreou, G., Kokkinos, I., Murphy, K., Yuille, A.L.: DeepLab: semantic image segmentation with deep convolutional nets, atrous convolution, and fully connected CRFs. IEEE TPAMI **40**(4), 834–848 (2016)
4. Zhou, Q., et al.: Multi-scale deep context convolutional neural networks for semantic segmentation. World Wide Web-Internet Web Inf. Syst. **22**(2), 555–570 (2019)
5. Isola, P., Zhu, J.-Y., Zhou, T., Efros, A.A.: Image-to-image translation with conditional adversarial networks. In: IEEE CVPR, pp. 5967–5976 (2017)
6. Zhu, J.-Y., Park, T., Isola, P., Efros, A.A.: Unpaired Image-to-image translation using cycle-consistent adversarial networks. In: IEEE ICCV, pp. 2380–7504 (2017)
7. Wang, T.-C., Liu, M.-Y., Zhu, J.-Y., Tao, A., Kautz, J., Catanzaro, B.: High-resolution image synthesis and semantic manipulation with conditional GANs. In: IEEE CVPR (2018)
8. Ballé, J., Laparra, V., Simoncelli, E.P.: End-to-end optimized image compression. In: ICLR (2016)
9. Rippel, O., Bourdev, L.: Real-time adaptive image compression. In: IEEE ICML, vol. 70, pp. 2922–2930 (2017)
10. Ballé, J., Minnen, D., Singh, S., Hwang, S.J., Johnston, N.: Variational image compression with a scale hyperprior. In: ICLR (2018)
11. Santurkar, S., Budden, D., Shavit, N.: Generative compression. arXiv preprint arXiv:1703.01467 (2017)
12. Sneyers, J., Wuille, P.: FLIF: free lossless image format based on maniac compression. In: IEEE ICIP, pp. 66–70 (2016)
13. Bellard, F.: BPG image format (2017). http://bellard.org/bpg
14. Mirza, M., Osindero, S.: Conditional generative adversarial nets. arXiv preprint arXiv:1411.178 (2014)
15. Ronneberger, O., Fischer, P., Brox, T.: U-Net: convolutional networks for biomedical image segmentation. In: Navab, N., Hornegger, J., Wells, W.M., Frangi, A.F. (eds.) MICCAI 2015. LNCS, vol. 9351, pp. 234–241. Springer, Cham (2015). https://doi.org/10.1007/978-3-319-24574-4_28
16. Goodfellow, I., et al.: Generative adversarial nets. In: NIPS, pp. 2672–2680 (2014)
17. Simonyan, K., Zisserman, A.: Very deep convolutional networks for large-scale image recognition. In: ICLR (2015)
18. Tyleček, R., Šára, R.: Spatial pattern templates for recognition of objects with regular structure. In: Weickert, J., Hein, M., Schiele, B. (eds.) GCPR 2013. LNCS, vol. 8142, pp. 364–374. Springer, Heidelberg (2013). https://doi.org/10.1007/978-3-642-40602-7_39
19. Kingma, D., Ba, J.: Adam: a method for stochastic optimization. arXiv preprint arXiv:1412.6980 (2014)
20. Zhang, R., Isola, P., Efros, A.A., Shechtman, E., Wang, O.: The unreasonable effectiveness of deep features as a perceptual metric. In: CVPR (2018)

AVE-WLS Method for Lossless Image Coding

Grzegorz Ulacha[1] and Ryszard Stasinski[2(✉)]

[1] West Pomeranian University of Technology, Szczecin, Poland
gulacha@wi.zut.edu.pl
[2] Poznan University of Technology, Poznań, Poland
ryszard.stasinski@put.poznan.pl

Abstract. In the paper currently the most efficient from the data compaction point of view image lossless coding method is presented. Being computationally complex the algorithm is still more time efficient than its main competitors. The method is based on weighted LS (WLS) technique idea with many improvements introduced, e.g. its main stage is followed by a two-step NLMS predictor. Prediction error is coded by a completely new highly efficient binary context arithmetic coder. Its performance is compared with that of other coders for a set of widely used benchmark images.

Keywords: Image coding · Lossless coding · Arithmetical coder

1 Introduction

Samples of multimedia signals are usually strongly correlated, which means that entropy coders do not compress them effectively. Correlation can be significantly reduced by signal prediction, but then another problem emerges, changes in signal statistical properties. The first image coder that dealt with these problems relatively well was the context coder CALIC [1]. At that time it was considered as too complex for practical purposes, nevertheless, the standardized JPEG-LS was a context coder, too [2]. Then followed more efficient, but also more complex techniques: TMW^{LEGO} [3], Multi-WLS [4], MRP 0.5 [5]. The more recent best algorithms were Blend-20 [6], and then improved versions of MRP 0.5: GPR-BP [7], and MRP-SSP [8].

In this paper currently the best image lossless coding algorithm is presented, AVE-WLS. It can be seen from Table I and II that it is clearly better than any older method, including the newest GPR-BP, and MRP-SSP. This is an extended version of WLS technique, which also formed a basis for very good Multi-WLS algorithm [4]. The first version of AVE-WLS was introduced in [9], the current one is significantly improved (several new formulas, additional NLMS stages, enhanced cumulated prediction error cancellation stage, new arithmetic coder).

The paper is organized as follows: The next section provides some insight into the research that led to construction of new AVE-WLS algorithm. Then, in Sect. 3 pixel numbering in predictor formulas is explained. In Sect. 4 predictors forming the structure of AVE-WLS algorithm are described, and note on prediction error cancelling is done. Section 5 is devoted to the new binary context arithmetic coder, with newly introduced two-stage prediction error coding. Finally, Sect. 6 provides results of

Y. Zhao et al. (Eds.): ICIG 2019, LNCS 11903, pp. 23–34, 2019.
https://doi.org/10.1007/978-3-030-34113-8_3

algorithm test, as well as their comparison to those for some other techniques, including the noted above most advanced ones, Tables 1 and 2.

2 Conceptual Background

In [10] it has been observed that minimization of mean square error is not equivalent to minimization of zero-order entropy and mean bit rate of a coded image. This observation prompted us to search for best from this point of view global static predictors for each of some 45 test images using Minkowsky vector distance criterion [11]:

$$L_M = \left(\sum_{i\,\text{range}} |x_i - \hat{x}_i|^M \right)^{1/M} \tag{1}$$

$x_i, \hat{x}_i$ are reference and actual vector elements, e.g. actual samples and their estimates (3). It appeared that best predictors were obtained for M values between 0.6 and 0.9, for comparison, used in [10] MMAE criterion meant that $M = 1$, and (1) was equivalent to MMSE for $M = 2$. Indeed, also in [10] some improved with respect to MMSE results were obtained, however, they were not as clear for coder final mean bit rate as for prediction error entropy. This was due to extremely difficult task of joint optimization of coder modeling and coding stages, at least for on-line methods. In the case of advanced off-line techniques like MRP [5] the optimization resulted simply in iterative nature of such algorithms, but also in their high computational complexity. Moreover, replacing MMSE by some version of Minkovsky criterion led to important increase of enhanced method computational complexity.

Nevertheless, we modified in this way predictor optimization formulas of several techniques in search for optimal M values, and it appeared that this value can be strongly variable. We started with OLS prediction followed by an adaptive arithmetic coder, and the value jumped from approximately 0.75 in [11] to 1.3 (partly due to locality of OLS predictors). After adding some kind of cumulated predictor error removal (compare Sect. 4.4) the value has grown to 1.5. 3ST-OLS technique [12] had additional NLMS+ stage (compare Sect. 4.3), and for it optimal $M = 1.7$. Finally, for presented here AVE-WLS version best M value is 1.9, and the gain in output data entropy with respect to MMSE criterion is very small and unlikely to be exploited in practice (in the paper we are presenting the algorithm for MMSE, i.e. for $M = 2$).

How this research can be summarized? Seeking for the best data compacting algorithms is in a sense like roaming in the darkness, testing for best version of Minkovsky criterion for predictor optimization seems to be like a ray of light somehow pointing at proper direction. For example, our study shed some light on a non-obvious fact that multi-stage multimedia lossless coders are often better than one-stage ones, in accordance with what is known about predictor construction the added stages could even deteriorate the result (the combined total linear predictor length is prolonged beyond limits given by length criteria, like Akaike, MDL, etc.). But as in examples above optimum M value for one-stage coder may happen to be wildly different from $M = 2$, while it is not the case of its multi-stage version.

In line with this research the presented in the paper AVE-WLS algorithm seems to be very close to the optimal one for Minkovsky criterion, has advantages of on-line approach, and indeed, is performing in an outstanding way, see Sect. 6.

3 Predictors

A linear predictor is used to estimate a value of a sample:

$$\hat{x}_n = \sum_{j=1}^{r} b_j \cdot P(j) \tag{2}$$

where in this paper $P(j)$ are pixels from the coded pixel x_n neighborhood (Fig. 1), and b_j are predictor coefficients [13]. The coded pixel estimate (rounded to closest integer) is subtracted from the true pixel value, and the difference (prediction error e_n) coded:

$$e_n = x_n - \hat{x}_n \tag{3}$$

Usually the closest pixels provide most information about the coded one, hence, neighboring pixels are ordered in accordance with their Euclidean distance from x_n, Fig. 1.

			26	24	27			
	29	20	16	14	17	21	30	
	19	11	8	6	9	12	22	
25	15	7	3	2	4	10	18	28
23	13	5	1	x_n				

Fig. 1. Numbering of neighborhood pixels.

4 Predictors Used

AVE-WLS is based on WLS concept, hence, the section begins with its description. Then follow AVE-WLS presentation and that of special version of NLMS used in the algorithm. The section ends with a brief note on prediction error cancelling stage, fully described in another paper [12].

4.1 Weighted Least-Squares (WLS)

In the most general case vector of least-squares predictor coefficients **B** is computed from the following formula [13]:

$$\mathbf{B} = (\mathbf{R} + u_{\text{bias}} \cdot \mathbf{I})^{-1} \cdot \mathbf{P} \tag{4}$$

where $\mathbf{R}$ is the "measured" estimate of signal autocorrelation matrix:

$$\mathbf{R}(j, i) = \sum_{y \in Q} \sum_{x \in Q} \psi_{(y,x)} \cdot P_{(y,x)}(i) \cdot P_{(y,x)}(j), \tag{5}$$

and vector $\mathbf{P}$ is:

$$\mathbf{P}(j) = \sum_{y \in Q} \sum_{x \in Q} \psi_{(y,x)} \cdot P_{(y,x)}(0) \cdot P_{(y,x)}(j), \tag{6}$$

pixels P are taken from a training window Q around the coded pixel located at position (y, x), Ψ is a weighting function, Q is an area extending W pixels to the left and up from the coded one, and to the right in rows preceding it, Fig. 2, finally, u_{bias} is a small number, term $u_{bias}\mathbf{I}$ guaranties non-singularity of (4). In WLS-related algorithms weighting function Ψ embodies concept of similarity between neighborhoods around the coded pixel $P(0)$ and some other one $P_{off}(0)$ [4, 9], see Fig. 2. Initial form of the function was relatively simple [4]:

$$\psi = \frac{1}{1 + \sum_{j=1}^{m} (P(j) - P_{\text{off}}(j))^2} \tag{7}$$

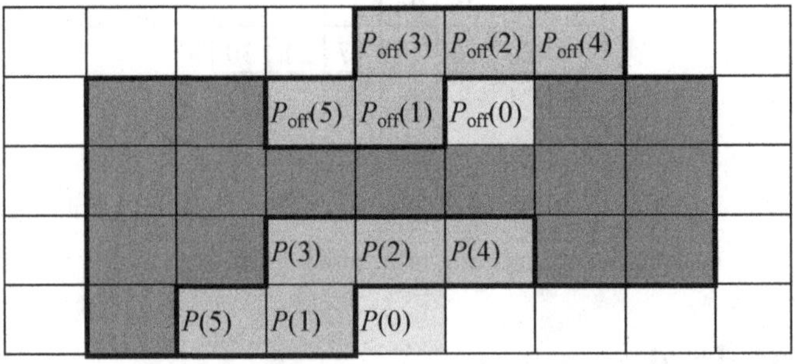

Fig. 2. Neighborhoods of pixels $P(0)$, and $P_{off}(0)$ for $m = 5$, $Q = 3$.

4.2   AVE-WLS Method

Previous (and this) paper on AVE-WLS [9] followed suggestions from [14, 15] concerning optimal form of LS predictors. First one was a statement that for each coded pixel it existed an optimal predictor rank [14]. It is not known a priori, so in [9] instead of seeking for it we proposed to compute averaged value of WLS predictor vectors for ranks from r_{min} to r_{max}:

$$\mathbf{B}_{\text{ave}} = \frac{1}{r_{\text{max}} - r_{\text{min}} + 1} \cdot \sum_{j=r_{\text{min}}}^{r_{\text{max}}} \mathbf{B}_j. \tag{8}$$

Implemented here predictors ranks are from $r_{min} = 4$ to $r_{max} = 24$, additionally, $W = 14$, Fig. 2. Vectors $\mathbf{B}_j$ should be extended to r_{max}, it is done by zero-padding.

In this paper a complex weighting function is proposed, compare (7), being an enhanced version of formula from [9]:

$$\psi_{(y,z)} = \alpha \cdot \frac{\lambda_2 + 0.8\sqrt{(\Delta y)^2 + (\Delta z)^2}}{\left(\lambda_1 + \sum\limits_{j=1}^{m} \left(\bar{d}_j \cdot (P(j) - P_{\text{off}}(j))\right)^2\right)^{\gamma}} \cdot \qquad (9)$$

where $\lambda_1 = 64$, $\lambda_2 = 0.25$, $\bar{d}_j = 1/\sqrt{(\Delta x_j)^2 + (\Delta y_j)^2}$, i.e. inverse of Euclidean distance between pixels, neighborhood size $m = r_{max}$, see (8), and $\gamma = 1.18$. Scaling factor α depends on two threshold values:

$t_1 = \max(P_{off}(0) - P_{off}(i))$, for $i = \{1, 2, -1\}$ (for indices i see Fig. 1 with pixel $P(0)$ replaced by $P_{off}(0)$)

$t_2 = \max(P_{off}(0) - P_{off}(i))$, for $i = \{3, 4\}$

Then:

$$a = 1$$
$$\text{if } (t_1 \geq 12)\ \alpha = t_1^{-0.25}$$
$$\text{else if } (t_2 \geq 25)\ \alpha = t_2^{-0.25}$$

Second suggestion concerning LS predictors optimization [15] was a proposition to use in basic prediction formula (2) not all, but only r_{max} "most similar" (correlated) pixels taken from a range of r_{ext} ones, $r_{ext} > r_{max}$. In this paper it is proposed to set $r_{ext} = 48$, but similarity is tested using only 10 pixels having indices from 15 to 48, and located in Q, Fig. 2, the similarity being here the smallest cumulated absolute distance of the pixels from Q origin:

$$\rho_{dist}(j) = \sum_{y \in Q} \sum_{z \in Q} \left| P_{(y,z)}(0) - P_{(y,z)}(j) \right| \qquad (10)$$

Apart from the chosen in this way 10 pixels the remaining ones in the modified predictor formula are the closest ones to the coded pixel.

Finally, the u_{bias} is also optimized in this paper. Firstly, initial vector $\mathbf{B}_{ave}$ is computed for $u_{bias} = 0$. Then the following term is computed:

$$u_{bias} = c \cdot \frac{\sum\limits_{y \in Q} \sum\limits_{z \in Q} \psi_{(y,z)} \cdot e^2_{(y,z)}}{\sum\limits_{i=1}^{r_{max}} b_i^2} \qquad (11)$$

where e, b_i are defined in (3), (2), b_i are coefficients of the mentioned above initial vector $\mathbf{B}_{ave}$. Constant c can be evaluated as $4 \cdot r_{max}/W^2 \approx 0.5$.

4.3   Normalized LMS (NLMS) Algorithm [12]

The general coefficient update formula for NLMS algorithm is [13]:

$$b_{\text{NLMS}(j)}(n+1) = b_{\text{NLMS}(j)}(n) + \mu \cdot \bar{e} \cdot P(j), \tag{12}$$

where here:

$$\bar{e} = \text{sgn}(e) \cdot \min\{|e|, \varphi\} \tag{13}$$

is the bounded prediction error, the bound is equal to φ. In NLMS approach the learning coefficient μ adapts to signal, here an enhanced formula for it is proposed [12]:

$$\mu_j = \frac{\bar{d}_j}{2^3 \cdot \sqrt{\bar{\sigma}^2} \cdot \left(10 + \sum\limits_{i=1}^{r_{\text{NLMS}}} \sqrt{\bar{d}_i} \cdot e_{\text{NLMS}}^2(i)\right)}, \tag{14}$$

where $e(j)$ is the j-th signal sample, here – the prediction error from the preceding stage of algorithm, $\bar{\sigma}^2$ is the mean value of all variances $\tilde{\sigma}^2$:

$$\tilde{\sigma}^2 = \frac{1}{\delta} \sum\limits_{j=1}^{m} \bar{d}_j \cdot (P(j) - \tilde{p})^2 \tag{15}$$

where $m = 10$, $\tilde{p} = \frac{1}{\delta} \sum\limits_{j=1}^{m} \bar{d}_j \cdot P(j)$, and $\delta = \sum\limits_{j=1}^{m} \bar{d}_j$.

Similarly as in [12] we implement here two stages of NLMS, one of rank $r_{\text{NLMS}} = 106$, and the following one of rank $r_{\text{NLMS+}} = 42$, the ranks in [12] are different. More details can be found in [12].

4.4   Cancelling Cumulated Prediction Error [12]

It has been discovered in [1] that predictors tend to produce DC error component, which diminish their efficiency. Then, algorithm for computing correction value used for cancelling this component was proposed. In the case of the proposed method highly sophisticated technique of computing this correction value is done, it is described in [12]. The value is:

$$C_{mix} = \sum\limits_{j=1}^{12} \alpha_j \cdot C_j[i_k] \tag{16}$$

where C_j are computed using error bias correction methods: $j = 1, 2, 3, 4$ for JPEG-LS, $j = 5, 6, 7, 8$ for CALIC, and $j = 9, 10, 11, 12$ for modified median algorithms. Indices i_k point at context systems (i) applied to each method (k), $j = 4(k - 1) + i$. Moreover, the formula (16) is adaptive, for more details see [12].

4.5 Data Modeling Part of the Coder

Final prediction error of the coder is obtained at the output of a cascade structure shown in Fig. 3. It is given by the formula:

$$\dot{e}(0) = P(0) - (\hat{x}_{\text{WLS}} + \hat{x}_{\text{NLMS}+} + C_{\text{mix}}) \tag{17}$$

where $\hat{x}_{\text{WLS}}$, $\hat{x}_{\text{NLMS}+}$ are signal estimates provided by AVE-WLS, and NLMS+ predictors, respectively, and C_{mix} is defined by (16). When preceded by AVE-WLS it is reasonable to increase order of first NLMS+ predictor up to $r_{\text{NLMS}} = 106$, which is not true in the case of 3ST-OLS algorithm [12].

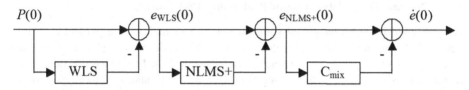

Fig. 3. Cascade of predictors forming the data modeling part of the coder. In fact, NLMS+ consists of two cascaded NLMS coders [12].

5 Arithmetic Coder

Entropy coding is done by a completely new binary context arithmetic coder. Absolute error value $|e(0)|$ is coded by an adaptive Golomb code, then compressed by two arithmetic coders, additionally, if error is non-zero, then third coder for sign compression is activated. Such a two-stage approach to coding significantly improves coder adaptability to quickly changing properties of image prediction error.

5.1 Short Term Estimation of Probability Distribution

Firstly, values ω_1 and ω_2 are computed:

$$\omega_1 = \max\{2.3|e(1)|, 2|e(2)|, 1.6|e(4)|, 0.95(|e(3)| + |e(4)|), 1.25(|e(5)| + |e(10)|),$$

$$1.3|e(3)|, 1.375(|e(1)| + |e(2)|), 0.4(|e(6)| + |e(7)|), 0.4(|e(8)| + |e(9)|)\}$$

$$\omega_2 = \frac{1}{\delta}\sum_{j=1}^{m} \bar{d}_j \cdot |e(j)| \tag{18}$$

where $\delta = \sum_{j=1}^{m} \bar{d}_j$, $m = 28$, for $\bar{d}_j$ see (9). Next computed parameters are:

$$\omega_3 = \max\{2.1 \cdot \omega_1, 10.2 \cdot \omega_2\} \tag{19}$$

$$\omega_4 = \max\{|P(1) - P(3)|, |P(2) - P(4)|, 1.1|P(1) - P(2)|, 0.7|P(2) - P(3)|,$$
$$0.9|P(1) - P(4)|, 0.9|P(3) - P(4)|\} \tag{20}$$

used for final calculation of ω:

$$\omega = \omega_3 + 0.48 \cdot \omega_4 \tag{21}$$

Value ω is quantized using $t - 1$ thresholds $T_h(j)$, which for $t = 16$ gives 4-bit number b_{medium} of short-term probability distribution, $T_h = \{3, 7, 12, 18, 24, 31, 39, 49, 59, 72, 90, 115, 140, 170, 210\}$.

5.2 Medium Term Estimation of Probability Distribution

Golomb code is particularly well suited for coding of data having geometric distribution [16]. Group number m_G (Golomb code rank) is chosen in such a way that for p being parameter of geometric probability distribution $p^m \approx 1/2$. The group number is searched for each coded $|e(0)|$ among 6 probability distributions of the form $G(i) = (1 - p)p^i$. They are defined by m_G values $\mathbf{m} = \{1, 1, 2, 3, 4, 12\}$.

The current p parameter is calculated as $p = (S - 1)/S$, where $S = \omega_2$ for $m = 48$ (17). Then m_G is evaluated [16]:

$$m_G = \left\lceil -\frac{\log_{10}(1+p)}{\log_{10} p} \right\rceil \tag{22}$$

According to observation from [17]: $m_G \approx \ln(2)S$. Then, value $\ln(2)S$ is quantized using thresholds $\{0.01, 1.5, 3.6, 11.0, 16.0\}$, the obtained index b_{Golomb} having values $0, 1, \ldots, 5$ is used to select element of set $\mathbf{m}$. The value b_{Golomb} is a part of context number, and is constant when coding bits of Golomb word representing current $|e(0)|$. Golomb word consists of unary coded group number $v_G = |e(0)| - u_G \cdot m_G$ and group element number $v_G = |e(0)| - u_G \cdot m_G$ coded using phased-in binary code [16].

5.3 Context Number Calculation

Binary sequences u_G and v_G are coded by separate arithmetic coders. Context number for u_G is computed as follows $ctx_u = 6 \cdot (2^4 \cdot b_{Golomb} + b_{medium}) + b_{unary}$, value b_{unary} is from the range $0 \ldots 5$, and denotes number of currently coded u_G bit (starting with most significant one), if there are more than six bits, then $b_{unary} = 5$. Hence, there are 576 ctx_u contexts.

The number of contexts for v_G is 192:

$$ctx_v = 2^4 \cdot (2 \cdot b_{Golomb} + b_{phased-in}) + 2^3 \cdot b_\omega + 2^2 \cdot b_{binary} + b_{unary2} \tag{23}$$

where $b_{unary2} = \min\{b_{unary}, 3\}$, b_{binary} is the most significant bit of v_G, b_ω is a one-bit number obtained by quantizing ω using threshold 49, and $b_{phased-in}$ is 0 for the first coded bit of v_G and 1 otherwise. If $b_{phased-in} = 0$, then $b_{binary} = 0$.

5.4   Long Term Adaptation of Probability Distribution

Each context number is associated with counters of its zeros and ones: $n(0)$ and $n(1)$. The counter values cannot grow infinitely, when sum $n(0) + n(1)$ reaches a value N_{max} both counts are halved. For u_G used $N_{max} = 2^{10}$, and counters initial values are $n(0) = n(1) = 1$. For v_G the values are $N_{max} = 2^{11}$, and at the beginning $n(0) = n(1) = 16$.

5.5   Sign Coding

Separate sign coding is rather uncommon in binary arithmetic coders, hence, it is a particular feature of the coder presented in the paper. There are 32 contexts for sign coding. Bits of the context number are: signs of neighbor errors $\text{sgn}(e(1))$ and $\text{sgn}(e(2))$, see Fig. 1, then bit b_ω, see comment to (23), finally two last bits are obtained from quantization of $|e(0)|$ using thresholds $\{1, 3, 16\}$. Initial counts of zeros and ones are set to 2. For the coder $N_{max} = 2^{10}$.

Table 1. Mean bit per pixel values for selected image lossless coding algorithms

Images	JPEG-LS	CALIC [1]	GLICBAWLS [18]	3ST-OLS [12]	TMW^{LEGO} [3]	MRP 0.5 [5]	Multi-WLS [4]	Blend-20 [6]	AVE-WLS
Balloon	2.889	2.78	2.640	2.580	2.60	2.579	2.60	2.566	**2.549**
Barb	4.690	4.31	3.916	3.832	3.84	3.815	3.75	3.768	**3.712**
Barb2	4.684	4.46	4.318	4.219	4.24	4.216	4.18	4.175	**4.134**
Board	3.674	3.51	3.392	3.296	3.27	3.268	3.27	3.272	**3.242**
Boats	3.930	3.78	3.628	3.544	3.53	3.536	3.53	3.520	**3.495**
Girl	3.922	3.72	3.565	3.471	3.47	3.465	3.45	3.449	**3.411**
Gold	4.475	4.35	4.276	4.208	4.22	4.207	4.20	4.185	**4.170**
Hotel	4.378	4.18	4.177	4.047	4.01	4.026	4.01	4.007	**3.979**
Zelda	3.884	3.69	3.537	3.504	3.50	3.495	3.51	3.498	**3.485**
Average	4.058	3.864	3.717	3.633	3.631	3.623	3.611	3.605	**3.575**

Table 2. Mean bit per pixel values for selected image lossless coding algorithms

Images	SWAP [19]	RALP [20]	TMW [21]	GLICBAWLS [18]	BMF [5]	xMRP [22]	MRP 0.5 [5]	GPR-BP [7]	MRP-SSP [8]	AVE-WLS
Airplane	3.58	3.71	3.601	3.668	3.602	3.590	3.591	**3.451**	3.536	3.550
Baboon	5.86	5.81	5.738	5.666	5.714	5.662	5.663	5.641	5.635	**5.623**
Balloon	2.49	2.55	2.649	2.640	2.649	2.613	2.579	**2.544**	2.548	2.549
Barb	4.12	4.12	4.084	3.916	3.959	3.817	3.815	3.821	3.764	**3.712**
Barb2	4.55	4.51	4.378	4.318	4.276	4.226	4.216	4.184	4.175	**4.140**
Camera	4.39	4.24	4.098	4.208	4.060	3.971	3.949	3.964	**3.901**	3.919
Couple256	3.75	3.63	3.446	3.543	3.448	3.389	3.388	3.339	**3.323**	3.350
Gold	4.30	4.32	4.266	4.276	4.238	4.216	4.207	4.178	4.173	**4.170**
Lennagrey	3.95	3.95	3.908	3.901	3.929	3.885	3.889	3.880	3.877	**3.847**
Peppers	4.25	4.27	4.251	4.246	4.241	4.208	4.199	4.170	4.163	**4.105**
Average	4.124	4.111	4.042	4.038	4.012	3.958	3.950	3.917	3.910	**3.896**

6 Performance Analysis

Tables 1 and 2 contain comparison of AVE-WLS performance to that provided in literature for other efficient lossless image coding techniques. Methods in Table 1 are faster than AVE-WLS, but are clearly worse: Blend-20 is nearly four times faster, 3ST-OLS is coding Lennagray image in 6.38 s, in contrast to 145.6 s for AVE-WLS (Pentium i5 3.4 GHz). This is still 2.88 times less than for MRP 0.5. GPR-BP, MRP-SSP, and TMW^{LEGO} are even more computationally complex. As can be seen, being not as complex AVE-WLS is on average better than these algorithms. It should be noted, however, that decoders for MRP 0.5, and hence, GPR-BP, and MRP-SSP are relatively time-efficient, while AVE-WLS decoder complexity is similar to that of a coder. Despite being a newer method lossless JPEG-2000 is less efficient than the JPEG-LS, hence, the results for the latter coder are shown in Table 1. AVE-WLS files are on average 11,9% shorter than those for JPEG-LS. It appears that computational time of the new arithmetic coder forms less than 1% of the coding procedure duration.

7 Conclusion

When compared to the best algorithms, on average the presented in the paper AVE-WLS lossless image coding technique is currently the most efficient one, at least if data compaction property is taken into consideration. At the same time the algorithm is less computationally complex than its main competitors. It is based on WLS approach, and has cascade form, where AVE-WLS predictor is followed by two-stage NLMS section. The new sophisticated binary context arithmetic coder is much less computationally complex than the preceding it data modeling stage, hence, it can be used in other image compression methods, too.

Some readers may be interested in notes on relations between Minkovsky distance, final prediction error zero-order entropy, and eventual coder mean data rate given in Sect. 2 of the paper. The presented AVE-WLS algorithm construction was influenced by these observations.

Acknowledgement. The work has been supported by Polish Ministry of Science and Education grant "Uwidacznianie i modelowanie informacji zawartej w sygnałach".

References

1. Wu, X., Memon, N.D.: CALIC – a context based adaptive lossless image coding scheme. IEEE Trans. Commun. **45**, 437–444 (1996)
2. Weinberger, M.J., Seroussi, G., Sapiro, G.: LOCO-I: lossless image compression algorithm: principles and standardization into JPEG-LS. IEEE Trans. Image Proces. **9**, 1309–1324 (2000)
3. Meyer, B., Tischer, P.: TMWLego - an object oriented image modeling framework. In: Proceedings Data Compression Conference, p. 504 (2001)

4. Ye, H., Deng, G., Devlin, J.C.: A weighted least squares method for adaptive prediction in lossless image compression. In: Proceedings Picture Coding Symposium, pp. 489–493 (2003)
5. Matsuda, I., Ozaki, N., Umezu, Y., Itoh, S.: Lossless Coding Using Variable Blok-Size Adaptive Prediction Optimized for Each Image. In: Proceedings EUSIPCO-05 (on CD) (2005)
6. Ulacha, G., Stasiński, R.: Performance optimized predictor blending technique for lossless image coding. In: Proceedings of the 36th International Conference on Acoustics. Speech and Signal Processing ICASSP 2011, Prague, Czech Republic, 22–27 May 2011, pp. 1541–1544 (2011)
7. Dai, W., Xiong, H.: Gaussian process regression based prediction for lossless image coding. In: Proceedings of Data Compression Conference, Snowbird, Utah. USA, March 2014, pp. 93–102 (2014)
8. Dai, W., Xiong, H., Wang, J., Zheng, Y.F.: Large discriminative structured set prediction modeling with max-margin Markov network for lossless image coding. IEEE Trans. Image Proces. 23(2), 541–554 (2014)
9. Ulacha, G., Stasiński, R.: Enhanced lossless image coding methods based on adaptive predictors. In: Proceedings of the International Conference on Systems. Signals and Image Processing IWSSIP 2010, Brazil, 17–19 June 2010, pp. 312–315 (2010)
10. Hashidume, Y., Morikawa, Y.: Lossless image coding based on minimum mean absolute error predictors. In: Proceedings of SICE Annual Conference 2007, Kagawa University, Japan, 17–20 September 2007, pp. 2832–2836 (2007)
11. Ulacha, G., Stasiński, R.: Paths to future image lossless coding. In: Proceedings of 54th International Symposium - ELMAR-2012, Zadar, Croatia, 12–14 September 2012, pp. 63–66 (2012)
12. Ulacha, G., Stasiński, R.: Three-Stage OLS method for improved lossless image coding. In: International Conference on Systems. Signals and Image Processing (IWSSIP), Maribor, Slovenia, 20–22 June 2018, pp. 1–4 (2018)
13. Sayood, K.: Introduction to Data Compression, 5th edn. Morgan Kaufmann Publication /Elsevier Inc., Cambridge (2018)
14. Deng, G., Ye, H., Marusic, S., Tay, D.: A method for predictive order adaptation based on model averaging. In: Proceedings IEEE International Conference on Image Processing ICIP 2003, Barcelona, Catalonia, Spain, 14–17 September 2003, vol. 2, pp. 189–192 (2003)
15. Wu, X., Zhai, G., Yang, X., Zhang, W.: Adaptive sequential prediction of multidimensional signals with applications to lossless image coding. IEEE Trans. Image Proces. 20(1), 36–42 (2011)
16. Salomon, D.: Data Compression. The Complete Reference, 4th edn. Springer, New York (2006). https://doi.org/10.1007/978-1-84628-603-2
17. Sugiura, R., Kamamoto, Y., Harada, N., Moriya, T.: Optimal Golomb-rice code extension for lossless coding of low-entropy exponentially distributed sources. IEEE Trans. Inf. Theor. 64(4), 3153–3161 (2018)
18. Meyer, B., Tischer, P.: GLICBAWLS - grey level image compression by adaptive weighted least squares. In: Proceedings of Data Compression Conference 2001, Snowbird, Utah, p. 503 (2001)
19. Kau, L.-J., Lin, Y.-P., Lin, C.-T.: Lossless image coding using adaptive. switching algorithm with automatic fuzzy context modelling. In: IEEE Proceeding Vision. Image and Signal Processing, October 2006, vol. 153, no. 5, pp. 684–694 (2006)

20. Kau, L.-J., Lin, Y.-P.: Least squares-adapted edge-look-ahead prediction with run-length encodings for lossless compression of images. In: Proceedings of International Conference on Acoustics. Speech and Signal Processing ICASSP 2008, Las Vegas, Nevada, USA, 31 March–4 April 2008, pp. 1185–1188 (2008)
21. Meyer, B., Tischer, P.: TMW – a new method for lossless image compression. In: Proceedings of International Picture Coding Symposium (PCS97), Germany, Berlin, September 1997, pp. 533–538 (1997)
22. Hsieh, F.-Y., Wang, C.-M., Lee, C.-C., Fan, K.-C.: A lossless image coder integrating predictors and block-adaptive prediction. J. Inf. Sci. Eng. 24(5), 1579–1591 (2008)

MHEF-TripNet: Mixed Triplet Loss with Hard Example Feedback Network for Image Retrieval

Xuebin Yang[1], Shouhong Wan[1,2(✉)], Peiquan Jin[1,2], Chang Zou[1], and Xingyue Li[1]

[1] School of Computer Science and Technology,
University of Science and Technology of China, Hefei 230027, China
yangxb@mail.ustc.edu.cn
[2] Key Laboratory of Electromagnetic Space Information,
Chinese Academy of Science, Hefei 230027, China

Abstract. Image retrieval has made significant advances, fueled mainly by deep convolutional neural networks, but their training procedure is not efficient enough. Because of the large imbalance between easy examples and hard examples, networks lack direct guidance information from hard examples. In this paper, we solve the problem by developing an effective and efficient method, called mixed triplet loss with hard example feedback network (MHEF-TripNet). Since the proportion of hard examples is small, a sample selection probability matrix is introduced to select hard examples, which assists a network to focus more on enlarging the gap between the confusing categories in triplet loss. And it will be adjusted according to the feedback of test results after each training iteration. Furthermore, a mixed triplet loss function is proposed, which combines triplet loss with category loss to take advantage of association information between images and category information. The effectiveness of MHEF-TripNet is confirmed by experimentation on UC Merced Land Use and Kdelab Airplane datasets. Compared with previous image retrieval approaches, our approach obtains superior performance.

Keywords: Triplet loss · Probability matrix of sample selection · Image retrieval

1 Introduction

Image retrieval is one of the greatly worthwhile computer vision tasks. It pays more attention to the image similarity, and is suitable for retrieving images from a massive image database, Content based Image Retrieval (CBIR) [5–7] is the mainstream method for image retrieval at present. The idea of CBIR is as follows. First, extract features from the query image. After that, use features to calculate the similarity between the query images and the images in database. And then sort the images in descending order by similarity. Finally, regard the result as the feedback to further improve the performance of feature extraction. Particularly, feature extraction and

Y. Zhao et al. (Eds.): ICIG 2019, LNCS 11903, pp. 35–46, 2019.
https://doi.org/10.1007/978-3-030-34113-8_4

similarity measurement are two important processes in CBIR, which determine the accuracy and efficiency of image retrieval methods.

CBIR approaches are often trained through a reduction that converts image retrieval into an image classification problem, and then take an intermediate bottleneck layer as extracted feature representation used to retrieving images. Although classification loss could increase the difference between classes, it cannot narrow the inner-class distance effectively. To solve this dilemma, FaceNet [1] proposes a novel triplet loss which calculates loss by learning a Euclidean embedding, it makes a great progress especially in face recognition. This method uses the squared L2 distance according to the image similarity: the larger the distance between two images, the less the similarity. The key of the method is to enlarge the distance between the images from different categories and narrow the distance between the images from the same category. However, new problem has arisen: the training set is distinguished by a large imbalance between easy examples and hard examples, where easy examples are the images with distinguishable deep features from different categories, while hard examples are the images with similar deep features from confusing categories.

Many studies [2, 3] have shown that hard examples (samples which are difficult to be distinguished by models) are beneficial to network convergence, since network frequent misclassify hard examples, which propagates back more loss. Thus, mining hard examples play an important role in model training. However, [1] selects training dataset in a random way, which might be inefficient to get hard examples, because the proportion of hard examples is small. The straightforward way to choose hard examples is to traverse the entire dataset, but the complexity of this method is too high to be directly applied. To tackle this issue, Hermans et al. [4] propose a variant triplet loss that provides a new hard examples selection method, which select hard examples by traversing a batch of data. Although it reduces the randomness of sample selection, it only considers the images in each batch and the complexity of this method is still too high. Wherefore mining hard examples is still a challenge for network training in triplet loss. In addition, triplet loss only utilizes the associated information between images, which does not make full use of the classification information.

To circumvent the limitations embedded in the existing triplet loss networks, we propose a novel network for image retrieval called mixed triplet loss with hard examples feedback network (MHEF-TripNet). Different from triplet networks, our method introduces a sample selection probability matrix to select hard examples. The matrix is used to select a different category that has the maximum similarity of the known category. After each iteration, we adjust the sample selection probability matrix according to the feedback of test results, and then the matrix can select hard examples more accurately. Also, we propose a mixed loss function [17], which combines triplet loss with category loss to extract discriminative features. The two main contributions of proposed method can be summarized as follows.

- A probability matrix of sample selection is introduced to choose hard example pairs. Additionally, the probability matrix will be updated according to the test results of the model after each iteration.

- The proposed mixed triple loss takes advantage of association information between images and category information simultaneously, so that more distinctive features can be learned.

The remainder of this paper is organized as follows: we summarize the related work of image retrieval in Sect. 2. The formulation of proposed MHEF-TripNet is described in Sect. 3. Section 4 shows our experimental results and their corresponding analysis. At last, we give the conclusion of this work in Sect. 5.

2 Related Work

Image feature extraction is very important for image retrieval. The ability of extracting features has made significant advances riding on the wave of convolutional neural network (CNN), which has achieved great success in target recognition [8], target detection, image segmentation [9], natural language understanding [10] and other fields. Previous image retrieval approaches based on deep networks use a classification layer [11–13] trained over a set of known categories and then take an intermediate bottleneck layer as a representation used to retrieving images. The downsides of this approach are its indirectness and its inefficiency: the bottleneck representation cannot generalize well to new categories. Triplet loss is proposed to solve this dilemma.

Triplet loss [1] is a metric learning method which is first introduced by Google along with FaceNet. The sketch of triple loss learning target is illustrated in Fig. 1. Triplet consists of the following components: a sample which is randomly selected from the training set is regarded as an anchor, other two samples which have the same class as the anchor denotes a positive and with different class represents a negative. Before training, the relationship between the three may be similar to the left part of the figure, where the negative is closer to the anchor than the positive. After training, the positive becomes much closer to the anchor, like the right part of the figure. In a word, the triplet loss aims to narrow the distance between an anchor and a positive and enlarge the distance between the anchor and a negative. The traditional triplet model randomly selects three samples from the training set, which is simple but too random. The key point in triple training is to find out the hard triplets, that is, an anchor together with a remote positive (hard positive) and a close negative (hard negative). Since the proportion of hard triplets is low, randomly selection might not effectively get the hard triplet, causing poor performance.

Hermans et al. [4] propose a variant of triplet loss that provides a new hard examples selection based on batch training. The main idea of this method is to select hard triplet from batches. First, randomly select P classes, and then randomly select K images from each class, thus forming a batch of $P * K$ images. As for each sample in the batch, a selected triplet can be consisted of the sample and its hardest negative and hardest positive within the batch. In this way, the selection randomness of the traditional method can be reduced to a certain extent, making it more conducive to model training. Although this approach avoids the randomness of triple sampling to a certain extent, it only enlarges the sampling range locally, and cannot guarantee that the difficult sample pair is optimal.

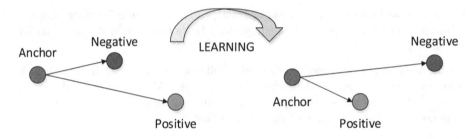

Fig. 1. Sketch of triple loss learning target

3   MHEF-TripNet

We propose MHEF-TripNet for effective image retrieval. We argue that single triplet loss is inefficient and the current way of triple sampling is suboptimal. Our method introduces a sample selection probability matrix to select hard examples and a mixed loss function combines triplet loss with category loss to extract discriminative features.

The framework of the proposed method is shown in Fig. 2, and the network is called MHEF-TripNet. In the training stage, similar to the traditional triple training, three images are transmitted at the same time, but the selection of the three images is different. Specifically, an image is randomly selected from the training data as an anchor. The category of the positive is consistent with the anchor, while the category of the negative is selected according to the probability matrix. The probability matrix is an $N \times N$ matrix, where N denotes the number of categories, the element V_{ij} denotes the probability of choosing j as a category of a negative when the anchor category is i. And each row adds up to 1. The selected three images are simultaneously fed into the same convolution neural network for feature extraction. After that, the network parameters are optimized by the mixed loss which consists of triplet loss and classification loss.

In order to better demonstrate the experimental results of our method, Table 1 presents details of a simple network architecture which is the backbone of MHEF-TripNet.

3.1   Sample Selection Probability Matrix

Although there exist some methods for hard example sampling in recent years, most of these methods focus on expanding the sampling range locally which only partly improve the sampling performance. Instead, in this paper, the selection is guided by f sample selection probability matrix globally to get hard examples with high generalization and pertinent. The training set and validation set are regarded as the input, while the network parameters for feature extraction are considered as the output.

Firstly, the images are preprocessed, including size clipping and normalization. In addition, the sample selection probability matrix is initialized as follows:

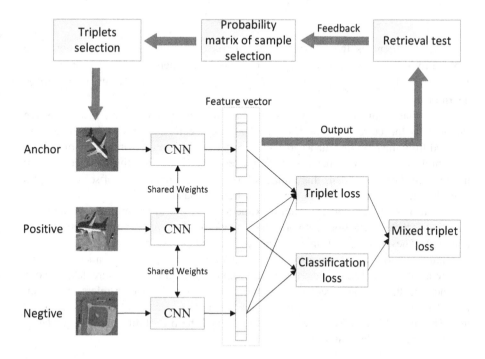

Fig. 2. The framework of MHEF-TripNet

Table 1. Network architecture: the backbone of MHEF-TripNet.

Layer name	Input size	Kernel	Stride	Padding	Output size
Conv_1	$128 \times 128 \times 3$	4×4	2	1	$64 \times 64 \times 32$
BN_1	$64 \times 64 \times 32$	–	–	–	$64 \times 64 \times 32$
Conv_2	$64 \times 64 \times 32$	4×4	2	1	$32 \times 32 \times 64$
BN_2	$32 \times 32 \times 64$	–	–	–	$32 \times 32 \times 64$
Conv_3	$32 \times 32 \times 64$	4×4	2	1	$16 \times 16 \times 128$
BN_3	$16 \times 16 \times 128$	–	–	–	$16 \times 16 \times 128$
Conv_4	$16 \times 16 \times 128$	4×4	2	1	$8 \times 8 \times 256$
BN_4	$8 \times 8 \times 256$	–	–	–	$8 \times 8 \times 256$
Conv_5	$8 \times 8 \times 256$	4×4	2	1	$4 \times 4 \times 512$
BN_5	$4 \times 4 \times 512$	–	–	–	$4 \times 4 \times 512$
Conv_6	$4 \times 4 \times 512$	4×4	2	1	$1 \times 1 \times 1024$
BN_6	$1 \times 1 \times 1024$	–	–	–	$1 \times 1 \times 1024$
Feature layer	$1 \times 1 \times 1024$	1×1	1	0	128
Classification layer	128	1×1	1	0	N

$$\begin{bmatrix} 0 & \frac{1}{N-1} & \cdots & \frac{1}{N-1} \\ \frac{1}{N-1} & 0 & \cdots & \frac{1}{N-1} \\ \cdots & \cdots & 0 & \cdots \\ \frac{1}{N-1} & \cdots & \cdots & 0 \end{bmatrix} \tag{1}$$

Where N denotes the number of categories of training images, V_{ij} denotes the probability of choosing j as a category of a negative when the anchor category is i. $V_{ii} = 0$, $i \in (1, N)$, $V_{ij} = \frac{1}{N-1}$, $i \neq j$, $i,j \in (1, N)$, since the probability is uniformly distributed.

After that is the iterative process of training. In each iteration, the triples are sampled by the current probability matrix. More specifically, a sample is randomly selected from the training data as an anchor. Suppose the category of the anchor is i, the probability of sampling a negative with j category is V_{ij}. A positive is selected from images with i category. This three images form a triple. The number of selected triples in each iteration is consistent to the size of training batch.

The triples are fed into the feature extraction network to optimize the parameters, and the feature extraction network parameters of the current iteration times are obtained. The training set image features are extracted from the current feature extraction network as a temporary feature database. For the verification set, the same feature is extracted. The image retrieval tests are carried out on the feature database one by one, and the relevant feedback data are counted. Feedback data refers to the statistical results of the misclassification of each image in this round of image retrieval test. The result of misclassification is analyzed and the probability matrix is updated. The updated formula is as follows:

$$V_{ij} = P(W) \times \frac{Num_j}{M}, i \neq j$$
$$V_{io} = \frac{P(R)}{N-1-M}, i \neq o, j \neq o \tag{2}$$

Where N denotes the number of categories of training images, i denotes the category of the current test sample, M denotes the number of categories which is result sequence retrieval, $P(R)$ is the accuracy, $P(W)$ is the error, Num_j represents the number of images which category is j.

Take a test sample belonging to i category as example, suppose there are W images being misclassified among K images from two categories ($M = 2$), and W_1 images belong to the p category, W_2 images belong to the q category ($W = W_1 + W_2$). The probability of correct classification is $P(R) = \frac{K-W}{K}$, and the probability of misclassification is $P(W) = \frac{W}{K}$, where p and q account for $\frac{W_1}{W}$ and $\frac{W_2}{W}$, respectively. Consequently, the probability matrix is updated as follows:

$$V_{ip} = P(W) \times \frac{W_1}{W}$$
$$V_{iq} = P(W) \times \frac{W_2}{W}$$
$$V_{io} = \frac{P(R)}{N-1-2} \tag{3}$$

The total probability is:

$$\begin{aligned} Total &= V_{ip} + V_{iq} + V_{io} \times (N - 1 - 2) \\ &= P(W) + P(R) \\ &= 1 \end{aligned} \qquad (4)$$

Each modification of the probability matrix is a positive feedback of the test results. In this way, MHEF-TripNet focuses more on enlarge the gap between the confusing categories, thus improve the distinction of features, and finally improves the accuracy of image retrieval.

3.2 Mixed Triplet Loss

After extracting image features, the traditional triple method iteratively updates the network parameters by using the loss of distance comparison between feature vectors. This method is suitable for the situation that the number of image categories is constantly changing, or the training data does not contain the category label information, only whether the two images belong to the same category of comparative information. For most of image datasets, the number of image categories is fixed, and all of them have image label information. Therefore, MHEF-TripNet considers to integrate the category loss of images into the training process of the network, and combines the comparative loss to form a hybrid loss training network.

The classification loss is defined as follows:

$$C_{loss} = J(p) + J(n) \qquad (5)$$

Where J denotes softmax loss, p and n represent the features of the positive and the negative, respectively. And the mixed loss is defined as follows:

$$M_{loss} = \alpha T_{loss} + \rho C_{loss} \qquad (6)$$

Where T_{loss} and C_{loss} denote triplet loss and classification loss, respectively. α, ρ are the corresponding weights. Particularly, in order to balance this two losses, we set $\alpha = 2.0$, $\beta = 1.0$, since the classification loss consists of two parts of softmax loss.

4 Experiments and Analysis

To evaluate the performance of MHEF-TripNet, we design a set of image retrieval experiments on two datasets: UC Merced Land Use and Kdelab Airplane. UC Merced Land Use dataset is land use image dataset meant for research purposes. It is a remote sensing dataset provide by [14] and include 21 classes. Kdelab Airplane dataset is created by our laboratory focus on retrieval airplane, which contains 11 different airplane types. We choose mean average precision (mAP), top 5 precision (P@5), top 10 precision (P@10), top 50 precision (P@50) and 100 precision (P@100) as evaluation criteria. In our retrieval results tables, TripNet denotes the image retrieval network based on triplet loss, M-TripNet denotes the TripNet with mixed triplet loss, HEF-TripNet denotes the TripNet with Hard Example Feedback and MHEF-TripNet represents the combination of the last two. The parameters of the training stage are set as follows: batch size is 64, iteration number is 100, learning rate is 10^{-4}.

4.1   Retrieval Results on UC Merced Land Use

The UC Merced Land Use is one of the most widely used remote sensing image datasets in the field of remote sensing. The dataset contains 2100 images, covering 21 different remote sensing scene categories, each with 100 images. The size of each image is 256 * 256. Figure 3 shows sample images of the dataset. The experiment is divided into two parts. The first part is the comparison with methods based on deep networks use a classification layer. The second part is ablation experiments based on the method proposed in this paper.

Fig. 3. Sample images of UC Merced Land Use dataset

To further evaluate the power of these methods, we have fine-tuned the networks to the remote sensing domain by using 80% of AID [16] dataset as training set. AID is a remote sensing dataset which is made of aerial image dataset collected from Google Earth imagery. It has a number of 10000 images within 30 classes and about 200 to 400 samples of size 600 * 600 in each class. Afterwards we use 100% of the UC Merced Land Use dataset as the test set. The experimental results are shown in Table 2. VGG16, VGG19, GoogleNet, ResNet-50, ResNet-101, and ResNet-152 are all experimental data from the [15] which is a summary of CBIR in remote sensing images. After comparative analysis, MHEF-TripNet proposed in this paper is the best in the most evaluation criteria, and the mAP is about 1.0% higher than other method. This indicates that MHEF-TripNet extracts discriminative features effectively on the UC Merced Land Use dataset.

Table 2. UC Merced Land Use dataset retrieval results of different approaches

Algorithm	mAP(%)	P@5(%)	P@10(%)	P@50(%)	P@100(%)
VGG16 [15]	52.46	83.91	78.34	61.38	49.78
VGG19 [15]	51.95	82.84	77.60	60.69	49.16
GoogleNet [15]	55.86	85.36	80.96	64.71	52.36
ResNet-50 [15]	56.57	88.26	84.00	65.92	52.69
ResNet-101 [15]	56.63	88.49	83.53	65.69	52.83
ResNet-152 [15]	56.03	88.42	83.08	64.65	52.50
TripNet [1]	57.04	88.95	84.58	66.06	53.09
M-TripNet	59.93	**90.24**	84.61	67.13	54.97
HEF-TripNet	58.31	89.05	84.43	66.73	54.23
MHEF-TripNet	**60.88**	89.42	**84.61**	**67.57**	**55.82**

The second part of the experiment used 80% of the UC Merced Land Use data as the training set and 20% of the UC Merced Land Use data as the test set. The experimental results are shown in Table 3.

Table 3. UC Merced Land Use test retrieval results of ablation experiments

Algorithm	mAP(%)	P@5(%)	P@10(%)	P@50(%)
TripNet [1]	44.70	51.48	51.48	20.09
M-TripNet	48.05	56.76	56.26	22.20
HEF-TripNet	46.60	53.67	52.86	20.67
MHEF-TripNet	**49.31**	**57.52**	**56.31**	**22.21**

The results of three modified algorithms are analyzed as follows:

1. M-TripNet: compared with TripNet, the mAP of M-TripNet is about 3% higher, and the accuracy of the first 5 and 10 are about 5% higher. The result indicates that M-TripNet performs better while training, and the additional label information in M-Triplet help to extract more robust features from remote sensing images.
2. HEF-TripNet: the mAP of HEF-TripNet is about 2% higher than that of TripNet. The P@5 and P@10 are about 2% and 1% higher than TripNet, respectively. It shows that the feedback plays a role in guiding feature extraction network to train hard examples by enlarge the distance of negative samples which are difficult to distinguish, hence improving the distinction of features.
3. MHEF-TripNet: compared to TripNet, the mAP of MHEF-TripNet is about 4.6% higher. P@5 and P@10 are about 6% and 5% higher, respectively. This means that MHEF-TripNet effectively integrates the above two modifications.

4.2   Retrieval Results on UC Merced Land Use

Due to the small number of images in UC Merced Land Use, where only 100 images of each class are available, we cannot measure P@100 in ablation experiments on UC

Merced Land Use dataset. Therefore, ablation experiments on Kdelab Airplane dataset are added. The Kdelab Airplane dataset is created by the Kdelab Laboratory of the University of Science and Technology of China. The dataset contains 2,200 images covering 11 different aircraft types, and 200 images of size 128 * 128 in each class. Figure 4 shows sample images of the dataset. Kdelab Airplane dataset is used to ablation experiments.

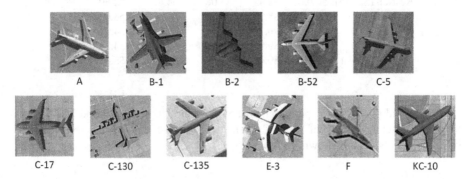

Fig. 4. Sample images of Kdelab Airplane dataset

In this experiment, 80% of the Kdelab Airplane dataset are used as training set and 20% as test set. Since there are 160 training images in each class of the dataset, the overall retrieval performs better than the UC Merced Land Use dataset. The result of retrieval is shown in Table 3 in detail. Comparing the mentioned three algorithms with TripNet, M-TripNet gets 3% higher in mAP, and about 1.5% higher in both P@5 and P@10. As for HEF-TripNet, the mAP is about 1% higher than that of TripNet, and the P@5 and P@10 are about 1.2% and 0.7% higher than TripNet, respectively. Regarding THEF-TripNet, it gets 4.4% higher in mAP, and about 2.2% higher in P@5 as well as in P@10. As can be seen, THEF-TripNet outperforms among other algorithms in all evaluation indicators, which suggests its effectiveness for feature extraction on Kdelab Airplane dataset (Table 4).

Table 4. Kdelab Airplane test retrieval results of ablation experiments

Algorithm	mAP(%)	P@5(%)	P@10(%)	P@50(%)	P@100(%)
TripNet [1]	76.41	79.18	89.00	76.81	74.17
M-TripNet	79.60	80.59	80.48	79.28	78.49
HEF-TripNet	77.44	80.32	79.68	77.81	75.57
MHEF-TripNet	**80.86**	**81.50**	**81.18**	**80.51**	**79.74**

As a result, THEF-TripNet can effectively improve the performance of TripNet in image retrieval. For one thing, the mixed loss not only considers the triplet loss, but also takes the label information of the image into account, which elaborately introduces the label information into the training of the triple. In fact, according to the label information, the cluster center is utilized to make training easier. For another, the feedback-based triple is a process of continuous iteration and adjustment. After each round of training, there is an image retrieval validation. THEF-TripNet evaluates the generalization of the current model, and finds out the hard examples at present, which will be improved pertinently in the next round. Therefore, the model can learn the most discriminative information from the triple, so as to improve the feature availability. Differentiation improves the performance of target retrieval.

5 Conclusion

In this paper, we propose mixed triplet loss with hard example feedback network. The method extracts more discriminative features based on mixed triple loss, focus on the correlation information and category information of images. At the same time, it introduces sample selection probability matrix to select hard triplets according to probability matrix. After each iteration, it adjusts the probability matrix according to the test results of the model, and then improves the effect of difficult sample selection from a global perspective. The experimental results show that this method is superior to the traditional triple method and can effectively improve the accuracy of remote sensing image retrieval.

References

1. Schroff, F., Kalenichenko, D., Philbin, J.: Facenet: a unified embedding for face recognition and clustering. In: Proceedings of the IEEE Conference on Computer Vision and Pattern Recognition, pp. 815–823 (2015)
2. Felzenszwalb, P.F., Girshick, R.B., McAllester, D., et al.: Object detection with discriminatively trained part-based models. IEEE Trans. Pattern Anal. Mach. Intell. **32**(9), 1627–1645 (2010)
3. Shrivastava, A., Gupta, A., Girshick, R.: Training region-based object detectors with online hard example mining. In: Proceedings of the IEEE Conference on Computer Vision and Pattern Recognition, pp. 761–769 (2016)
4. Hermans, A., Beyer, L., Leibe, B.: In defense of the triplet loss for person re-identification. arXiv preprint arXiv:1703.07737 (2017)
5. Smeulders, A.W.M., Worring, M., Santini, S., et al.: Content-based image retrieval at the end of the early years. IEEE Trans. Pattern Anal. Mach. Intell. **12**, 1349–1380 (2000)
6. Rui, Y., Huang, T.S., Ortega, M., et al.: Relevance feedback: a power tool for interactive content-based image retrieval. IEEE Trans. Circuits Syst. Video Technol. **8**(5), 644–655 (1998)
7. Liu, Y., Zhang, D., Lu, G., et al.: A survey of content-based image retrieval with high-level semantics. Pattern Recogn. **40**(1), 262–282 (2007)

8. Krizhevsky, A., Sutskever, I., Hinton, G.E.: Imagenet classification with deep convolutional neural networks. In: Advances in Neural Information Processing Systems, pp. 1097–1105 (2012)

9. Girshick, R., Donahue, J., Darrell, T., et al.: Rich feature hierarchies for accurate object detection and semantic segmentation. In: Proceedings of the IEEE Conference on Computer Vision and Pattern Recognition, pp. 580–587 (2014)

10. Zhang, Y., Wallace, B.: A sensitivity analysis of (and practitioners' guide to) convolutional neural networks for sentence classification. arXiv preprint arXiv:1510.03820 (2015)

11. Sun, Y., Wang, X., Tang, X.: Deeply learned face representations are sparse, selective, and robust. In: Proceedings of the IEEE Conference on Computer Vision and Pattern Recognition, pp. 2892–2900 (2015)

12. Taigman, Y., Yang, M., Ranzato, M.A., et al.: Deepface: closing the gap to human-level performance in face verification. In: Proceedings of the IEEE Conference on Computer Vision and Pattern Recognition, pp. 1701–1708 (2014)

13. Kumar, N.S., Arun, M., Dangi, M.K.: Remote sensing image retrieval using object-based, semantic classifier techniques. Int. J. Inf. Commun. Technol. 13(1), 68–82 (2018)

14. Yang, Y., Newsam, S.: Bag-of-visual-words and spatial extensions for land-use classification. In: Proceedings of the 18th SIGSPATIAL International Conference on Advances in Geographic Information Systems, pp. 270–279. ACM (2010)

15. Napoletano, P.: Visual descriptors for content-based retrieval of remote-sensing images. Int. J. Remote Sens. 39(5), 1343–1376 (2018)

16. Xia, G.S., IEEE, et al.: AID: a benchmark data set for performance evaluation of aerial scene classification. IEEE Trans. Geosc. Remote Sens. 55(7), 3965–3981 (2017)

17. Yan, Y., Wang, X., Yang, X., Bai, X., Liu, W.: Joint classification loss and histogram loss for sketch-based image retrieval. In: ICIG (2017)

Towards Joint Multiply Semantics
Hashing for Visual Search

Yunbo Wang[1,2(✉)] and Zhenan Sun[1,2]

[1] Institute of Automation, Chinese Academy of Sciences, Beijing, China
wang.yuenbo@gmail.com, znsun@nlpr.ia.ac.cn
[2] University of Chinese Academy of Sciences, Beijing 100190, China

Abstract. With the rapid growth of visual data on the web, deep hashing has shown enormous potential in preserving semantic similarity for visual search. Currently, most of the existing hashing methods employ pairwise or triplet-wise constraint to obtain the semantic similarity or relatively similarity among binary codes. However, some potential semantic context cannot be fully exploited, resulting in a suboptimal visual search. In this paper, we propose a novel deep hashing method, termed Joint Multiply Semantics Hashing (JMSH), to learn discriminative yet compact binary codes. In our approach, We jointly learn multiply semantic information to perform feature learning and hash coding. To be specific, the semantic information includes the pairwise semantic similarity between binary codes, the pointwise binary codes semantics and the pointwise visual feature semantics. Meanwhile, three different loss functions are designed to train the JMSH model. Extensive experiments show that the proposed JMSH yields state-of-the-art retrieval performance on representative image retrieval benchmarks.

Keywords: Deep hashing · Binary codes · Multiply semantics · Visual search

1 Introduction

With the explosive growth of image or video on the web, it is highly desirable that the data should be organized and indexed efficiently and accurately. As an approximate nearest neighbor (ANN) search technique, hashing [3,15,24,25] has shown superior potentials for dealing with large-scale visual data, which has received increasing attention in both the academia and industry. Generally, hashing employs a set of hashing functions to transform each data into compact binary codes, meanwhile retaining the semantic similarity of original data. Due to the encouraging efficiency in both search speed and storage [3,22], more and more hashing methods are proposed for visual retrieval tasks recently [2,26,29–31].

Generally, hashing methods could be divided into two main categories based on the type of hash functions: data-independent hashing [3,10,20] and data-dependent hashing (also known as learning-based hashing) [8,23,29]. Data-independent hashing methods always require long codes to achieve satisfying

© Springer Nature Switzerland AG 2019
Y. Zhao et al. (Eds.): ICIG 2019, LNCS 11903, pp. 47–58, 2019.
https://doi.org/10.1007/978-3-030-34113-8_5

performance, while data-dependent hashing methods are prone to learning more compact binary codes by utilizing a batch of training data. In this paper, we focus on learning-based hashing with the application in visual search [21].

A fruitful of learning-based hashing methods have been designed for efficient ANN search, where the efficiency comes from the compact binary codes that are orders of magnitude smaller than high-dimensional feature descriptors. Based on the generated binary codes, the similarity between the query and the database can be efficiently computed. Meanwhile, the storage cost can be distinctly decreased. According to whether the supervision information is available, the learning-based hashing can be roughly grouped into unsupervised and supervised approaches. In contrast to unsupervised hashing [4,15,17,27] where no supervision information is provided, supervised hashing mainly leverages supervision information (e.g., pointwise semantic labels, pairwise similarity affinity) to perform hash learning. The supervised approaches have obtained better accuracy in real-world visual search. Some representative works include Minimal Loss Hashing [19], Supervised Discrete Hashing [22], Fast Supervised Discrete Hashing [18]. Recently, some approaches [2,13,29,32,33] have shown that convolutional neural network (CNN) [6,9] can be used as nonlinear hash functions to learn end-to-end feature representations and binary codes, achieving state-of-the-art results on public datasets.

The first proposed deep hashing work is Convolutional Neural Network Hashing (CNNH) [28], which adopts the well-known architecture in [9] to learn discriminative and compact binary codes with a pairwise constraint. CNNH consists of two stages to learn the feature representations and binary codes. Nevertheless, the feature representations cannot make feedback to hash coding and it cannot fully show the efficiency of CNN in hash learning. On the basis of CNNH, Network In Network Hashing (DNNH) [11] integrates image representations and hash coding in a unified framework. Besides, DNNH employs a triplet-based ranking constraint to maximize the margin between a similar pair and dissimilar pair, and it designs a divide-and-encode module to reduce the redundancy among binary codes. Furthermore, Deep Hashing Network (DHN) [33] is a representative pairwise deep hashing work in a unified framework. It employs a cross-entropy loss to enforce similar(dissimilar) pairs to have small(large) hamming distance and formally controls the pointwise quantization error by a designed smooth surrogate of the l_1-norm. To better control quantization error, HashNet [1] proposes a continuous scale strategy to approximately approach the discrete binary codes, and takes into consideration class imbalance to obtain small(large) hamming distance between data pair. DPH [2] also takes into consideration class imbalance for supervised hashing, and integrates the prior information into getting binary codes. Other typical deep hashing methods can be found in [2,12,15,16].

Among these methods above, they generally construct data pairs' similarity affinity as the ground truth for supervised hash learning. Specifically, the similarity is defined as 1 if two samples share at least one label information, and otherwise −1, then they employ the defined similarity affinity to obtain similarity-preserving binary codes in Hamming space. However, the defined similarity affinity fails to employ the high-level semantic information offered by label information, and the generated binary codes cannot show the high-level semantics. In addition, although existing hashing works perform feature learning and hash coding in an end-to-end way, they little make effort about extracting discriminative feature, as well as the effect on binary codes.

In this paper, we propose a joint multiply semantics hashing approach to address the above challenges. Specifically, we jointly learn three semantic properties to generate discriminative yet compact binary codes, including preserving the semantic similarity between a pair of binary codes, guaranteeing the pointwise codes' high-level semantics and learning the semantic visual feature.

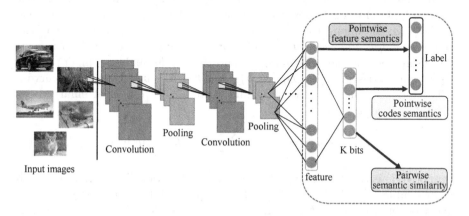

Fig. 1. An overview of the proposed deep hashing termed JMSH, which accepts image pairs as its input. In this framework, The AlexNet network is employed for extracting image feature, followed by a hashing layer with K neural units, which transforms the feature into K-bit binary codes. For each pair of binary codes, we utilize their similarity affinity to preserve the semantic similarity in Hamming space. Besides, we attempt to employ the label information to exploit the pointwise codes and feature semantic property.

2   Joint Multiply Semantics Hashing

Learning-based hashing has become an important research topic in multimedia retrieval, which trades off efficacy from efficiency. In this section, we will introduce our proposed joint multiply semantics hashing approach. The framework of the JMSH is shown in Fig. 1, which accepts paired images as the input and processes them through the deep feature learning and hash coding. In this framework, we learn multiple semantic properties, including the pairwise codes semantic similarity, the pointwise codes semantics and the pointwise feature semantics.

2.1   Problem Formulation

Given a training set of N points $\boldsymbol{I} = \{\boldsymbol{I}_i\}_{i=1}^N$, the goal of learning-based hashing is to learn a set of hashing functions to encode each data point $\boldsymbol{I}_i$ into a compact K-bit binary code $\boldsymbol{B} = \{\boldsymbol{b}_i\}^{N \times K}$, $\boldsymbol{b}_i \in \{-1,1\}^K$. The corresponding label matrix is denoted as $T = \{\boldsymbol{t}_i\}_i^N \in R^{N \times C}$ and C denotes the number of classes. The term $\boldsymbol{t}_{im}$ is the m-th element of $\boldsymbol{t}_i$ and $\boldsymbol{t}_{im} = 1$ if $\boldsymbol{I}_i$ is from class m, and otherwise $\boldsymbol{t}_{im} = 0$. Then, existing hashing generally denotes the paired similarity $s_{ij} = 1$ if two samples share at least one class label, and otherwise $s_{ij} = -1$ [23].

For training sample pairs $\{(I_i, I_j, s_{ij}), s_{ij} \in \boldsymbol{S}\}$, the discrete binary codes should preserve their similarity in Hamming space. Although several different objective functions can be leveraged to achieve this goal, the widely-used one is to leverage the inner product of two binary codes [2,23] to approximate the discrete semantic similarity. Specifically, for a pair of codes $\boldsymbol{b}_i$ and $\boldsymbol{b}_j$, the close relationship between their Hamming distance $D_H(\boldsymbol{b}_i, \boldsymbol{b}_i)$ and their inner product $\boldsymbol{b}_i^T \cdot \boldsymbol{b}_j$ can be described as: $D_H(\boldsymbol{b}_i, \boldsymbol{b}_j) = \frac{1}{2}(k - \boldsymbol{b}_i^T \cdot \boldsymbol{b}_j)$. Given the pairwise similarity relationship S_{ij}, the maximum posterior estimation of binary codes can be described as:

$$p(\boldsymbol{B}|\boldsymbol{S}) \propto p(\boldsymbol{S}|\boldsymbol{B})p(\boldsymbol{B}) = \sum_{s_{ij}} p(s_{ij}|(\boldsymbol{b}_i, \boldsymbol{b}_j))p(\boldsymbol{b}_i, \boldsymbol{b}_j), \qquad (1)$$

where $p(\boldsymbol{S}|\boldsymbol{B})$ is the likelihood function; $p(\boldsymbol{B})$ is the prior distribution. For each pair of sample, $p(s_{ij}|\boldsymbol{b}_i, \boldsymbol{b}_j)$ is the conditional probability of similarity s_{ij} given a pairwise binary codes $(\boldsymbol{b}_i, \boldsymbol{b}_j)$. In particular, $p(s_{ij}|\boldsymbol{b}_i, \boldsymbol{b}_j)$ can be defined as follows:

$$p(s_{ij}|\boldsymbol{b}_i, \boldsymbol{b}_j) = \begin{cases} \sigma(\theta_{ij}), & s_{ij} = 1 \\ 1 - \sigma(\theta_{ij}), & s_{ij} = 0 \end{cases} \qquad (2)$$

where $\sigma(x) = 1/(1+e^{-x})$ is the $sigmiod(\cdot)$ function; $\theta_{ij} = \eta \boldsymbol{b}_i^T \cdot \boldsymbol{b}_j$, and η is used to balance the saturation of $\sigma(x)$ in terms of different length of binary codes [1]. We can observe that the meaning of Eq. 2 is highly consistent with the Hamming distance $d_H(\boldsymbol{b}_i, \boldsymbol{b}_j)$.

2.2   The Pairwise Semantic Similarity

Since deep learning [10] based hashing methods have shown superior performance over the traditional handcrafted feature [2], we construct an end-to-end framework based on Convolutional Neural Network to simultaneously perform feature learning and hash coding. In order to have a fair comparison with other deep hashing methods, we choose the widely-used AlexNet [10] as our basic network. The CNN model consists of 5 convolutional layers and 2 fully connected layers for extracting image feature $\boldsymbol{f}_i$. The hashing layer followed the connected layers is designed to encode $\boldsymbol{f}_i$ into binary codes $\boldsymbol{b}_i$. Specifically, the binary codes can be obtained by following formula:

$$\boldsymbol{b}_i = sign(\boldsymbol{W}_h \cdot \boldsymbol{f}_i), \qquad (3)$$

where $\boldsymbol{W}_h$ is the weight of hashing layer and we omit its bias term for simplicity; $sign(\cdot)$ is the sign function, $sign(x) = 1$ if $x > 0$, and otherwise $sign(x) = -1$.

By taking the negative log-likelihood of the Eq. 2, we can get the following optimization problem:

$$min \sum_{s_{ij}} (log(1 + e^{\theta_{ij}}) - s_{ij}\theta_{ij}), \tag{4}$$

It is easy to find that the above optimization problem can make the Hamming distance between two similar points as small as possible, and simultaneously make the Hamming distance between two dissimilar points as large as possible. This exactly matches the goal of supervised hashing with pairwise labels.

Due to the binary discrete constraint $\boldsymbol{b}_i \in \{-1, 1\}^K$, it is hard to optimize the Eq. 4. As in existing hashing methods [16,33], continuous relaxation is applied to the binary constraints. Meanwhile, we resort to l_2 regularizer to narrow the gap between the relaxation term and its corresponding binary codes:

$$min \, \mathcal{L}_{pair} = \sum_{s_{ij}} (log(1 + e^{\Omega_{ij}}) - s_{ij}\Omega_{ij}) + \frac{\alpha}{2} \sum_{i}^{N} ||\boldsymbol{h}_i - \boldsymbol{b}_i||^2 + \frac{1}{2}||\boldsymbol{W}_h||_F^2, \tag{5}$$

where $\boldsymbol{h}_i = \boldsymbol{W}_h \boldsymbol{f}_i$; $\Omega_{ij} = \eta \boldsymbol{h}_i^T \cdot \boldsymbol{h}_j$; $||\cdot||_F$ denotes the Frobenius norm.

2.3 The Pointwise Semantics

The label information offers rich high-level semantics of a raw image. The above similarity learning only employs the course similarity affinity for hash coding, resulting in the generated binary codes failing to show the rich semantic property of an image. Existing hashing methods make less research to exploit the relationship between the generated binary codes and label information.

To obtain specific-semantics binary codes, we attempt to reconstruct the label information by the generated binary codes:

$$min \, \mathcal{L}_b = \frac{1}{2} \sum_{i}^{N} ||\boldsymbol{W}_c \boldsymbol{b}_i - \boldsymbol{t}_i||_2^2 + \frac{1}{2}||\boldsymbol{W}_c||_F^2, \tag{6}$$

where $\boldsymbol{W}_c$ is a line projection matrix, and $\boldsymbol{W}_c \boldsymbol{b}_i$ denotes the reconstructed label information. Due to $\boldsymbol{t}_i \in \{0, 1\}^C$, we input the $\boldsymbol{W}_c \boldsymbol{b}_i$ into the $sigmiod(\cdot)$ function to obtain approximated 0 or 1.

By Eq. 6, we establish a non-linear relationship to link the binary codes and its corresponding label information, and the final binary codes can show the high-level semantic property of an image.

Since the proposed hashing method performs feature extracting and hash coding in an end-to-end way, the discriminative ability of feature inevitably makes an effect on the quality of hash coding. Although Most of existing deep hashing approaches simultaneously perform feature extracting and hash coding in a unified framework, they do nothing on how to extracting discriminative feature. As our above analysis, the image label provides supervised information for mining semantic structures in images.

In this paper, in order to make the feature have more discriminative power, we intentionally build a semantic relationship between feature representations and its label information:

$$min \ \mathcal{L}_f = \frac{1}{2}\sum_i^N ||\boldsymbol{W}_f\boldsymbol{f}_i - \boldsymbol{t}_i||^2 + \frac{1}{2}||\boldsymbol{W}_f||_F^2, \qquad (7)$$

where the $\boldsymbol{W}_f$ is a line projection matrix, and $\boldsymbol{W}_f\boldsymbol{f}_i$ denotes the predicted label information. Noting that we input $\boldsymbol{W}_f\boldsymbol{f}_i$ into the $sigmiod(\cdot)$ to obtain approximated 0 or 1. By the Eq. 7, the feature is characteristic of the semantic property of an image, and the final feature representations have more discriminative power.

2.4   Joint Optimization

The proposed framework simultaneously perform feature learning and hash coding, the final objective of the proposed JMSH is formulated as follow:

$$
\begin{aligned}
min \ &\mathcal{L}_{pair} + \beta_1 \mathcal{L}_b + \beta_2 \mathcal{L}_f \\
&= \sum_{s_{ij}} (log(1 + e^{\Omega_{ij}}) - s_{ij}\Omega_{ij}) + \frac{\alpha}{2}\sum_i^N ||\boldsymbol{h}_i - \boldsymbol{b}_i||^2 + \frac{1}{2}||\boldsymbol{W}_h||_F^2 \\
&+ \frac{\beta_1}{2}(\sum_i^N ||\boldsymbol{W}_c\boldsymbol{h}_i - \boldsymbol{t}_i||^2 + ||\boldsymbol{W}_c||_F^2) + \frac{\beta_2}{2}(\sum_i^N ||\boldsymbol{W}_f\boldsymbol{f}_i - \boldsymbol{t}_i||^2 + ||\boldsymbol{W}_f||_F^2).
\end{aligned}
$$
$$(8)$$

By the above formula, we can obtain the discriminative yet compact binary code in terms of learning multiple semantic properties. Learning a discriminative feature is conducive to obtain compact binary codes, and learning specific-semantics binary codes would improve the quality of binary codes. In Optimization, we adopt the stochastic gradient descent algorithm to update all these above parameters until convergence.

3   Experiments and Analysis

To evaluate the effectiveness of the proposed JMSH, extensive experiments are conducted on two benchmarks against the state-of-the-art hashing methods.

3.1   Datasets

CIFAR-10 is a benchmark image dataset for similarity retrieval, consisting of 60,000 color images. Each image belongs to one of the ten categories, and the size of each image is 32×32. Following the setting in [33], we sample 100 images per

class as the query set. For the unsupervised methods, all the rest of the images are used as the training set. For the supervised methods, 5,000 images (500 images per class) are further selected from the rest of the images for training.
NUS-WIDE is a public web image dataset downloaded from Flickr.com, and it contains nearly 270,000 images with one or multiple labels of 81 semantic concepts. Following the setting in HashNet [1], the subset of 195,834 images that are associated with the 21 most frequent concepts are used, where each concept consists of at least 5,000 images. We sample 100 images per class as the query set. For the unsupervised methods, all the rest of the images are used for training. For the supervised methods, 500 images per class are further selected from the rest images for training.

3.2 Experimental Setting and Protocols

As in standard evaluation protocol in [1,2,16], the similarity information for hash learning and for ground-truth evaluation is based on image class labels: if images i and j share at least one label, they are similar and $s_{ij} = 1$; otherwise, they are dissimilar and $s_{ij} = 0$. In addition, to avoid the effect caused by a class-imbalance problem between similar and dissimilar similarity information, we empirically set the weight of the similar pair as the ratio between the number of dissimilar pairs and the number of similar pairs in image batch.

For the traditional hashing methods, each image is represented by a 4096-dim deep feature extracted from AlexNet [9] as the input. For the deep hashing methods, the raw image pixels are used as input. All deep methods adopt the AlexNet [7] as its basic architecture. In the JMSH, we fine-tune the front five convolutional layers and two fully-connected layers copied from the AlexNet model pre-trained on ImageNet2012 and train the semantic hashing layer. As the hashing layer is trained from scratch, we set its learning rate to be 10 times that of the lower layers. The initial learning rate is set to 10^{-5} and the weight decay parameter is 0.0005. The mini-batch size is fixed to be 200 and the input image is normalized to 256×256. For the hyper-parameters α, β_1 and β_2, we first fix $\beta_1 = 0$ and $\beta_2 = 0$, we conduct cross-validation to search α from 10^1 to 10^{-4}. We find that the optimal result can be obtained when setting α to be 10^{-1}. Then we search β_1 and β_2 from 10^1 to 10^{-5}, and we find the result is optimal when setting β_1 and β_2 to be 10^{-2} and 10^{-3}, respectively.

We compare retrieval performance of the **JMSH** with the classical state-of-the-art hashing methods, including the traditional hashing and deep hashing. The former includes **LSH** [3], **SH** [27], **ITQ** [5], **KSH** [10], **FastH** [14] and **SDH** [22]. The latter includes **DNNH** [11], **DHN** [33], **HashNet** [1] and **DPH** [2], where most of these methods obtains similarity-preserving binary codes according to the pairwise similarity affinity, such as DPH, HashNet, DHN, FastH and SH.

In the evaluation, several metrics are adopted to measure the quantitative performance. All methods are evaluated with four lengths of binary codes (8-bit, 16-bit, 24-bit and 32-bit), and under four standard evaluation metrics:

Mean Average Precision (**MAP**), Precision-Recall curves (**PR**) and Precision curves within Hamming distance 2 (**P@H $\leq$ 2**). For fair comparisons, all methods use identical training and test sets, which are sampled from the dataset.

Table 1. Mean Average Precision (MAP) of Hamming Ranking for different number of bits on two image datasets.

Method	CIFAR-10				NUS-WIDE			
	8 bits	16 bits	24 bits	32 bits	8 bits	16 bits	24 bits	32 bits
LSH [3]	0.1280	0.1368	0.1474	0.1637	0.1658	0.1867	0.2127	0.2494
SH [27]	0.1200	0.1254	0.1215	0.1277	0.1684	0.1694	0.1653	0.1765
ITQ [5]	0.1834	0.1997	0.2035	0.2087	0.2649	0.3142	0.3289	0.3407
KSH [10]	0.3860	0.4551	0.4701	0.4914	0.4696	0.5564	0.5684	0.5855
FastH [14]	0.4190	0.5006	0.5353	0.5436	0.5054	0.5962	0.6257	0.6386
SDH [22]	0.3192	0.5026	0.5318	0.5458	0.3608	0.5876	0.6080	0.6212
DNNH [11]	0.5561	0.6041	0.5876	0.5857	0.6121	0.6456	0.6574	0.6586
DHN [33]	0.5918	0.6554	0.6586	0.6601	0.6713	0.6823	0.6835	0.6871
HashNet [1]	0.6568	0.6925	0.7234	0.7401	0.6772	0.7001	0.7122	0.7239
DPH [2]	0.6672	0.6922	0.7243	0.7448	0.6852	0.7121	0.7199	0.7265
JMSH	**0.6962**	**0.7214**	**0.7326**	**0.7454**	**0.6916**	**0.7221**	**0.7316**	**0.7328**

3.3 Results and Discussions

Table 1 shows the MAP scores for different lengths of binary code on the CIFAR-10 and NUS-WIDE dataset, respectively. It is observed that our method constantly outperforms the baselines, including traditional hashing methods with CNN feature and deep learning based hashing methods.

Specifically, on the CIFAR-10 dataset, we can achieve an average MAP absolute increase of 24.88% compared to the traditional hashing method SDH [22] for different lengths of binary codes, and achieve an average MAP absolute increase of 2.04% and 1.65% compared to the state-of-the-art deep hashing methods HashNet [1] and DPH [2], respectively. For the NUS-WIDE dataset, the proposed JMSH shows a certain MAP improvement over these baselines, and the specific average MAP absolute increase can be up to 1.61% and 0.46% compared to the state-of-the-art hashing HashNet and DPH, respectively. The reason is that this dataset has in total of 21 class concepts and the structure information is more complicated among data pairs. Combined with the above analysis, the proposed JMSH show better results compared to the current hashing, the reason is that existing hashing methods mainly employ the pairwise similarity affinity to obtain similarity-preserving binary codes, overlooking the rich semantic information offered by label information. However, in the proposed JMSH, we further integrate the high-level semantic label information into the feature learning and binary codes learning, and improve the quality of the final binary codes.

The performance in terms of Precision within Hamming radius 2 (P@H=2) is very important for efficient retrieval with binary codes since such Hamming ranking only requires O(1) time for each query. As shown in Figs. 2 and 3(a), JMSH consistently achieves the best precision on two datasets. With the length of code becoming longer, P@H=2 of JMSH can still show a decreasing tendency. This validates that the JMSH can learn more compact binary codes than these baselines. As using longer codes, the Hamming space will become sparse and few data points fall within the Hamming ball with radius 2. This is why most hashing methods achieve the best accuracy with moderate code lengths.

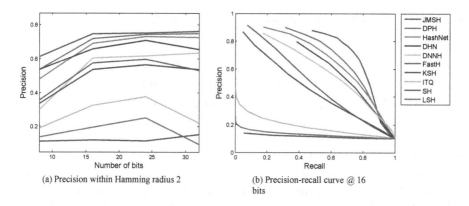

Fig. 2. Comparative evaluations on the CIFAR-10 dataset. (a) Precision curves within Hamming distance 2; (b) Precision-recall curves with 16 bits.

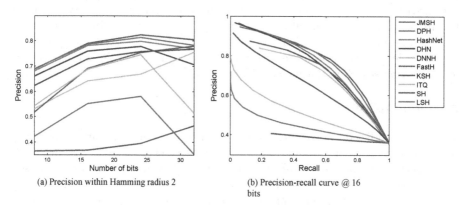

Fig. 3. Comparative evaluations on the NUS-WIDE dataset. (a) Precision curves within Hamming distance 2; (b) Precision-recall curves with 16 bits.

The retrieval performance in terms of Precision-Recall curves (PR) is shown in Figs. 2 and 3(b), respectively. It is clear that the JMSH shows a certain improvement compared to these comparison methods. Specifically, in low or high recall ratio, our method obtains a higher precision, which is desirable for precision-first practical retrieval systems. on the CIFAR-10, it shows a relatively higher initial recall over these baselines, and the reason is that the JMSH can put more similar pairs into the Hamming ball with low radius r, where the r increases from the minimum of 1 to the maximum of K (the code length). These obtained best results benefit from two components. First, We integrate the high-level semantics into the learning of binary codes. Second, We further learn the discriminative feature with the help of label information, and it is conducive to generate compact binary codes.

Table 2. Comparison of different loss terms in terms of MAP scores @ 16-bit binary codes.

	$\mathcal{L}_{pair}$	$\mathcal{L}_{pair} + \mathcal{L}_b$	$\mathcal{L}_{pair} + \mathcal{L}_f$	$\mathcal{L}_{pair} + \mathcal{L}_b + \mathcal{L}_f$
CIFAR-10	0.6986	0.7162	0.7059	0.7214
NUS-WIDE	0.7018	0.7155	0.7062	0.7221

3.4   Empirical Analysis

Table 2 reports the MAP scores of JMSH on two datasets about different loss functions. Each loss is corresponding to learning a semantic component, and reflects their individual effect in the objective function. The pairwise similarity learning loss $\mathcal{L}_{pair}$ is used to generate similarity-preserving binary codes in Hamming space; the pointwise codes semantics learning loss $\mathcal{L}_b$ explores the specific-semantics binary codes for enhancing the robust; the pointwise visual feature learning loss $\mathcal{L}_f$ facilitates the discriminative power of feature representations, and improves the quality of binary codes. It is observed that the three semantics learning can promote each other, generating the optimal binary codes for improving search performance.

4   Conclusion

This paper studies deep learning-based hashing approaches by learning multiply semantic properties to support efficient and effective visual search. The proposed deep hashing method, i.e., JMSH, can generate more compact binary codes based on three components: (1) learning the pairwise codes semantic similarity; (2) exploiting the pointwise codes high-level semantic property; (3) extracting more discriminative visual feature in an end-to-end framework. Extensive experimental results have shown the effectiveness of the proposed JMSH on two widely-used image retrieval datasets, compared with the state-of-the- art methods. In the future, we further exploit the multiple semantics learning on cross-modal datasets, improving cross-modal retrieval accuracy.

Acknowledgement. This work is supported by the National Natural Science Foundation of China (Grant No. U1836217, 61427811, 61573360) and the National Key Research and Development Program of China (Grant No. 2017YFC0821602, 2016YFB1001000).

References

1. Cao, Z., Long, M., Wang, J., Philip, S.Y.: Hashnet: deep learning to hash by continuation. In: Proceedings of the IEEE International Conference on Computer Vision, pp. 5609–5618 (2017)
2. Cao, Z., Sun, Z., Long, M., Wang, J., Yu, P.S.: Deep priority hashing. In: Proceedings of the ACM Multimedia Conference on Multimedia, pp. 1653–1661. ACM (2018)
3. Gionis, A., Indyk, P., Motwani, R., et al.: Similarity search in high dimensions via hashing. In: Proceedings of International Conference on Very Large Data Bases, pp. 518–529 (1999)
4. Gong, Y., Lazebnik, S.: Iterative quantization: a procrustean approach to learning binary codes. In: Proceedings of the IEEE Conference on Computer Vision and Pattern Recognition, pp. 817–824 (2011)
5. Gong, Y., Lazebnik, S., Gordo, A., Perronnin, F.: Iterative quantization: a procrustean approach to learning binary codes for large-scale image retrieval. IEEE Trans. Pattern Anal. Mach. Intell. **35**(12), 2916–2929 (2013)
6. He, K., Zhang, X., Ren, S., Sun, J.: Deep residual learning for image recognition. In: Proceedings of the IEEE Conference on Computer Vision and Pattern Recognition, pp. 770–778 (2016)
7. Hinton, G.E., Srivastava, N., Krizhevsky, A., Sutskever, I., Salakhutdinov, R.R.: Improving neural networks by preventing co-adaptation of feature detectors. arXiv preprint arXiv:1207.0580 (2012)
8. Jegou, H., Douze, M., Schmid, C.: Product quantization for nearest neighbor search. IEEE Trans. Pattern Anal. Mach. Intell. **33**(1), 117–128 (2011)
9. Krizhevsky, A., Sutskever, I., Hinton, G.E.: Imagenet classification with deep convolutional neural networks. In: Advances in Neural Information Processing Systems, pp. 1097–1105 (2012)
10. Kulis, B., Grauman, K.: Kernelized locality-sensitive hashing. IEEE Trans. Pattern Anal. Mach. Intell. **34**(6), 1092–1104 (2012)
11. Lai, H., Pan, Y., Liu, Y., Yan, S.: Simultaneous feature learning and hash coding with deep neural networks. In: Proceedings of the IEEE Conference on Computer Vision and Pattern Recognition, pp. 3270–3278 (2015)
12. Li, Q., Sun, Z., He, R., Tan, T.: Deep supervised discrete hashing. In: Advances in Neural Information Processing Systems, pp. 2482–2491 (2017)
13. Li, W.J., Wang, S., Kang, W.C.: Feature learning based deep supervised hashing with pairwise labels. In: Proceedings of the Twenty-Fifth International Joint Conference on Artificial Intelligence, pp. 1711–1717 (2016)
14. Lin, G., Shen, C., Shi, Q., Van den Hengel, A., Suter, D.: Fast supervised hashing with decision trees for high-dimensional data. In: Proceedings of the IEEE Conference on Computer Vision and Pattern Recognition, pp. 1963–1970 (2014)
15. Lin, K., Lu, J., Chen, C.S., Zhou, J.: Learning compact binary descriptors with unsupervised deep neural networks. In: Proceedings of the IEEE Conference on Computer Vision and Pattern Recognition, pp. 1183–1192 (2016)

16. Liu, H., Wang, R., Shan, S., Chen, X.: Deep supervised hashing for fast image retrieval. In: Proceedings of the IEEE Conference on Computer Vision and Pattern Recognition, pp. 2064–2072 (2016)
17. Liu, W., Mu, C., Kumar, S., Chang, S.F.: Discrete graph hashing. In: Advances in Neural Information Processing Systems, pp. 3419–3427 (2014)
18. Luo, X., Nie, L., He, X., Wu, Y., Chen, Z.D., Xu, X.S.: Fast scalable supervised hashing. In: The International ACM SIGIR Conference on Research and Development in Information Retrieval, pp. 735–744 (2018)
19. Norouzi, M., Blei, D.M.: Minimal loss hashing for compact binary codes. In: Proceedings of the International Conference on Machine Learning, pp. 353–360 (2011)
20. Raginsky, M., Lazebnik, S.: Locality-sensitive binary codes from shift-invariant kernels. In: Advances in Neural Information Processing Systems, pp. 1509–1517 (2009)
21. Shen, F., Gao, X., Liu, L., Yang, Y., Shen, H.T.: Deep asymmetric pairwise hashing. In: Proceedings of the 25th ACM International Conference on Multimedia, pp. 1522–1530. ACM (2017)
22. Shen, F., Shen, C., Liu, W., Tao Shen, H.: Supervised discrete hashing. In: Proceedings of the IEEE Conference on Computer Vision and Pattern Recognition, pp. 37–45 (2015)
23. Shen, F., Wei, L., Zhang, S., Yang, Y., Shen, H.T.: Learning binary codes for maximum inner product search. In: Proceedings of IEEE International Conference on Computer Vision, pp. 4148–4156. IEEE (2015)
24. Tang, J., Li, Z., Wang, M., Zhao, R.: Neighborhood discriminant hashing for large-scale image retrieval. IEEE Trans. Image Process. **24**(9), 2827–2840 (2015)
25. Wang, J., Zhang, T., Sebe, N., Shen, H.T., et al.: A survey on learning to hash. IEEE Trans. Pattern Anal. Mach. Intell. **40**(4), 769–790 (2018)
26. Wang, Y., Liang, J., Cao, D., Sun, Z.: Local semantic-aware deep hashing with hamming-isometric quantization. IEEE Trans. Image Process. **28**(6), 2665–2679 (2018)
27. Weiss, Y., Torralba, A., Fergus, R.: Spectral hashing. In: Advances in Neural Information Processing Systems, pp. 1753–1760 (2009)
28. Xia, R., Pan, Y., Lai, H., Liu, C., Yan, S.: Supervised hashing for image retrieval via image representation learning. In: Proceedings of the Twenty-Eighth AAAI Conference on Artificial Intelligence, vol. 1, pp. 2156–2162 (2014)
29. Yang, H.F., Lin, K., Chen, C.S.: Supervised learning of semantics-preserving hash via deep convolutional neural networks. IEEE Trans. Pattern Anal. Mach. Intell. **40**(2), 437–451 (2018)
30. Zhang, D., Wang, J., Cai, D., Lu, J.: Self-taught hashing for fast similarity search. In: Proceedings of the ACM SIGIR conference on Research and Development in Information Retrieval, pp. 18–25 (2010)
31. Zhang, P., Zhang, W., Li, W.J., Guo, M.: Supervised hashing with latent factor models. In: Proceedings of ACM SIGIR Conference on Research and Development in Information Retrieval, pp. 173–182. ACM (2014)
32. Zhang, R., Lin, L., Zhang, R., Zuo, W., Zhang, L.: Bit-scalable deep hashing with regularized similarity learning for image retrieval and person re-identification. IEEE Trans. Image Process. **24**(12), 4766–4779 (2015)
33. Zhu, H., Long, M., Wang, J., Cao, Y.: Deep hashing network for efficient similarity retrieval. In: Proceedings of the Thirtieth AAAI Conference on Artificial Intelligence, pp. 2415–2421 (2016)

Fine Granular Parallel Algorithm for HEVC Encoding Based on Multicore Platform

Yi Li[3(✉)], Dong Hu[1,2,3(✉)], Chuanwei Yin[3], and Yingcan Qiu[3]

[1] Education Ministry's Key Lab of Broadband Wireless Communication
and Sensor Network Technology, Nanjing University of Posts
and Telecommunications, Nanjing 210003, China
[2] Education Ministry's Engineering Research Center of Ubiquitous Network
and Health Service, Nanjing University of Posts and Telecommunications,
Nanjing 210003, China
[3] Jiangsu Province's Key Lab of Image Procession and Image Communications,
Nanjing University of Posts and Telecommunications, Nanjing 210003, China
{1217012311, hud}@njupt.edu.cn

Abstract. Compared with the previous standards, the coding efficiency and complexity of High Efficiency Video Coding (HEVC) have been greatly improved. Parallel encoding scheme based on CTU rows like wavefront parallel processing (WPP) and inter-frame wavefront (IFW) can efficiently reduce the encoding time of HEVC. However, due to the coding complexity of CTU within various rows may be quite different, WPP and IFW have the problem of unbalanced load among threads for parallel encoding tasks. To address this issue, in this paper, factors affecting coding efficiency are found by analyzing the data dependence and load relationship of intra- and inter-frame CTUs, and we propose a fine granular parallel strategy accordingly. In the meanwhile, refine the parallel granularity while maintaining the accuracy of symbol prediction requires additional context information in CABAC encoding, which leads to higher bit rate, and will reduce the efficiency of CABAC encoding. In order to decrease the bit rate without affecting the quality, we also making some modifications for the CABAC encoding. The proposed method is implemented on the Tilera-GX36 multicore platform. Experiment results show that our algorithm achieves up to 1.6 and 2.8 times speedup improvement compared with IFW and WPP respectively.

Keywords: HEVC encoding · CTU · IFW · WPP · CABAC · Multicore platform

1 Introduction

In order to achieve a range of 50% bit-rate reduction for equal perceptual video quality [1] and about 40% bit-rate reductions at similar PSNR [2] compared to its previous standard–H.264/AVC, some new features have been introduced into HEVC, which also bring great increments of computational complexity [3]. HEVC provides several parallel schemes to cope with the high-speed processing demands, which make parallel coding on multicore platform possible. A representative method is slice-based

© Springer Nature Switzerland AG 2019
Y. Zhao et al. (Eds.): ICIG 2019, LNCS 11903, pp. 59–69, 2019.
https://doi.org/10.1007/978-3-030-34113-8_6

parallelism, which has been introduced in H.264/AVC [4]. Two new parallel methods are introduced in HEVC, which are tiles [5] and wavefront parallel processing (WPP) [6]. Tiles splits a picture horizontally and vertically into multiple rectangular regions for parallel processing, which is removing the parsing and prediction dependency. WPP splits a picture into coding tree unit (CTU) rows, and processes these rows in parallel.

Several related works focus on improving parallelism of HEVC based on WPP have been proposed, Chi et al. [7] presented an approach called overlapped wavefront (OWF) to address ramping inefficiencies in WPP for HEVC decoding. Chen et al. [8] proposed a novel parallel encoding scheme called Inter-frame wavefront (IFW) using the dependence of inter-frame CTU, realizing the multi-frame parallel encoding. Although these methods well exploit parallelism in HEVC, since the coding complexity of CTUs within various CTU rows may be quite different, WPP and IFW have the problem of unbalanced load among threads for parallel encoding tasks. To handle this problem, in this paper, we focus on exploring the data dependence and load balancing between different CTUs within intra- and inter-frame, and propose a fine granular parallel encoding based on the exploration. To avoid the possible loss in coding efficiency, CABAC module is modified accordingly. Therefore, better parallel speedup ratio can be achieved while the image quality can be guaranteed.

The rest of this paper is organized as follows. Section 2 introduces the CTU row-level parallel schemes and analyzes its parallelism. In Sect. 3, our new fine granular parallel method is described in details. We evaluate performance of the proposed algorithm in Sect. 4, followed by a short conclusion in Sect. 5.

2 Related Works

In this section, the CTU data dependency and parallelism of CTU row-level parallel schemes are introduced and analyzed. In order to denote the dependencies between CTUs, $C_{i,j,k}$ is used here to represent the k-th CTU of the j-th CTU row in the i-th frame in the coding order, $\text{Dep}_{IFW,inter}(C_{i,j,k})$ and $\text{Dep}_{IFW,intra}(C_{i,j,k})$ is used to represent the CTU on which $C_{i,j,k}$ depends performing parallel inter- and intra-frame encoding using IFW respectively.

2.1 Analysis of CTU Data Dependency

The intra-frame CTU dependency of IFW is same as WPP, so that the current CTU will rely on the information of CTUs in its top, top right, top left and left directions, as is illustrated in Fig. 1, the specific dependence can be expressed as (1). The encoding of each CTU rows start only after coding from the second CTU of the previous row. As is indicated in Fig. 2, a picture is separated to multiple CTU row partitions, each CTU row is allocated to different threads for parallel processing.

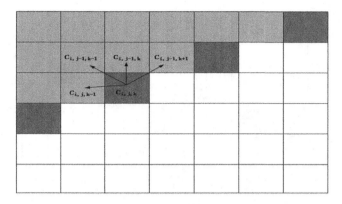

Fig. 1. The CTU data dependency of current CTU within a frame

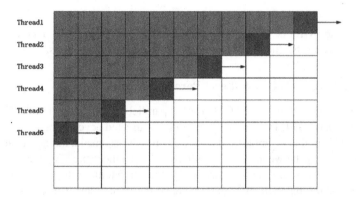

Fig. 2. Parallel processing of intra-frame in IFW

$$\text{Dep}_{IFW,intra}(C_{i,j,k}) = \text{Dep}_{wpp}(C_{i,j,k}) = \{C_{i,j-1,k-1}, C_{i,j-1,k}, C_{i,j-1,k+1}, C_{i,j,k-1},\} \quad (1)$$

The motion estimation is to find the best matching pixel block in the search range and get the best motion vector. All CTUs in the search range corresponding to the current coding CTU in the reference frame must be encoded before the optimal motion vector of the current CTU can be determined. The dependency relationship of inter-frame CTU in IFW is given by (2) and Fig. 3 shows the detail.

$$\text{Dep}_{IFW,inter}(C_{i,j,k}) = \{C_{i1,j1,k1} | i1 \in \text{ref}(I), 0 \le j1 < j + l_h, 0 \le k1 < l_w\} \quad (2)$$

l_h indicates the downward vertical component of the motion vector, it is usually set to 0 or 1 in IFW. l_w indicates the horizontal component of motion vector. The encoding process of $C_{i,j,k}$ will be started immediately after the encoding of $C_{i1,j1,k1}$ is completed,

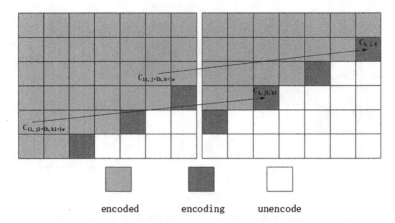

encoded   encoding   unencode

Fig. 3. Dependency of inter-frame CTU in IFW

instead of frame-by-frame CTU row-level parallel encoding in WPP. That is, CTUs in multiple frames can be encoded parallel after the dependencies are satisfied.

2.2 Parallelism of CTU Row-Level Parallel Schemes

Both the IFW and WPP using the CTU row as parallel unit. As shown in the Fig. 4, the dependencies between CTUs are represented by a directed acyclic graph (DAG), there are 4 × 5 CTUs in this example, and each CTU row is assigned a thread. It can be seen that most of the time between threads is idle, so the scheme using CTU rows as parallel unit wastes thread resources. Therefore, we propose a parallel scheme based on CTU. In this paper, using parallelism (PL) to evaluate the improvement of coding speed by parallel schemes and thread resource strategies. As shown in (3).

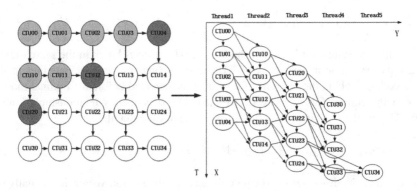

Fig. 4. DAG used to express the dependency between CTUs

$$PL = \frac{EncTime_{1,F}}{EncTime_{N,F}} \qquad (3)$$

$EncTime_{N,F}$ refers to the time spent using N cores to encode in the parallel algorithm F. We dividing a frame horizontally and vertically into (W × H) CTUs, assuming that the average encoding time of each CTU is a unit of time. According to the Fig. 4, there will be n units of time parallel processing when the thread resources are sufficient, n is given as (4).

$$n = 2 \times (H - 1) + W \qquad (4)$$

According to the relationship between the number of thread and CTU, we designing the scheduling strategies in two cases. Firstly, if the threads resources are sufficient, the H-th row begins to encode while the first row of CTU has not encoded yet, indicating that each CTU row has a designated thread to process. Therefore, when a thread encoding task is completed, the next frame will not be read due to the frame-level task has not been completed, so the core thread is not fully utilized and the parallelism is relatively low. (5) can express the PL.

$$PL = W \times H / (2H + W - 2) \qquad (5)$$

Secondly, if the threads resources are limited, in this case, $(2H - 2X - 2) < W < (2H - 2X)$, that is there are still X CTU rows that remain to be encoded when the first row encoding has been completed. As long as there are threads in the H − X CTU row threads has completed the corresponding row encoding, these threads will be transferred to deal with the remaining X rows, where the X threads are reused, the remaining H − X threads are not scheduled, so it is a waste of thread resources. (6) give the PL:

$$PL = W \times H / (2W + 2X - 2) \qquad (6)$$

2.3 Existing Problems

The possibility of load unbalance among CTU row threads exists in CTU row-level parallel schemes, like WPP and IFW, since the encoding complexity of CTUs within various CTU rows may be quite different. When these encoding threads are scheduled with each CTU row as the basic processing task, the encoding complexity of a CTU in the previous row is too high, which will lead to the blocking of the coding threads in the subsequent CTU rows, due to the data dependence between CTUs. This will cause considerable latency among encoding threads. Moreover, according to the two cases discussed in part 2.2, the parallelism are relatively low and thread resources has not be fully utilized. Discussion of more details and our method are in the Sect. 3.

3   Proposed Method

3.1   Analysis of CTU Load Balancing

As is shown in Fig. 5, suppose there are only two threads currently used to encode CTU03 and CTU11 respectively. Because the complexity of CTU03 is higher than CTU11, as a result, the second thread is blocked in CTU11, making it impossible to code CTU12. If using the CTU rows as parallel granularity and the threads are allocated to encode the CTU rows in parallel, the load of the coding threads will be unbalanced, which will lead to the blocking of the coding threads. Dependency DAG and (First in First out) FIFO queue are introduced to solve this issue. When the second thread is blocked, the coding condition of CTU20 has met in the meanwhile, thus, the second thread can be used to encode CTU20, thereby reducing the coding delay caused by load unbalance of encoding based on CTU rows. Similarly, if the CTU20 has a

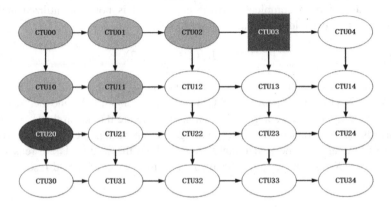

Fig. 5. Analysis of CTUs load balancing

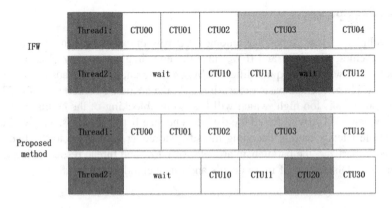

Fig. 6. The actual threads load

larger complexity, the thread that complete tasks first can be used to encode the CTU, which has no dependency in the queue. A main thread operates on the queue to schedule the threads pool; the DAG dependency matrix will be updated when a CTU encoding is completed. Figure 6 shows the actual thread load of IFW and our algorithm.

3.2   Specific Proposed Method

Threads scheduling strategy is described by adjacency matrix and in-degree matrix to solve the problem of CTU load unbalance. The dependency is expressed by the in-degree matrix, and the matrix will be updated every time a CTU has been encoded, when the dependencies of CTU are satisfied, idle threads can be invoked to realize multi-frame parallel encoding, thus solving the problem of thread blocking and low parallelism of frame-by-frame coding. DAG represents the dependency between CTUs, m is the serial number of CTUs, M is the number of CTUs within a frame, floor and mod are representing downward integral and modular function respectively.

The location of each CTU is represented by (i, j), that is:

$$i = \text{floor}\left(\frac{m}{M}\right) j = m \bmod M \tag{7}$$

For $DAG = (V, E)$, if the set of boundaries E contains $(V_{i,j}, V_{m,n})$, indicating that the CTU (m, n) depends on the CTU (i, j). When the CTU represented by $V_{i,j}$ is encoded, removing the boundaries containing $V_{i,j}$ from DAG. The entry of CTU, which has a boundary relationship with $V_{i,j}$, will be reduced by 1, and indicates a dependency is satisfied. When the entry of vertices becomes 0, the corresponding vertices can be processed in parallel. Therefore, the DAG and the in-degree matrix will be updated each time a CTU is encoded. Since the entrance values of different CTUs in the in-degree matrix are obtained from the DAG, the adjacency matrix is used to represent the DAG, and W and H are used to represent the number of CTUs in the horizontal and vertical directions of a frame respectively. The entry value D of each CTU is obtained by adjacent matrix A:

$$A_{(i,j),(m,n)} = \begin{cases} 1, (v_{i,j}, v_{m,n}) \in E \\ 0, else \end{cases} 1 \le i, m \le H, 1 \le j, n \le W \tag{8}$$

$$D_{m,n} = \sum_{i=1}^{H} \sum_{j=1}^{w} A(i,j), (m,n) \ 1 \le m \le H, 1 \le n \le W \tag{9}$$

Parallel granularity refinement makes CABAC encoding require additional context information if symbol prediction accuracy is to be maintained, which leads to higher bit rate. In order to reduce the bit rate, we divide the coding process at CTU level into two consecutive modules. The first module makes intra- and inter-frame prediction at CTU level according to the rate-distortion cost, and obtains the best partition and prediction mode of CTU. The second module to encode CTU according to the partition and prediction mode information. In the optimal mode decision-making stage, the best partition and optimal mode are obtained by parallel processing of multiple threads, the syntax information, however, will not be encoded by CABAC immediately, but will continue the encoding process of other CTUs. Independent CABAC encoding threads will encode the syntax elements of this optimal information. Consequently, the proposed scheme can be divided into two task levels, frame-level and CTU-level, as shown in Fig. 7. Frame-level tasks request threads to process the CTU-level task queue of the current frame for parallel processing. When the encoding process of a frame is finished, the thread resource for this frame is released and the code stream after CABAC is stored

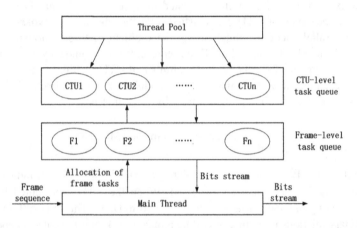

Fig. 7. Two task levels of the proposed scheme

4 Experiment

4.1 Experiments Design

The algorithm is implemented on the Tilera-GX36 multicore platform, and using x.265 as the reference software. Two sets of comparison experiments are set up in the meanwhile. The first one is the WPP that does not take into account the inter-frame correlation, and the second one is IFW, which takes into account the inter-frame correlation. Since the experiment involves the dependency of the CTU in the time domain, we dividing the coding frame type into two cases: IPPPP and IBBBP. The indicators used for evaluating the experimental performance are bit rate, PSNR, and parallel acceleration ratio. With the increase in the number of threads, the trend of the parallel acceleration of the three algorithms is compared. The size of LCU is 32 × 32 in the experiment, and the video sequence used in our experiment are 1600p Traffic, 1080p Kimono and 720p FourPeople. Parallel acceleration ratio is used to express the acceleration of parallel algorithm relative to serial encoding, which is represented by speedup.

$$Speedup = \frac{EncTime_{serial}}{EncTime_{parallel}} \qquad (10)$$

$EncTime_{serial}$ is the time required for single-core serial encoding and $EncTime_{parallel}$ is the time spend on multi-core parallel encoding.

4.2   Results and Discussion

Experimental results in Table 1 are obtained with the thread number is 32. It can be found from these data that compared with the two comparison algorithms, the PSNR of our method decreases and the parallelism degree improves. Furthermore, compared with the WPP, the IFW scheme also increases the bit rate slightly, because the improvement of the algorithm increases the syntax elements, but compared with IFW, our parallel algorithm reduces the bit rate due to the addition of the CABAC optimization scheme. The parallel acceleration ratio of our algorithm is much higher, which is achieves up to 1.6 and 2.8 times speedup improvement compared with IFW and WPP respectively for 720P FourPeople test sequence (Figs. 8, 9 and 10).

Table 1. Comparison results of three algorithms

Frame type	Sequences	WPP			IFW			Our method		
		PSNR (dB)	Bit rate (kbps)	Speed up	PSNR (dB)	Bit rate (kbps)	Speed up	PSNR (dB)	Bit rate (kbps)	Speed up
IPPPP	Traffic	31.422	3111.93	3.56	31.235	3286.68	6.31	31.081	3231.24	9.42
	Kimono	33.086	3098.74	3.37	32.863	3178.55	6.14	32.673	3145.16	9.13
	FourPeople	23.167	712.09	2.92	22.841	796.34	5.69	22.682	764.24	8.24
IBBBP	Traffic	32.087	3243.55	5.45	31.765	3395.56	7.43	31.584	3326.13	9.85
	Kimono	35.126	3122.88	4.39	34.839	3209.08	6.98	34.691	3186.24	9.61
	FourPeople	26.253	792.03	3.09	26.033	834.11	5.03	25.876	821.67	8.22

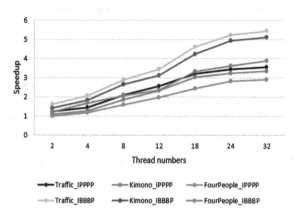

Fig. 8. Parallel acceleration ratio of WPP

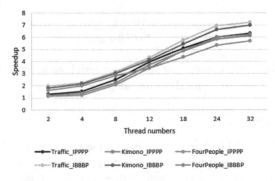

Fig. 9. Parallel acceleration ratio of IFW

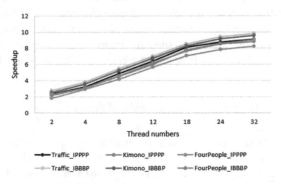

Fig. 10. Parallel acceleration ratio of proposed method

It can be found from these line charts that the parallel acceleration ratio for three methods increase gradually with the increasing thread numbers, the addition of B frames can improve the parallel acceleration ratio, because B frame is bidirectional predictive frame, which can enhance the efficiency of video sequence compression.

5   Conclusion

In this paper, we introducing the parallel algorithms based on CTU row firstly. Then, the dependency of CTUs on intra- and inter-frame and the load balancing among threads of CTU row-level parallel schemes are analyzed. A fine granular parallel coding model is established for the dependency relationship between CTUs, in-degree matrix and adjacent matrix are used to represent the update of dependency. Finally, we implementing the proposed method on the Tilera-GX36 multi-core platform. Experimental results show that the parallel acceleration ratio is further improved by our method.

References

1. Sullivan, G.J., et al.: Overview of the high efficiency video coding (HEVC) standard. IEEE Trans. Circuits Syst. Video Technol. **22**(12), 1649–1668 (2013)
2. Ohm, J., et al.: Comparison of the coding efficiency of video coding standards—including high efficiency video coding (HEVC). IEEE Trans. Circuits Syst. Video Technol. **22**(12), 1669–1684 (2012)
3. Bossen, F., et al.: HEVC complexity and implementation analysis. IEEE Trans. Circuits Syst. Video Technol. **22**(12), 1685–1696 (2012)
4. Zhao, L., et al.: A dynamic slice control scheme for slice-parallel video encoding. In: IEEE 19th International Conference on Image Processing 2012, pp. 713–716. IEEE, Florida (2012)
5. Baik, H., Song, H.: A complexity-based adaptive tile-partitioning algorithm for HEVC decoder parallelization. In: IEEE International Conference on Image Processing 2015, pp. 4298–4302. IEEE, Quebec (2015)
6. Radicke, S., et al.: A multi-threaded full-feature HEVC encoder based on wavefront parallel processing. In: 11th International Conference on Signal Processing and Multimedia Applications 2014, pp. 90–98. IEEE, Vienna (2014)
7. Chi, C.C., et al.: Improving the parallelization efficiency of HEVC decoding. In: IEEE 19th International Conference on Image Processing 2012, pp. 213–216. IEEE, Florida (2012)
8. Chen, K., et al.: A novel wavefront-based high parallel solution for HEVC. IEEE Trans. Circuits Syst. Video Technol. **22**(12), 181–194 (2016)

Block Partitioning Decision Based on Content Complexity for Future Video Coding

Yanhong Zhang[1,2(✉)], Yao Zhao[1,2], Chunyu Lin[1,2], and Meiqin Liu[1,2]

[1] Institute of Information Science, Beijing Jiaotong University,
Beijing 100044, China
{17120332,yzhao,cylin,mqliu}@bjtu.edu.cn
[2] Beijing Key Laboratory of Modern Information Science and Network
Technology, Beijing 100044, China

Abstract. Recently, a block partition structure of quadtree plus binary tree (QTBT) has been proposed. Compared with the quadtree structure in HEVC, the block partition of QTBT is more flexible and the encoding performance is better, but at the same time, the encoding complexity is greatly increased. In order to better balance coding performance and complexity, we propose a block partitioning decision algorithm based on content complexity. By analyzing the variation of the complexity range of different splitting modes of adjacent frames, the unnecessary iteration process is reduced, thereby reducing the coding time complexity. The experimental results show that compared with the joint exploration test model (JEM), the average coding time of this method is reduced by 9.0%, while the coding performance is only lost by about 0.55%.

Keywords: Block partitioning · Quadtree plus binary tree · Content complexity · JEM

1 Introduction

The high-efficiency video coding standard HEVC/H.265 [1] is an international video compression coding standard proposed in 2013. In HEVC, video frames are first divided into equally-sized Coding Tree Units (CTUs), which are 64×64 in size. Then, the CTU is iteratively partitioned into coding units (CUs) according to a quadtree structure to adapt to different local features. Each CU can further divided into prediction units (PUs) and transform units (TUs). Although the HEVC structure greatly improves its performance over previous coding standards, it still has some problems.

To further optimize HEVC, the next-generation video coding standard H.266/VVC has been researched and developed. The Joint Exploration Test Model (JEM) is the test model for H.266. Among them, a new quadtree plus binary tree (QTBT) [2] structure was adopted by the Joint Video Experts Group (JVET) and integrated in JEM 3.0 and higher [3, 4]. In the QTBT structure, a more flexible CU partition type is supported. The size of the coding tree unit (CTU) is 128×128. CTUs are further divided into CUs, which are the basic units of encoding. Unlike HEVC, one CU in QTBT can be square or rectangular in shape. Figure 1 is an example of a CTU partition, with solid lines representing quadtree partitioning and dashed lines representing binary tree

Y. Zhao et al. (Eds.): ICIG 2019, LNCS 11903, pp. 70–80, 2019.
https://doi.org/10.1007/978-3-030-34113-8_7

partitioning. As can be seen from the CTU is first divided by a quadtree structure. Quadtree leaf nodes are further divided by a binary tree structure. There are two types in binary tree partitioning: symmetric horizontal partitioning and symmetric vertical. CU is not further divided into PUs and TUs. Therefore, the CU is also the basic unit of prediction and transformation.

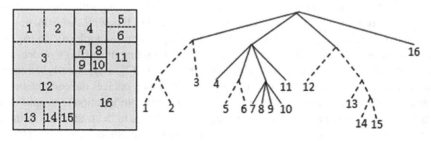

Fig. 1. Display of QTBT partition structure.

Due to the addition of the QTBT structure, in the JEM encoding, four types of partitioning attempts are required for each current block. They are unsplit, horizontal binary tree partitions, vertical binary tree partitions, and quadtree partitions. Among them, the type with the smallest RD cost is selected as the final division mode of the current block. The rate-distortion optimization process of JEM coding is shown in Fig. 2. As can be seen from the figure, when selecting the partition type for the current CU, in addition to the non-division mode, the other three partition types have to further recursively determine their own optimal partitions. The emergence of multiple partitioning structures allows CUs to be flexibly divided into different shapes to accommodate different video content. But it also leads to extremely high coding computation. Therefore, a fast algorithm needs to be proposed to reduce the consumption of coding time while ensuring stable coding performance.

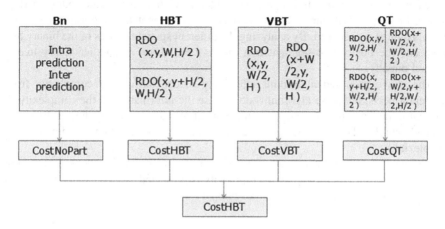

Fig. 2. Rate-distortion optimization process of JEM.

2 Related Work

After the above analysis, we know that the QTBT structure greatly improves the coding performance, but at the same time, the iterative process due to multiple partition types increases, which in turn leads to an increase in the encoding time. Therefore, an improved algorithm is needed to reduce the time complexity.

At this stage, many improvements have been proposed for algorithm acceleration. In [5], an algorithm is proposed to combine the CU coded bits with the reduction of unnecessary intra prediction modes to reduce the computational complexity. In [6], the author proposes a hybrid scheme consisting of a quick coding unit (CU) size decision and a fast prediction unit (PU) model decision process. In [7], a gradient-based intra-frame candidate mode clipping algorithm is proposed, which reduces the computational complexity by adaptive depth division and the use of spatial information to simplify the intra-frame prediction process. The above algorithm belongs to the traditional method. There are also some ways to use machine learning. In [8], the author proposes a HEVC inter-frame size decision algorithm. Several features that may be associated with the CU partition are selected by using an F-score based packaging method, and a three-output classifier is designed to control the risk of mispredictions by combining the classifier with the RD cost. In [9], an adaptive fast CU size decision algorithm is proposed. In this algorithm, firstly, the CU size decision process based on quadtree and the relationship between CU partition and image features are analyzed. Then, using Support Vector Machines, a three-output classification model is constructed based on CU complexity. Finally, the optimal CU size is predetermined by the model. The best CU size. In JEM, due to the appearance of the QTBT structure, the size and shape of the block division are different. Therefore, the above fast algorithm based on HEVC implementation cannot be directly applied to the QTBT structure.

Aiming at the QTBT structure, some improved algorithms are also proposed. In [10], a block segmentation technique based on probabilistic decision-making is proposed to identify unnecessary partition modes in terms of rate-distortion (RD) optimization. In [11], Wang et al. proposed an effective QTBT partition decision algorithm to achieve a good trade-off between computational complexity and coding performance. In [12], a fast intra-frame CU binary tree segmentation algorithm based on spatial features is proposed. By analyzing the different spatial features of the binary tree depth and the binary tree segmentation mode, the division of another binary tree is skipped directly.

The above proposed algorithms effectively reduce the coding complexity from different aspects, but these algorithms do not use the information of the complexity of adjacent frame content. We know that the content of video between adjacent frames is relatively similar. Therefore, we propose a fast partitioning algorithm based on content complexity.

The next part of the paper is organized as follows: In Sect. 3, block partitioning decision algorithm based on content complexity is presented. Experimental results and analysis are in Sect. 4. Section 5 is the summary of the paper.

3 Proposed Algorithm

In JEM coding, the partition size of a block is closely related to the complexity of the area to which the current block belongs. A region with a complex texture tends to split small blocks. Conversely, it tends to split large blocks. Then, the content of the image between adjacent frames does not change much, correspondingly, their partition structure is similar, which means that the content complexity and their splitting modes are similar between adjacent frames. In JEM coding, since the QTBT partition structure is added, the processing for the current block includes four cases. Therefore, it is desirable to reduce the coding time complexity by analyzing the variation of the complexity range of four different splitting modes of adjacent frames.

First, to get the complexity range of different partitioning methods, we calculate the complexity value of the current block first. Here, the standard deviation of the gray histogram of the current block is selected to represent its content complexity G. The specific calculation formula is as follows (1) and (2):

$$P_{average} = \frac{1}{H \times W} \sum_{i=1}^{H} \sum_{j=1}^{W} P_{i,j} \tag{1}$$

$$G = \frac{1}{H \times W} \sum_{i=1}^{H} \sum_{j=1}^{W} (|P_{i,j} - P_{average}|) \tag{2}$$

Where H and W represent the width and length of the current block, and $P_{i,j}$ represents the pixel value of the current block.

According to the above formula, we can get the content complexity of all CUs that select the same partition type in the same frame. The maximum and minimum values obtained constitute the complexity range of this kind of splitting. Here, the complexity of the four split methods is shown in Table 1:

Table 1. Complexity range representation of 4 partitioning methods.

(G_{MinBn}, G_{MaxBn})	The complexity range of all blocks that are not divided (Bn) in the same frame
(G_{MinHBT}, G_{MaxHBT})	The complexity range of all blocks that select horizontal binary tree partitioning (HBT) in the same frame
(G_{MinVBT}, G_{MaxVBT})	The complexity range of all blocks that select vertical binary tree partitioning (VBT) in the same frame
(G_{MinQT}, G_{MaxQT})	The complexity range of all blocks that select quadtree partitioning (QT) in the same frame

In order to oversee the variation of the complexity range of four different partitioning modes between adjacent frames of a video sequence, we calculate the complexity range of the BasketballPass video sequence. Table 2 shows the complexity range of four different partitioning modes in the first five frames of the sequence. From Table 2, we can see that the complexity range of selecting different partitioning modes is not exactly the same in the same frame. At the same time, the complexity range of selecting the same splitting method is similar between adjacent frames. Therefore, we can effectively reduce the coding complexity based on these two characteristics.

First, we can encode the first frame according to the original encoding process and obtain the complexity range corresponding to different partition modes. This is shown in Fig. 3. Among them, the shade of the color in the figure indicates the number of split modes that need to be tried. From deep to shallow, there are four, three, two, and one. In the next frame coding process, the unnecessary partitioning mode is directly skipped by judging the scope of the current block complexity. For example, the complexity value of the current block is 160. Since it is in the range of 158 to 165, it is only necessary to perform three partitioning attempts on the current block without splitting by the horizontal binary tree. If the complexity value is greater than 165, then only one of the partitioning modes of the current block can be tried, thereby reducing the time consumption caused by the other three partitions.

Table 2. Complexity range G of 4 divisions of the first 5 frames of BasketballPass.

	Bn	HBT	VBT	QT
Frame 1	(4,165)	(6,158)	(8,165)	(10,524288)
Frame 2	(3,166)	(8,149)	(10,158)	(18,524288)
Frame 3	(4,165)	(8,143)	(10,157)	(18,524288)
Frame 4	(4,157)	(8,138)	(8,157)	(18,524288)
Frame 5	(4,165)	(6,147)	(7,157)	(18,524288)

Fig. 3. The number of split modes that need to be tried corresponding to different complexity ranges of the first frame of BasketballPass (Colors from deep to shallow indicate that it need to try four, three, two and one.).

Through the above analysis, we know that due to the content correlation of adjacent video frames, the time consumption caused by unnecessary iterations can be reduced according to the complexity range of different partitioning modes. However, the above-mentioned complexity range does not consider different depth cases. The partitioning of the current block is closely related to its depth. For example, as the depth increases, the partitioning of the quadtree may be less used. Therefore, in order to make block partitioning decisions more accurately, the quadtree plus binary tree depth (uiQTBT-Depth) is taken into consideration. In other words, the complexity values calculated by selecting the same partitioning mode in one frame are separately counted according to different depths. Table 3 is a representation of the complexity range of four different partitioning modes with a depth of 2 in one frame of the BasketballPass video sequence. We compare the two situations with or without considering depth Fig. 4. Figure 4(a) is a complexity range when depth is not distinguished. When the depth is 2, we display the range of 10 to 158 according to the data in Table 3, as shown in Fig. 4 (b). It can be seen from the figure, for the complexity value calculated by the current block, in two cases, the required number of partitioning iterations may be different. For example, the content complexity of the current block is 48. When the depth is not distinguished, the four partitioning modes need to be tried once. When the depth is distinguished, only two partitioning attempts are required.

Table 3. The complexity range of different partitioning modes when the first frame of BasketballPass Depth = 2.

	Bn	HBT	VBT	QT
Depth = 2	(0,0)	(22,46)	(26,66)	(22,524288)

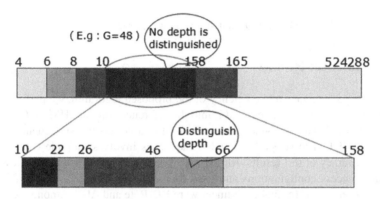

Fig. 4. Display of the number of divisions of the same complexity value in two cases. (a) Depth considered. (b) Without regard to depth.

Based on the above analysis, this paper proposes a partitioning decision algorithm based on content complexity. The overall process is shown in Fig. 5. In this algorithm, by counting the complexity ranges of different depths in the first frame, unnecessary partitioning attempts are reduced, thereby reducing coding time complexity. First, for each current block, its complexity G is calculated and its current partition depth d is obtained. If the current block belongs to the first frame, encode according to the original encoding process and update the corresponding complexity range. For other frames, if the current frame is entered for the first time, the complexity range corresponding to the depth d in the previous frame is obtained. Otherwise, the complexity range of the current frame depth d is obtained. Next, the unnecessary partitioning process is eliminated according to the range to which G belongs. Of course, if G is not within any complexity range, then the original encoding process is still performed. Similarly, in order to make the subsequent block partitioning more precise and efficient, the G value of the current block is also updated according to its corresponding complexity range.

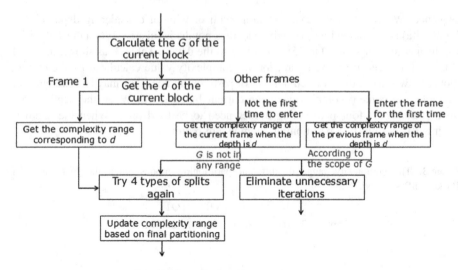

Fig. 5. Overall algorithm work process.

4 Experimental Results

To verify the performance and efficiency of the proposed algorithm, we performed the following experiments. We integrated it into the reference software HM-16.6-JEM-4.2 released by JVET. The test video sequence used is a common test sequence recommended by JVET. The selection of video sequences involves multiple categories to ensure the accuracy of test results. All the experiment was performed in both lowdelay and random access configurations and used four different QPs (22, 27, 32, 37). The evaluation criteria used for this experiment were BD-Rate and ΔET. Among them, BD-Rate represents the reduction of bit rate when the peak signal-to-noise ratio between the anchor and the algorithm is equal. ΔET is compared with the anchor, the algorithm reduces the time ratio as the formula (3) shown. Where T_{JEM} represents the time spent under the JEM source code and T_{Prop} represents the time used in the method.

$$\Delta ET = \frac{1}{4} \sum_{i=1}^{4} \frac{T_{JEM} - T_{Prop}}{T_{JEM}} \times 100\% \tag{3}$$

Compared with the JEM encoding process, the performance evaluation are shown in Table 4. Positive value of BD-Rate indicates a decrease in coding performance, and negative value of ΔET indicates a decrease in coding time. Under the Random Access configuration, the encoding time is reduced by an average of 8.3%, and the loss of encoding performance is only 0.2%. In the Lowdelay configuration, the encoding time is reduced by an average of 9.5%, and the loss of encoding performance is only 0.89%. From the data in the table, we can also see that the sequence RaceHorses can save more time than the sequence BQSquare and FourPeople. This is because the texture is complex in RaceHorses. Correspondingly, it needs to divide more blocks, so the time saved by the proposed algorithm is more. At the same time, because of its intense motion, the deviation between adjacent frames is slightly larger than other sequences, so the performance degradation is relatively large. For sequences with a simple background and slow motion, such as Kimono, performance degradation is negligible. This is because the slow motion makes the similarity between adjacent frames extremely high, and the resulting block partition structure is more accurate.

Table 4. Performance of the proposed algorithm.

Sequence	Proposed random access BD-rate	ΔET	Lowdelay BD-rate	ΔET
Cactus	+0.51%	−6.58%	+0.72%	−5.86%
Kimono	+0.10%	−4.91%	−0.08%	−5.10%
BQMall	+0.14%	−8.32%	+1.29%	−7.09%
BasketballDrill	+0.16%	−9.56%	+2.72%	−24.92%
BQSquare	+0.04%	−6.36%	+1.45%	−10.21%
RaceHorses	+1.02%	−17.30%	+1.04%	−16.75%
BasketballPass	−0.01%	−11.09%	+0.70%	−12.98%
FourPeople	+0.15%	−2.97%	+0.01%	−2.46%
KristenAndSara	−0.31%	−7.59%	+0.16%	−0.17%
Average	+0.20%	−8.30%	+0.89%	−9.50%

Figure 6 shows the rate-distortion comparison between the algorithm and JEM encoding in the RaceHorses sequence in two different configurations. The figure shows the rate savings for the two methods at the same objective quality, and the difference in PSNR-Y between the two methods at the same code rate. It can be seen from the figure that the performance difference between the algorithm and the original JEM encoding is not large, and the performance loss can be neglected.

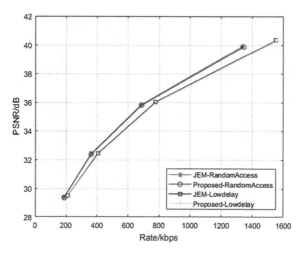

Fig. 6. The rate distortion curve of RaceHorses in both configurations.

Figure 7 shows the number of iterations reduced in frames 2 through 8 of the RaceHorses video sequence, respectively. As can be seen from the figure, the method can reduce the number of iterations of hundreds or even thousands for each frame. At the same time, we can also see that the later the frame to be encoded, the more the number of iterations is reduced. This is because, as the block is divided, the later the current frame is, the more information it can refer to.

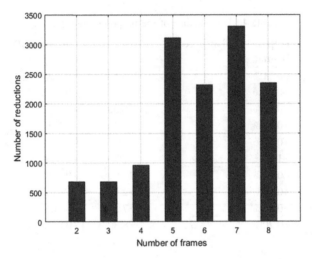

Fig. 7. The number of iterations reduced in the 2nd to 8th frames of RaceHorses.

In order to more objectively demonstrate the impact of the algorithm on the block partition structure, the number of different partition types for the same size CU is demonstrated for the JEM and the proposed algorithm. The statistical result of all

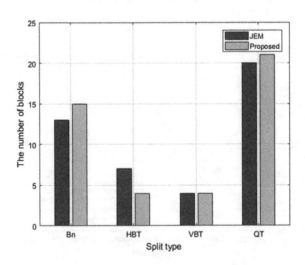

Fig. 8. Number of different partition types of 64×64 blocks in the 5th frame of BasketballPass.

64×64 sized blocks in the 5th frame of the BasketballPass sequence is shown in Fig. 8. It can be seen from the figure that the structure of block partitioning is similar in the two modes. Only a few of the blocks are selected in different types. Therefore, it is further proved that the current fast algorithm saves time while the selected mode is basically the same as JEM.

5 Conclusion

In this paper, we propose a block partitioning decision algorithm based on content complexity that is used to reduce encoding complexity while ensuring encoding performance. By analyzing the relationship between the content complexity of the video content and the four partition methods, the partial splitting mode attempt is terminated in advance, thus the coding complexity is achieved. Experimental results show that the average encoding time of the algorithm is reduced by 9.0%, while the coding performance loss is about 0.55%. This method achieves a good balance of coding performance and complexity.

Acknowledgment. This work was supported in part by the Fundamental Research Funds for the Central Universities (2018JBZ001), and by National Natural Science Foundation of China (No. 61772066).

References

1. Sullivan, G.J.: Overview of the high efficiency video coding (HEVC) standard. IEEE Trans. Circ. Syst. Video Technol. **22**(12), 1649–1668 (2012)
2. An, J.: Quadtree plus binary tree structure integration with JEM tools. JVET-B0023. In: Joint Video Exploration Team (JVET), San Diego, USA (2016)
3. Li, X.: JEM software development (AHG3). Document JVET-J0003-v1. In: Joint Video Exploration Team (JVET), San Diego, USA (2018)
4. Alshina, E.: Performance of JEM 1 tools analysis. Document JVET-B0022. In: Joint Video Exploration Team (JVET), San Diego, USA (2016)
5. Zhang, M.: Fast algorithm for HEVC intra prediction based on adaptive mode decision and early termination of CU partition. In: 2018 Data Compression Conference, Snowbird, UT, USA, p. 434 (2018)
6. Lu X.: A fast HEVC intra-coding algorithm based on texture homogeneity and spatio-temporal correlation. EURASIP J. Adv. Sig. Process. 1–14 (2018)
7. Shi, Z.: Gradient-based and intra-frame adaptive depth decision algorithm. J. Shanghai Normal Univ. (Nat. Sci.) **47**, 248–252 (2018)
8. Gao, X.: A fast HEVC inter CU size decision algorithm based on multi-class learning. In: 2018 10th International Conference on Intelligent Human-Machine Systems and Cybernetics (IHMSC), Hangzhou, China, pp. 64–68 (2018)
9. Liu, X.: An adaptive CU size decision algorithm for HEVC intra prediction based on complexity classification using machine learning. IEEE Trans. Circ. Syst. Video Technol. **29**(1), 144–155 (2019)
10. Wang, Z.: Probabilistic decision based block partitioning for future video coding. IEEE Trans. Image Process. **27**(3), 1475–1486 (2018)

11. Wang, Z.: Effective quadtree plus binary tree block partition decision for future video coding. In: 2017 Data Compression Conference, Snowbird, UT, USA, pp. 27–32 (2017)
12. Lin, T.: Fast binary tree partition decision in H.266/FVC intra coding. In: IEEE International Conference on Consumer Electronics, Taichung, Taiwan, pp. 1–2 (2018)

Multi-view and Stereoscopic Processing

No-Reference Stereoscopic Video Quality Assessment Based on Spatial-Temporal Statistics

Jiufa Zhang[✉], Lixiong Liu, Jiachao Gong, and Hua Huang

Beijing Laboratory of Intelligent Information Technology,
Beijing Institute of Technology, Beijing, People's Republic of China
{zhangjf,lxliu,jc_gong,huahuang}@bit.edu.cn

Abstract. Stereoscopic video quality assessment (SVQA) has become the necessary support for 3D video processing while the research on efficient SVQA method faces enormous challenge. In this paper, we propose a novel blind SVQA method based on monocular and binocular spatial-temporal statistics. We first extract the frames and the frame difference maps from adjacent frames of both left and right view videos as the spatial and spatial-temporal representation of the video content, and then use the local binary pattern (LBP) operator to calculate spatial and temporal domains' statistical features. Besides, we simulate binocular fusion perception by performing weighted integration of generated monocular statistics to obtain binocular scene statistics and motion statistics. Finally, all the computed features are utilized to train the stereoscopic video quality prediction model by a support vector regression (SVR). The experimental results show that our proposed method achieves better performance than state-of-the-art SVQA approaches on three public databases.

Keywords: Stereoscopic video quality assessment · Spatial-temporal · Structural statistics · No-reference

1 Introduction

In recent years, more and more 3D video contents have been demanded and produced. The need for efficient 3D video quality prediction approaches is significantly increasing. The quality representation methods for 3D video mainly include Quality of Service (QoS) and Quality of Experience (QoE). Since human is the ultimate receiver of video contents, the research on QoE becomes particularly important in the field of 3D video perception. Therefore, it is of great significance to study the perceptual quality evaluation methods of 3D video, especially objective methods.

Depending on whether pristine stereo videos can be used, objective stereoscopic video quality assessment (SVQA) methods can be divided into full-reference (FR), no-reference (NR) and reduced-reference (RR) methods. Since it is difficult to guarantee available pristine stereo videos, making it more practical to study the NR SVQA method. In this paper, we consider addressing the problem of NR stereoscopic video quality prediction.

Y. Zhao et al. (Eds.): ICIG 2019, LNCS 11903, pp. 83–94, 2019.
https://doi.org/10.1007/978-3-030-34113-8_8

Some SVQA algorithms have been developed, which have good prediction performance in recent years. However, there still exists room for improving on SVQA methods in terms of prediction performance and compute complexity. The initial SVQA methods simply utilize existing IQA methods such as PSNR and SSIM [1], by obtaining per frame's evaluation score from a video, then using average pooling method to obtain the video's quality score. Obviously, these methods only focus on the spatial information in the video but ignoring the temporal features, depth information, or binocular effects in human visual system (HVS). Consequently, their quality scores are unsatisfactorily consistent with the subjective perception scores. To address this issue, some researchers considered the above aspects to design an efficient SVQA model. Han et al. [2] proposed a FR SVQA method 3D-STS, which utilized structural tensor for salient areas from adjacent frames to predict video quality scores. Yu et al. [3] considered salient frames and binocular perception according to the internal generative mechanism of HVS, and designed a RR SVQA framework. However, these two methods rely on the salient regions and take into account spatial changes on video quality, but ignore the impact of temporal changes on video quality.

Very recently, several SVQA methods have been presented by integrating temporal information. Qi *et al.* [4] proposed a stereo just-noticeable difference model which mainly considers the masking effect in both spatial and temporal domains to evaluate the perceptual quality for stereo videos. Galkandage *et al.* [5] used IQA methods based on a HVS model that considers binocular suppression and recurrent excitation to evaluate frame quality, and then introduced an optimized temporal pooling method to associate the frame quality with the video quality. Yang *et al.* [6] utilized spatial and temporal information in curvelet domain and spatial-temporal optical flow features, and proposed a blind SVQA model named BSVQA. In addition, Yang *et al.* [7] jointly focused on spatial-temporal salient model and sparse representation to calculate the decorrelated features and then predicted stereo video's quality scores by using the deep-learning network. Chen *et al.* [8] integrated natural scene statistics and auto-regressive prediction-based disparity entropy measurement to propose a NR SVQA method. These methods fully consider the video spatial information and even the binocular perceptual characteristics, but utilize less temporal information or just use it as the pooling strategy for spatial features. Besides, these methods execute complex spatial-temporal domain transforms or train deep learning networks for predicting stereo video quality scores, which makes them time-consuming and complex. Considering the impact of binocular perception based on weighted fusion [9, 10] and enriched structural information in image, we attempt to simulate spatial-temporal processing by simply computing monocular and binocular spatial-temporal statistics in our proposed SVQA method.

In this paper, we propose a blind SVQA method that uses enriched structural statistics of spatial-temporal video content. The method firstly extracts the monocular structural statistics from both left and right stereo video frames in spatial domain. We then account for the impact of binocular fusion and weight generated monocular features, yielding binocular statistical features of left and right videos. In addition, following recent evidence regarding the measurement of temporal information of stereoscopic videos by motion intensity features [6], we utilize the frame difference maps from adjacent frames of both view videos as motion representation in spatial-temporal domain. Similar to the process of the spatial information, we perform binocular integration on the monocular features extracted from the frame difference maps. We finally use both monocular and binocular features obtained from the left and right video frames and corresponding frame difference maps to train the stereoscopic video quality prediction model by a support vector regression (SVR) [11].

The rest of this paper is organized as follows. Section 2 details the framework of our proposed method and features extracted from stereoscopic video sequences. In Sect. 3 we test the performance of our method on three public SVQA databases. We conclude the paper and discuss future work in Sect. 4.

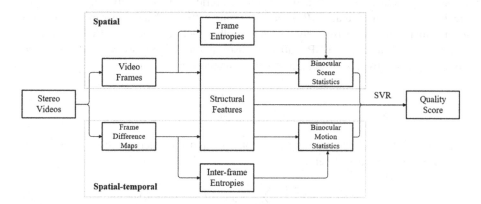

Fig. 1. Framework of our proposed NR SVQA method.

2 Proposed Method

In this section, we present our proposed NR SVQA and show its framework in Fig. 1. As shown in Fig. 1, stereo videos are first processed into video frames associated with monocular spatial information and frame difference maps corresponding to spatial-temporal motion information. We then use the local binary pattern (LBP) operator to calculate the monocular structural statistical features in spatial and spatial-temporal domain. Considering that the binocular perception, especially binocular fusion, plays an important role in the human visual perception of 3D contents, we further integrate the spatial/spatial-temporal statistics by weighting them to obtain binocular scene/motion statistics. Finally, a SVR is used to map all the monocular and binocular statistical features to stereoscopic video quality predictions.

2.1 Overview of LBP

Since HVS is sensitive to structural information in natural scene [1] and local descriptors can effectively represent scene's structural information [6], we utilize the LBP operator, an efficient structural texture descriptor, to process the structural information obtained from the stereo videos. Different from the traditional LBP calculation, here we simply consider the binary relationship of values between the central pixel and its neighborhood pixels in the local image region to obtain the non-uniform LBP operator. For a local region of image, we define the LBP operator through calculating the binary relationship between central pixel p_c and its neighborhood pixels p_i as

$$LBP_{P,R} = \sum_{p=0}^{P-1} \begin{cases} 1, & p_c - p_i \geq 0 \\ 0, & p_c - p_i < 0 \end{cases} \tag{1}$$

where P means the number of neighborhood pixels, R is the radius of the neighborhood, and i denotes the positional order of neighboring pixels. In our proposed method, we set the parameters $P = 8$ and $R = 1$ to empirically simplify the algorithm complexity. It is obvious that $LBP_{P,R}$ has 9 output patterns. Thus, we can transform a natural image into an LBP statistical map with structure patterns between 0 and 8. Finally, we calculate the LBP statistical distribution features as the features of the stereoscopic videos. The structural statistical features are given by

$$h(k) = \frac{G(k)}{\sum_{k=0}^{P} G(k)} \tag{2}$$

where k denotes the possible structure patterns, and $G(\cdot)$ denotes the number each pattern occurs, which is given by

$$G(k) = \sum_{m=1}^{M} \sum_{n=1}^{N} f\left(LBP_{P,R}(m,n), k\right) \tag{3}$$

where M and N mean image size, (m, n) are the coordinates of image pixels, and $f(\cdot)$ is used to calculate the correspondence as

$$f(x,y) = \begin{cases} 1, & x = y \\ 0, & else \end{cases} \tag{4}$$

2.2 Spatial Statistical Features

Due to the complexity of stereo videos, different types and degrees of distortion may occur symmetrically or asymmetrically in both left and right view videos, causing the change of structural information in spatial domain [2]. Consequently, for a stereo video, we first extract its left and right video frames, which can maximize the retention of spatial information. Then, we utilize the LBP operator described above to extract spatial statistical features of left and right video frames, respectively. Different from viewing 2D videos, human eyes perceive differences of binocular perception, such as binocular fusion, binocular rivalry and binocular suppression when viewing stereoscopic videos [3]. Since the binocular perception which has been fully studied in SIQA can greatly influence the perceptual quality when viewing stereo scenes [9, 10], it is valuable to imitate the binocular perception during processing the stereo videos' spatial and temporal information. Since the hybrid combination of features can model 3D image quality based on Bayesian theory [20], instead of directly merging left and right view video frames, we simplify the binocular fusion by pooling monocular spatial statistics to represent binocular perception, which is inspired by [19, 20]. Considering that the entropy can effectively represent the spatial changes caused by distortion [12] or scene changes occurring in left and right frames, we further integrate computed spatial statistics of left and right video frames with the weighted global entropy to generate binocular spatial statistics h_s:

$$h_s = \frac{\varepsilon_{sl} + C}{\varepsilon_{sl} + \varepsilon_{sr} + C} \cdot h_{sl} + \frac{\varepsilon_{sr} + C}{\varepsilon_{sl} + \varepsilon_{sr} + C} \cdot h_{sr} \tag{5}$$

where h_{sl} and h_{sr} are the monocular statistical features of the left and right video frames respectively, C is a constant to avoid the instability, and ε_{sl} and ε_{sr} are the entropy of the corresponding left and right video frames respectively, which is defined as

$$\varepsilon = -\sum_v p(v) log_2 p(v) \tag{6}$$

where v mean the pixel value from 0 to 255 in an image, while $p(\cdot)$ means the empirical probability density. Exemplar left and right video frames from the SVQA database [4] and corresponding calculated spatial statistics h_{sl}, h_{sr} and h_s are shown in Fig. 2. It can be seen that there exists strong correlation between binocular statistics and monocular features.

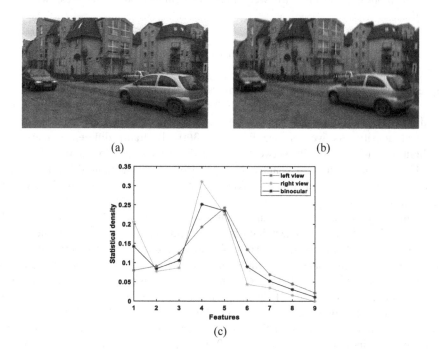

(a)   (b)

(c)

Fig. 2. Video frames and their corresponding statistical feature density. (a) The left video frame (b) the right video frame, and (c) the statistical feature density of monocular and binocular statistics.

2.3 Spatial-Temporal Statistical Features

Considering that videos contain rich temporal information such as motion intensity, which can affect visual perception significantly [6, 13], several SVQA methods have been developed to address the Stereoscopic VQA problem by using temporal information. Since the frame difference map as a widely used spatial-temporal representation, can be used to highlight motion information that exists in the video [6], we also calculate a frame difference map I_d from both adjacent frames of left and right view videos to show temporal changes. The frame difference map is defined as

$$I_d = |I_t - I_{t+1}| \tag{7}$$

where I_t and I_{t+1} denote two adjacent frames at times t and $t+1$ from left or right view video, respectively.

Extracting structural statistical features from frame difference maps can effectively represent the intensity of motion in the scene [6]. Thus, like the spatial statistical feature extraction, the spatial-temporal statistical features of frame difference maps of both videos, which are denoted as h_{dl} and h_{dr}, are calculated by using LBP structural operator firstly. Then, considering the pooling of monocular features can simulate binocular perception [20] and the motion perception is an important part of binocular perception, we assume that the binocular motion statistics h_d is integrated to reflect binocular motion perception by weighting monocular motion statistics, which is defined as

$$h_d = \frac{\varepsilon_{dl} + C}{\varepsilon_{dl} + \varepsilon_{dr} + C} \cdot h_{dl} + \frac{\varepsilon_{dr} + C}{\varepsilon_{dl} + \varepsilon_{dr} + C} \cdot h_{dr} \tag{8}$$

where ε_{dl} and ε_{dr} are the entropy of the corresponding frame difference maps of left and right view videos, respectively. Figure 3 shows the frame difference maps computed on two different stereo videos from the SVQA database and their corresponding binocular statistical density. As we can see from Fig. 3(a)–(d), frame difference maps can highlight the motion intensity between adjacent frames and possible temporal distortion. The binocular statistical features extracted from different frame difference maps can also show the feature distribution diversity for different motion scenes as shown in Fig. 3(e).

In summary, we extract monocular statistics h_{sl}, h_{sr}, h_{dl} and h_{dr} from the left and right view video frames, and weighted binocular statistics h_s and h_d from their corresponding frame difference maps. These features are calculated from frame-level in video sequence. In this paper, we simply take the average of each frame's features as the video-level features. Furthermore, considering multiscale processing has been proved to improve the efficacy of IQA algorithms [9], we extract 9 features computed on all six types of statistics at two scales, yielding $6 \times 2 \times 9 = 108$ features. All these features are empirically trained a SVR, whose kernel function is RBF (Radial Basis Function), margin of tolerance defaults to 0.001 and penalty factor is set to 5, to predict stereoscopic video quality scores [11].

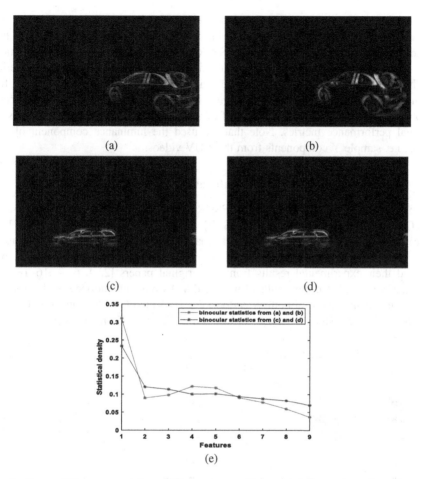

Fig. 3. Frame difference maps from different stereo videos and their corresponding binocular motion statistical feature density. (a) The left frame difference map and (b) the right frame difference map of Poznan Street sequence, (c) the left frame difference map and (d) the right frame difference map of Outdoor sequence, and (e) the statistical feature density of binocular statistics from two groups of frame difference maps.

3 Experimental Results

We verified the performance of our proposed model on three public SVQA databases. These databases are the SVQA database [4], the Waterloo-IVC 3D Video Quality Databases Phase I [14] and Phase II [15]. The SVQA database mainly contains two distortion types: Blur and improper H.264 compression. There exist 450 stereo video sequences of frame rates 25 fps. The Waterloo-IVC 3D Video Quality Database Phase I database contains totally 176 stereo video sequences which are obtained from 4 pristine stereo video sequences by compressing symmetrically or asymmetrically. Besides, the Waterloo-IVC 3D Video Quality Database Phase II contains 528 stereo video sequences obtained from different types of coding and levels of low-pass filtering symmetrically or asymmetrically. We used the Pearson linear correlation coefficient (PLCC), the Spearman rank correlation coefficient (SRCC), the Kendall rank-order correlation coefficient (KRCC) and the Root mean squared error (RMSE) as the evaluation criteria. All three databases were randomly divided into two independent subsets: 80% for training and the remaining 20% for testing. We repeated the training-testing process 1000 times and used the median values of evaluation criteria across 1000 iterations as the final performance metrics. Note that we used the luminance component of the videos, i.e. sample Y components from the YUV videos.

3.1   Performance on Three SVQA Databases

We selected the popular IQA algorithms PSNR and SSIM [1], and several state-of-the-art VQA models PHVS-3D [16], 3D-STS [2], SJND-SVA [4], VQM [17], Sliva [18], Yang [6], and Yang [7], to make the performance comparison on all three databases. Since the source codes of these SVQA approaches are not publicly available, we obtained their experimental results from the original papers [2, 4, 6, 7, 16–18]. In particular, we also listed the results of weighted VQA model mentioned in [15] for the performance comparison on both Waterloo-IVC 3D Video Quality Databases Phase I and Phase II. The results are shown in Fig. 4 and Tables 1, 2 and 3, respectively.

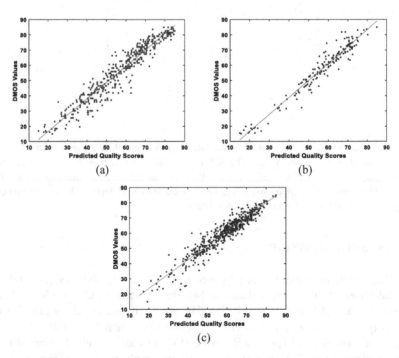

Fig. 4. Scatter plots of predicted quality scores of our proposed method against DMOS on the (a) SVQA, (b) Waterloo-IVC 3D Video Quality Phase I, and (c) Waterloo-IVC 3D Video Quality Phase II.

Table 1. Comparison of seven methods on the SVQA database.

Metric	SRCC	PLCC	KRCC	RMSE
PSNR	0.5319	0.5395	0.3767	0.8374
SSIM	0.4988	0.5025	0.3488	0.8598
PHVS-3D [16]	0.7195	0.7082	0.5353	0.7021
3D-STS [2]	0.8338	0.8311	0.6553	0.5520
SJND-SVA [4]	0.8379	0.8415	0.6650	0.5372
Yang [6]	0.9175	0.9208	0.7730	0.3709
Yang [7]	0.9111	0.9141	0.7605	0.4018
Proposed	0.9247	0.9300	0.7719	0.3625

Table 2. Comparison of seven methods on the Waterloo-IVC Phase I.

Metric	SRCC	PLCC	KRCC	RMSE
PSNR	0.5335	0.7085	0.3850	15.4516
SSIM	0.4789	0.5045	0.3436	18.9039
VQM [17]	0.6321	0.7912	–	13.3905
Weighted VQM [15]	0.8655	0.9191	–	8.6273
Silva [18]	0.6856	0.7416	–	14.6893
Proposed	0.8949	0.9383	0.7380	7.4890

Table 3. Comparison of seven methods on the Waterloo-IVC Phase II.

Metric	SRCC	PLCC	KRCC	RMSE
PSNR	0.3152	0.3286	0.2190	11.6362
SSIM	0.3374	0.3237	0.2432	11.6001
VQM [17]	0.6287	0.7019	–	8.7759
Weighted VQM [15]	0.8042	0.8496	–	6.4976
Silva [18]	0.5184	0.5566	–	10.1051
Proposed	0.8852	0.8814	0.7085	5.8018

Table 4. Performance of spatial and spatial-temporal features on the SVQA database.

Features	Spatial	Spatial-temporal	All
SRCC	0.9140	0.8875	0.9247

Table 5. Computational complexity of three methods on the SVQA database.

Metric	Time (s)
PSNR	4.4490
SSIM	41.0248
Proposed	105.3997

From Tables 1, 2 and 3, it may be shown that our proposed model performed better than all other metrics on the SVQA database, the Waterloo-IVC 3D Video Quality Phase I and Phase II databases. The scatter plot distribution in Fig. 4 shows the scatter plots of predicted quality scores of our proposed method versus DMOS on the three SVQA database. It may be observed that our proposed method correlated well with human subjective judgements on all three databases.

3.2   Performance of Spatial and Spatial-Temporal Features

We tested the performance of spatial and spatial-temporal separately on the SVQA database to verify the validity of the computed features. The SROCC results are listed in Table 4. Clearly, both spatial and spatial-temporal features can capture space-time distortion well, and a combination of these feature achieves better performance.

3.3   Computational Complexity

We also tested the compute complexity of our proposed method on the SVQA database, using a PC with i5-3.2 GHz CPU and 16 GB RAM. Since the source codes of all of selected VQA algorithms are not publicly available and there are no compute complexity experiments in their literatures, only the compute complexity of PSNR and SSIM are analyzed here. We tested three methods on a same pair of videos, and the running time results are listed in Table 5. Clearly, our method is slower than PSNR and SSIM. Considering that our method has better prediction as compared with all of selected methods performance and is not computed in transform domain, our model may be referred to as a relatively fast SVQA method.

4   Conclusion

In this paper, we propose a blind SVQA method based on monocular and binocular spatial-temporal statistics. We utilize the frames of left and right view videos as the spatial representation and extract monocular statistics and weighted binocular scene statistics by using LBP operator. The generated binocular statistics only computed on low-level content makes it possible to design a fast algorithm. Since temporal changes such as motion intensity have a significant impact on stereoscopic video perception, similar to spatial statistical feature extraction, we further extract monocular statistics and binocular motion statistics from frame difference maps as spatial-temporal features. The proposed model was validated on three public SVQA databases, and shown to achieve significant performance improvement. In near future, we will pay more attention on the binocular perceptual mechanism of HVS and design more effective SVQA models.

Acknowledgments. This work is supported by the National Natural Science Foundation of China under grant 61672095 and grant 61425013.

References

1. Wang, Z., Bovik, A.C., Sheikh, H.R., Simoncelli, E.P.: Image quality assessment: from error visibility to structural similarity. IEEE Trans. Image Process. **13**(4), 600–612 (2004)
2. Han, J., Jiang, T., Ma, S.: Stereoscopic video quality assessment model based on spatial-temporal structural information. In: Proceedings IEEE Conference on Visual Communication and Image Processing, pp. 1–6. IEEE, Sarawak (2013)
3. Yu, M., Zheng, K., Jiang, G., Shao, F., Peng, Z.: Binocular perception based reduced-reference stereo video quality assessment method. J. Vis. Commun. Image Represent. **38**, 246–255 (2016)
4. Qi, F., Zhao, D., Fan, X., Jiang, T.: Stereoscopic video quality assessment based on visual attention and just-noticeable difference models. Signal Image Video Process. **10**(4), 737–744 (2016)
5. Galkandage, C., Calic, J., Dogan, S., Guillemaut, J.Y.: Stereoscopic video quality assessment using binocular energy. IEEE J. Sel. Top. Signal Process. **11**(1), 102–112 (2017)
6. Yang, J., Wang, H., Lu, W., Li, B., Badii, A., Meng, Q.: A no-reference optical flow-based quality evaluator for stereoscopic videos in curvelet domain. Inform. Sci. **414**, 133–146 (2017)
7. Yang, J., Ji, C., Jiang, B., Lu, W., Meng, Q.: No reference quality assessment of stereo video based on saliency and sparsity. IEEE Trans. Broadcast. **64**(2), 341–353 (2018)
8. Chen, Z., Zhou, W., Li, W.: Blind stereoscopic video quality assessment: from depth perception to overall experience. IEEE Trans. Image Process. **27**(2), 721–734 (2018)
9. Liu, L., Liu, B., Su, C., Huang, H., Bovik, A.C.: Binocular spatial activity and reverse saliency driven no-reference stereopair quality assessment. Signal Process. Image Commun. **58**, 287–299 (2017)
10. Geng, X., Shen, L., Li, K., An, P.: A stereoscopic image quality assessment model based on independent component analysis and binocular fusion property. Signal Process. Image Commun. **52**, 54–63 (2017)
11. Chang, C.-C., Lin, C.-J.: LIBSVM: a library for support vector machines. ACM Trans. Intell. Syst. Technol. 2(3), 27 (2011). http://www.csie.ntu.edu.tw/~cjlin/libsvm
12. Liu, L., Liu, B., Huang, H., Bovik, A.C.: No-reference image quality assessment based on spatial and spectral entropies. Signal Process. Image Commun. **29**(8), 856–863 (2014)
13. Jiang, G., Liu, S., Yu, M., Shao, F., Peng, Z., Chen, F.: No reference stereo video quality assessment based on motion feature in tensor decomposition domain. J. Vis. Commun. Image Represent. **50**, 247–262 (2018)
14. Wang, J., Wang, S., Wang, Z.: Quality prediction of asymmetrically compressed stereoscopic videos. In: Proceedings IEEE International Conference Image Processing, pp. 1–5. IEEE, Quebec City (2015)
15. Wang, J., Wang, S., Wang, Z.: Asymmetrically compressed stereoscopic 3D videos: quality assessment and rate-distortion performance evaluation. IEEE Trans. Image Process. **26**(3), 1330–1343 (2017)
16. Jin, L., Boev, A., Gotchev, A., Egiazarian, K.: 3d-DCT based perceptual quality assessment of stereo video. In: Proceedings Eighteenth IEEE International Conference Image Processing, pp. 2521–2524. IEEE, Brussels (2011)
17. Pinson, M., Wolf, S.: A new standardized method for objectively measuring video quality. IEEE Trans. Broadcast. **50**(3), 312–322 (2004)
18. De Silva, V., Arachchi, H.K., Ekmekcioglu, E., Kondoz, A.: Toward an impairment metric for stereoscopic video: a full-reference video quality metric to assess compressed stereoscopic video. IEEE Trans. Image Process. **22**(9), 3392–3404 (2013)

94 J. Zhang et al.

19. Fan, Y., Larabi, M.C., Cheikh, F.A., Fernandez-Maloigne, C.: No-reference quality assessment of stereoscopic images based on binocular combination of local features statistics. In: Proceedings IEEE Conference on Image Processing, pp. 3538–3542. IEEE, Athens (2018)
20. Shao, F., Li, K., Lin, W., Jiang, G., Yu, M.: Using binocular feature combination for blind quality assessment of stereoscopic images. IEEE Signal Process. Lett. 22(10), 1548–1551 (2015)

CNN-Based Stereoscopic Image Inpainting

Shen Chen[✉], Wei Ma[✉], and Yue Qin[✉]

Beijing University of Technology, 100 Pingleyuan, Chaoyang District, Beijing, China
{chenshen,qinyue1992}@emails.bjut.edu.cn, mawei@bjut.edu.cn

Abstract. CNN has proved powerful in many tasks, including single image inpainting. The paper presents an end-to-end network for stereoscopic image inpainting. The proposed network is composed of two encoders for independent feature extraction of a pair of stereo images with missing regions, a feature fusion module for stereo coherent structure prediction, and two decoders to generate a pair of completed images. In order to train the model, besides a reconstruction and an adversarial loss for content recovery, a local consistency loss is defined to constrain stereo coherent detail prediction. Moreover, we present a transfer-learning based training strategy to solve the issue of stereoscopic data scarcity. To the best of our knowledge, we are the first to solve the stereoscopic inpainting problem in the framework of CNN. Compared to traditional stereoscopic inpainting and available CNN-based single image inpainting (repairing stereo views one by one) methods, our network generates results of higher image quality and stereo consistency.

Keywords: Stereoscopic vision · Image inpainting · Convolutional Neural Network

1 Introduction

With the development of 3D technology and AR/VR glasses, stereoscopic vision is playing an important role in people's daily life. In the near future, it can be imagined that the scene in the film "Ready Player One" will come true. The soaring of stereoscopic visual data and applications foster research based on such data. Many research topics, targeting at processing the left and right views of stereo images, simultaneously and consistently, have emerged as required, such as stereoscopic image editing [2,15], stereoscopic style transfer [4,10], and stereoscopic image segmentation [17–19].

Before deep learning, inpainting [29] was achieved mainly by searching and copying appropriate local patches from the remaining parts of a given image to

This research is supported by National Natural Science Foundation of China (61771026), Beijing Municipal Natural Science Foundation (4152006), the Open Project Program of the National Laboratory of Pattern Recognition (NLPR), and International Research Cooperation Seed Fund of Beijing University of Technology (No. 2018A02).

© Springer Nature Switzerland AG 2019
Y. Zhao et al. (Eds.): ICIG 2019, LNCS 11903, pp. 95–106, 2019.
https://doi.org/10.1007/978-3-030-34113-8_9

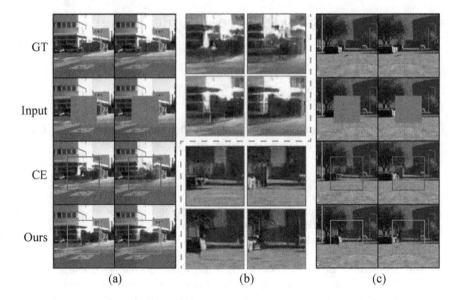

Fig. 1. Results obtained by Context Encoder (CE in the figure) [24] and the proposed method. Groundtruth (GT in the figure) and inputs are presented in the first and second rows, respectively. (a) Results on KITTI [9] images; (b) Close-up views of the results; (c) Results on Driving [20] images.

be repaired. In order to deal with stereo images, consistency between the left and right views was formulated into the inpainting process [21,22,27]. Despite great progress, it is hard for these patch-based methods to complete large missing areas correctly. This is because they can hardly perceive the global context of a given image to guide structure prediction. Moreover, source patches used for filling the hole are limited to coming from the remaining parts of the image.

In recent years, CNN (Convolutional Neural Network), acknowledged for its strong ability in feature representation after being well trained on large dataset, has been widely used in many tasks, including image inpainting. For example, Pathak et al. [24] presented a CNN-based encoder-decoder network, called Context Encoder, which captures image context into a compact latent feature representation. It was demonstrated to have better performances than traditional patch-based methods in semantic hole-filling [24]. However, up to now, there is no related work trying to solve the problem of stereoscopic image inpainting in the framework of deep learning.

Of course, stereo images could be inpainted one by one, by using networks for single images, e.g. Context Encoder [24]. However, as shown in Fig. 1, stereoscopic repairing without considering consistency between left and right views produces inconsistent contents. The paper therefore proposes a stereoscopic image inpainting network, which takes both views into consideration simultaneously with the information aggregation in a feature level. Meanwhile, the consistency in pixel level is also be improved by minimizing stereo matching cost according to the disparity map.

On the other hand, CNN based image inpainting is a data-hungry task [24]. Previous monocular networks [24] are generally pre-trained on *ImageNet* [25] for better performance and generalization. Unfortunately, there is no such huge stereoscopic dataset like *ImageNet*. In order to overcome this obstacle, our network is designed to be pre-trainable on monocular images.

The main contributions of this paper are summarized as follows:

1. A CNN-based stereoscopic image inpainting network, called Stereo Inpainting Net, is proposed. To the best of our knowledge, we are the first to solve the stereoscopic image inpainting problem in the framework of deep learning;
2. Our network encodes stereo consistency in both structure and detail levels, via a specially designed feature fusion module and a local correspondence loss, respectively. We validate the effectiveness of the feature fusion module and the consistency loss via ablation study;
3. Under the circumstance of stereoscopic data scarcity for training the network, we find a way to pre-train the network with single images, specifically being the huge *ImageNet* dataset. We validate the pre-training strategy via comparison experiments. This strategy could be generalized to other stereoscopic image processing tasks.

2   Related Work

Our work is directly related to traditional patch-based stereoscopic inpainting approaches in topics and CNN-based image inpainting in frameworks. Besides, the proposed method is also relevant to those involving stereoscopic consistency constrains. Therefore, we introduce related works from the above three aspects.

Patch-Based Stereoscopic Image Inpainting. Given a pair of stereo images, traditional methods [21,22,27], specifically being those without using deep learning, find usable patches only from the remaining parts and fill holes with stereo consistency constraints. For example, Wang et al. [27] completed RGB images and disparity maps jointly via greedy patch searching. The disparity maps were then used for consistency check to refine RGB completion. Morse et al. [21] firstly completed the disparity maps while maintaining mutual consistency by using a coupled Partial Differential Equation (PDE). Then, they used the completed disparity maps to guide cross-image patch search to fill RGB images. The above methods, limited by available data in the remaining parts and the quality of the completed disparity maps, are not good at repairing large missing areas and foreground with abrupt depth changes. Luo et al. [16] proposed a method which could edit both foreground and background. However, it needs users to manually provide a target depth map, thereby not being used for performance comparison in our experiments. The two automatic patch-based methods [21,27] are tested and demonstrate poorer performances than our CNN-based method in filling foreground and large holes.

CNN-Based Image Inpainting. Inspired by the ability of CNN in feature representation, global structure extraction and image generation [7], Pathak et al. [24] proposed Context Encoder for single image inpainting. It is an encoder-decoder network with an adversarial loss. After sufficient training on extensive image dataset, Context Encoder is able to extract semantic features from input images with holes and generate completed images. Compared to traditional patch-based methods, Context Encoder is good at perceiving and recovering image structures. Besides, this network is able to generate novel contents, which might not appear in input images. Based on Context Encoder, several other approaches were proposed. For example, Yang et al. [30] and Wu et al. [28] improved its performance in dealing with high-resolution images. Demir et al. [5] polished the residual after initial restoration. Iizuka et al. [14] combined global and local consistency to make images more natural and plausible. These CNN-based methods perform well in monocular image inpainting. Based on these works, we develop a new network for stereo image inpainting, which successfully models consistency in both structure and detail levels. Moreover, we solve the stereoscopic data scarcity problem by a pre-training strategy.

Stereoscopic Consistency Constraints. Keeping consistency among different views is essential when processing multi-view images [1,26]. Baek et al. [1] used structure propagation for consistent space topology across images. For stereoscopic image inpainting, disparities computed by left and right correspondences are widely used to form consistency constraints in the patch-based framework. For example, Wang et al. [27] inpainted images and their disparities together and then refined the results via disparity-determined consistency, iteratively. Morse et al. [21] and Luo et al. [16] filled stereo images based on their disparity maps which were completed in advance. Although there are no CNN-based stereoscopic inpainting methods according to our investigation, other tasks targeting at processing stereo images under the framework of CNN have appeared and certainly used consistency constraints. For instance, Chen et al. [4] and Gong et al. [10] adopted disparity maps to guide feature aggregation in a middle level for stereoscopic style transfer. Our methods are much different from the above ones in frameworks or tasks. However, the above works inspire us much in modeling stereo consistency in the proposed Stereo Inpainting Net.

3   Stereoscopic Inpainting Network

3.1   Overview

The overall architecture of the proposed network, called Stereo Inpainting Net, is given in Fig. 2. It has two encoders sharing parameters with each other. Each encoder captures the context of the left/right view of an input image pair and expresses the context in a semantic feature representation. The feature representations of the two views are concatenated and fused via a fusion layer. Two decoders ($Decoder_l$ and $Decoder_r$) take the fused features and generate a pair

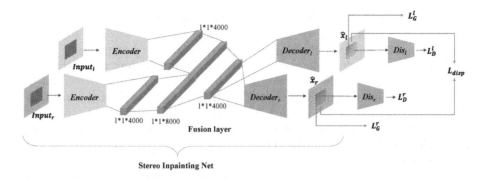

Fig. 2. Architecture overview.

of completed images ($\hat{x}_l$ and $\hat{x}_r$), simultaneously. Decoding based on the fused features achieves coherent structure repairing.

As illustrated in Fig. 2, the total loss, denoted as L_{total}, is composed of three parts:

$$L_{total} = \sum_{d \in \{l,r\}} (\alpha L_G^d + \beta L_D^d) + \gamma L_{disp}. \tag{1}$$

Here, $d \in \{l, r\}$ denotes a current view (left or right). L_G, L_D are an $L2$ reconstruction loss and an adversarial loss, respectively. L_{disp} is a local consistency loss. α, β and γ are weights balancing the three. The $L2$ reconstruction loss captures the overall structures of the missing regions in relation to the context, while the adversarial loss, making prediction of the discriminators (Dis_l and Dis_r) look real, drives the Stereo Inpainting Net to produce sharper predictions [24]. The local consistency loss, constraining the left and right views to look similar in details, is a complementary of the feature fusion layer in enforcing stereo consistency. We train the Stereo Inpainting Net with parts of or all the losses in multiple stages. Since there is no enough stereoscopic data available, a training strategy based on transfer learning is proposed.

The encoders, decoders, and the discriminators have the same architectures with those in Context Encoder [24], thereby being skipped in this paper. In the following, we will introduce the fusion layer for structure consistency, the local consistency loss, and the transfer-learning based training strategy, in detail.

3.2 Feature Fusion for Structure Consistency

For stereo coherent inpainting, the network is supposed to take both views into consideration, comprehensively. An intuitive way to achieve this is to pile the two RGB views into six channels and send them into a single network. As demonstrated in [3,23], composition in a semantic feature level is more robust than that in the original image level. Thus, we feed the two views into encoders separately and fuse their features for coherent inpainting. Moreover, this design enables us to transfer parameters of the pre-trained Context Encoder [24], as we will explain in Sect. 3.4. Inspired by the Siamese network [32] used to calculate stereo matching costs, the two encoders share weights, in order to reduce parameters and produce unified feature representations for feature fusion.

Through the encoders, the two views are turned into feature vectors of 4000 channels. To aggregate the information of both views, we concatenate the two feature vectors into one of 8000 channels. After that, we apply a channel-wise convolution to the combined vector to blend features from different channels and produce a fused feature vector of 4000. Based on the fused feature vector, two independent decoders are employed to generate unique contents for the left and right views, respectively.

Both the reconstruction loss and the adversarial loss will be used for training the feature fusion layer. The former measures the $L2$ distance between generated images by Stereo Inpainting Net and ground truth. The reconstruction loss for view d is given by:

$$L_G^d = \|(G(M \odot x_d) - x_d) \odot (1 - M)\|_2. \tag{2}$$

Here, x_d is a ground-truth view. $M \odot x_d$ denotes the input for training. M is a mask, in which a missing area is filled with 0 and the other pixels are set to be 1. $\odot$ is the element-wise product operation. $G(input_d)$ is the generation function represented by Decoder$_d$. The adversarial loss [11] is computed after the discriminators in Fig. 2. The discriminators receive generated images or ground truth as input and make a judgement whether the input is real. Two discriminators sharing weights have been tried in our experiments. However, it results in poor convergence because the derivatives provided by left and right branches are not symmetric. More generally, when dealing with stereoscopic images with GANs [11], it is a good practice to use two branches of decoders and discriminators, in order to make the training process easier and more stable. The adversarial loss for view d is computed by binary cross entropy over the judgements $D()$ and ground-truth labels:

$$L_D^d = \max_D \mathbb{E}_{x \in X}[\log D((1 - M) \odot x_d) + \log(1 - D(G(M \odot x_d)))]. \tag{3}$$

3.3 Local Consistency Loss

The local consistency loss, L_{disp}, measures the differences between corresponding patches in the generated left and right views of contents. The loss computation is illustrated in Fig. 3. For each pixel i in the filled areas (indicated by the dashed boxes) of the left view, i.e. $i \in (1 - M) \odot \hat{x}_l$, we take a 3×3 patch $P_l(i)$ around i and warp the patch to the right image by the disparity of i. The disparity map of the left view is computed by DispNet [20]. Through warping, we find the corresponding patch of $P_l(i)$ in the right view.

We denote the corresponding patch of $P_l(i)$ as $\overleftarrow{W}(P_l(i), x_{disp}(i))$. L_{disp} is defined as:

$$L_{disp} = \frac{1}{|(1 - M) \odot x_l|} \sum_{i \in (1-M) \odot x_l} cost(P_l(i), \overleftarrow{W}(P_l(i), x_{disp}(i))) \tag{4}$$

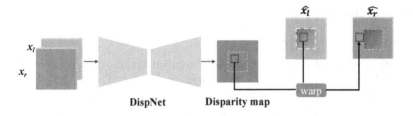

Fig. 3. Patch matching for local consistency loss.

Here, $cost()$ measures the distance between the two patches. According to [12], many stereo matching costs, e.g. Sum of Squared Differences (SSD), Sum of Absolute Differences (SAD), mutual information [8], rank and census transforms [31], could be used. Unfortunately, some of them, such as rank transform and hierarchical mutual information, are unable to propagate derivatives backward. In this paper, we choose Normalized Cross-Correlation (NCC) [12] as the stereo matching cost.

3.4 Transfer-Learning Based Training

Due to the stereoscopic data limit, we present a transfer-learning based training strategy, which is summarized in Algorithm 1.

Algorithm 1. Transfer & Train

1: train Context Encoder on *ImageNet*
2: transfer parameters of the encoder and decoder from Context Encoder to ours
3: **while** iterations $t < T_{train}$ **do**
4:   **if** $t < T_{fusion}$ **then**
5:     lock encoders and decoders
6:     update fusion layer with L_G loss
7:   **else if** $t < T_D$ **then**
8:     lock Stereo Inpainting Net
9:     update discriminator with L_D loss
10:   **else if** $t < T_G$ **then**
11:     update Stereo Inpainting Net and discriminator with $\alpha L_G + \beta L_D$
12:   **else**
13:     generate disparity maps by DispNet [20]
14:     update the whole network in Fig 2 with the total loss L_{total}
15:   **end if**
16: **end while**

Here, $T_{train} = 2500$, $T_{fusion} = 100$, $T_D = 300$, and $T_G = 1000$. T_{fusion}, $T_D - T_{fusion}$, $T_G - T_D$ denote individually trained epochs for the fusion layer, the discriminator and the Stereo Inpainting Net plus discriminator, respectively. The whole network in Fig. 2 is trained for $T_{train} - T_G$ epochs.

4   Experiments

4.1   Implementation Details

Experimental Settings. We use Adam for optimization with a learning rate of 0.0002 and without weight decay. The batch size is 128. The weights balancing the three losses in Eq. 1 are set to be $\alpha = 1, \beta = 0.001, \gamma = 0.1$.

Dataset. In Algorithm 1, the baseline net, Context Encoder, is trained on *ImageNet* [25] which has $1,260,000$ monocular images. The remaining training steps are performed on *KITTI* [9]. The original *KITTI* dataset contains $42,382$ rectified stereo pairs from 61 scenes. Images in this dataset are captured at 10 Hz and their resolution is 1242×375 pixels. In our experiments, we resample the dataset with 1/5 of the original frequency to avoid high correlation among image pairs and generate 8476 stereo pairs, in which 8176 pairs for training our network and the left 300 pairs for the validation in Sect. 4.2 and the qualitative evaluation in Sect. 4.3. The images are resized to be 640×384 for computation convenience of DispNet [20]. At each training iteration or testing step, we randomly crop a pair of 128×128 pixels in the resized image pairs as input. Quantitative evaluation in Sect. 4.3 is carried out on *Driving* dataset [20], which has 4392 frames with accurate disparity. The dataset is resampled (with lower frequency and removal of too dark images) to be 600 pairs, 400 for fine tuning the network on this dataset and 200 for quantitative test.

4.2   Evaluation on Transfer-Learning Based Training

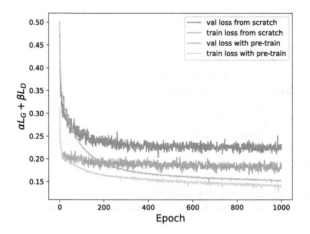

Fig. 4. Loss curves with and without transfer learning on both training and validation datasets.

To verify the performance of the transfer learning strategy, comparison is made between the network trained from scratch by ignoring step 2 in Algorithm 1 and our network trained based on transfer learning. Figure 4 presents the reconstruction-plus-adversarial loss curves of the two networks, on the *KITTI* training and validation datasets, respectively. From the figure, it can be seen that our network with transfer learning achieves much lower loss on both training and validation data than the one trained from scratch. In addition, with transfer learning, the performance of the network on the validation data is closer to that on the training data, which means the network is better in generalization [6].

4.3 Evaluation on the Proposed Network with Ablation Study

Quantitative Evaluation. In order to demonstrate the effectiveness of our method sufficiently, we present quantitative evaluation and comparison with the other methods in aspects of stereo consistency and image quality. Results are given in Table 1. The stereo consistency is quantified with SSD and SAD of corresponding patches (1×1 pixels in this evaluation). In order to avoid influences from disparity noises, we carry out the evaluation on the *Driving* dataset [20] with ground truth disparity maps. Note that Context Encoder and our models are fine-tuned on the dataset in advance with parts of the *Driving* dataset (refer to Sect. 4.1). PSNR (Peak Signal-to-Noise Ratio) and SSIM (Structural Similarity Index) [13] are employed to measure the image quality of the generated contents in pixels and local structures, respectively.

Table 1. Quantitative results in stereoscopic inconsistency and image quality.

Method	Inconsistency		Image quality	
	SAD	SSD	PSNR	SSIM
Wang et al. [27]	1572.7	762.1	14.947	0.2652
Morse et al. [21]	1522.4	743.6	16.835	0.2729
Context Encoder [24]	1783.6	936.4	17.132	0.2811
Ours (without L_{disp})	1569.2	760.9	17.554	0.2966
Ours (complete)	**1466.1**	**715.4**	**17.910**	**0.3117**

As it can be seen from Table 1, Context Encoder performs poorly in keeping consistency. To be noticed, lower SAD/SSD means higher consistency while higher PSNR/SSIM means better quality. In contrast, patch-based methods are better at keeping consistency, but cannot produce images with high quality. Our network, even the one with only feature fusion, generates contents with high quality and consistency, simultaneously.

Qualitative Evaluation. We compare the results of our method with Context Encoder [24] and two traditional patch-based stereoscopic inpainting methods [21,27]. Context Encoder is used to repair stereo images view by view, independently. Parts of the results on the *KITTI* and *Driving* validation dataset are given in Figs. 1 and 5. From Fig. 5, it can be seen that patch-based stereoscopic methods can restore missing areas and keep the consistency of these areas to some extent. However, their performances are limited by existing patches in the source images and they are prone to destroy the structure integrity. For example, in Fig. 5(a), patch-based methods break the window structure seriously because the window is partly missing in both views.

In contrast, Context Encoder is better at predicting content structures in the missing parts than patch-based methods, as it can be seen from Fig. 5. However, view-by-view repairing often leads to stereo inconsistency. For example, in the results of Context Encoder in Fig. 5(b), the yellow car appearing in the right view is absent in the left view.

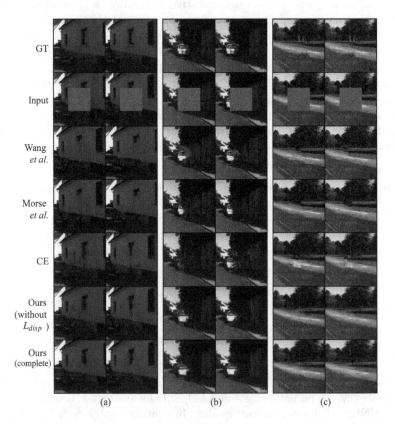

Fig. 5. Results obtained by Wang et al. [27], Morse et al. [21], Context Encoder [24] and our method without and with disparity loss. The first and second rows are ground truth (GT in the figure) and inputs, respectively. (Color figure online)

From these figures, it can be seen that our network improves the consistency of structures by employing feature fusion. The disparity-determined local consistency loss helps coherent inpainting in detail level. In all, compared with the patch-based methods and Context Encoder, our network obtains better inpainting results in stereo consistency. In the meanwhile, the quality of each image generated by our network also looks better than those obtained by existing methods. Due to page limit, only few examples are listed. More results are provided in the supplementary material.

5   Conclusion

In this paper, a stereoscopic image inpainting network was proposed. The network was endowed with a specially assigned feature fusion layer and a local correspondence loss. The two played essential roles in coherent stereoscopic inpainting in structures and details, respectively. Besides, a transfer-learning based training strategy was presented, which conquered the problem of stereoscopic data scarcity. Contents predicted by the proposed network demonstrated higher stereo consistency and image quality than state-of-the-art methods.

References

1. Baek, S.H., Choi, I., Kim, M.H.: Multiview image completion with space structure propagation. In: IEEE Conference on Computer Vision and Pattern Recognition, pp. 488–496 (2016)
2. Chang, C.H., Liang, C.K., Chuang, Y.Y.: Content-aware display adaptation and interactive editing for stereoscopic images. IEEE Trans. Multimedia 13(4), 589–601 (2011)
3. Chen, D., Liao, J., Yuan, L., Yu, N., Hua, G.: Coherent online video style transfer. In: IEEE International Conference on Computer Vision, pp. 1114–1123 (2017)
4. Chen, D., Yuan, L., Liao, J., Yu, N., Hua, G.: Stereoscopic neural style transfer. In: IEEE Conference on Computer Vision and Pattern Recognition (2018)
5. Demir, U., Ünal, G.B.: Deep stacked networks with residual polishing for image inpainting. arXiv:1801.00289 (2017)
6. Domingos, P.: A few useful things to know about machine learning. Commun. ACM 55(10), 78–87 (2012)
7. Dosovitskiy, A., Springenberg, J.T., Brox, T.: Learning to generate chairs with convolutional neural networks. In: IEEE Conference on Computer Vision and Pattern Recognition, pp. 1538–1546 (2015)
8. Egnal, G.: Mutual information as a stereo correspondence measure. Technical reports (2000)
9. Geiger, A., Lenz, P., Stiller, C., Urtasun, R.: Vision meets robotics: the KITTI dataset. Int. J. Robot. Res. 32(11), 1231–1237 (2013)
10. Gong, X., Huang, H., Ma, L., Shen, F., Liu, W.: Neural stereoscopic image style transfer. arXiv:1802.09985 (2018)
11. Goodfellow, I.J., et al.: Generative adversarial nets. In: International Conference on Neural Information Processing Systems, pp. 2672–2680 (2014)
12. Hirschmüller, H., Scharstein, D.: Evaluation of cost functions for stereo matching. In: IEEE Conference on Computer Vision and Pattern Recognition, pp. 1–8 (2007)
13. Horé, A., Ziou, D.: Image quality metrics: PSNR vs. SSIM. In: International Conference on Pattern Recognition, pp. 2366–2369 (2010)

14. Iizuka, S., Simo-Serra, E., Ishikawa, H.: Globally and locally consistent image completion. ACM Trans. Graph. **36**(4), 107:1–107:14 (2017)
15. Lo, W.Y., van Baar, J., Knaus, C., Zwicker, M., Gross, M.: Stereoscopic 3D copy & paste. ACM Trans. Graph. **29**(6), 147:1–147:10 (2010)
16. Luo, S.J., Sun, Y.T., Shen, I.C., Chen, B.Y., Chuang, Y.Y.: Geometrically consistent stereoscopic image editing using patch-based synthesis. IEEE Trans. Visual Comput. Graph. **21**(1), 56–67 (2015)
17. Ma, W., Qin, Y., Xu, S., Zhang, X.: Interactive stereo image segmentation via adaptive prior selection. Multimedia Tools Appl. **77**, 28709–28724 (2018)
18. Ma, W., Qin, Y., Yang, L., Xu, S., Zhang, X.: Interactive stereo image segmentation with RGB-D hybrid constraints. IEEE Signal Process. Lett. **23**, 1533–1537 (2016)
19. Ma, W., Yang, L., Zhang, Y.L., Duan, L.: Fast interactive stereo image segmentation. Multimedia Tools Appl. **75**, 10935–10948 (2015)
20. Mayer, N., et al.: A large dataset to train convolutional networks for disparity, optical flow, and scene flow estimation. In: IEEE Conference on Computer Vision and Pattern Recognition, pp. 4040–4048 (2016)
21. Morse, B.S., Howard, J., Cohen, S., Price, B.L.: PatchMatch-based content completion of stereo image pairs. In: International Conference on 3D Imaging, Modeling, Processing, Visualization & Transmission, pp. 555–562 (2012)
22. Mu, T.J., Wang, J.H., Du, S.P., Hu, S.: Stereoscopic image completion and depth recovery. Vis. Comput. **30**(6–8), 833–843 (2014)
23. Oquab, M., Bottou, L., Laptev, I., Sivic, J.: Learning and transferring mid-level image representations using convolutional neural networks. In: IEEE Conference on Computer Vision and Pattern Recognition, pp. 1717–1724 (2014)
24. Pathak, D., Krähenbühl, P., Donahue, J., Darrell, T., Efros, A.A.: Context encoders: feature learning by inpainting. In: IEEE Conference on Computer Vision and Pattern Recognition, pp. 2536–2544 (2016)
25. Russakovsky, O., et al.: Imagenet large scale visual recognition challenge. Int. J. Comput. Vis. **115**(3), 211–252 (2015)
26. Thaskani, S., Karande, S.S., Lodha, S.: Multi-view image inpainting with sparse representations. In: IEEE International Conference on Image Processing, pp. 1414–1418 (2015)
27. Wang, L., Jin, H., Yang, R., Gong, M.: Stereoscopic inpainting: joint color and depth completion from stereo images. In: IEEE Conference on Computer Vision and Pattern Recognition, pp. 1–8 (2008)
28. Wu, H., Zheng, S., Zhang, J., Huang, K.: GP-GAN: towards realistic high-resolution image blending. arXiv:1703.07195 (2017)
29. Xu, Z., Sun, J.: Image inpainting by patch propagation using patch sparsity. IEEE Trans. Image Process. **19**(5), 1153–11657 (2010)
30. Yang, C., Lu, X., Lin, Z., Shechtman, E., Wang, O., Li, H.: High-resolution image inpainting using multi-scale neural patch synthesis. In: IEEE Conference on Computer Vision and Pattern Recognition, pp. 4076–4084 (2017)
31. Zabih, R., Woodfill, J.: Non-parametric local transforms for computing visual correspondence. In: Eklundh, J.-O. (ed.) ECCV 1994. LNCS, vol. 801, pp. 151–158. Springer, Heidelberg (1994). https://doi.org/10.1007/BFb0028345
32. Zbontar, J., LeCun, Y.: Computing the stereo matching cost with a convolutional neural network. In: IEEE Conference on Computer Vision and Pattern Recognition, pp. 1592–1599 (2015)

Edge Orientation Driven Depth Super-Resolution for View Synthesis

Chao Yao[1(✉)], Jimin Xiao[2], Jian Jin[3], and Xiaojuan Ban[1(✉)]

[1] Beijing Advanced Innovation Center for Materials Genome Engineering,
School of Computer and Communication Engineering,
University of Science and Technology Beijing, Beijing 100083, China
{yaochao,banxj}@ustb.edu.cn
[2] The Department of Electrical and Electronic Engineering,
Xi'an Jiaotong-Liverpool University, Suzhou 215123, China
[3] Institute of Information Science,
Beijing Jiaotong University, Beijing 100044, China

Abstract. The limited resolution of depth images is a constraint for most of practical computer vision applications. To solve this problem, in this paper, we present a novel depth super-resolution method based on machine learning. The proposed super-resolution method incorporates an edge-orientation based depth patch clustering method, which classifies the patches into several categories based on gradient strength and directions. A linear mapping between the low resolution (LR) and high resolution (HR) patch pairs is learned for each patch category by minimizing the synthesis view distortion. Since depth maps are not viewed directly, they are used to generate the virtual views, our method takes synthesis view distortion as the optimization strategy. Experimental results show that our proposed depth super-resolution approach performs well on depth super-resolution performance and the view synthesis compared to other depth super-resolution approaches.

Keywords: View synthesis · Depth-image-based rendering · Linear mapping · Edge orientation

1 Introduction

Depth super-resolution is one of important research topics in the image processing and computer vision field. In practical applications, since depth information is always captured in a low resolution, depth images have to be interpolated to the full size corresponding to the texture images. For example, the resolution of depth image captured by the Swiss Range SR4000 is only QCIF format (176×144 pixels). Even for Kinect, the resolution of captured depth image is only 640×480 (512×424 for Kinect v2), which is much lower than its corresponding color image (1920×1080 for Kinect v2). Hence, interpolation and other image enhancement techniques are essential to improve the resolution and

© Springer Nature Switzerland AG 2019
Y. Zhao et al. (Eds.): ICIG 2019, LNCS 11903, pp. 107–121, 2019.
https://doi.org/10.1007/978-3-030-34113-8_10

quality of depth images. For the applications like 3D viewpoint reconstruction, action recognition and object detection [28], high resolution and accuracy depth information can help to improve the system performance.

Reconstructing High Resolution (HR) images from Low Resolution (LR) images is an ill-posed inverse problem [14,36]. It is difficult to produce high quality. Nevertheless, for depth super-resolution, it could be slightly easier because depth image has more homogeneous regions and more similar structures than the natural images. Generally speaking, researches on depth super-resolution can be divided into two categories: single depth super-resolution and depth super-resolution with multiple images. For single depth super-resolution, depth maps are directly interpolated into the full size of the corresponding color images, without other side information. Consequently, depth super-resolution is equivalent with the general image super-resolution, some classical interpolation filters including bi-linear, bi-cubic interpolation filter can be used. However, since filter-based method rarely consider the property of depth maps, i.e. the importance of edges, the performance of the depth super-resolution is largely limited. Therefore, to preserve depth edges in the interpolation process, optimization based methods which regard depth super-resolution as a Markov Random Field (MRF) or least squares optimization problem are proposed. *Kim et al.* proposed a novel MRF-based depth super-resolution method taking the noise characteristics of depth map into account [13]. *Zhu et al.* further extended the traditional spatial MRF by considering temporal coherence [39]. In [6], depth super-resolution was formulated as a convex optimization problem which utilizes anisotropic total generalized variation. Then, patch-based features in a depth map were employed to optimize depth super-resolution. [9] proposed to exploit the self-similar patch in the rigid body to reconstruct the high resolution depth maps. In [16], depth edges were preserved in the interpolation process by adding geometric constraints from self-similar structures. In [4,7,11,33,35], sparse representation of depth image patches were introduced by imposing a locality constraint. Unfortunately, the performance of the above methods could be limited due to the failure of establishing patch correspondences either from the external dataset or within the same depth map, which leads to edge artifacts between patches or incorrect depth pattern estimation.

To eliminate the edge artifacts after depth super-resolution operation, the corresponding color images are utilized as geometric constraints [20]. A classical method is to apply bilateral filter to enhance depth quality [24,30], in which color information are jointly utilized as weights of bilateral filter. In [3] and [32], color images were directly used to guide the depth image super-resolution. In [17] and [18], the edge and structure similarity between depth images and color images are considered for depth images up-sampling. *Park et al.* extended the nonlocal mean filtering with an edge weighting term in [23]. *Xie et al.* proposed an edge-guided depth super-resolution, which produces sharp edges [34]. Then, *Yang et al.* proposed to use multiple views to assist the depth super-resolution in [37]. *Choi et al.* proposed a region segmentation based method to tackle the texture-transfer and depth-bleeding artifacts in [2]. Recently, some convolutional neural network based depth super-resolution methods are also proposed to learn the texture-depth mapping [19,31], however, these methods still need to use the classical interpolation methods to obtain HR depth in the first stage, ignoring the relations between LR-depth and HR-texture. And most importantly, only depth distortion is considered which is similar as the learning based super-resolution method.

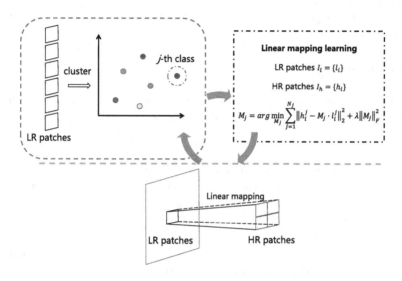

Fig. 1. Flowchart of learning-based image super-resolution.

In fact, for most depth based applications, depth images are generally not provided for watching but for enhancing the applicability. For instance, in 3D video framework, depth images are used to assist virtual views synthesis, instead of being watched by users. Hence, integrating view synthesis quality into depth super-resolution problem is necessary. *Jin et al.* design a natural image super-resolution framework, in which depth images are utilized to synthesize the image, and the synthesis artifacts are used as a criteria to guide the image super-resolution [12]. [10] introduces the difference between color image and synthesized images as a regularization term for depth super-resolution. In [17], the fractal dimension and texture-depth boundary consistencies are jointly considered in depth super-resolution.

In this paper, we present a depth super-resolution method based on the relations between HR and LR depth patches. Considering the sharpness of depth edge, the LR-depth patches are firstly clustered based on their edge orientations into different edge-orientation classes. Here, the edge-orientation feature is extracted based on our designed gradient operators, in which the edge strength and direction are employed as the basis for the LR patches cluster. Then for each edge-orientation class, a class-dependent linear mapping function is learned using LR-HR patch pairs. Moreover, the view synthesis distortion is integrated into the linear mapping learning process. Therefore, depth super-resolution problem is formulated as view synthesis distortion driven linear mapping learning optimization. Experimental results show that our proposed depth super-resolution method achieves superior performance for the synthesized virtual view compared with other depth super-resolution approaches.

The paper is organized as follows: Sect. 2 describes the proposed depth super-resolution framework, along with details. Section 3 shows the settings of our experiment and the performance of our proposed approach. At last, we conclude this paper in Sect. 4.

2   Methodology

Typically, learning-based image super-resolution aims to learn a linear mapping relation between LR-HR patch pairs. For example, as shown in Fig. 1,

$$\mathbf{x} = \mathbf{My}, \tag{1}$$

where $y \in \mathbb{R}^m$, $x \in \mathbb{R}^n$, $m \le n$, $\mathbf{M}$ is a linear mapping operator.

For LR-to-HR conversions, the linear mapping between LR-HR pairs should be learned. Specifically, the LR image $\mathbf{I_l}$ is denoted as

$$\mathbf{I_l} = \{l_i\}_{i=1}^N, \tag{2}$$

where l_i is i−th LR image patch, N is the total number of depth image patches in $\mathbf{I_l}$. Similarly, the HR image is also represented as

$$\mathbf{I_h} = \{h_i\}_{i=1}^N. \tag{3}$$

Then, the LR-HR patch pairs are classified into different classes based on the specified rule. U is the number of the classes, N_j is the number of patches which belong to j−th class, $\sum_{j=1}^U N_j = N$. For each class j, the linear mapping can be learned from an error minimization equation as follows [14]

$$M_j = \arg \min_{M_j} \sum_{j=1}^{N_j} \|h_i^j - M_j \cdot l_i^j\|_2^2 + \lambda \|M_j\|_F^2, \tag{4}$$

where h_i^j, l_i^j are the concatenate matrix of the vectorized HR, LR patches which belong to the j−th class, M_j is the mapping kernel of the j−th class. $\|M_j\|_F^2$ is a regularization term with Frobenius norm which can prevent overfitting, and λ is a penalty factor which is empirically set to 1 in general. Therefore, the learning-based image super-resolution is expressed as a multivariate regression problem. The goal of the regression is to minimize the Mean Squared Error (MSE) between the ground-truth HR patches and the patches which are interpolated from the corresponding LR patches,

$$J = \min \frac{1}{N_j} \sum_{j=1}^N \|h_i^j - M_j \cdot l_i^j\|_2^2. \tag{5}$$

Nevertheless, depth images are different from the natural images, they are just used to assist various applications, i.e. view synthesis, object recognition and action recognition etc. Hence, the goal of depth image super-resolution should be different from the traditional image super-resolution. In this work, we assume that depth images are used for view synthesis. In the following of this paper, we are addressing the depth image super-resolution problem in the framework of view synthesis.

2.1   Depth Patches Classification Based on Edge Orientation

The published super-resolution methods [1,27,29] use edge-orientation information to implement the LR-to-HR interpolation for texture images. However, since color images usually poss very complicated texture, the edge-orientation information is difficult to extract for patch clustering. Compared to texture images, depth images represent the distance between the camera and objects in a scene and generally have more homogeneous regions and sharp edges, without much texture. Consequently, edge information in depth images is vivid and the corresponding features are easily extracted. Motivated by this observation, we design a new edge-orientation feature based on the above conventional learning-based super-resolution scheme to learned the mapping between the LR patches and the HR patches, which aims to preserve the depth edge in the LR-to-HR conversion process.

To find edge orientation of depth LR image patches, we employ two simple gradient operators as

$$K_h = [1 \ -1] \text{ and } K_v = \begin{bmatrix} 1 \\ -1 \end{bmatrix} \tag{6}$$

where K_h and K_v indicate horizontal and vertical gradient operators, respectively. Here, considering that (5) calculates the pixel-level statistical error between the interpolated patches and the ground-truth patches, we take the pixel variations as the basis for patch classification. In theory, LR depth patches with similar gradient variations between adjacent-pixel pairs are likely to share similar linear mappings in LR-to-HR conversions.

For demonstration, let us take a 2×2 LR depth patch as an example, which is

$$P = \begin{bmatrix} p_{1,1} & p_{1,2} \\ p_{2,1} & p_{2,2} \end{bmatrix}. \tag{7}$$

The edge orientation is determined in terms of the edge strength and edge directions. Both of two operators K_h and K_v are applied to obtain the horizontal and vertical edge strength, as

$$\begin{aligned} g_h &= K_h * P \\ g_v &= K_v * P, \end{aligned} \tag{8}$$

where $*$ indicates the convolutional operator. g_h and g_v are horizontal and vertical gradients, respectively. Then, the edge strength and edge direction can be computed as

$$S = \sqrt{g_h^2 + g_v^2}$$
$$\phi = \tan^{-1}(\tfrac{g_h}{g_v}) + \tfrac{\pi}{2} \tag{9}$$

where S indicates the edge strength and ϕ is the edge direction for the given LR depth patch.

To correctly distinguish the edge and the homogeneous parts of depth images, we set a threshold T to constrain the edge strength. When the edge strength is lower than T, the corresponding regions in depth patch are regarded as the homogeneous regions. Then,

$$S = \begin{cases} S & \text{if } S > T \\ 0 & \text{otherwise} \end{cases} \tag{10}$$

The edge direction in (9) takes on values from 0 to 2π. Note that, each edge direction and its opposite direction can be seen as the same edge direction. Therefore, we map the direction information to a range of value $[0, \pi]$ obtaining a new field

$$\hat{\phi} = \begin{cases} \phi & 0 \le \phi < \pi \\ \phi - \pi & \pi \le \phi < 2\pi \end{cases} \tag{11}$$

Finally, the edge orientation feature can be represented using the following formula

$$\mathbf{\Phi} = S e^{j\hat{\phi}}. \tag{12}$$

The calculated feature points for the pre-given LR depth patches are clustered into different classes using K-means [8].

2.2   Depth Super-Resolution in View Synthesis

View synthesis technique is often employed to generate the extra virtual viewpoints in 3D video system [12]. In this framework, depth images are used to describe the distance between the camera and objects in a scene. Based on depth information, the virtual view images are synthesized by applying DIBR [5]. Consequently, depth images are only a sort of supplement data for view synthesis rather than an independent image data. The quality of depth images would not linearly affect the quality of the synthesized view images, and the relation varies according to its corresponding texture image information as mentioned in [21,22]. Thereby, in the learning based depth super-resolution problem, the goal of regression should consider the property of depth images in view synthesis. Instead, the distortion of the synthesized view introduced by the possible depth distortion in super-resolution process can be integrated, which is written as

$$SSD = \sum |V - \tilde{V}|^2$$
$$= \sum |f_w(C, D) - f_w(C, \tilde{D})|^2, \tag{13}$$

where C and V indicate the texture images and its virtually synthesized view, respectively. D is the ground-truth full size depth images, and $\tilde{D}$ denotes the corresponding interpolated HR depth images. For the synthesized view, it is synthesized based on C and D by the pre-defined warping function, f_w.

Based on (5) and (13), the goal of the learning-based depth super-resolution problem can be expressed as a view synthesis distortion minimization problem, as

$$
\begin{aligned}
J &= \sum_M |V - \tilde{V}|^2 \\
&= \sum_M |f_w(C, D) - f_w(C, \tilde{D})|^2, \\
&\text{where } \tilde{D} = M \cdot d
\end{aligned}
\tag{14}
$$

here, M denotes the learned mapping functions.

To further simplify this distortion, following [22], (13) can be approximately written as

$$
\begin{aligned}
SSD &= \sum_{\forall(x,y)} |f_w(C, D) - f_w(C, \tilde{D})|^2 \\
&\approx \sum_{\forall(x,y)} |C_{x,y} - C_{x-\triangle p(x,y),y}|^2,
\end{aligned}
\tag{15}
$$

where (x, y) represents pixel position, and $\triangle p$ denotes the translational rendering position, which has been proven to be proportional to the depth image error

$$
\triangle p(x, y) = \alpha \cdot (D_{x,y} - \tilde{D}_{x,y}),
\tag{16}
$$

where α is a proportional coefficient determined by the following equation

$$
\alpha = \frac{f \cdot L}{255} \cdot \left(\frac{1}{Z_{near}} - \frac{1}{Z_{far}} \right)
\tag{17}
$$

here, f is the focal length and L is the baseline between the current view and the synthesized view. Z_{near} and Z_{far} are the values of the nearest and the farthest depth of the scene, respectively. Therefore, (14) can be further simplified according to [22] as

$$
J \approx \sum_{\forall(x,y)} \left[|\triangle p(x,y)| \frac{|C_{x,y} - C_{x-1,y}| + |C_{x,y} - C_{x+1,y}|}{2} \right]^2.
\tag{18}
$$

Finally, to learn the linear mapping from LR examples to the HR examples, for depth images (4) can be rewritten based on (18) as

$$
\begin{aligned}
M_j = \arg\min_{M_j} \| &\left[\alpha(D_i^j - M_j d_i^j) \right] \frac{|C_{x,y} - C_{x-1,y}| + |C_{x,y} - C_{x+1,y}|}{2} \|_2^2 \\
&+ \lambda \|M_j\|_F^2,
\end{aligned}
\tag{19}
$$

where D_i^j denotes the HR depth patches which belong to the same class j, and d_i^j are for the LR depth patches of class j. This is known as multi-variate regression, and according to [38], this optimization problem can be approximately solved as

$$
M_j = \alpha^2 A^T A D_i^j {d_i^j}^T \left(d_i^j {d_i^j}^T + \lambda \mathbf{I} \right)^{-1},
\tag{20}
$$

where $A = \frac{|C_{x,y} - C_{x-1,y}| + |C_{x,y} - C_{x+1,y}|}{2}$, $\mathbf{I}$ is the identity matrix. Based on (20), the linear mapping can be learned off-line and used to reconstruct HR patches for class j. The complete training process are summarized in Algorithm 1.

Algorithm 1. Training phase of linear mapping learning for depth super-resolution

---

Input: external HR depth images **H**

1: Generate LR depth images **L** from **H**
2: Generate 2×2 LR patch l and 4×4 HR patch **h** pairs.
3:
4: **for** each LR depth patch l **do**
5:     Apply 2 operators (8) to obtain g_h and g_v
6:     Calculate the edge-orientation information as (12)
7: **end for**
8: For all LR patches, using K-means to cluster different classes using the edge-orientation features
9: Put the patch l into the corresponding cluster
10: **for** each cluster of class j **do**
11:     Compute the linear mappings $\mathbf{M_j}$ by using (20)
12: **end for**

Output: learned linear mappings **M**

Based on the calculated linear mappings M_j for each class j, the given LR depth images for testing are firstly divided into a set of LR patches with size 2×2. Then, using (9) and (12), the edge-orientation feature of each patch $\mathbf{\Phi_p}$ can be calculated and matched with the cluster centers $\mathbf{\Phi_c}$. The matching procedure of edge-orientation class can be described as searching the minimal distance between the given LR depth patch and each cluster centers, and the distance metric is

$$d = sin(|\mathbf{\Phi_p} - \mathbf{\Phi_c}|), \tag{21}$$

which is based on the Sine of the local angular distance. At last, the corresponding linear mapping can be found. The super-resolution phase is summarized in Algorithm 2.

3   Experimental Results

In this section, the proposed depth super-resolution method is compared with the other 3 depth super-resolution methods, which include a filter-based method which is joint bilateral up-sampling algorithm (JBU) [15], a guidance information assistant method called the color-based depth up-sampling method (CBU) [32] and a learning-based method which is edge-guided depth super-resolution method (EDU) [34]. To train the linear mappings, the depth images from 17 image pairs in the Middlebury Stereo dataset [25] are used. Each image pair consists of 2 views (left and right views, and the corresponding texture and depth image pairs) taken under several different illuminations and exposures. For testing, the realistic depth images from MPEG Standardization Test Dataset are applied to evaluate the performance of depth super-resolution,

---

Algorithm 2. Super-resolution phase of proposed depth super-resolution

Input: LR depth images **L**, and pre-learned linear mappings **M**

 1: Generate 2×2 LR patch l
 2:
 3: **for** each LR depth patch l **do**
 4:     Apply 2 operators (8) to obtain g_h and g_v
 5:     Calculate the edge-orientation information as (12)
 6:     Find the corresponding LR patch class j by using (21)
 7:     Apply the obtained linear mapping $\mathbf{M_j}$ to the current LR patch to reconstruct its HR version **h**
 8: **end for**
 9: Combine all reconstructed HR patches **h**

Output: HR image **H**

---

which include "Newspaper", "Balloons", "Kendo", "Dancer", "Poznan_hall2" and "Poznan_street". The details about the test sequences are shown in Table 1. For both of training and testing, the depth images are down-sampled with the scale factor is 2 by using the "Bicubic" filter. The results are evaluated in PSNR for quality assessments. To evaluate the view synthesis performance, the given depth images from two different views are firstly down-sampled and then up-sampled by using different depth super-resolution methods, in prior to view synthesis. The standard software VSRS 3.5 [26] is employed to generate the synthesized views by using the interpolated depth images and the corresponding texture images. Moreover, the ground-truth depth images are used as reference.

Table 1. Details of test dataset.

Sequence	Resolution	Left view	Right view	Synthesized view
Newspaper	1024×768	2	4	3
Balloons	1024×768	1	3	2
Kendo	1024×768	1	3	2
Dancer	1920×1088	1	5	3
Poznan_hall2	1920×1088	5	7	6
Poznan_street	1920×1088	3	5	4

For quantitative evaluations, we firstly evaluate the depth super-resolution results on test dataset. Table 2 lists the objective quality of depth super-resolution for each view in the test dataset. As reported in Table 2, the objective quality of the proposed depth super-resolution is limited, because the designed target function (19) is not for minimizing the distortion between up-sampled depth images and the ground-truth ones, as [34]. But the PSNR values of up-sampled depth images obtained by using the proposed method are also near to the other benchmark baselines. By evaluating the synthesized view quality, as shown in Table 3, the proposed depth super-resolution method performs much better than the other 3 methods. Compared with JBU and EDU which both utilize the edge information to guide depth super-resolution without employing the color information, the average PSNR gain on synthesize quality is near to 2 dB. Considering the synthesize distortion as (18), the color information should be considered. Thereby, CBU method shows a good performance on synthesize quality, but the average PSNR is still near to 1.2 dB lower than the proposed method.

Table 2. Objective quality of depth super-resolution.

Sequence	View	JBU [15]	CBU [32]	EDU [34]	Proposed
Newspaper	Left	38.2	40.39	41.06	40.72
	Right	38.68	40.52	40.71	40.05
Balloons	Left	41.66	41.17	41.74	41.27
	Right	41.71	41.31	42.28	41.44
Kendo	Left	45.1	46.6	45.46	45.24
	Right	45.67	46.46	47.92	45.37
Dancer	Left	39.4	37.31	40.54	37.92
	Right	39.64	37.48	40.61	37.37
Poznan_hall2	Left	52.23	52.45	53.75	53.25
	Right	53.26	53.41	55.78	55.85
Poznan_street	Left	46.53	46.82	46.8	45.76
	Right	47.49	46.94	46.8	47.17

Table 3. Objective quality of synthesized views by using interpolated depth images with scale factor 2.

Sequence	JBU [15]	CBU [32]	EDU [34]	Proposed
Newspaper	36.63	39.26	36.44	**39.88**
Balloons	40.81	41.89	38.48	**43.07**
Kendo	43.86	44.16	47.39	**48.25**
Dancer	37.17	37.75	37.03	**38.08**
Poznan_hall2	44.13	44.16	43.77	**44.88**
Poznan_street	41.18	41.26	40.75	**41.77**

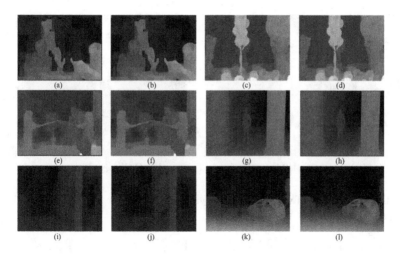

Fig. 2. The comparison of visual results of depth images: (a) *Newspaper* [34]; (b) *Newspaper* by proposed; (c) *Balloons* [15]; (d) *Balloons* by proposed; (e) *Kendo* [32]; (f) *Kendo* by proposed; (g) *Dancer* [34]; (h) *Dancer* by proposed; (i) *Poznan_hall2* [32]; (j) *Poznan_hall2* by proposed; (k) *Poznan_street* [15]; (l) *Poznan_street* by proposed.

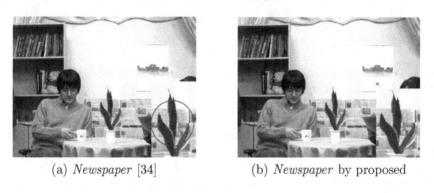

(a) *Newspaper* [34]   (b) *Newspaper* by proposed

Fig. 3. The comparison of visual results of synthesized view for *Newspaper*: (a) EDU [34]; (b) Proposed depth super-resolution.

We also evaluate our proposed method visually in Figs. 2, 3, 4 and 5. The depth visual results are shown in Fig. 2. Note that, not all interpolated depth images by using the baseline methods are shown in Fig. 2 due to the space limitation. Refer to Table 2, we select several depth images which are generated using the baseline methods, to compare with the generated ones by using our proposed method. Visually, the proposed method focus on the transition regions between foreground objects and background, which means that not all edges would be preserved in the super-resolution process. In comparison, JBU [15], CBU [32] and EDU [34] introduce the edge guidance information from texture images or self depth image to optimize the depth super-resolution. Thereby, the texture/depth edge would be sharped. Moreover, Figs. 3, 4 and 5 show the

(a) *Balloons* [34]   (b) *Balloons* by proposed

Fig. 4. The comparison of visual results of synthesized view for *Balloons*: (a) EDU [34]; (b) Proposed depth super-resolution.

(a) *Dancer* [34]   (b)*Dancer* by proposed

Fig. 5. The comparison of visual results of synthesized view for *Dancer*: (a) EDU [34]; (b) Proposed depth super-resolution.

synthesized views by utilizing the interpolated depth images, and some details are shown with zoomed cropped regions. To clearly distinguish the differences of synthesized views, we select the visual results based on Table 3. EDU [34] method has the best objective quality, so the subjective comparison is mainly between EDU [34] and our proposed method. The red circle lines in Figs. 3, 4 and 5 shows the comparison regions between the EDU method [34] and the proposed method.

4   Conclusion

In this paper, we present a depth super-resolution method based on the linear mapping relations between HR and LR depth patch pairs. Motivated by the idea that depth images are not directly watched by viewers, just for assisting different vision tasks, we convert the traditional super-resolution problem as view synthesis driven depth super-resolution optimization. We design an edge-orientation feature based learning method to learn the possible linear mappings, and interpolate the LR depth image to HR version by utilizing the learned mappings. In a realistic test dataset, our proposed method can generate the synthesized views with competitive quality in terms of PSNR, compared to the other depth super-resolution methods.

Acknowledgement. This research was supported in part by the National Key Research and Development Program of China (2016YFB0700502) National Natural Science Foundation of China (61873299, 61702036, 61572075).

References

1. Choi, J.S., Kim, M.: Super-interpolation with edge-orientation-based mapping kernels for low complex 2× upscaling. IEEE Trans. Image Process. **25**(1), 469–483 (2016)
2. Choi, O., Jung, S.W.: A consensus-driven approach for structure and texture aware depth map upsampling. IEEE Trans. Image Process. **23**(8), 3321–3335 (2014)
3. Deng, H., Yu, L., Qiu, J., Zhang, J.: A joint texture/depth edge-directed upsampling algorithm for depth map coding. In: 2012 IEEE International Conference on Multimedia and Expo (ICME), pp. 646–650. IEEE (2012)
4. Dong, Y., Lin, C., Zhao, Y., Yao, C., Hou, J.: Depth map up-sampling with texture edge feature via sparse representation. In: Visual Communications and Image Processing (VCIP), pp. 1–4. IEEE (2016)
5. Fehn, C.: Depth-image-based rendering (DIBR), compression, and transmission for a new approach on 3D-TV. In: Stereoscopic Displays and Virtual Reality Systems XI, vol. 5291, pp. 93–105. International Society for Optics and Photonics (2004)
6. Ferstl, D., Reinbacher, C., Ranftl, R., Rüther, M., Bischof, H.: Image guided depth upsampling using anisotropic total generalized variation. In: Proceedings of the IEEE International Conference on Computer Vision, pp. 993–1000 (2013)
7. Guo, C., Li, C., Guo, J., Cong, R., Fu, H., Han, P.: Hierarchical features driven residual learning for depth map super-resolution. IEEE Trans. Image Process. **28**(5), 2545–2557 (2019)
8. Hartigan, J.A., Wong, M.A.: Algorithm as 136: a k-means clustering algorithm. J. Roy. Stat. Soc.: Ser. C (Appl. Stat.) **28**(1), 100–108 (1979)
9. Hornácek, M., Rhemann, C., Gelautz, M., Rother, C.: Depth super resolution by rigid body self-similarity in 3D. In: IEEE Conference on Computer Vision and Pattern Recognition (CVPR) (2013)
10. Hu, W., Cheung, G., Li, X., Au, O.: Depth map super-resolution using synthesized view matching for depth-image-based rendering. In: 2012 IEEE International Conference on Multimedia and Expo Workshops (ICMEW), pp. 605–610. IEEE (2012)
11. Jiang, Z., Hou, Y., Yue, H., Yang, J., Hou, C.: Depth super-resolution from RGB-D pairs with transform and spatial domain regularization. IEEE Trans. Image Process. **27**(5), 2587–2602 (2018)
12. Jin, Z., Tillo, T., Yao, C., Xiao, J., Zhao, Y.: Virtual-view-assisted video super-resolution and enhancement. IEEE Trans. Circ. Syst. Video Technol. **26**(3), 467–478 (2016)
13. Kim, D., Yoon, K.J.: High-quality depth map up-sampling robust to edge noise of range sensors. In: 2012 19th IEEE International Conference on Image Processing (ICIP), pp. 553–556. IEEE (2012)
14. Kim, K.I., Kwon, Y.: Single-image super-resolution using sparse regression and natural image prior. IEEE Trans. Pattern Anal. Mach. Intell. **32**(6), 1127–1133 (2010)

15. Kopf, J., Cohen, M.F., Lischinski, D., Uyttendaele, M.: Joint bilateral upsampling. ACM Trans. Graph. (ToG) **26**(3), 96 (2007)
16. Li, J., Lu, Z., Zeng, G., Gan, R., Zha, H.: Similarity-aware patchwork assembly for depth image super-resolution. In: IEEE Conference on Computer Vision and Pattern Recognition (CVPR), pp. 3374–3381 (2014)
17. Liu, M., Zhao, Y., Liang, J., Lin, C., Bai, H., Yao, C.: Depth mapup-samplingwith fractal dimension and texture-depth boundary consistencies. Neurocomputing **257**, 185–192 (2017)
18. Liu, M.Y., Tuzel, O., Taguchi, Y.: Joint geodesic upsampling of depth images. In: IEEE Conference on Computer Vision and Pattern Recognition (CVPR), pp. 169–176 (2013)
19. Liu, X., Zhai, D., Chen, R., Ji, X., Zhao, D., Gao, W.: Depth super-resolution via joint color-guided internal and external regularizations. IEEE Trans. Image Process. **28**(4), 1636–1645 (2019)
20. Ni, M., Lei, J., Cong, R., Zheng, K., Peng, B., Fan, X.: Color-guided depth map super resolution using convolutional neural network. IEEE Access **5**, 26666–26672 (2017)
21. Oh, B.T., Lee, J., Park, D.S.: Depth map coding based on synthesized view distortion function. IEEE J. Sel. Top. Sign. Process. **5**(7), 1344–1352 (2011)
22. Oh, B.T., Oh, K.J.: View synthesis distortion estimation for AVC-and HEVC-compatible 3-D video coding. IEEE Trans. Circ. Syst. Video Technol. **24**(6), 1006–1015 (2014)
23. Park, J., Kim, H., Tai, Y.W., Brown, M.S., Kweon, I.: High quality depth map upsampling for 3D-TOF cameras. In: IEEE International Conference on Computer Vision (ICCV), pp. 1623–1630. IEEE (2011)
24. Riemens, A., Gangwal, O., Barenbrug, B., Berretty, R.P.: Multistep joint bilateral depth upsampling. In: Visual Communications and Image Processing 2009, vol. 7257, p. 72570M. International Society for Optics and Photonics (2009)
25. Scharstein, D., et al.: High-resolution stereo datasets with subpixel-accurate ground truth. In: Jiang, X., Hornegger, J., Koch, R. (eds.) GCPR 2014. LNCS, vol. 8753, pp. 31–42. Springer, Cham (2014). https://doi.org/10.1007/978-3-319-11752-2_3
26. Tanimoto, M., Fujii, T., Suzuki, K.: View synthesis algorithm in view synthesis reference software 3.5 (VSRS3. 5) document M16090, ISO/IEC JTC1/SC29/WG11 (MPEG) (2009)
27. Timofte, R., De, V., Van Gool, L.: Anchored neighborhood regression for fast example-based super-resolution. In: 2013 IEEE International Conference on Computer Vision (ICCV), pp. 1920–1927. IEEE (2013)
28. Tsai, C.Y., Tsai, S.H.: Simultaneous 3D object recognition and pose estimation based on RGB-D images. IEEE Access **6**, 28859–28869 (2018)
29. Wang, L., Xiang, S., Meng, G., Wu, H., Pan, C.: Edge-directed single-image super-resolution via adaptive gradient magnitude self-interpolation. IEEE Trans. Circ. Syst. Video Technol. **23**(8), 1289–1299 (2013)
30. Wang, Y., Ortega, A., Tian, D., Vetro, A.: A graph-based joint bilateral approach for depth enhancement. In: IEEE International Conference on Acoustics, Speech and Signal Processing (ICASSP), pp. 885–889. IEEE (2014)
31. Wen, Y., Sheng, B., Li, P., Lin, W., Feng, D.D.: Deep color guided coarse-to-fine convolutional network cascade for depth image super-resolution. IEEE Trans. Image Process. **28**(2), 994–1006 (2019). https://doi.org/10.1109/TIP.2018.2874285
32. Wildeboer, M.O., Yendo, T., Tehrani, M.P., Fujii, T., Tanimoto, M.: Color based depth up-sampling for depth compression. In: Picture Coding Symposium (PCS), pp. 170–173. IEEE (2010)

33. Xie, J., Chou, C.C., Feris, R., Sun, M.T.: Single depth image super resolution and denoising via coupled dictionary learning with local constraints and shock filtering. In: IEEE International Conference on Multimedia and Expo (ICME), pp. 1–6. IEEE (2014)
34. Xie, J., Feris, R.S., Sun, M.T.: Edge-guided single depth image super resolution. IEEE Trans. Image Process. **25**(1), 428–438 (2016)
35. Xie, J., Feris, R.S., Yu, S.S., Sun, M.T.: Joint super resolution and denoising from a single depth image. IEEE Trans. Multimedia **17**(9), 1525–1537 (2015)
36. Yang, J., Wright, J., Huang, T.S., Ma, Y.: Image super-resolution via sparse representation. IEEE Trans. Image Process. **19**(11), 2861–2873 (2010)
37. Yang, Y., Gao, M., Zhang, J., Zha, Z., Wang, Z.: Depth map super-resolution using stereo-vision-assisted model. Neurocomputing **149**, 1396–1406 (2015)
38. Yao, C., Xiao, J., Tillo, T., Zhao, Y., Lin, C., Bai, H.: Depth map down-sampling and coding based on synthesized view distortion. IEEE Trans. Multimedia **18**(10), 2015–2022 (2016)
39. Zhu, J., Wang, L., Gao, J., Yang, R.: Spatial-temporal fusion for high accuracy depth maps using dynamic mrfs. IEEE Trans. Pattern Anal. Mach. Intell. **32**(5), 899–909 (2010)

Robust Dynamic 3D Shape Measurement with Hybrid Fourier-Transform Phase-Shifting Profilometry

Jiaming Qian[1,2,3], Tianyang Tao[1,2,3], Shijie Feng[1,2,3], Qian Chen[1,2],
and Chao Zuo[1,2,3(✉)]

[1] School of Electronic and Optical Engineering, Nanjing University of Science
and Technology, Nanjing 210094, Jiangsu Province, China
surpasszuo@163.com
[2] Jiangsu Key Laboratory of Spectral Imaging and Intelligent Sense, Nanjing
University of Science and Technology, Nanjing 210094, Jiangsu Province, China
[3] Smart Computational Imaging (SCI) Laboratory, Nanjing University of Science
and Technology, Nanjing 210094, Jiangsu Province, China
zuochao@njust.edu.cn
http://www.scilaboratory.com/

Abstract. In this work, we propose a novel hybrid Fourier-transform phase-shifting profilometry method to integrate the advantages of Fourier-transform profilometry (FTP) and phase-shifting profilometry (PSP). The motion vulnerability of multi-shot PSP can be significantly alleviated through the combination of single-shot FTP, while the high accuracy of PSP can also be preserved when the object is motionless. We design a phase-based pixel-wise motion detection strategy that can accurately outline the moving object regions from their motionless counterparts. The final measurement result is obtained by fusing the determined regions where the PSP or FTP is applied correspondingly. To validate the proposed hybrid approach, we develop a real-time 3D shape measurement system for measuring multiple isolated moving objects. Experimental results demonstrate that our method achieves significantly higher precision and better robustness compared with conventional approaches where PSP or FTP is applied separately.

Keywords: Fourier-transform profilometry · Phase-shifting profilometry · Motion detection

1 Introduction

The fringe projection profilometry (FPP) [1,2] is one of the most popular three-dimensional (3D) surface measurement technologies due to its advantages in terms of high measurement accuracy, simple hardware configuration, and being easy to implement. With the recent advances in high speed imaging sensors and digital projection technology, it now becomes possible to achieve high-precision, high-speed real-time 3D shape measurement of dynamic scenes [3].

© Springer Nature Switzerland AG 2019
Y. Zhao et al. (Eds.): ICIG 2019, LNCS 11903, pp. 122–133, 2019.
https://doi.org/10.1007/978-3-030-34113-8_11

The phase-shifting profilometry (PSP) [4,5] and Fourier-transform profilometry (FTP) [6] are two mainstream fringe analysis approaches of FPP. FTP retrieves phase information from only one single high-frequency fringe image, so it is well-suited for dynamic 3D sensing [7]. However, the frequency band overlapping problem limits its measurement precision, which can be improved by the π phase-shifting FTP [8], modified FTP [9], or background normalized FTP [10]. On the other hand, PSP typically requires a minimum of three fringe images to provide high-accuracy pixel-wise phase measurement, the advantages of which are higher spatial resolution, measurement accuracy, and robustness towards ambient illumination and varying surface reflectivity [11,12]. However, when measuring dynamic scenes, motion will lead to phase distortion artifacts and make the accuracy of PSP lower than that of FTP, that is an intrinsic and inevitable problem of PSP.

During recent years, dynamic 3D shape measurement using FPP has attracted a great deal of research interest, which can be roughly categorized in the following three directions: (1) Increasing the speed of hardware (projector and camera); (2) Reducing the number of required patterns per 3D reconstruction; (3) Improving the measurement quality and reducing the motion artifacts. The first direction focuses on the projector defocusing technique that allows the projector to cast binary fringe patterns close to the sinusoidal ones to maximize the speed of the projector [10,13]. When the high-speed projector is synchronized with a high-speed camera, motion-induced error on the phase reconstruction can be reduced accordingly, depending on the frame rate of the projector-camera pair. The second direction is to improve the measurement efficiency, i.e., to reduce the number of patterns required per measurement. Essentially, the dominant challenge affecting the measurement efficiency is the phase ambiguity. To recover the absolute phase, a common practice is to use temporal phase unwrapping (TPU) algorithm [14,15]. However, additional multi-wavelength fringes should be used in TPU, which decreases the measurement efficiency. Recently, stereo phase unwrapping (SPU) methods based on geometric constraint [16] can be used to solve the phase ambiguity problem without using additional auxiliary patterns [17–19], which is well-suitable to high-speed real-time 3D shape measurement of dynamic scenes. The third direction focuses on enhancing the dynamic measurement capability of PSP with use of post-processing algorithm. These motion compensation methods [17,20–24] can improve the accuracy of PSP in dynamic scenes to some extent. However, most of them adopt iterative methods, which makes the computational efficiency relatively low, and some other methods are restricted to certain assumptions and are not suitable for non-rigid motion compensation. In addition, Yang et al. [25] proposed the methods of combining single-frame method and multi-frame method, where the motion regions of the object are detected, and different imaging methods are used according to different regions. In contrast to other methods, the method is more targeted, i.e., the motion compensation algorithm is only performed in the motion regions, while the high precision of multi-frame method in the still regions is preserved. However, only local rather than pixel-by-pixel motion state can be judged by this method, because this method is susceptible to ambient light noise.

The goal of this paper is to develop a new 3D shape measurement technique which can measure 3D shapes robustly in real time for rigid and non-rigid objects in complex scenes consisting of both static and dynamic objects. To this end, we propose a novel hybrid Fourier-transform phase-shifting profilometry method for motion-induced error reduction. First of all, four patterns are projected onto the objects, from which the absolute phase information can be simultaneously calculated by both PSP and FTP. Then, the motion regions of the measured objects are automatically detected with a pixel-wise motion detection strategy based on phase information. At last, the results of PSP and FTP are fused according to the detected motion regions. In order to prove the feasibility of the proposed method, a real-time 3D shape measurement system based on our method is developed. Experiments show that our method can integrate the advantages of PSP and FTP to achieve higher measurement precision than traditional real-time algorithms based on PSP or FTP.

2   Principle

2.1   Basic Principles of 3-Step PSP and SPU

A typical 3D imaging system based on SPU is composed of two cameras and one projector [18]. Taking three-step phase-shifting fringe patterns for example, the patterns captured by the camera can be expressed by the following formulas:

$$I_1^c (u^c, v^c) = A^c (u^c, v^c) + B^c (u^c, v^c) \cos (\Phi^c (u^c, v^c)), \tag{1}$$

$$I_2^c (u^c, v^c) = A^c (u^c, v^c) + B^c (u^c, v^c) \cos \left(\Phi^c (u^c, v^c) + \frac{2\pi}{3} \right), \tag{2}$$

$$I_3^c (u^c, v^c) = A^c (u^c, v^c) + B^c (u^c, v^c) \cos \left(\Phi^c (u^c, v^c) + \frac{4\pi}{3} \right), \tag{3}$$

where the superscript c denotes the camera, (u^c, v^c) is a point in the camera, I_1^c, I_2^c and I_3^c represent the three captured fringe patterns, A^c is the average intensity map, B^c is the amplitude intensity map, and Φ^c is the absolute phase map. Because of the truncation feature of the $arctan$ function, only the wrapped phase can be obtained with Eqs. (1)–(3):

$$\phi^c (u^c, v^c) = \arctan \left(\frac{\sqrt{3} (I_2^c (u^c, v^c) - I_3^c (u^c, v^c))}{2I_1^c (u^c, v^c) - I_2^c (u^c, v^c) - I_3^c (u^c, v^c)} \right), \tag{4}$$

where ϕ^c represents the wrapped phase. The absolute phase map and the wrapped phase map satisfy the following relation:

$$\Phi^c (u^c, v^c) = \phi^c (u^c, v^c) + 2k^c (u^c, v^c) \pi, \quad k^c (u^c, v^c) \in [0, N - 1], \tag{5}$$

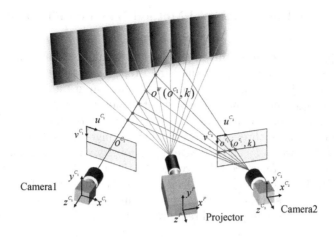

Fig. 1. The principle of SPU.

where k^c is the fringe order, and N denotes the number of fringes. The process of obtaining the fringe orders is called phase unwrapping.

The principle of SPU is shown in Fig. 1. For an arbitrary point o^{c_1} in the Camera 1, it has N possible fringe orders corresponding to N possible absolute phases, with which the horizontal coordinates of the corresponding points in the projector can be obtained. Then the N corresponding 3D candidates can be retrieved by the parameter matrices derived from calibration parameters between the Camera 1 and the projector. The retrieved N 3D candidates can be projected into the Camera 2 to get their corresponding 2D candidates just like the red and green points in the Camera 2 in Fig. 1. There is a correct matching point which should have the more similar wrapped phase to o^{c_1} among these 2D candidates. Then a phase similarity check will be carried out to find the matching point, and the phase ambiguity of o^{c_1} will also be removed.

However, conventional SPU is not enough to robustly eliminate phase ambiguities when high-frequency fringes are used. Depth constraint [16,19] is a popular method to improve the stability of SPU. The strategy of adaptive depth constraint (ADC) proposed by Tao et al. [18] can provide and update the pixelwise depth range automatically according to the real-time measurement results, which is especially suitable for the measurement where the object is moving constantly. So, in this work, we utilize this method to assist SPU to improve the stability of the measurement.

Although PSP based on SPU can robustly remove phase ambiguity in the static scene, the motion-caused phase error and unwrapping error in motion introduced scene make it necessary to compensate for the motion-induced error of PSP.

2.2   Composite Phase Retrieval Method Based on FTP and PSP

To reduce the sensitivity to motion, PSP with as few fringe patterns as possible should be applied. Therefore, three-step phase-shifting method is chosen in this work. We use the second fringe of the three-step phase-shifting images to perform FTP. Meanwhile, in order to improve the measurement precision of FTP, we use the background-normalized Fourier transform profilometry (BNFTP) [10], where a pure white map is cast the light intensity of which is equal to the average intensity of the three-step phase-shifting fringes. By taking the normalized difference between I_2^c and the average intensity, the zero-frequency term as well as the effect of surface reflectivity variations can be effectively removed before the Fourier transform. Considering both the efficiency of PSP and the precision of FTP, the fringe strategy selected in this work is a $1+3$ strategy which is one pure white map and three three-step phase-shifting fringe patterns.

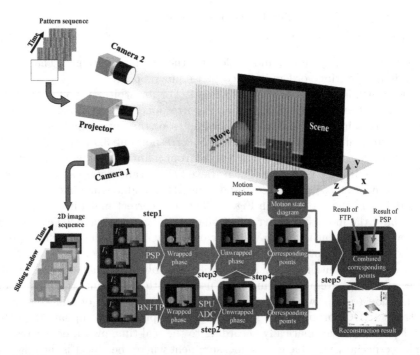

Fig. 2. Fusion algorithm flow diagram (The dark blue region indicates the result of the PSP, the dark red region indicates the result of the FTP and the dark green region indicates the combined result). (Color figure online)

The entire algorithm process is discussed next. Firstly, the wrapped phases are respectively calculated by PSP and FTP. SPU is implemented to achieve phase unwrapping of the FTP phase with the assistance of ADC, while the ambiguity of the wrapped phase of PSP is removed by means of the absolute FTP phase. Then, the matching points of the Camera 1 of PSP and FTP can be respectively obtained. Finally, the results of PSP and FTP are fused by the determined motion regions of the object. For the still regions, the result of PSP is reserved, while the result of the motion regions, is replaced with that of FTP. The whole algorithm flow is shown in Fig. 2.

The steps of the whole algorithm are summarized as follows:

Step 1: Obtain the wrapped phases by PSP and FTP respectively;
Step 2: Unwrap the wrapped phase of FTP by SPU, with the assistance of ADC;
Step 3: Unwrap the wrapped phase of PSP by means of the absolute phase of FTP;
Step 4: Obtain the matching points of the Camera 1 of PSP and FTP respectively;
Step 5: Fuse the matching points of PSP and FTP with the detected motion areas and achieve 3D reconstruction;
Step 6: Update the range of the next cyclic dynamic depth constraint with the obtained depth information;
Step 7: Return back to *Step* 1 and repeat the above process;

3   Motion Detection and Judgment

The key to the proposed algorithm is how to analyze the state of motion of the object pixel by pixel. In this paper, we propose the phase frame different method (PFDM), which is a motion detection method based on phase differentials from frame to frame. Firstly, the absolute value of the phase difference introduced by motion between the FTP phases of two adjacent moments is calculated. Then, the phase change of each point is compared with a certain threshold. If the phase change is greater than the threshold, it is considered to be in motion and the corresponding point of the output motion state map is 1, otherwise judged to be stationary and the corresponding output is 0. In order to eliminate some individual stationary points judged to be moving and to correct some individual undetermined motion points, we perform Gaussian filtering on the output motion state map. After filtering, if the output of a certain point is less than 1/2, it is considered to be stationary, otherwise judged to be in motion.

In order to accurately determine the motion regions, the threshold of motion judgment needs to be reasonably designed. The process of the determination of the threshold is as shown in Fig. 3. Firstly, we measure a flat panel in a static environment and obtain its absolute phase. We record the phase values of a fixed area as shown by the red dashed box in Fig. 3 of successive n moments $t_0 \sim t_{n-1}$, and then sum and average them. The resulting average phase can be approximated as the phase value measured without ambient light noise. Then the histogram of the difference between the average phase and the phase at time t_{n-1} is obtained. Areas with a value of less than e in the histogram are removed, such as the red areas of the histogram in Fig. 3, and then the two areas with the greatest difference are acquired, such as the green ones of the histogram in Fig. 3. Here e represents a smaller constant, which is 10 in this work. The

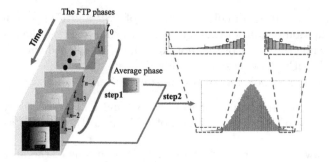

Fig. 3. Threshold determination process. (Color figure online)

absolute values are obtained for these two regions, and the upper limit of the larger region is taken as the phase threshold.

4   Experiment

We establishe a quad-camera real-time 3D imaging system based on the proposed method, which is shown in Fig. 4, where Fig. 4(a) is the outline structure, and Fig. 4(b) is the internal structure. This set-up includes a LightCrafter 4500Pro (912×1140 resolution), three Basler acA640-750um cameras (640×480 resolution) used for SPU and one Basler acA640-750uc camera (640×480 resolution) used for colorful texture. In our experiments, the projection speed is 100 Hz, and all the cameras are synchronized by the trigger signal from the projector and 48-period phase-shifting fringe patterns are used.

Fig. 4. The quad-camera color real-time 3D imaging system.

4.1   Comparison of Two Methods of Motion Judgment

In the first experiment, two different scenes are designed to compare the performance of PFDM and the Yang's method [25] which is frame difference method (FDM). In the first scene, a rigid object is measured in the first scene as shown in

Fig. 5(a). The measurement results are shown Figs. 5(b)–(c). These results indicate that PFDM performs better than FDM in judging the motion of rigid object. In the second scene, a freely moving hand is measured as shown in Fig. 5(d). Figures 5(e)–(f) display the motion regions detected by FDM and PFDM. Obviously, for the motion of non-rigid objects, the detection accuracy of PFDM is still better than that of FDM.

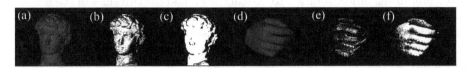

Fig. 5. The motion regions determined by FDM and PFDM. (a) The first measurement scene. (b) The result of FDM of the first scene (A rigid object in translational motion). (c) The result of PFDM of the first scene. (d) The second measurement scene (A hand in arbitrary motion). (e) The result of FDM of the second scene. (f) The result of PFDM of the second scene.

4.2 Quantitative Evaluation

In the second experiment, a rotating flat plate is measured. For the rotating object, the portion near the center of rotation can be considered to be stationary, and those on both sides of the center of rotation are moving, which presents two different motion states. The measurement results are shown in Fig. 6, where Fig. 6(a) is the background map, Fig. 6(b) is the detected motion areas, Figs. 6(c), (e) and (g) are the results measured by a real-time algorithm based on stereo phase unwrapping using only the PSP algorithm [19] (for simplicity, the method

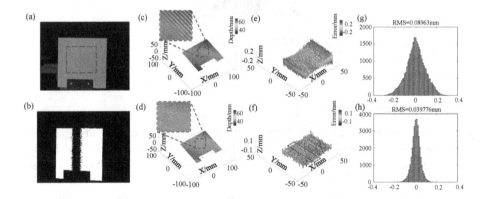

Fig. 6. Measurement results in the second complex scenario. (a) The background map collected. (b) The detected motion areas. (c) The results measured by the conventional PSP. (e) The error distribution of the flat plate data of (c). (g)The histogram of (e). (d) The results measured by our method. (f) The error distribution of the flat plate data in (e). (h) The histogram of (f).

is hereinafter referred to as "traditional PSP"), and Figs. 6(d), (f) and (h) are those of the proposed method. The plane fittings on the measured plate data of a certain area, as shown in the area inside the red dotted frame in Fig. 6(a) are performed. Figures 6(e) and (f) are the errors between the measured data of the two methods and the fitted data and Figs. 6(g) and (h) are the histograms of Figs. 6(e) and (f), respectively. It can be seen from Fig. 6(b) that PFDM judges the center of the object rotation to be stationary, and the two sides of the center of the rotation are judged to be moving. The RMS of the measurement error of the conventional PSP is 89 um. The results measured by our method combine the results of PSP and FTP, in which the data in the red dashed box as shown in Fig. 6(f) is that of PSP while that of other region is the result of FTP. The RMS of the measurement error of our method is 40 um, which is better than that of the traditional PSP.

4.3 Qualitative Evaluation

In this experiment, a moving hand is measured, which is a non-rigid body with complex motion. Figure 7 shows the measured results, where Figs. 7(a) and (c) are the results of PSP and our method respectively, and Fig. 7(b) is the motion regions detected by PFDM. We can see from the measurement results that the proposed method can eliminate the motion-induced ripples of non-rigid object.

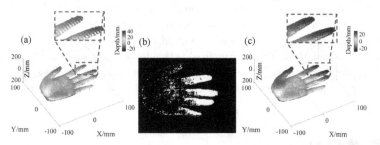

Fig. 7. The measurement results of the second scene). (a) The measurement results of conventional PSP. (b) The motion areas determined by PFDM. (c) The measurement results of our method.

4.4 Real-Time Experiments

In the final experiment, the established quad-camera real-time 3D imaging system based on the proposed method is used to measure the small fan and David model in motion by conventional PSP and our method respectively. We use a HP Z230 computer (Intel Xeon E3-1226 v3 CPU, NVIDIA Quadro K2200 GPU). The visual interface is developed with Qt and all core algorithms are written based on CUDA. The real-time measurement results are shown in Fig. 8. It can be observed from the measurement results that for the motion regions, the results of PSP have obvious motion ripples, while those of our method have no motion ripples in which the results of PSP are replaced by those of FTP. About 30 fps reconstructed speed can be achieved by our method.

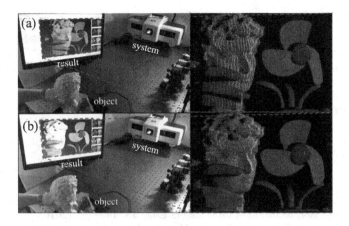

Fig. 8. The real-time measurement processes and results based on (a) conventional PSP and (b) our method.

5   Conclusion

In this paper, we present a novel hybrid Fourier-transform phase-shifting profilometry method for rigid and non-rigid objects in the complex scenes which contain both static and dynamic motions. Firstly, we use a $1+3$ fringe strategy to retrieve the phase information of the measured objects with both PSP and FTP assisted by ADC which can efficiently achieve phase unwrapping of the high frequency fringes. Then, we develop a phase-based motion detection strategy to accurately determine the motion state of each pixel. Finally, based on the detected regions of motion, we combine the results of PSP and FTP. Several experiments have verified that the proposed method can obtain more precise 3D reconstruction than traditional real-time strategy based on PSP or FTP. Compared to other motion-compensation methods such as Lu's method [20], which can significantly eliminate the effects of 3D motion on PSP by redefining the motion-affected fringe pattern and the use of an iterative least-squares algorithm but is only applicable to a single movement of non-rigid objects, our approach is suitable for objects under both rigid and non-rigid motion, showing the higher feasibility for more kinds of scenes, and easier to implement.

Funding. National Natural Science Fund of China (61722506, 61705105, 111574152); National Key R&D Program of China (2017YFF0106403); Final Assembly '13th Five-Year Plan' Advanced Research Project of China (30102070102); Equipment Advanced Research Fund of China (61404150202), The Key Research and Development Program of Jiangsu Province, China (BE2017162); Outstanding Youth Foundation of Jiangsu Province of China (BK20170034); National Defense Science and Technology Foundation of China (0106173); 'Six Talent Peaks' project of Jiangsu Province, China (2015-DZXX-009); '333 Engineering' research project of Jiangsu Province, China (BRA2016407, BRA2015294); Fundamental Research Funds for the Central

Universities (30917011204, 30916011322); Open Research Fund of Jiangsu Key Laboratory of Spectral Imaging & Intelligent Sense (3091601410414); China Postdoctoral Science Foundation (2017M621747), and Jiangsu Planned Projects for Postdoctoral Research Funds (1701038A).

References

1. Geng, J.: Structured-light 3D surface imaging: a tutorial. Adv. Opt. Photonics **3**, 128–160 (2011)
2. Gorthi, S.S., Rastogi, P.: Fringe projection techniques: whither we are? Opt. Lasers Eng. **48**, 133–140 (2010)
3. Zhang, S.: Recent progresses on real-time 3D shape measurement using digital fringe projection techniques. Opt. Lasers Eng. **48**, 149–158 (2010)
4. Zuo, C., Feng, S., Huang, L., Tao, T., Yin, W., Chen, Q.: Phase shifting algorithms for fringe projection profilometry: a review. Opt. Lasers Eng. **109**, 23–59 (2018)
5. Srinivasan, V., Liu, H.-C., Halioua, M.: Automated phase-measuring profilometry of 3-D diuse objects. Appl. Optics **23**, 3105–3108 (1984)
6. Su, X., Zhang, Q.: Dynamic 3-D shape measurement method: a review. Opt. Lasers Eng. **48**, 191–204 (2010)
7. Takeda, M., Ina, H., Kobayashi, S.: Fourier-transform method of fringe-pattern analysis for computer-based topography and interferometry. JosA **72**, 156–160 (1982)
8. Li, J., Su, X., Guo, L.: Improved fourier transform profilometry for the automatic measurement of three-dimensional object shapes. Opt. Eng. **29**, 1439–1445 (1990)
9. Guo, H., Huang, P.S.: 3-D shape measurement by use of a modified fourier transform method. In: Proceedings of SPIE -International Society for Optical Engineering, vol. 7066 (2008)
10. Zuo, C., Tao, T., Feng, S., Huang, L., Asundi, A., Chen, Q.: Micro fourier transform profilometry (FTP): 3D shape measurement at 10,000 frames per second. Opt. Lasers Eng. **102**, 70–91 (2018)
11. Li, J., Hassebrook, L.G., Guan, C.: Optimized two-frequency phase-measuring-profilometry light-sensor temporal-noise sensitivity. JOSA A **20**, 106–115 (2003)
12. Su, X.-Y., Von Bally, G., Vukicevic, D.: Phase-stepping grating profilometry: utilization of intensity modulation analysis in complex objects evaluation. Opt. Commun. **98**, 141–150 (1993)
13. Zhang, S., Van Der Weide, D., Oliver, J.: Superfast phase-shifting method for 3-D shape measurement. Opt. Express **18**, 9684–9689 (2010)
14. Zuo, C., Huang, L., Zhang, M., Chen, Q., Asundi, A.: Temporal phase unwrapping algorithms for fringe projection profilometry: a comparative review. Opt. Lasers Eng. **85**, 84–103 (2016)
15. Zhang, Z., Towers, C.E., Towers, D.P.: Time eÿcient color fringe projection system for 3D shape and color using optimum 3-frequency selection. Opt. Express **14**, 6444–6455 (2006)
16. Bräuer-Burchardt, C., Munkelt, C., Heinze, M., Kühmstedt, P., Notni, G.: Using geometric constraints to solve the point correspondence problem in fringe projection based 3D measuring systems. In: Maino, G., Foresti, G.L. (eds.) ICIAP 2011. LNCS, vol. 6979, pp. 265–274. Springer, Heidelberg (2011). https://doi.org/10.1007/978-3-642-24088-1_28

17. Weise, T., Leibe, B., Van Gool, L.: Fast 3D scanning with automatic motion compensation. In: IEEE Conference on Computer Vision and Pattern Recognition. CVPR 2007, pp. 1–8. IEEE (2007)
18. Tao, T., et al.: High-speed real-time 3D shape measurement based on adaptive depth constraint. Opt. Express 26, 22440–22456 (2018)
19. Tao, T., Chen, Q., Feng, S., Hu, Y., Zhang, M., Zuo, C.: High-precision real-time 3D shape measurement based on a quad-camera system. J. Opt. 20, 014009 (2017)
20. Lu, L., Xi, J., Yu, Y., Guo, Q.: Improving the accuracy performance of phase-shifting profilometry for the measurement of objects in motion. Opt. Lett. 39, 6715–6718 (2014)
21. Feng, S., et al.: Robust dynamic 3-D measurements with motion-compensated phase-shifting profilometry. Opt. Lasers Eng. 103, 127–138 (2018)
22. Li, B., Liu, Z., Zhang, S.: Motion-induced error reduction by combining fourier transform profilometry with phase-shifting profilometry. Opt. Express 24, 23289–23303 (2016)
23. Cong, P., Xiong, Z., Zhang, Y., Zhao, S., Wu, F.: Accurate dynamic 3D sensing with fourier-assisted phase shifting. IEEE J. Sel. Top. Signal Process. 9, 396–408 (2015)
24. Liu, Z., Zibley, P.C., Zhang, S.: Motion-induced error compensation for phase shifting profilometry. Opt. Express 26, 12632–12637 (2018)
25. Yang, Z., Xiong, Z., Zhang, Y., Wang, J., Wu, F.: Depth acquisition from density modulated binary patterns. In: Proceedings of the IEEE Conference on Computer Vision and Pattern Recognition, pp. 25–32 (2013)

An Improved Clustering Method
for Multi-view Images

Yang Dong[✉], Dazhao Fan, Qiuhe Ma, and Song Ji

Information Engineering University, Zhengzhou, China
wenku34@163.com

Abstract. Existing algorithms do not meet the requirements of multi-view image clustering under big data conditions. Here, we design a multi-view clustering algorithm for massive and unstructured images. To meet the multi-view requirements, improve speed and accuracy, a response layer is introduced to the self-organizing map neural network. An online self-organizing map neural network with simple parameters and without prior training is proposed and used for the multi-view clustering process. Experiments are performed using multiple datasets. The results show that the proposed algorithm is capable of multi-view clustering of image data with high accuracy, low error rate and favorable stability.

Keywords: Image clustering · Multi-view · Self-organizing map neural network

1 Introduction

In recent years, the widespread application of information network technology has promoted changes in lifestyle. The Internet, the Internet of Things, knowledge services, and intelligent services have become indispensable parts of people's lives. These components form a huge sensor network collecting unsustainably massive amounts of image data that are complex in type, huge in volume, critical in time, and have prominent big data features; such data have become an important research object. The first step in processing these inaccurate, unstructured big image data is to conduct autonomous clustering of images to find a collection of images with similar content in the same target area. Image clustering can be classified into two steps: generating the global description of each image and clustering the image descriptors using a clustering method. The global descriptor of an image is typically obtained through the aggregation of local image descriptors. Many scholars have conducted related studies [1–6]. This part work has been done in our previous conference papers [7].

For image clustering methods, it can be divided into various types according to the clustering characteristics, including the following: clustering algorithms based on partitioning, such as the k-means algorithm [8–10]; hierarchical clustering algorithms, such as the clustering using representatives (CURE) algorithm [11]; density-based clustering algorithms, such as the density-based spatial clustering of applications with noise (DBSCAN) algorithm [12]; grid-based clustering algorithms, such as the statistical information grid (STING) algorithm [13]; and model-based clustering algorithms,

© Springer Nature Switzerland AG 2019
Y. Zhao et al. (Eds.): ICIG 2019, LNCS 11903, pp. 134–144, 2019.
https://doi.org/10.1007/978-3-030-34113-8_12

such as the self-organizing map (SOM) algorithm [14]. Current clustering algorithms mostly consider clustering between similar content, but there is little research on multi-view image clustering between the same target. Finding multi-view image of the same target has important applications in three-dimensional reconstruction, image registration, and data fusion, etc. Therefore, achieving better clustering of multi-view images has important research significance.

In this study, an improved clustering method is proposed, achieving an accurate multi-view clustering process. The traditional SOM neural network is extended, and a response layer is introduced to produce a three-layer online SOM neural network clustering algorithm to comprehensively cluster multi-view image data. We introduce the response layer, simplify the input parameters and eliminate the pre-training process, thereby improving the accuracy of the overall multi-view clustering results and achieving a suitable performance and stability of the multi-view clustering process.

2   Materials and Methods

Most current clustering algorithms do not consider multi-view images. Some of the image content between multi-view images may be completely different, which brings great difficulties to clustering. Therefore, we improved SOM neural network to achieve this task, in the hope of obtaining complete multi-view clustering results.

2.1   Online SOM Neural Network

The SOM neural network is a method used to numerically simulate human brain neural function. This network is an unsupervised competitive learning feedforward neural network that can achieve unsupervised self-organized learning in training [14]. The traditional SOM is a two-layer neural network: the first layer is the input layer, which accepts input eigenvectors, and the second layer is the competing layer (in which each node is a neuron) that outputs the classification result of the input samples. The basic working principle is that when the sample data enter the input layer, the distance between each input sample data value and the neuron's weight is calculated and that the neuron with the smallest distance to the input sample data becomes the competitive neuron. The weights of the competitive neuron and the adjacent neuron are adjusted to attain values similar to the input sample data values. After many rounds of training, the neurons are divided into various regions that can map the input sample and cluster the input data.

The SOM method is a model-based clustering algorithm whose strategy is to construct the data model based on prior knowledge and use the model to cluster the new data; this strategy has unique advantages for high-dimensional data processing. However, the traditional SOM neural network must be trained based on prior knowledge, making this network type unsuitable for clustering multi-view, massive and disordered image data. It is important to optimize the SOM network to achieve the characteristics of online learning and multi-view clustering.

Considering the existence of nerve endings in the actual brain model, an improved SOM neural network is proposed for obtaining an online self-organizing map neural network (OSOM). The OSOM is designed as a three-layer neural network. The first two layers are similar to those of the traditional SOM and correspond to the data input and competition layers. The additional layer responds to the nerve endings and corresponds to the response layer. In Fig. 1, the first layer is illustrated as light yellow cells, which represent input data; the neurons of the second layer are illustrated as large circles, of which the blue circles represent inactive neurons and the yellow circles represent the neurons that have won the competition; and the third layer consists of small circles that represent nerve endings, where red circles correspond to inactivated nerve endings and yellow to neurons that have successfully entered the activated state. To meet the requirements of performance and accuracy, this approach uses the input of high-dimensional data based on stream mode and incremental learning using an improved SOM neural network to realize multi-view clustering of data and online learning of the neural network.

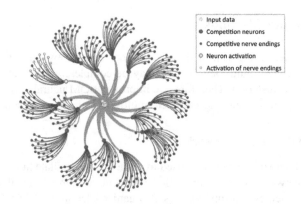

Fig. 1. OSOM neural network diagram. (Color figure online)

The OSOM can continuously generate neurons and nerve endings during data processing and does not need to perform prior training or initialize the network in advance. This is an important reason that why OSOM could get complete multi-view clustering results. The specific process is as follows:

1. Input the data stream from the input layer. The input data stream consists of two parts, namely, the global image descriptor $x = \{x_1, x_2, \ldots, x_m\}$ and the local image descriptor set $Y = \{y_1, y_2, \ldots, y_n\}$, where x is a single vector, m is its dimension, Y is a vector set, n is the number of local image feature points, and $y_i = \{\gamma_1, \gamma_2, \ldots, \gamma_h\}$ is the i-th descriptor of the local feature point of the image, which is of dimension h;

2. Enter the neuronal competition mode. Calculate the distance between the input global descriptor x and each competing neuron connection weight ω, and identify the nearest N neurons, that is, impose the following condition

$$N\|x - \omega\| = \min_i(N\|x - \omega_i\|) \tag{1}$$

where N represents the first N nearest neuron sets, and ω_i represents the connection weight of the i-th competing neuron;

3. The first N competitive neurons enter the response mode in turn, which is called the response to competitive neurons. Calculate the shortest distance l between each local descriptor y in set Y and nerve end ϖ under each competitive neuron, that is,

$$l_{ik} = \min_j\|y_j - \varpi_{ik}\| \tag{2}$$

where y_j denotes the j-th input local descriptor that traverses set Y, ϖ_{ik} denotes the connection weight of the k-th nerve terminal under the i-th responding competitive neuron, and l_{ik} denotes the shortest distance between the corresponding nerve endings and set Y.

If distance l_{ik} is less than a threshold value α, the corresponding nerve endings determine that the response is successful. If the number of successes of the nerve endings in responding to the i-th responsive neurons is greater than a threshold value β, then the overall response is judged to be successful, and the other neurons no longer respond.

$$\sum_{k=1}^{K} \xi(\alpha - l_{ik}) > \beta \tag{3}$$

where k is the total number of nerve endings under the i-th competitive neuron and $\xi(x)$ is the response function, which is expressed as

$$\xi(x) = \begin{cases} 1 & x > 0 \\ 0 & x \leq 0 \end{cases} \tag{4}$$

4. Enter the feedback learning mode. If there is a neuron and nerve ending overall response to the success of the corresponding neurons and nerve terminals using a certain learning efficiency to learn the data.

$$\begin{cases} \Delta\omega_i = \chi_i(x - \omega_i) \\ \Delta\varpi_{ij} = \chi_{ij}(y_g - \varpi_{ij}) \end{cases} \tag{5}$$

$$\begin{cases} \omega_i(t+1) = \omega_i(t) + \Delta\omega_i(t) \\ \varpi_{ij}(t+1) = \varpi_{ij}(t) + \Delta\varpi_{ij}(t) \end{cases} \tag{6}$$

where t is the number of learning rounds, χ is the learning efficiency, x is the global descriptor for neuron response, and y_g is the local descriptor for obtaining the nerve ending response. Then, a new descriptor within each neuron is generated using a local descriptor that failed to successfully obtain the nerve ending response.

$$\varpi_{i(k+1)} = \chi_{i(k+1)} y_d \tag{7}$$

After learning, the learning efficiency χ of the neuron and the corresponding nerve endings decreases by a specified step size, which is designated δ.

$$\chi_i(t_i + 1) = \begin{cases} \chi_i(t_i) - \delta & t_i \leq m \\ E & t_i > m \end{cases} \tag{8}$$

where δ is the step-down rate of each learning rate; m is the upper limit on the number of reductions in the learning rate, which satisfies $m \leq \chi_i(0)/\delta$; and E is the learning termination rate. If all the nerve endings that correspond to the first N winning neurons fail to respond to the learning process, generate new neurons and nerve endings.

$$\begin{cases} \omega_r = \chi_r x \\ \varpi_{i(k+1)} = \chi_{i(k+1)} y_d \end{cases} \tag{9}$$

5. Continue to enter the data stream, and return to 2 until all the data have been processed.

Each neuron that corresponds to the image constitutes a category, thereby completing the multi-view clustering process for image data. In practice, to control the growth of the number of neurons under constant input, old neurons can be merged after a specified amount of time to yield more accurate clustering results.

2.2   Multi-view Clustering Algorithm

Using the OSOM neural network, a multi-view clustering algorithm for image data is proposed. The specific process is illustrated in Fig. 2.

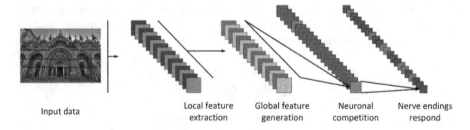

| Input data | Local feature extraction | Global feature generation | Neuronal competition | Nerve endings respond |

Fig. 2.   Multi-view clustering algorithm diagram.

First, the global descriptor are extracted from the input image, which is designated u. Then, descriptor u is inputted into the OSOM neural network, and the N nearest neurons are identified. Finally, the corresponding nerve ending responses are calculated, and learning and rules generation are performed to produce the image clustering results. Additionally, to improve the processing efficiency, parallel input of the images can be performed.

3   Results and Discussion

Clustering analysis of image data is conducted to identify images of the same target automatically. Therefore, there are two main indices for evaluating the clustering algorithm: the ratio of the number of correct clustering results to the total number of clustering results, that is, the accuracy rate (AR), and the number of correctly clustered images lost from the clustering result, that is, the negative true rate (NTR). The former index evaluates the locality of the clustering results and characterizes the in-class performance of the clustering algorithm. The latter index evaluates the integrity of the clustering results and characterizes the inter-class performance of the clustering algorithm. In the experiments, we use these two indicators as the main criteria. To evaluate the proposed OSOM neural network, it is designed for comparison with the classical k-means algorithm. To evaluate the performance and accuracy of the overall algorithm flow, 10,000 unordered and cluttered Internet images are used as inputs to conduct experiments, and the final clustering results are analyzed and evaluated.

3.1   OSOM Neural Network Experiments

The OSOM neural network is tested and compared using the classical k-means clustering algorithm. The specific experimental design is as follows: Clustering experiments are conducted using 10 categories of data from the BMW dataset [15]. A total of 100 images of the BMW dataset are used in the experiments, each of which contains 10 images of the same scene from different angles. VELAD [7] is used to obtain a global description of the images. Clustering experiments are performed using OSOM and k-means, respectively.

To describe the clustering results more intuitively, the AR, the NTR and false positive rate (FPR) of each method for each type of data clustering result are calculated. The cluster type defined as the main component in the clustering results. The AR of the calculation is $\eta = m/M$, where m is the number of correctly clustered images in the class, and M is the total number of clustered images in the class. The NTR γ $\gamma = w/I$ is the true-negative rate, where w is the number of images that cannot be divided into the class, and I is the total number of images that should be assigned to the class. The FPR ε is expressed as $\varepsilon = r/M$, where r is the number of correctly clustered images in the class. According to the above definition, the higher AR, the lower FPR and NTR, and the better the overall performance of the method.

The results are shown in Fig. 3, Tables 1 and 2. The OSOM threshold is set to 25, the learning efficiency is set to 1.0, the learning step is set to 0.3, the number of clusters in the k-means clustering process is set to 10. The image type that is the main component of the specified clustering result is the final representative result of the cluster type.

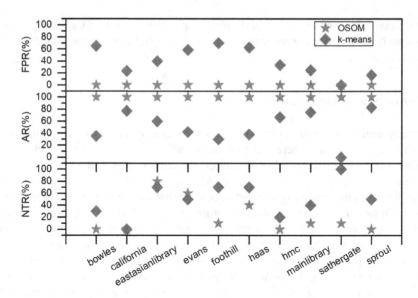

Fig. 3. Clustering results of comparative analysis.

Table 1. OSOM clustering statistics table.

Class name	Total number of clusters	Correct number	AR	FPR	NTR
Bowles	10	10	100.00%	0.00%	0.00%
California	10	10	100.00%	0.00%	0.00%
East asian library	2	2	100.00%	0.00%	80.00%
Evans	4	4	100.00%	0.00%	60.00%
Foothill	9	9	100.00%	0.00%	10.00%
Haas	6	6	100.00%	0.00%	40.00%
HMC	10	10	100.00%	0.00%	0.00%
Main library	9	9	100.00%	0.00%	10.00%
Sathergate	9	9	100.00%	0.00%	10.00%
Sproul	10	10	100.00%	0.00%	0.00%

According to the data in Table 1 and Fig. 3, for the BMW dataset, the OSOM clustering AR remains at 100%, which is much higher than that of the k-means algorithm. However, the correctness of k-means clustering is generally low, and the clustering of the 'sathergate' class is fully incorrect. According to the data in Table 2 and Fig. 3, the ER of OSOM is consistently 0%, which is lower than that of k-means clustering. The OSOM FPR and NTR values are also lower than those of k-means clustering. Overall, the experiments on the BMW dataset show that OSOM achieves a higher overall clustering performance than traditional k-means clustering and exhibits a higher clustering AR and better stability.

Table 2. K-means clustering statistics table.

Class name	Total number of clusters	Correct number	AR	FPR	NTR
Bowles	20	7	35.00%	65.00%	30.00%
California	13	10	76.92%	23.08%	0.00%
East asian library	5	3	60.00%	40.00%	70.00%
Evans	12	5	41.67%	58.33%	50.00%
Foothill	10	3	30.00%	70.00%	70.00%
Haas	8	3	37.50%	62.50%	70.00%
HMC	12	8	66.67%	33.33%	20.00%
Main library	8	6	75.00%	25.00%	40.00%
Sather gate	0	0	0.00%	0.00%	100.00%
Sproul	6	5	83.33%	16.67%	50.00%

3.2 Multi-view Clustering Algorithm Experiments

To evaluate the multi-view clustering algorithm for practical applications, the following experiments are designed: Using a dataset of 10,000 cluttered Internet images, the multi-view clustering experiments of this method are conducted. The images are downloaded from Flickr [16]. The VELAD parameters and the OSOM parameters are set to the same values as in the previous experiments. The final clustering result contains 81 image classes, each containing 20 or more images. Partial clustering results are shown in Fig. 4. The clustering result in Fig. 4 contains multi-view images of the same scene. As shown in the red box in the Fig. 4, it can be seen that the content in the red frame is different side images of the same building, and the content is completely different. This shows that our method can achieve the clustering of multi-view images well.

Fig. 4. Experimental clustering results for ten thousand images. (Color figure online)

In the experiments, the image type that constitutes the main component of the specified clustering result is the final representative of the clustering type, and the AR of the clustering results is calculated, as shown in Fig. 5.

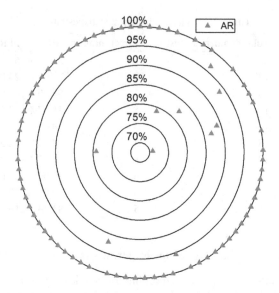

Fig. 5. AR chart for the results of clustering experiments on ten thousand images.

The ARs of the 81 clustering results obtained in the clustering experiment on 10,000 images are relatively high. The ARs of 71 clustering results are 100%, and the ARs of 3 clustering results are as low at 80%. The lowest AR of the clustering results is 70.8%, and the average correct classification rate is 98.33%. According to the results of the clustering experiments on ten thousand images, the clustering results obtained by the method proposed here exhibit high correctness and favorable stability and can satisfy the clustering requirements of images under multi-view data conditions.

3.3   Discussion and Analysis

With the continuous formation of big image data, clustering between multi-view images has gradually become a hot research field. However, the existing algorithms mostly consider clustering of the same content, there is little discussion about clustering between different angle images of the same target. Although some content may vary greatly among multi-view images, there may be some content crossover between images. With this assumption, we have improved SOM. OSOM does not need to specify the number of clusters and does not require prior training. Through the online learning in the clustering, the multi-view feature of the same target is obtained. Thus, a better multi-view clustering result is obtained. From the 10,000 Internet images experiments, we can see that OSOM can complete multi-view clustering tasks, obtain a good result. However, this paper only proposes a multi-view processing method, the application of the method in actual engineering needs to continue to be optimized (processing time, hardware consumption, etc.).

4   Conclusions

We have designed an OSOM neural network to achieve an accurate multi-view clustering processing. Considering the multi-view clustering process, a three-layer OSOM neural network algorithm without prior training is proposed. This algorithm simplifies the clustering process and satisfies the accuracy and speed requirements. The experimental results of the BMW dataset and a dataset of 10,000 Internet images show that the proposed algorithm offers high accuracy and favorable stability and can accomplish clustering tasks for multi-view image data.

References

1. Csurka, G., Dance, C., Fan, L., Willamowski, J., Bray, C.: Visual categorization with bags of keypoints. In: Proceedings of the European Conference on Computer Vision, Prague, pp. 1–2 (2004)
2. Lazebnik, S., Schmid, C., Ponce, J.: Beyond bags of features: spatial pyramid matching for recognizing natural scene categories. In: Proceedings of the IEEE Conference on Computer Vision and Pattern Recognition, New York, pp. 2169–2178 (2006)
3. Yang, J., Yu, K., Gong, Y., Huang, T.: Linear spatial pyramid matching using sparse coding for image classification. In: Proceedings of the IEEE Conference on Computer Vision and Pattern Recognition, Miami, pp. 1794–1801 (2009)
4. Wang, J., Yang, J., Yu, K., Lv, F., Huang, T., Gong, Y.: Locality-constrained linear coding for image classification. In: Proceedings of the IEEE Conference on Computer Vision and Pattern Recognition, San Francisco, pp. 3360–3367 (2010)
5. Perronnin, F., Sánchez, J., Mensink, T.: Improving the fisher kernel for large-scale image classification. In: Daniilidis, K., Maragos, P., Paragios, N. (eds.) ECCV 2010. LNCS, vol. 6314, pp. 143–156. Springer, Heidelberg (2010). https://doi.org/10.1007/978-3-642-15561-1_11
6. Russakovsky, O., Lin, Y., Yu, K., Fei-Fei, L.: Object-centric spatial pooling for image classification. In: Fitzgibbon, A., Lazebnik, S., Perona, P., Sato, Y., Schmid, C. (eds.) ECCV 2012. LNCS, pp. 1–15. Springer, Heidelberg (2012). https://doi.org/10.1007/978-3-642-33709-3_1
7. Dong, Y., Fan, D., Ma, Q., Ji, S., Lei, R.: Edge-based locally aggregated descriptors for image clustering. Int. Arch. Photogram. Remote Sens. Spat. Inf. Sci. **XLII-3**, 303–308 (2018)
8. MacQueen, J.: Some methods for classification and analysis of multivariate observations. In: Proceedings of the Fifth Berkeley Symposium on Mathematical Statistics and Probability, Berkeley, pp. 281–297 (1967)
9. Wang, H.X., Jin, H.J., Wang, J.L., Jiang, W.S.: Optimization approach for multi-scale segmentation of remotely sensed imagery under k-means clustering guidance. Acta Geodaetica Cartogr. Sin. **44**, 526–532 (2015)
10. Jiayao, W., Mingxia, X., Jianzhong, G.: Improved high dimensional data clustering algorithm based on similarity preserving and feature transformation. Acta Geodaetica Cartogr. Sin. **40**, 269–275 (2011)
11. Guha, S., Rastogi, R., Shim, K.: CURE: an efficient clustering algorithm for large databases. In: Proceedings of the ACM SIGMOD International Conference on Management of Data, Washington, pp. 73–84 (1998)

12. Ester, M., Kriegel, H.P., Sander, J., Xu, X.: A density-based algorithm for discovering clusters in large spatial databases with noise. In: Proceedings of the International Conference on Knowledge Discovery and Data Mining, Portland, pp. 226–231 (1996)
13. Wang, W., Yang, J., Muntz, R.: STING: a statistical information grid approach to spatial data mining. In: Proceedings of the International Conference on Very Large Data Bases, Athens, pp. 186–195 (1997)
14. Kohonen, T.: Self-organization and associative memory. Appl. Opt. **8**, 3406–3409 (1989)
15. BMW Images Dataset. http://download.csdn.net/detail/wmgd85/9700927
16. Flickr. https://www.flickr.com

Common Subspace Based Low-Rank and Joint Sparse Representation for Multi-view Face Recognition

Ziqiang Wang[1,2], Yingzhi Ouyang[1,2], Weidan Zhu[1,2], Bin Sun[1,2(✉)], and Qiang Liu[1,2]

[1] School of Aeronautics and Astronautics, University of Electronic Science and Technology of China, Chengdu 611731, China
{201721190135, 20171901011027, 201622190334}@std.uestc.edu.cn,
{sunbinhust, lqiang}@uestc.edu.cn

[2] Aircraft Swarm Intelligent Sensing and Cooperative Control Key Laboratory of Sichuan Province, Chengdu 611731, China

Abstract. Multi-view face data are very common in real-world application, since different viewpoints and various types of sensors attempt to better represent face data. However, these data have large pose variation, which dramatically degrades the performance of multi-view face recognition. To address this, we propose a common subspace based low-rank and joint sparse representation (CSLRJSR) method, which provides a framework encompassing divergence mitigation and feature fusion. In CSLRJSR method, common subspace is learnt to bridge the view, then low-rank and joint sparse representation are exploited to learn and then fuse the discriminative features. Experiments on multi-view face dataset demonstrate that CSLRJSR outperforms the state-of-the-art methods both in two-view and multi-view situations.

Keywords: Multi-view face recognition · Common subspace · Low-rank representation · Joint sparse

1 Introduction

Multi-view face recognition has been receiving a great deal of attention recently. Multi-view face data provide complementary information of the same object from multiple different views, which have positive effect on multi-view face recognition, compared to single-view face data. Researchers have already realized that fusing multi-view information can greatly improve face recognition performance [1, 2]. However, multi-view face recognition confronts a challenge of the wide variations of pose, illumination, and expression often encountered in realities. Therefore pursing effective methods is still an urgent problem.

Sparse representation is explored extensively in face recognition [3, 4] and super resolution [5] due to its good performance in revealing underlying structure. Some sparse representation based methods are used for multi-view recognition tasks, which improve recognition performance by indirectly exploiting the inherent relationships

© Springer Nature Switzerland AG 2019
Y. Zhao et al. (Eds.): ICIG 2019, LNCS 11903, pp. 145–156, 2019.
https://doi.org/10.1007/978-3-030-34113-8_13

between multi-view data. Wang et al. [6] assumed one view can be represented sparsely by another view through a pair of dictionaries. Huang et al. [7] combined coupled dictionary and feature space learning (CDL) for two-view recognition and synthesis. Mandal et al. [8] proposed a generalized coupled dictionary learning (GCDL) method which learns dictionaries from two different views in a coupled manner, so that in the two views, the sparse coefficients of corresponding classes are correlated maximally. However, these methods are not suitable for scenarios more than two views, due to that they excessively rely on the coupling between views.

Subspace learning based methods have been introduced in pattern classification and data mining. These methods directly apply a specific low-rank projection to different view data. They can reduce differences between views and flexibly deal with scenarios more than two views. Several recognition approaches based on subspace learning were proposed recently, aiming at seeking for a common subspace where the data from multi-view can be compared [9]. The typical subspace learning method-principal component analysis (PCA) [10], is a technology of seeking a subspace in which the variance of the projected samples is maximized. Supervised regularization based robust subspace (SRRS) [11] presented a unified framework for subspace learning and data recovery. Ding et al. [12] proposed low-rank common subspace for multi-view learning (LRCS), which reserves compatible information among each view, through seeking a common discriminative subspace with a low-rank constraint. Robust multi-view data analysis through collective low-rank subspace (CLRS) proposed by Ding et al. [13] in 2018 complemented LRCS with a regularizer to further maximize the correlation within classes with the help of supervised information. Subspace learning methods perform well when reducing the divergence between views, but ignore the full use of extracted features, which actually limit the performance of recognition.

Recently, low-rank representation [14–17] and joint sparse [1, 18] are adopted in sparse representation. Low-rank representation based method has shown promising performance in capturing underlying low-rank structure as well as noise robustness. A joint sparse representation (SMBR) was proposed in [18] that enforce joint sparse constraints to the extracted features. SMBR took fully advantage of the extracted feature information to improve recognition performance.

Aforementioned multi-view face recognition methods still exist some intrinsic problems. To address these issues, we propose a novel multi-view face recognition algorithm, the contributions of this work are as follows:

- This paper focuses on the shared information across different views in order to handle the negative situation brought by multi-view face recognition, and puts forward common subspace based low-rank and joint sparse representation (CSLRJSR) method which unifies domain divergence mitigation and feature fusion.
- The method we propose is a more general algorithm that can be easily extended to handle more than two-view scenarios. Different scenarios of experiments were conducted to demonstrate the effectiveness of our algorithm. In many cases, our method outperforms the state-of-the-art multi-view recognition algorithms.

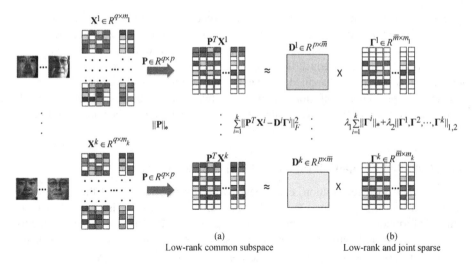

Fig. 1. Framework of our proposed CSLRJSR algorithm. (a) A common projection P for multi-view data to reduce divergences between views. (b) Low-rank and joint sparse constraints are imposed on sparse coefficients to reveal the global structure of multi-view data and fuse extracted features.

2 The Proposed Algorithm

In this section, we briefly present our motivation, and then propose our CSLRJSR method for the task of multi-view face recognition. Finally, we present the design of the optimization solution.

2.1 Motivation

Multi-view face data are ubiquitous in the real world, as the same objects are usually observed at different viewpoints, or even captured with different sensors. Therefore, the data of the same class but different views will show a big difference, which brings great challenges to the analysis of multi-view data. However, some research work [12, 13, 19] shows that the data of different views of the same class have a close relationship in the feature space. Some algorithms based on sparse representations [6–8] handle the task of multi-view recognition by integrating the inherent connection of multi-view data in the algorithm. The main idea of these methods is to learn the dictionary of two views in a coupled way, so that the same classes from the two views are most correlated in some transform space. These algorithms greatly improve the recognition performance of multi-view data. Unfortunately, these algorithms can only handle two views.

Subspace-based algorithms [12, 13, 20] directly process data from multiple views. The core idea of these methods is to directly apply a specific low-rank projection to different view data. In this way, the low-rank common subspace is learned, so that more shared information in different view data of the same class can be found. These algorithms take advantage of the relationship between multi-view data to improve recognition performance and to generalize the processing of multiple views. However, feature information extracted by these algorithms is not further utilized. Following the core idea of subspace learning, we bridge different view data of the same class based on the common subspace to reduce the divergence between views. And the low-rank and joint sparse constraints are applied to the extracted features to achieve feature fusion, so that the complementary information of the features can be better utilized. Figure 1 shows an overview of the proposed algorithm. Next, we will introduce our algorithm in detail.

2.2   Common Subspace Based Sparse Representation

In multi-view face recognition, each view owns several classes and there are same classes across different views. Between these same classes, there is shared low-rank similar information. Thus, a low-rank common projection $\mathbf{P}$ is utilized in our method to preserve this shared information, so that a same class from different views can be aligned into common subspace. Suppose there is k-view data $\mathbf{X} = [\mathbf{X}^1, \cdots, \mathbf{X}^k]$, and each view $\mathbf{X}^i \in \mathbb{R}^{q \times m_i}$ includes m_i training samples and c same classes, where q is the original feature dimension of face sample. For each view $i = 1, \cdots, k$, $\mathbf{D}^i$ and $\mathbf{\Gamma}^i$ represent the corresponding dictionary and sparse coefficients, respectively. Therefore, the objective function is defined as:

$$\arg \min_{\mathbf{P}, \mathbf{D}^i, \mathbf{\Gamma}^i} \sum_{i=1}^{k} ||\mathbf{P}^T \mathbf{X}^i - \mathbf{D}^i \mathbf{\Gamma}^i||_F^2 + rank(\mathbf{P}) \tag{1}$$

$$s.t. \quad \mathbf{P}^T \mathbf{P} = \mathbf{I}, \quad ||\mathbf{d}_j^i||_2 \leq 1, \quad (i = 1, 2, \ldots, k)$$

where $rank(P)$ denotes the rank operator of matrix $\mathbf{P} \in \mathbb{R}^{q \times p}$ (p is the reduced dimensionality). The orthogonal constraint $\mathbf{P}^T \mathbf{P} = \mathbf{I}$ ($\mathbf{I}$ is a unit matrix) in Eq. (1) is applied to ensure the obtained $\mathbf{P}$ is a valid solution. $\mathbf{d}_j^i$ is an atom at the j-th column of dictionary $\mathbf{D}^i$. $||\mathbf{M}||_F = \sqrt{\sum_{i,j} \mathbf{M}_{i,j}^2}$ denotes the Frobenius norm of matrix $\mathbf{M}$. Since rank minimization problem is a NP-hard problem in Eq. (1), recent researches adopt nuclear norm as a good surrogate [17]. However, after reducing the divergence between views and obtaining the ability to deal with scenarios more than two views, we notice that the extracted features haven't been fully used yet. Thus, we propose a common subspace based low-rank and joint sparse representation method to further exploit them, which is presented in Sect. 2.3.

2.3   Common Subspace Based Low-Rank and Joint Sparse Representation

In order to fully exploit the extracted features and improve the recognition performance, joint sparse constraints are imposed on the representation coefficients to achieve feature-level fusion. Hence, we formulate the final objective function by unifying domain divergence mitigation and feature fusion as

$$\arg\min_{\mathbf{P},\mathbf{D}^i,\mathbf{\Gamma}^i} \sum_{i=1}^{k}\left(||\mathbf{P}^T\mathbf{X}^i - \mathbf{D}^i\mathbf{\Gamma}^i||_F^2 + \lambda_1||\mathbf{\Gamma}^i||_*\right) + \lambda_2||\mathbf{\Gamma}||_{1,2} + ||\mathbf{P}||_* \tag{2}$$

$$s.t.\quad \mathbf{P}^T\mathbf{P} = \mathbf{I},\quad ||\mathbf{d}_j^i||_2 \le 1,\quad (i = 1, 2, \ldots, k)$$

where we concatenate k coefficient matrices as $\mathbf{\Gamma} = [\mathbf{\Gamma}^1, \cdots, \mathbf{\Gamma}^k]$. And $||\mathbf{\Gamma}||_{1,2}$ denotes a joint sparse constraint calculated via $||\mathbf{\Gamma}||_{1,2} = \sum_i ||\boldsymbol{\gamma}^i||_2$ ($\boldsymbol{\gamma}^i$ denotes a vector on the i-th row of matrix $\mathbf{\Gamma}$), which is used to seek sparse nonzero rows so that all views can have similar sparse representations. And features are fused through this way. As for $||\bullet||_*$, it denotes a low-rank constraint that is applied to the sparse coefficient $\mathbf{\Gamma}^i$ in order to better expose the global structure of the data, by this way, learnt features become more discriminative. λ_1 and λ_2 are two positive tradeoff parameters. The detailed solution of the proposed algorithm is presented in Sect. 2.4.

2.4 Optimization

In this part, the alternating direction method of multipliers (ADMM) [21, 22] algorithm is used to deal with the optimization problem, as it converges well even several variables are non-smooth. We first introduce three auxiliary variables $\mathbf{Z}$, $\mathbf{L}^i$ and $\mathbf{W}$, and then transform Eq. (2) into its equivalent constrained optimization problem as

$$\arg\min_{\mathbf{D},\mathbf{P},\mathbf{\Gamma},\mathbf{Z},\mathbf{L}^i,\mathbf{W}} \sum_{i=1}^{k}(||\mathbf{P}^T\mathbf{X}^i - \mathbf{D}^i\mathbf{\Gamma}^i||_F^2 + \lambda_1||\mathbf{L}^i||_*) + \lambda_2||\mathbf{Z}||_{1,2} + ||\mathbf{W}||_* \tag{3}$$

$$s.t.\quad \mathbf{\Gamma} = \mathbf{Z}, \mathbf{P} = \mathbf{W}, \mathbf{\Gamma}^i = \mathbf{L}^i, i = 1, \ldots, k$$

Equation (3) can be addressed using the Augmented Lagrangian Method (ALM) [21]. The Augmented Lagrangian function $f_{\alpha_{\mathbf{Z}},\alpha_{\mathbf{L}},\alpha_{\mathbf{W}}}(\mathbf{P}, \mathbf{D}^i, \mathbf{\Gamma}, \mathbf{Z}, \mathbf{L}_i, \mathbf{W}; \mathbf{A}_{\mathbf{Z}}, \mathbf{A}_{\mathbf{L}}^i, \mathbf{A}_{\mathbf{W}})$ is defined as:

$$\arg\min_{\mathbf{D}^i,\mathbf{P},\mathbf{\Gamma},\mathbf{Z},\mathbf{L}^i,\mathbf{W}} \sum_{i=1}^{k}(||\mathbf{P}^T\mathbf{X}^i - \mathbf{D}^i\mathbf{\Gamma}^i||_F + \lambda_1||\mathbf{L}^i||_* + \langle\mathbf{A}_{\mathbf{L}}^i, \mathbf{\Gamma}^i - \mathbf{L}^i\rangle + \frac{\alpha_{\mathbf{L}}}{2}||\mathbf{\Gamma}^i - \mathbf{L}^i||_F^2)$$

$$+ \lambda_2||\mathbf{Z}||_{1,2} + \langle\mathbf{A}_{\mathbf{Z}}, \mathbf{\Gamma} - \mathbf{Z}\rangle + \frac{\alpha_{\mathbf{Z}}}{2}||\mathbf{\Gamma} - \mathbf{Z}||_F^2 \tag{4}$$

$$+ ||\mathbf{W}||_* + \langle\mathbf{A}_{\mathbf{W}}, \mathbf{P} - \mathbf{W}\rangle + \frac{\alpha_{\mathbf{W}}}{2}||\mathbf{P} - \mathbf{W}||_F^2$$

where $\mathbf{A}_{\mathbf{Z}}$, $\mathbf{A}_{\mathbf{L}}^i$, $\mathbf{A}_{\mathbf{W}}$ are three Lagrange multipliers and $\alpha_{\mathbf{Z}}$, $\alpha_{\mathbf{L}}$, $\alpha_{\mathbf{W}}$ are the positive penalty parameters, $\langle\mathbf{A}, \mathbf{B}\rangle$ denotes $tr(\mathbf{A}^T\mathbf{B})$, and $\mathbf{A}_{\mathbf{Z}} = [\mathbf{A}_{\mathbf{Z}}^1, \mathbf{A}_{\mathbf{Z}}^2, \ldots, \mathbf{A}_{\mathbf{Z}}^k]$.

The truth is that it is difficult to jointly optimize the variables in Eq. (4). Fortunately, we can get optimization results in an iterative way. That is, we solve each variable by keeping the others fixed. Moreover, we denote $\mathbf{P}_t$, $\mathbf{D}_t^i$, $\mathbf{\Gamma}_t$, $\mathbf{Z}_t$, $\mathbf{L}_t^i$, $\mathbf{W}_t$, $\mathbf{A}_{\mathbf{Z},t}$,

$\mathbf{A}^i_{\mathbf{L},t}$, $\mathbf{A}_{\mathbf{W},t}$, $\alpha_{\mathbf{Z},t}$, $\alpha_{\mathbf{L},t}$ and $\alpha_{\mathbf{W},t}$ as the solutions optimized in the t-th iteration $(t > 0)$. Then in the $(t+1)$-th iteration, those solutions are updated as follows:

Updating $\mathbf{L}^i$:

$$\mathbf{L}^i_{t+1} = \arg\min_{\mathbf{L}^i} \frac{\lambda_2}{\alpha_{\mathbf{L},t}} ||\mathbf{L}^i||_* + \frac{1}{2} ||\mathbf{L}^i - (\mathbf{\Gamma}^i_t + \frac{\mathbf{A}^i_{\mathbf{L},t}}{\alpha_{\mathbf{L},t}})||^2_F \quad (5)$$

Updating $\mathbf{\Gamma}^i$:

$$\mathbf{\Gamma}^i_{t+1} = (\mathbf{D}^{i^T}_t \mathbf{D}^i_t + \alpha_{\mathbf{Z},t}\mathbf{I} + \alpha_{\mathbf{L},t}\mathbf{I})^{-1}(\alpha_{\mathbf{Z},t}\mathbf{Z}^i_t + \alpha_{\mathbf{L},t}\mathbf{L}^i_{t+1} - \mathbf{A}^i_{\mathbf{Z},t} - \mathbf{A}^i_{\mathbf{L},t} + \mathbf{D}^{i^T}_t \mathbf{P}^T_t \mathbf{X}^i) \quad (6)$$

Updating $\mathbf{D}^i$:

$$\mathbf{D}^i_{t+1} = \arg\min_{\mathbf{D}^i} ||\mathbf{P}^T_t \mathbf{X}^i - \mathbf{D}^i \mathbf{\Gamma}^i_{t+1}||^2_F \quad s.t. \quad \left\|\mathbf{d}^i_j\right\|_2 \le 1 \quad (7)$$

Updating $\mathbf{W}$:

$$\mathbf{W}_{t+1} = \arg\min_{\mathbf{W}} \frac{1}{\alpha_{\mathbf{W},t}} ||\mathbf{W}||_* + \frac{1}{2} ||\mathbf{W} - (\mathbf{P}_t + \frac{\mathbf{A}_{\mathbf{W},t}}{\alpha_{\mathbf{W},t}})||^2_F \quad (8)$$

Updating $\mathbf{P}$:

$$\mathbf{P}_{t+1} = (\sum_{i=1}^k \mathbf{X}^i \mathbf{X}^{i^T} + \alpha_{\mathbf{W},t})^{-1}(\sum_{i=1}^k \mathbf{X}^i \mathbf{\Gamma}^{i^T}_{t+1} \mathbf{D}^{i^T}_{t+1} - \mathbf{A}_{\mathbf{W},t} + \alpha_{\mathbf{W}}\mathbf{W}_{t+1}) \quad (9)$$

Updating $\mathbf{Z}$:

$$\mathbf{Z}_{t+1} = \min_{\mathbf{Z}} \frac{\lambda_1}{\alpha_{\mathbf{Z},t}} ||\mathbf{Z}||_{1,2} + \frac{1}{2} ||\mathbf{Z} - (\mathbf{\Gamma}_{t+1} + \alpha^{-1}_{\mathbf{Z}}\mathbf{A}_{\mathbf{Z},t})||^2_F \quad (10)$$

We use Singular Value Thresholding (SVT) [23] to solve Eqs. (5) and (8), and a quadratic problem solver [24] to address Eq. (7). Since the structure of Eq. (10) is separable, we solve it separately with respect to each row of $\mathbf{Z}$. For each row, we follow the method used in [18] to solve the following sub-problems:

$$\mathbf{z}_{i,t+1} = \min_{\mathbf{z}} \frac{1}{2} ||\mathbf{n} - \mathbf{z}||^2_2 + \frac{\lambda}{\alpha_{\mathbf{z}}} ||\mathbf{z}||_2 \quad (11)$$

where $\mathbf{n} = \gamma_{i,t+1} + \alpha^{-1}_{\mathbf{z}}\mathbf{a}_{z_i,t}$, $\gamma_{i,t+1}$, $\mathbf{a}_{z_i,t}$, $\mathbf{z}_{i,t+1}$ represent the i-th row of matrix $\mathbf{\Gamma}_{t+1}$, $\mathbf{A}_{\mathbf{Z},t}$ and $\mathbf{Z}_{t+1}$, respectively.

In conclusion, we present the detailed optimization procedure of CSLRJSR in Algorithm 1, in which $\alpha_{\mathbf{Z}}$, $\alpha_{\mathbf{L}}$ and $\alpha_{\mathbf{W}}$ are set empirically, while tuning the two tradeoff parameters λ_1 and λ_2 via experiments elaborated in the next section. We initialize $\mathbf{P}$ randomly in the same way as [12] and initialize dictionary $\mathbf{D}$ via an online dictionary learning method that used in [8]. To determine the influence of different initialization methods, we use several traditional methods to initialize $\mathbf{P}$, which turns out that the final recognition performance tends to be exceedingly similar.

Algorithm 1 Solving Problem (CSLRJSR) by ADMM

Input: $\mathbf{X}^i\,(i=1,\cdots,k)\,,\lambda_1\,,\lambda_2$

Initialization: $\mathbf{L}_0^i = 0\,,\mathbf{Z}_0 = \mathbf{\Gamma}_0 = 0\,,\mathbf{W}_0 = 0\,,\mathbf{A}_{Z,0} = 0\,,\mathbf{A}_{L,0}^i = 0\,,\ \ \mathbf{A}_{W,0} = 0$

$$\alpha_Z = \alpha_L = \alpha_W = 0.9\times10^{-4}\,,\rho = 1.1\,,\varepsilon = 10^{-5}\,,t = 0$$

While not converged **do**

1. Fix other variables and optimize $\mathbf{L}^i$ through Eq.(5).
2. Fix other variables and optimize $\mathbf{\Gamma}^i$ through Eq.(6).
3. Fix other variables and optimize $\mathbf{D}^i$ through Eq.(7).
4. Fix other variables and optimize $\mathbf{W}$ through Eq.(8).
5. Fix other variables and optimize $\mathbf{P}$ through Eq.(9).
6. Fix other variables and optimize $\mathbf{Z}$ through Eq.(10).
7. Optimize the multipliers $\mathbf{A}_{Z,t+1}$, $\mathbf{A}_{L,t+1}^i$, $\mathbf{A}_{W,t+1}$ through

$$\mathbf{A}_{Z,t+1} = \mathbf{A}_{Z,t} + \alpha_Z(\mathbf{\Gamma}_{t+1} - \mathbf{Z}_{t+1});$$
$$\mathbf{A}_{L,t+1}^i = \mathbf{A}_{L,t}^i + \alpha_{Z,t}(\mathbf{\Gamma}_{t+1}^i - \mathbf{Z}_{t+1}^i);$$
$$\mathbf{A}_{W,t+1} = \mathbf{A}_{W,t} + \alpha_{W,t}(\mathbf{P}_{t+1} - \mathbf{W}_{t+1}).$$

8. Optimize the penalty parameter $\alpha_{Z,t+1}$, $\alpha_{L,t+1}$, $\alpha_{W,t+1}$ through:

$$\alpha_{\lambda,t+1} = \rho\alpha_{\lambda,t} \quad (\lambda = \mathbf{Z},\mathbf{L},\mathbf{W})$$

9. Check the convergence conditions

$$\| \mathbf{A}_{t+1} - \mathbf{Z}_{t+1} \|_\infty < \varepsilon,$$
$$\| \mathbf{P}_{t+1} - \mathbf{W}_{t+1} \|_\infty < \varepsilon.$$

10. $t = t + 1$
11. **end while**

---

output: $\mathbf{L}^i\,,\mathbf{\Gamma}\,,\mathbf{D}^i\,,\mathbf{W}\,,\mathbf{P}\,,\mathbf{Z}$

---

3   Experiments

In this section, a public multi-view dataset named CMU-PIE face dataset and experimental protocols are first introduced. Secondly, we demonstrate the comparison results of our proposed algorithm and the state-of-the-art algorithms. Lastly, for a comprehensive evaluation, several properties of our CSLRJSR approach are evaluated.

3.1   Dataset and Experimental Setting

The CMU-PIE Face dataset [25] consists of 68 subjects, each of which has multiple poses. Examples for each subject have 21 various illumination variations. In the experiments, we use face images of 7 poses (C02, C05, C07, C09, C14, C27, C29), where there are large differences between every subject in different poses (Fig. 2). Different numbers of poses are selected to build multiple evaluation subsets.

Furthermore, face images are cropped into size of 64×64 and only the raw features are used as the input. We randomly choose 10 samples from each subject each pose to construct the training set, whilst the remaining samples are used for testing.

3.2   Comparison Results

To demonstrate the effectiveness of our approach, we compare the proposed method with sparse representation based methods and subspace learning based methods. All of these methods directly or indirectly exploit the inherent characteristics of the relationship between multi-view data to improve recognition performance. Sparse representation based methods include SCDL [6], CDL [7], GCDL1&GCDL2 [8]; and subspace learning based methods include PCA [10], SRRS [11], LRCS [12] and CLRS [13]. Actually, SCDL, CDL, GCDL1 and GCDL2 are specially designed for two-view cases, thus, only the recognition performances of two-view cases are presented. While PCA, SRRS, LRCS and CLRS are used to process multi-view cases by seeking a robust subspace.

For all comparison algorithms, we adopt the nearest neighbor classifier to evaluate the final recognition performance. We conduct five random selections and average the results. Table 1 depicts recognition performance of different methods on CMU-PIE datasets, where Case1: {C02, C14}, Case2: {C05, C07}, Case3: {C05, C29}, Case4: {C07, C09}, Case5: {C09, C27}, Case6: {C09, C29}, Case7: {C05, C07, C29}, Case8: {C05, C27, C29}, Case9: {C07, C09, C27}, Case10: {C07, C09, C29}, and Case11: {C05, C07, C09, C29}.

From the experimental results, we obtain the following observations. (1) All methods based on sparse representation show good performance. SCDL, CDL, GCDL1 and GCDL2 are to learn the dictionary for the two-view cases in a coupled manner, so that for the corresponding classes from the two views, the sparse coefficients of them are maximally correlated in a certain transformed space. However, these methods are only applicable to two-view cases. While our method is completely compatible for multi-view cases, which applies low-rank common subspace constraint to different views to mitigate the differences between views. And the recognition performance of our proposed algorithm is better than the above algorithms in most case. (2) Comparing with other subspace learning methods, we apply low-rank and joint sparse constraints to learn and fuse discriminative features so that the recognition performance is improved.

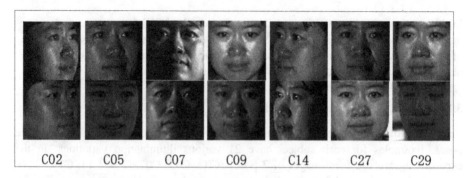

| C02 | C05 | C07 | C09 | C14 | C27 | C29 |

Fig. 2. Face samples from different views of one subject in CMU-PIE dataset. We can notice the differences across different views of the same subject.

Table 1. Comparison results between 9 algorithms on CMU-PIE dataset

Methods	SCDL	CDL	GCDL1	GCDL2	PCA	SRRS	LRCS	CLRS	Ours
Case1	85.18	84.43	84.38	84.54	66.47	74.52	86.35	86.03	**87.69**
Case2	**90.35**	88.97	88.91	88.43	63.22	61.14	88.27	88.06	90.14
Case3	89.71	88.81	88.75	88.17	64.93	74.36	88.70	76.33	**91.68**
Case4	90.41	89.66	88.97	88.75	68.28	76.39	90.72	80.06	**91.10**
Case5	90.09	89.13	88.49	88.75	73.13	78.31	90.19	87.26	**90.41**
Case6	89.93	89.45	88.86	89.07	69.08	71.96	91.10	86.57	**91.95**
Case7	/	/	/	/	64.39	72.96	85.18	75.41	**91.22**
Case8	/	/	/	/	64.53	72.67	83.01	75.27	**91.26**
Case9	/	/	/	/	73.77	72.03	87.74	88.91	**90.41**
Case10	/	/	/	/	68.12	66.56	87.63	88.77	**91.65**
Case11	/	/	/	/	66.07	63.09	84.81	75.88	**91.68**

3.3 Convergence Analysis and Parameters Analysis

In this part, we analyze several properties of our proposed method, i.e., convergence and parameter influence.

First, we carry out server experiments on convergence curve and recognition performance of different iterations. Specifically, we evaluate on two-view case {C02, C14} and the performance is presented in Fig. 3. From the results, we can see our algorithm converges pretty well. Also, we find that the recognition performance goes up quickly and keeps a relatively stable point.

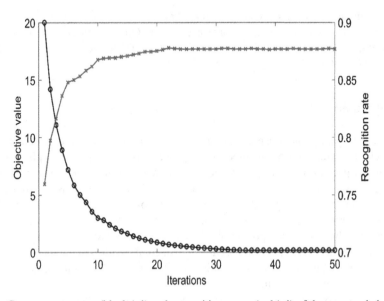

Fig. 3. Convergence curve (black 'o') and recognition curve (red 'x') of the proposed algorithm in two-view Case1 (C02&C14), where the dimensionality is set to 200 and the parameter values λ_1 and λ_2 to 10 and 0.1, respectively. (Color figure online)

Second, because there are two tradeoff parameters λ_1, λ_2 in our method, we simultaneously analyze them on Case1 (C02&C14) and the results are presented in Fig. 4.

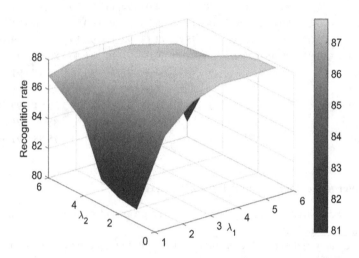

Fig. 4. We evaluate the recognition performance of our proposed algorithm on the two tradeoff parameters influence $\{\lambda_1, \lambda_2\}$ using two-view case (C02&C14). The value from 0 to 6 denotes [0.1, 0.5, 1,5, 10, 20], respectively.

According to the results, we can see that when λ_1 and λ_2 both are set small or large at the same time, the recognition performance is poor. On the contrary, we notice when $\lambda_1 \in [5, 15]$, it provides a much better performance. Therefore, we set $\lambda_1 = 10$ and $\lambda_2 = 0.1$ during the whole experiments.

4   Conclusion

In this paper, a common subspace based low-rank and joint sparse representation for multi-view face recognition method is proposed. Specifically, we apply low-rank common subspace projection to multi-view data to reduce differences between views of the same class, so that the discriminative ability of learnt features is improved. Furthermore, joint sparse is imposed to get a representation consistent across all the views, and then low-rank representation uncovers the global structure of data and further improves the discriminative power of the features. And finally, the discriminative features are learnt and efficiently fused. Experimental results on multi-view dataset, demonstrate the effectiveness and accuracy of the proposed algorithm, compared to several state-of-the-art algorithms.

Our future work will mainly focus on evaluating our method on more different multi-view datasets and improving the accuracy and robustness of our method on noisy datasets which are more common in real-world applications.

Acknowledgments. The work was supported by National Natural Science Foundation of China (No. 61803075). We thank the anonymous reviewers for their comments and suggestions which make the paper much improved.

References

1. Yuan, X., Liu, X., Yan, S.: Visual classification with multitask joint sparse representation. IEEE Trans. Image Process. **21**(10), 4349–4360 (2012)
2. Cao, L., Luo, J., Liang F., Huang, T.: Heterogeneous feature machines for visual recognition. In: IEEE International Conference on Computer Vision (2009)
3. Wright, J., Yang, A., Ganesh, A., Sastry, S., Ma, Y.: Robust face recognition via sparse representation. IEEE Trans. Pattern Anal. Mach. Intell. **31**(2), 210–227 (2009)
4. Jiang, X., Lai, J.: Sparse and dense hybrid representation via dictionary decomposition for face recognition. IEEE Trans. Pattern Anal. Mach. Intell. **37**(5), 1067–1079 (2015)
5. Yang, J., Wright, J., Huang, T., Ma, Y.: Image super-resolution as sparse representation of raw image patches. In: 2008 Conference on Computer Vision and Pattern Recognition (CVPR), pp. 1–8 (2008)
6. Wang, S., Zhang, L., Liang, Y., Pan, Q.: Semi-coupled dictionary learning with applications to image super-resolution and photo-sketch synthesis. In: 2012 IEEE Conference on Computer Vision and Pattern Recognition (CVPR), pp. 2216–2223 (2012)
7. Huang D., Wang, Y.: Coupled dictionary and feature space learning with applications to cross-domain image synthesis and recognition. In: IEEE International Conference on Computer Vision, pp. 2496–2503 (2013)
8. Mandal, D., Biswas, S.: Generalized coupled dictionary learning approach with applications to cross-modal matching. IEEE Trans. Image Process. **25**(8), 3826–3837 (2016)
9. Ouyang, S., Hospedales, T., Song, Y., et al.: A survey on heterogeneous face recognition: sketch, infra-red, 3D and low-resolution. Image Vis. Comput. **56**, 28–48 (2016)
10. Turk, M., Pentland, A.: Eigenfaces for recognition. Cogn. Neurosci. **3**(1), 71–86 (1991)
11. Li, S., Fu, Y.: Learning robust and discriminative subspace with low-rank constraints. IEEE Trans. Neural Netw. Learn. Syst. **27**(11), 2160–2173 (2016)
12. Ding, Z., Fu, Y.: Low-rank common subspace for multi-view learning. In: Proceedings of the IEEE International Conference on Data Mining, pp. 110–119 (2014)
13. Ding, Z., Fu, Y.: Robust multiview data analysis through collective low-rank subspace. IEEE Trans. Neural Netw. Learn. Syst. **29**(5), 1986–1997 (2018)
14. Li, J., Kong, Y., Zhao, H., Yang, J., Fu, Y.: Learning fast low-rank projection for image classification. IEEE Trans. Image Process. **25**(10), 4803–4814 (2016)
15. Li, L., Li, S., Fu, Y.: Learning low-rank and discriminative dictionary for image classification. Image Vis. Comput. **32**(10), 814–823 (2014)
16. Zhang, H., Patel, V., Chellappa, R.: Robust multimodal recognition via multitask multivariate low-rank representations. In: 11th IEEE International Conference and Workshops on Automatic Face and Gesture Recognition (FG), pp. 1–8 (2015)
17. Liu, G., Lin, Z., Yan, S., Sun, J., Yu, Y., Ma, Y.: Robust recovery of subspace structures by low-rank representation. IEEE Trans. Pattern Anal. Mach. Intell. **35**(1), 171–184 (2013)
18. Shekhar, S., Patel, V., Nasrabadi, N., Chellappa, R.: Joint sparse representation for robust multimodal biometrics recognition. IEEE Trans. Pattern Anal. Mach. Intell. **36**(1), 113–126 (2014)
19. Kan, M., Shan, S., Zhang, H., Lao, S., Chen, X.: Multi-view discriminant analysis. IEEE Trans. Pattern Anal. Mach. Intell. **38**(1), 188–194 (2016)

20. Li, S., Fu, Y.: Robust subspace discovery through supervised low-rank constraints. In: Proceedings of SIAM International Conference on Data Mining, pp. 163–171 (2014)
21. Yang, J., Zhang, Y.: Alternating direction algorithms for l1 problems in compressive sensing. SIAM J. Sci. Comput. **33**(1), 250–278 (2011)
22. Afonso, M., Bioucas-Dias, J., Figueiredo, M.: An augmented lagrangian approach to the constrained optimization formulation of imaging inverse problems. IEEE Trans. Image Process. **20**(3), 681–695 (2011)
23. Cai, J., Candès, E., Shen, Z.: A singular value Thresholding algorithm for matrix completion. SIAM J. Optimiz. **20**(4), 1956–1982 (2010)
24. Schölkopf, B., Platt, J., Hofmann, T.: Efficient sparse coding algorithms. In: Advances in Neural Information Processing Systems, pp. 801–808 (2007)
25. Sim, T., Baker, S., Bsat, M.: The CMU pose, illumination, and expression (PIE) database of human faces. In: Proceedings of Fifth IEEE International Conference on Automatic Face Gesture Recognition, pp. 53–58 (2002)

Target Positioning Based on Binocular Vision

Ronghua Zhu[1](✉) and Enyu Hou[2]

[1] School of Physical Science and Information Engineering, Liaocheng University, Liaocheng 252000, China
1045104740@qq.com
[2] SAS Medical Technology (Beijing) Co., LTD, Beijing 100044, China
houey@qq.com

Abstract. In order to improve the accuracy of workpiece positioning in the manufacturing process, this paper presents a binocular vision technology to identify the target object and locate the target area. Firstly, a novel and effective HALCON-based stereo calibration method is proposed to solve the problem of non-standard external polar line geometry of binocular system. Subpixel-accurate-based template matching with scaling and image pyramid algorithm are presented, and target objects are identified accurately and feature points are extracted accurately. Secondly, the stereo matching of feature points can be completed quickly according to the polar line constraint and gray-value-based template matching using the normalized cross-correlation (NCC). Finally, stereo reconstruction of feature points is completed by the combination of the binocular parallax principle and 3D coordinate affine transformation. The experimental results show that the detection radius error is less than 0.4 mm, and the error rate is less than 3%; the positioning depth error is less than 0.2 mm, and the error rate is less than 0.5%.

Keywords: Stereo vision · System calibration · Sub-pixel shape template matching with scaling · Pyramid search strategy · Stereo matching · Stereo reconstruction binocular system calibration

1 Introduction

With the rise of the industrial 4.0 strategy, the combination of vision and robotic systems has become an important means to improve the intelligence of robots [1]. In the current practical industrial applications, 2D vision technology is often used in combination with robots, but the two-dimensional image almost loses all the depth information of the object and it is difficult to obtain the three-dimensional information of the target. Therefore, it is necessary to reconstruct the three-dimensional information of the target from the two-dimensional image, for more comprehensive and true reflection of objective objects, and further improving the intelligence of the robot system [2]. Because binocular vision has the advantages of high efficiency, high precision, non-contact and depth information, it can be widely used in target recognition and positioning, and has important research significance for the precise positioning of mass production workpieces.

© Springer Nature Switzerland AG 2019
Y. Zhao et al. (Eds.): ICIG 2019, LNCS 11903, pp. 157–168, 2019.
https://doi.org/10.1007/978-3-030-34113-8_14

In this paper, we propose an recognition and localization algorithm based on HALCON binocular stereo vision technology. The main contribution of this paper is in three respects. First, the stereo correction of the target image is achieved by binocular system calibration. Second, considering various linear, nonlinear illumination changes and occlusion factors, this paper propose a pyramid search strategy and sub-pixel shape template matching algorithm with scaling to achieve accurate extraction of feature points. This algorithm can effectively cope with various linear and nonlinear illumination changes according to the gradient correlation of the edge of the object and it has strong resistance to occlusion and partial deletion. Lastly, we can quickly complete stereo matching of feature points through a normalized cross-correlation (NCC) based grayscale template matching algorithm, even if there is illumination variation in the image. The experimental results show that the proposed algorithm can realize the high-precision positioning of the target object under the premise of real-time and high efficiency, and the feasibility of the method can be verified by experiments.

2   Binocular Stereo Vision Positioning Principle

Binocular stereo vision can perceive the depth information of the three-dimensional world by simulating human eyes. By using any point in the space at the imaging position of the left and right cameras, the feature point matching relationship and the principle of triangular geometry, the parallax can be calculated to obtain the information of the object's three-dimensional space [3].

In this experiment, we use an axis parallel system structure consisting of two cameras. The physical map is displayed in Fig. 1a, and the binocular system model is shown in Fig. 1b. Assume that the focal lengths of both cameras are f, and the distance between the projection centers is b (also called the baseline). $O_l uv$, $O_r uv$ are two imaging plane coordinate systems whose coordinate directions coincide with the x-axis and y-axis directions, respectively. To simplify calculations, we take the coordinate system of the left camera as the world coordinate system $O - XYZ$. The image coordinates of the space point $P(x, y, z)$ on the left and right camera imaging planes are $P(u_l, v_l)$ and $P(u_r, v_r)$, respectively. The coordinates in the left and right camera coordinate systems are $P(x_l, y_l, z_l)$ and $P(x_r, y_r, z_r)$, respectively. Since the imaging planes of the two cameras are on the same plane, the image coordinates of the spatial point $P(x, y, z)$ have the same v coordinates, that is, $v_l = v_r = v$. According to the triangular geometry, we have:

$$u_l = f\frac{x_l}{z_l} \quad u_r = f\frac{(x_l - b)}{z_l} \quad v_l = v_r = f\frac{y_l}{z_l} \tag{1}$$

Since the left and right images are on the same plane, the disparity value of the corresponding point is defined as the difference between the coordinates of the corresponding point column in the left and right images. Hence, disparity can be computed:

$$D = u_l - u_r = \frac{b \times f}{z_l} \tag{2}$$

Combining (1) and (2), the formula for calculating the three-dimensional coordinates of the spatial point can be represented by the Eq. (3):

$$x = x_l = \frac{b \times u_l}{d} \quad y = y_l = \frac{b \times v}{d} \quad z = z_l = \frac{b \times f}{d} \tag{3}$$

Where $z = z_l$ is the depth distance of the space point P From the above formula, we can see that before the three-dimensional coordinates of the spatial point are obtained, the task to be solved by stereo vision positioning is to determine camera parameters and conjugate points.

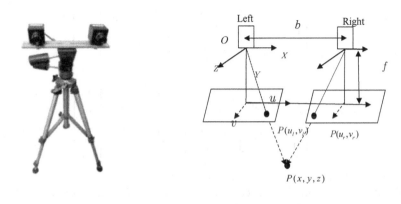

a Binocular stereo system physical map   b Binocular camera model

Fig. 1. Binocular stereo system

3 Binocular System Calibration and Stereo Rectification

3.1 System Calibration

Define camera calibration is a crucial step in stereo imaging [4]. Camera calibration in binocular system is similar to single camera calibration. Firstly, the internal and external parameters of the two cameras are obtained by single camera calibration, and then the positional relationship between two cameras is obtained by using the external parameters of the two cameras.

Camera calibration refers to establish the relationship between the pixel coordinates of the camera image and the three-dimensional coordinates of the scene point. According to the camera model, the internal and external parameters of the camera are solved by the image coordinates and world coordinates of the known feature points [5]. Establishing a camera imaging model, that is, the model parameters is solved by projection relationship, experiment and calculation method. Throughout the projection process, the conversion relationship between the image pixel coordinate system and the world coordinate system is:

$$
Z_c \begin{bmatrix} u \\ v \\ 1 \end{bmatrix} = Z_c \begin{bmatrix} \frac{1}{d_x} & 0 & u_0 \\ 0 & \frac{1}{d_y} & v_0 \end{bmatrix} \begin{bmatrix} x \\ y \\ 1 \end{bmatrix}
$$

$$
= \begin{bmatrix} \frac{1}{d_x} & 0 & u_0 \\ 0 & \frac{1}{d_y} & v_0 \\ 0 & 0 & 1 \end{bmatrix} \begin{bmatrix} f & 0 & 0 & 0 \\ 0 & f & 0 & 0 \\ 0 & 0 & 1 & 0 \end{bmatrix} \begin{bmatrix} X_c \\ Y_c \\ Z_c \\ 1 \end{bmatrix}
$$

$$
= \begin{bmatrix} \frac{1}{d_x} & 0 & u_0 \\ 0 & \frac{1}{d_y} & v_0 \\ 0 & 0 & 1 \end{bmatrix} \begin{bmatrix} f & 0 & 0 & 0 \\ 0 & f & 0 & 0 \\ 0 & 0 & 1 & 0 \end{bmatrix} \begin{bmatrix} R & t \\ 0 & 1 \end{bmatrix} \begin{bmatrix} X_w \\ Y_w \\ Z_w \\ 1 \end{bmatrix} \qquad (4)
$$

$$
= \begin{bmatrix} \frac{f}{dx} & 0 & u_0 \\ 0 & \frac{f}{dy} & v_0 \\ 0 & 0 & 1 \end{bmatrix} \begin{bmatrix} R & t \\ 0 & 1 \end{bmatrix} \begin{bmatrix} X_w \\ Y_w \\ Z_w \\ 1 \end{bmatrix} = M_1 M_2 \begin{bmatrix} X_w \\ Y_w \\ Z_w \\ 1 \end{bmatrix}
$$

Where: uv is the image pixel coordinate system, d_x, d_y is the pixel unit and f is the distortion coefficient. $O_c X_c Y_c Z_c$ is the camera coordinate system and $O_w X_w Y_w Z_w$ represents the world coordinate system, M_1, M_2 represents the internal and external parameters of the camera.

This experiment uses Zhengyou Zhang calibration method to calibrate the system. We use two identical cameras and lenses, which is the M-1614MP2 industrial lens and model MV-VS120 CCD color industrial cameras by Vision Digital Image Technology Co., Ltd. Combined with the HALCON software platform, calibration of the camera is achieved via using its algorithmic dynamic library. The calibration plate processing is shown in Fig. 2. The internal and external parameters of the two cameras and the relative positional relationship between the cameras are determined by averaging 20 calibrations. The internal parameter calibration results are shown in Table 1. Table 2 shows the external parameters of the two cameras before and after calibration.

Fig. 2. Calibration plate image processing

Table 1. Calibration results of internal parameter

Internal parameter	f(mm)	k	s_x(m)	s_y(m)	Row (pixel)	Column (pixel)
C1 before correction	14.85	−1080.1	4.6240e−6	4.6500e−6	674.067	685.180
C2 before correction	14.83	−1081.1	4.6256e−6	4.6500e−6	687.468	580.303
C1 after correction	14.15	0.0	4.6500e−6	4.6500e−6	647.319	670.510
C2 after correction	14.15	0.0	4.6500e−6	4.6500e−6	2220.34	670.510

Table 2. Calibration results of external parameter

External parameter	Translation matrix T			Rotation matrix R		
	x	y	z	x	y	z
Before correction	10.37	0.05	0.03	336.4	358.8	0
After correction	10.97	0	0	0	0	0
Error (pixel)	0.29					

According to the above data, the error level is lower than one pixel, and the calibration accuracy is high. After correction, the column coordinates of the pixel points of the two images are equal, and the position of the right image relative to the left image is only translated in the X-axis direction. This shows that the corrected binocular positioning system is a standard external polar line geometry [6], which can greatly save the time of stereo matching.

3.2 Stereo Rectification

After the system calibration, we can calculate the two correction maps by using the internal and external parameters of the two cameras and the relative positional relationship between the two cameras. The two map images combining functions map_image() is used to rectify the acquired stereo image pairs to the polar standard geometry. The rectified images of two cameras are shown in Fig. 3.

Fig. 3. Stereo rectification

4   Target Recognition and Feature Point Extraction

To improve the accuracy and speed of the matching algorithm in the process of object identification and position detection, subpixel-accurate-based template matching with scaling and image pyramid algorithm are applied in this paper, which is robust to occlusion, chaos, nonlinear illumination changes and contrast global inversion.

4.1   Subpixel Edge Extraction

For subpixel accurate contour extraction, the edge is extracted by a combination of canny operator and subpixel edge detection, which takes the image as input and returns to the XLD contour. Through the edges_sub_pix() operator, the canny filter is used to detect the gradient edge, and the canny operator repeats the gray value at the image boundary to obtain the optimal filter width by the Alpha option. This maintains greater noise invariance and enhances the ability to detect small details. The edge detection effect is shown in Fig. 4.

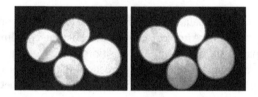

Fig. 4. Edge detection

In this paper, the Tukey weight function is used to fit through three iterations. The Tukey weight function is defined as:

$$\omega(\sigma) = \begin{cases} [1 - (\frac{\sigma}{\tau})^2], & |\sigma| \leq \tau \\ \frac{\tau}{|\sigma|}, & |\sigma| > \tau \end{cases} \tag{5}$$

Where: parameter τ represents the distance threshold. When the distance from the point to the circle is greater than the threshold, the weight function is equal to the reciprocal of the distance multiplied by the threshold. When the distance from the point to the circle is less than or equal to the threshold, the weight is the square of the difference between the square of the distance divided by the threshold and 1.

4.2   Shape Template Matching and Feature Point Extraction

To improve the speed and accuracy of the matching algorithm, support X/Y direction scaling and nonlinear illumination changes, subpixel-accurate-based template matching with scaling algorithm to detect position are applied in this paper. The algorithm is based on the direction vector of the edge point obtained by Sobel filtering, and defines the similarity measure. Furthermore, combined with the image pyramid hierarchical search strategy, the shape information is used for template matching.

The similarity measure of the shape-based template matching algorithm is the sum of the gradient vector of the point in the template and the gradient vector of the point in the image, the similarity measure s:

$$S = \frac{1}{n} \sum_{i=1}^{n} d_i^T e_{q+p} = \frac{1}{n} \sum_{i=1}^{n} t_i v_{r+r_i,c+c_i} + u_i w_{r+r_i,c+c_i} \tag{6}$$

Where: d is the gradient vector of the point in the template, and e is the gradient vector of the point in the image.

Normalized similarity measure s:

$$S = \frac{1}{n} \sum_{i=1}^{n} \frac{d_i^T e_{q+p}}{\|d_i^T\| \|e_{q+p}\|} = \frac{1}{n} \sum_{i=1}^{n} \frac{t_i v_{r+ri,c+ci} + u_i w_{r+ri,c+ci}}{\sqrt{t_i^2 + u_i^2} \sqrt{v_{r+ri,c+ci}^2 + w_{r+ri,c+ci}^2}} \tag{7}$$

Since the gradient vector is normalized, the similarity measure s will return a value less than or equal to 1. When $s = 1$, the template corresponds to the image one-to-one.

In the image matching process, each potential point of the search image is subjected to a normalization calculation of one traversal, the calculation amount is very large. Therefore, to improve the speed of the algorithm, it is necessary to try to reduce the number of poses examined and the points in the template, and the pyramid hierarchical search strategy can simultaneously reduce the two parts to improve the operation speed [7]. The image pyramid is shown in Fig. 5.

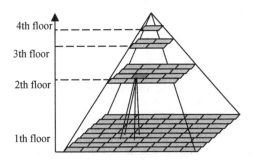

Fig. 5. Pyramid image

Performing the same edge detection and filtering on each layer of image when creating the template, and then searching from top to bottom layer by layer until the similarity measure is greater than the threshold, and finally we can get the row and column coordinates of the matching template. The results of workpiece recognition and center extraction are shown in Fig. 6a. The cross mark is the central feature point The fitted XLD edge is segmented by a basic geometric element such as a straight line and an arc by a Ramer [8] algorithm for a large number of subpixel edge coordinate data. The edge feature points obtained are shown in Fig. 6b.

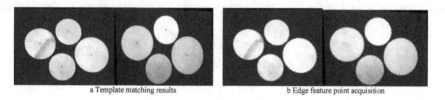

a Template matching results   b Edge feature point acquisition

Fig. 6. Feature point extraction

5   Target Three-Dimensional Position

5.1   Stereo Matching

Stereo matching is the most critical step in the binocular vision algorithm. Its main task is to find the corresponding relationship of the same point in space in different images under different observation angles [9]. To complete the stereo matching of feature points quickly, we use the polar line constraint and region matching algorithm based on normalized cross-correlation (NCC). Since the two cameras have different viewing angles, the illumination will also have a certain difference, and a method that does not change with the change of illumination is needed, that is, the normalized cross-correlation (NCC) [7]. The NCC is defined as:

$$NCC(x,y,d) = \frac{1}{(2n+1)(2m+1)} \frac{\sum_{i=-n}^{n}\sum_{j=-m}^{m}([I_L(x+i,y+j) - \overline{I_L(x,y)}][I_R(x+i,y+j+d) - \overline{I_R(x,y+d)}])}{\sqrt{\delta^2(I_L) \times \delta^2(I_R)}}$$

(8)

Here, $\overline{I(x,y)} = \frac{\sum_{i=-n}^{n}\sum_{j=-m}^{m} I(x+i,y+j)}{(2n+1)(2m+1)}$ is the average gray value of all pixels in the

neighborhood of the current location search point, $\delta(I) = \sqrt{\frac{\sum_{i=-n}^{n}\sum_{j=-m}^{m} I^2(x,y)}{(2n+1)(2m+1)} - I(y,y)}$

represents the variance. The value of NCC is $[-1, 1]$. When the absolute value of NCC is larger, it indicates that the sub-window is more closely matched with the neighborhood of the search point. When $NCC = 1$ it indicates that the two polarities are the same; when $NCC = -1$ the two polarities are opposite, this means that the results of the normalized correlation coefficients are not affected by linear illumination changes [10].

The stereo matching procedure can be summarized as the following steps: Centering the pixel point P_L to be matched in the image, and interceping a rectangular sub-window B_L. In the image to be matched searching for window B_R, which is most similar to the gray value of B_L according to the principle from left to right and from top to bottom. Calculating the center P_R of the window B_R, and getting the matching pixel points P_L and P_R in the left and right image (see Fig. 7).

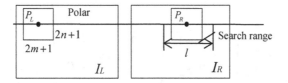

Fig. 7. Template matching schematic

According to the above steps, the point to be matched of the first feature point of the left image is searched; the point to be matched of the second feature point is searched... until the feature points of the left image are traversed, that is, the stereo matching task is completed. The stereo matching result is shown in Fig. 8.

Fig. 8. Stereo matching

5.2 Stereo Reconstruction and 3D Affine Transformation

After the system calibration, stereo correction and stereo matching are completed, our next task is to calculate the depth information of the target. The three-dimensional reconstruction of the binocular system is to acquire two images of the scene simultaneously by two cameras and find the matching point pairs of the same point in the two images in space. The three-dimensional coordinates of the point can be obtained by combining the principle of binocular vision imaging [11]. The three-dimensional point cloud map is shown in Fig. 9.

Fig. 9. The three-dimensional point cloud map

To improve the accuracy of the evaluation positioning system, we need to perform 3D affine transformation on the 3D point cloud coordinates of 3D reconstruction and convert it into the world coordinates under the left camera as the reference coordinate system. The principle expression is given by:

$$
\begin{pmatrix} Q_z \\ Q_y \\ Q_x \\ 1 \end{pmatrix} = \begin{bmatrix} R & T \\ 0 & 1 \end{bmatrix} \cdot \begin{pmatrix} P_z \\ P_y \\ P_x \\ 1 \end{pmatrix} = \left(R \cdot \begin{pmatrix} P_z \\ P_y \\ P_x \\ 1 \end{pmatrix} + T \right)
\tag{9}
$$

Where (P_x, P_y, P_z) is the input point and returns the resulting point to (Q_x, Q_y, Q_z).

6 Experimental Results and Analysis

To detect the size of the target object, each edge point and the corresponding center can be calculated by the space curve fitting formula $l = \sqrt{(x_1 - x_2)^2 + (y_1 - y_2)^2 + (z_1 - z_2)^2}$ to complete the detection of the workpiece radius. The experimental results are shown in Fig. 10.

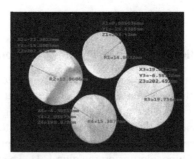

Fig. 10. 3D spatial information and detect results

To analyze the reconstruction accuracy of the algorithm, we compute the error between the four target detection data and the actual data. Table 3 shows comparison results. The measured actual radius error of the workpiece is less than 0.4 mm, and the error rate is less than 3%; the actual depth of the workpiece is less than 0.2 mm, and the error rate is less than 0.5%. It shows that the target positioning method can accurately locate the target object with high precision, which verifies the feasibility and accuracy of the method under certain conditions.

Table 3. Comparison of test results with actual results

Number	Measuring Z(mm)	Actual Z (mm)	Error (mm)	Error rate (%)	Measuring R(mm)	Actual R (mm)	Error (mm)	Error rate (%)
1	203.520	204.5	1.020	0.499	14.8032	15.00	0.1968	1.312
2	202.621	202.0	0.621	0.307	18.9606	18.75	0.2106	1.123
3	202.491	203.5	1.009	0.496	19.7364	20.00	0.2636	1.318
4	198.878	199.3	0.422	0.212	15.3877	15.00	0.3877	2.585

7 Conclusion

In this paper, we study the whole process of target recognition and localization based on binocular vision. In the target recognition and feature point extraction stage, the canny sub-pixel edge extraction, edge fitting and sub-pixel shape template matching algorithm with scaling are used to target the target area, which has a great improvement in feature point extraction speed. In the target positioning stage, we use the polar line constraint and region matching algorithm based on NCC gray correlation to complete the stereo matching of the feature positioning points, which solves the problem that the target feature points in the left and right images do not match. Finally, the three-dimensional positioning of the target object is realized by the principle of three-dimensional reconstruction. The experimental results show that the whole process method improves the speed of target recognition and the accuracy of feature point extraction, reduces the possibility of matching errors or repeated matching, and effectively achieves accurate positioning of the target object. The accuracy can be better satisfied in the working space of the robot, which is more conducive to the three-dimensional reconstruction and positioning of the robot vision system.

According to the current experimental research situation, and for the complex and varied manufacturing environment of the workpiece, we need further research and experimentation to realize a more general and effective image recognition and localization algorithm. It is necessary to improve the existing experimental positioning results and obtain more accurate position information of the target object in three-dimensional space.

References

1. Huang, N., Liu, G., Zhang, Y., et al.: Unmanned aerial vehicle vision navigation algorithm. Infrared Laser Eng. **45**(7), 269–277 (2016)
2. Men, Y., Ma, Y., Zhang, G., et al.: A stereo matching algorithm based on Census transform and improved dynamic programming. J. Harbin Inst. Technol. **47**(3), 60–65 (2015)
3. Shen, T., Liu, W., Jing, W.: Target ranging system based on binocular stereo vision. Electron. Measur. Technol. **38**(4), 52–54 (2015)
4. Chen, X., Wei, Y.: Target positioning based on binocular stereo vision. Autom. Technol. Appl. **56**(2), 224–229 (2017)
5. Yu, D., Wang, Y., Mao, J., et al.: Vision-based object tracking method of mobile robot. J. Optoelectron.·Laser **40**(1), 227–235 (2019)

6. Zhang, X., Wu, B.: Research on three-dimensional information acquisition technology of small field using integral imaging. J. Optoelectron. Laser **28**(11), 1240–1245 (2017)
7. Ruru, Z., Guangying, G., Zhe, S., et al.: 3D reconstruction based on binocular stereo vision. J. Yangzhou Univ. (Natural Sci. Ed.) **21**(3), 5–10 (2018)
8. Lin, H., Pan, W.: Research and application of image edge feature extraction algorithm based on variable weighted least squares method. Combined Mach. Tool Autom. Process. Technol. **6**(2), 66–71 (2015)
9. Zhang, J., Wu, S., Chen, B., et al.: Binocular vision based multi-dimensions on-line measuring system for workpieces. Instrum. Tech. Sensor **32**(10), 75–80 (2018)
10. Guo, A., Xiao, D., Zou, X.: Computation model on image segmentation threshold of litchi cluster based on exploratory analysis. J. Fiber Bioeng. Inform. **7**(3), 441–452 (2014)
11. Lu, B., Liu, Y., Sun, L.: Error analysis of binocular stereo vision system based on small scale measurement. Acta Photonica Sinica **8**(2), 232–237 (2015)

An Efficient Quality Enhancement Solution for Stereo Images

Yingqing Peng[1], Zhi Jin[1,2], Wenbin Zou[1(✉)], Yi Tang[1], and Xia Li[1]

[1] College of Electronics and Information Engineering, Shenzhen University,
Shenzhen, People's Republic of China
`zouszu@sina.com`
[2] School of Intelligent Systems Engineering, Sun Yat-sen University,
Guangzhou, People's Republic of China

Abstract. Recently, with additional information in the disparity variant, quality enhancement for stereo images has become an active research field. Current methods generally adopt cost volumes for stereo matching methods to learn correspondence between stereo image pairs. However, with the large disparity in the different viewpoints of stereo images, how to learn the accurate corresponding information remains a challenge. In addition, as the network deepens, traditional convolutional neural networks (CNNs) adopt cascading methods, which results in the high computational cost and memory consumption. In this paper, we propose an end-to-end effective CNN model. Channel-wise attention-based information distillation and long short-term memory (LSTM) are the basic components, which contribute to reconstruct high quality image (DCL network). Within a stereo image pair, we use high quality (HQ) image to guide the image reconstruction of low quality (LQ). To incorporate the stereo correspondence, information fusion-based LSTM module can be used to learn the disparity variant in stereo images. Specially, in order to distill and enhance effective features map, we introduce channel-wise attention-based a long distillation information module with the consideration of interdependencies among feature channels. Experimental results demonstrate that the proposed network achieves the best performance with comparatively less parameters.

Keywords: Quality enhancement · Stereo image · Information distillation · Channel attention · LSTM

1 Introduction

With the different views of additional information, stereo images are used in various ranges of applications including 3D model reconstruction [1] and autonomous driving for vehicles [2]. Since the seminal work of super resolution convolutional neural network (SRCNN) [3] had proposed, learning-based methods [4,5] are

---

Y. Peng and W. Zou—Equal contribution.

Y. Zhao et al. (Eds.): ICIG 2019, LNCS 11903, pp. 169–180, 2019.
https://doi.org/10.1007/978-3-030-34113-8_15

widely adopted to improve image quality. As CNN-based methods resize input before sending them in the network, and adopt a deeper and recursive network to gain better reconstruction performance. But it demands large computational cost and memory consumption, which are hard to applied in mobile phones and embedded devices. Moreover, the traditional convolutional methods [6,7] design networks by cascading technologies, which lead to the features redundancy because features map of each layer sending to the sequence layer without difference. However, Hu *et al.* [8] demonstrated that the representational power of a network can be improved by recalibrating channel-wise feature responses. Recent video quality enhancement method [9] focuses on the exploitation of correspondence between adjacent frames in local region. Video quality enhancement methods cannot be directly applied to stereo image quality enhancement, since stereo images have a long-range dependency and non-local characteristic. Current stereo images enhancement methods leverage stereo matching [10–12] to learn correspondence between a stereo image pair. They use cost volumes to model long-range dependency in the network. But these methods are insufficient for estimating accurate correspondence in the large disparity.

To address these problems, we propose an end-to-end CNN model (DCL network) to incorporate stereo correspondence for the task of quality enhancement. Given a stereo image pair, a feature extraction block is firstly used to separately extract features from input images. Secondly, we employ long information distillation blocks (LDBlock) on the LQ image to distill useful information, and information distillation blocks (DBlock) [13] on the HQ image. Because the LQ image requires deeper network to learn more features than HQ image. Features are extracted from LQ and HQ image, and then fed to information fusion based LSTM [14] module to capture stereo correspondence. In addition, we use channel-wise attention following and embedded the information distillation block, which focuses on key information and neglects irrelevant information by considering interdependencies among channels.

The main contributions can be summarized as follows:

1. HQ image is used to guide the image reconstruction of LQ image within stereo image in our network.
2. The proposed long information distillation block extracts the LQ features and combines with channel-wise attention to distill and enhance useful and efficient features.
3. We propose information fusion based LSTM to handle the disparity variations between two viewpoints in one stereo image pair.

2   Related Work

Stereo images quality enhancement methods have been extensively studied in the computer vision community. In this section, we focus on the works related to quality enhancement and long-range dependency learning.

2.1 Quality Enhancement

CNNs have shown to be the state-of-the-art methods for the task of quality enhancement over recent years. Model SRCNN [3], as a pioneer in image reconstruction by using deep learning, is an end-to-end CNN model with three layers: patch extraction and representation, non-linear mapping, reconstruction. But the feature extraction uses only one layer so that it has small receptive field and gets local features. To address this problem, Dong et al. [4] introduced Artifacts Reduction Convolutional Neural Network (called ARCNN), which added a feature enhancement layer. Yu et al. [5] proposed a faster CNN with five layers (FastARCNN). With the employment of deeper and wider networks, CNN-based methods [7] suffer from computational complexity and memory consumption in practice. Hui et al. [13] proposed information distillation block, and used few filters per layer. Although the information distillation block is deep, the convolutional network is compact. Thus, it achieves better results with higher speed and accuracy. In addition, to address the problem of noticeable visual artifacts with a high compression ratio, based on quality enhancement, Jin et al. [15] introduced a fully convolutional neural network. They extracted the corresponding high frequency information in HQ image and fused it with LQ image, which can enhance the LQ image quality in asymmetric stereo images by exploiting inter-view correlation.

2.2 Long-Range Dependency Learning

To leverage the disparity information from both right and left views in stereo images, long-range dependency learning has become an important concept in deep neural networks. With the development of a great number of algorithms for stereo correspondence, related works with stereo matching mainly aim to strive for better performance [16–18]. In recent years, Zbonta et al. [19] concatenate the left and right features using CNNs to compute the stereo matching cost by learning a similarity on small image patches. To address the problem that current networks depend on path-based network, these methods [10,12] employ 4D cost volume to effectively exploit global context information. However, with the challenges of computational complexity and memory consumption, Liang et al. [11] proposed 4D cost volume by incorporating all steps into a single network for stereo matching with sharing the same features.

Attention mechanisms have been widely applied in diverse prediction tasks including localization and understanding in images [20,21], image captioning [22] and so on. It was first introduced by Bahdanau et al. [23]. Visual attention can be seen as a dynamic feature extraction mechanism [24,25]. These methods [26,27] can process data in parallel and model complex contexts. SCA-CNN [28] demonstrated that existing visual spatial attention is only applied in the last conv-layer, where the size of receptive field will be quite large and the differences between each receptive field region are quite limited. Therefore, they proposed to incorporate spatial and channel-wise attention in a CNN model.

Inspired by visual attention model, and that stereo images can be seen as the consecutive frames in videos, we propose to combine attention with LSTM to learn the disparity variations in different stereo images. In particular however, our work directly extends [13,15].

3   Proposed Method

In this section, we describe the proposed model architecture and the long information distillation module. In the following, we introduce the loss function adopted in our network.

3.1   Network Structure

Our method takes a stereo image pair as input, which contains a LQ (right) image and a HQ (left) image. The output is the enhanced LQ (right) image. The architecture of our network is illustrated in Fig. 1 and Table 1. The network comprises of four modules: features extraction, information distillation, information fusion and image reconstruction.

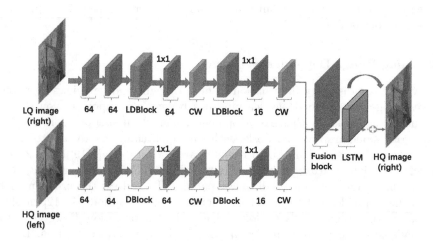

Fig. 1. The architecture of the proposed network

Firstly, We adopt two 3×3 convolutions to extract original features of input image by features extraction module (FBlock) [13]. The extracted features map is fed to the information distillation module to distill more useful information, whose results are 64 features map. Each information distillation module combines channel-wise attention module to focus on the key information. In order to reduce data dimension and further distill relevant information for following network, we use a 1×1 convolutional layer. In addition, it can increase the nonlinear characteristics while maintaining the size of the image features. This process can be formulated as:

Table 1. The proposed network architecture includes four stages

Stage	Layer	Output shape
	Input	$300 \times 300 \times 1$
Stage 0	FBlock	$160 \times 160 \times 64$
Stage 1	DB/LDBblock1	$160 \times 160 \times 80$
	Channel-wise	$160 \times 160 \times 64$
Stage 2	DB/LDBblock2	$160 \times 160 \times 80$
	Channel-wise	$160 \times 160 \times 64$
Stage 3	Fusion block	$160 \times 160 \times 1$
Stage 4	LSTM	$160 \times 160 \times 1$

$$D_i = C(D_{i-1}(f(x))), i = 1, ..., n, \tag{1}$$

$$P_i = P(D_i) \tag{2}$$

Where x denotes the input of right LQ image and left HQ image; f represents the operation of feature extraction; D_i indicates the i-th LDBlock or DBlock function; C, P represent the operation of the channel-wise attention and compression respectively.

Then, the extracted features of two streams for LQ and HQ image make a information fusion by a 4-layer CNN. The operation of these layers can be formulated as:

$$F_0 = F(I_{low} + I_{high}) \tag{3}$$

where I_{low}, I_{high} denote the output of longer information distillation module and information distillation module, respectively; F represents the information fusion of the left HQ features and right LQ features; F_0 denotes the output of information fusion module.

Finally, we use a LSTM network [14] that focuses on learning the corresponding information at the different views of location using features similarities, and keep the left and right of a stereo image pair in location consistency. In order to improve features utilization, we combine the previous features map from the input of LSTM with some current information, which can effectively reconstruct a HQ image. Here, the final enhanced LQ image can be expressed as:

$$y = F_0 + L(F_0) \tag{4}$$

where L denotes the function of LSTM, y represents a output of the network.

3.2   Long Information Distillation

Motivated by an enhancement unit in the IDN [13], we use stacked information distillation blocks to effectively extract image features. And inspired by inception model in GoogLeNet [29], we try to design a deeper and wider network to generate more features maps. Combined the above methods, we design a deeper and wider information distillation block called long information distillation (LDBlock). It is shown in Fig. 2. Based on enhancement unit in the DBlock, we use stacked convolution operation respectively after slicing features map to extract more information in LQ image. In order to reduce the parameters of our network, we leverage the grouped convolutional layers in the second convolutional layer in each enhancement unit with 4 groups. Specially, we adopt the channel-wise attention to adaptively rescale features by considering interdependencies among feature channels.

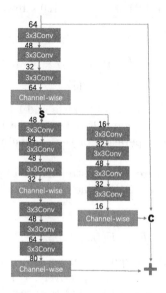

Fig. 2. The architect of enhancement unit in long information distillation. s indicates the slice operation and c represents the channel concatenation

3.3 Loss Function

Our network is optimized with loss function. We design two loss functions including total loss L_{total} and LSTM loss L_{lstm}. The total loss L_{total} is to measure the difference of predicted LQ image I_{low} and the corresponding uncompressed ground-truth image I_{GT}. We use the mean square error (MSE) as our total loss, which is most widely applied in image restoration. To optimize the difference of left and right image location, we introduce LSTM loss L_{lstm}. Aiming at improving the effectiveness of our network, we choose to optimize the same loss function as previous works.

$$L_{total}(\Theta) = \frac{1}{N} \sum_{i=1}^{N} \| F(I_{low}^i, I_{high}^i; \Theta) - I_{GT}^i \|_2^2 \tag{5}$$

$$L_{lstm} = \frac{1}{N} \sum_{i=1}^{N} \| I_{lstm}^i - I_{GT}^i \|_2^2 \qquad (6)$$

Where Θ contains the parameter set of the network, including both weights and biases. F represents network to generate the predicted images. I_{lstm}^i denotes the reconstructed images in a LSTM module. Therefore, the overall loss function is formulated as:

$$Loss = \lambda_1(L_{total}) + \lambda_2(L_{lstm}) \qquad (7)$$

Where λ is the weight balancing two losses. Here, λ_1, λ_2 is set to 0.8 and 0.2 in our experiment, respectively. More details of training is shown in Sect. 4.2.

4 Experiment

In this section, we first introduce the datasets and implementation details, and then analyze the proposed network architecture. We further compare our network to the state-of-the-art networks on two multiview datasets.

4.1 Dataset

To train the proposed network, we follow [15] and adopt the Middlebury 2014 stereo image dataset including 18 images as our training data. For testing, we use 5 remaining images. Taking into account the training complexity, we leverage the small patch training strategy to crop the image size with 300×300. Meanwhile, the corresponding patches in HQ images and ground-truth images are also obtained. There are 942×2 images in the total training. In order to evaluate the performance of the proposed network, JPEG quality is set to 10 and 20 to generate image of a different compression quality. However, for testing, the larger size testing image is unable to process. We crop the test image into a set of l_{sub} x l_{sub} with same equal proportion in different sizes of the image.

4.2 Implementation Details

To improve the robustness and generalization ability of model, data augmentation is adopted in four ways: (1) rotate the image randomly by 90°; (2) crop in a 160 size image; (3) flip images horizontally; (4) flip images vertically. In this work, our model is trained by Adam optimizer with $\beta_1 = 0.9$, $\beta_2 = 0.999$ and the batch size is 12. There are 800 epochs in total, since the learning rate approaches to zero if there are too many epochs. The learning rate is initially set to 0.0001 and decreases by the factor of 10 during fine-tune phase. In addition, the LeakyReLU is applied after each convolution operation, and the negative scope is set to 0.05. In order to focus on the quality enhancement of the image luminance, we adopt a single channel image. We conduct our experiment on a Nvidia GTX 1080Ti GPU and to train a model it need half a day. We implement our network on the Pytorch platform, where its flexibility and efficiency enable us to easily develop the network.

4.3   Network Architecture Analysis

Stereo Image vs Single Image. In order to validate the effectiveness of stereo information for image quality enhancement, we do an experiment based on our network to use a single image (i.e., LQ images), stereo image pairs (HQ and LQ) from the different view as the input. The result is shown in Table 2. It is demonstrated that HQ image contributes to improve LQ image reconstruction. Compared to use a LQ image as the input, restructured image trained by this network decreases 0.74 dB (from 41.12 to 41.38) in terms of peak signal-to-noise ratio (PSNR).

Table 2. Comparative results achieved on the Middlebury 2014 stereo image dataset by our network with different inputs at q20.

Model	Input	PSNR (dB)	SSIM	Para (k)
Our net with single input	Left	41.38	0.9863	51
Our net with two stream input	Left-Right	**42.12**	**0.9873**	79

Effectiveness of Channel-Wise Attention. Information distillation module is utilized to distill and enhance features map from the feature extraction. More importantly, channel-wise attention is employed inside and outside of the information distillation block, which can learn the more representative features. To demonstrate its effectiveness, we introduce some implementations by removing channel-wise (CW) in different conditions. From the Table 3, our network only has 41.36 dB in PSNR and 0.9861 in structural similarity values (SSIM) by removing the CW inside the information distillation module of both LQ and HQ image stream. After inserting CW into the DBlock or LDBlock, the performance reaches 41.47 dB and 41.48 dB, respectively. As the same implementation, Table 4 also indicates that LQ image performance benefits from CW outside the information distillation. The increase of parameters is rarely though CW. Theses comparisons show that CW is essential to focus on the effective features in information distillation for deep networks. The results in Tables 3 and 4 denote that the channel-wise features really improve the performance.

Table 3. Comparative results achieved on the Middlebury 2014 by our network with the CW inside DBlock/LDBlock at q20.

Model	DBlock	LDBlock	PSNR	SSIM	Para (k)
CW	×	×	41.36	0.9861	78
	×	√	41.47	0.9863	79
	√	×	41.48	0.9864	79
	√	√	**42.12**	**0.9873**	79

Table 4. Comparative results achieved on the Middlebury 2014 by our network with the CW outside DBlock/LDBlock for q20.

Model	DBlock	LDBlock	PSNR	SSIM	Para (k)
CW	×	×	41.36	0.9862	79
	×	√	41.42	0.9864	79
	√	×	41.40	0.9863	79
	√	√	**42.12**	**0.9873**	79

Effectiveness of Long Short-Term Memory. In order to validate the effectiveness of LSTM module for image quality enhancement, we do a comparative experiment after the information fusion. From Table 5, it is shown that our network with LSTM gets a better performance. The PSNR value is higher than network without LSTM by 0.38 dB.

Table 5. Comparative results achieved on the Middlebury 2014 stereo image dataset by our network with different inputs at q20.

Model	LSTM	PSNR (dB)	SSIM	Para (k)
Our net with two stream input	×	41.54	0.9866	78
Our net with two stream input	√	**42.12**	**0.9873**	79

4.4 Comparison to State-of-the-Art Approaches

In order to evaluate the performance of our network, we compare with other methods including JPEG [30], SA-DCT [31], ARCNN [4], FastARCNN [5], Fusion-4 and Fusion-8 [15]. The comparison results of the PSNR and SSIM on the Middlebury dataset at JPEG quality 10 and 20 are shown in Table 5. Further more, the number of network parameters for the deep learning based methods are also given. From these results, it is clear that our method achieves the best performance than other methods except Fusion-8 because of the input of Fusion method [15] with the same view. It [15] neglects the different stereo images with large disparity variations. However, our method captures the more reliable correspondence. It can be observed that SSIM achieves the best performance. Compared with Fusion-8, our method reduces the parameters by three times while guaranteeing a higher PSNR (Table 6).

Table 6. Quality enhancement comparison with the state-of-the-art algorithm on the Middlebury.

Dataset	Algorithm	Q10		Q20		Para(k)
		PSNR	SSIM	PSNR	SSIM	
Middlebury	JPEG [30]	34.68	0.9065	38.28	0.942	–
	SA-DCT [31]	36.52	0.9768	39.94	0.993	–
	ARCNN [4]	36.69	0.9422	39.85	0.959	106
	FastARCNN [5]	36.91	0.9426	40.11	0.960	56
	Fusion-4 [15]	38.60	0.9635	41.29	0.972	75
	Fusion-8 [15]	**39.28**	0.9681	**42.16**	0.975	223
	proposed	38.82	**0.9801**	42.12	**0.987**	79

5   Conclusion

In this paper, an efficient deep-learning-based method is proposed to enhance LQ image quality by exploiting from a stereo image pair. We design a deeper and wider information distillation combined with channel-wise attention to extract abundant and efficient features for the LQ image reconstruction. Moreover, our method using information fusion based LSTM module can handle disparity in different views of stereo images. Experiments demonstrate that our method can capture correspondence in stereo image, and achieves the state-of-the-art performance.

Acknowledgement. This work was supported in part by the NSFC Project under Grants 61771321, 61701313, and 61871273, in part by the China Postdoctoral Science Foundation under Grants 2017M622778, in part by the Key Research Platform of Universities in Guangdong under Grants 2018WCXTD015, in part by the Natural Science Foundation of Shenzhen under Grants KQJSCX20170327151357330, JCYJ20170818091621856 and JSGG20170822153717702, and in part by the Interdisciplinary Innovation Team of Shenzhen University, in part by the China Postdoctoral Science Foundation Grants (2017M622778).

References

1. Chen, X., et al.: 3D object proposals for accurate object class detection. In: Advances in Neural Information Processing Systems, pp. 424–432 (2015)
2. Zhang, C., Li, Z., Cheng, Y., Cai, R., Chao, H., Rui, Y.: Meshstereo: a global stereo model with mesh alignment regularization for view interpolation. In: Proceedings of the IEEE International Conference on Computer Vision, pp. 2057–2065 (2015)
3. Dong, C., Loy, C.C., He, K., Tang, X.: Image super-resolution using deep convolutional networks, vol. 38, pp. 295–307. IEEE (2015)
4. Dong, C., Deng, Y., Loy, C.C., Tang, X.: Compression artifacts reduction by a deep convolutional network. In: Proceedings of the IEEE International Conference on Computer Vision, pp. 576–584 (2015)

5. Yu, K., Dong, C., Loy, C.C., Tang, X.: Deep convolution networks for compression artifacts reduction. arXiv preprint arXiv:1608.02778 (2016)
6. Kim, J., Lee, J.K., Lee, K.M.: Deeply-recursive convolutional network for image super-resolution. In: Proceedings of the IEEE Conference on Computer Vision and Pattern Recognition, pp. 1637–1645 (2016)
7. Kim, J., Lee, J.K., Lee, K.M.: Accurate image super-resolution using very deep convolutional networks. In: Proceedings of the IEEE Conference on Computer Vision and Pattern Recognition, pp. 1646–1654 (2016)
8. Hu, J., Shen, L., Sun, G.: Squeeze-and-excitation networks. In: Proceedings of the IEEE Conference on Computer Vision and Pattern Recognition, pp. 7132–7141 (2018)
9. Tao, X., Gao, H., Liao, R., Wang, J., Jia, J.: Detail-revealing deep video super-resolution. In: Proceedings of the IEEE International Conference on Computer Vision, pp. 4472–4480 (2017)
10. Chang, J.-R., Chen, Y.-S.: Pyramid stereo matching network. In: Proceedings of the IEEE Conference on Computer Vision and Pattern Recognition, pp. 5410–5418 (2018)
11. Liang, Z., et al.: Learning for disparity estimation through feature constancy. In: Proceedings of the IEEE Conference on Computer Vision and Pattern Recognition, pp. 2811–2820 (2018)
12. Kendall, A., et al.: End-to-end learning of geometry and context for deep stereo regression. In: Proceedings of the IEEE International Conference on Computer Vision, pp. 66–75 (2017)
13. Hui, Z., Wang, X., Gao, X.: Fast and accurate single image super-resolution via information distillation network. In: Proceedings of the IEEE Conference on Computer Vision and Pattern Recognition, pp. 723–731 (2018)
14. Hochreiter, S., Schmidhuber, J.: Long short-term memory. Neural Comput. $9(8)$, 1735–1780 (1997)
15. Jin, Z., Luo, H., Luo, L., Zou, W., Lil, X., Steinbach, E.: Information fusion based quality enhancement for 3D stereo images using CNN. In 2018 26th European Signal Processing Conference (EUSIPCO), pp. 1447–1451. IEEE (2018)
16. Barnard, S.T.: Stochastic stereo matching over scale. Int. J. Comput. Vis. $3(1)$, 17–32 (1989)
17. Scharstein, D., Szeliski, R.: A taxonomy and evaluation of dense two-frame stereo correspondence algorithms. Int. J. Comput. Vision $47(1–3)$, 7–42 (2002)
18. Lee, S.H., Kanatsugu, Y., Park, J.-I.: Map-based stochastic diffusion for stereo matching and line fields estimation. Int. J. Comput. Vision $47(1–3)$, 195–218 (2002)
19. Zbontar, J., LeCun, Y., et al.: Stereo matching by training a convolutional neural network to compare image patches. J. Mach. Learn. Res. $17(1–32)$, 2 (2016)
20. Jaderberg, M., Simonyan, K., Zisserman, A., et al.: Spatial transformer networks. In: Advances in Neural Information Processing Systems, pp. 2017–2025 (2015)
21. Cao, C., et al.: Look and think twice: capturing top-down visual attention with feedback convolutional neural networks. In: Proceedings of the IEEE International Conference on Computer Vision, pp. 2956–2964 (2015)
22. Xu, K., et al.: Show, attend and tell: Neural image caption generation with visual attention. arXiv preprint arXiv:1502.03044 (2015)
23. Bahdanau, D., Cho, K., Bengio, Y.: Neural machine translation by jointly learning to align and translate. arXiv preprint arXiv:1409.0473 (2014)
24. Mnih, V., Heess, N., Graves, A., et al.: Recurrent models of visual attention. In: Advances in Neural Information Processing Systems, pp. 2204–2212 (2014)

25. Stollenga, M.F., Masci, J., Gomez, F., Schmidhuber, J.: Deep networks with internal selective attention through feedback connections. In: Advances in Neural Information Processing Systems, pp. 3545–3553 (2014)

26. Xu, H., Saenko, K.: Ask, attend and answer: exploring question-guided spatial attention for visual question answering. In: Leibe, B., Matas, J., Sebe, N., Welling, M. (eds.) ECCV 2016. LNCS, vol. 9911, pp. 451–466. Springer, Cham (2016). https://doi.org/10.1007/978-3-319-46478-7_28

27. You, Q., Jin, H., Wang, Z., Fang, C., Luo, J.: Image captioning with semantic attention. In: Proceedings of the IEEE Conference on Computer Vision and Pattern Recognition, pp. 4651–4659 (2016)

28. Chen, L., et al.: SCA-CNN: spatial and channel-wise attention in convolutional networks for image captioning. In: Proceedings of the IEEE Conference on Computer Vision and Pattern Recognition, pp. 5659–5667 (2017)

29. Szegedy, C., Ioffe, S., Vanhoucke, V., Alemi, A.A.: Inception-v4, inception-resnet and the impact of residual connections on learning. In: Thirty-First AAAI Conference on Artificial Intelligence (2017)

30. Wallace, G.K.: The JPEG still picture compression standard. IEEE Trans. Consum. Electron. **38**(1), xviii–xxxiv (1992)

31. Foi, A., Katkovnik, V., Egiazarian, K.: Pointwise shape-adaptive dct for high-quality denoising and deblocking of grayscale and color images. IEEE Trans. Image Process. **16**(5), 1395–1411 (2007)

Camera Pose Free Depth Sensing Based on Focus Stacking

Kai Xue, Yiguang Liu$^{(\boxtimes)}$, Weijie Hong, Qing Chang, and Wenjuan Miao

Vision and Image Processing Lab(VIPL), College of Computer Science,
Sichuan University, Chengdu 610065, People's Republic of China
`lygpapers@aliyun.com`

Abstract. Binocular or multi-view depth imaging usually fails when camera pose is fixed, but depth need to be sensed with single fixed camera in some scenarios. To tackle this problem, we present a camera pose free depth sensing based on focus stacking. We first compute the mapping between scene depth and focus ring. A sharpness function based on discrete Fourier transform (DFT) is provided to calculate the in-focus parts, and parallax method is used to obtain the mapping between object space and image space. After the camera mapping calculation, we calculate the depth of the scene from the image distance map (IDM), which is generated by fusing in-focus areas of different images in the focal stacks. To reconstruct the scene, a depth map and an all-in-focus (AiF) image are combined from the focal stacks and IDM. Experimental results show that the proposed method is effective and robust compared to some binocular stereo and focus stacking method, and the depth sensing accuracy of our method is over 98%.

Keywords: Depth sensing · Focus staking · Camera pose

1 Introduction

Depth sensing from images is a traditionally hot research field. Generally, the depth information is computed by stereo matching, in which the pixels are matched between images, and the depth are obtained by solving the geometry relation between the camera poses and matched pixels. The stereo matching-based methods are facing many difficulties in practice, such as mutual occlusion, textureless region, none diffuse reflection, etc. In this paper, we propose a novel method for depth sensing with better convenience in general use, since it avoids solving the geometry relation of the cameras and it does not need the time-consuming pixel-wise matching. The proposed method is based on focus stacking, which is primally designed to gain large depth of field (DoF) in one image by fusing images captured at different focusing distances. It is especially useful to compute AiF images when the DoF is limited [1,8,14]. Focus stacking

---

Supported by NSFC under Grant 61860206007 and 61571313.

Y. Zhao et al. (Eds.): ICIG 2019, LNCS 11903, pp. 181–192, 2019.
https://doi.org/10.1007/978-3-030-34113-8_16

has been used in many other applications in image processing and computational photography [2,4,5], such as image denoising [17] and 3D surface profiling [3]. And there are also some works proposed to improve its efficiency [13].

Camera imaging is a bijection from object space, generating an inverted, shrunken and distorted real image to image space. Taking photos is a sampling process of the image space with the shift of image sensor. However, it is not a standard sampling process, for the image sensor receive and block all the light beams casting on it at any location, as shown in Fig. 1. In-focus parts produce the best sharpness when the objects are exactly on the focal plane. Others are differently blurred into circles of confusion (CoC) related to the distance to the camera.

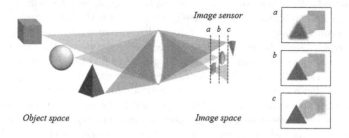

Fig. 1. A simplified model of camera imaging. Three objects in object space at different depth and their images in image space. a–c are 3 positions of the image sensor, and right are pictures taken at these positions.

As shown in Fig. 2, in-focus points in image space can be described as $(h_0, v_0) = (Hf_0/(d - f_0), df_0/(d - f_0))$, where H and h_0 are radial distances from the object points and its corresponding image points to the optical axis respectively. The in-focus image distance v_0 is related to the depth d and focal length f_0. In this condition, all light beams from objects converge to a single sensor point, which leads to image pixels with best sharpness. With the altering of image distance, defocus blur is generated. The defocus amount of a pixel denoted by c is defined as the diameter of CoC [10], which is positive related to the image distance v when v_0 is fixed. N_s is the f-stop number:

$$c = \frac{f_0(v - v_0)}{N_s v_0} \tag{1}$$

The defocus blur can be denoted by a convolution of a sharp image with the point spread function (PSF). The PSF is usually approximated by a Gaussian function. And the standard deviation σ measures the diameter of CoC.

The approach we present is to reconstruct the image in image space, and invert the camera mapping from image space to the object space. Figure 3 shows the framework of the presented method. There are two key points to reconstruct the scene. We first calculate the inverse mapping $(H, d) = (h_0 f_0/(v_0 - f_0), v_0 f_0/v_0 - f_0)$ between image distance and scene depth, in which sharpness

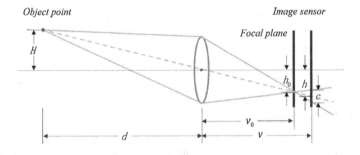

Fig. 2. Description of in-focus and defocus image points.

evaluation function and parallax method are used to confirm the position of the image sensor plane. Then we reconstruct the scene with the focal stacks. A defocus blur estimation method [18] is improved to segment in-focus regions of the focal stacks and fuse an IDM to mark the in-focus patches and an AiF image to record their colors. Now we have all the 3D information which is used to reconstruct the scene.

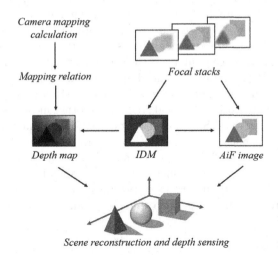

Fig. 3. Framework of the proposed depth sensing method.

2 Camera Mapping Calculation

We calculated the inverse mapping between image distance and object distance in the INTRODUCTION, which is undifferentiated to each camera. But the positions of image sensor are complicated to learn which is related to camera types and conditions. Camera mapping calculation is to confirm the relation between scene depth and its corresponding focus ring positions. In this section, we use the parallax method to calculate the image distance. Before this, sharpness evaluation function is used to evaluate the clarity of local areas and confirm the in-focus parts in the focal stacks.

2.1 Sharpness Evaluation Function

Image sharpness is a measurement of the focus degree. There are more details and edge features in focused images compared to defocused ones. In the view of pixels on the images, clear images change dramatically especially at complex texture areas. The defocus blur modeled as a convolution of a sharp image with the PSF. We can evaluate the sharpness of images by the complexity of pixels at a certain area. Sharpness evaluation function is used for filtering the in-focus parts in the focal stacks.

Two objects with complex texture and flat plane are chosen as aim objects in the experimental scene. The planes perpendicular to the optical axis provide homogeneous depth areas and the complex textures offer more features. Positions of the camera and two aim objects in different depth were fixed. Shift the image plane and focus on two aim objects respectively. During this process, we assume $a_s(x, y)$ as the aim object area on the image plane, and s is the displacement of focusing ring. It is always hard to distinguish the best in-focus position with human eyes. There are many sharpness evaluation functions to solve this problem, especially in space domain, such as gradient square function, Roberts gradient function, Brenner function and Laplacian function [15,16].

We employ the DFT in frequency domain into the sharpness evaluation function, which shows superiorities to focal stacks than other methods. For the defocus blur can be treated as a PSF convolution of the in-focus image, and the degree of the defocus blur is related to diameter of CoC. In the frequency domain, PSF like a lowpass filtering (LSP) reduce the high frequency parts. And with the expansion of CoC, more high frequency parts are abandoned. We obtain the frequency image of $a_s(x, y)$ after Fourier transformation $A_s(x, y) = \mathcal{F}\{a_s(x, y)\}$. Then we compare the aim parts with different s and calculate our sharpness evaluation function

$$
\begin{cases}
f_s(x, y) = \sum_{x=0}^{Max(x)} \sum_{y=0}^{Max(y)} A_s(x, y) W(x, y) \\
W(x, y) = \left(\frac{Max(x)-x}{\sum_{x=0}^{Max(x)} x}, \frac{Max(y)-y}{\sum_{y=0}^{Max(y)} y} \right)
\end{cases}
, \qquad (2)
$$

where $W(x, y)$ is weight matrix to provide higher weights to the high frequency parts. In this subsection, we obtain the best in-focus positions of two aim objects with their corresponding focus ring positions denoted by s_a and s_b respectively.

2.2 Parallax Method

To distinguish the two image planes, we invert the aim1 image plane at v_a in front of the optic center, as shown in Fig. 4. Two objects reflect their images at

(x_{1L}, y_1) and (x_{2L}, y_2) on the left camera sensor respectively, and reflect their images at (x_{1R}, y_1) and (x_{2R}, y_2) on the right camera sensor respectively. As the focus ring positions are known, we calculate the corresponding image distances v_a and v_b using parallax method in Eq. (3), where Δ is unit pixel length of the image sensor plane.

$$\begin{cases} v_a = \frac{(x_{1L} - x_{1R})\Delta + B}{B} f_0 \\ \\ v_b = \frac{(x_{2L} - x_{2R})\Delta + B}{B} f_0 \end{cases} \tag{3}$$

We obtain the two best image distances of in-focus image planes with their

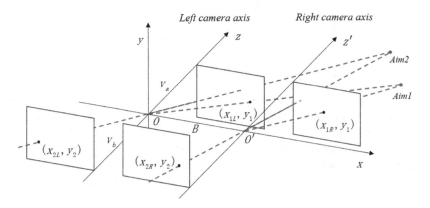

Fig. 4. The model of parallax method. World coordinate system with the left optic center as origin is established, whose x-axis is horizontal direction, y-axis is vertical direction and z-axis is depth direction. O' is the right camera optic center and B is the baseline between the two optic centers. v_a and v_b are the optimum image plane distances of two aim points.

responding focus ring displacements s_a and s_b. The relation between them is a liner mapping $v = k'(s - s_b) + v_b$, $k' = (v_a - v_b)/(s_a - s_b)$. Combining the inverse mapping function, we can acquire the position of the focus ring and their corresponding scene depth.

$$u = \frac{f_0^2}{k'(s - s_a) + v_a - f_0} + f_0 \tag{4}$$

It should be noted that the mapping calculation only needs to conduct once for every camera, when the mapping between in-focus images plane and responding focus ring displacement is unknown. If camera mapping calculation is finished during the camera manufacturing process, no more camera mapping calculation is needed to users and depth sensing can be directly conducted.

3   Depth Sensing

3.1   Defocus Model of Focus Stacks

By shifting the image plane of an aperture camera and coaxially photograph-ing the scene, we can obtain the focal stacks with different image distances. Accord-ing to Eq. (1), the same image coordinates in focal stacks will be defocus blurred with different sizes of PSF caused by the image distance. The defocus blur image can be described as a sharp image convoluted by a PSF, which is usually approximated by a Gaussian function. We assume the defocus blur as follows:

$$\begin{cases} I_i(x,y) = P(x,y) \star g_i(x,y) \\ \\ g_i(x,y) = \frac{1}{2\pi\sigma_i^2} exp[-\frac{(x-x_0)^2+(y-y_0)^2}{2\sigma_i^2}] \\ \\ \sigma_i(x,y) = \frac{kf_0[v_i - v_0(x,y)]}{N_s v_0(x,y)}, i = 1, 2, \cdots, n \end{cases} \qquad (5)$$

where i is the serial number of image in the focal stacks and v_i is the image dis-tance of the $No.i$ image. $v_0(x, y)$ is the latent in-focus parts at (x, y) of the image, which is only related to the depth of the scene. $I_i(x, y)$ is the blurred image, mod-eled as a convolution of the latent sharp image $P(x, y)$ and the Gaussian function map $g_i(x, y)$ of the whole $No.i$ image with different σ_i sizes, which is related to the image coordinates. k is a coefficient measures the defocus blur amount c.

3.2   IDM

We improve Zhuo et al.'s method [18] to select the in-focus parts, which is an effective approach to estimate the amount of spatially varying defocus blur at edge locations. Zhuo et al.'s method [18] can produce a continuous defocus map with less noise, which is quite robust especially in detecting the spatially adjacent in-focus objects. However, it can't distinguish defocus blur between front and back areas. We add a contrast section to compare adjacent images of the focal stacks to verify the spatial adjacent parts.

By propagating the blur amount at edge locations to the entire image based on Gaussian gradient ratio, a full defocus map obtained. Then Canny edge detec-tor is used to perform the edge detection, and calculate the standard deviation of the PSF to obtain the sparse depth map. Finally, we apply the joint bilat-eral filtering (JBF) [12] to correct defocus estimation errors and interpolate the sparse depth to full defocus map [9,11].

In our method, we use the JBF method [12] to deal with the focal stacks first. And then a threshold is given to dispose the most defocus parts, especially effective on the spatially adjacent objects. A comparation is used to select the most in-focus parts among the neighbor areas. Every image corresponding to one focus ring position, and with which an IDM is fused from the defocus map stacks.

Values on the IDM are labels, which mark the clearest parts on all images in the focal stacks. Need to know that "the best image" is unequal to "the clearest image" because of the discrete sampling illustrated in the INTRODUCTION. Therefore, the sample frequency determines the IDM accuracy. It can be an index to guide the most in-focus parts in the stacks and by which an AiF image is fused. We can calculate the coordinates of the points in world space according to Figs. 2 and 4:

$$(X, Y, Z) = (\frac{-x \Delta f_0}{v - f_0}, \frac{-y \Delta f_0}{v - f_0}, \frac{v f_0}{v - f_0}), \tag{6}$$

where Z is the depth of the scene. Then we reconstruct the scene with these conditions.

4 Experiments and Analysis

In this section, the proposed method is evaluated on the real scene. The main devices we used are Cannon EOS 80D SLR camera with a 135 mm focus, a camera holder whose moving unit is up to 0.01 mm, and a PC to control the images sensor shifts. Besides, two bookends clamped with two printed leopard pictures are used as the mapping calculation targets. A pavilion and a path in Sichuan University in China are chosen for camera mapping calculation and depth sensing respectively.

4.1 Camera Mapping Calculation

A software from the Cannon official website on a PC are used to control the camera shift, reducing shakes during photographing and improving the accuracy of focal plane's movements. Camera mapping calculation is conducted in a pavilion in Sichuan University in China.

We divide the image sensor moving distance into sparse unit displacements and we fix the camera and coaxially photograph at every unit to obtain focal stacks. Top two rows of Fig. 5 show some of the focal stacks. We can see the focal plane move from the camera nearby to the white wall behind including the two bookends. Then we choose the aim area of the front bookend at the same position in the stacks, as the yellow boxes shown in the top row. The aim area is processed with DFT shown in the bottom row of Fig. 5, and we can see it's apparently different in the frequency domain of the images with different sizes of CoC, especially in the high frequency areas. Then we do the same process to the back bookend and the frequency domain maps of the two aim areas are obtained.

We compare the frequency domain of the aim areas in the focal stacks with the Eq. (2), where the higher frequency parts share more weights. Figure 6 left one shows the sharpness of the focal stacks of the front and back bookend planes. Two target objects are combined into one coordinate system to illustrate focal position relations of the two objects, and we know that the peak of sharpness

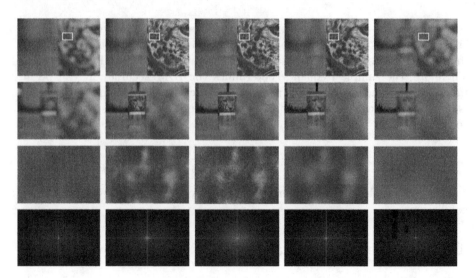

Fig. 5. Top row: several images of the front bookend at different image distances, which are 165.25 mm, 163.35 mm, 161.45 mm, 159.55 mm and 157.65 mm from left to right. Second row: several images of the back bookend at different image distances, which are 144.35 mm, 142.45 mm, 140.55 mm, 138.65 mm and 136.75 mm from left to right. Third row: the responding details boxed out in the top row. Bottom row: the DFT of the third row.

evaluation function curve is single and symmetrical. That is because the diameter of CoC c positively correlates to the distance between focal plane and image plane (see Eq. (1)), which make the blur degree symmetrical about the in-focal image plane.

We get the two sharpest image positions from the curve in Fig. 6 left and photograph the scene at in-focus plane. Shift the camera holder to simulate the parallax method. Images from left and right camera can be seen in Fig. 6 right. The yellow lines connect corresponding points between the two cameras. We calculate image distances of the two bookends with parallax method from Eq. (3) and the depth of the front and back bookends. The two in-focus distances of the two bookends are $v_a = 140.02$ mm and $v_b = 161.77$ mm, and the object distances are $Z_a = 815.72$ mm and $Z_b = 3763.22$ mm. The depth between them that we measured with tape is $d_{ab} = 2900$ mm, which is close to the computation and the accuracy is 98.36%. The linear relation between image plane shift and image distance is $v = -0.38s/\delta + 176.65$, where δ is the unit displacement of the focus ring.

4.2 Depth Sensing

A path scattered with several stones and branches at different depth are chosen as the test scene. Devices are still the Cannon EOS 80D SLR camera with a 135 mm fixed focus and a PC to control the shift of the image plane.

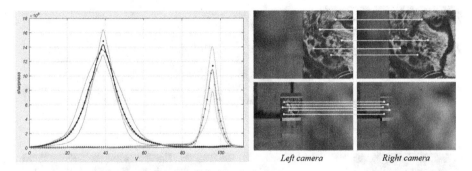

Fig. 6. Left: the sharpness evaluation function curve. Two peaks represent the front and back bookends respectively. The left peak is the front one, and right peak is the behind one. The yellow and light blue lines are some sample points we chosen. The orange and dark blue lines are their mean values respectively. Right: top two are images of the front bookend from right and left cameras at in-focus distance v_a and bottom two are images of the back bookend from right and left cameras at in-focus distance v_b. (Color figure online)

In our experiments, we photograph the scene with the image plane moving far away gradually and some of the results shown in the top row of Fig. 7. The focal stacks are $\{P_i, s_i\}, \forall_i = 1, 2, ..., N$. As shown in the bottom row of Fig. 7, defocus maps of images in focal stacks darken the aim depth areas and light up the adjacent defocus areas. We exclude the defocus light patches and compare with the contiguous defocus map to select the most in-focus parts of the whole image. The final IDM, depth map and the AiF image calculated from the IDM as shown in Fig. 8.

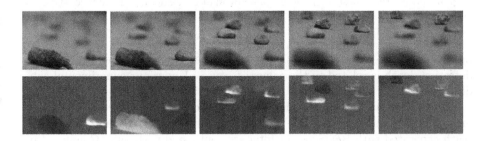

Fig. 7. Top row: samples of focal stacks. Bottom row: our defocus maps of the top row.

Figure 9 shows the experimental scene and the different views of the reconstruction of the scene. We can see the final scene reconstruction illustrates the spatial relationship of the fused image, which is similar to the real scene. Objects close to the camera show more details because of the depth and image distance mapping. Layered reconstructed road is caused by the discrete sampling, but

Fig. 8. Left: the IDM. Middle: depth map. Right: defocus map.

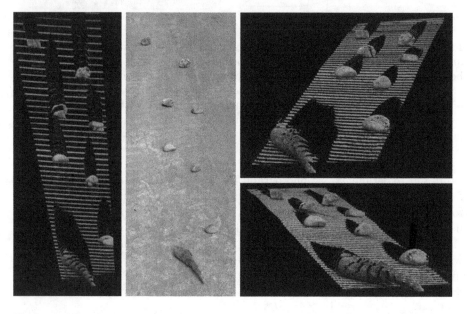

Fig. 9. Middle: the test scene photographed by another camera. Others: reconstructed scene in different directions.

provide a precise distance detection of each object without camera poses. The detection depth is related to the camera features. Under our experimental conditions, the best sensing range is from 0.4 m to 25 m.

To demonstrate the effectiveness of our method, we present contrast experiments and results are shown in Fig. 10. Three methods [6,7,10] and the ground truth generated with RealSense of Intel are contrasted with ours. Compared to the binocular methods, our method provides complete outlines. Compared to the Levin et al.'s method [10] which we experimented on focal stacks, our method provides clear boundaries and more layers from the stacks. Bisides, we calculate the real distance between objects in space compared with the real depth obtained from the RealSense, which shows that depth sensing accuracy of in-focus areas is over 98% in the experimental scope.

Fig. 10. Top row: the experimental scene photographed via binocular stereo, and the focal stacks of the same scene. Bottom row: depth map of ground truth, three depth sensing method [6,7,10] and ours.

5 Conclusion

In this paper, we proposed a camera pose free depth sensing method, in which the depth information was inferred from differently blurred images captured by aperture camera with focus stacking. DFT sharpness evaluation function and parallax method were employed in the camera mapping calculation. Then we realized depth sensing by fusing an IDM and an AiF image with focus stacking. The experimental results show that the proposed method is robust and accurate for depth sensing compared to the binocular and other focus stacking methods. In the future, we will concentrate on improving spatial continuity of the reconstructed scene, less focal stacks and better calculation algorithm.

References

1. Akira, K., Kiyoharu, A., Tsuhan, C.: Reconstructing dense light field from array of multifocus images for novel view synthesis. IEEE Trans. Image Process. **16**(1), 269 (2007). A Publication of the IEEE Signal Processing Society
2. Alonso, J.R., Fernández, A., Ferrari, J.A.: Reconstruction of perspective shifts and refocusing of a three-dimensional scene from a multi-focus image stack. Appl. Opt. **55**(9), 2380 (2016)
3. Fan, C., Weng, C., Lin, Y., Cheng, P.: Surface profiling measurement using varifocal lens based on focus stacking. In: 2018 IEEE International Instrumentation and Measurement Technology Conference (I2MTC), pp. 1–5, May 2018. https://doi.org/10.1109/I2MTC.2018.8409820
4. Grossmann, P.: Depth from focus. Pattern Recogn. Lett. **5**(1), 63–69 (1987)
5. Gulbins, J., Gulbins, R.: Photographic Multishot Techniques: High Dynamic Range, Super-Resolution, Extended Depth of Field, Stitching. Rocky Nook, Inc., Santa Barbara (2009)
6. Heiko, H.: Stereo processing by semiglobal matching and mutual information. IEEE Trans. Pattern Anal. Mach. Intell. **30**(2), 328–341 (2007)
7. Konolige, K.: Small vision systems: hardware and implementation. In: Shirai, Y., Hirose, S. (eds.) Robotics Research, pp. 203–212. Springer, London (1998). https://doi.org/10.1007/978-1-4471-1580-9_19

8. Kuthirummal, S., Nagahara, H., Zhou, C., Nayar, S.K.: Flexible depth of field photography. IEEE Trans. Pattern Anal. Mach. Intell. **33**(1), 58–71 (2010)
9. Levin, A., Lischinski, D., Weiss, Y.: Colorization using optimization. ACM Trans. Graph. **23**(3), 689–694 (2004)
10. Levin, A., Lischinski, D., Weiss, Y.: A closed form solution to natural image matting. IEEE Trans. Pattern Anal. Mach. Intell. **30**, 228–242 (2007)
11. Lischinski, D., Farbman, Z., Uyttendaele, M., Szeliski, R.: Interactive local adjustment of tonal values, pp. 646–653 (2006)
12. Petschnigg, G., Szeliski, R., Agrawala, M., Cohen, M.F., Toyama, K.: Digital photography with flash and no-flash image pairs. ACM Trans. Graph. **23**(3), 664–672 (2004)
13. Sakurikar, P., Narayanan, P.J.: Focal stack representation and focus manipulation. In: 2017 4th IAPR Asian Conference on Pattern Recognition (ACPR) (2017)
14. Xu, G., Quan, Y., Ji, H.: Estimating defocus blur via rank of local patches. In: Proceedings of the IEEE International Conference on Computer Vision, pp. 5371–5379 (2017)
15. Zhang, L.X., Sun, H.Y., Guo, H.C., Fan, Y.C.: Auto focusing algorithm based on largest gray gradient summation. Acta Photonica Sinica **42**(5), 605–610 (2013)
16. Zhao, H., Bao, G.T., Wei, T.: Experimental research and analysis of automatic focusing function for imaging measurement. Opt. Precis. Eng. **12**, 531–536 (2004)
17. Zhou, S., Lou, Z., Yu, H.H., Jiang, H.: Multiple view image denoising using 3D focus image stacks. In: Signal & Information Processing (2016)
18. Zhuo, S., Sim, T.: Defocus map estimation from a single image. Pattern Recogn. **44**(9), 1852–1858 (2011)

Objective Quality Assessment for Light Field Based on Refocus Characteristic

Chunli Meng, Ping An[(⊠)], Xinpeng Huang, and Chao Yang

Shanghai Institute for Advanced Communication and Data Science,
School of Communication and Information Engineering,
Shanghai University, Shanghai 200444, China
anping@shu.edu.cn

Abstract. The light filed (LF) is emerging as a new form of 3D content due to its super dense-view and refocus properties. The compression algorithms of LF have been developed maturely; however, few metrics are published to measure the performance of coding algorithm. At present, the metrics widely used to evaluate the quality of LF is limited to average the objective scores on the whole sub-aperture images (SAI), but this time-consuming process cannot represent the overall quality of LF well. The refocus images are mapped from the original LF, and the distortion measure of the refocus images reflects the overall quality of LF. Therefore, we unprecedentedly utilize the refocus character of LF to build a new image quality assessment framework, named RIQA. The results show that RIQA can improve most of objective metrics than SAI method. Furthermore, the RIQA framework can save the running time extremely.

Keywords: Light field · Image quality assessment · Refocus

1 Introduction

In recent years, the light field imaging has been the most promising means for virtual reality, due to the abundant information recorded from three-dimensional (3D) scene. The light field (LF) describes the set of light rays traveling in every direction through every point in 3D space [1]. Such light filed is expressed as a seven-dimensional (7D) function when published initial. However, the 7D light field model is difficult to realize, so it is simplified to four-dimensional (4D) representation for practicability [2]. Generally, the 4D light field can be parameterized by the coordinates of their interaction with two planes in arbitrary position. The two parameterized coordinates refer to the planes of micro lens and pixels under micro-lens, which denote the space and angular information respectively.

This paper analyzes the images captured by the cameras with micro-lens array. The pixels behind each micro lens named super-pixel which records the ray direction, the number of pixels on the super-pixel expresses the angular resolution [3]. In addition, the sub-aperture images (SAI) are formed by extracting the same position pixels from super-pixel, and the number of micro-lens represents space resolution of light field [4]. The most common applications of light field images process are related to SAI, especially for compression and reconstruction of light field [5–8]. The light field

Y. Zhao et al. (Eds.): ICIG 2019, LNCS 11903, pp. 193–204, 2019.
https://doi.org/10.1007/978-3-030-34113-8_17

images containing abundant detailed information, which benefits from its multiple angles of views. Accordingly, the process system of light field needs much larger storage than general 3D content, so many researchers devote to study with the efficaciously compression and reconstruction algorithms for light field. LF compression and reconstruction need the metrics to assess the artifacts induced by the process algorithms. In addition, the research on acquisition and display of light field also desires the appropriate metrics to evaluate the quality accurately for the more stunning visual experience. However, there is still no standard subjective evaluation method and suitable objective metrics for light field.

A few subjective perception quality assessment databases have been designed in [9–11], which serve as ground truth for questing objective metrics. Subjective assessment spends lots of manpower and material resource, and it is time-consuming because of the large data contained. Furthermore, it cannot be built in encoder algorithm, hence it is urgent to study objective metrics specialized for light field.

There are few objective metrics for LF in the state-of-the-art. At present, the classic algorithms like PSNR and SSIM are mostly used to evaluate the performance of compression and reconstruction algorithms. The final objective score for the overall quality is obtained by averaging the score of each image in SAI. Although the resolution of the light field image is not high enough, nevertheless, the number of SAI is general 15×15. As a result, the quality assessment of SAI consumes time seriously. So the most urgent task of light field image quality assessment (LFIQA) is not only to improve the accuracy but also save time as far as possible. In addition, there are also other objective metrics published. The computation efficiency is promoted in [12] by extracting views on a circle motion animation of the scene around the central view, but it ignores the vignetting effect on edges of micro-lens, which affects the quality of light field images at great extent. A reduced reference LFIQA metric is proposed in [13] based on depth map of origin and distorted LF images. It saves the running time, but its results are dependent on the depth estimation method and do not fit well with the subjective scores.

The SAI has been researched a lot for quality evaluating, while the refocus image is only used to picture segmentation or depth estimation. We are illuminated by light refocus properties in solving depth map [14], the light intensity distribution can be refocused nearby the original focused scenes according to the ray tracing theory [4]. The refocused image can represent the properties of light field due to the mapping process.

In this paper, the refocus character of LF is taken into account because the refocus images contain the distortion information mapped from lenslet images We find that multiple images which focus at different objects in scene can be obtained via setting different depth resolution. The paper demonstrates a framework of image quality assessment based on refocus to represent the properties of light field.

The rest of the paper is organized as follows: Sect. 2 briefly describes the two frameworks of LF image quality evaluation. Section 3 analyzes and compares two frameworks through several objective metrics, and finally in Sect. 4 concluding remarks are drawn.

2 LFRIQA Framework

The most researches of objective evaluation for light field are conducted based on the sub-aperture image quality assessment (SAIQA) framework. The objective evaluation of light field image is mainly applied to assess the artifacts induced by compression and reconstruction algorithm. The procedure of SAIQA framework contains three steps. Firstly, the sub-aperture images can be extracted from the 4DLF images, and the 4DLF image can be obtained from lenslet image through remapping process. It needs to be noticed that it is reversible for conversion between 4DLF and sub-aperture images. Secondly, the selected objective metrics are used to compute the score of each image from sub-aperture images. Finally, the final score of light field are expressed by averaging the array scores of sub-aperture images, and the details of SAIQA frame are visualized in Fig. 1, indicting with blue lines. The conventional objective metric using sub-aperture frame is expressed as follows:

$$LF_{SAIQA} = \frac{1}{kl} \sum_{i=1}^{k} \sum_{j=1}^{l} f_{(i,j)} \left(SAI_{ref}, SAI_{dis} \right) \tag{1}$$

Where LF_{SAIQA} is the final perceived quality value, k and l denote the index value with row and column $f(\cdot)$ n of sub-aperture image, and $k = l = 9$ in the following contrast test. Then the is used to represent the selected image quality metric such as PSNR or SSIM, SAI_{ref} and SAI_{dis} indicate referenced and distorted SAI of corresponding position respectively.

In addition to the usage of sub-aperture image in subjective LFIQA, the refocus image has also been used as an evaluation strategy considering that the perception of depth information attracts observer easier than pictures on sub-aperture, that is to say, the artifacts appeared in refocus image has more influence on the properties of light filed. We suppose that the images on the border of sub-aperture are more annoying to the viewers than those on any other area. Averaging the whole images quality cannot fit well with human visual system (HVS), while it may be solved by drawing a weight array to the sub-aperture images. Then the artifacts induced to sub-aperture images from encoder algorithm also impact on depth information which can be sliced into several refocus images. Moreover, the refocus model can maximize the weight of border distortion as far as possible. The refocused images can be acquired by refocus process with 4DLF images, as shown in Fig. 1 with red lines.

Considering the effect of vignetting to perspective views at the border of the sub-aperture images array, the viewpoint is more legible when its position is closer to the center. The perception of observer is generally affected by the border images according to the assumption of most apparent distortion [15], so that the quality of effective viewpoint of light field can be pulled down by the useless corner view. Therefore, most of subjective quality assessment methods select the central 9 × 9 views. We choose the same views for subjective assessment, and take the distortion of border into account as far as possible.

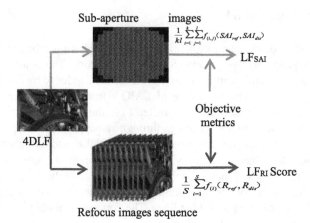

Sub-aperture   images

$$\frac{1}{kl}\sum_{i=1}^{k}\sum_{j=1}^{l}f_{(i,j)}(SAI_{ref}, SAI_{dis})$$

LF$_{SAI}$

4DLF

Objective
metrics

LF$_{RI}$ Score

$$\frac{1}{S}\sum_{i=1}^{S}f_{(i)}(R_{ref}, R_{dis})$$

Refocus images sequence

Fig. 1. The diagram of SAIQA and RIQA frameworks. (Color figure online)

The comparison of two objective quality evaluation frameworks in the following study adopts the 4D LF synthesized with the central 9×9 views. The expression (2) demonstrates the framework of LFIQA based on refocus. It is worked by averaging the objective score with each refocus image.

$$LF_{RIQA} = \frac{1}{S}\sum_{i=1}^{S}f_{(i)}\left(R_{ref}, R_{dis}\right) \tag{2}$$

where S is the amount of refocus images, $f(\cdot)$ is used to represent the selected image quality metric such as PSNR or SSIM, R_{ref} and R_{dis} indicate referenced and distorted refocus image of corresponding refocus position respectively.

In this paper, the light field images are refocused at different positions with same interval. In the following implementation, considering that the parameter variation of positive defocus is not remarkable compared with the negative defocus, so we choose 0.1 times of focal length as the smaller negative defocus value and 1.6 times of focal length as the positive defocus value. In addition, the refocusing interval is set to 0.15 for saving time and algorithm stability. We use 10 refocus images to take place of the 81 sub-aperture images, and then compute the objective score with those refocus images, and average them to the last score.

3   Performance Analysis of RIQA Framework

There have been a few subjective evaluate methods for light field images currently, which may be slightly different, but they are basically based on the sub-aperture images and refocus images. In this paper, we compared the performance of SAIQA and RIQA frame with subjective LFIQA database of Shanghai University (SHU) [9, 10] and VALID [11]. The details of two databases are shown in Table 1.

Table 1. Comparison of existing IQA datasets of LFIs

Dataset	Year	Content	Distortion		Total
VALID	2018	5 (Lytro Illum)	8bit	HEVC, VP9	40
			10bit	HEVC, VP9, [16–18]	100
SHU	2018	8 (Lytro Illum)	Gaussian blur, JPEG, JPEG2000, Motion blur, White noise		240

The SHU includes eight contents with five compression algorithms at six compression ratios (CR), The database contains artifacts such as gaussian blur, JPEG, JEPG2000, motion blur and white noise those artifacts Then VALID includes five contents with five compression algorithms at four quantization parameters (QPs), which containing of HEVC, VP9, [16–18] artifacts. The VALID contains 10bit depth (the original bit depth of images) and 8bit depth. Although the 8bit part just have HEVC and VP9, there are three subjective evaluations, therefore, both bit depths above will be tested later. The angular resolutions of SHU and VALID are 15×15, 13×13 respectively, and the corresponding spacial resolutions are 625×434 and 626×434. For the purpose of validity and practicability, the analysis of objective metrics on two frameworks employed the central 9×9 viewpoints and 625×434 resolution.

In order to compare the performance of two frameworks, we used nine representative full reference IQA metrics, including peak signal to noise ratio (PSNR), structural similarity index metric (SSIM) [19], multi-scale SSIM (MS-SSIM) [20], information content weighting SSIM (IW-SSIM) [21], feature similarity index metric (FSIM) [22], gradient similarity metric (GSM) [23], visual information fidelity (VIF) [24], visual saliency index (VSI) [25], and sparse feature fidelity (SFF) [26]. For a better understanding of the correlation between the mean opinion score (MOS) and the objective metrics above. Figure 2(a–i) shows the scatter distributions of MOS versus the predicted scores by nine objective metrics for SAIQA frameworks on the SHU database. Correspondingly, the Fig. 2(j–r) show the homologous scatter diagrams under RIQA framework. The black lines are curves fitted with the five-parameter logistic function. The results show that, compared with SAIQA framework, the objective score predicted by RIQA has a stronger correlation with MOS In the scatter diagrams of RIQA, the scatter points around the fitting curves are more aggregated than that of SAIQA.

The correlation between the predicted score and MOS was calculated using root-mean-square error (RMSE), Pearson linear correlation coefficient (PLCC), Spearman rank order correlation coefficient (SROCC), and Kendall rank order correlation coefficient (KROCC) metrics. The first two metrics need to undergo the nonlinear regression process before fitting with MOS, which denote the accuracy of correlation between MOS and the predicted score. Moreover, the KROCC and SROCC are used to measure the monotonicity of objective IQA metrics. A better objective metric is expected to have a higher absolute value of PLCC, KROCC, SROCC a lower RMSE.

The performance of the above two frameworks in the SHU database is shown in Table 2. It can be seen that the performance of most objective metrics in RIQA is

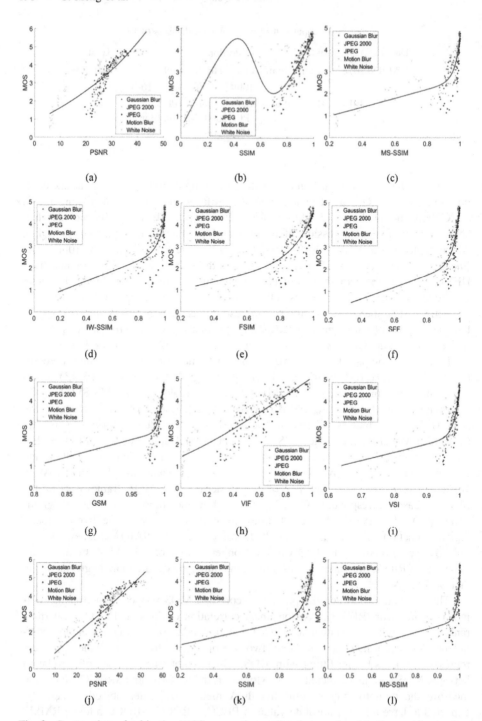

Fig. 2. Scatter plots of subjective MOS versus the predicted scores by objective metrics on the SAIQA-SHU (a–i) and RIQA-SHU database (j–r).

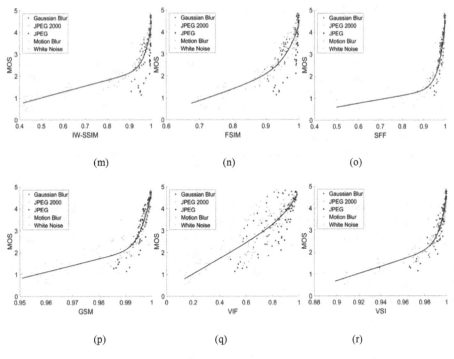

Fig. 2. (*continued*)

outperform the SAIQA framework. Judging from the above four indexes, RIQA framework can improve the performance both in terms of accuracy and monotonicity. The best results for two frameworks are in bold front. For the SAIQA method, the SFF obtained the best result than other metrics (measured in terms of four indexes above). This result could be due to the fact that the SFF takes into account the independent component analysis (PCA), which simulates the sparse representation of images by primary visual cortex. SFF performs better than SAIQA in the RIQA framework, while VSI outperforms others with RIQA framework in SHU database. The VSI combines the excellent visual saliency (VS) map and gradient map as feature maps as well as VS map employed as weighted function to reflect the importance of the local regions. To some extent, the saliency map plays an important role in the evaluation of refocused images, which can be researched in the future. In addition, GSM is also superior to the best result of SAIQA. This can be explained in part by the effectiveness of IQA using refocused images.

The performance of RIQA and SAIQA for two bit-depth forms in VALID is listed in Table 3. For the length reasons, we do not show the specific fitted scatter diagram for the single distortion type. The 8bit part of VALID contains three subjective evaluation methodologies (interactive, passive, passive-interactive). It can be seen that different subjective evaluation strategies have different fitting results, indicating that it is very important to study the subjective evaluation. The objective metrics still improved by RIQA though it is not as prominent as SHU. It can be seen that SAIQA is much more

Table 2. Performance of RIQA and SAIQA in SHU database

SHU		PSNR	SSIM	MS-SSIM	IW-SSIM	FSIM	SFF	GSM	VIF	VSI
SAIQA	**RMSE**	0.6309	0.5973	0.5165	0.5081	0.5400	**0.4725**	0.5340	0.5791	0.5040
	PLCC	0.8194	0.8399	0.8831	0.8870	0.8713	**0.9031**	0.8744	0.8504	0.8890
	SROCC	0.8861	0.8575	0.8937	0.8919	0.8868	**0.9168**	0.8903	0.8689	0.9069
	KROCC	0.7318	0.6976	0.7182	0.7216	0.7097	**0.7544**	0.7323	0.6876	0.7411
RIQA	**RMSE**	0.4586	0.5024	0.4524	0.4874	0.4811	0.3814	0.3575	0.5619	**0.3353**
	PLCC	0.9090	0.8897	0.9116	0.8966	0.8994	0.9380	0.9458	0.8598	**0.9525**
	SROCC	0.9228	0.8900	0.9128	0.8942	0.8915	0.9313	0.9457	0.8421	**0.9471**
	KROCC	0.7658	0.7184	0.7484	0.7300	0.7251	0.7845	0.8030	0.6681	**0.8097**

consistent with passive subjective evaluation method, while RIQA has great consistency with interactive subjective evaluation method. In addition, there is still a lot of room for improvement in the study of LFIQA with refocus properties, such as locating the refocus range as well as extracting the key refocus location. In a word, the RIQA framework can realize the improvement of most of objective metrics than traditional IQA based on SAI. Besides, using RIQA framework takes much less running time than SAIQA. Table 4 records the detailed time of two frameworks with different objective metrics under different database.

Table 3. Performance of RIQA and SAIQA in VALID database

VALID-8bit		PSNR	SSIM	MS-SSIM	IW-SSIM	FSIM	SFF	GSM	VIF	VSI
SAIQA (interactive)	**RMSE**	0.3795	0.3970	0.3444	0.2927	0.3028	0.2780	0.2983	**0.2300**	0.2961
	PLCC	0.9590	0.9550	0.9663	0.9758	0.9741	0.9782	0.9749	**0.9851**	0.9752
	SROCC	0.9194	0.9490	0.9601	0.9658	0.9720	0.9555	0.9690	**0.9735**	0.9679
	KROCC	0.7693	0.8080	0.8339	0.8546	0.8649	0.8339	0.8598	**0.8753**	0.8598
RIQA (interactive)	**RMSE**	0.2848	0.3493	0.3145	0.2823	0.3208	0.2275	0.2842	**0.2273**	0.2807
	PLCC	0.9771	0.9654	0.9720	0.9775	0.9709	**0.9855**	0.9772	**0.9855**	0.9778
	SROCC	0.9621	0.9576	0.9608	0.9662	0.9625	0.9664	0.9680	0.9679	**0.9725**
	KROCC	0.8520	0.8261	0.8313	0.8520	0.8417	0.8648	0.8598	0.8675	**0.8753**
SAIQA (passive)	**RMSE**	0.4848	0.3741	0.2992	0.2505	0.2556	0.3225	0.2955	**0.2342**	0.2851
	PLCC	0.9442	0.9672	0.9791	0.9854	0.9848	0.9757	0.9796	**0.9873**	0.9811
	SROCC	0.9253	0.9421	0.9538	0.9589	0.9642	0.9676	0.9640	**0.9702**	0.9648
	KROCC	0.7703	0.7910	0.8195	0.8376	0.8479	0.8609	0.8428	**0.8635**	0.8479
RIQA (passive)	**RMSE**	0.3156	0.3366	0.2887	0.2632	0.2928	0.2594	0.2828	**0.2438**	0.2790
	PLCC	0.9767	0.9735	0.9806	0.9839	0.9800	0.9843	0.9814	**0.9862**	0.9819
	SROCC	0.9614	0.9510	0.9531	0.9576	0.9570	0.9655	**0.9678**	0.9641	0.9668
	KROCC	0.8376	0.8169	0.8195	0.8376	0.8324	0.8528	0.8557	0.8531	**0.8583**
SAIQA (passive-interactive)	**RMSE**	0.4209	0.3950	0.3379	0.2803	0.3066	0.2666	0.3062	**0.2391**	0.2985
	PLCC	0.9498	0.9559	0.9679	0.9780	0.9737	0.9802	0.9737	**0.9841**	0.9751
	SROCC	0.9102	0.9527	0.9658	0.9717	0.9729	0.9680	0.9691	**0.9755**	0.9679
	KROCC	0.7617	0.8187	0.8550	0.8731	0.8757	0.8601	0.8653	**0.8861**	0.8627
RIQA (passive-interactive)	**RMSE**	0.2825	0.3406	0.3086	0.2760	0.3116	0.2210	0.2805	**0.2173**	0.2731

(continued)

Table 3. (*continued*)

VALID-8bit		PSNR	SSIM	MS-SSIM	IW-SSIM	FSIM	SFF	GSM	VIF	VSI
	PLCC	0.9777	0.9674	0.9733	0.9787	0.9728	0.9864	0.9780	**0.9869**	0.9792
	SROCC	0.9645	0.9631	0.9648	0.9706	0.9672	0.9707	0.9740	**0.9774**	0.9753
	KROCC	0.8653	0.8498	0.8524	0.8731	0.8576	0.8678	0.8757	**0.8912**	0.8835
VALID-10bit		PSNR	SSIM	MS-SSIM	IW-SSIM	FSIM	SFF	GSM	VIF	VSI
SAIQA (passive)	**RMSE**	0.4110	0.3895	0.3167	0.2752	0.2901	0.3246	0.3162	**0.2425**	0.3132
	PLCC	0.9042	0.9145	0.9443	0.9582	0.9535	0.9414	0.9445	**0.9677**	0.9456
	SROCC	0.8866	0.9028	0.9345	0.9450	0.9473	0.9266	0.9350	**0.9560**	0.9305
	KROCC	0.7150	0.7284	0.7760	0.7984	0.7988	0.7691	0.7862	**0.8257**	0.7776
RIQA (passive)	**RMSE**	0.4029	0.3777	0.3122	0.2828	0.3049	0.3400	0.3127	**0.2428**	0.3289
	PLCC	0.9082	0.9198	0.9459	0.9558	0.9485	0.9355	0.9458	**0.9677**	0.9398
	SROCC	0.8743	0.9069	0.9230	0.9351	0.9340	0.9035	0.9324	**0.9494**	0.9195
	KROCC	0.7015	0.7304	0.7610	0.7809	0.7732	0.7394	0.7789	**0.8102**	0.7610

The execution time here is calculated by averaging all the content, all the distorted types and all the distorted levels for each objective metric. All of the experiments were run on a PC with 3.70-GHz Intel Core i7-8700K CPU and 32 GB of RAM. Figure 3 shows that the RIQA framework can save more time for the metrics that consume more time. Considering that the sub-aperture images extraction from 4DLF is more time consuming than the refocus process, the paper does not calculate the time of extracting process.

It is easily to comprehend the consume time is longer with SAIQA frame, because the light field images have 15 * 15 viewpoints in general. Although the paper just use the central 9 * 9 viewpoints for the effectiveness, it still needs to calculate more images, so it is inevitable to spend a lot of time. It is terrible for real time evaluating process of light field images. However, the refocused images only a few pieces, which is the most important reason to save time on such a large extent. It should be noted that even if we compute the average execution time, there will be also different results on the different

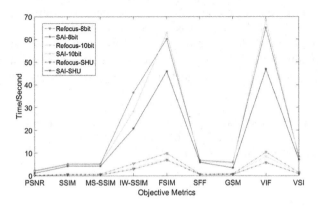

Fig. 3. Execution time of RIQA and SAIQA frameworks on different objective metrics under different databases

databases with the same metrics, which can be ascribed to the reason of different databases have different contents as well as the difference in the allocation of running memory by the computer. However, the overall tendency is close to the distribution of broken lines in Fig. 3. The objective metrics suitable to the light field not only require the high correlation with MOS, but also call for the relatively short time.

The Q in Table 4 represents the quotient of corresponding objective metrics between two frameworks. Obviously, the refocus character of light field can solve this problem to a great extent. One interesting thing is that the database with more images takes less time for single LF image, this could be caused by the link of calling images, but it does not affect the comparison of running time between two frameworks. based on the consideration of performance and time, refocusing image, as a form of light field, obviously has a broad research prospect in the field of LFIQA.

Table 4. The average running time of RIQA and SAIQA frameworks on different objective metrics and different databases

Database time (second) metrics	PSNR	SSIM	MS-SSIM	IW-SSIM	FSIM	SFF	GSM	VIF	VSI
SAIQA-SHU	1.2037	4.2360	4.2395	20.7247	45.8991	5.9124	3.4505	46.8835	7.0562
RIQA-SHU	0.1371	0.3752	0.3881	2.9444	6.8849	0.5568	0.5233	5.8577	0.8640
Q	8.8	11.3	10.9	7.0	6.7	10.6	6.6	8.0	8.2
SAIQA-10BIT	2.0798	4.7011	5.0028	28.4175	62.9268	6.0589	5.6069	68.4277	7.9130
RIQA-10BIT	0.1740	0.5126	0.5199	3.5165	7.4347	0.7271	0.6074	8.5050	1.1237
Q	11.9	9.2	9.6	8.1	8.5	8.3	9.2	8.0	7.0
SAIQA-8BIT	2.2607	5.1654	5.1999	36.5598	60.0967	6.7400	5.8998	65.0990	8.4084
RIQA-8BIT	0.2082	0.7248	0.7712	5.3528	9.8296	0.7441	0.7944	10.3800	1.4287
Q	10.8	7.1	6.7	6.8	6.1	9.1	7.4	6.3	5.9

4   Conclusion

In this paper, we proposed a new LFIQA framework based on refocus property of light field. The new method is demonstrated by various objective metrics with SHU and VALID databases. The RIQA frame has two advantages than general SAIQA frame. Firstly, it improves the performance of most objective metrics, even to the different distortion. Secondly, the RIQA frame saves the time at a large extent. In addition, the RIQA frame can deal with the assessment of compressed or reconstructed algorithm based on lenslet images directly.

Acknowledgment. This work was supported in part by the National Natural Science Foundation of China, under Grants 61571285 and 61828105, and Shanghai Science and Technology Commission under Grant 17DZ2292400 and 18XD1423900.

References

1. Wu, G., Masia, B., Jarabo, A., et al.: Light field image processing: an overview. IEEE J. Sel. Top. Sign. Proces. **11**(7), 926–954 (2017)
2. Levoy, M., Hanrahan, P.: Light field rendering. In: Computer Graphics (1996)
3. Lim, J.G., et al.: Improving the spatial resolution based on 4D light field data. In: 16th International Conference on Image Processing. IEEE, Cairo, Egypt (2009)
4. Ren N.: Digital light field photography. Ph.d. Thesis, Stanford University **115**(3), 38–39 (2006)
5. Helin, P., Astola, P., Rao, B., et al.: Sparse modelling and predictive coding of subaperture images for lossless plenoptic image compression. In: 2016 3DTV-Conference: The True Vision - Capture, Transmission and Display of 3D Video (3DTV-CON). IEEE, Hamburg, Germany (2016)
6. Huang, X., An, P., Shan, L., et al.: View synthesis for light field coding using depth estimation. In: 2018 IEEE International Conference on Multimedia and Expo (ICME). IEEE Computer Society, San Diego, USA (2018)
7. Yoon, Y., Jeon, H.G., Yoo, D., et al.: Learning a deep convolutional network for light-field image super-resolution. In: 2015 IEEE International Conference on Computer Vision Workshop (ICCVW). IEEE, Santiago, Chile (2015)
8. Farrugia, R.A., Galea, C., Guillemot, C.: Super resolution of light field images using linear subspace projection of patch-volumes. IEEE J. Sel. Top. Sig. Process. **11**(7), 1 (2017). PP (99)
9. Shan, L., An, P., et al.: Subjective evaluation of light field images for quality assessment database. In: 14th International Forum IFTC 2017: Digital TV and Wireless Multimedia Communication, pp. 267–276, Shanghai, China (2017)
10. Shan, L., et al.: Research on subjective quality assessment of light field images. In: 7th International Conference on Network, Communication and Computing, pp. 278–282. ACM, Taiwan, China (2018)
11. Viola, I., Ebrahimi, T.: VALID: visual quality assessment of light field images dataset. In: 2018 Tenth International Conference on Quality of Multimedia Experience (QoMEX), pp. 1–3. IEEE, Sardinia, Italy (2018)
12. Perra, C.: Assessing the quality of experience in viewing rendered decompressed light fields. Multimedia Tools Appl. **77**(16), 21771–21790 (2018)
13. Paudyal, P., Battisti, F., Carli, M.: Reduced reference quality assessment of light field images. IEEE Trans. Broadcast. **65**(1), 152–165 (2019)
14. Tao, M.W., Hadap, S., Malik, J., et al.: Depth from combining defocus and correspondence using light-field cameras. In: 2013 IEEE International Conference on Computer Vision (ICCV), pp. 673–680. IEEE Computer Society. IEEE, Sydney, NSW, Australia (2013)
15. Chandler, D.M.: Most apparent distortion: full-reference image quality assessment and the role of strategy. J. Electron. Imaging **19**(1), 011006 (2010)
16. Zhao, S., Chen, Z.: Light field image coding via linear approximation prior. In: IEEE International Conference on Image Processing, pp. 4562–4566. IEEE, Beijing, China (2017)
17. Ahmad, W., Olsson, R., Sjostrom, M.: Interpreting plenoptic images as multi-view sequences for improved compression. In: IEEE International Conference on Image Processing, pp. 4557–4561. IEEE, Beijing, China (2017)
18. Tabus, I., Helin, P., Astola, P.: Lossy compression of lenslet images from plenoptic cameras combining sparse predictive coding and JPEG2000. In: IEEE International Conference on Image Processing. IEEE, Beijing, China (2017)

19. Wang, Z., Bovik, A.C., Sheikh, H.R., et al.: Image quality assessment: from error visibility to structural similarity. IEEE Trans. Image Process. **13**(4), 600–612 (2004)
20. Wang, Z., Simoncelli, E.P., Bovik, A.C.: Multi-scale structural similarity for image quality assessment. In: 36th ASILOMAR Conference on Signal Systems and Computers, vol. 5, pp. 1398–1402. IEEE, Pacific Grove, CA, USA (2002)
21. Wang, Z., Li, Q.: Information content weighting for perceptual image quality assessment. IEEE Trans. Image Process. **20**(5), 1185–1198 (2011)
22. Zhang, L., Mou, X., et al.: FSIM: a feature similarity index for image quality assessment. IEEE Trans. Image Process. **20**(8), 2378 (2011)
23. Liu, A., Lin, W., Narwaria, M.: Image quality assessment based on gradient similarity. IEEE Trans. Image Process. **21**(4), 1500–1512 (2012)
24. Sheikh, H.R., Bovik, A.C.: Image information and visual quality. IEEE Trans. Image Process. **15**(2), 430–444 (2006)
25. Zhang, L., Shen, Y., Li, H.: VSI: a visual saliency-induced index for perceptual image quality assessment. IEEE Trans. Image Process. **23**(10), 4270–4281 (2014)
26. Chang, H.W., Yang, H., Gan, Y., et al.: Sparse feature fidelity for perceptual image quality assessment. IEEE Trans. Image Process. **22**(10), 4007–4018 (2013)

Fast Stereo 3D Imaging Based on Random Speckle Projection and Its FPGA Implementation

Yuhao Shang[1,2], Wei Yin[1,2], Shijie Feng[1,2], Tianyang Tao[1,2], Qian Chen[2], and Chao Zuo[1,2(✉)]

[1] Smart Computational Imaging (SCI) Laboratory, Nanjing University of Science and Technology, Nanjing, Jiangsu 210094, China
zuochao@njust.edu.cn

[2] Jiangsu Key Laboratory of Spectral Imaging and Intelligent Sense, Nanjing University of Science and Technology, Nanjing, Jiangsu 210094, China

Abstract. In this paper, we propose a fast stereo 3D imaging technique based on random speckle projection and its FPGA implementation. Stereo vision, as a classic passive method for 3D shape measurement based on the multi-view geometric constraints, can realize the 3D reconstruction of the tested scene using a pair of images captured through the binocular cameras. In addition, some complicated matching techniques, such as graph cut and block matching, are used to obtain a global disparity map but it leads to massive computing overhead. To solve this problem, we developed a fast stereo vision system based on FPGA. Benefiting from the full parallel architecture of FPGA, the complete computational framework is based on a full pipeline design, that is, the storage and calculation of data are performed under the system clock to implement different works of stereo vision (including stereo rectify and stereo matching) at the same time, promoting calculation speed and measurement efficiency. In order to further improve the accuracy of 3D measurement, by introducing structured light illumination into the existing system, a projection system based on random speckle is designed where fast speckle projection and synchronous acquisition are realized on the FPGA hardware. Experimental results verify that our method can achieve high-speed and robust 3D shape measurement.

Keywords: 3D imaging · Speckle · FPGA

1 Introduction

The acquisition of 3D information has extremely high significance in the fields of AR, VR, military, industrial inspection, robotics, and aerospace. Among plenty of state-of-the-art methods of achieving the 3D reconstruction of the tested scene (including binocular stereo vision (BSV), TOF, and structured light illumination [1–4]), BSV, which is based on the principle of triangulation, has been proven to be one of the most promising techniques due to its inherent advantages of non-contact, high efficiency, and low cost. In a conventional measurement system based on BSV only consisting of the binocular cameras, a series works of stereo vision (including stereo rectify, stereo

© Springer Nature Switzerland AG 2019
Y. Zhao et al. (Eds.): ICIG 2019, LNCS 11903, pp. 205–216, 2019.
https://doi.org/10.1007/978-3-030-34113-8_18

matching, and left-right consistency check) are performed sequentially to get a global disparity map with high quality, but the measurement efficiency and speed of the system based on BSV are limited by the inherent instruction cycle delay within traditional computers to bring massive computing overhead, which leads to the limits on the application of BSV. Meanwhile, different from the traditional computer and specified integrated circuit, FPGA offers high flexibility and programmability to meet the stringent requirements of parallelism and internal bandwidth [5], that makes many FPGA-based stereo vision systems have good performance like real-time. Dunn et al. [6] propose a stereo vision system based on multi-chip FPGA with the time required for a stereo matching of 256×256 resolution images only 34 ms. FPGA-based stereo vision systems on custom boards have been developed by Nishihara [7] using the Laplacian-of-Gaussian Sign-Correlation algorithm and a stereo vision system with the correlation-based algorithm is designed by Ding et al. [8] with a high processing speed. Jin et al. [9] propose a fully pipelined stereo vision system providing a dense disparity image with additional sub-pixel accuracy in real-time. Hariyama [10] proposes a processor architecture for high-speed and reliable stereo matching based on adaptive window-size control of SAD computation.

However, due to the limited accuracy obtained using BSV, we bring speckle pattern projection into the 3D measurement system based on BSV in order to improve the accuracy of the measurement. Meanwhile, researchers have also done a lot of work on structured light illumination measurement, such as Pan et al. [11] propose an improved DIC combining a 2D digital image correlation technique with the projection of a random speckle pattern using a conventional LCD projector, and Axel et al. [12] propose a fast and accurate method with a correlation technique which takes only the area of one pixel into account, used to locate the homologous points. Furthermore, the projection pattern design is also a critical step for the structured light illumination measurement. Hua et al. [13] study the quality of the speckle pattern used in image correlation technique using the mean subset fluctuation parameter. A method for designing a composite pattern, in which the speckle pattern is embedded into the conventional phase-shifting fringe pattern with a simple and effective evaluation criterion for the correlation quality of the designed speckle pattern in order to improve the matching accuracy significantly, is proposed by Yin et al. [14]. In addition, the 3D imaging method based on speckle projection in our system is similar to the temporal correlation method Schaffer et al. [15] have proposed in this paper, and the 3D imaging system is realized on FPGAs.

2   FPGA-Based Data Transmission Framework

2.1   Image Data Transferred from Cameras to SDRAM

In our system, the digital image sensor used in the binocular cameras is MT9V034, which is a 1/3-Inch wide-VGA CMOS chip and can capture 10-bit grayscale image with the resolution of 752×480 at 60 Hz. In order to process and transmit the image data quickly and conveniently, we fine-tune the register configuration of MT9V034 to make our binocular cameras capture images with the resolution of 640×480 at 75 Hz under a camera clock with the frequency of 27 MHz. In the acquisition process of images, the whole image data are transmitted pixel by pixel and row by row into FPGA. On the basis of MT9V034's datasheet, it is obvious that 224 clock intervals will be needed in the transmission between two adjacent rows of an image, which means that the data transmission of images by cameras can be equivalent to the transmission without interruption under a pixel clock of 20 MHz. Meanwhile, the SDRAM in our FPGA development board, which consists of two IS42S16320B chips with the memory size of 32 M $\times$ 16 bit, makes the system has enough storage for a pair of images and is able to refresh the stored data of images in real time to guarantee the efficiency of the data processing.

In order to make full use of the SDRAM, the read/write clock frequency is set to 100 MHz. However, the transmission of image data, between binocular cameras and SDRAM, needs to transfer data from 20 MHz clock domain to 100 MHz clock domain, which may lead to image data overflow or loss. To avoid this problem, two FIFOs (each with the size of 213 $\times$ 8 bit) are set between the two different clock domains, achieving the transmission of image data normally without losing or overflowing data, as shown in Fig. 1(a). In addition, according to the storage characteristics of SDRAM, the data stored in SDRAM will not disappear unless the power is turned off, SDRAM is cleared, or new data is read in and overwrites the old data, so the image data will be stored and read out by Ping-Pong switching.

2.2 Data Transferred from SDRAM to Post-processing Module

The clock signal used in the post-processing modules is set to 20 MHz, which aims at making the image post-process operation and the image acquisition equivalent to real-time handling of the original pixel data from the camera each clock. There is also a mismatch between the clock domain of SDRAM and the clock domain of the post-processing module, so two more FIFOs need to be set between the two modules to deal with the problems mentioned above, as shown in Fig. 1(a).

Therefore, the data transmission between the two modules is that SDRAM will receive a read request from the back-end FIFOs after storing the data of a pair of images, and then will write the image data to these FIFOs. The post-processing module deals with the data from back-end FIFOs when those back-end FIFOs have stored enough data. In addition, the important point is that when the post-processing module starts reading data from the two back-end FIFOs these FIFOs will be not cleared until the data of the entire image has been read, ensuring that the order of the transferred data is consistent with the order in which the image data is entered from cameras.

2.3 Ethernet Transfers Data to Computers

In this system, due to its wide transmission bandwidth that enables Ethernet to realize efficient data transmission, the processed data is transferred by Gigabit Ethernet using TCP/IP protocol to send UDP packets to computers under the clock signal with a frequency of 125 MHz. There into, except the preamble code, each UDP packet contains 1328 bytes, including a 42-byte header, a 2-byte image row number flag, 1280-byte image data that are the data of the same row in the pair of images, and a check code of 4 bytes, as shown in Table 1. Similar to the four front-end and back-end FIFOs, two FIFOs, of which each at least stores data with the amount M (M could be obtained by Eq. (1)), are set between the post-processing and Ethernet modules.

Through the FPGA-based system, the computer handles the data packets received, and saves the data in the form of image, as shown in Fig. 1(b)–(c).

$$(44 + 640)/125 = (640 - M)/20 \tag{1}$$

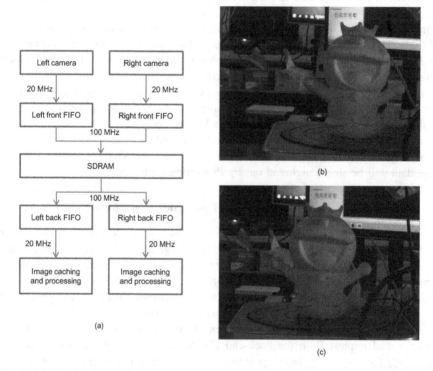

(a)

(b)

(c)

Fig. 1. (a) The data transmission between each module in this system. (b)–(c) There are two images captured by cameras. (b) The image is captured by left camera. (c) The image is captured by right camera.

Table 1. UDP packet contents (in byte).

Name	Preamble code	Ethernet header	IP header	UDP header
Length	8	14	20	8
Name	Image row number	Left image data	Right image data	Check code
Length	2	640	640	4

The key of the system implemented on FPGAs will be clearly stated in Sect. 4.

3   Image Processing

3.1   Speckle Pattern Design

In order to further improve the accuracy of 3D measurement, by introducing structured light illumination into the existing system, a projection system based on random speckle is designed where fast speckle projection and synchronous acquisition are realized on the FPGA hardware. Three-dimensional imaging technology based on optical structure is applied in more and more fields such as biomechanics, intelligent monitoring, robot navigation, industrial quality control, and human-computer interaction. In order to improve the three-dimensional imaging technology, researchers have carried out research on many factors that may have influence on the quality of the 3D imaging results, including the coding of projected structured light pattern. In order to accurately match the two images, a random encoding method will be proposed below.

Zhou et al. [16] propose a novel design method of color binary speckle pattern, and we will use this idea to design speckle patterns according to the relative position of the camera, tested object and the projector (see Fig. 2), as well as camera and projector parameters.

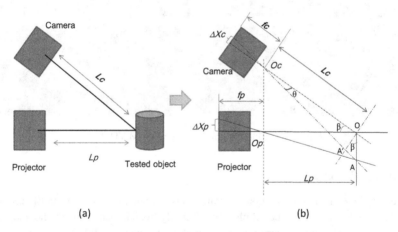

(a)   (b)

Fig. 2. Relationship between BWBSP design and system parameters. (a) Schematic binocular stereo measurement system. (b) Geometric relationship of the system.

According to the parameters of the projector and cameras, the relationship of the size between the speckle projected by the projector and the speckle captured by the camera can be known through Eq. (2), where $\Delta\delta_p$ is the pixel size of the projector (in mm), m_p is the width of the projected speckle, L_p is the projection distance of the projector, and f_p is the focal length of the projector, $\Delta\delta_c$, m_c, and L_c are related parameters of the camera similarly.

$$m_p \Delta \delta_p = \frac{L_c^2 f_p}{L_p^2 f_c} (m_c \Delta \delta_c) \tag{2}$$

In addition, in order to satisfy the sampling theorem and obtain good image contrast, the allowable range of m_c value should belong to 3 to 5 [17]. In this design, the ratio of the camera distance L_c to the projection distance L_p is about 6/5; the size of a pixel of the camera sensor is 6.0 μm; the focal length f_c is 12 mm; the size of the pixel of the projector is 7.6 μm; and the focal length f_p of the projector is about 15 mm. If $m_c = 3$, then m_p is calculated as 4.

Speckle generation is generated by using MATLAB R2017a. The method is generated by referring to the method of Pan et al. [18]. The generated speckle pattern is shown in Fig. 3.

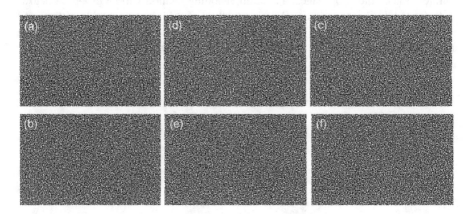

Fig. 3. Speckle patterns generated by MATLAB.

3.2   Image Rectification

Between binocular image acquisition and stereo matching, stereo rectification of binocular images needs to be implemented firstly which can narrow the matching range, thereby reducing the amount of computation generated by the matching algorithm, and indirectly speeding up the matching speed. Before image rectification, the work of camera calibration, which determines the parameters of the binocular cameras that facilitate the subsequent association of the world coordinate with the camera coordinate based on the relationship in the geometric models, would be done by Zhang's camera calibration method [19]. And then the polar line rectification of the images can be performed.

Camera Calibration and Inverse Mapping Pixel Calculation. The camera coordinate system and the world coordinate system can be converted to each other by rotation and translation transformations. In addition to the parameters required for the rotation and translation transformations, determining the relationship between the world coordinate system and the camera coordinate system also requires the precise focal length and focus of the camera. The rotation matrix R and the translation matrix T are the external parameters of the camera, each having three parameters, while the focal length f and the focus c are the internal parameters of the camera, each of which consists of two parameters, so the calibration of a camera is to determine 10 variables of the camera. The conversion relationship between the world coordinate M_{world} and the camera coordinate M_{camera} of the object could be defined by Eq. (3). Then we can get the relationship between left and right cameras, as shown in Eq. (4), where R_{lr} is the rotation matrix and T_{lr} is the translation matrix between the binocular cameras, M_{right} and M_{left} are the coordinates of the object in the right and left camera coordinate systems, respectively.

$$M_{world} = R(M_{camera} - T) \tag{3}$$

$$M_{right} = R_{lr}(M_{left} - T_{lr}) \tag{4}$$

The rectification of the images is the calculation of the inverse mapping pixel. Before the value of pixels in the rectified images is calculated, the inverse mapping coefficient must be calculated before the subsequent calculation. However, the inverse mapping coefficient is the decimal part of the pixel coordinate, and the inverse pixel coordinates p are calculated by Eqs. (5) to (8).

$$p = [p_x \ p_y]^T \tag{5}$$

$$[PX \ PY \ PZ]^T = H'[x \ y \ 1]^T \tag{6}$$

$$H' = [H_x \ H_y \ H_z]^T = R^T K K^{-1} \tag{7}$$

$$p_x = f_x \frac{PX}{PZ} + c_x, \quad p_y = f_y \frac{PY}{PZ} + c_y \tag{8}$$

(f_x, f_y) and (c_x, c_y) are the focal length and principal point in x-axis and y-axis respectively, KK is the inherent parameters matrix, and R is the rotation matrix between right and left cameras.

It is easy to find that eight multiplications, two indispensable divisions, and eight additions are required in the process of calculating the inverse coordinates. However, the time required for calculating a multiplication in an FPGA is long, with the used resources large. In order to simplify the calculation of the inverse mapping pixel on the FPGA, the calculation process is reorganized, which makes Eqs. (4) to (7) changing into Eqs. (9) to (11).

$$H'' = \begin{bmatrix} f_x & f_x & f_x \\ f_y & f_y & f_y \\ 1 & 1 & 1 \end{bmatrix} .* H' \tag{9}$$

$$[X' \ Y' \ Z']^T = H''[x \ y \ 1]^T \tag{10}$$

$$p_x = \frac{X'}{Z'} + c_x, \quad p_y = \frac{Y'}{Z'} + c_y \tag{11}$$

Bilinear Interpolation Module. The equation for bilinear interpolation is given (see Eq. (12)). According to the principle of linear interpolation method, the integer part of the calculation result is the inverse mapping pixel coordinate, and the decimal part is the inverse mapping coefficient α_x and α_y, and the design of bilinear interpolation module [20] is shown in Fig. 4(a). The image correction result is shown in Fig. 4(b) and (c).

$$Pix_{rec} = (1 - \alpha_x)(1 - \alpha_y)Pix_{LU} + \alpha_x(1 - \alpha_y)Pix_{RU} + (1 - \alpha_x)\alpha_y Pix_{LD} + \alpha_x\alpha_y Pix_{RD} \tag{12}$$

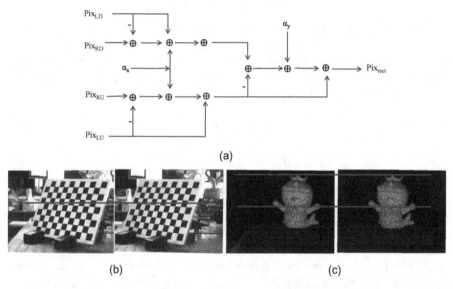

(a)

(b)   (c)

Fig. 4. (a) The design of bilinear interpolation module; (b) Simulation results of the rectification algorithm on MATLAB; (c) The rectified images obtained from FPGA.

3.3   Image Matching

Statistical Pattern. Since the two images captured by cameras have been rectified in the previous work, the matching area of the images could be reduced from the whole frame to one line which means that potential wrong matching points are reduced, and it can be found that the disparity between the two images is within a certain range (about

100 or so) in Fig. 1 (b)–(c). Therefore, we can set the disparity value in the range from 80 to 144.

The temporal correlation method for statistical pattern is to project multiple speckle patterns on the tested object, and then the correlation between the two gray value sequences of the reference point and the point to be matched is obtained, among which the point with the largest correlation value is the matching point. According to the paper [15], the image related equation is shown in Eq. (13), where $g_i(p_j, t)$ denotes the gray value of the pixel p_j in the t-th image by camera i, and $\bar{g}_i(p_j)$ stands for the mean gray value of the pixel p_j in camera i over all the N images.

$$\rho(p_1, p_2) = \frac{\sum_{t=1}^{N}[g_1(p_1, t) - \bar{g}_1(p_1)] \cdot [g_2(p_2, t) - \bar{g}_2(p_2)]}{\sqrt{\sum_{t=1}^{N}[g_1(p_1, t) - \bar{g}_1(p_1)]^2 \cdot \sum_{t=1}^{N}[g_2(p_2, t) - \bar{g}_2(p_2)]^2}} \quad (13)$$

Algorithm Optimization. The number of speckle patterns projected in this experiment is small (only 6 different speckle patterns). Therefore, the quality of the result matched by Eq. (13) is very poor, the results have many wrong matching points, and the environmental interference can be found very serious, as shown in Fig. 5(a).

Therefore, the images are filtered by a simple filter that does not damage the image data before the matching is performed, and the background interference is filtered out (shown in Fig. 5(b)). After removing the background and then using Eq. (13) to correlate with 24 speckle patterns, it is found that the quality of the matching result is still poor as shown in Fig. 5(c), and by the method of spatial correlation we get the result shown in Fig. 5(d), of which the accuracy is not well. Therefore, we add the gray value of the neighboring pixels around this pixel for high quality matching, that is, the temporal correlation method is optimized by combining with spatial correlation method, with Eq. (13) changing into Eq. (14), where the radius of the added window centered on the pixel p_j to be matched is set to r, and $\bar{g}_i(p_j)$ means the average gray value of all the pixels in this window on all N images captured by camera i. And we can obtain disparity maps, as shown in Fig. 5(e)–(f). The result shown in Fig. 5(g) is the disparity map after left-right consistency check and occlusion area filling processing, and the result shown in Fig. 5(h) is the disparity map obtained by the median filter.

$$\rho(p_1, p_2) = \frac{\sum_{j=-r}^{r}\sum_{i=-r}^{r}\sum_{t=1}^{N}[g_1(p_1(i,j), t) - \bar{g}_1(p_1)] \cdot [g_2(p_2(i,j), t) - \bar{g}_2(p_2)]}{\sqrt{\sum_{j=-r}^{r}\sum_{i=-r}^{r}\sum_{t=1}^{N}[g_1(p_1(i,j), t) - \bar{g}_1(p_1)]^2 \cdot \sum_{j=-r}^{r}\sum_{i=-r}^{r}\sum_{t=1}^{N}[g_2(p_2(i,j), t) - \bar{g}_2(p_2)]^2}}$$

$$(14)$$

This optimized algorithm is realized on MATLAB with all experiments conducted on a 2.5 GHz Intel Core i7-6500U CPU, 8 GB of RAM and no GPU optimization, and the running time of processing single image with the resolution of 640 × 480 is about 8 min, that means it could not meet the requirement of real-time. Meanwhile, the operation using this proposed algorithm needs to get the data of all images with different speckle patterns at the same time and make correlation operation. So, on our FPGA development board, DE2-115, it is extremely difficult for this optimized algorithm to implement due to the limited storage capacity, limited data bandwidth and the limited internal resources of FPGA chip. In our follow-up work, the problems mentioned above will be studied.

4   FPGA-Based Image Matching

Since temporal correlation algorithm is extremely difficult to implement on FPGAs, the stereo vision system is based on the Census transform matching method, by which the image data could be transformed into Census binary vectors to achieve the image matching, and the Census vectors are suit for the parallel computing mode of FPGA. Due to the space limitations, the details of the principle about the Census transform are omitted here. In order to better achieve the image matching module on FPGA, the pipeline design is introduced into the system, seen in Fig. 6(a), where the Hamming distances are stored in the registers with the corresponding disparity value after the exclusive OR operation is implemented on the Census binary vectors stored in shift registers, and the disparity value with the smallest Hamming distance is the desired.

The disparity maps obtained from the 3D imaging system built on the FPGA are shown in Fig. 6(b)–(e), where the result shown in Fig. 6(b) is obtained directly from FPGA board, the result shown in Fig. 6(c) is obtained after the left-right consistency check, and the result shown in Fig. 6(d) is the disparity map after the occlusion area filling processing with the result shown in Fig. 6(e) obtained after median filtering.

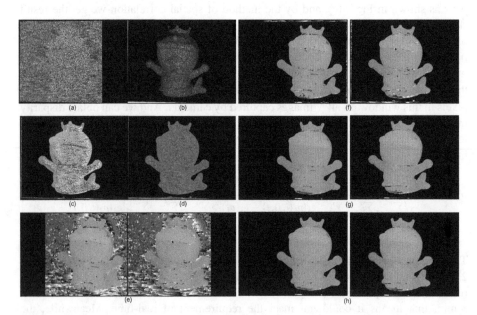

Fig. 5. Matching results. (a) The result is obtained by temporal correlation method; (b) The result is obtained by filtering out the background interference. (c) The result is obtained by temporal correlation method. (d) The result is obtained by spatial correlation method. (e)–(f) The results are obtained by the optimized method. (g)–(h) The results are obtained by left-right consistency check and the median filter.

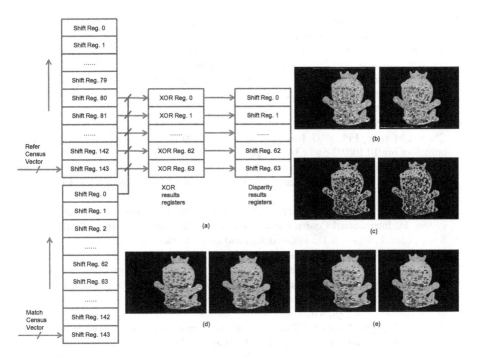

Fig. 6. (a) The pipeline design introduced on FPGA. (b)–(e) Disparity maps.

5   Conclusion

In this work, the 3D imaging technology based on random speckle projection is studied, and the hardware implementation of 3D imaging system is realized on FPGAs. The system can rectify and match the images acquired by the binocular cameras and use Gigabit Ethernet to transmit data. Then the correlation method is optimized by combining the spatial correlation method with temporal correlation method, by which the accuracy of the image matching results obtained with 6 speckle patterns is much higher than the results only by spatial correlation method or temporal correlation method (even more speckle patterns). Finally, the image process module of 3D imaging system realized by Census transform on FPGA could achieve real-time 3D measurement at 75 frames per second for the images with a resolution of 640 × 480 under a global 27 MHz clock signal.

References

1. Gorthi, S.S., Rastogi, P.: Fringe projection techniques: whither we are? Opt. Laser Eng. **48** (2), 133–140 (2010)
2. Feng, S., Zhang, L., Zuo, C., Tao, T., Chen, Q., Gu, G.: High dynamic range 3-D measurements with fringe projection profilometry: a review. Meas. Sci. Technol. **29**(12), 122001 (2018)

3. Zuo, C., Feng, S., Huang, L., Tao, T., Yin, W., Chen, Q.: Phase shifting algorithms for fringe projection profilometry: a review. Opt. Laser Eng. **109**, 23–59 (2018)
4. Yin, W., et al.: High-speed three-dimensional shape measurement using geometry-constraint-based number-theoretical phase unwrapping. Opt. Laser Eng. **115**, 21–31 (2019)
5. Zhang, L., Zhang, K., Chang, T.: Real-time high-definition stereo matching on FPGA. In: Proceedings of the ACM/SIGDA 19th International Symposium on Field Programmable Gate Arrays (2011)
6. Dunn, P., Corke, P.: Real-time stereopsis using FPGAs. In: Luk, W., Cheung, P.Y.K., Glesner, M. (eds.) FPL 1997. LNCS, vol. 1304, pp. 400–409. Springer, Heidelberg (1997). https://doi.org/10.1007/3-540-63465-7_245
7. Nishihara, H.K.: Real-time stereo- and motion-based figure ground discrimination and tracking using LOG sign correlation. In: Conference on Signals, Systems & Computers. IEEE (2002)
8. Ding, J., Du, X., Wang, X.: Improved real-time correlation-based FPGA stereo vision system. In: International Conference on Mechatronics & Automation. IEEE (2010)
9. Jin, S., Cho, J., Pham, X.D.: FPGA design and implementation of a real-time stereo vision system. IEEE Trans. Circuits Syst. Video Technol. **20**(1), 15–26 (2010)
10. Hariyama, M.: FPGA implementation of a stereo matching processor based on window-parallel-and-pixel-parallel architecture. In: Symposium on Circuits & Systems. IEEE (2005)
11. Pan, B., Xie, H., Gao, J.: Improved speckle projection profilometry for out-of-plane shape measurement. Appl. Opt. **47**(29), 5527–5533 (2008)
12. Axel, W., Holger, W., Richard, K.: Human face measurement by projecting bandlimited random patterns. Opt. Express **14**(17), 7692–7698 (2006)
13. Hua, T., Xie, H., Wang, S.: Evaluation of the quality of a speckle pattern in the digital image correlation method by mean subset fluctuation. Opt. Laser Technol. **43**(1), 9–13 (2011)
14. Yin, W., et al.: High-speed 3D shape measurement using the optimized composite fringe patterns and stereo-assisted structured light system. Opt. Express **27**, 2411–2431 (2019)
15. Schaffer, M., Marcus, G., Harendt, B.: Statistical patterns: an approach for high-speed and high-accuracy shape measurements. Opt. Eng. **53**(11), 112205 (2014)
16. Zhou, P., Zhu, J., Jing, H.: Optical 3-D surface reconstruction with color binary speckle pattern encoding. Opt. Express **26**(3), 3452 (2018)
17. Lionello, G., Cristofolini, L.: A practical approach to optimizing the preparation of speckle patterns for digital-image correlation. Meas. Sci. Technol. **25**(10), 107001 (2014)
18. Pan, B., Lu, Z., Xie, H.: Mean intensity gradient: an effective global parameter for quality assessment of the speckle patterns used in digital image correlation. Opt. Lasers Eng. **48**(4), 469–477 (2010)
19. Zhang, Z.: A flexible new technique for camera calibration. IEEE Trans. Pattern Anal. Mach. Intell. **22**(11), 1330–1334 (2000)
20. Ma, J., Yin, W., Zuo, C., Feng, S., Chen, Q.: Real-time binocular stereo vision system based on FPGA. In: ICOPEN 2018, p. 108271U (2018)

Security

A Novel Robust Blind Digital Image Watermarking Scheme Against JPEG2000 Compression

Zheng Hui[✉] and Quan Zhou

Xi'an Institute of Space Radio Technology, Xi'an 710000, Shaanxi, China
358971616@qq.com

Abstract. In this paper, a novel robust blind digital image water marking scheme is proposed by jointly using discrete wavelet transform (DWT), stationary wavelet transform (SWT), discrete cosine transform (DCT) and singular value decomposition (SVD). Firstly host image is decomposed by DWT and the obtained approximation coefficient is portioned into non-overlapping blocks. For each block, SWT is applied to affine redundant low frequency sub-bands which are subsequently processed by DCT and SVD. Watermark bit is embedded through quantifying the obtained greatest singular value. Extraction of proposed scheme is blind without any referring to the original image or watermark. Experimental result show that watermarked image is visually invisible of which peak signal to noise ratio (PSNR) is above 44 dB. Besides, by comparing with other DWT-SVD robust watermarking approaches, proposed scheme significantly outperforms in robustness against JPEG2000 compression. Performance of proposed scheme is also superior or competitive against other attacks such as rotation, filter or scaling.

Keywords: Blind image watermarking · Discrete wavelet transform · Stationary wavelet transform · Singular value decomposition · JPEG2000

1 Introduction

With the popularization and ripeness of the Internet, efficient storage management, rapid transmission and sharing, and real-time analysis and processing of digital multimedia data have gradually become an indispensable part of people's daily life. Due to the openness and compatibility of Internet, it's simple and convenient for people to access and obtain digital resources. However, under such circumstance, security of digital media has been greatly threatened and challenged for numerous digital products being copied, tampered and spread without the permission of copyrights' owners. Through illegal copying, huge profits have been made by criminals, which heavily threaten the development of digital media industry.

Digital watermarking, as an efficient authentication approach for copyright protection, is an important brunch of information security. Digital image is a key part of digital multimedia resources, thus digital image watermarking has been the essential aspects of watermarking technology. Digital watermarking protects the copyright of digits images by embedding watermarks into host images. In the implement of

© Springer Nature Switzerland AG 2019
Y. Zhao et al. (Eds.): ICIG 2019, LNCS 11903, pp. 219–230, 2019.
https://doi.org/10.1007/978-3-030-34113-8_19

copyright protection, the visual quality of watermarked image should not be significantly reduced; on the other hand, watermarking information should be robust of which most part can be detected and extracted after interference and attacking.

Since to deliver raw image greatly challenges storage and transmission bandwidth, it's necessary to have digital images compressed. JPEG2000 is discrete wavelet based still-image compression standard proposed by Joint Photographic Expert Group (JPEG). Taking advantages of discrete wavelet transform (DWT) and EB2COT encoding, JPEG2000 supports multi-resolution progressive representation and outperforms JPEG standard in reconstruction quality and compression ratio. However, in most scenes, JPEG2000 is applied as lossy compression scheme which brings distortion to watermarked image. In this paper, we focus in designing an efficient watermarking scheme against JPEG2000 compression.

According to the embedding domain of host images, digital image watermarking can be roughly categorized into two aspects, namely the spatial domain watermarking and the transform domain watermarking. Generally, digital watermarking in spatial domain is implemented by directly altering pixels within host image, which is characterized by simplicity and low computational complexity. The least significant bit substitution (LSB) [1] is a classic spatial domain watermarking algorithm implement by replacing host images' LSB with watermarking bits. Other typical spatial watermark includes pixel value differencing (PVD) [2], exploiting modification direction (EMD) [3] and reversible approaches such as histogram shifting (HS) [4] and difference expansion (DE) [5].

However, spatial watermark is not robust enough to resist attacks such as affine transformation or image compression in most scenes. Therefore research focusing on watermarking withstands compression has been continuously worked out for decades [6, 7]. The transform domain based watermarks is one of the efficient schemes resists to digital image compression. Compared with spatial domain watermarking, watermarks embedded in transform domain, such as discrete Fourier transform (DFT) [8, 9], discrete cosine transform (DCT) [10–12], discrete wavelet transform (DWT) [13, 14] and singular vale decomposition (SVD) [15–17] exploits better performance in both imperceptivity and robustness.

As mentioned, characteristics of mentioned transforms make them eligible for robust watermarking—most energy of natural signals (including images) is concentrated in low frequency coefficient and correlation between DCT coefficients is very low; DWT is a multi-resolution analysis in both spatial domain and frequency domain which characterizes the local properties in both domains; in addition, SVD is a powerful numeric tools for watermarking which effectively withstands attacks like geometric transform and noise. Therefore, research of robust watermarking [18–21] in hybrid domains involving DWT, DCT and SVD has been continually proposed in recent years which combines advantages of each transform. In Zear et al. [18], a back propagation Neural Network (BPNN) is applied in the watermark extraction phase to compensate the distortion induced by various attacks. In Fazli et al. [19], a watermarking scheme is proposed by combing DWT, DCT and SVD. The host image is firstly into four non-overlapping blocks and a 64 bit/128 bit binary watermark is embedded into each block four times respectively to enhance robustness. However, their approach is non-blind and its watermarking capacity is limited. In [21], Hu et al.

embeds multiple watermarking bits into host images by adjusting feature parameters obtained from DWT-SVD-DCT domain via the progressive quantization index modulation technique, which effectively withstands JPEG2000 compression attack.

Despite the mentioned transforms—DWT, DCT and SVD, another transform called stationary wavelet transform (SWT) is induced in this paper to implement robust watermarking scheme. SWT is an improved wavelet transform version aimed at overcoming the shortage of translation-invariance of DWT by removing downsamplers and up-samplers in original DWT algorithm. The salient features of SWT are redundancy and translation invariance. In this article, host image is firstly decomposed by 1-level DWT to obtained four sub-bands $[LL, LH, HL, HH]$. Then LL is portioned into 4×4 non-overlapping blocks, for each block a 1-level SWT is applied to obtain the low approximation coefficients LL_{SWT}. DCT and SVD are successively executed in LL_{SWT}, watermarking bits are embedded into the largest singular value via quantization.

The rest of this paper is organized as follows. In Sect. 2 describes the algorithm of both embedding and extraction algorithm. In Sect. 3, we gave out the experimental results and comparison between proposed Scheme and prior works. Eventually conclusion is presented in Sect. 4.

2 Proposed Blind Watermarking Scheme

2.1 Watermarking Embedding

The detailed embedding process of proposed scheme is given as follow:

(1) Using Haar wavelets, one-level 2-dimension DWT is applied on host image I. Therefore, four sub-bands are obtained namely LL, LH, HL and HH. Size of each sub-band will be $M/2 \times N/2$ Considering the demand of watermarking robustness, the embedding will be executed in sub-band LL.

$$[LL, LH, HL, HH] = \text{DWT}(I) \tag{1}$$

(2) Then the obtained LL is portioned into 4×4 non-overlapping block $LL(m, n)$ of which total amount is $M/8 \times N/8$. Each sub-block is decomposed by 2-dimension SWT; therefore a newly generated sub-band is obtained with size being the same as $LL(m, \text{n})$

$$LL = \bigcup_{m}^{M/8} \bigcup_{n}^{N/8} LL(m, n) \tag{2}$$

$$[A, H, V, D] = \text{SWT}(LL(m, n)) \tag{3}$$

(3) Then each stationary wavelet approximation A is transformed by DCT to obtain new coefficients A^{DCT} then apply SVD to A^{DCT}, therefore a singular value matrix $\mathbf{S}$ is acquired.

$$A^{DCT} = \text{DCT}(A) \tag{4}$$

$$[U, S, V] = \text{SVD}(A^{DCT}) \tag{5}$$

(4) According to formulas (5) and (6), watermarking bits $b \in \{0, 1\}$ is embedded into the maximum singular value $S(1, 1)$

$$S_W(1, 1) = round\left(\frac{S(1, 1) - d(b)}{\delta}\right)\delta + d(b) \tag{6}$$

Where, δ denotes quantization step, $d(0)$ is the quantization dither which is a random value within interval $[0, \delta]$ and $d(1) = d(0) + \delta/2$.

(5) Then calculate the watermarked A_W^{DCT} as follow:

$$A_W^{DCT} = U * S_W * V^T \tag{7}$$

(6) Inverse DCT and SWT operation is successively applied to 4×4 non-overlapping blocks, therefore the watermarked $LL_W(m, n)$ sub-band is obtained:

$$A_W = \text{Inverse\_DCT}(A_W^{DCT}) \tag{8}$$

$$LL_W(m, n) = \text{Inverse\_SWT}(A_W, H, V, D) \tag{9}$$

(7) These modified $LL_W(m, n)$s are put back to relevant position; therefore the watermarked approximation coefficient LL_W is obtained. Then apply inverse DWT transform by using Haar filter to LL_W and the rest detailed sub-bands which remain unchanged to acquire watermarked image I_W

$$LL_W = \bigcup_m^{M/8} \bigcup_n^{N/8} LL_W(m, n) \tag{10}$$

$$I_W = \text{Inverse\_DWT}(LL_W, LH, HL, HH) \tag{11}$$

2.2 Watermarking Extraction

The watermark extraction is basically the inverse operation against embedding process that contains similar operations, which are:

(1) By using Haar wavelet, two dimension DWT transform is applied to the water-marked image I_W, therefore a series of decomposed coefficients are obtained according to:

$$[LL_W, LH_W, HL_W, HH_W] = \text{DWT}(I_W) \tag{12}$$

(2) Divide acquired approximation sub-band LL_W into 4×4 non-overlapping blocks $LL_W(m, n)$s of which amount is $M/8 \times N/8$. Each sub-block is decomposed by 2-demsion SWT, therefore newly generated sub-bands are obtained with size being the same as $LL_W(m, n)$.Similarly, DCT and SVD operation are also successively applied to obtained singular value

$$LL_W = \bigcup_m^{M/8} \bigcup_n^{N/8} LL_W(m, n) \tag{13}$$

$$[A_W, H_W, V_W, D_W] = \text{SWT}(LL(m, n)) \tag{14}$$

$$A_W^{DCT} = \text{DCT}(A_W) \tag{15}$$

$$[U_W, S_W, V_W] = \text{SVD}\left(A_W^{DCT}\right) \tag{16}$$

(3) To extract the watermark bit b, firstly the modified maximum singular value $S_W(1, 1)$ is modulated by a pair of quantization dither $d(i), i \in \{0, 1\}$ respectively:

$$e_i = round\left(\frac{S_W(1, 1) - d(i)}{\delta}\right)\delta + d(i) \tag{17}$$

Then b will be extracted according to the comparison of distance derived by demodulation in (17), which is

$$b = \underset{i \in \{0,1\}}{\arg\min}(S_W(1, 1) - e_i)^2 \tag{18}$$

Based on (18), the modulated $e_i, i \in \{0, 1\}$ of which distance is less will be judged as proper watermark bit as index $i_{\min}$ as $b = i_{\min}$.

3   Experimental Results

In this paper, five 512×512 gray-scale image namely are served as host images, namely 'Lena', 'Pepper', 'Boat', 'Jet' and 'Tiffany'. In addition, a binary logo with size 64×64 is used as watermark. The watermarking logo is 20 times Arnold transformed before embedding. Host images and watermarking logo are displayed as follow:

(a)   (b)   (c)   (d)   (e)

Fig. 1. Host images: (a) Lena; (b) Pepper; (c) Boat; (d) Jet; (e) Tiffany

Fig. 2. Watermarking logo and its permutation by Arnold transform

3.1   Index of Quality Evaluation

In order to evaluate performance of proposed watermarking scheme, two metrics are induced namely peak signal to noise ratio (PSNR) and bit error rate (BER), among which PSNR indicates the imperceptivity of proposed scheme which is the variation between original host image and BER evaluates the robustness of extracted watermark under various attack types (Figs. 1 and 2).

PSNR between image I_1 and I_2 with size $M \times N$ is defined as below:

$$\text{PSNR} = 10 \log_{10} \left(\frac{255}{\text{MSE}} \right) (dB) \tag{19}$$

Where, MSE denotes the mean square error of which definition is as follow:

$$\text{MSE} = \frac{1}{MN} \sum_{x=1}^{M} \sum_{y=1}^{N} (I_1(x,y) - I_2(x,y))^2 \tag{20}$$

Definition of BER between $m \times n$ sized original watermark w and extracted w^* is shown as follow:

$$\text{BER} = \sum_{x=1}^{m} \sum_{y=1}^{n} \frac{(w(x,y) \oplus w^*(x,y))}{mn} \tag{21}$$

Where, $\oplus$ is exclusive or operation.

3.2   Selection of Quantization Step δ

As described in Sect. 2, it figures out that relation between imperceptivity of watermarked image and robustness of watermark is a compromise both affected by quantization step δ; which is greater δ enhances the robustness of watermark, yet impacts the invisibility of watermarked host images negatively.

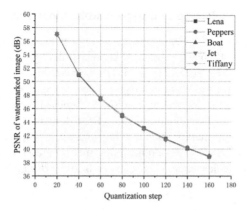

Fig. 3. Curves of watermarked images PSNR varying with different quantization steps

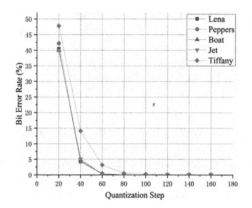

Fig. 4. Bit error rate of extracted watermark under JPEG 2000 compression with compression ratio set to 4

Figure 3 illustrates the trend how PSNR of watermarked images varies with different quantization steps. Figure 4 indicates the BERs of the extracted watermarks in case of JPEG2000 compression of which compression ratio (CR) is 4. From Fig. 4, it figures out that when quantization step $\delta \geq 80$ BERs of extracted watermarks of test images is very close to zero ($\leq 0.1\%$). The improvement in BER is very slight when step δ keeps increasing. However, performance of extracted watermarks' BERs deteriorates when quantization step $\delta \leq 60$. Moreover, from Fig. 3, it points out that when δ equals 80 the average PSNR of watermarked images is approximately 46 dB, which according to Human Vision System (HVS) [22], is excellent in vision quality and extremely invisible. Therefore, we intensively set quantization step $\delta = 80$ to achieve a trade-off between imperceptivity and robustness of proposed watermarking scheme.

3.3 Experimental Results and Comparison with Prior Works

In order to evaluate proposed scheme, a series of prior watermarking scheme of which watermark scales are all 4096 bits is induced as comparative groups, including Su et al. [17], Patra et al. [12] and Hu et al. [21]. In [17], watermark bits are embedded into non-overlapping blocks of host image by modifying some elements within U component of SVD decomposition. In [12], Patra et al. employs a Chinese Remainder Theorem-based (CRT) technology to embed watermark bits into DCT domain of host images. Hu et al. [21] embeds multiple watermarking bits into host images by adjusting obtained feature parameters from DWT-SVD-DCT domain via the progressive quantization index modulation technique, which effectively withstands JPEG2000 compression attack.

Table 1. Resulting PSNR (dB) of watermarked images for different schemes

Images	Watermarking schemes			
	Su et al. [17]	Patra et al. [12]	Hu et al. [21]	The proposed
Lena	41.55	42.49	43.60	44.88
Peppers	39.35	42.12	42.78	45.07
Boat	37.36	42.47	42.96	44.87
Jet	36.21	42.50	42.71	44.90
Tiffany	35.99	42.33	42.65	44.88

Table 1 indicates PSNR resulting from various watermarking schemes. It's obvious that PSNR achieved by proposed scheme is approximately 44.90 dB, which is significantly higher than other three approaches. Furthermore, unlike Su et al. PSNR achieved by different varies very slight for proposed scheme, which is, relevance of watermarked image quality to specific images is very little. Overall, imperceptivity of proposed algorithm stays in a relatively high level.

Subsequently, in order to test the robustness of proposed scheme, some types of attacks are taken into consideration, which are displayed in Table 2:

Attacks applied in this article mainly focus on JPEG2000 compression with a range of different compression ratio. Besides, other types of attack including noise, filter, rotation, scaling and pixels intensity variation are also explored to test the robustness of proposed scheme. Comparison between our work and prior research is displayed in Table 3.

Table 3 displays the average BER of extracted watermarks for test images under various types of attack, from which we can tell, proposed scheme significantly outperforms the other three works against JPEG2000 standard with all compression ratio employed. Besides, robustness of proposed scheme also has superiority under Median filter, scaling and rotation attack. However, not all of BER obtained by proposed algorithm is statistically competitive, for example, performance against Gaussian filter and pixels intensity variation is just general among four schemes and proposed scheme underperforms among all four works against salt & pepper noise. Figure 5 presents the extracted watermark visually.

Table 2. Attack types applied

Index	Attack type	Description
1–3	JPEG2000 compression	JPEG2000 compression with compression ratio of {2, 4, 8} is successively applied
4	Salt & pepper noise (1%)	Watermarked images are corrupted by salt & pepper noise with 1% intensity
5	Median filter (3 × 3)	Water marked images are filtered by a 3 × 3 median mask
6	Gaussian filter (3 × 3)	Watermarked images are filtered by a 3 × 3 Gaussian mask
7	Scaling	Watermarked images are shrunk into 256 × 256, then enlarged back to 512 × 512
8	Rotation	Watermarked images are rotated by $\pi/4$, then rotated back by $-\pi/4$
9	Cropping	Left upper corners with 256 × 256 pixels of watermarked images are cropped
10	Brighten	Intensity of watermarked images is added by 20
11	Darken	Intensity of watermarked images is subtracted by 20

Table 3. Average BER (%) of extracted watermarks for various schemes

Attack Type	Watermarking scheme			
	Su et al. [17]	Patra et al. [12]	Hu et al. [21]	The proposed
None	0	0	0	0
1	1.82	3.76	0	0
2	7.95	10.41	0.66	0.02
3	27.93	20.98	7.78	1.07
4	11.61	20.17	22.60	25.88
5	27.18	27.96	9.35	7.30
6	11.77	17.49	0.40	4.66
7	23.45	24.50	4.24	1.29
8	25.76	35.75	22.29	17.43
9	12.01	12.34	12.55	6.81
10	0.22	15.82	0.08	1.12
11	1.5	17.11	1.41	6.08

Fig. 5. Extracted watermark under various types of attack (a) None; (b–d) JPEG2000 compression with CR = 2, 4, 8; (e) Salt & pepper noise; (f) Median filter; (g) Gaussian filter; (h) Scaling; (i) Rotation; (j) Cropping; (k) Brighten; (h) Darken;

4   Conclusion

In this paper, we propose a novel robust blind watermarking scheme by jointly using DWT, SWT, DCT and SVD. The robustness is guaranteed by taking advantages of multi-resolution analysis offered by DWT, the translation invariance provided by SWT and the algebraic invariance furnished by SVD. Host images is firstly decomposed by DWT. Subsequently the approximation coefficient LL is portioned into non-overlapping blocks. For each block, SWT is applied to obtain the redundant low frequency coefficient LL_{SWT}. After successively applying DCT and SVD, multiple watermarks are embedded into the obtained greatest singular value of LL_{SWT} blindly using quantization. Experimental results show that the watermarked image is visually invisible of which peak signal to noise ratio (PSNR) is above 44 dB. Besides, by comparing with other DWT-SVD robust watermarking approaches, proposed scheme significantly outperforms in robustness against JPEG2000 compression. Performance of proposed scheme is also superior or competitive against other attacks such as rotation, filter or scaling.

Acknowledgement. This work is supported by the National Natural Science Foundation of China (No. 61372175) and National Key Laboratory Foundation (No. 2018SSFNKLSMT-13, No. HTKJ2019KL504006, No. HTKJ2019KL504007).

References

1. Muhammad, K., Sajjad, M., Mehmood, I., Rho, S., Baik, S.W.: A novel magic LSB substitution method (M-LSB-SM) using multi-level encryption and achromatic component of an image. Multimed. Tools Appl. **75**, 14867–14893 (2016). https://doi.org/10.1007/s11042-015-2671-9

2. Sahu, A.K., Swain, G.: An optimal information hiding approach based on pixel value differencing and modulus function. Wirel. Pers. Commun. (2019). https://doi.org/10.1007/s11277-019-06393-z

3. Kieu, T.D., Chang, C.-C.: A steganographic scheme by fully exploiting modification directions. Expert Syst. Appl. **38**, 10648–10657 (2011). https://doi.org/10.1016/j.eswa.2011.02.122

4. Chen, H., Ni, J., Hong, W., Chen, T.-S.: Reversible data hiding with contrast enhancement using adaptive histogram shifting and pixel value ordering. Signal Process. Image Commun. **46**, 1–16 (2016). https://doi.org/10.1016/j.image.2016.04.006

5. Vinoth Kumar, C., Natarajan, V.: Hybrid local prediction error-based difference expansion reversible watermarking for medical images. Comput. Electr. Eng. **53**, 333–345 (2016). https://doi.org/10.1016/j.compeleceng.2015.11.033

6. Wu, H., Huang, J.: Secure JPEG steganography by $LSB^{+;}$ matching and multi-band embedding. In: 2011 18th IEEE International Conference on Image Processing. pp. 2737–2740. IEEE, Brussels (2011). https://doi.org/10.1109/ICIP.2011.6116235

7. Wu, H.-T., Liu, Y., Huang, J., Yang, X.-Y.: Improved steganalysis algorithm against motion vector based video steganography. In: 2014 IEEE International Conference on Image Processing (ICIP), pp. 5512–5516. IEEE, Paris (2014). https://doi.org/10.1109/ICIP.2014.7026115

8. Cedillo-Hernandez, M., Garcia-Ugalde, F., Nakano-Miyatake, M., Perez-Meana, H.: Robust watermarking method in DFT domain for effective management of medical imaging. Signal Image Video Process. **9**, 1163–1178 (2015). https://doi.org/10.1007/s11760-013-0555-x

9. Urvoy, M., Goudia, D., Autrusseau, F.: Perceptual DFT watermarking with improved detection and robustness to geometrical distortions. IEEE Trans. Inf. Forensics Secur. **9**, 1108–1119 (2014). https://doi.org/10.1109/TIFS.2014.2322497

10. Hsu, L.-Y., Hu, H.-T.: Robust blind image watermarking using crisscross inter-block prediction in the DCT domain. J. Vis. Commun. Image Represent. **46**, 33–47 (2017). https://doi.org/10.1016/j.jvcir.2017.03.009

11. Liu, S., Pan, Z., Song, H.: Digital image watermarking method based on DCT and fractal encoding. IET Image Process. **11**, 815–821 (2017). https://doi.org/10.1049/iet-ipr.2016.0862

12. Patra, J.C., Phua, J.E., Bornand, C.: A novel DCT domain CRT-based watermarking scheme for image authentication surviving JPEG compression. Digit. Signal Process. **20**, 1597–1611 (2010). https://doi.org/10.1016/j.dsp.2010.03.010

13. Keshavarzian, R., Aghagolzadeh, A.: ROI based robust and secure image watermarking using DWT and Arnold map. AEU Int. J. Electron. Commun. **70**, 278–288 (2016). https://doi.org/10.1016/j.aeue.2015.12.003

14. Singh, A.K., Dave, M., Mohan, A.: Multilevel encrypted text watermarking on medical images using spread-spectrum in DWT domain. Wirel. Pers. Commun. **83**, 2133–2150 (2015). https://doi.org/10.1007/s11277-015-2505-0

15. Makbol, N.M., Khoo, B.E., Rassem, T.H.: Security analyses of false positive problem for the SVD-based hybrid digital image watermarking techniques in the wavelet transform domain. Multimed. Tools Appl. **77**, 26845–26879 (2018). https://doi.org/10.1007/s11042-018-5891-y

16. Vaishnavi, D., Subashini, T.S.: Robust and invisible image watermarking in RGB color space using SVD. Procedia Comput. Sci. **46**, 1770–1777 (2015). https://doi.org/10.1016/j.procs.2015.02.130

17. Su, Q., Niu, Y., Zhao, Y., Pang, S., Liu, X.: A dual color images watermarking scheme based on the optimized compensation of singular value decomposition. AEU Int. J. Electron. Commun. **67**, 652–664 (2013). https://doi.org/10.1016/j.aeue.2013.01.009

18. Zear, A., Singh, A.K., Kumar, P.: A proposed secure multiple watermarking technique based on DWT, DCT and SVD for application in medicine. Multimed. Tools Appl. **77**, 4863–4882 (2018). https://doi.org/10.1007/s11042-016-3862-8

19. Fazli, S., Moeini, M.: A robust image watermarking method based on DWT, DCT, and SVD using a new technique for correction of main geometric attacks. Optik. **127**, 964–972 (2016). https://doi.org/10.1016/j.ijleo.2015.09.205

20. Dong, H., He, M., Qiu, M.: Optimized gray-scale image watermarking algorithm based on DWT-DCT-SVD and chaotic Firefly algorithm. In: 2015 International Conference on Cyber-Enabled Distributed Computing and Knowledge Discovery. pp. 310–313. IEEE, Xi'an (2015). https://doi.org/10.1109/CyberC.2015.15

21. Hu, H.-T., Hsu, L.-Y.: Exploring DWT–SVD–DCT feature parameters for robust multiple watermarking against JPEG and JPEG2000 compression. Comput. Electr. Eng. **41**, 52–63 (2015). https://doi.org/10.1016/j.compeleceng.2014.08.001

22. Panetta, K., Gao, C., Agaian, S.: Human-visual-system-inspired underwater image quality measures. IEEE J. Ocean. Eng. **41**, 541–551 (2016). https://doi.org/10.1109/JOE.2015.2469915

JPEG Reversible Data Hiding with Matrix Embedding

Fangjun Huang[(⊠)] and Jiayong Li

Guangdong Provincial Key Laboratory of Information Security Technology,
School of Data and Computer Science, Sun Yat-sen University,
Guangzhou 510006, GD, China
huangfj@mail.sysu.edu.cn, lijy393@foxmail.com

Abstract. Joint photographic experts group (JPEG) image is the most popular image format used in our daily life. Different from the reversible data hiding (RDH) in spatial domain image, JPEG RDH needs to consider not only the visual quality, but also the file storage size of the marked image. In this paper, we firstly implement the matrix embedding (which is originated from steganography) strategy into the field of JPEG RDH. Via considering the philosophy behind the JPEG encoder, those quantized discrete cosine transform (DCT) coefficients that may introduce less distortion are adaptively selected for modification in the embedding process. Experimental results demonstrate that higher visual quality and less storage size of the marked JPEG image can be obtained compared with the state-of-the-art methods.

Keywords: Reversible data hiding · JPEG · Distortion

1 Introduction

Reversible data hiding (RDH) is a discipline developed at the end of last century [1]. It can imperceptibly hide data into digital images, and more importantly, the original image can be reconstructed completely while extracting the embedded data.

The RDH algorithms have been proposed on the basis of three fundamental strategies: lossless compression (LC) [2, 3], difference expansion (DE) [4, 5], and histogram shifting (HS) [6, 7]. Recently, some HS based strategies, such as two-dimensional histogram modification [8], multiple histograms modification [9, 10], and optimized histogram modification [11–13] were proposed, which have been approaching the rate distortion (*i.e.*, the embedding rate vs. visual distortion) upper bound. However, those methods designed for uncompressed image cannot be applied to JPEG image directly, since they may lessen the visual quality or increase the storage size of the marked JPEG image unpredictably.

In [2], Fridrich and Goljan firstly proposed a JPEG RDH algorithm. With dividing some elements of the quantization table by an integer, space can be created for embedding information, which was further improved by Wang *et al.* [14]. These methods can preserve the visual quality of the marked image well. However, the storage size of the marked JPEG image may greatly increase. In [15], Mobasseri *et al.* proposed a JPEG RDH algorithm via modifying the Huffman table of the JPEG file,

© Springer Nature Switzerland AG 2019
Y. Zhao et al. (Eds.): ICIG 2019, LNCS 11903, pp. 231–243, 2019.
https://doi.org/10.1007/978-3-030-34113-8_20

which was further improved by Qian and Zhang [16], and Hu *et al.* [17]. These methods can preserve the visual quality and storage size of the JPEG file perfectly. However, the embedding capacity is limited, and this may restrict its application. In [18], Huang *et al.* extended the HS strategy from spatial domain into JPEG domain. Through expanding the quantized DCT (qDCT) coefficients with values 1 and −1 to carry message bits, and with a new adaptive selection (*i.e.*, block selection) strategy, a tradeoff between the embedding capacity and distortion (including visual quality and storage space of the marked image) can be obtained. Recently, some new adaptive selection (*i.e.*, block selection and frequency selection) strategies were proposed by Wedaj *et al.* [19] and Hou *et al.* [20].

In this paper, we present a new JPEG RDH algorithm with matrix embedding [21, 22]. As we know, matrix embedding is a technique initially proposed for in the field of steganography. Through using it, less alternation needs to be made to the cover image while embedding the same amount of information bits. However, matrix embedding is designed for secret communication and can only ensure the successful extraction of the embedded information bits. If it is utilized in RDH directly, the original carrier image cannot be restored after data hiding. In this paper, we firstly design a new approach to apply matrix embedding technology to JPEG RDH, which can restore the original carrier image completely while extracting the embedded message bits. Experimental results demonstrate that compared with the state-of-the-art algorithms, good visual quality can be easily obtained. Meanwhile, the storage size of the original JPEG file can be well preserved.

The remainder of this paper is organized as follows. In Sect. 2, the proposed matrix embedding based RDH scheme for JPEG image is introduced. Experimental results and the comparison study are discussed in Sect. 3. Finally, we conclude in Sect. 4.

2   Proposed Scheme

In this section, an overview of HS-based RDH is introduced first, and then, we give our proposed RDH scheme for JPEG images.

2.1   Introduction of HS-Based RDH

HS is the most widely used RDH approach nowadays. As introduced in [18], the HS-based JPEG RDH algorithm consists of four steps, which are shown in Fig. 1.

The first step is to generate a sequence with a small entropy from the host image, which is shown in Fig. 1(a). The sequence can be realized by using the original qDCT coefficient histogram, the difference histogram, or the prediction error histogram. As pointed out in [18], the original qDCT coefficient histogram of JPEG image is quite sharp, and the data hiding can be easily performed on the qDCT coefficient histogram.

The second step is to divide the obtained histogram into two regions, *i.e.*, inner region and outer region, which is shown in Fig. 1(b). In general, some higher bins are divided into the inner region, while the remaining bins are divided into the outer region. For example, in Fig. 1(b) the histogram bins corresponding to coefficients with value 0,

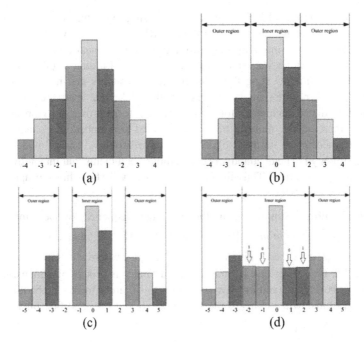

Fig. 1. The illustration of inner and out regions of HS method. (a) The original qDCT coefficient histogram of JPEG image, (b) the inner region and outer region, (c) shifting step, (d) expansion step.

1 and -1 are simply divided into inner region, and the remaining are divided into the outer region.

The third step is shifting, which is shown in Fig. 1(c). In this step, the bins in the outer region are shifted on both sides. Note that the shifting (and the subsequent expansion) of bins is achieved by modifying the corresponding qDCT coefficient values of the carrier image.

The fourth step is expansion, which is shown in Fig. 1(d). That is, the bins in the inner region are expanded to carry data. For example, for the coefficient with value 1, if message bit 1 is embedded, the coefficient becomes 2; otherwise if message bit 0 is embedded, the coefficient remains unchanged. Note that in this step, the coefficients with value 0 are not expanded to carry message bits.

As seen, in the third step the bins in the outer region are shifted to both sides, so that the inner and outer regions are still separate from each other after data hiding. In the receiving end, the receiver can easily extract the message bits and restore the original image.

2.2   Proposed JPEG RDH

As seen, for HS based JPEG RDH, the distortion mainly comes from two aspects, *i.e.*, shifting and expansion. Previously, the researchers mainly focused on how to reduce the number of shiftings and expansions, such as using more accurate prediction algorithms to generate PEE histograms, and using adaptive selection strategies. However, for JPEG image, even though the two RDH methods have the same number of shiftings and expansions, they may result in different visual qualities and storage sizes due to the quantization, run length coding and Huffman coding in the compressing process. Thus locating those modification positions that may introduce less distortion is another important factor. As mentioned before, matrix embedding is a previously introduced technique for steganography to improve the embedding efficiency (*i.e.*, increase the number of bits embedded per embedding change). It can decrease the necessary number of changes. Furthermore, some modern matrix embedding strategy [22] can adaptively select those coefficients that may introduce less distortion for modification. Thus in this section, we will show how to apply matrix embedding to JPEG RDH.

Matrix Embedding. Suppose that the message sequence to be embedded is $m = (m_1, \ldots, m_p)^T$, where $m_i \in \{0, 1\}$. The least significant bits (LSBs) of the qDCT coefficients selected for data hiding is $x = (x_1, \ldots, x_q)^T$, where $x_i \in \{0, 1\}$ and $q \geq p$. It is assumed that the sender and recipient share a binary matrix A of dimension $p \times q$, which can be generated randomly or according to different matrix embedding strategies. The data hider will modify some bits in x, so that the modified binary column $x' = (x'_1, \ldots, x'_q)^T$ satisfies:

$$Ax' = m \tag{1}$$

Thus, the sender needs to solve a system of linear equations over Galois field GF (2). According to the law of matrix embedding, the rank of the generated matrix A should be equal to p in general. Since the binary matrix A is with the dimension $p \times q$ and $q > p$ generally, the above equation may have multiple solutions. Therefore, the sender can select the solution that may result in higher visual quality and less file size increments.

After data hiding, the embedded message should be extracted without error. With sharing a secret key with the sender, the recipient can extract the modified LSB sequence $x' = (x'_1, \ldots, x'_q)^T$, the decoding is very simple because the recipient can extract the embedded message according to Eq. (2) directly, *i.e.*,

$$m = Ax' \tag{2}$$

However, the philosophy behind the matrix embedding can only ensure that the embedded message is extracted without error. As we know, in the field of RDH, the carrier image should also be restored completely. How to restore the carrier image will be explained in the next.

Distortion Function Designing. As introduced before, Eq. (1) may have many solutions, and the sender can select the solution that may result in minimal distortion. However, which solution can lead to minimal distortion?

Figure 2 illustrates the standard JPEG quantization table [23] corresponding to the quality factor (QF) of 80. It is known that the inverse discrete cosine transform (IDCT) is a linear transformation. Thus the modification to the qDCT coefficient associated with smaller quantization step may result in less visual distortion in the marked image [24, 25]. Based on this observation, in JPEG RDH, the message bits should be embedded into those coefficients belonging to the relatively low frequencies.

$$\begin{bmatrix} 6 & 4 & 4 & 6 & 10 & 16 & 20 & 24 \\ 5 & 5 & 6 & 8 & 10 & 23 & 24 & 22 \\ 6 & 5 & 6 & 10 & 16 & 23 & 28 & 22 \\ 6 & 7 & 9 & 12 & 20 & 35 & 32 & 25 \\ 7 & 9 & 15 & 22 & 27 & 44 & 41 & 31 \\ 10 & 14 & 22 & 26 & 32 & 42 & 45 & 37 \\ 20 & 26 & 31 & 35 & 41 & 48 & 48 & 40 \\ 29 & 37 & 38 & 39 & 45 & 40 & 41 & 40 \end{bmatrix}$$

Fig. 2. Standard JPEG quantization table corresponding to QF = 80.

Without loss of generality, the non-zero qDCT coefficients selected for RDH are represented by $c = (c_1, c_2, \ldots, c_N)$, where N represents the number of coefficients. Those selected coefficients are divided into two groups, *i.e.*, wet group (WG) and dry group (DG) [26]. In our method, all the coefficients with values 1 and -1 are divided into DG, and the rest are divide into WG. The coefficients in WG are assigned a large cost value and should be kept unchanged as many as possible; the coefficients in DG can be modified and assigned a cost value that is closely related to its associated quantization step. Suppose the quantization step associated with c_i is q_i. The distortion is represented as follows.

$$d_{c_i} = \begin{cases} q_i^\alpha & \text{if } c_i \in DG \\ \infty & \text{if } c_i \in WG \end{cases} \tag{3}$$

where α is a parameter that controls the impact of the quantization step. For all coefficients $(c_1, c_2, \ldots, c_N)$, the distortion values $(d_{c_1}, d_{c_2}, \ldots, d_{c_N})$ can be computed according to Eq. (3).

2.3   Embedding, Extraction, and Restoration

As before, the nonzero qDCT coefficients selected for RDH are represented by $c = (c_1, c_2, \ldots, c_N)$. Note that in our algorithm, the direct current (DC) coefficients are excluded, and only some non-zero alternating current (AC) coefficients are selected for matrix embedding. The number (N) of coefficients selected for RDH is determined by the number of message bits to be embedded and the distribution of AC coefficients.

Suppose the number of message bits is L, the number of coefficients with values 1 or -1 (*i.e.*, the dry coefficients) in the selected sequence c should be no less than $\beta \times L(\beta \geq 1)$, where β is a control parameter. With an appropriately selected β value, the efficiency of the matrix embedding can be improved, whereas less wet coefficients (*i.e.*, the coefficients do not have values 1 and −1) need to be modified in the embedding process. For the selected coefficient sequence (note that how to select the coefficient sequence c will be introduced in Sect. 2.4), a coefficient histogram can be constructed. The Bin 1 and Bin −1 are grouped into the inner region, and the rest of the bins into the outer region. Our algorithm has the following four steps.

The first step is to shift all outer coefficients to both sides as follows.

$$\tilde{c}_i = \begin{cases} c_i & \text{if } |c_i| = 1 \\ c_i + sign(c_i) & \text{if } |c_i| > 1 \end{cases} \tag{4}$$

where

$$sign(x) = \begin{cases} 1 & \text{if } x > 0 \\ 0 & \text{if } x = 0 \\ -1 & \text{if } x < 0 \end{cases} \tag{5}$$

After that, the shifted sequence $\tilde{c} = (\tilde{c}_1, \tilde{c}_2, \ldots, \tilde{c}_N)$ can be obtained.

The second step is to embed the message with matrix embedding. Suppose the message sequence to be embedded is $m = (m_1, m_2, \ldots, m_L)$, where L represents the number of message bits to be embedded and $m_i \in \{0, 1\}$. The LSB sequence of the shifted sequence $\tilde{c}$ is represented with $x = (x_1, \ldots, x_N)^T$., where $x_i \in \{0, 1\}$ and $N \geq L$. In our algorithm, the Syndrome-trellis Codes (STCs) [22] will be selected to embed the message bits because of its high embedding efficiency. According to our above analysis, when applying matrix embedding to the LSB sequence of those selected non-zero AC coefficients, the coefficients with minimal distortion, *i.e.*, those dry coefficients in DG will be preferentially modified. Suppose that the modified LSB sequence corresponding to the minimal distortion is $y = (y_1, \ldots, y_N)$. The distortion is computed as follows.

$$D(x, y) = \sum_{i=1}^{N} d_c f(x_i \neq y_i) \tag{6}$$

where

$$f(x) = \begin{cases} 1 & \text{if } x \text{ is true} \\ 0 & \text{if } x \text{ is false} \end{cases} \tag{7}$$

After achieving the optimal binary column y, the shifted coefficient sequence $\tilde{c}$ is modified as follows.

$$\tilde{\tilde{c}}_i = \begin{cases} \tilde{c}_i + sign(\tilde{c}_i) & \text{if } x_i \neq y_i \text{ and } |\tilde{c}_i| = 1 \\ \tilde{c}_i & \text{else} \end{cases} \tag{8}$$

In Eq. (8), the modified coefficient sequence is represented with $\tilde{\tilde{c}} = \left(\tilde{\tilde{c}}_1, \tilde{\tilde{c}}_2 \ldots, \tilde{\tilde{c}}_N \right)$. Note that in Eq. (8), when $x_i = y_i$, no modification needs to be made. In the case of $x_i \neq y_i$

and $\left|\widetilde{C_i}\right| = 1$, the corresponding coefficient $\widetilde{c}_i$ needs to be expanded to carry the message bits. Since $\left|\widetilde{C_i}\right| = 1$, the introduced distortion may be small according to our distortion definition in Eq. (3). In the case of $x_i \neq y_i$ and $\left|\widetilde{C_i}\right| \neq 1$, the LSB of corresponding coefficient $\widetilde{c}_i$ may also need to be modified in the matrix embedding process, otherwise the embedded message may fail to be extracted correctly. However, according to Eq. (3), the coefficient not equal to 1 or -1 (i.e., the wet coefficients) may introduce a large distortion while being modified. Thus in the case of $x_i \neq y_i$ and $\left|\widetilde{C_i}\right| \neq 1$, the coefficient will remain unchanged during the embedding process. But we will record the position of such coefficient, and the location will be embedded into some DC coefficients of the carrier image later as side information. In the experiments, we will demonstrate that with careful selection of the parameter β, few wet coefficients need to be modified in the embedding process.

In the extraction process, the side information are extracted first. Then locate the modified coefficient sequence $\widetilde{c}$. Suppose the LSB sequence of $\widetilde{\widetilde{c}}_i$ is represented by $\widetilde{\widetilde{y}}_i = \left(\widetilde{\widetilde{y}}_i, \widetilde{\widetilde{y}}_2 \ldots, \widetilde{\widetilde{y}}_N\right)^T$. Note that according to the extracted side information, if there are some wet coefficients which need to be modified in the matrix embedding process (these coefficients are not really modified and only the locations are recorded), we need to flip those elements in the extraction process. After flipping, suppose the coefficient sequence is $\tilde{y} = (\tilde{y}_1, \tilde{y}_2 \ldots, \tilde{y}_q)$. The message extraction and image restoration can be described as follows:

$$m' = A\tilde{y}^T \tag{9}$$

$$c'_i = \begin{cases} sign\left(\widetilde{\widetilde{c}}_i\right) & \text{if } 1 \leq \left|\widetilde{\widetilde{c}}_i\right| \leq 2 \\ \widetilde{\widetilde{c}}_i - sign\left(\widetilde{\widetilde{c}}_i\right) & \text{if } \left|\widetilde{\widetilde{c}}_i\right| \geq 3 \end{cases} \tag{10}$$

where $\tilde{y}^T$ represents the transpose of $\tilde{y}$, m' is the extracted message bit, and $c' = (c'_1, c'_2 \ldots, c'_N)$ is the restored quantized coefficient sequence, respectively.

2.4 Adaptive Selection Strategy

As shown, in our proposed method, the outer coefficients (with magnitude greater than 1) are shifted so that the inner and outer regions of the coefficient histogram are still kept separate from each other after data hiding. However, the inner coefficients are not expanded directly as that in the HS-based RDH scheme. As we know, if the number of the message bits to be embedded is L, in the HS-based RDH scheme, generally about $L/2$ inner coefficients need to be expanded since the message bits to be embedded are assumed to be uniformly distributed. When matrix embedding is adopted, the inner coefficients that need to be modified is generally less than $L/2$ because of the efficiency of the matrix embedding. That is the main reason why our new method may introduce less distortion. Secondly, according to our analysis previously, when some adaptive matrix embedding strategy is adopted, those coefficients that may introduce less distortion (including visual quality and file size) will be chosen for modification preferentially. That is the second reason that our method may have better performance.

However, as discussed in [22], the efficiency of matrix embedding has a close relationship with the relative wetness and relative payload, where the relative wetness represents the number of wet coefficients (*i.e.*, the coefficients not with values 1 and −1) per those coefficients selected for matrix embedding, and the relative payload represents the number of bits to be embedded per those dry coefficients (*i.e.*, the coefficients with values 1 and −1) selected for matrix embedding. In order to make sure that the number of wet coefficients is as few as possible (though those wet coefficients are kept unchanged, the locations of some wet coefficients may need to be recorded in the matrix embedding process according to the introduction above), the relative wetness or relative payload should be decreased as low as possible. Moreover, the outer coefficients do not carry any information, but they need to be shifted; this invalid shifting may lead to worse visual quality and larger storage size of the marked image.

Thus, for our block selection strategy, the first goal is to find the 8×8 blocks with fewer outer coefficients, and the coefficients belonging to these coefficient blocks will take precedence for data hiding. As described in [18], the 8×8 blocks with more zero coefficients will have fewer outer coefficients in general. Moreover, even the two blocks have the same number of non-zero coefficients, they may result in different distortion because those non-zero coefficients may be associated with different quantization steps.

Suppose that in one 8×8 block B_i, the non-zero qDCT coefficients are represented with $(NZ_1, \ldots, NZ_K)$, and the quantization steps associated with those coefficients are $(Q_1, \ldots, Q_K)$, where $K \leq 63$. Thus for each block, the distortion value is represented by

$$D_{B_i} = Q_1^{\gamma} + Q_2^{\gamma} + \cdots + Q_K^{\gamma} \tag{11}$$

where the parameter γ is selected as 2 in all our experiments. Those 8×8 blocks with less D_{B_i} will be chosen for RDH preferentially in our proposed algorithm.

Note that in the proposed algorithm, all the zero AC coefficients remain unchanged in the embedding process, and the distortion of each 8×8 block will never change in the data hiding process according to Eq. (11). The receiver can easily locate the blocks utilized for data hiding, then extract the embedded information and restore the host image.

2.5   Embedding, Extraction, and Restoration Steps

In the embedding process, side information such as message length, the parameter of STCs, the number of wet coefficients that need to be modified, and the positions of these wet coefficients, are embedded in the key determined l DC coefficients with LSB substitution. The original LSBs of those DC coefficients are appended as part of the payload before embedding. In the extraction and recovery process, the LSBs of the DC coefficients are read first to find the side information.

The embedding steps are as follows.

Step (1) Entropy-decode the original JPEG file to get the qDCT coefficients. Then, Compute d_{c_i} for each coefficient c_i according to Eq. (3), and calculate D_{B_i} according to Eq. (11) as well as the number of AC coefficients with values 1 and -1 for each 8×8 block B_i.

Step (2) Find the minimum threshold value T_D, and the corresponding 8×8 blocks whose distortion values computed according to Eq. (11) are no less than T_D. Note that the number of ± 1 coefficients (represented by S) belonging to those blocks should satisfy the following condition, *i.e.*, $S \geq \beta \times (L+l)$, where L denotes the number of message bits to be embedded, l represents the number of side information bits. For the ease of explanation, the nonzero AC coefficients in those blocks utilized for matrix embedding (ME) are called **ME coefficients** in the following.

Step (3) Scan all nonzero AC coefficients in a secret key determined order. If the coefficient to be visited is a **ME coefficient**, it will be shifted according to Eq. (4). When the number (represented by S) of visited coefficients is equal to $\beta \times (L+l)$, the scanning is completed.

Step (4) Extract all the LSBs of the **ME coefficients** visited in step 3, and embed the information bits (*i.e.*, the message bits to be embedded and the LSBs of the predetermined DC coefficients) with matrix embedding using the STCs [22]. The modified LSB sequence can be obtained, and the marked coefficient sequence can be computed according to Eq. (8). Note that in this step, all the wet coefficients are kept unchanged and the positions of those wet coefficients that may need to be modified in the matrix embedding process are recoded, which will be embedded into those predetermined DC coefficients in the next step.

Step (5) After all information bits (including the message bits and the LSBs of the predetermined DC coefficients) are embedded into the AC coefficients, the message length, the wet coefficient positions that may needed to be changed, and some other side information are embedded into the predetermined DC coefficients with LSB substitution.

Step (6) Entropy-encode the obtained coefficients to get the marked JPEG file.

The extraction and restoration steps are as follows.

Step (1) Entropy-decode the marked JPEG file to get the quantized DCT coefficients.

Step (2) Locate the predetermined DC coefficients, and extract the side information.

Step (3) Locate **ME coefficients** according to the key determined order, extract the information bits having been embedded and restore the original AC coefficients according to Eqs. (9) and (10), respectively.

Step (4) Restore the LSBs of the DC coefficients via using the extracted information bits.

Step (5) After all the qDCT (including DC and AC) coefficients are restored, entropy-encode the restored coefficients again to get the original JPEG file.

3 Experimental Results

In our experiments, the secret message bits are randomly generated, and the JPEG images are compressed with the optimized Huffman table by using the IJG toolbox [23]. The 1,000 images randomly selected from BOSSbase [27] are utilized in our testing.

To evaluate the performance of the proposed new scheme, the state-of-the-art RDH scheme [18] designed for JPEG images is selected for comparison. Note that, the main difference between our new proposed method and the scheme in [18] is the utilization of ME technology. The parameters regarding to ME are selected as $\alpha = 2, \beta = 1.25$, $\gamma = 2$ and $h = 16$, where α is a parameter to control the impact of the quantization step in Eq. (3), β is a parameter to control the message length, γ is a block selection parameter, and h regarding to the efficiency of ME [22]. In addition, in order to demonstrate the efficiency of the proposed block selection strategy, experimental results corresponding to the proposed algorithm without using the old block selection strategy [18] is also illustrated, which are represented with the label "Old Adaptive".

Two aspects, namely visual quality and file size preservation, are discussed. The peak signal-to-noise ratio (PSNR) value, which is calculated between the original JPEG

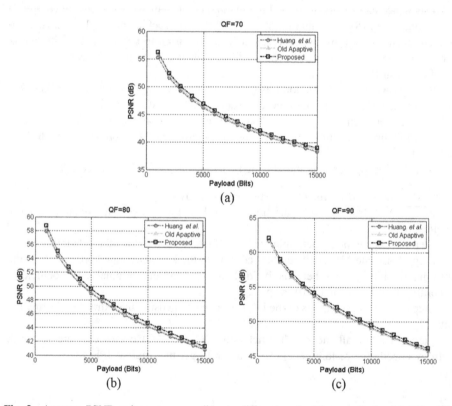

Fig. 3. Average PSNR values corresponding to different embedding payloads: (a) QF = 70 (b) QF = 80 (c) QF = 90.

image and the marked JPEG image, is used as a measure to evaluate the visual quality of the marked JPEG image.

3.1 Visual Quality

Three widely used image quality factors, *i.e.*, QF = 70, 80, 90 are tested. The testing results are shown in Fig. 3(a)–(c), where the horizontal axes represent the embedding payloads and the vertical axes represent the average PSNR values. The quality factor is shown in the title of each sub-figure. It is observed from Fig. 3 that the average PSNR values obtained by the proposed method are larger than those obtained by Huang *et al.*'s method [18] in general. However, without use of the block selection strategy (labeled as "Old adaptive"), the average PSNR values obtained by the proposed method will decrease, which implies the efficiency of our new adaptive selection strategy.

3.2 File Size Preservation

Figure 4 shows the average increased file sizes between the marked images and the original images. In Fig. 4(a)–(c), the horizontal axes represent the embedding payloads

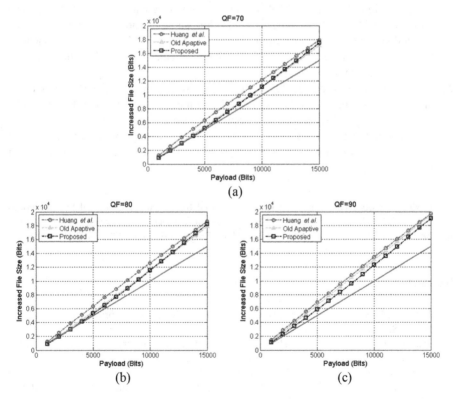

Fig. 4. Average increased file sizes corresponding to different embedding payloads: (a) QF = 70 (b) QF = 80 (c) QF = 90.

and the vertical axes represent the increased file sizes (bits). The solid magenta line in each sub-figure is used as a reference; every point on the line represents that the length of the embedded message bits is equal to the increased file size. As discussed earlier, the corresponding image quality factor is shown in the title of each sub-figure.

It is observed from Fig. 4 that the proposed method can preserve the file size constantly better than Huang *et al.*'s method [18]. Even if the block selection strategy is not applied in the embedding process, the increased file size of the proposed method is still less than that of Huang *et al.*'s methods. This implies that the proposed method can preserve the file size better than Huang *et al.*'s method.

4 Conclusions

Although a remarkable progress has been made in the field of JPEG RDH nowadays, compared to that in the airspace, there are still many shortcomings. Regardless of the visual quality or file size preservation, the performance of current methods is far from the upper bound. What's more, what is the upper bound for JPEG image, is still a problem. New JPEG RDH algorithms are called for. In this paper, we present a new RDH scheme for JPEG images. The main contributions of this paper are as follows:

(1) We firstly introduce matrix embedding (which is originated from steganography) into JPEG RDH. Via using matrix embedding strategy, more message bits can be embedded with less modifications. Moreover, those qDCT coefficients that may introduce less distortion can be adaptively selected for modifications in the embedding process.
(2) A novel block selection strategy has been proposed in this paper, which may result in better visual quality and less storage size of the marked JPEG file. It can also be utilized by other RDH schemes to improve their performance.
(3) Experimental results demonstrate that higher visual quality and less storage size of the marked JPEG image can be obtained compared with the state-of-the-art methods.

Acknowledgements. This work is partially supported by the National Natural Science Foundation of China (61772572), the NSFC-NRF Scientific Cooperation Program (61811540409), and the Natural Science Foundation of Guangdong Province of China (2017A030313366).

References

1. Barton, J.M.: Method and apparatus for embedding authentication information within digital data. U.S. Patent 5646997 (1997)
2. Fridrich, J., Goljan, M.: Lossless data embedding for all image formats. In: SPIE Proceedings of Photonics West, Electronic Imaging, Security and Watermarking of Multimedia Contents, vol. 4675, pp. 572–583 (2002)
3. Celik, M., Sharma, G., Tekalp, A., Saber, E.: Lossless generalized-LSB data embedding. IEEE Trans. Image Process. **14**(2), 253–266 (2005)

4. Tian, J.: Reversible data embedding using a difference expansion. IEEE Trans. Circuits Syst. Video Technol. **13**(8), 890–896 (2003)
5. Alattar, A.M.: Reversible watermark using the difference expansion of a generalized integer transform. IEEE Trans. Image Process. **13**(8), 1147–1156 (2004)
6. Ni, Z., Shi, Y., Ansari, N., Wei, S.: Reversible data hiding. IEEE Trans. Circuits Syst. Video Technol. **16**(3), 354–362 (2006)
7. Li, X., Li, B., Yang, B., Zeng, T.: General framework to histogram-shifting-based reversible data hiding. IEEE Trans. Image Process. **22**(6), 2181–2191 (2013)
8. Ou, B., Li, X., Zhao, Y., Ni, R., Shi, Y.-Q.: Pairwise prediction-error expansion for efficient reversible data hiding. IEEE Trans. Image Process. **22**(12), 5010–5021 (2013)
9. Li, X., Zhang, W., Gui, X., Yang, B.: Efficient reversible data hiding based on multiple histograms modification. IEEE Trans. Inf. Forensics Secur. **10**(9), 2016–2027 (2015)
10. Wang, J., Ni, J., Zhang, X., Shi, Y.-Q.: Rate and distortion optimization for reversible data hiding using multiple histogram shifting. IEEE Trans. Cybern. **47**(2), 315–326 (2017)
11. Zhang, X.: Reversible data hiding with optimal value transfer. IEEE Trans. Multimedia **15**(2), 316–325 (2013)
12. Hu, X., Zhang, W., Li, X., Yu, N.: Minimum rate prediction and optimized histograms modification for reversible data hiding. IEEE Trans. Inf. Forensics Secur. **10**(3), 653–664 (2015)
13. Zhang, W., Hu, X., Li, X., Yu, N.: Optimal transition probability of reversible data hiding for general distortion metrics and its applications. IEEE Trans. Image Process. **24**(1), 294–304 (2015)
14. Wang, K., Lu, Z.-M., Hu, Y.-J.: A high capacity lossless data hiding scheme for JPEG images. J. Syst. Software **86**, 1965–1975 (2013)
15. Mobasseri, B.G., Berger, R.J., Marcinak, M.P., NaikRaikar, Y.J.: Data embedding in JPEG bitstream by code mapping. IEEE Trans. Image Process. **19**(4), 958–966 (2010)
16. Qian, Z., Zhang, X.: Lossless data hiding in JPEG bitstream. J. Syst. Softw. **85**, 309–313 (2012)
17. Hu, Y., Wang, K., Lu, Z.-M.: An improved VLC-based lossless data hiding scheme for JPEG images. J. Syst. Softw. **86**, 2166–2173 (2013)
18. Huang, F., Qu, X., Kim, H.J., Huang, J.: Reversible data hiding in JPEG images. IEEE Trans. Circuits Syst. Video Technol. **26**(9), 1610–1621 (2016)
19. Wedaj, F.T., Kim, S., Kim, H.J., Huang, F.: Improved reversible data hiding in JPEG images based on new coefficient selection strategy. EURASIP J. Image Video Process. **63**, 1–11 (2017)
20. Hou, D., Wang, H., Zhang, W., Yu, N.: Reversible data hiding in JPEG image based on DCT frequency and block selection. Signal Process. **148**, 41–47 (2018)
21. Fridrich, J., Soukal, D.: Matrix embedding for Large Payloads. IEEE Trans. Inf. Forensics Secur. **1**(3), 390–395 (2006)
22. Filler, T., Judas, J., Fridrich, J.: Minimizing additive distortion in steganography using Syndrome-Trellis Codes. IEEE Trans. Inf. Forensics Secur. **6**(3), 920–935 (2010)
23. Wallace, G.K.: The JPEG still picture compression standard. IEEE Trans. Consumer Electron. **38**(1), xviii–xxxiv (1992)
24. Huang, F., Huang, J., Shi, Y.Q.: New channel selection rule for JPEG steganography. IEEE Trans. Inf. Forensics Secur. **7**(4), 1181–1191 (2012)
25. Huang, F., Kim, H.J.: Framework for improving the security performance of ordinary distortion functions of JPEG steganography. Multimedia Tools Appl. **75**, 281–296 (2016)
26. Fridrich, J., Goljan, M., Lisonek, P., Soukal, D.: Writing on wet paper. IEEE Trans. Inf. Forensics Secur. **53**(10), 3923–3935 (2005)
27. http://www.agents.cz/boss/BOSSFinal/

Detection and Localization of Video Object Removal by Spatio-Temporal LBP Coherence Analysis

Shanshan Bai[1,2], Haichao Yao[1,2], Rongrong Ni[1,2(✉)], and Yao Zhao[1,2]

[1] Institute of Information Science, Beijing Jiaotong University, Beijing 100044, China
rrni@bjtu.edu.cn
[2] Beijing Key Laboratory of Advanced Information Science and Network Technology, Beijing 100044, China

Abstract. Local object removal on video can directly affect our understanding and cognition of the video content without changing the motion continuity of other moving objects in the same video frame. Forgers can use video editing tools or certain inpainting techniques to remove undesired objects easily for covering up the truth. In this paper, we present a new approach based on spatio-temporal LBP coherence analysis for detection and localization of forged regions, which are generated by removing unwanted objects from the video. The proposed method starts with frames alignment to handle camera motion. And then the coherence analysis on the spatial LBP operator between two adjacent frames is performed to find the possible forged region. Finally, the temporal LBP operator is utilized to remove the false positives so as to obtain the final abnormal area. Two common region-level inpainting methods are adopted to simulate two different types of forgery processes for performance evaluation of our scheme. The experimental results prove that our method is effective in detecting and locating the forged regions and superior to the existing two approaches.

Keywords: Video forensics · Video inpainting detection · LBP · Coherence analysis

1 Introduction

Videos are generally regarded as unbiased and reliable records of events, and they have been widely used to provide basic evidences in many different fields. However, with the rapid development of digital media editing and inpainting techniques, it becomes easier for forgers to change the facts by removing undesired target from the video. Compared with the schemes that directly delete video frames containing the target, local removal of object does not destroy the continuity of other moving objects in the same frame. Tampered videos transmitted through the Internet can disrupt people's daily lives, and even interfere with the normal social order.

© Springer Nature Switzerland AG 2019
Y. Zhao et al. (Eds.): ICIG 2019, LNCS 11903, pp. 244–254, 2019.
https://doi.org/10.1007/978-3-030-34113-8_21

Over the past few years, several video forensic methods for object removal have been proposed. Hsu et al. [1] proposed an approach for detecting and locating the forged regions using block based correlation of noise residue. This method is based on the observation that correlation between temporal noise residue in forged regions of the frame is significantly different from that in the normal regions of a frame. While the noise correlation is unstable if the test videos suffer from abrupt illumination variations and sensitive to quantization noise. And the noise-residue correlation was also used to locate forgeries in [2–4]. Singh et al. [5] proposed a sensor pattern noise based detection scheme, which is an improved and forensically stronger version of noise-residue based technique. Wang et al. [6] developed a technique to uncover copy-paste forgeries in de-interlaced and interlaced videos using correlation coefficients. For de-interlaced video, tampering will destroy the correlations introduced by de-interlacing algorithms. Bestagini et al. [7] proposed a similar approach to solve this problem and locate the forgeries in the spatio-temporal domain. Zhang et al. [8] detected video forgery based on the ghost shadow artifact which is usually introduced when objects are removed by video inpainting technology. However, this method cannot accurately locate the forged regions and is vulnerable to the effects of noise. The technique proposed by Li et al. [9] is to uncover object removal of surveillance videos with stationary background using motion vector correlation analysis. And it is based on the observation that the distribution of the motion vectors in the foreground area between the authentic video and the forged are quite different. Lin et al. [10] analyzed the abnormalities in the spatio-temporal coherence between successive frames to detect and locate forged regions. But this approach only works well on uncompressed forged videos.

Inpainting techniques are used to fill the missing holes in a visually reasonable manner when unwanted objects are removed from the video. Temporal copy-and-paste (TCP) and exemplar-based texture synthesis (ETS) are two typical inpainting methods. The TCP method replaces the forged region with the most coherent area from the nearest frame, which leads to unnaturally high temporal coherence in the forged area. The ETS inpainting method proposed in [11] individually fills in the regions from sample textures for each frame, which leads to abnormally low temporal coherence in the forged region.

This paper aims to address the problem of detecting and locating forged regions based on the coherence analysis of spatio-temporal local binary patterns (LBP). LBP is a popular operator for describing the spatial structure of image texture, and it is not affected by illumination variations because of its invariance to monotonic gray level changes. It is robust to video compression since LBP describes the distribution of regional gray space, and compression does not change this relationship significantly. In view of its simplicity and effectiveness in image representation and classification, LBP and its variants have been applied in many research fields, such as facial image analysis and digital image/video forensics [12,13]. The major procedures of the proposed algorithm are as follows: (i) the motion vector (MV) of the background for each frame is computed to align video frames so as to realize the preprocessing of video captured by mobile camera; (ii) the coherence analysis on the spatial LBP operator between

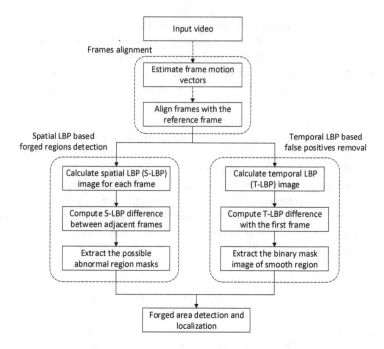

Fig. 1. Flowchart of our proposed method.

two adjacent frames is performed to find the possible forged region; (iii) the temporal LBP is utilized to remove false positives and the final abnormal region is located. Our method can be applied to videos taken by moving cameras. And the experimental results prove that it is effective and relatively robust to detect the forged region manipulated by well known inpainting methods such as TCP and ETS in video sequences.

The remainder of this paper is organized as follows. Section 2 gives the details of the proposed video forgery detection scheme based on spatio-temporal LBP coherence analysis. The experimental results are presented in Sect. 3. Finally, Sect. 4 summarizes the highlights and discusses the future work.

2   Proposed Method

The proposed method aims to expose the traces of object removal forgery in static and dynamic scene videos. Our idea is to detect the forged regions manipulated by TCP and ETS by means of finding the region with abnormal temporal correlation, because video subjected to such forgery exhibits unnaturally high or low correlation between region of successive video frames. As shown in Fig. 1, the proposed detection scheme consists of three major steps: (i) frames alignment, (ii) spatial LBP (S-LBP) based forged regions detection, and (iii) temporal LBP (T-LBP) based false positives removal. The details of the proposed method are given in following subsections.

2.1   Frames Alignment

In order to handle video motion caused by camera movement or shaking of the mobile phone, we adopt a simple block matching motion estimation algorithm to obtain the motion vector of each video frame to achieve frames alignment. In this paper, we use $\{F_1, F_2, \cdots, F_L\}$ to represent a video sequence V of length L, $L \in \mathbb{Z}^+$. And F_t represents the tth frame, $\mathbb{Z}^+$ is the set of positive integers. It is obvious that the background motion vector (Vx_t, Vy_t) of tth frame can be utilized as the tth frame motion vector.

For computational efficiency, we first convert the video sequence from three-dimensional color space to two-dimensional grayscale space. Then each frame is divided into non-overlapping b blocks with $M \times N$ pixels, and the motion vector of the ith block of tth frame can be denoted by (vx_t^i, vy_t^i). We use the exhaustive search (ES) algorithm and mean absolute deviation (MAD) matching criterion for each block between successive frames F_{t-1} and F_t to find the most similar block, and then obtain the motion vector of each block. In typical applications, the area of foreground regions is usually much smaller than that of the background region. Based on this assumption, choose the most frequent (vx_t^i, vy_t^i) as the background motion of F_t as follows:

$$V x_t = mode\{vx_t^1, vx_t^2, \cdots, vx_t^b\} \tag{1}$$

$$V y_t = mode\{vy_t^1, vy_t^2, \cdots, vy_t^b\} \tag{2}$$

where $mode(\cdot, \cdot, \cdots, \cdot)$ denotes that the value with the highest frequency in parentheses will be selected as the result. After the motion vector of each frame is obtained, the pixels in frame F_t are shifted by the cumulative vector (Cx_t, Cy_t) of the motion vectors of all frames before F_t. Cx_t and Cy_t can be calculated as follows:

$$Cx_t = \sum_{j=1}^{t} V x_j \tag{3}$$

$$Cy_t = \sum_{j=1}^{t} V y_j \tag{4}$$

2.2   Spatial LBP Based Forged Regions Detection

The spatial LBP (S-LBP) based forged regions detection is performed on the aligned frames. In this section, S-LBP is defined in 3×3 window as shown in Fig. 2. We take the center pixel of the window as the threshold and compare the gray values of 8 adjacent pixels with it: if the surrounding pixel value is greater than the center, then the binary code of the corresponding position is 1, otherwise 0. Finally, the S-LBP coded frame SL of each original video frame is obtained. The definition of SL is given by Eqs. (5) and (6).

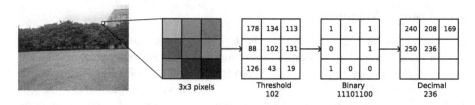

Fig. 2. The computation process of LBP.

$$SL(x_c, y_c) = \sum_{p=0}^{P-1} s(g_p - g_c)2^p \tag{5}$$

$$s(x) = \begin{cases} 1, & x \geq 0 \\ 0, & otherwise \end{cases} \tag{6}$$

where (x_c, y_c) represent the coordinates of center pixel, p denotes the serial number of the sampling point around (x_c, y_c), and g_c, g_p represent the gray value of (x_c, y_c) and its adjacent pixel respectively. P is the number of pixels around the center pixel, which is set to 8 here.

For analyzing the correlation between the previous frame F_{t-1} and the current frame F_t, we first calculate the frame difference S_d of two adjacent LBP frames. Then S_d is divided into non-overlapping blocks, and the number of zeros in the histogram vector for each block is counted. If a block is forged, the number of zeros in the block varies (increased or decreased) substantially depending on the forgery scheme (TCP or ETS). Figure 3 shows the average distribution of histograms of block-level (8 × 8 block) differences between every two consecutive LBP frames in three different cases. Note that the ordinates of the three figures are different. Obviously, the numbers of zeros and the distributions of histograms in forged region are significantly different from those of the original area. As a result, the forged region and non-forged one can be distinguished by analyzing the number of zeros Q in the histogram vector in each block of S_d. The preliminary classification is defined as follows:

$$Class_i = \begin{cases} 0, & T_1 < Q < T_2 \\ 1, & otherwise \end{cases} \tag{7}$$

where $Class_i$ denotes the binary classification mask of the ith block, and a value of 1 indicates that the block has been forged. T_1 and T_2 are thresholds for dividing the forged region and the normal. Finally, the pre-classification mask image of every original video frame is obtained by combining these block-level binary mask. Since the large smooth areas like sky can also lead to abnormally high correlation between two adjacent frames and interfere with the detection result, we elaborate the scheme for removing the false positive areas in the next section.

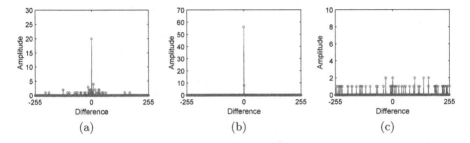

Fig. 3. The comparison of the histograms of block-level differences between every two consecutive LBP frames in three different cases: (a) normal region, (b) the block inpainted by TCP, and (c) the block inpainted by ETS. The abscissa represents the difference of pixels between adjacent LBP frames (ranging from -255 to 255), and the ordinate represents the number of zeros in the 8×8 block of S_d.

2.3 Temporal LBP Based False Positives Removal

In this section, temporal LBP (T-LBP) operator extended from the spatial domain is utilized to remove the false positives. The value of each pixel in the aligned frame obtained by Sect. 2.1 is computed by weighting the symmetric pixels within the range of 8 adjacent frames in temporal domain. That is, each T-LBP coded frame TL_t carries the information of video frames within 8 neighborhoods (16 frames in total). The mathematical definition of TL_t is as follows:

$$TL_t(x, y) = \sum_{r=1}^{R} s(G_{t-r}(x, y) - G_{t+r}(x, y))2^{r-1} \tag{8}$$

where R is the neighborhood radius in temporal domain, which is set to 8 here. $G_t(x, y)$ represents the gray value of pixel point whose coordinates are (x, y) in the tth aligned frame. Figure 4 shows the pixel pairs and their weights in the process of calculating $TL_t(x, y)$. Thus, the TL sequence of length $L - 16$ consisting of LBP-coded frames with the same size as the original video frames are obtained.

Large smooth areas causing false alarms are found by means of extracting the regions that remain stable for a period of time in TL sequence. The specific method is described as follows: similar to the previous section, we first calculate the frame difference between each current frame TL_t and the first LBP-coded frame to obtain the difference sequence of length $L - 17$. Then each difference frame is divided into non-overlapping blocks, and the number of zeros in the histogram vector of each block is counted. Finally, we convert each difference frame to a binary image based on a proper threshold as follows:

$$Class_i' = \begin{cases} 1, & Q' > T_3 \\ 0, & otherwise \end{cases} \tag{9}$$

where $Class_i'$ denotes the binary classification mask of the ith block, and a value of 1 indicates that the block belongs to the large smooth area. The binary mask

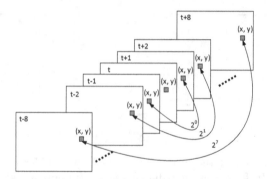

Fig. 4. Pixel pairs and their weights in the process of calculating $TL_t(x,y)$.

image of each difference frame is obtained by combining these block-level binary mask. And the mask image of the smooth region is obtained after OR operation and mathematical morphological processing as follows:

$$smooth = ((B_1 \bigcup B_2 \bigcup \cdots \bigcup B_{L-17}) \oplus E) \ominus E \qquad (10)$$

where B_t is the binary image filtered by the threshold of each difference frame. $\bigcup$ is the logical OR operator. E is a structuring element. $\oplus$ and $\ominus$ represent the morphological close and open respectively. Finally, the false positives removal operation is performed on each pre-classification mask image given in Sect. 2.2 according to binary mask image of the smooth region, and the final binary classification image and the localization result are obtained, as shown in Fig. 5.

3   Experimental Results

To evaluate the performance of our method, twenty test video sequences were prepared for the experiments. We classify these videos into three groups according to their sources and the states of the video background: group I contains 7 test videos with still background which were obtained from SULFA data set [14], and the resolution of each frame is 320×240 pixels. Group II contains 8 test videos that we have taken with static camera and group III contains the

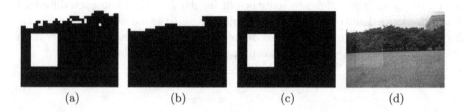

Fig. 5. The process of locating the forged region in a frame: (a) pre-classification mask image, (b) mask image of the smooth area in video, (c) final binary classification image, and (d) localization result.

remaining 5 videos with dynamic background taken by ourselves. The resolution of each frame in group II and III is 352×288 and the frame rate for all test videos is 30 fps. All the videos were forged by TCP and ETS inpainting methods respectively, and then re-encoded to H.264/AVC (with bitrates in the range of 1 Mbps to 5 Mbps) after the forgery. Through a large number of experiments, T_1, T_2 and T_3 are empirically set to 18, 63 and 30 for 8×8 blocks.

As shown in Table 1, the detection performance is measured by precision rate P, recall rate R, and F1-score $F1$, which are calculated as below:

$$P = TP/(TP + FP) \tag{11}$$

$$R = TP/(TP + FN) \tag{12}$$

$$F1 = (2 \times P \times R)/(P + R) \tag{13}$$

where TP denotes the number of correct detections, FP represents the number of false positives, and FN is the number of misses. Table 1 shows the average values of the experimental results for all videos in each group at 5 different bitrates. And it can be seen that the proposed method achieves high precision for both two video inpainting attacks, especially for TCP scheme. The performance of ETS tampered videos with a large amount of dynamic background is degraded because the errors of frames alignment operation make the authentic regions to be falsely classified as forged. Figure 6 shows the screenshots of the original frames, their inpainted frames forged by two inpainting schemes, and the corresponding localization results using the proposed method. The red blocks indicate the forged regions detected.

Table 1. Average performance of the proposed method for videos forged by TCP and ETS.

Group	TCP inpainting			ETS inpainting		
	Precision	Recall	F1	Precision	Recall	F1
I	0.9677	0.8937	0.9274	0.9483	0.8513	0.8969
II	0.9441	0.8640	0.9021	0.9243	0.8925	0.9077
III	0.9724	0.8623	0.9134	0.8271	0.7767	0.8002
Average	0.9614	0.8733	0.9143	0.8999	0.8402	0.8683

In addition, we make a comparison between the proposed approach and the existing methods presented by Hsu et al. [1] and Lin et al. [10], and the comparison results are shown in Table 2. It can be seen that our approach outperforms the other two algorithms and it achieves higher performance especially for ETS inpainting attack. There is no mechanism to remove false positive regions in the noise residual based method [1], so the performance of data set in group II with large smooth areas is obviously decreased. And since it is not available to dynamic background, we have not shown the relevant experimental results

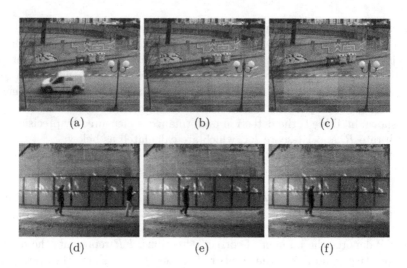

Fig. 6. Screenshots of the test video sequences: (a), (d) original frames, (b) the inpainted frame forged by TCP, (e) the inpainted frame forged by ETS, and (c), (f) the corresponding detection result. (Color figure online)

of group III. The performance of [10] drops significantly for videos forged by ETS inpainting compared with TCP since this method relies heavily on the edge detection of forgery region, and it is difficult to accurately extract the region boundary forged by ETS. The LBP operator and its variants used in our method are not affected by the change of illumination due to their invariance to monotonic gray level changes. In addition, the frames alignment operation enables video captured by the mobile camera to be detected.

Table 2. Comparison results between our method and two existing schemes presented by Hsu *et al.* [1] and Lin *et al.* [10].

Group	TCP inpainting			ETS inpainting		
	Hsu *et al.*	Lin *et al.*	Ours	Hsu *et al.*	Lin *et al.*	Ours
I	0.8672	0.9278	0.9677	0.8860	0.8521	0.9483
II	0.5448	0.9076	0.9441	0.8947	0.8148	0.9243
III	–	0.9311	0.9724	–	0.7238	0.8271
Average	0.7060	0.9222	0.9614	0.8904	0.7969	0.8999

In-depth analysis of the literatures revealed that the primary factors affecting the performance of inpainting detection techniques are the bitrates and compression quality of the test videos. Therefore, we present the forgery detection capabilities of these three forensic schemes for video sequences with bitrates in

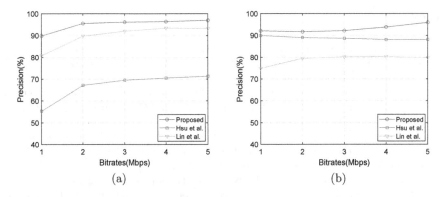

Fig. 7. Comparison of detection precision under different bitrates settings: (a) forged by TCP inpainting scheme, and (b) forged by ETS inpainting scheme.

the range of 1 Mbps to 5 Mbps as shown in Fig. 7. It can be seen that the spatio-temporal LBP based approach still has high precision rate in the case of decreasing the bitrate. This is because the LBP operator and its variants describe the distribution of regional gray space, which does not change significantly during the compression process.

4   Conclusion

In this paper, we have presented a detection and localization method for video object removal forgery based on spatio-temporal LBP coherence analysis. We first perform frames alignment to handle camera motion. Then we use spatial LBP operator making coherence analysis to find the possible abnormal areas. Finally, the temporal LBP operator is utilized to remove the authentic regions that are falsely classified as forged to locate the final forged areas. In our experiments, two video inpainting schemes (TCP and ETS) are used to simulate two different types of tampering processes for performance evaluation. The experimental results prove that our method can detect and locate the forged regions effectively and keep stability with respect to decreased bitrates. It can also be applied to videos taken by mobile cameras or handheld phones. However, great shaking and even slightly rotating of the forged video will cause unsatisfactory experimental results. The main reason is that the coherence analysis does not work well under the above conditions because the difference between two normal frames can be very large. In the future, we will explore ways to solve the problems above and improve the scope of the applicability.

Acknowledgements. This work was supported in part by the National Key Research and Development of China (2016YFB0800404), National NSF of China (61672090, 61532005), and Fundamental Research Funds for the Central Universities (2018JBZ001).

References

1. Hsu, C.-C., Hung, T.-Y., Lin, C.-W., Hsu, C.-T.: Video forgery detection using correlation of noise residue. In: 2008 IEEE 10th Workshop on Multimedia Signal Processing, pp. 170–174. IEEE (2008)
2. Chetty, G.: Blind and passive digital video tamper detection based on multimodal fusion. In: Proceedings of 14th WSEAS International Conference on Communications, Corfu, Greece, pp. 109–117 (2010)
3. Goodwin, J., Chetty, G.: Blind video tamper detection based on fusion of source features. In: 2011 International Conference on Digital Image Computing: Techniques and Applications, pp. 608–613. IEEE (2011)
4. Pandey, R.C., Singh, S.K., Shukla, K.K.: Passive copy-move forgery detection in videos. In: 2014 International Conference on Computer and Communication Technology (ICCCT), pp. 301–306. IEEE (2014)
5. Singh, R.D., Aggarwal, N.: Detection and localization of copy-paste forgeries in digital videos. Forensic Sci. Int. **281**, 75–91 (2017)
6. Wang, W., Farid, H.: Exposing digital forgeries in video by detecting duplication. In: Proceedings of the 9th Workshop on Multimedia & security, pp. 35–42. ACM (2007)
7. Bestagini, P., Milani, S., Tagliasacchi, M., Tubaro, S.: Local tampering detection in video sequences. In: 2013 IEEE 15th International Workshop on Multimedia Signal Processing (MMSP), pp. 488–493. IEEE (2013)
8. Zhang, J., Su, Y., Zhang, M.: Exposing digital video forgery by ghost shadow artifact. In: Proceedings of the First ACM Workshop on Multimedia in Forensics, pp. 49–54. ACM (2009)
9. Li, L., Wang, X., Zhang, W., Yang, G., Hu, G.: Detecting removed object from video with stationary background. In: Shi, Y.Q., Kim, H.-J., Pérez-González, F. (eds.) IWDW 2012. LNCS, vol. 7809, pp. 242–252. Springer, Heidelberg (2013). https://doi.org/10.1007/978-3-642-40099-5_20
10. Lin, C.-S., Tsay, J.-J.: A passive approach for effective detection and localization of region-level video forgery with spatio-temporal coherence analysis. Digit. Invest. **11**(2), 120–140 (2014)
11. Criminisi, A., Pérez, P., Toyama, K.: Region filling and object removal by exemplar-based image inpainting. IEEE Trans. Image Process. **13**(9), 1200–1212 (2004)
12. Li, L., Li, S., Zhu, H., Chu, S.-C., Roddick, J.F., Pan, J.-S.: An efficient scheme for detecting copy-move forged images by local binary patterns. J. Inf. Hiding Multimedia Signal Process. **4**(1), 46–56 (2013)
13. Zhang, Z., Hou, J., Ma, Q., Li, Z.: Efficient video frame insertion and deletion detection based on inconsistency of correlations between local binary pattern coded frames. Secur. Commun. Netw. **8**(2), 311–320 (2015)
14. Qadir, G., Yahaya, S., Ho, A.T.S.: Surrey university library for forensic analysis (SULFA) of video content (2012)

An Image Splicing and Copy-Move Detection Method Based on Convolutional Neural Networks with Global Average Pooling

Qian Zhang[1,2], Jun Sang[1,2(✉)], Weiqun Wu[1,2], Bin Cai[1,2],
Zhongyuan Wu[1,2], and Haibo Hu[1,2]

[1] Key Laboratory of Dependable Service Computing in Cyber Physical Society
of Ministry of Education, Chongqing University, Chongqing 40004, China
jsang@cqu.edu.cn
[2] School of Big Data and Software Engineering, Chongqing University,
Chongqing 401331, China

Abstract. Splicing and copy-move are two well-known methods of image tampering, while detection of image splicing and copy-move forgery is an important research topic in image forensics. In this paper, a method based on convolutional neural network with global average pooling was proposed for splicing and copy-move tampering detection. To detect image tampering, the inconsistency between the authentic images and the tampered images should be captured regardless of the image contents. So, the existing strategy using high-pass filter in SRM as initialization of the first layer was improved to reduce the influence of image content and make the features more diverse on each channel at the same time. In order to reduce the number of parameters in the fully connected layers and avoid overfitting, global average pooling was utilized before fully connected layers in the proposed model. Experiments on three public image tampering datasets demonstrated that the proposed method outperformed some state-of-the-art methods.

Keywords: Image tampering detection · Image splicing · Copy-move ·
Convolutional neural networks (CNNs) · SRM (Spatial Rich Model) · Global
average pooling

1 Introduction

With the development of digitization and informatization, digital image has become an important information carrier. At the same time, the emergence of more and more powerful and sophisticated image processing software makes it easy to modify and manipulate images without leaving any traceable proof. However, illegal use of the forged images results in negative impact on human cognition and judgment of the objective world. Therefore, image forensics is an urgent problem to be solved, and a research hotspot in the field of information security.

Among many image tampering methods, splicing and copy-move are the most commonly used. In image splicing forgery, one region is cut and pasted to another image; while in copy-move forgery, one region is copied and pasted over other region

© Springer Nature Switzerland AG 2019
Y. Zhao et al. (Eds.): ICIG 2019, LNCS 11903, pp. 255–265, 2019.
https://doi.org/10.1007/978-3-030-34113-8_22

in the same image [1]. Many splicing detection methods [2–5] and copy-move detection approaches [1, 6–8] based on handcrafted features have been proposed to detect these two kinds of image tampering, respectively.

In recent years, some researchers have applied deep learning to image tampering detection. Rao et al. [9] proposed a convolutional neural network (CNN) to automatically learn feature from images, and used the high-pass filters in Spatial Rich Model (SRM) [10] as the initialization of the first layer to suppress the image content. In [11], a Stacked Autoencoder model was used to learn the complex feature to detect tampered images with different image formats. Chen et al. [12] proposed a new technique based on the analysis of the camera response functions combining with CNN for splicing and copy-move detection and localization. In [13], resampling features and deep learning were used to detect and localize image manipulations. Pomari et al. [14] combined the high representation power of Illuminant Maps with CNN to eliminated the laborious feature engineering process and locate forgery region. In [15], the noise features were extracted from a SRM filter layer to discover the noise inconsistency for tampered regions detection.

In this paper, a CNN model referencing to VGGNet [16] for image splicing and copy-move detection was proposed by analyzing the structure in [9]. Inspired by [9, 15], our initialization strategy of the first layer using 30 high-pass filters in SRM ensured not only suppression for image content, but also more diverse features on each channel. In addition, as there were too many parameters in the 5×5 convolutional layer in [9], two 3×3 convolutional layers were stacked to replace the 5×5 convolutional layer. In order to further reduce overfitting and improve network performance, global averaging pooling was applied before the fully connected layer of the network. Experimental results showed that the proposed method outperformed some existing methods on 3 public datasets.

The rest of the paper is organized as follows. In Sect. 2, the proposed method is described in detail. Section 3 presents and discusses experimental results and analysis. Finally, Sect. 4 contains the conclusion and future work.

2   The Proposed Method

2.1   Global Average Pooling

Convolutional neural networks (CNNs) usually use the fully connected layer in the last several layers to weight the features of the convolutional layer. Each neuron in the fully connected layer is connected to all of the neurons in the previous layer, so the fully connected layers usually have many parameters. Also, the fully connected layers tend to overfitting because of too many parameters, thus hampering the generalization ability of the overall network.

In [17], global average pooling (GAP) was proposed to replace fully connected layers, which required the last convolutional layer to output the same number of feature maps as the number of categories. The global average pooling calculates the average value for each feature map as the output, and there is no parameter to optimize. However, the number of the output feature maps of the last convolutional layer was inconsistent with the number of categories in our proposed method. So, the global average pooling could not directly replace the fully connected layer and was added before the fully connected layer to decrease the dimension of the feature and reduce the parameters in fully connected layers. Figure 1 shows the difference between the fully connected layer and GAP.

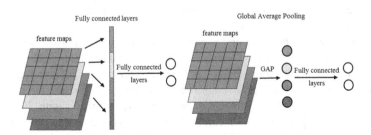

Fig. 1. The difference between the fully connected layer and GAP.

In Fig. 1, suppose there are four feature maps with size of 5×5, and the final output category is 2. Without applying GAP, the feature maps are constructed into a 100-dimensional vector, and then the vector is fully connected with the output. In this way, there are 200 parameters. By applying GAP, the global average value of each feature map is calculated to get a 4-dimensional vector, and then the vector is fully connected with the output. So, only 8 parameters are needed. By using GAP, the number of parameters for fully connected layer is greatly reduced.

Considering the finiteness of training data and the subtlety of tampering features, global averaging pooling was applied in our proposed network to avoid overfitting and improve performance.

2.2 High Pass Filtering

In 2012, Fridrich et al. [10] proposed a steganalysis method based on SRM, which constructed a set of high-pass filters of linear and nonlinear to obtain a variety of residual images. The image steganalysis methods based on SRM model the residual image rather than directly model the image itself, aiming at suppressing the influence of image content on steganalysis and strengthen the steganographic signal. There were 30 basic filters in a set of high-pass filters and they were divided into six categories, including "1st", "2nd", "3rd", "SQUARE", "EDGE3 $\times$ 3", and "EDGE5 $\times$ 5".

Image forgery detection, like image steganalysis, does not focus on the content of image, but only on the subtle artifacts (noise) introduced by the tampering operations. So the high pass filters in SRM have been used in image forgery detection to suppress the image content. Cozzolino et al. [18] and Verdoliva et al. [19] computed the residuals with a third-order ("3rd") linear high-pass filter to ensure a good performance for forgery detection. Based on the high-pass filter residuals, tampering detection and localization were carried out through a series of operations such as quantization and computation of co-occurrences histogram.

High-pass filters in SRM were not only used in image forgery detection based on traditional methods, but also in the deep learning based methods. Rao et al. [9] proposed a 10-layer CNN using the 30 basic high-pass filters in SRM for initialization of the first layer to detect splicing and copy-move images. The initialization served as a regularizer to suppress the image content and capture the subtle artifacts introduced by the tampering operations. Zhou et al. [15] proposed a two-stream Faster R-CNN for image tampering detection and localization, in which three high-pass filters in SRM were also used to extract noise features.

In our proposed method, the first convolutional layer was initialized with 30 high-pass filters in SRM to focus on the subtle tampering artifacts referencing to [9]. But compared with the initialization strategy in [9], our strategy was simpler and made the features diverse on each channel for color image. For grayscale images, the input image had only one channel, and the first layer was initialized directly with 30 high-pass filters. For color images, the input includes 3 channels and the weight of each channel was initialized with 30 high-pass filters. The initialization of each channel weight is defined as follows:

$$W_{CNN}(x, y) = W_{SRM}(x, y) \tag{1}$$

Where W_{CNN} and W_{SRM} are the weight matrix of size 5×5 used on every channel and the filter kernels of size 5×5 in SRM, respectively, and $x, y = 1, 2, 3, 4, 5$.

2.3   Network Architecture

In [9], a 10 layers CNN (denote as RaoNet) was designed for image splicing and copy-move detection, which can automatically learn feature representations from the input images. The 10-layer CNN structure was shown in Fig. 2. It consisted of 8 convolutional layers, 2 pooling layers and a fully connected layer with a softmax classifier. The first and second convolutional layers had 30 filters of size 5×5, while other convolutional layers all had 16 filters of size 3×3. The first convolutional layer was initialized with 30 basic high-pass filters in SRM, while other layers were initialized with "xavier". The stride of the second convolutional layer was set to 2, and the stride of other convolutional layers was set to 1. Max pooling with filter of size 2×2 was used

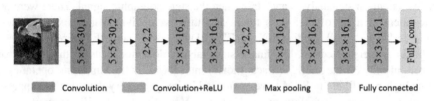

Fig. 2. The architecture of RaoNet [9]. $\{5 \times 5 \times 30, 1\}$ denotes 30 convolution kernels of 5×5, and the stride is 1. $\{2 \times 2, 2\}$ denotes pooling of 2×2, and the stride is 2.

after the second and fourth convolutional layers. Activation function was Rectified Linear Units (ReLU), and fully connected layer was followed by dropout technique.

Three observations can be drawn from Fig. 2. Firstly, there were two convolutional layers with 5 × 5 filter in the RaoNet. It was verified in VGGNet that the stack of two 3 × 3 convolutional layers had an equivalent receptive field of 5 × 5, and the number of parameters was also decreased. Therefore, we replaced the second 5 × 5 convolutional layer in RaoNet with two 3 × 3 convolutional layers. In order to further reduce the number of parameters, the number of convolutional kernels was also modified to 16. Secondly, it was noted that the convolutional layer with a stride 2 was followed by the pooling layer with a stride 2 in RaoNet, which made the size of the feature map rapidly reduced and the feature information seriously lost. To solve this problem, the structure of RaoNet was improved by adjusting the location of pooling layer and increasing the number of network layers. Lastly, only one necessary fully connected layer in RaoNet was used at the end of the network aiming at reducing parameters. To further reduce the number of parameters and avoid overfitting, we used global average

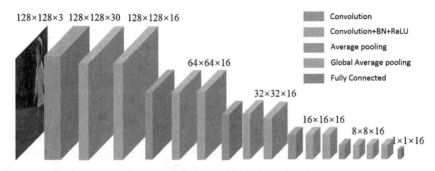

Fig. 3. The proposed CNN architecture.

pooling before the fully connection layer in the proposed model. Based on the above analysis, we proposed a CNN model as shown in Fig. 3.

The proposed network model contained 11 convolutional layers, 4 average pooling, 1 global average pooling, and 1 fully connected layer with 2-way softmax classifier. The first convolutional layer had 30 filters of size 5 × 5 and was initialized with 30 basic high-pass filters in SRM. Other convolutional layers had 16 filters of size 3 × 3 and were initialized with "xavier". Except for the first layer, BN and ReLU were used after other convolutional layers. Average pooling was used in the proposed model, and global average pooling was applied before the fully connected layers. RaoNet had 41,390 parameters to be trained, while our proposed model had 27,338 parameters. Compared with RaoNet, the layer number of the proposed network model was increased, but the number of parameters was only 66.03% of RaoNet. The number of parameters in the fully connected layer were also reduced from 800 to 32. The detailed network structure of the proposed model was shown in Table 1.

Table 1. The detailed structure of the proposed CNN.

Layer	Input size	Process	Kernels size	Output size
1	128 × 128 × 3	High pass filtering	30 × 5 × 5 (stride 1)	128 × 128 × 30
2	128 × 128 × 16	Conv-BN-ReLU	16 × 3 × 3 (stride 1)	128 × 128 × 16
3	128 × 128 × 16	Conv-BN-ReLU	16 × 3 × 3 (stride 1)	128 × 128 × 16
4	128 × 128 × 16	Average pooling	2 × 2 (stride 2)	64 × 64 × 16
5	64 × 64 × 16	Conv-BN-ReLU	16 × 3 × 3 (stride 1)	64 × 64 × 16
6	64 × 64 × 16	Conv-BN-ReLU	16 × 3 × 3 (stride 1)	64 × 64 × 16
7	64 × 64 × 16	Average pooling	2 × 2 (stride 2)	32 × 32 × 16
8	32 × 32 × 16	Conv-BN-ReLU	16 × 3 × 3 (stride 1)	32 × 32 × 16
9	32 × 32 × 16	Conv-BN-ReLU	16 × 3 × 3 (stride 1)	32 × 32 × 16
10	32 × 32 × 16	Average pooling	2 × 2 (stride 2)	16 × 16 × 16
11	16 × 16 × 16	Conv-BN-ReLU	16 × 3 × 3 (stride 1)	16 × 16 × 16
12	16 × 16 × 16	Conv-BN-ReLU	16 × 3 × 3 (stride 1)	16 × 16 × 16
13	16 × 16 × 16	Average pooling	2 × 2 (stride 2)	8 × 8 × 16
14	8 × 8 × 16	Conv-BN-ReLU	16 × 3 × 3 (stride 1)	8 × 8 × 16
15	8 × 8 × 16	Conv-BN-ReLU	16 × 3 × 3 (stride 1)	8 × 8 × 16
16	8 × 8 × 16	GAP	16 × 8 × 8	1 × 1 × 16
17	1 × 1 × 16	Fully connected	–	1 × 1

3   Experiments

The CPU and GPU of the experimental computer were Intel (R) Xeon CPU e5-2683 v3@2.00 GHz and NVIDIA TESLA K80, respectively. The experimental platform was equipped with 64 bit ubuntu14.04, Anaconda3.4, CUDA Toolkit9.0, Opencv3.4. The proposed model was implemented using TensorFlow framework.

3.1   Dataset for Experiments

The datasets used in our experiment to analyze the accuracy of proposed method were the CASIA v1.0 [20], CASIA v2.0 [20] and Columbia gray datasets [21]. The CASIA v1.0 dataset consists of 800 authentic and 921 forged color images with size of 384 × 256. All of the images are in JPEG format without applying any post processing. The CASIA v2.0 dataset contains 7,491 authentic and 5,123 tampered color images with size ranging from 240 × 160 to 900 × 600 pixels in JPEG, BMP and TIFF formats. The geometric transforms, such as scaling and rotation, are applied for cropped image regions for the CASIA v1.0 and CASIA v2.0 datasets. In addition, post-processing is also adopted to forged image for the CASIA v2.0 datasets. The Columbia gray dataset contains 933 authentic and 912 spliced gray images with size of 128 × 128 in BMP format, and no post-processing is applied to the splicing image.

In the experiment, images in the CASIA v1.0 and CASIA v2.0 datasets were cropped to 128 × 128, which is helpful for CNN to learn more representative samples. For authentic image, a patch of 128 × 128 was cropped randomly from the image. For the tampered image, a patch of 128 × 128 was also cropped, while the ratio between the tampered region and the original region was kept as 1:1 as possible.

3.2   Experimental Settings

Due to the large difference between the number of the authentic images and that of the tampered images in the CASIA v2.0 dataset, 5123 authentic image were randomly selected from 7413 authentic images to keep balance between authentic and forged images. To evaluate the performance of the proposed method, 5/6 of the images were selected for training and 1/6 of the remaining images were used for testing. The training data were augmented by flipping horizontally and vertically for Columbia gray dataset. A six fold cross-validation evaluation protocol was adopted to validate the performance of proposed method. Adam was used to optimize the network. Initial learning rate, batch size and maximum epoch were set to 0.001, 32, and 500, respectively.

3.3   Results and Analysis

Effectiveness of Initialization with SRM. The first layer of the network was initialized with the 30 basic high-pass filters in SRM, which was helpful for the network to learn tampering features. Table 2 showed the comparison results between using SRM as the initialization of the first convolutional layer (denoted as CNN-SRM) and using "xavier" as the initialization of the first layer (denoted as CNN-xavier) for proposed model on Columbia gray, CASIA v1.0, and CASIA v2.0 datasets.

Table 2. Detection accuracy (%) with and without SRM initialization.

Method	Columbia gray	CASIA v1.0	CASIA v2.0
CNN-xavier	94.90	93.93	99.27
CNN-SRM	97.82	99.30	99.70

As can be seen from Table 2, when the high-pass filters were used to initialize the first convolutional layer, the detection accuracy was improved by 2.92%, 5.37% and 0.43% on Columbia gray, CASIA v1.0 and CASIA v2.0 datasets, respectively. Compared with the Columbia gray and CASIA v1.0 datasets, CASIA v2.0 dataset has more samples in it, and the improvement was not obvious for the CASIA v2.0 dataset.

We further compared the convergence of proposed model using SRM and not using SRM. Figure 4 showed the evolutions of training loss versus number of epochs on 3 datasets. It was observed that the CNN-SRM converged much faster and had smaller fluctuations than CNN-xavier in training loss.

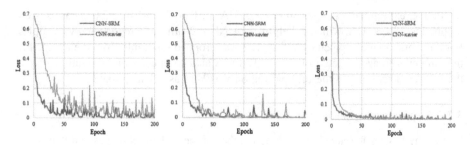

Fig. 4. The convergence comparison between CNN-SRM and CNN-xavier on Columbia gray, CASIA v1.0 and CASIA v2.0 datasets, respectively.

Performance Comparisons with Different Pooling Methods. Image tampering detection does not focus on the content of images, but on the noise features introduced by tampering. In order to explore the suitable pooling for image tampering detection, comparative experiments were conducted with average pooling and max pooling on Columbia gray, CASIA v1.0 and CASIA v2.0 datasets. Table 3 presented the detection accuracy of the comparison.

Table 3. Detection performance (%) of the proposed method with different pooling.

Method	Columbia gray		CASIA v1.0		CASIA v2.0	
	Average pooling	Max pooling	Average pooling	Max pooling	Average pooling	Max pooling
RaoNet	–	96.38	97.71	97.39	97.48	97.83
Ours	97.82	97.57	99.30	99.06	99.70	99.79

For Columbia gray dataset, the detection accuracy was 96.36% for RaoNet using max pooling, while it cannot obtain a decent result using average pooling. And the accuracy of the proposed model with average pooling was better than with max pooling on Columbia gray dataset. On CASIA v1.0 dataset, RaoNet and the proposed model achieved better performance using average pooling. While both RaoNet and the proposed model obtained higher accuracy using max pooling on CASIA v2.0 dataset. Overall, the difference of detection accuracy with average pooling or max pooling was not very obvious on the three datasets.

Effectiveness with GAP. In order to verify the effectiveness with GAP, the comparison results with and without GAP were shown in Table 4. The detection accuracy with GAP was higher than that of without GAP on Columbia gray, CASIA v1.0 and CASIA v2.0 datasets, regardless of whether the max pooling or average pooling were used. And it can be observed that the performance improvement with GAP was more obvious on the CASIA v1.0 dataset. It may be that there was less data in CASIA v1.0 dataset and the parameters in fully connected layer were not adequately trained, resulting in overfitting. Therefore, GAP can improve network performance by reducing the number of parameters.

Table 4. Detection accuracy (%) with and without GAP.

Method	Columbia gray		CASIA v1.0		CASIA v2.0	
	Average pooling	Max pooling	Average pooling	Max pooling	Average pooling	Max pooling
Ours (without-GAP)	97.07	97.45	96.11	96.10	99.33	99.45
Ours (with-GAP)	97.82	97.57	99.30	99.06	99.70	99.79

Performance Comparisons with Other Methods. Finally, to evaluate the performance of the proposed method, the proposed method was compared with other existing methods and the experimental results were shown in Table 5.

Table 5. Detection accuracy (%) compared with other methods on three datasets.

Methods	Columbia gray	CASIA v1.0	CASIA v2.0
Muhammad [7]	–	94.89	97.33
Goh [8]	–	90.18	96.21
Rao [9]	96.38	98.04	97.83
Prakash [1]	–	99.44	98.89
Han [5]	91.28	98.95	97.28
Ours	97.82	99.30	99.70

As shown in Table 5, the proposed method outperformed some existing methods with an accuracy of 97.82%, 99.30% and 99.70% on Columbia gray, CASIA v1.0 and CASIA v2.0 datasets, respectively. Since the Columbia gray dataset consists of grayscale images, the methods [1, 7, 8] based on *YCbCr* channels were not applicable. While the proposed method was applicable not only to color images, but also to grayscale images. The accuracy of our method was lower than that of the method in [1] by 0.14% on CASIA v1.0 dataset, but our proposed method outperforms the method in [1] by 0.81% on the more challenging CASIA v2.0 dataset. Compared with RaoNet in [9], the accuracy of the proposed method was higher by 1.44%, 1.26% and 1.87% on Columbia gray, CASIA v1.0 and CASIA v2.0 datasets, respectively.

4 Conclusions

In this paper, we presented a method based on CNN with GAP to detect image tampering, which could be applied to the splicing and copy-move tampering at the same time. The proposed CNN model included 11 convolutional layers, 4 average pooling, 1 global average pooling, and 1 fully connected layer. Every two 3×3 convolutional layers was followed by a pooling layer. In order to reduce the influence of image content on tampering features and made the features diverse on each channel, a simple strategy was adopted to initialize the first convolutional layer of the proposed CNN with 30 high-pass filters in SRM. Global average pooling was adopted before fully connected layers to reduce the parameters and avoid the network overfitting. The experiments demonstrated that the proposed method outperformed some existing methods. The detection accuracies were 97.82%, 99.30%, and 99.70% on Columbia gray, CASIA v1.0, and CASIA v2.0 datasets, respectively. In future work, the effectiveness of the proposed method will be tested on more complex dataset, and the proposed method will be introduced into other image tampering detection.

References

1. Prakash, C.S., Kumar, A., Maheshkar, S., Maheshkar, V.: An integrated method of copy-move and splicing for image forgery detection. Multimedia Tools Appl. **77**, 26939–26963 (2018)
2. Ng, T.T., Chang, S.F., Sun, Q.: Blind detection of photomontage using higher order statistics. In: IEEE International Symposium on Circuits and Systems 2004, vol. 5, pp. V–V. IEEE Computer Society, Washington (2004)
3. Fu, D., Shi, Y.Q., Su, W.: Detection of image splicing based on Hilbert-Huang transform and moments of characteristic functions with wavelet decomposition. In: Shi, Y.Q., Jeon, B. (eds.) IWDW 2006. LNCS, vol. 4283, pp. 177–187. Springer, Heidelberg (2006). https://doi.org/10.1007/11922841_15
4. Pun, C.M., Liu, B., Yuan, X.C.: Multi-scale noise estimation for image splicing forgery detection. J. Vis. Commun. Image Represent. **38**, 195–206 (2016)
5. Han, J.G., Park, T.H., Moon, Y.H., Eom, I.K.: Quantization-based Markov feature extraction method for image splicing detection. Mach. Vis. Appl. **29**(3), 543–552 (2018)
6. Huang, H., Guo, W., Zhang, Y.: Detection of copy-move forgery in digital images using SIFT algorithm. In: 2008 IEEE Pacific-Asia Workshop on Computational Intelligence and Industrial Application, vol. 2, pp. 272–276. IEEE Computer Society, Washington (2008)
7. Muhammad, G., Al-Hammadi, M.H., Hussain, M., Bebis, G.: Image forgery detection using steerable pyramid transform and local binary pattern. Mach. Vis. Appl. **25**(4), 985–995 (2014)
8. Goh, J., Thing, V.L.: A hybrid evolutionary algorithm for feature and ensemble selection in image tampering detection. Electron. Secur. Digit. Forensics **7**(1), 76–104 (2015)
9. Rao, Y., Ni, J.: A deep learning approach to detection of splicing and copy-move forgeries in images. In: IEEE International Workshop on Information Forensics and Security 2016, pp. 1–6. IEEE Computer Society, Washington (2016)
10. Fridrich, J., Kodovsky, J.: Rich models for steganalysis of digital images. IEEE Trans. Inf. Forensics Secur. **7**(3), 868–882 (2012)

11. Zhang, Y., Goh, J., Win, L.L., Thing, V.L.: Image region forgery detection: a deep learning approach. In: Mathur, A., Roychoudhury, A. (eds.) Singapore Cyber Security R&D Conference (SG-CRC) 2016, pp. 1–11. IOS, Berlin (2016)
12. Chen, C., McCloskey, S., Yu, J.: Image splicing detection via camera response function analysis. In: Proceedings of the IEEE Conference on Computer Vision and Pattern Recognition 2017, pp. 5087–5096. IEEE Computer Society, Washington (2017)
13. Bunk, J., et al.: Detection and localization of image forgeries using resampling features and deep learning. In: IEEE Conference on Computer Vision and Pattern Recognition Workshops (CVPRW) 2017, pp. 1881–1889. IEEE Computer Society, Washington (2017)
14. Pomari, T., Ruppert, G., Rezende, E., Rocha, A., Carvalho, T.: Image splicing detection through illumination inconsistencies and deep learning. In: 25th IEEE International Conference on Image Processing (ICIP) 2018, pp. 3788–3792. IEEE Computer Society, Washington (2018)
15. Zhou, P., Han, X., Morariu, V.I., Davis, L.S.: Learning rich features for image manipulation detection. In: IEEE Conference on Computer Vision and Pattern Recognition 2018, pp. 1053–1061. IEEE Computer Society, Washington (2018)
16. Simonyan, K., Zisserman, A.: Very deep convolutional networks for large-scale image recognition. arXiv preprint arXiv:1409.1556 (2014)
17. Lin, M., Chen, Q., Yan, S.: Network in network. arXiv preprint arXiv:1312.4400 (2013)
18. Cozzolino, D., Poggi, G., Verdoliva, L.: Splicebuster: A new blind image splicing detector. In: IEEE International Workshop on Information Forensics and Security (WIFS) 2015, pp. 1–6. IEEE Computer Society, Washington (2015)
19. Verdoliva, L., Cozzolino, D., Poggi, G.: A feature-based approach for image tampering detection and localization. In: IEEE International Workshop on Information Forensics and Security (WIFS) 2014, pp. 149–154. IEEE Computer Society, Washington (2014)
20. Dong, J., Wang, W.: CASIA tampered image detection evaluation (TIDE) database, v1.0 and v2.0 (2011). http://forensics.idealtest.org/
21. Ng, T.T., Hsu, J., Chang, S.F.: Columbia image splicing detection evaluation dataset (2009). http://www.ee.columbia.edu/ln/dvmm/downloads/AuthSplicedDataSet/AuthSplicedDataSet. htm

Digital Media Copyright and Content Protection Using IPFS and Blockchain

Kwame Opuni-Boachie Obour Agyekum[1], Qi Xia[1], Yansong Liu[1], Hong Pu[1], Christian Nii Aflah Cobblah[1], Goodlet Akwasi Kusi[1], Hanlin Yang[1], and Jianbin Gao[2]($\boxtimes$)

[1] Center for Cyber Security, University of Electronic Science and Technology of China, Chengdu 611731, China
obour539@yahoo.com, xiaqi@uestc.edu.cn, johnsonlys@outlook.com, puhong1997@outlook.com, kriscobblah@gmail.com, gkusikat@gmail.com, p1usj4de@gmail.com
[2] School of Resources and Environment, Center for Digital Health, University of Electronic Science and Technology of China, Chengdu 611731, China
gaojb@uestc.edu.cn

Abstract. With the development of the Internet, the total amount of digital media transmission and storage has been very large. However, traditional digital copyright solidification and rights protection are offline processes, which are time-consuming and labor-intensive. This paper focuses on digital fingerprint technology, Inter-planetary File System (IPFS) and Fabric Alliance blockchain technology to create a digital system to optimize traditional processes and improve the efficiency of digital media copyright solidification.

In this work, we build an IPFS system where all digital media files exist in the form of IPFS objects. Digital fingerprints, which reflect the characteristics of the digital media files are also designed. Finally, all files are recorded onto the Fabric blockchain, ensuring immutability and provenance. Our system proves to be efficient and accurate in ensuring complete ownership of digital media.

Keywords: Blockchain · Digital fingerprinting · Fabric · IPFS

1 Introduction

The massive Internet adoption has resulted in rapidly growing cases involving the protection of digital media, content copyright and access to patented multimedia files. These are now major concerns for authors and holders of copyrights [1]. The Internet is widely used to trade and distribute digital content such as music, software, games, footage, video, and text. At the same time, the traditional protection mechanism for copyright is difficult to adapt to the protection of digital content copyright requirements with the arrival of the information age [2].

Incidents regarding the infringement of digital content online are increasing as well as the infringement and piracy challenge of digital content on the Internet [2]. Users deliberately or accidentally disclose valuable copyrighted resources

Y. Zhao et al. (Eds.): ICIG 2019, LNCS 11903, pp. 266–277, 2019.
https://doi.org/10.1007/978-3-030-34113-8_23

when using and disseminating digital content, consume potential user resources and harm creators and related copyright holder's economic interests. Digital protection of copyright has become a key issue, which has received great attention.

It is essential for the creator of media files to have complete access, authorization and a secure medium for sharing their information to stop such incidents and to expose and punish actual guilty parties. The owner should be able to show copyright for its contents if information is leaked [3]. Online media like the DropBox or peer-to-peer (P2P) media are the best available tools for rapid and effective data sharing and privacy protection [2].

Existing solutions such as digital rights management, Micro-payments, paywalls, etc. have their merits and setbacks: no regard is given to the author. Consequently, our studies revealed that Blockchain technology in conjunction with Inter-planetary File Systems (IPFS), which is a P2P distributed file system that seeks to replace HTTP and build a much better web for all, can help alleviate some of the issues regarding digital content copyright. IPFS is a P2P file system that incorporates the knowledge gained from many previous successful systems [4]. It merges a distributed hash table, an incentivized block exchange and a name-space that certifies itself. IPFS is a P2P hypermedia protocol that renders the web faster, safer, and more open [4].

The concept behind decentralized copyright management is premised on the storage in an extensive blockchain of creative works and their metadata [3]. This would enable the distribution of digital content to be monitored in real time, licenses checked, certain applications permitted, and precisely calculated. This can also verify the authenticity of a work. This is already in progress, for example, pay-per-use offerings are available that use blockchain technology. Examples of such systems are PeerTracks, Ujo Music, Mediachain Attribution Engine, Blo [2].

In this paper, we introduce a novel idea of combining the advantages of IPFS and Blockchain technology to help protect the copyright of authors and copyright holders. To the best of our knowledge, this is the first of its kind.

The organization of the paper is as follows: Sect. 2 presents the works related to this study, with Sect. 3 introducing the technologies utilized in this work. Section 4 presents the model and implementation of the system, while Sect. 5 provides the operation and results obtained. Finally, Sect. 6 concludes the paper.

2   Related Works

The idea of utilizing the blockchain technology for licenses verification has been illustrated in some research works of which Herbert and Litchfield [3] stand to have a solid preposition based on their research works. They characterized the blockchain into two main forms for licenses permit verification. Within the Bitcoin transaction model, clients demonstrate possession by demonstrating that they have the bitcoin from an active software vendor they engage in the transaction. Another model of Bitcoin is the Bespoke model which is more advanced with the extra data fields that permit computer programmers, and software manufacturers alike to also subscribe and store their license information on the system such as permit expiration, permit limits, and others. Custom models are utilized for clients with a single permit. However, the limitation is to have these stakeholders to hold numerous licenses.

McConaghy and Holtzman [5] utilized Bitcoin blockchain to also record media data by focusing on image ownership by Legal Registry capacity terms, and timestamps are recorded as the image attributes. The registry is put in a blockchain network with proprietorship data; web crawlers utilize machine learning techniques to distinguish pictures put on websites without the owner's consent, which in so doing violates the data owner's rights and discredits the work since individuals can claim the sole ownership of such data as well as enjoying any benefits that come with it thereof.

Kishigami et al. [6] depict a distributed blockchain based system as a management hub for media files and documents. The key potential of their system is the use of blockchain to oversee rights for over 4k video in a distributed environment which permits copyright holders to manage their content licenses and simultaneously counting the connected client licenses for its content. Their design framework does not allow offline access of the content on the system and the clients also expect the online miners to exchange ID to facilitate decoding of the content of the media file.

Gao and Nobuhara [7] also proposed a strategy for putting away up to N times, 20 bytes in the blockchain and for creators and owners, computerized records technically don't need timestamp anonymity. The strategy can embed the hashes of electronic information and related data such as author name, file name, and comments. Mostly these comments and other related data can be accounted for by writing it in a plain text basically. The owner of the digital media file can ensure data protection and integrity by this approach. The limitation was the improvement in the application of subsequent intellectual property rights other than patent protection policies and obvious security.

"Mediachain", also made use of IPFS (Inter-planetary File System) record framework [8], enhances copyrights of computerized works. As of now, it's basically used for computerized picture copyright security applications. Mediachain, however, could be a collaborative solution that combines media metadata convention that gives copyright recognition for imaginative works. Copyright proprietors are able to sign metadata statements with cryptographic marks on their finished media file and with the use of timestamps on the blockchain, the records are stored in IPFS. These claims can be accessed by inputting a query that calls the data.

IPFS ideology as it stands can be acknowledged from many past effective systems and frameworks, and it has overcome numerous challenges and constraints. Nevertheless, we think a few perspectives of IPFS can be improved with the coupling of blockchain, and until presently, this thought has not yet been realized.

3 Background

3.1 Inter Planetary File System (IPFS)

IPFS [4] is a file sharing platform, which identifies files through its content. A distributed hash table (DHT) is used to recover file locations and node connectivity data. When a file is fed into the IPFS system, it is divided into chunks, with each chunk containing a maximum of 256 kbs of data and/or connections to other chunks. Each chunk is recognized by a cryptographic hash, also referred to as content identifier, which is calculated from its content [11].

The connections also comprise contents' identifiers, forming a Merkle directed acyclic graph (DAG) that explains the entire file and can be used to recreate any file from its chunks. Due to the Merkle DAG, the root hash can be used to identify a complete file. The node is registered as a provider through DHT once the node is divided into chunks, and the Merkle DAG has been formed. The DHT [12] is basically a distributed store of key-value pairs. It utilizes node identifiers and keys, with a distance metric to store and collect data readily, both having to be the same length. As a result of the use of IPFS's content identifiers, it is particularly appropriate for blockchain use in order to locate, verify and transfer chunks and files [11].

Indeed, the root hash of a Merkle DAG file can be sent via a transaction to the blockchain and thus, does not expand the chain. Simultaneously, no information other than the hash is needed to retrieve the file from IPFS. This is distinct to file sharing schemes that do not depend on cryptographic hashes for content identification, as they need a file whose hash is discovered in the blockchain with extra name resolution mechanisms.

Moreover, it is difficult to create a second, separate file with the same hash so IPFS cannot be flooded with files with a specific target file identifier [11]. In conclusion, an IPFS-based file can be checked readily and it is hard to thwart a user with the same name/identifier in several files. The issue of decentralized storage of large files is resolved with IPFS. When you upload a new file to IPFS, it is divided into several chunks of data. Each chunk has a hash value for its content to be clearly identified. Finally, for the whole file, a hash value is created which can be downloaded by any node.

3.2 Blockchain

Blockchain [10] is a decentralized infrastructure and a distributed computing paradigm which uses cryptographic chained block structures to validate and store data, consensus algorithms to generate and update data, and smart contracts, programmable scripts, to program and manipulate data.

Blockchain management is achieved by multiple participants, with each participant providing nodes and storing data on the chain. This enables an easy sharing of data. The use of a time-stamped chain of data makes for easy verification and traceability. Each modification to the data is recorded and can be tracked on the blockchain. The utilization of Merkle trees and blockchain hash tables enables an irreversible modification of the data. Information recorded in the blockchain cannot be tampered with, after reaching a consensus.

Blockchain transactions only hold very small amounts of data, wherefore it is crucial to choose what data should be placed On-chain and what should be kept Off-chain [11]. There are many off-chain storage solutions customized for blockchain such as IPFS [4]. These solutions share the concept of a distributed peer-to-peer file system where the information is split into different chunks, encrypted and disseminated across various network nodes to guarantee security and accessibility.

4   System Design and Implementation

4.1   System Model

In this section, we outline the various components, and also illustrate the flow, of the system.

Users upload files and metadata information through the web-client. The web client is written in JavaScript, and node.npm and yarn, which are tools that ensure the efficient functioning of the system. The server-side, which is designed by the Flask framework and based on python programming language, finds the file transfer port through the HTTP response and saves the file at the localhost. The server-side transfers the file to IPFS by invoking the HTTP protocol, and IPFS returns the hash for the corresponding file. Meanwhile, the digital fingerprint extraction module is used to extract the digital fingerprint of the corresponding file (digital fingerprint is a string of binary characters). After the hash characters and digital fingerprint are received at the server-side, fabric network is called remotely through the Remote Procedure Call (gRPC) service to take the digital fingerprint as the key, and combines the hash characters and the metadata information after re-decoding as the value. The key-value pairs are then uploaded to the fabric network. The data in fabric network are synchronized and updated by kafka consensus algorithm.

When other users want to upload the same file to the system (which can be interpreted as a copyright infringement), the system extracts the digital fingerprint after receiving the file, and sends the digital fingerprint as the key to the fabric network for a thorough search. If the digital fingerprint already exists, the system will report an error, roll back the upload operation of the current user and remind the user that the same file already exists.

4.2   System Implementation

IPFS provides a new platform for writing and deploying applications, as well as a new distribution system for versioning big data. So the sum is greater than the parts. Like all decentralized systems, IPFS is point-to-point, with no privileged nodes. The node stores the object IPFS in local storage. These files or other data structures are then linked and transmitted through the nodes.

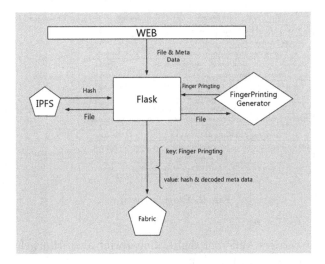

Fig. 1. System model

By transferring files with private information off-line, some weaknesses of blockchain can be overcome. This guarantees that files can be removed when necessary and that the chain does not expand too quickly. However, the guarantee that files have not been edited or modified must be maintained for information sharing between participants on the network. In addition, the Fabric blockchain monitors which participants have access to which data.

IPFS stores data in a dispersed manner by dividing them into pieces that can be asked for, and transmitted between nodes. With its cryptographic hash, each file is identified. This makes it simple to verify that the right information is obtained by creating the hash of the file chunks and ensuring that it matches the required hash. IPFS hashes identifying files that contain personal data can be stored on the blockchain instead of the data itself.

The blockchain containing the hash guarantees that the file has not been altered. The file itself being stored in IPFS means it can be removed as required, by nodes deleting it from their local storage. File hashes can be used to connect owner's files with access permissions. Thus, the growth of the chain is significantly decreased as hashes are normally smaller than the data they represent. The combination of blockchain security and a private-network IPFS guarantees data protection and decrease in storage costs. The structure of the block is given in Fig. 2.

4.3 Digital Fingerprint Generation

The digital fingerprint generation, which has been presented by several authors in literature [14]–[18], is the key component of this system, and it marks the unique key of identifying copyright information from the system. The requirement for the algorithm is to be reliable, fast and accurate. For digital media

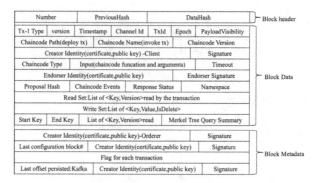

Number			PreviousHash			DataHash			Block header

Tx-1 Type	version	Timestamp	Channel Id	TxId	Epoch	PayloadVisibility
Chaincode Path(deploy tx)		Chaincode Name(invoke tx)		Chaincode Version		
Creator Identity(certificate,public key) -Client						Signature
Chaincode Type		Input(chaincode funcation and arguments)				Timeout
Endorser Identity(certificate,public key)					Endorser Signature	
Proposal Hash		Chaincode Events		Response Status		Namespace
Read Set:List of <Key,Version>read by the transaction						
Write Set:List of <Key,Value,IsDelete>						
Start Key	End Key	List of <Key,Version>read			Merkel Tree Query Summary	

(Block Data)

Creator Identity(certificate,public key)-Orderer				Signature
Last configuration block#	Creator Identity(certificate,public key)			Signature
Flag for each transaction				
Last offset persisted:Kafka	Creator Identity(certificate,public key)			Signature

(Block Metadata)

Fig. 2. Block structure

files of different carriers, different digital fingerprint algorithms should be used to reflect the uniqueness of the files.

1. **Perceptual hash algorithm used by an image:** An image is composed of pixels. Each pixel has its own color, and we can use the rgb channel to describe this color. But if the color of the pixel of each image is described as the digital fingerprint of the picture, the length of this fingerprint will be very large. It's difficult to use this in specific projects, and not conducive for communication. Since each picture has different image features, if we can digitally describe these features, it can also be used as a digital fingerprint of this picture.

   To make a distinction between two similar photos, we can use the encryption hash algorithm. The calculated hash will output a fixed length hash-key according to different inputs (different binary arrangements). If the two images are the same, then their hash-key will be the same. This paper uses the perceptual hash algorithm. The perceptual hash algorithm mainly includes ahash, phash, and dhash, and is not a strict hash calculation method, but a hash value is calculated in a relative manner. This similarity can be used to digitize image features.

   – **ahash:** average hash, faster, but generally accurate.
   – **phash:** perceives hash, with higher accuracy, but at a fair speed.
   – **dhash:** difference value hash, higher precision, faster.

2. **Video Segmentation Key-frame dhash algorithm:** The video processing method in this paper adopts the dhash algorithm mainly for the consideration of processing speed and accuracy. But a video has a few more steps than dealing with a single image. The video is formed by a continuous playback of each frame of the picture, but like the picture, we can't say that each frame of the picture is included in the calculation range. We can extract the picture number of the specific frame by equally dividing the key frame. The picture dhash fingerprint of a specific frame is calculated, and then all the fingerprints are spliced. The result of this stitching is the dhash fingerprint of the video.

3. **Audio fingerprinting:** After the whole audio is divided into blocks, Fourier transform is performed on each block respectively, and then the molecular band extracts the subscript of the highest energy point.

4.4 Fabric Consensus Algorithm

The essence of each node of Fabric is a state machine that is replicated, and the same ledger needs to be stored between the nodes. In Fabric, the consensus process is used to achieve the consistency of distributed nodes and the consistency of ledger state. Fabric's consensus process has three phases: endorsement, sorting, and verification. The fabric network is started and the chaincode is successfully invoked. The fabric network guarantees that nobody can tamper with the data, and that ensures traceability.

In order not to limit links or data flow between nodes, the IPFS is intended to communicate information as broadly as possible. The situation in question concerns personal information. Thus, IPFS cannot exchange files with any entity that asks for it. In accordance with permissions registered on the Fabric blockchain by the data owners, only participants with access permissions must be allowed access. As such, the provided solution is an IPFS that makes use of a chaincode (smart contract) which has the ability of adding, deleting and updating file ownership and accesses. Participants of the system are identified by their public keys and files are identified by their unique cryptographic hash.

5 Operation Manual and Results

In this section, we discuss the operable nature of the setup and show some results obtained. For the setup of the system, the following are the steps we adhered to.

We first initiate the IPFS setup. Once a *Daemon is ready* message appears, it indicates a successful setup. Next, we start the Fabric blockchain network. We pre-install Docker and docker-compose, and also pull the images beforehand. All startup steps needed for the complete functionality of the Fabric network are already written in the script file, so the file is run once the path that contains the script file is located. Once the network has been started, the chaincode is invoked. We then start the gRPC service, by entering the path where the gRPC files are located. The gRPC service connects the server-side and the Fabric blockchain network. Next, we start the Flask server and run the main function. Figures 3 to 5 illustrate the setup processes and the results obtained.

For an owner who wants to publish his copyrighted work on the blockchain network, s/he has to send the name and possibly, remarks on the work. Once the file exists on the network, an error message will be generated once anyone tries to claim ownership of that same work and publishes it on the blockchain network.

We further compare our system to other related systems by taking into consideration some performance metrics such as data security, bandwidth efficiency,

Fig. 3. Setup of the system: 1. gRPC 2. IPFS 3. Fabric 4. Network

access control, provenance and auditing, privacy and storage costs. Table 1 provides a summary of the comparison, with the following notations: Y - Yes, N - No, H - High, M - Moderate, and L - Low. The figure depicts that our system performs very well as compared to other related existing systems.

Figure 3 illustrates the interfaces in starting the system, while Fig. 4 represents the interface for uploading the files onto the system. The first picture of

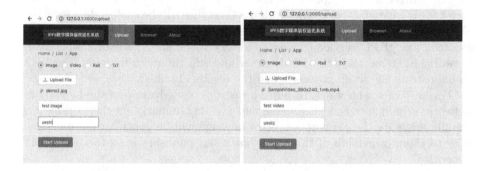

Fig. 4. Data upload onto server: 1. image 2. video

Fig. 5. 1. Interface showing finger printing, metadata and hash of uploaded files 2. Records on the fabric blockchain

Table 1. Comparison between proposed and other related systems

Metric	[3]	[5]	[6]	[7]	[8]	Our system
Blockchian copyright protection	Y	Y	Y	Y	Y	Y
Data security	Y	Y	Y	Y	Y	Y
Bandwidth efficiency	N	Y	N	N	N	Y
Access control	Y	N	N	N	Y	Y
Provenance and auditing	N	Y	N	Y	Y	Y
Privacy	N	Y	Y	N	N	Y
Storage costs	H	H	M	H	M	L

Fig. 4 illustrates an image upload while the second one illustrates a video upload. Once the file has been uploaded onto the server, there is an interface that shows the fingerprint of the uploaded file, the name of the file and the generated hash value of the file. This can be seen in the first image of Fig. 5. The second image shows the details of the uploaded files after querying the IPFS server.

6 Conclusion

Digital media is a very sensitive data and can easily be stolen or copied by third parties. The copyright holders should be able to own and monitor their data without compromising safety instead of trusting a third party to storing or distributing the data. Similarly, traditional digital copyright protection mechanisms are inefficient simply because notarization is done offline and it takes a very long time before it's completed.

This paper therefore proposes a system that incorporates the use of a digital fingerprint technology, IPFS and Blockchain technology (Fabric) as its core constituents, to optimize the traditional processes and help protect digital media copyright and ensure complete ownership. This ensures that copyright holders or authors know when their data is being accessed and how it is used, so that they don't have to trust any third party. Moreover, investigations into the using IPFS and Blockchain in the protection of digital media copyright has a high potential value, which is important in improving the current situation of digital media copyright protection. Copyright organizations should also cooperate actively in support of Blockchain's digital copyright efforts and development policies.

Acknowledgment. This work was supported in part by the programs of International Science and Technology Cooperation and Exchange of Sichuan Province under Grant 2017HH0028, Grant 2018HH0102 and Grant 2019YFH0014.

References

1. Vishwa, A., Hussain, F.K.: A blockchain based approach for multimedia privacy protection and provenance. In: IEEE Symposium Series on Computational Intelligence (SSCI), Bangalore, India, vol. 2018, pp. 1941–1945 (2018). https://doi.org/ 10.1109/SSCI.2018.8628636
2. Qi, Y., Liu, X.: Digital copyright protection based on blockchain technology. In: 2018 International Journal of Knowledge and Language Processing, vol. 9, no. 2, pp. 61–70 (2018)
3. Bhowmik, D., Feng, T.: The multimedia blockchain: a distributed and tamper-proof media transaction framework. In: 2017 22nd International Conference on Digital Signal Processing (DSP), London, pp. 1–5 (2017). https://doi.org/10.1109/ICDSP. 2017.8096051
4. Benet, J.: IPFS - Content Addressed, Versioned, P2P FileSystem, July 2014
5. McConaghy, M., McMullen, G., Parry, G., McConaghy, T., Holtzman, D.: Visibility and digital art: blockchain as an ownership layer on the Internet. Strateg. Change **26**(5), 461–470 (2017)
6. Kishigami, J., Fujimura, S., Watanabe, H., Nakadaira, A., Akutsu, A.: The blockchain-based digital content distribution system. In: 2015 IEEE Fifth International Conference on Big Data and Cloud Computing, Dalian, pp. 187–190 (2015). https://doi.org/10.1109/BDCloud.2015.60
7. Gao, Y., Nobuhara, H.: A decentralized trusted timestamping based on blockchains. IEEJ J. Ind. Appl. **2017**, 252–257 (2017). https://doi.org/10.1541/ ieejjia.6.252
8. How Mediachain Works. http://www.mediachain.io/
9. Baumgart, I., Mies, S.: S/Kademlia: a practicable approach towards secure key-based routing. In: 2007 International Conference on Parallel and Distributed Systems, Hsinchu, pp. 1–8 (2007). https://doi.org/10.1109/ICPADS.2007.4447808
10. Nakamoto, S.: Bitcoin: a peer-to-peer electronic cash system, October 2008. (cited on pp. 15 and 87) (2017). http://www.bitcoin.org/bitcoin.pdf
11. Steichen, M., Pontiveros, B.F., Norvill, R., Shbair, W., et al.: Blockchain-based, decentralized access control for IPFS. In: The 2018 IEEE International Conference on Blockchain (Blockchain-2018), pp. 1499–1506. IEEE (2018)
12. Maymounkov, P., Mazières, D.: Kademlia: a peer-to-peer information system based on the XOR metric. In: Druschel, P., Kaashoek, F., Rowstron, A. (eds.) IPTPS 2002. LNCS, vol. 2429, pp. 53–65. Springer, Heidelberg (2002). https://doi.org/10. 1007/3-540-45748-8_5
13. J. Herbert and A. Litchfield, A Novel Method for Decentralised Peer-to-peer Software License Validation Using Cryptocurrency Blockchain Technology, ACSC 2015, 2015(27)
14. Cappelli, R., Erol, A., Maio, D., Maltoni, D.: Synthetic fingerprint -image generation. In: Proceedings 15th International Conference on Pattern Recognition, Barcelona, vol. 3, pp. 475–478, September 2000
15. Cappelli, R., Maio, D., Maltoni, D.: Synthetic fingerprint -database generation. In: Proceedings 16th International Conference on Pattern Recognition, Quebec City, vol. 3, pp. 744–747, August 2002

16. Bontrager, P., Togelius, J., Memon, N.: Deepmasterprint: generating fingerprints for presentation attacks. https://arxiv.org/abs/1705.07386 (2017)
17. Abdelnur, H.J., State, R., Festor, O.: Advanced network fingerprinting. In: Lippmann, R., Kirda, E., Trachtenberg, A. (eds.) RAID 2008. LNCS, vol. 5230, pp. 372–389. Springer, Heidelberg (2008). https://doi.org/10.1007/978-3-540-87403-4_20
18. Minaee, S., Abdolrashidi, A.: Finger-GAN: generating realistic fingerprint images using connectivity imposed GAN. arXiv preprint arXiv:1812.10482 (2018)

Surveillance and Remote Sensing

TQR-Net: Tighter Quadrangle-Based Convolutional Neural Network for Dense Building Instance Localization in Remote Sensing Imagery

Kaiyu Jiang and Qingpeng Li[✉]

State Key Laboratory of Virtual Reality Technology and Systems, School of
Computer Science and Engineering, Beihang University, Beijing 100191, China
{kyjiang,liqingpeng}@buaa.edu.cn

Abstract. Building localization in remote sensing imagery (RSI) is
widely applied in many geoscience and remote sensing areas. However,
many existing methods cannot generate accurate building contours. In
this paper, we propose an effective convolutional neural network (CNN)
framework, Tighter Quadrangle Network (TQR-Net), to locate buildings
with quadrangular contours in RSI. Here, TQR-Net can generate regular contours for each of building targets using a CNN branch which can
predict tighter quadrangles in parallel. Then, we train and test TQR-
Net on a large building dataset collected from Google Earth, and the
experiment results demonstrate that the proposed method can generate high-quality building contours and significantly outperforms other
CNN-based detectors.

Keywords: Deep learning · Convolutional neural network · Building
instance localization · Remote sensing · Tighter quadrangle

1 Introduction

With the rapid development of spaceborne and airborne imaging technology, the
high-resolution remote sensing imagery (RSI) can be more and more accessible to
make the spatial structure, texture and other information of geographic objects
abundant. Thus, automatic building localization can potentially achieve higher
accuracy, which is helpful to many remote sensing applications, such as land
planning, environment management and disaster assessment.

Therefore, developing automatic methods of building localization is a significant task. Over the past decades, many approaches have been proposed for automatic building localization. For example, in the early days, low-level handcrafted
features were applied for feature extraction to locate buildings. Kim et al. [1]
extracted the edge segments and detected possible building structures based on
graph search strategy. Jung et al. [2] proposed a Hough transform-based method
to extract the rectangular building roofs.

© Springer Nature Switzerland AG 2019
Y. Zhao et al. (Eds.): ICIG 2019, LNCS 11903, pp. 281–291, 2019.
https://doi.org/10.1007/978-3-030-34113-8_24

Fig. 1. Example of building localization results from TQR-Net in Google Earth image of Calgary, Alberta, Canada (51.05°N, 114.07°W).

Moreover, in order to obtain building contours, image segmentation can also be utilized to partition RSI into many regions and classify each pixel into a fixed set of categories [3], distinguishing buildings from their surrounding background. For example, Kampffmeyer et al. [4] combined different deep architectures including patch-base and pixel-to-pixel approaches, to achieve good accuracy for small object segmentation in urban remote sensing. Wu et al. [5] proposed a multi-constraint fully convolutional network to improve the performance of the U-Net model in building segmentation from aerial imagery. Troya-Galvis et al. [6] presented two different extensions of a collaborative framework called CoSC which outperform hybrid pixel-object oriented approach as well as a deep learning approach. Insufficiently, such methods can generate roughly building segmentation boundary, however, they are always irregular and can not differentiate building instances.

In recent five years, the CNN-based object detectors [7–10] have made a great improvement for detecting remotely sensed targets [11–17]. Consequently, the CNN-based building detectors have also made a breakthrough. For example, Zhang et al. [18] proposed a CNN-based detector using multi-scale saliency-based sliding window and improved non-maximum suppression (NMS) to detect suburban buildings. Li et al. [19] presented a cascaded CNN architecture utilizing Hough transform to guide CNN to extract mid-level features of the building. Chen et al. [20] proposed a two-stage CNN-based detector for multi-sized building localization, in which a multi-sized fusion region proposal network (RPN) and a novel dynamic weighting algorithm were used to generate and classify multi-sized region proposals, respectively. Although such object detection-based methods can classify individual buildings, they denote detection via rectangular bounding boxes and can not generate building contour. To tackle this problem,

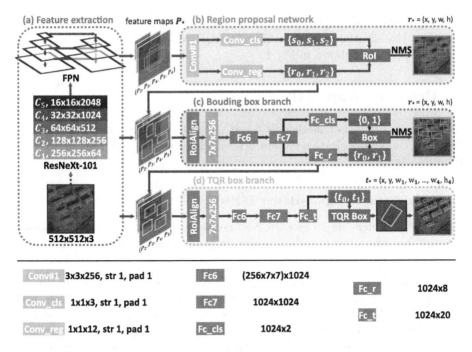

Fig. 2. The architecture of the proposed multi-stage TQR-Net is as follows: (a) Feature extraction stage generates a rich and multi-scale feature pyramid. (b) Region proposal network outputs a set of object proposals with objectness scores s_i (e.g., $i = 0, 1, 2$ denotes three aspect ratios). (c) Bounding box branch regresses rectangular bounding boxes of each pyramid level. (d) TQR box branch predicts quadrangle bounding boxes and obtains building contours.

some instance segmentation-based methods [21–23] can be adopted to detect buildings in RSI, but the generated contours are still irregular in the instance segmentation-based approaches.

As aforementioned, generally, there are two kinds of bounding boxes to locate building targets. One is rectangular, which cannot generate the contours of buildings. The other is polygonal, based on instance segmentation detectors (e.g., Mask R-CNN [10]), which can locate buildings via predicting their segmentation and polygonal contours. However, such polygonal contours are always inaccurate due to their uncertain nodes and irregular shapes.

In this paper, aiming to make a trade-off between these two kinds of bounding boxes, we propose to use quadrangular bounding boxes, which are generated by a tighter quadrangle-based convolutional neural network (TQR-Net) directly. Considering that most buildings are quadrilateral, we adopt quadrangular bounding boxes with four nodes, which can not only avoid irregular shapes but also keep certain structural restrictions.

Without bells and whistles, the experiment results prove that the proposed TQR-Net can improve the feature extraction domain of corner and contour in building targets with higher precision of building localization. Here, we give an example of localization results acquired by TQR-Net in Google Earth urban area image of Calgary is shown in Fig. 1.

2   Proposed Approach

As shown in Fig. 2, our method is based on a multi-stage region-based object detection framework. In this section, we will elaborate the proposed network in the subsections.

2.1   Multi-stage Region-Based TQR-Net

There are four main stages in TQR-Net, i.e., feature extraction, region proposal network, bounding box branch, and tighter quadrangle box branch, and we will detail each stage as follows.

Feature Extraction. A feature extraction network can extract features from the input image. Here we utilize ResNeXt-101 [24] for feature extraction, and such multi-scale feature maps are extracted on five levels, which can be defined as $\{C_1, C_2, C_3, C_4, C_5\}$. At each level, convolutional layers generate feature maps of the same size. In order to detect buildings in different scales, we use Feature Pyramid Network (FPN) [25] in the convolutional backbone which utilizes top-down lateral connections to build an in-network feature pyramid. The FPN can take $\{C_2, C_3, C_4, C_5\}$ as input and generate the final set of feature maps defined as follows:

$$P_* = \{P_2, P_3, P_4, P_5, P_6\}. \tag{1}$$

Region Proposal Network. A region proposal network (RPN) can generate region of interests (RoIs) on feature maps P_* by the anchors which are predefined in five scales and three aspect ratios. In RPN, classification and bounding box regression are performed by a 3×3 convolutional layer, followed by two sibling 1×1 convolutions, subsequently.

Bounding Box Branch. After RPN, feature maps of size 7×7 from RoIs are extracted by using RoIAlign [10] on $\{P_2, P_3, P_4, P_5\}$, and they are fed into bounding box branch which performs classification and rectangular bounding box regression, respectively.

Tighter Quadrangle Box Branch. In the proposed network, a tighter quadrangle (TQR) box branch is applied to generate building contours using quadrangular bounding boxes. Similar to the sequential protocol of coordinates proposed in [26], via ordering the coordinates, we can define the quadrangular bounding box with four nodes uniquely. By default, the four nodes are arranged clockwise, and the node closest to the grid origin is set to be the first. In particular, if there are two nodes at the same distance with the grid origin, we set the node which

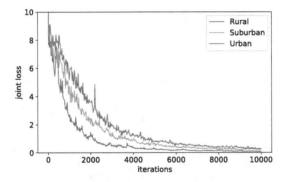

Fig. 3. Joint loss curves of TQR-Net with ResNeXt-101 in three typical areas.

owns smaller value x as the first one. After determining the order of the nodes, inspired by the coordinates of rectangle bounding box as follows:

$$r_* = (x, y, w, h), \tag{2}$$

the 8-coordinate TQR box can be represented as follows:

$$t_* = (x, y, w_1, h_1, w_2, h_2, w_3, h_3, w_4, h_4). \tag{3}$$

Here, variables x, y denote the center coordinates of the TQR box's minimum bounding rectangle, and w_n, h_n represent the n-th $(n = 1, 2, 3, 4)$ relative position to the center coordinates.

As aforementioned, in order to generate the TQR box, $\{P_2, P_3, P_4, P_5\}$ are fed into TQR box branch, which uses RoiAlign to extract 7×7 feature maps from boxes (x_b, y_b, w_b, h_b) output by bounding box branch. Then, three fully-connected layers are utilized to collapse the small feature maps into two 10-d vectors $\{t_0, t_1\}$, where t_0 corresponding to the background class is ignored in the loss computation, and t_1 represents the predicted TQR box. For TQR box regression, we adopt the parameterizations of the 10-coordinate as follows:

$$\begin{aligned}
d_x &= (x - x_b)/w_b, & d_{w_n} &= w_n/w_b, \\
d_y &= (y - y_b)/h_b, & d_{h_n} &= h_n/h_b, \\
d_x^* &= (x^* - x_b)/w_b, & d_{w_n}^* &= w_n^*/w_b, \\
d_y^* &= (y^* - y_b)/h_b, & d_{h_n}^* &= h_n^*/h_b,
\end{aligned} \tag{4}$$

where x^*, y^*, w_n^*, h_n^* $(n = 1, 2, 3, 4)$ stand for the ground-truth TQR box.

2.2   Loss Function

For end-to-end training, we utilize a joint loss to optimize our network. Here, the joint loss is combined of L_{rpn}, L_{bbox} and L_{tqr}, for region proposal network,

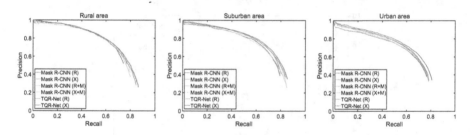

Fig. 4. Precision-recall comparisons of bounding box between TQR-Net and other baseline methods with different backbones on Qinghai Province dataset in three different kinds of areas. (IoU = 0.5). Key: R = ResNet-101-FPN; X = ResNeXt-101-FPN; M = Mask Branch.

bounding box branch and TQR box branch, respectively. Formally, we compute the joint loss function L for each mini-batch as follows:

$$L = \sum_{\theta}^{\Theta} L_{rpn}^{(\theta)} + \sum_{\theta}^{\Theta} L_{bbox}^{(\theta)} + \sum_{\theta}^{\Theta} L_{tqr}^{(\theta)} + \varphi \parallel \mathbf{w} \parallel^2, \qquad (5)$$

where φ is a hyper-parameter, $\mathbf{w}$ is a vector of network weights and, the definition of RPN loss $L_{rpn}^{(\theta)}$ and bounding box branch loss $L_{bbox}^{(\theta)}$ can refer to [9,10], for the θ-th image in a mini-batch (e.g., batch size $\Theta = 3$ in our experiments). Moreover, the TQR box branch loss L_{tqr} for one image is defined as follows:

$$L_{tqr}(\{d_i\}, \{d_i^*\}) = \lambda \frac{1}{N_{tqr}} \sum_i smooth_{L_1}(d_i - d_i^*),$$

$$smooth_{L_1}(x) = \begin{cases} 0.5x^2 & \text{if } |x| < 1 \\ |x| - 0.5 & \text{otherwise} \end{cases} . \qquad (6)$$

Here, i and N_{tqr} are the index and number of the TQR boxes, and d_i and d_i^* represent the 10 parameterized coordinates of the predicted and ground-truth TQR boxes, respectively. For the regression loss, we use $smooth_{L_1}$ which is the robust loss function defined in [8].

In this paper, we set the weight decay $\varphi = 0.0001$, $N_{tqr} = 1000$, and the loss weight $\lambda = 10$. The joint loss curves of TQR-Net with ResNeXt-101 in three typical kinds of areas are shown in Fig. 3.

3   Experiments and Discussion

3.1   Dataset

In order to evaluate our method, we collect a large building dataset from Google Earth, in which all buildings are manually labeled by minimum bounding rectangles. The RGB images in this dataset are from rural, suburban and urban

Fig. 5. Building localization results in Qinghai Province, China. First two rows (urban): Tianjun Dist. in Haixi Mongolian T.A.P ($37.30°N$, $99.02°E$) and Xinghai Dist. in Hainan T.A.P ($35.58°N$, $99.99°E$). Key: T.A.P = Tibetan Autonomous Prefecture; E.A = Ethnic Autonomous Dist. Second two rows (suburban): Tu E.A.D in Haidong City ($36.82°N$, $101.99°E$) and Tongde Dist. in Hainan T.A.P ($35.26°N$, $100.55°E$). Last two rows (rural): Gonghe Dist. in Hainan T.A.P ($36.40°N$, $100.97°E$) and Datong Hui and Tu E.A.D in Xining City ($37.03°N$, $101.50°E$).

areas in Qinghai Province, China. Statistically, there are 48222 labeled buildings (7628, 16533 and 24061 in rural, suburban and urban areas) in 1660 images

Table 1. Comparisons of bounding box $AP^{bb}(\%)$ and $AR^{bb}(\%)$ among the baseline methods and the proposed method on Qinghai Province dataset in three different kinds of areas. Key: M.R. = Mask R-CNN [10]; R = ResNet-101-FPN; X = ResNeXt-101-FPN; M = Mask Branch.

Area	Method	AP^{bb}	AP_{50}^{bb}	AP_{75}^{bb}	AR^{bb}
Rural	M.R. (R)	32.5	64.9	29.0	41.4
	M.R. (X)	34.7	66.7	33.3	43.8
	M.R. (R+M)	34.3	67.0	32.7	44.7
	M.R. (X+M)	35.1	67.7	33.2	45.8
	TQR-Net (R)	38.2	68.9	38.7	49.8
	TQR-Net (X)	**38.8**	**70.7**	**39.7**	**51.3**
Suburban	M.R. (R)	33.4	65.3	30.9	44.5
	M.R. (X)	34.9	67.3	32.9	46.2
	M.R. (R+M)	35.4	67.6	34.1	49.7
	M.R. (X+M)	37.0	69.3	36.7	49.3
	TQR-Net (R)	38.7	69.3	39.9	50.8
	TQR-Net (X)	**39.8**	**70.4**	**41.4**	**52.0**
Urban	M.R. (R)	28.8	58.3	25.6	42.0
	M.R. (X)	31.1	61.0	29.1	43.2
	M.R. (R+M)	30.5	59.9	28.5	43.8
	M.R. (X+M)	32.0	61.3	31.1	44.7
	TQR-Net (R)	33.7	61.6	33.5	46.8
	TQR-Net (X)	**35.4**	**64.3**	**36.6**	**48.5**

(296, 631 and 733 in rural, suburban and urban areas). For each area, images are randomly split into 50% for training and 50% for testing.

3.2 Implementation and Results

All models are implemented with PyTorch on 3 NVIDIA GeForce GTX 1080 Ti of 11 GB on board memory. We evaluate ResNet-101 [27] and ResNeXt-101 [24] pre-trained on ImageNet [28] as backbone. As for the parameters in the new layers, we adopt the weight initialization strategy introduced in [29]. In order to train our network, we use stochastic gradient descent (SGD) with a fixed learning rate of 0.002, and the momentum is set to 0.9.

The proposed TQR-Net is compared with Mask R-CNN [10] in three typical areas. We also compare the TQR box branch with the mask branch. Table 1 shows the comparison results of COCO-style bounding box average precision (AP^{bb}) and average recall (AR^{bb}), following the definitions in [30].

In Table 1, we can see that TQR-Net outperforms the baseline methods in both AP^{bb} and AR^{bb} indicators in all three areas. For example, compared to Mask R-CNN with the mask branch, TQR-Net improves 3.7% in AP^{bb} and 5.5%

in AR^{bb} while using ResNeXt-101 as backbone in rural area. Moreover, we show precision-recall curves comparisons of our method and other competitors with different backbones in three different kinds of areas, respectively, in Fig. 4 (for convenience, we draw precision-recall curves according to PASCAL VOC format here). Some localization results generated by TQR-Net with ResNeXt-101 as backbone can be seen in Fig. 5. Thus, our method preserves more geometric information with maintaining certain structural restrictions, which can aid building localization.

4   Conclusion

In this paper, a multi-stage CNN-based method called TQR-Net has been proposed to locate buildings with quadrangle bounding boxes, which can be trained end-to-end by a joint loss function. We make a trade-off between rectangular and polygonal bounding boxes to acquire high-quality building contours in our method. Different from traditional object detection-based and instance segmentation-based methods, TQR-Net can directly generate TQR boxes with more flexibility of freedom than bounding boxes, while avoiding irregular shapes, extra time and resource overheads, associated with predicting masks. Experiments on a large Google Earth dataset of three typical kinds of areas demonstrate its effectiveness for building instance localization task.

References

1. Kim, T., Muller, J.-P.: Development of a graph-based approach for building detection. Image Vis. Comput. **17**(1), 3–14 (1999)
2. Jung, C.R., Schramm, R.: Rectangle detection based on a windowed Hough transform. In: Proceedings, 17th Brazilian Symposium on Computer Graphics and Image Processing, pp. 113–120 (2004)
3. He, L., et al.: A comparative study of deformable contour methods on medical image segmentation. Image Vis. Comput. **26**(2), 141–163 (2008)
4. Kampffmeyer, M., Salberg, A.-B., Jenssen, R.: Semantic segmentation of small objects and modeling of uncertainty in urban remote sensing images using deep convolutional neural networks. In: Proceedings of the IEEE Conference on Computer Vision and Pattern Recognition Workshops, pp. 1–9 (2016)
5. Wu, G., et al.: Automatic building segmentation of aerial imagery using multi-constraint fully convolutional networks. Remote Sens. **10**(3), 407 (2018)
6. Troya-Galvis, A., Gançarski, P., Berti-Équille, L.: Remote sensing image analysis by aggregation of segmentation-classification collaborative agents. Pattern Recogn. **73**, 259–274 (2018)
7. Girshick, R., Donahue, J., Darrell, T., Malik, J.: Rich feature hierarchies for accurate object detection and semantic segmentation. In: Proceedings of the IEEE Conference on Computer Vision and Pattern Recognition, pp. 580–587 (2014)
8. Girshick, R.: Fast R-CNN. In: Proceedings of the IEEE International Conference on Computer Vision, pp. 1440–1448 (2015)

9. Ren, S., He, K., Girshick, R., Sun, J.: Faster R-CNN: towards real-time object detection with region proposal networks. In: Advances in Neural Information Processing Systems, pp. 91–99 (2015)

10. He, K., Gkioxari, G., Dollár, P., Girshick, R.: Mask R-CNN. In: Proceedings of the IEEE International Conference on Computer Vision, pp. 2980–2988 (2017)

11. Ševo, I., Avramović, A.: Convolutional neural network based automatic object detection on aerial images. IEEE Geosci. Remote Sens. Lett. **13**(5), 740–744 (2016)

12. Cheng, G., Zhou, P., Han, J.: Learning rotation-invariant convolutional neural networks for object detection in VHR optical remote sensing images. IEEE Trans. Geosci. Remote Sens. **54**(12), 7405–7415 (2016)

13. Ren, Y., Zhu, C., Xiao, S.: Small object detection in optical remote sensing images via modified Faster R-CNN. Appl. Sci. **8**(5), 813 (2018)

14. Chen, F., et al.: Fast automatic airport detection in remote sensing images using convolutional neural networks. Remote Sens. **10**(3), 443 (2018)

15. Li, K., Cheng, G., Bu, S., You, X.: Rotation-insensitive and context-augmented object detection in remote sensing images. IEEE Trans. Geosci. Remote Sens. **56**(4), 2337–2348 (2018)

16. Li, Q., Mou, L., Jiang, K., Liu, Q., Wang, Y., Zhu, X.X.: Hierarchical region based convolution neural network for multiscale object detection in remote sensing images. In: IEEE International Geoscience and Remote Sensing Symposium, pp. 4355–4358 (2018)

17. Li, Q., Mou, L., Liu, Q., Wang, Y., Zhu, X.X.: HSF-Net: multiscale deep feature embedding for ship detection in optical remote sensing imagery. IEEE Trans. Geosci. Remote Sens. **56**(12), 7147–7161 (2018)

18. Zhang, Q., Wang, Y., Liu, Q., Liu, X., Wang, W.: CNN based suburban building detection using monocular high resolution Google earth images. In: IEEE International Geoscience and Remote Sensing Symposium, pp. 661–664 (2016)

19. Li, Q., Wang, Y., Liu, Q., Wang, W.: Hough transform guided deep feature extraction for dense building detection in remote sensing images. In: International Conference on Acoustics, Speech and Signal Processing, pp. 1872–1876 (2018)

20. Chen, C., Gong, W., Chen, Y., Li, W.: Learning a two-stage CNN model for multisized building detection in remote sensing images. Remote Sens. Lett. **10**(2), 103–110 (2019)

21. Pinheiro, P.O., Collobert, R., Dollár, P.: Learning to segment object candidates. In: Advances in Neural Information Processing Systems, pp. 1990–1998 (2015)

22. Dai, J., He, K., Sun, J.: Instance-aware semantic segmentation via multi-task network cascades. In: Proceedings of the IEEE Conference on Computer Vision and Pattern Recognition, pp. 3150–3158 (2016)

23. Li, Y., Qi, H., Dai, J., Ji, X., Wei, Y.: Fully convolutional instance-aware semantic segmentation. In: Proceedings of the IEEE Conference on Computer Vision and Pattern Recognition, pp. 2359–2367 (2017)

24. Xie, S., Girshick, R., Dollár, P., Tu, Z., He, K.: Aggregated residual transformations for deep neural networks. In: Proceedings of the IEEE Conference on Computer Vision and Pattern Recognition, pp. 5987–5995 (2017)

25. Lin, T.-Y., Dollár, P., Girshick, R., He, K., Hariharan, B., Belongie, S.: Feature pyramid networks for object detection. In: Proceedings of the IEEE Conference on Computer Vision and Pattern Recognition, vol. 1, no. 2, p. 4 (2017)

26. Liu, Y., Jin, L.: Deep matching prior network: toward tighter multi-oriented text detection. In: Proceedings of the IEEE Conference on Computer Vision and Pattern Recognition, pp. 3454–3461 (2017)

27. He, K., Zhang, X., Ren, S., Sun, J.: Deep residual learning for image recognition. In: Proceedings of the IEEE Conference on Computer Vision and Pattern Recognition, pp. 770–778 (2016)
28. Russakovsky, O., et al.: ImageNet large scale visual recognition challenge. Int. J. Comput. Vision **115**(3), 211–252 (2015)
29. He, K., Zhang, X., Ren, S., Sun, J.: Delving deep into rectifiers: surpassing human-level performance on imagenet classification. In: Proceedings of the IEEE International Conference on Computer Vision, pp. 1026–1034 (2015)
30. Lin, T.-Y., et al.: Microsoft COCO: common objects in context. In: Fleet, D., Pajdla, T., Schiele, B., Tuytelaars, T. (eds.) ECCV 2014. LNCS, vol. 8693, pp. 740–755. Springer, Cham (2014). https://doi.org/10.1007/978-3-319-10602-1_48

A Semantic Segmentation Approach Based on DeepLab Network in High-Resolution Remote Sensing Images

Hangtao Hu[1,2], Shuo Cai[1], Wei Wang[1,2(✉)], Peng Zhang[2], and Zhiyong Li[2]

[1] Changsha University of Science and Technology,
School of Computer and Communication Engineering, Changsha 410076, China
wangwei@csust.edu.cn
[2] Hunan Shenfan Technology Co., Ltd., Changsha 410000, China

Abstract. Recently, more and more applications for high-resolution remote sensing image intelligent processing are required. Therefore, the semantic segmentation based on deep learning has successfully attracted people's attention. In this paper, the improved Deeplabv3 network is used in the application of image semantic segmentation. The problem of segmenting objects of multiple scales of high-resolution remote sensing image is handled, and the Chinese GaoFen NO. 2(GF-2) remote sensing image is taken as the main research object. Firstly, the original image is pre-processed. Next, use data augmentation and expansion for the pre-processed training image to avoid over-fitting. Finally, it is studied the adaptability and accuracy of the model of high-resolution remote sensing images, while is found the appropriate parameters to improve the precise of the result models compared. And explore the effectiveness of the model in the case of a fewer samples. This model is demonstrated that could be achieved the well classification result.

Keywords: Remote sensing image classification · Deep learning · Semantic segmentation

1 Introduction

In recent years, convolutional neural networks have attracted widespread attention to the academic circles once again, which are actively applied for image classification and recognition. The basic idea of the neural network method is to train the multi-layer perceptron to obtain the decision function, and then utilize it to classify the pixel [1]. This method requires a large amount data, and the deep neural network has a huge number of connections, so it is easy to be applied for spatial information and can better solve the noise and unevenness in the image. Nowadays, the application of deep learning in remote sensing image processing has become more widespread.

So far, The GaoFen(high-resolution) earth observation system have launched GF-1 high-resolution and wide-amplitude satellite, GF-2 sub-meter Panchromatic satellite, GF-3 1 m radar satellite, GF-4 synchronous gaze satellite and others. Among them, there are different spatial resolution, coverage width, spectrum segment and other

Y. Zhao et al. (Eds.): ICIG 2019, LNCS 11903, pp. 292–304, 2019.
https://doi.org/10.1007/978-3-030-34113-8_25

performance parameters, which have enhanced the data source of China's Earth observation system. High-resolution remote sensing image classification has been extensively used in various fields such as land planning, surveying and mapping, national defense security, agriculture, disaster prevention and mitigation [2].

With the development of deep learning, the remote sensing image processing has also been established to some extent. However, its application of industrialization is still in a low stage. A crucial reason is that machine learning methods are inefficiency. Thus, the semantic segmentation based on deep learning has become a research hotspot in this field [3]. The deep convolutional network model is trained by using big data, and it is used to solve automatic extraction of surface geomorphology information in high-resolution remote sensing images. Concurrently, using deep learning to extract the complex information that contained in big data could make more accurate predictions of unknown data [4]. Thus, the academic circle began to apply the deep learning theory about the high-resolution remote sensing images, and explored the multi-layer expression of the potential distribution of high-resolution remote sensing images through the deep neural network, extracting deep features. Therefore, semantic segmentation is incorporated into the deep learning framework, used in high-resolution remote sensing image classification [5].

In this paper, The DeepLabv3 network is used to deal with the GF-2 image of Chenzhou, Hunan Province. We are studied and improved the semantic segmentation method. According to the local geomorphological features labeled the original image and augmented dataset, so could be trained model. The model suitable for GF-2 image data is explored in terms of network layer setting, image input size mode and network parameter setting.

2 Related Work

Semantic segmentation refers to dividing into the pixels of the same object in the image of the same class, and segmenting the different objects to predict the category of each pixel in the image. In semantic segmentation, visual input needs to be divided into distinct semantically interpretable categories [6].

The fully convolutional network proposed by Long [7], which adjusted the general convolutional network structure to enable dense prediction without the fully connected layer. The fully convolutional network replaces the fully connected layers of convolutional layers. This model could arbitrarily segment the inputted image to obtain the expected output size, and it also greatly reduces the running time compared with traditional image block classification method. Therefore, most subsequent semantic segmentation network models to be used in this structure.

One of the main challenges to semantic segmentation based on deep convolutional networks is to solve the problem about pixel loss caused by the pooling layer. Although the pooling layer can further extract abstract features to increase the receptive field [8], the spatial location information on the pixels is lost. Semantic segmentation requires the classification target output image and the input image to have the same resolution and size, so it is necessary to reintroduce the spatial position information on the pixel. There is a different structure that can solve the pixel loss problem.

Atrous convolution [9] structure: This structure used the Atrous convolutional layer to replace pooling layer. It is a feature sampling method. From the dense sampling to the sparse sampling of data, so it can be effortlessly in the pre-trained basic network. There is no necessary to change the structure of the network, and the training parameters will not be greatly improved. In the case of a given convolution kernel, it is increased the receptive field of subsequent convolution. Since the parameters of the large convolution kernel are inefficient, this method is better than increasing the size of the convolution kernel. It could significantly expand receptive field while does not reduce the spatial dimension [10]. Representative neural network: DeepLab, PSPNet, and RefineNet (Fig. 1).

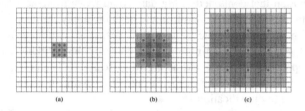

Fig. 1. (a) dilation rate 1 (b) dilation rate 2 (c) dilation rate 4.

3   Method

DeepLabv3 is taken advantage of the second generation residual network (ResNet) as the basic network. The residual network contains 4 residual blocks. Each block contains a different number of residual units, which a residual standard unit consisting of two 1 * 1 convolution kernels and one 3 * 3 convolution kernels. Assuming the neural network input is x and its expected output is H(x), the goals that can be learned now are:

$$F(x) = H(x) - x \qquad (1)$$

The original output is F(x) + x. The residual is equivalent to changing the learning goal, instead of learning a complete output H(x), but the difference between the output and the input H(x) − x [11] (Fig. 2).

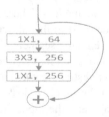

Fig. 2. Residual unit structure

In order to deal with multi-scale feature learning, DeepLabv3 effectively extracts multi-scale context information by using different dilation rate (step size) atrous convolution parallel architecture. The last residual block uses the atrous convolution instead of a regular convolution [12]. In addition, each convolution in this residual block utilized the atrous spatial pyramid pooling (ASPP), which utilized multiple atrous convolution kernels and batch normalization in the atrous convolution block, capturing multi-scale context information, and use image-level feature information improvement to optimize the training performance of the network [13], and further improve the classification effect. The block diagram of the initial implementation of the algorithm is as follows (Fig. 3).

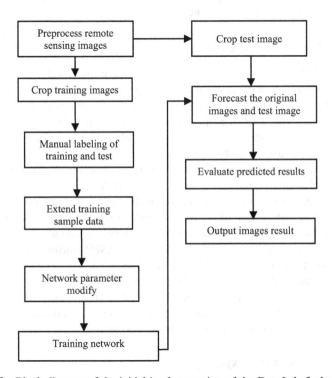

Fig. 3. Block diagram of the initial implementation of the DeepLabv3 algorithm

3.1 Atrous Convolution for Detail Feature Extraction

The deep neural network of fully convolutional structure fashion has shown to be effective for the task of semantic segmentation. However, the repeated combination of max-pooling and striding convolution at successive layers of these networks significantly reduces, Which these operations in the network reduce the spatial resolution of the output feature map, so the deconvolution layer is used to recover the spatial resolution. DeepLabv3 is used atrous convolution instead of deconvolution.

Assuming a two-dimensional signal [14], for each location i on pixel, the corresponding output y and a convolution kernel weight w, the dilation rate r, and the output kernel size k, the atrous convolution calculation is performed on the input feature map x

$$y[i] = \sum_k x[i + r \cdot k]w[k] \qquad (2)$$

The input x and the upsampled convolution kernel obtained by inserting 0 of $r - 1$ along each spatial dimension between two consecutive convolution kernel weight values are convolved. The standard convolution is a special form of $r = 1$. The atrous convolution allows us to modify the receptive field of the convolution kernel by changing the setting of the dilation rate r.

3.2 Atrous Spatial Pyramid Pooling

ASPP is showed that it is effective to resample features of multi-scales for precisely and efficiently classifying area of an arbitrary scale. Multiple parallel atrous convolutions with different dilation rates are applied on top of the feature map, and are obtained feature maps of diverse sizes of output. Then, the feature map is pooled to generate a fixed-length representation. Therefore, it is possible to be robustly segmented one object of multiple scales, thereby capturing context information on the image. The features extracted from each dilation rate could be processed in separate branches of a single scale, and finally merged to produce a result [15].

To incorporate global context information on the model, it is applied global average pooling on the last feature map of the model, feed the resulting image-level features in a 1×1 convolution with 256 filters, and then bilinearly upsample the feature of the desired spatial dimension. In the end, our improved ASPP consists of (a) one 1×1 convolution and three 3×3 convolutions with rates = (6, 12, 18) when all with 256 filters and batch normalization, and (b) the image-level features. The resulting features from all the branches are then concatenated and pass through another 1×1 convolution before the final 1×1 convolution recovery to the desired the resolution [16]. In the end, it could be produced the final classification result.

3.3 Improved DeepLabv3 Model

According to the characteristics of the GF-2 image, the network model is adjusted, majorly to modify the ASPP structure.

DeepLabv3 is replicated several copies of the residual blocks 4 to be cascaded up to the residual block 7. However, this consecutive cascade design is detrimental to semantic segmentation, destroys the detail information on the image and requires higher computational performance and memory, reducing the running rate. After removing the cascading block, it was found that the impact on the results was limited, so the cascading block was not used in this model.

DeepLabv3 is processed the feature map using four parallel atrous convolutions of different dilation rates. ASPP has different sampling rates and can extract information of multiple scales very efficiently. However, it is found that the effective convolution weight in the convolution kernel becomes smaller as the dilation rate increases. Therefore, according to the multi-scales feature of GF-2 image, the dilation rate is reduced, and the number of parallel atrous convolutions (rate (3, 6, 9, 12)) is increased, so that a wider range of context information can be well (Fig. 4).

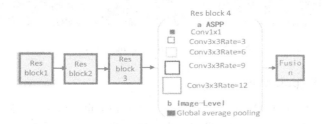

Fig. 4. Improved DeepLabv3 atrous spatial pyramid pooling layer structure

4 Experiments

The operating system running is Ubuntu, which is used the pre-trained residual network of ImageNet as the basic network framework. The training device GPU is NVIDIA GTX1080Ti. We use Tensorflow to build a deep neural network that dealt with GF-2 images. It is trained and used for data processing. Furthermore, the control variable method is used to study the influence of the parameters of the network on the classification results, which find the appropriate combination of parameters.

4.1 Dataset Introduction

The dataset is derived from the image of the GF-2, which is a satellites developed and launched by China. The dataset is based on the GF-2 image of the Chenzhou area in 2016. There is complex and preserved with intact primary secondary forest communities and low-altitude broad-leaved forests in the Nanling Mountains. The forest plant resources are rich and diverse. This dataset has a spatial resolution of 0.8 meters, specific latitude and longitude is 112°623′112°188′ east longitude and 26°535′−25° 882 north latitude, and the number of bands is 4. The original GF-2 image is preprocessed with ENVI, and then it is cropped and is marked in the range of 2000 * 2000 pixels, which is marked by Matlab. It can be made a ground true image of an annotation the different image types with diverse colors by manual labeling.

According to the geomorphological characteristics, the classification categories are divided into seven categories, which are forest, others, water, house, road, furrow (farmland as background), except that the background has a corresponding color covering it (Fig. 5).

Fig. 5. Manually annotating images

4.2 Image Preprocessing

The original dataset of the GF-2 image is included 12 training images (6 of which are processed for the original image) and 1 test image. The GF-2 image size is too large, so these images cannot be directly sent to the network for training. The running memory of the device is limited and the input image size is different, thence the training image is cropped. On the other hand, the significant feature of the deep neural network model need a larger number of training samples. In order to avoid the neural network over-fitting in part of dataset, the solution is to augment and expand the existing training dataset, thereby enriching the GF-2 image training dataset and improving the generalization ability of the semantic segmentation model. Therefore, for a GF-2 image, it is cropped into small image blocks for use as a training dataset, implemented using OpenCV.

(1) First dataset the 2000 * 2000 training image to a specific size output image according to requiring.
(2) Then it is sampled and cropped, wherein the sampling method is random window sampling and then obtaining a small image of a definite size output under the coordinate.
(3) Data augmentation is performed on the cropped image, which is produced by random rotation, horizontal and vertical flipping, gamma transformation, blurring, erode, adding noise, and bilinear filtering.
(4) Observation data reveal imbalances between categories, such as fewer roads. Therefore, it is necessary to extra augment a fewer categories. Before the network starts to train, search for the cropped data, find images of more roads, and increase the number of such samples by image transformation. This gave rise to a large amount of extended data used as a training dataset.

4.3 Semantic Segmentation Performance Evaluation Method

The following four standards are commonly used in image semantic segmentation to measure the accuracy of an algorithm [17].

(1) Pixel Accuracy (PA, Pixel Accuracy): The ratio of the correct pixels in the test image to the total pixels of the ground true image.
(2) Mean Pixel Accuracy (MPA, Average Pixel Accuracy): It is calculated the proportion of correctly classified pixels in each class, and then averages all classes.
(3) Mean Intersection over Union (MIoU): a standard measure of semantic segmentation. It is calculated the intersection of the two sets and the union of the two sets. In the problem of semantic segmentation, the two sets are the ground true image and the test image, respectively. IoU is calculated on each class and then averaged.
(4) Frequency Weighted Intersection over Union (FWIoU): An enhancement to MIoU that sets the weight of each class in its frequency.

4.4   Comparative Analysis of Network Training and Prediction Results

4.4.1   DeepLabv3 Network Training and Prediction Results

The improved network parameters are fine-tuned according to the characteristics of GF-2 image. The basic network selects the residual 101 layers network (Res101). The network training parameters are as follows: where batch norm decay = 0.997, batch

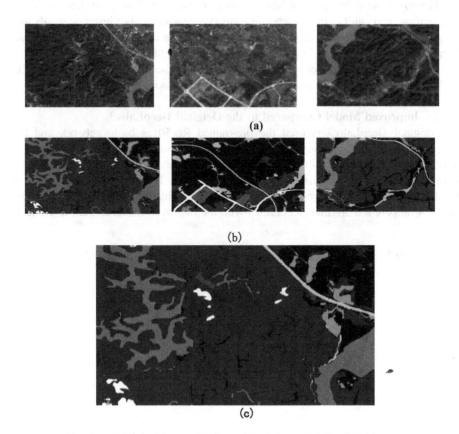

Fig. 6. (a) Original image (b) Ground truth image (c) Predicted image

size = 4, learning rate = 0.0001, weight decay = 0.00001, 100000 iterations, of which the learning rate was reduced to one tenth to 40,000 and 80,000 times, and the data concentration training and testing ratio is 4:1.

The test image is then placed into the trained model for prediction. The test remote sensing image is too large, usually 2000 * 2000. Therefore, in the prediction program, first the test image is cropped into small image blocks, moving window sampling to predict each image block, and then combine the predicted image blocks to get the final predicted image (Fig. 6).

By comparing the predicted image and the ground true image, the image information that can be accurately classified. DeepLabv3 is utilized the diverse step size atrous convolution parallel method to effectively extract multi-scales context information. This improved the ASPP structure's ability to extract global context information by combining image-level information to augmented the effect Image boundaries and details are smoother, without blurring and aliasing. It is classified each pixel and considered the relationship between pixels and pixels, where does not was neglected the spatial regularization used in the usual pixel classification based segmentation method. Thus, it has spatial consistency. For example, large areas of rivers, buildings and forests can be effectively identified.

The downside is the case that ASPP is not sensitive enough to some slender objects information, and can't extract context information efficiently. For instance, roads and streams are not completely recognized by the model. The atrous convolution is sparse. The slender object fills the blank space with zero weight in the atrous convolution. Therefore, the partial convolution result is zero, and the pixel is recognized as the background, resulting in an incorrect classification decision.

4.4.2   Improved Model Compared to the Original DeepLabv3

The original DeepLabv3 is used the pre-trained Res50 as basic network and the learning rate for the poly strategy, while the batch norm decay of the BN layer is 0.9997, with an initial learning rate of 0.007, and the size of the images is 513, using PASCAL VOC 2012. The dataset is a near-view image. The improved model has five parallel atrous convolution pooling structures with a dilation rate (3, 6, 9, 12,) and others. Compare the original DeepLabv3 with the improved model to get the Table 1.

Table 1. Performance evaluation of original DeepLabv3 and improved models

	PA	MPA	MIoU	FWIoU
Original model	86.7	75.2	66.7	72.4
Rate 1, 2, 3, 4	87.1	78.1	70.3	75.5
Rate 2, 4, 6, 8	87.8	80.9	71.7	78.1
Rate 3, 6, 9, 12	88.6	83.8	73.4	80.2
Rate 6, 12, 18, 24	86.9	80.4	69.6	77.5

The improved network is at least the performance better than the original network. The original network is used a larger dilation rate, and the effective convolution weight in the convolution kernel is getting smaller and smaller. The global context information on the image cannot be extracted efficiently. The improved model has more parallel atrous convolutions, which facilitates the extraction of deeper details of the image, to solve complex remote sensing landform information. From the performance indicators of the results of the dataset, it can be concluded that the dilation rate (3, 6, 9, 12) set of data performs best.

4.4.3   Network Depth and Input Size Impact on the Network

The improved DeepLabv3 is trained using the residual 24 layers, the residual 50 layers, the residual 74 layers and the residual 101 layers as the basic network framework. The input image sizes in training are 512 * 512 or 256 * 256, respectively. The test images were not trained in the neural network versatility of the model. It is predicted using a prediction program, and then it is passed through the image quality evaluation program to obtain the following Table 2.

Table 2. Performance evaluation of different depth residual networks and input sizes

	PA	MPA	MIoU	FWIoU
256Res24	83.9	77.3	66.1	72.8
512Res24	84.1	77.7	67.3	73.1
256Res50	85.3	78.2	67.8	74.3
512Res50	86.1	78.7	68.3	75.7
256Res74	86.3	78.3	68.1	76.8
512Res74	86.7	79.3	68.8	77.1
256Res101	87.8	81.3	71.8	78.8
512Res101	88.6	83.8	73.4	80.2

Through the above Table 2, it is found that the basic network is the Res101, and the training input image size is 512 * 512 that is the best.

(1) The depth of the residual neural network plays a major role in the performance index of the classification objects, because it determines the feature quality of the GF-2 image of different aspects such as invariance and abstraction [18]. Following consideration of the complexity of the network calculation, the depth also affects the running time of the global network training. Res101 runtime is generally more time than the Res24, and the maximum size of the batch size of Res24 can be set to 16, and the memory requirements for the GPU will be reduced.

(2) On the other hand, the input image size of the same basic network framework has a little effect on image quality evaluation, and there is a definite improvement on the same basic network. The proportion of each classification objects in training dataset is not balanced, so some categories occupy the proportion is large and the proportion of others is small. If classify an image by moving window, one image should contain as many categories as possible. Generally, the 256 * 256 images

have less probability of containing the classification objects than the 512 * 512 images. The large image is divided, when the image is predicted. The cropped image size is larger. The fewer the number of cuts, the lower the error rate of the cutting edge recognition. This will have an effect on the final result.

4.4.4 Small Sample Impact on the Network

In order to explore the deviation of the prediction results of the model when the retraining samples are insufficient, the influence of network depth of its classification decision is tested for the case of a few samples. Reduce the number of training images to 4, and 2, with a sample size 512 * 512 of 30,000, and 10,000 The Res24 and the Res101 were respectively used for training, and the test images were predicted to obtain the following Table 3.

Table 3. Performance evaluation of Res24 and Res101

	PA	MPA	MIoU	FWIoU
10000Res24	61.2	66.3	42.1	42.7
10000Res101	63.8	66.3	44.1	51.2
30000Res24	81.4	72.1	63.8	70.9
30000Res101	82.1	74.3	64.5	71.8

In the case of reducing the number of samples, performance indicators have declined in various aspects. Due to insufficient training samples identify deviations in classification targets that different within the class and similar between classes.

(1) The training data has a significant decline in the classification of 10,000, and many categories have not been classified.
(2) The training data is 30,000 pieces that can get closer to the training values of all dataset, and can initially reach the classification effect.

From the table, the performance values of Res24 and Res101 are small gap. If only from the running rate, it is more suitable to select the Res24. In the case of limited samples, the higher efficiency of the running time and classification accuracy of the lightweight neural network is considered under balanced.

4.4.5 Analysis of Different Time-Phase Data

In addition, in order to verify the generalization ability of the model, the Chenzhou area of different time-phase is selected for verification. It is mainly to verify the model to learn image category information on different data samples. The verification images of different phases in other parts of Chenzhou are heterogeneous data, and the classification objects have large differences between the class, and the distribution of training images and verification images are inconsistent, which leads to training and verification of forest, buildings, and roads, are dissimilar. Moreover, the amount of category data on each classification objects is not balanced. The basic network is used as the Res 101, and the input image size 512 * 512.

Table 4. Performance indicators for different phases in other parts of Chenzhou

	PA	MPA	MIoU	FWIoU
Others 1	86.3	84.3	74.2	75.8
Others 2	85.7	82.3	73.4	74.3
Others 3	87.6	85.3	76.3	77.8

From the above Table 4, it can be seen that the partial evaluation index MPA of different phase in other regions is higher than the test image, and the PA is only slightly lower than the test image. It can be seen that the model has generality for the classification effect of GF-2 images in Chenzhou area and has well generalization ability.

5 Conclusions

In this experiment, the improved DeepLabv3 network is tested to perform image classification in the GF-2 image of Chenzhou area. Firstly, the original remote sensing image is pre-processed. Then it is labeled as the dataset. Next, the training dataset is cropped, augmented, and trained. Finally, the test image is predicted, and the performance of the result is numerically analyzed by image semantic segmentation evaluation.

By comparing the classification results of different model parameters, it is found that the classification of the Res101 network and the input image size of 512 * 512 is the best. Because the larger the training size, the fewer the number of segments is divided, which can reduce the identification of edge information and have sufficient classification objects. On the other hand, the shallow residual network is easy to converge, and it was fallen into a local optimal solution and cannot reach the best result. The deeper residual network can be extracted features the higher abstraction and captured more image details, so it can be beneficial to the deep network to optimize the classification result. Besides, the depth of the network is explored the impact on insufficient samples. When the training sample is few, the residual network is easily under-fit, and misjudgment occurs when encountering similar pixel and texture features between similar classes.

The model is verified by adding different time-phase images to test. Whether the classification effect is reduced due to factors such as intra-image differences and pixel differences, thereby verifying the generalization ability. Unfortunately, it is not sensitive enough to some slender objects in the image, like roads and streams. These objects are not fully recognized by this model. The next work will focuses on improving the recognition of slender objects.

Acknowledgment. This work was supported by the National Nature Science Foundation, P.R. China 61702052 and 61070040 and also supported by Hunan Provincial Education Department under grant 18A137 and 17C043.

References

1. FeiYan, Z., LinPeng, J., Dong, J.: Review of convolutional neural network. Chin. J. Comput. **40**(6), 1229–1251 (2017)
2. XiaoFei, H., ZhengRong, Z., Chao, T.: Combined saliency with multi-convolutional neural network for high resolution remote sensing scene classification. Acta Geodaetica Cartogr. Sin. **45**(9), 1073–1108 (2016)
3. ChuChu, Y., Xianxian, L., YuDan, Z., et al.: A review on image classification of remote sensing using deep learning. In: 2017 3rd IEEE International Conference on Computer and Communications, pp. 1947–1955 (2017)
4. Pan, B., Shi, Z., Xu, X.: MugNet: deep learning for hyperspectral image classification using limited samples. ISPRS J. Photogrammetry Remote Sens. **145**, 108–119 (2017)
5. Hamida, A., Benoît, A., Lambert, P.: Deep learning for semantic segmentation of remote sensing images with rich spectral content. In: IEEE International Geoscience and Remote Sensing Symposium, pp. 2569–2572 (2017)
6. Kemker, R., Salvaggio, C., Kanan, C.: Algorithms for semantic segmentation of multispectral remote sensing imagery using deep learning. ISPRS J. Photogrammetry Remote Sens. **145**, 60–77 (2018)
7. Long, J., Shelhamer, E., Darrell, T.: Fully convolutional networks for semantic segmentation. IEEE Trans. Pattern Anal. Mach. Intell. **39**(4), 640–651 (2014)
8. Xin, W., Yajing, G., Xin, G.: A new semantic segmentation model for remote sensing Images. In: 2017 IEEE International Geoscience and Remote Sensing Symposium, pp. 1776–1779 (2017)
9. Fisher, Y., Koltun, V.: Multi-Scale context aggregation by dilated convolution. In: International Conference on Learning Representations (ICLR) (2016)
10. Guosheng, L., Anton, M.: RefineNet: multi-path refinement networks for high-resolution semantic segmentation. In: 2017 IEEE Conference on Computer Vision and Pattern Recognition, pp. 5168–5177 (2017)
11. He, K., Zhang, X., Ren, S., et al.: Identity mappings in deep residual networks. In: European Conference on Computer Vision, pp. 630–645 (2016)
12. LiangChieh, C., Papandreou, G., Kokkinos, I., et al.: Semantic image segmentation with deep convolutional nets and fully connected CRFs. In: International Conference on Learning Representations (ICLR), no. 4, pp. 357–361 (2015)
13. Yang, Z., Mu, X., Fa, Z.: Scene classification of remote sensing image based on deep network grading transferring. Optik **168**, 127–133 (2018)
14. LiangChieh, C., Papandreou, G.: DeepLab: semantic image segmentation with deep convolutional nets Atrous convolution and fully connected CRFs. IEEE Trans. Pattern Anal. Mach. Intell. **40**(4), 834–848 (2017)
15. Zhao, H., Shi, J., Qi, J., et al.: Pyramid scene parsing network. In: 2017 IEEE Conference on Computer Vision and Pattern Recognition (CVPR), pp. 6230–6239 (2017)
16. LiangChieh, C., Papandreou, G., Schroff F.: et al.: Rethinking Atrous convolution for semantic image segmentation. arXiv:1706.05587 (2017)
17. Garcia, G., Alberto, O., Sergio O., et al.: A review on deep learning techniques applied to semantic segmentation. arXiv:1704.06857 (2017)
18. Wei, W., Yujing, Y., Xin, W., et al.: The development of convolution neural network and its application in image classification: a survey. Opt. Eng. **58**(4), 040901 (2019)

Modified LDE for Dimensionality Reduction of Hyperspectral Image

Lei He, Hongwei Yang, and Lina Zhao$^{(\boxtimes)}$

The Beijing University of Chemical Technology, Beijing 10029, China
{2018200881,yanghw,zhaoln}@buct.edu.cn

Abstract. Hyperspectral image (HSI) has shown promising results in many fields because of its high spectral resolution. However, redundancy and noise in spectral dimension seriously affect the classification of HSI. For this reason, many popular dimensionality reduction (DR) methods are proposed to solve the problem. The local discriminant embedding (LDE) as an effective non-linear method for DR can be more discriminative by constructing two neighborhood graphs. However, HSI is very easy influenced by noise, and the LDE algorithm based on K nearest neighborhood is highly susceptible to interference from extreme point, which may lead to inaccurate graph construction and poor performance of classification. To overcome the problem and retain the advantages of LDE, a modified local discriminant embedding (MLDE) is firstly applied on HSI by constructing neighborhood graphs on a new spectral feature space instead of the original space. We use variance to characterize the pixels similarity of the same class and use covariance to characterize the separation of different classes of pixels. The combination of variance and covariance makes pixels in the same class to be closer and makes greater separation of pixels from different classes, which enhances classification performance of HSI. The way of representing data by using variance and covariance can attenuate the effects of noise. The Log-Euclidean metric is used to capture the similarity between spectral vectors, which can provide a more accurate similarity evaluation than euclidean distance. The experimental results of two hyperspectral datasets demonstrate the effectiveness of our proposed MLDE method.

Keywords: Classification of hyperspectral image (HSI) ·
Dimensionality reduction (DR) · Local discriminant embedding
(LDE) · Log-Euclidean metric

1 Introduction

Hyperspectral image (HSI) usually consists of hundreds of spectral bands from the visible spectrum to the infrared spectrum [1]. Each pixel of HSI can be represented by a high dimensional spectral vector. It's because HSI's rich spectral

Supported by the National Natural Science Foundation of China, 11301021 and 11571031.

© Springer Nature Switzerland AG 2019
Y. Zhao et al. (Eds.): ICIG 2019, LNCS 11903, pp. 305–319, 2019.
https://doi.org/10.1007/978-3-030-34113-8_26

information that it has not only attracted the attention of the remote sensing community, but also aroused great interest in other fields, for instance, military [2], agriculture [3], urban planning, and environmental monitoring [4]. It is known that classification plays a crucial role in these fields. However, HSI generates a large amount of irrelevant or redundant data that causes a number of issues including significantly increased computation time, computational complexity and the classification performance especially when the training datasets are limited. A number of classical dimensionality reduction (DR) algorithms are explored to address these issues.

One of classic linear methods of DR is principle component analysis (PCA) [5]. But as an unsupervised methods, PCA doesn't take advantage of class label information. Another one of classic linear methods of DR is linear discriminant analysis (LDA) [6], as a supervised method, it often suffers from the small sample size problem. And the biggest disadvantage of these linear methods is the failure to discover the nonlinear structure inherent in HSI.

Since nonlinear techniques have the merit of preserving geometrical structure of data manifold, it can overcome the above-problem. Laplacian eigenmaps (LE) [7], local linear embedding (LLE) [8] and other manifold learning algorithms have been successfully applied to DR for HSI. Besides, as a linear version of LE, locality preserving projection (LPP) [9] has been introduced. In order to overcome the difficulty of LDA tending to produce undesirable results when the samples in a class is multimodal non-Gaussian class distributions [10], local Fisher's discriminant analysis (LFDA) [11] which having the advantages of LDA and LPP at the same time was introduced. After that, unlike LPP which uses only one graph to describe the geometry of the sample, local discriminant embedding (LDE) [12] method using two graphs to characterize the geometry structure of the sample was proposed. One as an intrinsic graph to characterize the compact nature of the sample, and the other as a penalty graph to describe the internal separation of the sample. Thus, LDE is more discriminative than LPP. The advantage of LDE is that it can make the data from the same class keep their intrinsic neighbor relations, and it also makes the data in different classes no longer close to each other. However, one thing in common among these above-mentioned methods is that the calculation of the affinity matrix is based on K nearest neighborhood, which is sensitive to outlier samples.

To overcome the above-problem, a graph embedding (GE) frame work [13] was proposed. In order to represent the sparse nature of the samples, a sparse graph embedding (SGE) [14] was developed. Later, a sparse graph-based discriminant analysis (SGDA) [15] model was developed by exploiting the class label information, resulting in a better performance than SGE. Above this, based on SGDA, sparse and low-rank graph discriminant analysis (SLGDA) [16] was proposed by increasing local information of samples. Recently, since considering curves changing description among spectral bands, a graph-based discriminant analysis with spectral similarity (GDA-SS) [17] method was proposed.

Each pixel of HSI is a high dimensional spectral vector that directly displays the spectral reflectance of the targets in different bands. Under an ideal condition, the same targets should have the same spectral characteristics. Nevertheless, HSI is very easy influenced by environment change (i.e. atmosphere and illumination) and instrument problem (i.e. senor) in the real word. And K nearest neighborhood based on euclidean distance is usually used to compute the similarity between two vectors, which is highly susceptible to interference from extreme point. These may lead to inaccurate graph construction and poor performance of classification. Inspired by the region covariance descriptor in [18] and the superiority of the second-order statistic representing data, a novel modified local discriminant embedding (MLDE) is proposed by constructing neighborhoods on a new spectral feature space instead of the original space. We use variance to characterize the pixel similarity of the same class and use covariance to characterize the separation of different classes of pixels. Considering the symmetric positive definite nature of covariance matrix lying on a Riemannan manifold, the Log-Euclidean metric is used to capture the similarity, which has a better effect than the euclidean distance. The main advantages in this paper are summarized as follows: (a) The combination of variance and covariance enables data points in the same class to be closer and enables greater separation of data points from different classes, which enhances classification performance of HSI. (b) The way of representing data by using variance and covariance can attenuate the effects of noise, which can better handle with noise in HSI. (c) The Log-Euclidean metric can provide a more accurate similarity evaluation than euclidean distance, which can better express the characteristics of spectral information.

2   Related Work

2.1   Local Discriminant Embedding (LDE)

Assume a hyperspectral dataset having N samples is denoted as $X = \{x_i\}_i^N$ existing in a $\mathbb{R}^{m \times 1}$ feature space, where m is the number of bands. And class labels $y_i \in 1, 2, ...C$, where C is the number of classes.

LDE which is defined for manifold learning and pattern classification tries to obtain an optimal projection matrix by considering the class label information of the data points and the local neighborhood information between data points. Specifically, the LDE algorithm can be described as follows.

Steps 1: Construct neighborhood graphs. An intrinsic graph G and a penalty graph G' can be constructed by K nodes of K nearest neighborhood (KNN) over all the data point.

Steps 2: Compute affinity weights. An affinity matrix W of the intrinsic graph G and an affinity matrix W' of the penalty graph G' can be computed as follows:

$$w_{ij} = \begin{cases} exp(-||x_i - x_j||^2/t) & x_j \in O(K, x_i) \\ & \text{or } x_i \in O(K, x_j) \\ & \text{and } y_i = y_j; \\ 0 & \text{otherwise} \end{cases} \tag{1}$$

and

$$w'_{ij} = \begin{cases} exp(-||x_i - x_j||^2/t) & x_j \in O(K, x_i) \\ & \text{or } x_i \in O(K, x_j) \\ & \text{and } y_i \neq y_j; \\ 0 & \text{otherwise} \end{cases} \quad (2)$$

where $O(K, x_i)$ represents the K nearest neighborhood of data x_i and the parameter t is a kernel width parameter.

The optimization problem of LDE is described as follows:

$$\arg\min_P \sum_{i,j} ||P^T x_i - P^T x_j||^2 w_{ij}$$

$$s.t. \sum_{ij} ||P^T x_i - P^T x_j||^2 w'_{ij} = 1 \quad (3)$$

Steps 3: Complete the embedding. The projection matrix P can be obtained by solving the eigenvectors corresponding to the H smallest nonzero eigenvalues of the following generalized eigenvalue problem:

$$X(D - W)X^T P = \wedge X(D' - W')X^T P \quad (4)$$

where $\wedge$ is a diagonal eigenvalue matrix. D and D' are diagonal matrices with $D_{ii} = \sum_{j=1}^N W_{i,j}$ and $D'_{ii} = \sum_{j=1}^N W'_{i,j}$.

2.2   Region Covariance Descriptor for HSI

As a robust and very novel data descriptor, region covariance descriptor has been successful and effectively applied to many computer vision problems [19, 20]. Consider a HSI data $\boldsymbol{X} \in \mathbb{R}^{l \times w \times m}$ with m representing the number of bands and $l \times w$ representing the spatial structure. Consider a three order spatial-spectral tensor $x \in \mathbb{R}^{(2n-1) \times (2n-1) \times m}$ as a small patch of $\boldsymbol{X} \in \mathbb{R}^{l \times w \times m}$, the central of x is a pixel, the rest of the central of x is its local region neighborhood. Therefore, the pixels of a HSI data $\boldsymbol{X} \in \mathbb{R}^{l \times w \times m}$ can be denoted as $\{x_i\}_{i=1}^N$, where $x_i \in \mathbb{R}^{(2n+1) \times (2n+1) \times m}$ denotes the ith pixel and N is the number of pixels [18]. And x_s ($s = 1, 2, ..., (2n + 1) \times (2n + 1)$) is a spectral vector in the region of interest around the ith hyperspectral pixel. Then, a spectral region covariance descriptor C_i can be obtained by the Eq. (5).

$$C_i = \frac{1}{S-1} \sum_{s=1}^S (x_s - \mu_i)(x_s - \mu_i)^T$$

$$\mu_i = \frac{1}{S} \sum_{s=1}^s x_s \quad (5)$$

where S is the number of spectral vectors in the region of interest, and μ_i is the mean vector. Meantime, C_i is considered to be the feature of $\boldsymbol{X}_i$.

3   Our Work

3.1   Variance and Covariance for HSI

Inspired by the region covariance descriptor in [18], we want to introduce the variance and covariance instead of the region covariance descriptor to attenuate the effects of noise, because in this paper the hyperspectral dataset is used as input in the form of a vector, not a tensor. Consider a hyperspectral dataset denoted as $X = \{x_i | x_{i1}, x_{i2}, ..., x_{im}\}_{i=1}^{N}$ existing in a $\mathbb{R}^{m \times 1}$ feature space, where m is the number of bands. Then, a spectral variance C_i ($i = 1, 2, ..., N$) and a covariance C_{ij} ($i, j = 1, 2, ..., N$) can be obtained by the Eq. (6).

$$C_i = \frac{1}{m-1} \sum_{k=1}^{m} (x_{ik} - \mu_i)(x_{ik} - \mu_i)^T$$

$$\mu_i = \frac{1}{m} \sum_{k=1}^{m} x_{ik} \tag{6}$$

$$C_{ij} = \frac{1}{m-1} \sum_{k=1}^{m} (x_{ik} - \mu_i)(x_{jk} - \mu_j)^T$$

where μ_i is the spectral mean value. Meantime, the variance C_i is considered to be the feature of x_i, and the covariance C_{ij} is considered to be the feature of between x_i and x_j.

3.2   Modified Local Discriminant Embedding (MLDE)

Suffered by the euclidean distance which is sensitive for noise and the data which contain inevitable noise created by environment change (i.e. atmosphere and illumination) and instrument problem (i.e. senor), the LDE algorithm may lead to inaccurate graph construction and a poor performance of classification. In this section, we propose an MLDE algorithm to overcome the problem.

Like LDE, the intrinsic graph G and the penalty graph G' should be constructed firstly. Nevertheless, in MLDE, the difference is that we use the variance features $\{C_i\}_{i=1}^{N}$ and the covariance features $\{C_{ij}\}_{i,j=1}^{N}$ obtained by Eq. (6) to construct the intrinsic graph and the penalty graph denoted as G_{var} and G'_{cov}, respectively. Due to the variance features and the covariance features lying on a Rimannian manifold, the Log-Euclidean metric is a good choice to compute the affinity.

$$D_{LE}(C_i, C_j) = |log(C_i) - log(C_j)| \tag{7}$$

Then, the affinity matrix W_{var} of the intrinsic graph G_{var} and the affinity matrix W_{cov} of the penalty graph G_{cov} can be computed as follows:

$$w_{var\ ij} = \begin{cases} exp(-D_{LE}(C_i, C_j)^2/t) & C_j \in O(K, C_i) \\ & \text{or } C_i \in O(K, C_j) \\ & \text{and } y_i = y_j; \\ 0 & \text{otherwise} \end{cases} \tag{8}$$

and

$$w'_{cov\ ij} = \begin{cases} exp(-|log(C_{ij})|^2/t) & C_{ij} \in O(K, C_{ii}) \\ & \text{or } C_{ii} \in O(K, C_{ij}) \\ & \text{and } y_i \neq y_j; \\ 0 & \text{otherwise} \end{cases} \quad (9)$$

where $O(K, C_i)$ represents the K nearest neighborhood of covariance feature C_i and the parameter t is a kernel width parameter.

The optimization problem of MLDE is described as follows:

$$J(P) = \arg\min_P \sum_{i,j} ||P^T x_i - P^T x_j||^2 w_{var\ ij}$$

$$s.t. \quad \sum_{ij} ||P^T x_i - P^T x_j||^2 w'_{cov\ ij} = 1 \quad (10)$$

Similarity to LDE, the optimization problem (10) can be rewritten as (11) by the nature of trace.

$$J(P) = \arg\min_P \sum_{i,j} ||P^T x_i - P^T x_j||^2 w_{var\ ij}$$

$$= \arg\min_P \sum_{i,j} tr\{(P^T x_i - P^T x_j)(P^T x_i - P^T x_j)^T\} w_{var\ ij} \quad (11)$$

$$= \arg\min_P \sum_{i,j} tr\{P^T (x_i - x_j)(x_i - x_j)^T P\} w_{var\ ij}$$

By $w_{var\ ij}$ is a scalar and the operation of trace is linear, the Eq. (11) can be rewritten as (12):

$$J(P) = \arg\min_P \ tr\{P^T \sum_{i,j} ((x_i - x_j) w_{var\ ij} (x_i - x_j)^T) P\}$$

$$= \arg\min_P \ tr\{P^T (2X D_{var} X^T - 2X W_{var} X^T) P\} \quad (12)$$

$$= \arg\min_P \ 2tr\{P^T X(D_{var} - W_{var}) X^T P\}$$

where D_{var} is a diagonal matrix with $D_{var\ ii} = \sum_{j=1}^{N} W_{var\ ij}$. Then, the optimization problem (10) can be rewritten as (13):

$$J(P) = \arg\min_P \ 2tr\{P^T X(D_{var} - W_{var}) X^T P\}$$

$$s.t. \quad 2tr\{P^T X(D_{cov} - W_{cov}) X^T P\} = 1 \quad (13)$$

The projection matrix P can be obtained by solving the eigenvectors corresponding to the H smallest nonzero eigenvalues of the following generalized eigenvalue problem:

$$X(D_{var} - W_{var}) X^T P = \wedge X(D_{cov} - W_{cov}) X^T P \quad (14)$$

Thus, MLDE for hyperspectral image classification is carried out following the steps in Algorithm 1.

Algorithm 1 MLDE-Based HSI Classification Algorithm

Input: Training set X_{train}, the class labels of training set y_{train}, testing set X_{test}, the class labels of testing set y_{test}, where $X_{train} = \{x_i | x_i \in R^{m \times 1}, i = 1, ..., N_{train}\}$, $X_{test} = \{x_i | x_i \in R^{m \times 1}, i = 1, ..., N_{test}\}$, $y_{train} \in \{1, ..., C\}$, and $y_{test} \in \{1, ..., C\}$.

Output: The class labels of testing set.

Initialize: $K = k$, $H = h$.

1: Structure the intrinsic graph G_{var} and the penalty graph G_{cov}.

2: Compute the affinity matrices W_{var} and W_{cov} by Eq. (8) and Eq. (9), respectively;

3: Compute the projection matrix P by Eq. (14).

4: Obtain the training set $B_{train} = \{b_i | b_i \in R^{h \times 1}, i = 1, 2, ..., N_{train}\}$ in a low dimensional space, where $B_{train} = P^T X_{trian}$.

5: Obtain the testing set $B_{test} = \{b_i | b_i \in R^{h \times 1}, i = 1, 2, ..., N_{test}\}$ in a low dimensional space, where $B_{test} = P^T X_{test}$.

6: Perform classification on the testing set B_{test} by support vector machine.

---

4   Experimental Results and Discussions

In this section, we will apply MLDE on two hyperspectral datasets. Firstly, we introduce the experimental datasets. Secondly, how to choose the best experimental parameters would be given. Finally, The classification accuracy and classification maps on compared algorithms and MLDE algorithm would be shown. The MLDE algorithm is implemented by matlab. The results are generated on a personal computer equipped with an Intel Core i7-3370 with 3.40 GHz. The personal computer's memory is 4 GB.

Table 1. Number of training and testing samples for the University of Pavia dataset

Class	Name	Training	Testing
1	Asphalt	530	6101
2	Meadows	1492	17157
3	Gravel	168	1931
4	Trees	245	2819
5	Painted Metal Sheets	108	1237
6	Bare Soil	402	4627
7	Bitumen	106	1224
8	Self-Blocking Bricks	295	3387
9	Shadows	76	871
Total		3422	39354

4.1   Experimental Dataset

The first experimental dataset was acquired by the Reflective Optics System Imaging Spectrometer (ROSIS) sensor over the University of Pavia in Italy. The image includes 610×340 pixels and 115 spectral bands in the wavelength

Table 2. Number of training and testing samples for the Salinas dataset

Class	Name	Training	Testing
1	Brocoli-green-weeds-1	100	1909
2	Brocoli-green-weeds-1	186	3540
3	Fallow	99	1877
4	Fallow-rough-plow	70	1324
5	Fallow-smooth	134	2544
6	Stubble	198	3761
7	Celery	179	3400
8	Grapes-untrained	564	10707
9	Soil-vinyard-develop	310	5893
10	Corn-senesced-green-weeds	164	3114
11	Lettuce-romaine-4wk	53	1015
12	Lettuce-romaine-5wk	96	1831
13	Lettuce-romaine-6wk	46	870
14	Lettuce-romaine-7wk	54	1016
15	Vinyard-untrained	363	6905
16	Vinyard-vertical-trellis	90	1717
Total		2706	51423

range $0.43 - 0.86 - \mu m$. In our experiments, 12 spectral bands covering noisy are removing. Then, a total of 103 bands is used. Thus, the image contains 9 different classes and a total of 42776 ground-truth samples (Table 1).

The second experimental dataset was acquired by the National Aeronautics and Space Administration's Airborne Visible/ Infrared Imaging Spectrometer (AVIRIS) sensor over Salinas Valley in California. The image includes 512×127 pixels and 204 bands afther 20 water-absorption bands are removed. Thus, the image cantains 16 different classes and a total of 54129 ground-truth samples.

8% and 5% samples in each class are randomly selected as training samples in the University of Pavia dataset and the Salinas dataset, respectively. And the rest are chosen as the testing samples. More detailed information of the number of training and testing samples is summarized in Tables 1 and 2.

4.2   Experiment Parameters

The SVM is used to verify the proposed MLDE algorithm. The SVM classifier is implemented by libsvm (the kernel is rbf, the penalty parameter is 1000 and the sigma is searched in {0.01, 0.05, 0.5, 1, 5, 10, 50, 100, 500, 1000}). And to demonstrate the benefits of MLDE algorithm, the experimental results would be compared with nine other classical algorithm of DR, i.e., PCA, LDA, LPP, LDE, LFDA, LGDA, SGDA, SLGDA, GDA-SS.

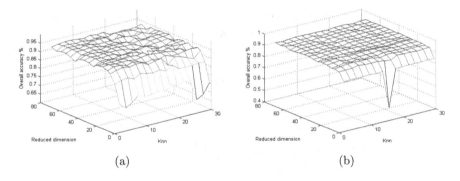

(a)   (b)

Fig. 1. The overall accuracy corresponding to different reduced dimensionality and different K for MLDE on two hyperspectral datasets

It is very easy to note that the reduced dimensionality and the value of the K nearest neighborhood are two important parameters, which have a significant influence on the performance of the classification.

If the K is too small, it may reduce classification accuracy. And if the K is too large, it would increase computational complexity, increase the noise and reduce the classification effect. To find a good value of K, the even numbers are chosen from 2 to 60, and the reduced dimensionality is searched in the range of $\{2, 7, 12, 15, 20, 25, 27, 30, 35, 40, 45, 50, 55, 60, 65, 70, 75\}$. To have a better presentation, we only show the range of 2–30 of the value of K in Fig. 1.

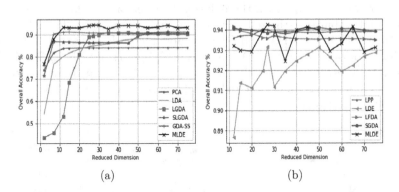

(a)   (b)

Fig. 2. The overall accuracy corresponding to different reduced dimensionality for MLDE on the University of Pavia dataset

Figure 1 shows the classification performances of MLDE in different K for two hyperspectral datasets. It can be seen from Fig. 1 that the overall accuracy would increase as K increasing when K is at a relatively small value, while the overall accuracy would decline as K increasing when K is at a relatively big value. It's noticed that the overall accuracy will be stable and less affected by k when the spectral number is in a high position. From Fig. 1, the highest value of overall accuracy are 94.28% and 93.30% in the University of Pavia dataset and the Salinas dataset, at the same time, K are 12 and 22, respectively.

Thus, the K is respectively fixed as 12 and 22 according to Fig. 1. Next, a good value of the reduced dimensionality would be searched in the above spectral range, the way in which other algorithms do, e.g. LFDA, SGDA, SLGDA.

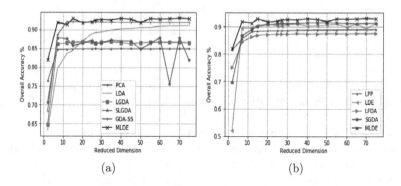

(a)   (b)

Fig. 3. The overall accuracy corresponding to different reduced dimensionality for MLDE on the Salinas dataset

Figure 2 illustrates the overall accuracy corresponding to the reduced dimensionality H for all the algorithms mentioned in the University of Pavia dataset. The performance is poor when the reduced dimensionality is low, and it would increase and stabilize as the reduced dimensionality increasing. From Fig. 2(a), PCA, LDA, LGDA, SLGDA, and GDA-SS apparently don't have a better classification performance than MLDE. Although the curves of LPP, LFDA, SGDA and MLDE alternatively rise, the highest point 94.28% can be found on the MLDE curve in Fig. 2(b). So, the reduced dimensionality being set as 27 can be considered a good choice.

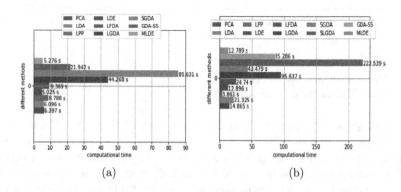

(a)   (b)

Fig. 4. The computational time of different methods in two hyperspectral datasets: (a) the University of Pavia dataset, (b): the Salinas dataset

Figure 3 also illustrates the overall accuracy corresponding to the reduced dimensionality H for all the algorithms mentioned in the Salinas dataset. The performance is poor when the reduced dimensionality is low, and it would increase and stabilize as the reduced dimensionality increasing. From Fig. 3 (b), LPP, LDE, LFDA, SGDA apparently don't have a better classification performance than MLDE. Excpet the curver of GDA-SS has some intersection with the curver of MLDE, the other methods don't have a better value than MLDE in Fig. 3(a), and the highest overall accuracy 93.12% will be found in the curve of MLDE. So, the reduced dimensionality being set as 70 can be considered a good choice.

From Fig. 4(a), the computational time of MLDE is 5.276 s and ranked second with a small difference of 0.251 s of the first place. Because the computational time of SLGDA is 1564.8 s is very big will cause the figure don't have a good presentation, it don't be shown in Fig. 4(a). And from Fig. 4(b), the computational time of MLDE is 12.879 s and ranked third.

4.3   Experimental Results

Through our experiments, for the University of Pavia dataset, the value of K would be set as 12, the reduced dimensionality would be set as 27, for the salinas datastet, the value of K would be set as 22, the reduced dimensionality would be set as 70.

The each class's accuracy, overall accuracy (OA), average accuracy (AA) and kappa coefficient of two hyperspectral datasets are listed in Tables 3 and 4.

From Table 3, the MLDE achieves the best classification performance in the class 3, the class 7, and the class 8, respectively. And the classification accuracy of OA, AA, and κ are all better than other compared methods. On details, the OA of MLDE increases from 0.44% to 10.89%, the AA of MLDE increases from 1% to 17.08%, and the κ of MLDE increases from 0.59% to 15.27%, when compared with other methods. Especially, the classification performance of the class 7 is 83.83% when the accuracy of other methods is basically no more than 80%, and the classification performance of the class 8 is 91.53% when the accuracy of other methods is basically no more than 90%. Meaawhile, when other methods achieve the best results in a certain class, the results of MLDE are not inferior, for instance, the class1, the class2, the class 5, and the class 9.

From Table 4, although the MLDE only achieves the best classification performance in the class 16, the classification performance of the other classes has a good performance, for example, the classification accuracy of the class 1 and the class 12 are also good. And the classification accuracy of OA is better than other compared methods. On details, the OA of MLDE increases from 3.64% to 7.21%.

Figure 5 illustrates the classification maps resulting from the classification of those methods in the University of Pavia dataset. In Fig. 5, the number of misclassified points in the class 3 (Gravel), the class 8 (Self-Blocking Bricks) of MLDE is significantly less than other methods, which further illustrates that the results in Table 3 are indeed believable.

Table 3. Classification accuracy (%) for the University of Pavia dataset

*	PCA	LDA	LPP	LDE	LFDA	LGDA	SGDA	SLGDA	GDA-SS	MLDE
1	89.78	89.93	87.42	94.03	**95.32**	92.02	95.81	89.61	93.55	94.81
2	94.69	95.55	**98.24**	96.60	97.21	96.21	97.62	95.60	96.16	97.61
3	23.96	43.83	54.12	72.61	74.75	62.32	70.13	33.40	66.89	**76.56**
4	77.97	85.87	78.49	88.25	**96.83**	91.68	95.82	88.97	92.69	94.32
5	98.66	99.78	99.26	99.63	97.17	**99.85**	99.85	99.78	99.78	99.55
6	59.00	72.06	32.95	83.69	**92.05**	78.29	90.59	75.66	80.41	90.91
7	68.05	30.45	62.63	74.29	72.48	64.06	82.63	38.65	72.26	**83.83**
8	89.33	76.91	88.10	90.55	87.64	81.10	87.72	84.27	85.55	**91.53**
9	**100.00**	80.89	99.79	99.79	97.47	99.47	99.79	99.47	99.79	99.89
OA	84.01	84.87	83.39	91.86	93.59	89.35	93.84	86.27	90.75	**94.28**
AA	77.94	75.03	77.89	88.83	90.10	85.00	91.11	78.38	87.45	**92.11**
κ	78.38	79.64	77.14	89.15	91.51	85.78	91.82	81.65	87.70	**92.41**

Table 4. Classification accuracy (%) for the salinas dataset

*	PCA	LDA	LPP	LDE	LFDA	LGDA	SGDA	SLGDA	GDA-SS	MLDE
1	97.31	99.15	97.90	96.91	99.30	98.80	99.60	**99.65**	98.70	97.71
2	96.91	99.00	**99.70**	97.42	94.60	90.31	99.06	99.35	99.06	96.70
3	86.13	96.00	91.29	84.91	**99.39**	69.88	84.15	90.73	75.35	95.29
4	98.78	98.49	99.06	98.70	**99.56**	99.42	98.78	96.84	93.68	97.13
5	92.15	91.97	94.24	94.36	95.07	92.49	**98.69**	96.82	98.65	96.00
6	98.91	**99.44**	99.19	98.40	99.11	98.56	98.68	98.86	99.36	97.17
7	99.13	99.46	99.10	99.49	98.91	99.16	**99.63**	99.38	99.74	97.59
8	87.33	86.09	**89.82**	88.53	84.38	85.53	83.09	78.14	77.51	83.10
9	96.16	99.01	99.06	97.64	98.85	95.38	**99.90**	99.50	**99.90**	95.87
10	79.01	89.38	85.96	79.22	80.81	82.45	64.88	63.51	**93.77**	86.12
11	72.00	93.25	82.86	88.01	**94.66**	89.88	94.10	91.10	90.91	87.27
12	96.83	77.58	98.02	97.66	61.13	84.12	**100.00**	99.63	97.71	99.01
13	98.58	97.27	98.03	98.25	99.01	99.12	99.01	**99.45**	**99.45**	93.77
14	88.69	90.56	89.71	90.46	86.72	81.58	**91.21**	82.61	88.41	84.01
15	40.05	55.71	44.12	347.8	63.34	63.01	63.47	70.58	**73.34**	61.64
16	88.43	95.84	83.50	97.39	86.22	91.09	98.50	97.67	98.61	**99.89**
OA	84.93	88.34	87.38	87.15	87.49	86.63	88.21	87.86	89.50	**92.14**
AA	88.53	91.77	90.73	90.95	90.07	88.80	92.05	91.49	**92.77**	91.77
κ	83.13	86.99	85.88	85.63	86.06	85.10	86.86	86.48	**88.32**	86.84

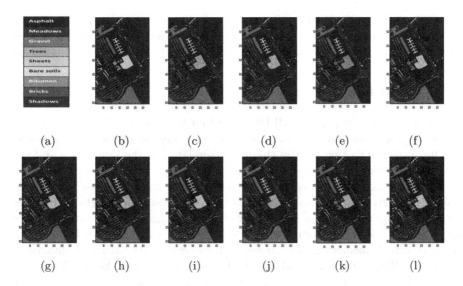

Fig. 5. Classification maps of different methods for the University of Pavia dataset: (a) legend (b) ground truth; (c) PCA: 84.01%; (d) LDA: 84.87%; (e) LPP: 83.39%; (f) LDE: 91.86%; (g) LFDA: 93.59%; (h) LGDA: 89.35%; (i) SGDA: 93.84%; (j) SLGDA: 86.27%; (k) GDA-SS: 90.75% (l) MLDE: 94.28%

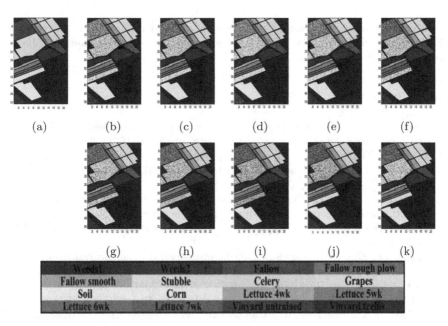

Fig. 6. Classification maps of different methods for the salinas dataset: (a) ground truth; (b) PCA: 84.93%; (c) LDA: 88.34%; (d) LPP: 87.38%; (e) LDE: 87.15%; (f) LFDA: 87.49%; (g) LGDA: 86.63%; (h) SGDA: 88.21%; (i) SLGDA: 87.86%; (k) GDA-SS: 89.50% (l) MLDE: 92.14%

Figure 6 illustrates the classification maps resulting from the classification of those methods in the salinas dataset. In Fig. 6, the number of misclassified points in the class 16 (Vinyard-vertical-trellis) is significantly less than other methods.

5   Conclusion

In this paper, we proposed a MLDE algorithm for HSI by constructing neighborhood graphs on a new spectral feature space instead of the original space. We use variance to characterize the pixels similarity of the same class and use covariance to characterize the separation of different classes of pixels. The combination of variance and covariance enables pixels in the same class to be closer and enables greater separation of pixels from different classes, which enhances classification performance of HSI. The way of representing data by using variance and covariance can attenuate the effects of noise, which can better handle with noise in HSI. Considering the symmetric positive definite nature of covariance lying on a Riemannan manifold, the MLDE algorithm using the Log-Euclidean metric to capture the similarity between spectral vectors, which can provide a more accurate similarity evaluation than euclidean distance and can better express the characteristics of spectral information. The experimental results of two hyperspectral datasets demonstrate the effectiveness of our proposed MLDE method.

Acknowledgement. We would like to thank Prof. Wei Li for sharing the codes of LFDA, LGDA, SGDA, and SLGDA. We would also like to thank Changming Jia for offering the code of GDA-SS.

References

1. Lianru, G., Bin, Y., Qian, D., et al.: Adjusted spectral matched filter for target detection in hyperspectral imagery. Remote Sensing **7**(6), 6611–6634 (2015)
2. Zhang, L., Zhang, L., Tao, D., et al.: Hyperspectral remote sensing image subpixel target detection based on supervised metric learning. IEEE Trans. Geosci. Remote Sens. **52**(8), 4955–4965 (2014)
3. Onoyama, H., Ryu, C., Suguri, M., et al.: Integrate growing temperature to estimate the nitrogen content of rice plants at the heading stage using hyperspectral imagery. IEEE J. Sel. Top. Appl. Earth Observations Remote Sensing **7**(6), 2506–2515 (2014)
4. Cheng, G., Zhu, F., Xiang, S., et al.: Semisupervised hyperspectral image classification via discriminant analysis and robust regression. IEEE J. Sel. Top. Appl. Earth Observations Remote Sensing **9**(2), 595–608 (2017)
5. Jolliffe, I.T.: Principal component analysis. J. Mark. Res. **87**(100), 513 (2002)
6. Bandos, T.V., Bruzzone, L., Camps-Valls, G.: Classification of hyperspectral images with regularized linear discriminant analysis. IEEE Trans. Geosci. Remote Sens. **47**(3), 862–873 (2009)
7. Zhang, X., Liang, Y., Cahill, N.: Using superpixels to improve the efficiency of Laplacian Eigenmap based methods for target detection in hyperspectral imagery. In: Geoscience & Remote Sensing Symposium, IEEE (2016)

8. Wang, M., Yu, J., Niu, L., et al.: Unsupervised feature extraction for hyperspectral images using combined low rank representation and locally linear embedding. In: IEEE ICASSP 2017–2017 IEEE International Conference on Acoustics, Speech and Signal Processing (ICASSP) - New Orleans, LA, USA, 5 March 2017–9 March 2017, pp. 1428–1431 (2017)

9. Zhang, M., Jia, P., Shen, Y., et al.: Hyperspectral image classification method based on orthogonal NMF and LPP. In: Instrumentation & Measurement Technology Conference, IEEE (2016)

10. Sugiyama, M.: Dimensionality reduction of multimodal labeled data by local fisher discriminant analysis. J. Mach. Learn. Res. **8**(1), 1027–1061 (2007)

11. Li, W., Prasad, S., Fowler, J.E., et al.: Locality-preserving dimensionality reduction and classification for hyperspectral image analysis. IEEE Trans. Geosci. Remote Sens. **50**(4), 1185–1198 (2012)

12. Chen, H.T., Chang, H.W., Liu, T.L.: Local discriminant embedding and its variants. In: IEEE Computer Society Conference on Computer Vision & Pattern Recognition (2005

13. Yan, S., Xu, D., Zhang, B., et al.: Graph embedding: a general framework for dimensionality reduction. IEEE Trans. Pattern Anal. Mach. Intell. **29**(1), 40 (2007)

14. Cheng, B., Yang, J., Yan, S., et al.: Learning with 1-graph for image analysis. IEEE Trans. Image Process. **19**(4), 858–866 (2010)

15. Ly, N.H., Du, Q., Fowler, J.E.: Sparse graph-based discriminant analysis for hyperspectral imagery. IEEE Trans. Geosci. Remote Sens. **52**(7), 3872–3884 (2014)

16. Li, W., Liu, J., Du, Q.: Sparse and low-rank graph for discriminant analysis of hyperspectral imagery. IEEE Trans. Geosci. Remote Sens. **54**(7), 1–12 (2016)

17. Fubiao, F., Wei, L., Qian, D., et al.: Dimensionality reduction of hyperspectral image with graph-based discriminant analysis considering spectral similarity. Remote Sensing **9**(4), 323 (2017)

18. Deng, Y.J., Li, H.C., Pan, L., et al.: Modified tensor locality preserving projection for dimensionality reduction of hyperspectral images. IEEE Geosci. Remote Sens. Lett. **15**(2), 277–281 (2018)

19. Yang, X., Tu, S., Bai, Y., et al.: Fusion of intensity/coherent information using region covariance features for unsupervised classification of SAR imagery. In: Geoscience & Remote Sensing Symposium, IEEE (2016)

20. Yang, J., Xing, C., Chen, Y.: Improving the ScSPM model with Log-Euclidean Covariance matrix for scene classification. In: 2016 International Conference on Computer on Information and Telecommunication Systems (CITS), IEEE (2016)

Mapping of Native Plant Species and Noxious Weeds in Typical Area of the Three-River Headwaters Region by Using Worldview-2 Imagery

Benlin Wang[1,2], Ru An[1(✉)], Yu Zhang[3], and Zetian Ai[1,2]

[1] Hohai University, Nanjing, Jiangsu, China
anrunj@163.com
[2] Chuzhou University, Chuzhou, Anhui, China
[3] Nanjing Urban Planning and Research Center, Nanjing, Jiangsu, China

Abstract. Mapping of native plant species and noxious weeds is critical to monitor grassland degradation in the Three-River Headwaters Region. The grass species in the study area were divided into native plant species and noxious weeds based on the applicability of grazing. Field data of the two kinds of grass species were collected and divided into ten coverage grades with an interval of 10%. The eight original bands were used to derive 37 features by Random Forest (RF) algorithm, including first derivative (FD), vegetation indexes (VI), biochemical indexes (BI), hat transform (KT) and gray level co-occurrence matrix (GLCM). The importance of each feature was calculated and 17 of them were selected by RF, reflecting their superiority in identifying native plant species and noxious weeds. The random forest algorithm was also used in classification of the native plant species with an overall accuracy (OA) of 43.2% (8 bands), 45.9% (37 features) and 51.3% (17 selected features) and an 10% grade expansion accuracy (GEA) of 59.4%, 64.8% and 70.2%, respectively. The noxious weeds with a higher overall accuracy (OA) of 62.1% (8 bands), 64.8% (37 features) and 67.5% (17 selected features) and an 10% grade expansion accuracy (GEA) of 86.4%, 83.7% and 89.1%, respectively. Therefore, the classification of native plant species and noxious weeds coverage grades with the interval of 10% demonstrated the potential of the WorldView-2 data for mapping native plant species and noxious weeds in the typical area of Three-River Headwaters Region.

Keywords: Coverage · Native plant species · Noxious weeds · Worldview-2 imagery · Random Forest algorithm · Three-River Headwaters Region · Qinghai-Tibet Plateau

1 Introduction

Grassland resource is an important component of agriculture and animal husbandry, which has a significant impact on the local ecological environment. In recent decades, the grassland in Three-River Headwaters Region has been in a long state of degradation. Compared with the 1950s, the yield per unit area has decreased by 30%–50%,

© Springer Nature Switzerland AG 2019
Y. Zhao et al. (Eds.): ICIG 2019, LNCS 11903, pp. 320–333, 2019.
https://doi.org/10.1007/978-3-030-34113-8_27

the proportion of high-quality forage grass decreased by 20%–30%, and the proportion of toxic and harmful weeds increased by 70%–80%. The vegetation coverage of grassland decreased by 15%–25%, the height of dominant pasture decreased by 30%–50%, and the height of grass decreased by more than 20% [1, 2].

From an ecological perspective, grassland species have been classified into categories (native plant species and noxious weeds) based on their grazing value and changes in their relative abundance in the presence or absence of grazing. The identification and mapping of native plant species and noxious weeds coverage is an important work for grassland monitoring. The native plant species (mainly *Kobresias*) are harmless and eatable for livestock while the noxious weeds (mainly *Compositaes, Labiataes and Gentianideas*) are uneatable or even poisonous that makes it not suitable for grazing. The degradation of grassland is not only the change of productivity, but also the change of population structure, such as the decrease of native plant species and the increase of the proportion of noxious weeds. Mapping the native plant species and noxious weeds can help direct resource managers to critical areas in need of conservation measures.

Mapping the spatial distribution of grass using traditional methods is a complex work and requires intensive field work, including the identification of species characteristics and the visual estimation of species percentage, all of which are costly and time-consuming and are sometimes impossible to accomplish due to poor accessibility [3]. With the development of sensor and image processing technology, remote sensing technology is widely used in grassland degradation monitoring.

Multi-spectral remote sensing has made great progress in the recognition of grassland vegetation for the advantages of high resolution, high quality and easy acquisition of data. Friedl et al. [4] used TM data and ground observation data to calculate many vegetation indexes and used the most accurate vegetation index to estimate the biomass change of grassland. Hostert et al. [5] used TM data and MSS data to monitor vegetation coverage in Crete, Greece, using linear spectral method. The results showed that it was feasible to monitor vegetation coverage in this region with Landsat image data. Elmore et al. [6] used 1991–1996 TM image data and normalized vegetation index (NDVI) data to monitor vegetation coverage in the Irvine valley, California, using a spectral hybrid analysis method. These studies show that multi-spectral data have great advantages in vegetation coverage and classification recognition.

With the development of high-resolution remote sensing images (WorldView-2 for example), the classification of grassland vegetation using high-resolution images has become a research hotspot at home and abroad. Meyer et al. [7] pointed out that when studying vegetation coverage on the Tibetan plateau, it is very effective to combine hyperspectral and multispectral methods and then use machine learning method to calculate vegetation coverage. Wiesmair et al. [8] used Worldview2 high-resolution images to calculate the NDVI and MXAVI2 indexes, and used the random forest algorithm to calculate the FVC of the Russian Georgian region. Santos et al. [9] pointed out that the four bands added to the high-resolution Worldview2 data contributed a lot to the research on urban vegetation extraction. From the perspective of grassland identification methods, the current research contents of grassland classification and identification are mostly the analysis and comparison of spectral reflection features

[10], and the identification research also stays on the establishment of grassland classification decision tree based on the simple analysis of spectral features [11].

Machine learning method (RF for example) has been widely used to identify species. Ham et al. [12] used hyperspectral remote sensing data to perform random forest classification by setting binary hierarchy structure in the multi-classifier system under the limited training data of hyperspectral data set. Wilschut et al. [13] defined different landscape units based on the distribution of rat holes, and used random forest to establish scene and classify images. RF has several advantages compared with other conventional classification trees, such as being able to provide better performance, having reasonable accuracies, and being relatively easy to implement, as well as its capability in ranking important prediction variables [14, 15].

Efforts have been made in grassland recognition and mapping using high resolution image and random forest algorithm. This high-resolution, multi-spectral and random forest algorithm has been proved to be effective. However, there are few studies on the identification of native plant species and noxious weeds in the Three-River Headwaters Region located in the hinterland of the Tibetan Plateau. The objective of this study was therefore to investigate the potential of WorldView-2 imagery in identifying the native plant species and noxious weeds and mapping their coverage.

2   Materials and Methods

2.1   Study Area and Mainly Native Plant Species and Noxious Weeds

This study area is located in the Tongtian river reserve of Yushu Tibetan autonomous prefecture, covering part of the southeast of Zhiduo county of Qinghai, China. The area was selected from the of Three-rivers Headwaters region, with a typical alpine and cold plateau continental climate. Annual temperatures average −0.4 °C with an annual rainfall ∼394 mm/year. The average altitude of the research area is above 4,000 m, with sufficient sunlight radiation. The cold season lasts nearly 10 months (Feb–Jun, Sep–Dec) with large temperature difference between day and night. About 70%–90% of the study area is covered by vegetation and the alpine meadow is the main grassland type in this region. The location of the research area is shown in Fig. 1.

In the study area, our field investigation showed that Kobresias (such as *K.pygmaea & K.humilis, K.capillifolia & K.tibetica*) were the main native plant species, accompanied by a variety of invasive noxious weeds (such as *Heteropappus Altaicus (Willd.) Novopokr, Lamiophlomis Rotata, Gentiana Straminea Maxim, Ajania Tenuifolia, Leontopodium Nanum, Morina Kokonorica Hao*). Although the native plant species and noxious weeds have been mix-living for years, we could still distinguish the two species from their leaf shape and texture. The leaves of native plant species are always slender and intricately textured, while the leaves of noxious weeds are always broader. Also, the colors of the native plant species in the growing season are light green with a little gray, while the colors of the noxious weeds are mainly dark green, milky white and yellow. The pictures of major native plant species and noxious weeds were shown in Fig. 2.

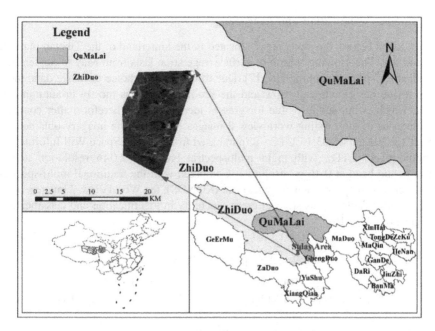

Fig. 1. Location of study area in the Three-River Headwaters Region of the Tibetan Plateau

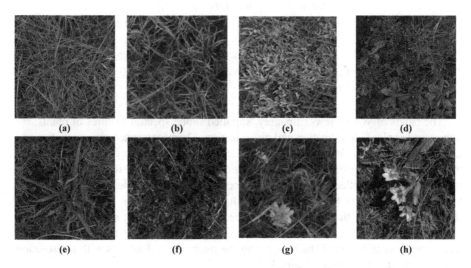

Fig. 2. Native plant species and noxious weeds in the study area **(a)** K. Pygmaea & K. Humilis **(b)** K. Capillifolia & K. Tibetica **(c)** Heteropappus Altaicus (Willd.) Novopokr. **(d)** Lamiophlomis Rotate **(e)** Gentiana Straminea Maxim **(f)** Ajania Tenuifolia **(g)** Leontopodium Nanum **(h)** Morina Kokonorica Hao (Color figure online)

2.2   Imagery Acquisition and Processing

As mentioned before, the study area is located in the hinterland of the Tibetan plateau, cold and dry. The growing season of surface vegetation lasts from May to September, thus ideal for species mapping [16, 17]. Due to the limited choice of image data, most of the image has clouds and snow and the shooting date was mostly in autumn and winter, which is not suitable time for grasses identification. Therefore, after comparative analysis of the existing worldview-2 images, we chose the imagery obtained on August 12, 2012 at 05:03:15 UTC +8 (purchased from Beijing Space Will Information Technology co. LTD), with eight multispectral bands at 2.0-m resolution and a panchromatic band at 0.46 m resolution. Compared with the traditional multi-spectral remote sensing imagery (such as Quickbird, IKONOS), the WorldView-2 imagery with unique bands (Table 1) has showed great capability in identification and classification of vegetations [18, 19].

Table 1.   Spectral wavelength properties for WorldView-2 multispectral image

Bands	Band name	Wave/nm	Resolution/m	Other
Multispectral band	Coastal blue	400–450	2	Unique band
	Blue	450–510	2	
	Green	510–580	2	
	Yellow	585–625	2	Unique Band
	Red	630–690	2	
	Red-edge	705–745	2	Unique Band
	NIR1	770–895	2	
	NIR12	860–1040	2	Unique Band
Panchromatic band	Pan	450–800	0.46	

The bands of Worldview-2 Imagery, supplied subtle spectral features of plants, are important for plant identification and classification. Therefore, space characteristics and texture characteristics from WorldView-2 data would be very useful for identification of the native plant species and noxious weeds. After converting the image data from radiance to surface reflectance by the fast line-of-sight atmospheric analysis of spectral hypercubes (FLAASH [20]) algorithm built-in Environment for Visualizing Images (ENVI 5.3) software, the accurate reflectance of both native plant species and noxious weeds was obtained. Gram-Schmidt (GS) method was used to fuse panchromatic bands and multi-spectral bands of the image, and the multi-spectral images with a resolution of 0.5 m and 8 bands were obtained.

2.3   Grassland Coverage Data Collection

Field data were obtained from two field surveys. The first field survey started on 16 August and finished on 28 August, 2013. The second field survey was from 10 to 19 August, 2017. South S750 hand-held sub-meter GPS was utilized to record sample location information with an accuracy of ~ 0.5 m after differential correction. An "X"

Sampling method was defined in 30 m × 30 m square. The collected samples, which were located in the vertices and center of the square, were 0.5 m × 0.5 m squares (Fig. 3).

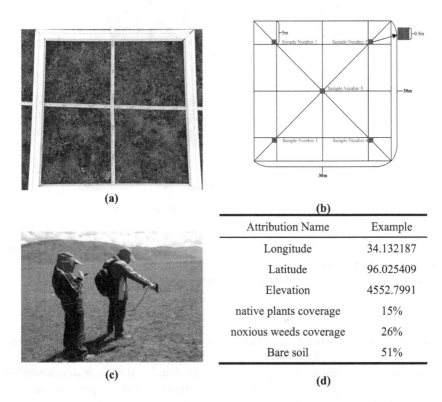

(a)

(b)

Attribution Name	Example
Longitude	34.132187
Latitude	96.025409
Elevation	4552.7991
native plants coverage	15%
noxious weeds coverage	26%
Bare soil	51%

(c)

(d)

Fig. 3. "X" sampling method sampling and spectrometer measurement **(a)** Field measurement of 0.5 m sample square **(b)** A schematic of "X" sampling method **(c)** Our team measured the spectrum of native plant species and noxious weeds using spectrometer **(d)** Main information attribute table structure of field collection.

Due to the harsh highland environment and unreachable in the study area, all-together 145 samples were collected along major roads and rivers in the study area as shown in Fig. 4. The first 30 samples were collected along the Tongtian river in the year 2013. The rest 115 samples, were collected in the year 2017 to expand the sample of our research. After filed data processing and analysis, 128 unduplicated and accurate samples were selected for classification. For each collected sample, location and grassland coverage information were recorded as shown in Fig. 3(d).

According to our field surveys, the grass coverage and component had not much changed, possibly because of sparsely populated and protective grazing policies in the study area. Although the time span of image acquisition and the second field investigation is 5 years long, we believed that the vegetation in the study area have not change much that the time span could be ignored. In addition, the influence of season is more

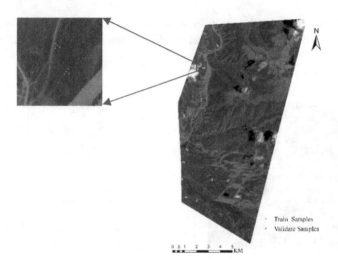

Fig. 4. Distribution of samples in the study area

significant than that of year for grass in the study area. Thus, the two field surveys were conducted in august, which was consistent with the acquisition time of the WorldView-2 imagery, to ensure the consistency of vegetation identification features.

2.4   The Random Forest Algorithm

Random forest (RF) classification algorithm has been widely used in the field of remote sensing data classification due to its characteristics of fast classification speed, high accuracy and high dimensional adaptability. The random forest classification algorithm model used in this study is based on enmap-box (Environmental Mapping and Analysis Program), which can be used in combination with ENVI5.1 plug-in. Enmap-box is a remote sensing data processing toolkit developed by the German environmental mapping and analysis program based on IDL [21]. 100 default classification trees with the Gini coefficient, samples and classification features parameters was adapted for creating the Random Forest Classification (RFC) model file. The RFC model was utilized to calculate variable importance of features and classify coverage grades of the native plant species and noxious weeds.

2.5   Features for Extraction

In this study, 6 types of features were calculated from the spectral values extracted fromWorldView-2 imagery. These features are 8 fused multispectral bands (FMB), first derivative (FD) spectrum of the 8 bands, 8 vegetation indexes (VI), 2 biochemical indexes (BI), 3 hat transform features (KT), 8 gray level co-occurrence matrix (GLCM), all together totaling 37 features (Table 2). The 8 FMBs, a 0.5 m high resolution for identifying the grasses, were obtained from the original panchromatic and multi-spectral bands using GS pan-sharping method. The spectral curve tends sharper in higher order derivative than the origin spectral curve, so that the Spectral differences between native plant species and noxious weeds would be more significant. Thus, first derivate spectrum was calculated for each band.

The 8 VIs were Normalized Difference Vegetation Index (NDVI), Visible Atmospherically Resistant Index (VARI), Worldview Improved Vegetative Index (WV-IVI), Worldview Built-Up Index (WV-BU), Worldview New Iron Index (WV-NII), Worldview Soil Index(WV-SI), Worldview Non-Homogenous Feature Difference Index (WV-NHFDI) and Worldview Water Index (WV-WI), generated by spectral index tools of ENVI5.3. The Worldview Indexes were designed especially for vegetable identification of Worldview image. We expected to distinguish the two types species by worldview exclusive vegetation index.

The biochemical and biophysical parameters of plant leaves and canopy, such as chlorophyll, carotene and anthocyanin, would be important factors affecting spectral reflectance of vegetation. Related research shows that anthocyanins and carotenoids are the most important biochemical indexes to distinguish the noxious weeds from native plant species in the Three-River Headwaters Region [22, 23]. Thus, the Anthocyanin Reflectance Index 1 (ARI1) and Carotenoid Reflectance Index 1 (CRI1) were calculated. The first three components of tasseled cap transformation, Soil Brightness, Greenness and Wetness, were selected for classification. The mean value of Gray-level Co-occurrence Matrix (GLCM) were also selected.

Table 2. All 6 type features (n = 37) derived from the WorldView-2 eight origin bands

Num	Feature type	Feature names
1	FMB	Coast, Blue, Green, Yellow, Red, Red-edge, NIR1, NIR2
2	FD	FD-Coast, FD-Blue, FD-Green, FD-Yellow, FD-Red, FD-Red-edge, FD-NIR1, FD-NIR2
3	VI	NDVI, VARI, WV-IVI, WV-BUI, WV-NII, WV-SI, WV-NHFDI, WV-WI
4	BI	ARI1, CRI1
5	KT	Soil Brightness, Greenness, Wetness
6	GLCM	Mean-Coast, Mean-Blue, Mean-Green, Mean-YellowMean-Red, Mean-Red-edge, Mean-NIR1, Mean-NIR2

3   Results

3.1   Definition of Grown Types for Native Plant Species and Noxious Weeds

The vegetation type in Three-River Headwaters Region is mainly alpine meadow, including about 10 kinds mix-living grasses. It is almost impossible to identify all the vegetation species one by one. We divided these meadows into two major categories: native plant species and noxious weeds and assumed that each pixel of the grass imagery was composed by the native plant species, noxious weeds and land. According the field investigation, the maximum of coverage of native plant species (CNPS) is 75%, while the minimum is 5%. The maximum of coverage of noxious weeds (CNW) is 55%, while the minimum is 0%. According to the expert experience, the grown types of native plant species coverage could be divided into 0−10% (10%), 10 −20%, 20−30%, 30−40%, 40−50%, 50−60%, 60−70% and 70−100%, a total of 8 grades. The grown types of noxious weeds coverage could be divided into 6 grades: 0 −10% (10%), 10−20%, 20−30%, 30−40%, 40−50%, 50−60%. Thus, the growing types of the study area is the arrangement and combination of all grades of native plant species and noxious weeds, forming the information of composition of grassland in 37 forms (Table 3).

Table 3. 37 grown types of native plant species and noxious weeds

CNPS (%)	CNW (%)	CNPS (%)	CNW (%)	CNPS (%)	CNW (%)
(1) 0–10	0–10	(3) 20–30	0–10	(5) 40–50	0–10
	10–20		10–20		10–20
	20–30		20–30		20–30
	30–40		30–40		30–40
	40–50		40–50		40–50
	50–60		50–60	(6) 50–60	0–10
(2) 10–20	0–10	(4) 30–40	0–10		10–20
	10–20		10–20		20–30
	20–30		20–30		30–40
	30–40		30–40	(7) 60–70	0–10
	40–50		40–50		10–20
	50–60		50–60		20–30
				(8) 70–100	0–10

3.2   Features' Importance

Using a smaller number of features may result in a non-inferior accuracy compared to the use of larger feature sets, and provides potential advantages regarding data storage and computational processing costs. Thus, RF was applied to measure the relative importance of the 6 types of features for mapping the native plant species and noxious weeds. The importance of all together 37 features was calculated by descending ordering. In this study, a threshold value of 0.3 was set for the normalized and raw variable importance of the RF. 17 features was selected as Table 4.

The selected features were divided into 6 types, with a total of 17 features: (1) 5 features of the original band, (2) 3 features of the first derivative, (3) 2 features of the hat transform, (4) 1 feature of the biochemical index, (5) 5 features of the texture, (6) 1 feature of the vegetation index.

Table 4. Importance of selected 17 feature calculated by RF (>=0.3)

Index	Band name	RFI importance	Index	Band name	RFI importance
1	Coast	0.47	10	Mean-NIR2	0.49
2	Yellow	0.31	11	FD-Green	0.44
3	Red	0.42	12	FD-NIR1	0.38
4	NIR1	0.63	13	FD-NIR2	0.35
5	NIR2	0.33	14	Brightness	0.33
6	Mean-Coast	0.46	15	Greenness	0.47
7	Mean-Green	0.51	16	CRI1	0.59
8	Mean-Red-edge	0.50	17	WV-IVI	0.48
9	Mean-NIR1	0.47			

3.3   Classification Result and Accuracy

In this study, the method of direct verification of measured points is used to evaluate the classification accuracy. The training samples and verification samples in this study were all from the field investigation in study area. All 128 samples were divided into training samples (n = 91) and verification samples (n = 37) according to the expert experience.

There is no overlap between the training samples and the verification samples, which are independent on each other. All the native plant species and noxious weeds coverage types need to be included to ensure the reliability and accuracy of the verification. These 37 samples were used to verify the pixel-based RF recognition results. However, when defining the category of "growth type" of native plant species and noxious weeds, the threshold value of grade interval of 10% was an experiential definition, and there was a certain deviation between the classification result and the actual coverage information. For example, assuming that the CNPS or CNW of sample A is 19% and B is 21%, A would be classified as 10−20% while B would be classified as 20−30% though the difference is only 2%. Considering the errors of the above self-defined coverage grade, this paper uses the direct verification accuracy results-"overall accuracy" (OA: exact match between estimated and measured grades) and overage difference of one grade (10%) for accuracy-"grade expansion accuracy" (GEA: for example, "20%–30%" grade is recognized as "30%–40%" grade or as "10%–20%" grade) to evaluate the classification accuracy.

The classification accuracy of native plant species is 43.2% (OA) and 59.4% (GEA) and the accuracy of noxious weeds is 62.1% (OA)and 86.4% (GEA) using 8 origin bands, while using 37 features extracted form Worldview-2, the accuracy of native plant species is 45.9% (OA) and 64.8% (GEA) and the accuracy of noxious weeds is 64.8% (OA) and 83.7% (GEA). After using the optimized 17 features, the accuracy of native plant species is 51.3% (OA) and 70.2% (GEA) and the accuracy of noxious weeds is 67.5% (OA) and 89.1% (GEA) as shown in Table 5.

Table 5. The OA&GEA of native plant species and noxious weeds using 8 bands, 37 features and 17 selected features

Different features	Accuracy	Native plant species	Noxious weeds
8 bands	OA ($\leq 10\%$)	43.2%	62.1%
	GEA ($\leq 20\%$)	**59.4%**	**86.4%**
37 features	OA ($\leq 10\%$)	45.9%	64.8%
	GEA ($\leq 20\%$)	**64.8%**	**83.7%**
17 selected feature	OA ($\leq 10\%$)	51.3%	67.5%
	GEA ($\leq 20\%$)	**70.2%**	**89.1%**

4 Discussion

4.1 Variables' Importance for Classifying Grasses in Study Area

WorldView-2 data offer 8 original bands to identify grassland. These bands and the derivative features (such as FD, VI, BI, KT and GLCM) have different characteristics with regard to grass classification. Feature selection is an effective method for selecting the optimal number of top-ranked features of WorldView-2 data for better classification.

For the 8 WorldView-2 bands, RF has successfully described and explored the relative importance of each individual band. Six selected bands (coast, yellow, red, NIR1, NIR2) might contribute more in reclassifying the native plant species and noxious weeds using RF than blue and green band. However, the importance of five derivative features did not seemed to be the exact same response as the corresponding band origin bands. For the FD features, the first derivative of green, NIR1 and NIR2 were more important than the other bands. Also, there is no obvious relativity of the feature importance between these derivative features and origin bands. As shown in Table 1, 17 features selected by RF reflected their superiority in identifying the native plant species and noxious weeds. The new band NIR1 was the most important feature for classifying the two kind of species. The variation in spectral reflectance of these species in the NIR1 portion (770 to 895 nm) may be due to significant variations in internal leaf structure and water content [24, 25]. CRI1 was the second important feature due to the differences between the native plant species and noxious weeds on chlorophyll a and b, β-carotene, α-carotene, and xanthophylls [26].

5 original bands, 5 GLCM features, 3 FD features, 2 KT features, 1BI features and 1 WI features were finally selected as the most suitable features for classification in the study. The use of RF for classification of the native plant species and noxious weeds with selected features confirmed its utility as a variable selection method [27]. As shown in Table 5, the noxious weeds have a greater potential for being distinguished than the native plant species using WorldView-2 imagery and its derivative features. This result also confirms the previous studies that RF has been applied in remote-sensing image classifications with much better performance.

4.2   Classification Assessment

RF classification for native plant species using 8 bands, 37 Features and 17 selected features yielded an OA of 43.2%, 45.9% and 51.3%, and GEA of 59.4%, 64.8% and 70.2%. This might verify the importance of the feature selection of RF classification on the impact of classification results (8 Bands < 37 Features < 17 selected features), which was also a similar phenomenon in the OA (62.1%, 64.8%, 67.5) and GEA (86.4%, 83.7%, 89.1%) of noxious weeds classification. As shown in Fig. 5, the identification accuracy of noxious weeds was better compared to the native plant species, both the OA and GEA. This could be due to more regular textures and relatively high variance of species' biochemical and biophysical properties such as chlorophyll a and b, β-carotene, α-carotene, and xanthophylls. Considering the continuity of native plant species and noxious weeds coverage, GEA seems to be more suitable for the evaluation of grass classification accuracy.

In summary, the results from this study demonstrate the possibility of classifying native plant species and noxious weeds using WorldView-2 data and confirm the robust of random forest algorithm for both variable selection and classification application.

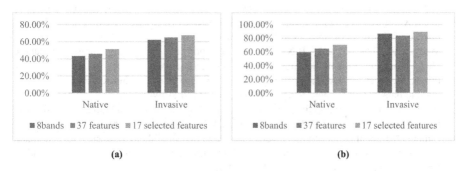

(a)   (b)

Fig. 5. (a) Histogram of OA for native plant species and noxious weeds (b) Histogram of GEA for native plant species and noxious weeds

5   Conclusions

In this study, Worldview-2 imagery was used to mapping the native plant species and noxious weeds in typical area of the Three-River Headwaters Region of China by Random Forest algorithm. The experimental results indicate that the classification using WorldView-2 data shows an GEA of 86.4%, 83.7%, 89.1% (noxious weeds) and GEA of 59.4%, 64.8% and 70.2% (native plant species) for 8 original bands, 37 derivate features, and 17 optimized features, respectively. Therefore, the multispectral and derivative data provided by WorldView2 could distinguish between native plant species and noxious weeds. RF algorithm could be applied to the feature optimization and mapping of native plant species and noxious weeds, and more features did not lead to better classifying precision. The 17 optimization features in this study generated higher classification accuracy than 34 features.

In summary, the invasion of noxious weeds poses a serious threat to the growth of native plant species and causes the instability of the ecosystem in the study area. In order to maintain the ecological balance, it is necessary to mapping for the native plant species and noxious weeds. In this regard, we expect that the results of this study can be used to support precision rangeland analysis and provide support for the treatment of invasive and degraded grassland in Three-River Headwaters Region.

Acknowledgements. This work is supported by the National Nature Science Foundation of China (No. 41871326; 41271361); Key Project in the National Science & Technology Pillar Program during the Twelfth Five-Year Plan Period (No. 2013BAC03B04); and Jiangsu Province Key R&D Plan (No. BE2017115). We express our heartfelt gratitude for Lijun Huang, Xiaoling Zhou, Yu Zhang, Jietong Liu, and Yinan Wang for their work of field samples collection.

References

1. Shuang, Y.U., et al.: Changing spring phenology dates in the Three-Rivers Headwaters Region of the Tibetan plateau during 1960–2013. Adv. Atmos. Sci. **35**(1), 116–126 (2018)
2. Shen, X., et al.: Vegetation changes in the Three-River Headwaters Region of the Tibetan Plateau of China. Ecol. Ind. **93**, 804–812 (2018)
3. Muchoney, D.M., Haack, B.N.: Change detection for monitoring forest defoliation. Photogram. Eng. Remote Sensing **60**(10), 1243–1251 (1994)
4. Friedl, M.A., et al.: Estimating grassland biomass and leaf area index using ground and satellite data. Int. J. Remote Sensing **15**(7), 1401–1420 (1994)
5. Hostert, P., et al.: Retrospective studies of grazing-induced land degradation: a case study in central Crete, Greece. Int. J. Remote Sensing **24**(20), 4019–4034 (2003)
6. Elmore, A.J., et al.: Quantifying vegetation change in semiarid environments: precision and accuracy of spectral mixture analysis and the normalized difference vegetation index. Remote Sensing Environ. **73**(1), 87–102 (2000)
7. Meyer, H., et al.: From local spectral measurements to maps of vegetation cover and biomass on the Qinghai-Tibet-Plateau: do we need hyperspectral information? Int. J. Appl. Earth Obs. Geoinf. **55**, 21–31 (2017)
8. Wiesmair, M., et al.: Estimating vegetation cover from high-resolution satellite data to assess grassland degradation in the Georgian Caucasus. Mt. Res. Dev. **36**(1), 56–65 (2016)
9. Santos, T., Freire, S.: Testing the contribution of worldview-2 improved spectral resolution for extracting vegetation cover in urban environments. Can. J. Remote Sensing **41**(6), 505–514 (2015)
10. Hong-fei, Y., et al.: Analysis of hyperspectral reflectance characteristics of three main grassland types in Xinjiang. Acta Prataculturae Sinica **21**(6), 258–266 (2012)
11. Everitt, J.H., et al.: Use of remote sensing for detecting and mapping leafy spurge (euphorbia esula). Weed Technol. **9**(03), 599–609 (1995)
12. Ham, J., et al.: Investigation of the random forest framework for classification of hyperspectral data. IEEE Trans. Geosci. Remote Sensing **43**(3), 492–501 (2005)

13. Wilschut, L.I., et al.: Mapping the distribution of the main host for plague in a complex landscape in Kazakhstan: an object-based approach using SPOT-5 XS, Landsat 7 ETM+ , SRTM and multiple Random Forests. Int. J. Appl. Earth Obs. Geoinf. ITC J. **23**(100), 81 (2013)

14. Archer, K.J., Kimes, R.V.: Empirical characterization of random forest variable importance measures. Comput. Stat. Data Anal. **52**(4), 2249–2260 (2008)

15. Diaz-Uriarte, R., Alvarez, D.A.S.: Gene selection and classification of microarray data using random forest. BMC Bioinform. **7**, 3 (2006)

16. Jin, L., et al.: Arbuscular mycorrhiza regulate inter-specific competition between a poisonous plant, Ligularia virgaurea, and a co-existing grazing grass, Elymus nutans. Tibetan Plateau Alpine Meadow Ecosystem. Symbiosis **55**(1), 29–38 (2011)

17. Wang, S., et al.: Timing and duration of phenological sequences of alpine plants along an elevation gradient on the Tibetan plateau. Agric. Forest Meteorol. **189–190**, 220–228 (2014)

18. Peerbhay, K., et al.: Mapping solanum mauritianum plant invasions using WorldView-2 imagery and unsupervised random forests. Remote Sensing Environ. **182**, 39–48 (2016)

19. Melville, B., Lucieer, A., Aryal, J.: Object-based random forest classification of Landsat ETM+ and WorldView-2 satellite imagery for mapping lowland native grassland communities in Tasmania, Australia. Int. J. Appl. Earth Obs. Geoinf. **66**, 46–55 (2018)

20. Anderson, G.P., et al.: FLAASH and MODTRAN4: state-of-the-art atmospheric correction for hyperspectral data, IEEE (1999)

21. Van Der Linden, S., et al.: The EnMAP-Box—a toolbox and application programming interface for enmap data processing. Remote Sensing **7**(9), 11249–11266 (2015)

22. Stylinski, C., Gamon, J., Oechel, W.: Seasonal patterns of reflectance indices, carotenoid pigments and photosynthesis of evergreen chaparral species. Oecologia **131**(3), 366–374 (2002)

23. Garrity, S.R., Eitel, J.U.H., Vierling, L.A.: Disentangling the relationships between plant pigments and the photochemical reflectance index reveals a new approach for remote estimation of carotenoid content. Remote Sensing Environ. **115**(2), 628–635 (2011)

24. Price, K.P., Guo, X., Stiles, J.M.: Optimal Landsat tm band combinations and vegetation indices for discrimination of six grassland types in eastern Kansas. Int. J. Remote Sensing **23**(23), 5031–5042 (2002)

25. Gitelson, A., Merzlyak, M.N.: Spectral reflectance changes associated with autumn senescence of aesculus hippocastanum l. and acer platanoides l. leaves. spectral features and relation to chlorophyll estimation. J. Plant Physiol. **143**(3), 286–292 (1994)

26. Frank, T.D.: The effect of change in vegetation cover and erosion patterns on albedo and texture of Landsat images in a semiarid environment. Ann. Assoc. Am. Geogr. **74**(3), 393–407 (1984)

27. Lawrence, R.L., Wood, S.D., Sheley, R.L.: Mapping invasive plants using hyperspectral imagery and Breiman Cutler classifications (Random Forest). Remote Sensing Environ. **100**(3), 356–362 (2006)

A New Smoothing-Based Farmland Extraction Approach with Vectorization from Raster Remote Sensing Images

Ruoxian Li, Kun Gao$^{(\boxtimes)}$, and Zeyang Dou

Key Laboratory of Photoelectronic Imaging Technology and System, Ministry of Education of China, Beijing Institute of Technology, Beijing 100081, China
gaokun@bit.edu.cn

Abstract. With the increasing resolution and application scene of remote sensing images, land and resource investigators begin to consider using these images to investigate crop species, cultivated area and ownership. Instead of manually drawing the boundary of the selected farmland region, an efficient edge-preserving smoothing method for automatically segmenting and extracting the area is proposed, which is performed according to the following three steps: (1) Remove the interference information by image preprocessing. The smoothing algorithm in this process was proposed according to features of the ideal smoothed image and using Maximum a Posteriori estimation model to preserve borderlines of farmland regions; (2) Image segmentation, including threshold and region segmentation using the fixed threshold and the hole removal based on the region growth method respectively after edge and whole image enhancement; (3) Information extraction, including region separation with the Flood Fill method and region vectorization which can reduce the amount of data and make the image to scale arbitrarily by contour tracking after thinning with the Freeman Chain Code. The final results of segmenting and extracting farmland objects with different features from raster remote sensing images demonstrate the correctness and efficiency of the proposed process.

Keywords: Remote sensing image · Edge-preserving smoothing · Farmland region · Image segmentation · Information extraction · Vectorization

1 Introduction

With the development of remote sensing (RS) technology, the accuracy of RS image has been continuously improved, and it has been widely used in military reconnaissance, land resource survey, disaster monitoring, etc. Nowadays, investigators are trying to investigate crop species, cultivated area and ownership through orthoimages of farmland in China. However, due to the complex environment, they need to draw the boundary of the area manually. In view of this inefficient work, automatic farmland extraction approach is in urgent need of research and application.

In order to extract the regional information of farmland, we have to remove the interference caused by the process of image transmission and the land or vegetation texture within the region first. Since the information of edges is important in most

© Springer Nature Switzerland AG 2019
Y. Zhao et al. (Eds.): ICIG 2019, LNCS 11903, pp. 334–346, 2019.
https://doi.org/10.1007/978-3-030-34113-8_28

cases, the traditional smoothing filters such as mean filter, Gaussian filter and median filter are gradually replaced by Laplacian of Gaussian (LoG) operator [1], Bilateral filter [2], total variation [3] and so on. Based on these algorithms, edge-preserving smoothing algorithms with better performance have been proposed. Farbman et al. [4] proposed a flexible filter using the weighted least square (WLS) framework. Zhang et al. [5] proposed the rolling guidance filter (RGF) to separate different scale structures. Dou et al. [6] proposed the truncated total variation to preserve only salient structures. In this paper, we finally designed a new algorithm which is more suitable for farmland based on the advantages of existing algorithms.

Image segmentation and information extraction of farmland should be the important process to realize the automatic farmland extraction. Most of the information extraction algorithms for RS images are oriented to the whole image [7], or segment and extract the region of interest according to the spectral characteristics [8]. The extraction methods for specific objects such as river [9] and road [10] networks are not effective in farmland due to their different object characteristics. Now there are algorithms to achieve fine farmland segmentation by stratified regionalization and local segmentation parameter estimation [11]. In order to draw the boundary of a piece of farmland automatically, we only need to extract the information of the designated one. Therefore, the fine segmentation of all farmland which requires a lot of work is not conducive to practical application. What's more, RS images are stored as raster images generally. Since they have a large amount of data and can not be arbitrarily scaled, we have to vectorize them through thinning-based, contour-based, run-graph-based or other classical vectorization algorithms to save the extraction results.

In this paper, we developed a new smoothing-based automatic farmland segmentation and extraction approach with vectorization from raster RS images. After the regions of interest in images are vectorized and stored, the investigators can directly edit the information of the regions, thus avoiding the influence of the subjective factors and reducing the time needed for information extraction and recording.

2   Methods

The proposed method of farmland segmentation and extraction with vectorization from raster RS images contains three steps: image preprocessing, image segmentation, and information extraction. The specific workflow is shown in Fig. 1. To begin with, the input raster RS image needs to be preprocessed. Then, threshold segmentation and region segmentation can be performed on preprocessed images. Finally, the region of interest is separated from the segmented image by region separation technique. After vectorization, the farmland information of the designated area is extracted, and the vectorized farmland image can be used by land investigators.

2.1   Image Preprocessing

As raster images scanned by aerial or scanner usually contain a lot of redundant information, image noise, etc., which will adversely affect subsequent image processing, it is necessary to preprocess the original image. Since the selected raster image

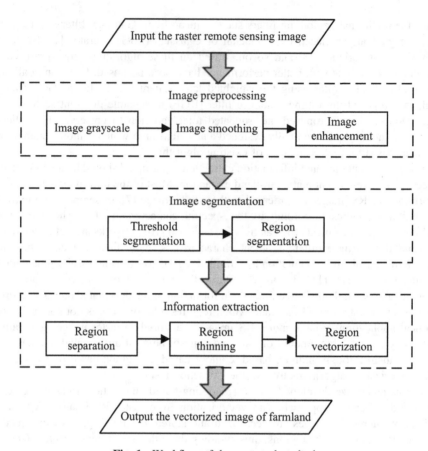

Fig. 1. Workflow of the proposed method.

is orthophoto, image correction is not required. In our proposed method, image pre-processing includes image grayscale, image smoothing and image enhancement to improve the quality of input original image.

Image Grayscale. Grayscale image processing can simplify the image information under the condition of ensuring the integrity of useful information. For the input color image, we use the weighted average method to process the three components of RGB and the result of the sample image can be seen in Fig. 2(a):

$$f(x, y) = 0.21R(x, y) + 0.72G(x, y) + 0.07B(x, y) \tag{1}$$

Image Smoothing. Smoothing images can minimize the ratio of image noise and texture. Since we want to preserve the information of edges, according to the introduction of smoothing algorithms at the beginning, we have tried a lot. Figure 2(b) and

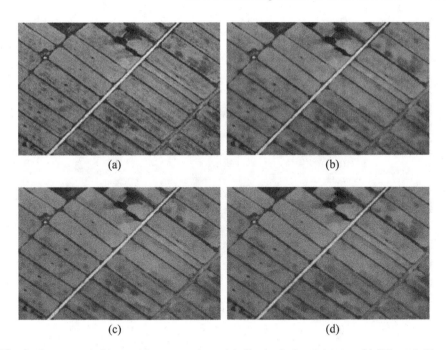

Fig. 2. Image smoothing results comparison. (a) Grayscale input image; (b) Bilateral filter; (c) Total variation; (d) Proposed method.

(c) show the smoothing results of the classical Bilateral filter and total variation algorithms.

Since these classical algorithms can not meet our needs that the texture in the region should be removed better, we consider first defining the characteristics of the ideal smoothed image of the farmland, and then choose the most appropriate method. We used Photoshop to draw the simulated farmland and its ideal smoothed image as shown in Fig. 3(a) and (c), and their histograms of gradient statistics are shown in Fig. 3(b) and (d) respectively.

The gradient of the original image conforms to the Laplace distribution, but that of the smoothed image does not. We denote the input image by f, the smoothed result by u and the pixel value of u is normalized to [0, 1]. The gradient distribution of the smoothed image can be expressed as

$$D(x) = \frac{1}{c}e^{-|T(\nabla u)|} \tag{2}$$

$$s.t. \ c = \frac{1}{\int_{\Omega} e^{-|T(\nabla u)|}dxdy} \tag{3}$$

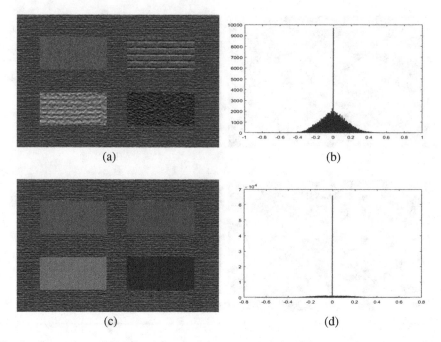

Fig. 3. Comparison of simulated farmland images and their histograms of gradient statistics before and after smoothing. (a) Original simulated image of farmland; (b) Histogram of gradient statistics of (a); (c) Ideal smoothed image of (a); (d) Histogram of gradient statistics of (c).

$$T(u) = \begin{cases} \nabla u = \sqrt{u_x^2 + u_y^2} & \nabla u < \varepsilon \\ \varepsilon & \text{otherwise} \end{cases} \tag{4}$$

$$s.t. \quad u(x, y) \in [0, 1]; \, x, y \in \Omega \tag{5}$$

Where $1/c$ is the normalization factor, ∇u is the gradient of u, Ω represents the region of the image. The formulas above indicate that only the gradient smaller than the threshold ε is calculated. The problem of obtaining the best smoothing result can be regarded as the Maximum a Posteriori estimation. When suppose the noise of image obeys zero mean Gaussian distribution $((f - u) \sim N(0, \sigma^2))$, it can be expressed as

$$\arg \max L(u) = \ln(\prod_{i=1}^{n} \frac{1}{\sigma\sqrt{2\pi}} e^{-\frac{(f_i - u_i)^2}{2\sigma^2}} \cdot \prod_{j=1}^{m} \frac{1}{c} e^{-|T(\nabla u)|})$$

$$= -\frac{1}{2\sigma^2} \sum_{i=1}^{n} (f_i - u_i)^2 - \sum_{j=1}^{m} |T(\nabla u)| - n \ln(\sigma\sqrt{2\pi}) - m \ln c \tag{6}$$

$$\arg\min l(u) = \lambda \sum_{i=1}^{n} (f_i - u_i)^2 + \sum_{j=1}^{m} |T(\nabla u)|$$
$$= \lambda \|f - u\|_2^2 + \|T(\nabla u)\|_1 \qquad (7)$$

The u that minimizes (7) is the smoothing result we want, which can be acquired by using the gradient descent algorithm to solve the corresponding Euler-Lagrange (E-L) equation. The E-L equation and its solving method are

$$2\lambda(u-f) - div(\frac{T(\nabla u)}{|T(\nabla u)|}) = 0 \qquad (8)$$

$$\begin{cases} \dfrac{\partial u}{\partial t} = div(\dfrac{T(\nabla u)}{|T(\nabla u)|}) - 2\lambda(u-f) \\[2mm] u|_{t=0} = f \\[2mm] \lambda = \dfrac{1}{\sigma^2 |\Omega|} \int_{\Omega} div(\dfrac{T(\nabla u)}{|T(\nabla u)|})(u-f)dxdy \end{cases} \qquad (9)$$

As shown in Fig. 2(d), the proposed image smoothing algorithm makes a good balance between the detail smoothing and the strong edge preserving.

Image Enhancement. In our proposed method, image enhancement includes two parts: region edge enhancement and overall image contrast enhancement.

In many natural scenes, the gray value of the region boundary varies a lot and may be close to the value inside each region. If we set the edges to the same grayscale value, some interference would be removed. Therefore, we apply edge detection and make the result fuses with smoothed image to achieve edge enhancement:

$$I = \alpha u + \beta e + \gamma \ (\alpha = 1, \ \beta \geq 1) \qquad (10)$$

Where I, u and e represent the result of edge enhancement, smoothing and edge detection respectively, α, β, γ are weight factors. If the boundaries' gray values of e are significantly different, β should be set greater than one.

In Fig. 4, we compare edge enhancement results using Laplace, Canny, Prewitt and Sobel operator. As we can see in (a), Laplace operator is very sensitive to edges, the edge of noise and texture are detected at the same time. When using Canny operator, there is no difference in strength of the edge it detects, as shown in (b). Since we hope as few edges as possible to be detected within the field area, Sobel operator is a better choice, it can overcome the defect of above two methods, as shown in (d). The result of using Prewitt operator is similar to Sobel, but it's not as accurate as that of Sobel. The effect of edge enhancement is achieved by merging smoothed image and multiple times of edge detection result using Sobel operator, which can be seen in Fig. 5(a).

Histogram equalization can be adopted to enhance the whole image contrast by expanding the distribution of pixel intensity, the result using this method is shown in

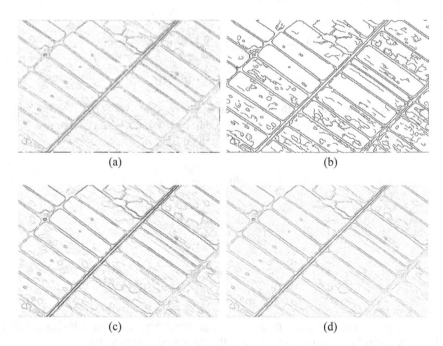

Fig. 4. Results comparison of edge detection for Fig. 1(a). (a) Laplace operator; (b) Canny operator; (c) Prewitt operator; (d) Sobel operator.

Fig. 5. Edge and whole image enhancement results. (a) Edge enhancement result with Sobel operator; (b) Image enhancement result with Histogram equalization.

Fig. 5(b). After image enhancement, the gray value of edges and other regions are clearly distinguished.

2.2   Image Segmentation

After the completion of image preprocessing, it is necessary to carry out the image segmentation before information extraction. We divide the process into two stages: threshold segmentation and region segmentation.

Threshold Segmentation. We want to make the edge and interior of regions in Fig. 5 (b) have the same gray value respectively, binarization in threshold segmentation is carried out first. However, the adaptive threshold algorithm which considered to have fine effect isn't perform better than fixed threshold segmentation when dealing with farmland images. The result after threshold segmentation is shown in Fig. 6(a).

Region Segmentation. After the fixed threshold segmentation, the edges of each region have been clearly depicted. However, there are some small black areas in the interior and white holes in the boundary line of individual regions, which are affected by the edge enhancement operation. If these interferences are removed, the farmland information extraction can achieve better. We adopted the region segmentation based on the region growth method to obtain the effect shown in Fig. 6(b). In order to retain valuable information, eight-neighborhood detection is selected to remove white holes, and four-neighborhood detection is selected to remove small black areas. If eight-neighborhood detection is still selected to remove the small black areas, the parts near the edge will not be easy to remove.

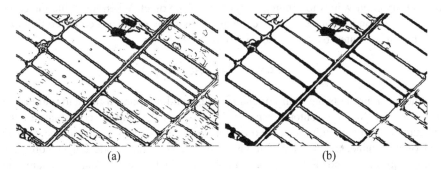

(a)   (b)

Fig. 6. Image segmentation results. (a) Fixed threshold segmentation result. (b) Region segmentation result.

2.3   Information Extraction

In order to extract the information of the region of interest from the segmented image, the region needs to be separated from the whole image. Since the images we got at first are rasterized, we need to consider the process of converting raster regions into vector to reduce the amount of data and store results easily. Therefore, the information extraction process can be divided into region separation and vectorization.

Region Separation. According to the actual characteristics of the research object, we chose Flood fill method to realize the region separation, as shown in Fig. 7(a). Specifically, the eight-neighborhood detection method is used to obtain the mask image of the connected region with the same gray value, thus accelerating the processing.

Region Vectorization. Before this step, the separated images should be optimized by removing small black areas that away from edges. The Closing operation in the Mathematical morphology can be used and the kernel size can be selected as (5, 5).

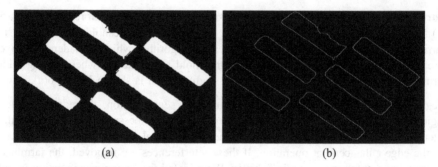

(a)   (b)

Fig. 7. Results of region separation and contours. (a) Region separation result; (b) Thinning contours of regions tracked by the Freeman Chain Code.

Considering the complexity and efficiency of the algorithm, we choose the Freeman chain code to track the contour of regions (shown in Fig. 7(b)) to achieve vectorization.

The Freeman chain code picks any pixel point as a reference point, and gives different direction values to different neighbors of the pixel. When the value increases one, the direction it indicates rotates counterclockwise by 45°. The connected thinning contour is represented by chain code as follows:

$$F = (s, x, y, d_0, d_1, \ldots, d_j, \ldots, d_n, p) \tag{11}$$

Where F represents the string of chain code, s and p represent the start and end of the connected thinning contour respectively, (x, y) is the starting coordinate of the connected thinning contour, d_j is the direction code connecting the j th and the $j + 1$ th pixel of the connected thinning contour. The Freeman chain code only records the starting coordinate and direction code numbers, so it has simple data structure and stores a small amount of data.

Contour tracking is performed with the Freeman chain code for each connected thinning contour, and the gray value of the encoded pixels is set to zero to avoid repetition. After all pixels of thinning contours are removed, we can decode the chain codes and connect the pixels with line segments to obtain the vectorized images. When pixels connected by line segments are separated by 30 and 5 pixels, the effect is shown in Fig. 8(a) and (b). The final result of the proposed method of farmland segmentation and extraction with vectorization from raster images can be seen in Fig. 9(a). Each pixel we tracked can be recorded in the file for drawing the region boundaries directly later.

3 Study Area and Experimental Data

The RS images published on National Catalogue Service For Geographic Information website of China in 2012 were used to evaluate the effectiveness of the proposed method. The study areas are located in the countryside of Xianning (29.87 °N, 114.28 °E), Hubei province and Jiuquan (39.71 °N, 98.5 °E), Gansu province, China.

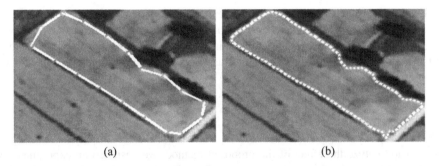

Fig. 8. Information extraction results at different sampling intervals. (a) Line segments separated by 30 pixels; (b) Line segments separated by 5 pixels.

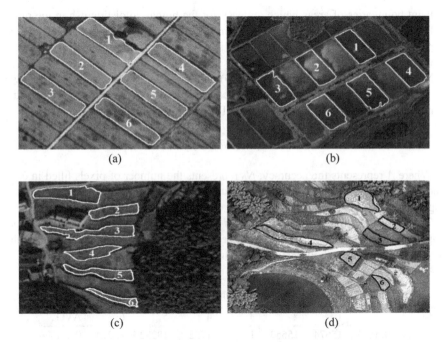

Fig. 9. Original aerial RS test images and the final results using the proposed method of regions selected randomly on the original images. (a), (b), (c), and (d) are typical rural landscape with different features of farmland captured by UCXP and are numbered on each region.

The typical images we chose to use are all parts of aerial RS images captured by UCXP, which has 0.1-m spatial resolution. As shown in Fig. 9, (a) is a part of farmland with colorful rectangular blocks in Jiuquan, (b) shows regular ponds with cloud reflections in Xianning, (c) is chosen to represent the irregular farmland, and (d) represents typical rural landscape with irregular farmland that has textural features, bending roads and randomly distributed trees.

Each image in Fig. 9 represents a typical farmland situation, as we can see, it is increasingly difficult to segment and extract the information of farmland areas we interested in. The more irregular the region is, the more textures there are in the region, and the more external disturbances such as vegetation and buildings are, the more complex the processing process will be.

4 Experimental Results

In order to analyze the effect of the proposed method, we designed an experiment to test the accuracy of information extraction. The experimental hypothesis is that the boundary of farmland region depicted manually is completely accurate and the extracted region information is complete. Experimental steps:

- Paint boundaries of areas which are easy for the human to distinguish in the raster RS image manually and obtain the boundaries of the same regions with the proposed method in this paper, then fill the interior of boundaries obtained in different ways.
- Number the regions (as shown in Fig. 9) and input the filling images of these two methods into the region separation process of the proposed method to obtain the number of pixels filled in each region. The way of calculating the accuracy is:

$$A = [1 - |(N - N_0)/N_0|] \times 100\% \qquad (12)$$

Where A represents the accuracy, N_0 represents the number of pixels filled in each hand-painted region, and N represents the number of pixels in the region filled with the proposed method.

The segmentation and extraction results using the proposed method of the sample images are shown in Fig. 9. According to the number of areas shown in each image, the above experimental method was applied, and statistical results are shown in Table 1.

Table 1. The experimental results of the method we presented.

		1	2	3	4	5	6	AVG
Fig. 9(a)	N_0	15674	15653	17235	17821	18252	15974	98.67%
	N	16294	15874	17069	17950	18357	16029	
	A	96.04%	98.59%	99.04%	99.28%	99.42%	99.66%	
Fig. 9(b)	N_0	10774	11296	11214	11389	12400	11818	97.48%
	N	11080	11601	11326	11703	12585	12333	
	A	97.16%	97.30%	99.00%	97.24%	98.51%	95.64%	
Fig. 9(c)	N_0	6582	3785	5520	3429	4791	2421	91.12%
	N	7077	4118	6277	4046	4560	2410	
	A	92.48%	91.20%	86.29%	82.01%	95.18%	99.55%	
Fig. 9(d)	N_0	6026	2398	3165	7189	3795	1856	89.53%
	N	6496	2554	3517	7353	2822	2032	
	A	92.20%	93.49%	88.88%	97.72%	74.36%	90.52%	

The average accuracy of the method proposed in this paper is 94.2%, but as we can see, the accuracy decreases with the increase of texture and shadow interference. The fifth region in Fig. 9(d) has the lowest accuracy because the method doesn't have the ability to think like a person that two parts with very different gray values are actually a region.

5   Conclusion

In this paper, we have presented a new approach for farmland segmentation and extraction from raster RS images. The experimental results demonstrate that the whole process proposed in this paper can achieve considerable success even regions are colorful, irregular and have textures inside. When the contrast between the interior and the boundary of a region is distinct, the accuracy of the extraction can be relatively high. However, when the boundary of a region is affected by the shadow of vegetation or farmland, or the gray value of texture within the region varies greatly, the extracted results will have much deviation, which is another important research topic to be solved. In a word, the proposed method has a considerable effect on the segmentation and extraction of farmland regions, and can be extended to other areas, such as roads, buildings, water areas, etc.

References

1. Marr, D., Hildreth, E.: Theory of edge detection. Proc. R. Soc. Lond. Biol. Sci. **207**(1167), 187–217 (1980)
2. Tomasi, C., Manduchi, R.: Bilateral filtering for gray and color images. In: Sixth International Conference on Computer Vision, pp. 839–846. IEEE, India (1998)
3. Rudin, L.I., Osher, S., Fatemi, E.: Nonlinear total variation based noise removal algorithms. Physica D **60**(1–4), 259–268 (1992)
4. Farbman, Z., Fattal, R., Lischinski, D., Szeliski, R.: Edge-preserving decompositions for multi-scale tone and detail manipulation. ACM Trans. Graph. **27**(3), 67 (2008)
5. Zhang, Q., Shen, X., Xu, L., Jia, J.: Rolling guidance filter. In: Fleet, D., Pajdla, T., Schiele, B., Tuytelaars, T. (eds.) ECCV 2014. LNCS, vol. 8691, pp. 815–830. Springer, Cham (2014). https://doi.org/10.1007/978-3-319-10578-9_53
6. Dou, Z., Song, M., Gao, K., et al.: Image smoothing via truncated total variation. IEEE Access **5**, 27337–27344 (2017)
7. Chen, Q., Luo, J., Zhou, C., et al.: A hybrid multi-scale segmentation approach for remotely sensed imagery. In: 2003 IEEE International Geoscience and Remote Sensing Symposium, pp. 3416–3419. IEEE, France (2003)
8. Yang, J., He, Y., John, C.: A self-adapted threshold-based region merging method for remote sensing image segmentation. In: 2016 IEEE International Geoscience and Remote Sensing Symposium, pp. 6320–6323. IEEE, Beijing (2016)
9. Song, Y., Wu, Y., Dai, Y.: A new active contour remote sensing river image segmentation algorithm inspired from the cross entropy. Digit. Sig. Process. **48**, 322–332 (2016)

10. Jin, H., Feng, Y., Li, B.: Road network extraction with new vectorization and pruning from high-resolution RS images. In: 2008 23rd International Conference Image and Vision Computing New Zealand, pp. 1–6. IEEE, New Zealand (2008)
11. Xu, L., Ming, D., Zhou, W., et al.: Farmland extraction from high spatial resolution remote sensing images based on stratified scale pre-estimation. Remote Sens. **11**(2), 108 (2019)

S³OD: Single Stage Small Object Detector from Scratch for Remote Sensing Images

Feng Yang[1,2,4(✉)], Wentong Li[1,2], Wanyi Li[3], and Peng Wang[3]

[1] Northwestern Polytechnical University,
Xi'an 710129, People's Republic of China
yangfeng@nwpu.edu.cn
[2] Key Laboratory of Information Fusion Technology, Ministry of Education,
Xi'an 710129, People's Republic of China
[3] Institute of Automation, Chinese Academy of Sciences, Beijing 100190,
People's Republic of China
[4] CETC Key Laboratory of Data Link Technology,
Xi'an 710129, People's Republic of China

Abstract. Small object detection is an important but challenge computer vision task in both natural scene and remote sensing scene. Due to the large difference of density, low contrast, sparse texture and arbitrary orientations, many advanced algorithms for small object detection in natural scene usually experience a sharp performance drop when directly applied to remote sensing images. In addition, most of state-of-the-art object detectors are fine-tuned from the off-the-shelf networks pretrained on large-scale classification dataset like ImageNet, which can incur learning bias and inconvenience of modification for remote sensing object detection tasks. In order to tackle these problems, a robust Single Stage Small Object Detector (S³OD) is trained from scratch, which can efficiently detect small-dense and small-dispersed objects in remote sensing images. The proposed S³OD adopts the small down-sampling factor to keep accurate location information and maintains high spatial resolution by introducing a new dilated residual block in deeper layers for small objects. Especially, the two-branch dilated feature attention module is proposed to enlarge the valid receptive field and make effective attention feature map for small-dense and small-dispersed object detection. S³OD can be trained from scratch stably while keeping the comparable performance by employing BatchNorm on both the backbone and detection head subnetworks. Experiments conducted on our built Remoting Sensing Small Object (RSSO) dataset shows that, our S³OD achieves the state-of-the-art accuracy for small objects detection and even performs better than several one-stage pretrained method.

Keywords: Object detection · Remote sensing images · Small objects · Convolutional neural networks

© Springer Nature Switzerland AG 2019
Y. Zhao et al. (Eds.): ICIG 2019, LNCS 11903, pp. 347–358, 2019.
https://doi.org/10.1007/978-3-030-34113-8_29

1 Introduction

Object detection of remote sensing images plays an important role in many real-world applications such as traffic control, environmental monitoring, and urban planning. Remarkable progresses have been made in object detection of remoting sensing images recently due to the convolutional neural networks (CNNs) [1]. However, the small object detection is still one of remaining challenge tasks in remote sensing images [2]. Lots of CNN-based object detectors have been proposed and achieve great success over natural scene. Those methods can be divided into two categories including one-stage detector, like YOLO [3], SSD [4], and two-stage detectors, like Faster R-CNN [5] and R-FCN [6]. It is found experimentally that these frameworks have poor performance for small objects, because they are based on high-level CNN features and fail to capture precise descriptions of small objects. For more advanced methods, FPN [7] introduces feature pyramids to combine multi-layer feature map by utilizing U-shape structure. RetinaNet [8] proposes a new focal loss to address class imbalance issue to make the object detection more accurate. YOLOv3 [9] introduces a powerful feature extraction backbone and adopts a similar concept to feature pyramid networks in detection layers. TridentNet [10] constructs a parallel multi-branch architecture with different receptive fields to detection multi-scale object. Those frameworks have achieved promising results for small objects detection to a certain extent. However, these methods often experience a sharp performance drop while directly applied to remote sensing images to detect small objects. The main reasons are as followed and illustrated in Fig. 1.

(1) Small objects in remote sensing images usually appear in dense cluster with overwhelmed feature information or in dispersed distribution with sparse feature information.
(2) Remote sensing objects viewed from over-head appear in arbitrary orientations. Such as the ship can have any degrees between 0 and 360 degrees, whereas the objects in ImageNet are often vertical.
(3) Remote sensing images are complex, not only because a large amount of various noises from remote sensors (like satellite sensors), but also because remote sensing objects usually lack visual clues such as texture details, image contrast.

For remote sensing images, many deep-learning-based detection methods also have been developed. R2-CNN [11] proposes a unified and self-reinforced network including Tiny-Net backbone, global attention block and final classifier and detector towards practical real-time remote sensing systems. YOLT [12] inspired by YOLOv2 [3] implements a unique network architecture with a denser final prediction grid to help differentiate between classes by yielding grained features in remote sensing images. Those methods mainly focus on how to implement a multi-class framework elegantly while the detection performance of small objects is not well. Small object detection seems much more difficult.

Besides, most of current impressive detectors are generally fine-tuned from the off-the-shelf networks with high accuracy classification, e.g. VGGNet [13], ResNet [14] pretrained on ImageNet dataset. Object detectors fine-tuned from pretrained networks often achieve better performance than those trained from scratch. But fine-tuning from

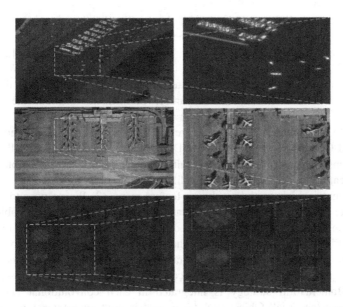

Fig. 1. Examples of small object detection including boat, airplane and oilcan. Illustration of density, sparse texture, arbitrary orientations, and low contrast in remote sensing images.

pretrained networks for object detection tasks has two main problems: (1) The classification and detection have different loss function, leading to the learning bias; (2) The architecture of backbone is limited by the classification network, resulting in the inconvenience of modification. DSOD [15] is the first to train the one-stage object detector from scratch and focuses on the deep supervision of DenseNet [16]. That introduces many principles to get the good performance. DetNet [17] analyzes the drawbacks of ImageNet pre-trained model for fine-tuning object detectors and presents a train-from-scratch backbone for object detection. ScratchDet [18] explores that BatchNorm is one of the key points for object detectors from scratch and presents a single-shot object detector which integrates BatchNorm to help the detector converge well from scratch. For object detection in remote sensing images, most state-of-art methods are fine-tuned from the pretrained on large-scale dataset ImageNet, which is unreasonable.

In this paper, we propose a Single Stage Small Object Detector (S³OD) for small object detection from scratch in remote sensing images. Firstly, a novel backbone aimed at small remote sensing objects is designed. A large down-sampling factor used by most classic methods with the down-sampling operations (e.g. max-pooling and convolution with stride 2) is not a reasonable option in remote sensing images with high resolution. We adopt a small down-sampling factor to keep more precise feature for small objects. To build a deep neural network which can maintain high resolution feature maps in deeper layer, we introduce a new dilated residual block structure. Secondly, we find out that small remote sensing objects can be divided into two categories, including small-dense objects and small-dispersed objects. To detect small objects effectively, we adopt a two-branch dilated feature attention module, one branch is designed for small-dense objects with the small dilatation rate in the relatively shallow layer, another one branch is designed for small-dispersed objects with the large dilatation rate in the relatively deep layer. In addition, as pointed out in [20], Batch-Norm is one of the key points in current trained-from-scratch detector. We integrate BatchNorm into both the backbone and detection head subnet which helps the detector converge well and achieves the comparable performance without the pretrained baseline.

The main contributions of this paper are summarized as follows. (1) A novel Single Stage Small Object Detector dubbed S^3OD is proposed to detect the small objects in remoting sensing images, in which a small down-sampling factor is adopted to keep accurate location information and a new dilated residual block is introduced in deeper layers to maintain high spatial resolution feature maps. (2) We propose to categorize small remote sensing objects into small-dense objects and small-dispersed objects. And a two-branch dilated feature attention module is designed, in which the first branch with small dilatation rate in the relatively shallow layer is for small-dense objects, while the other branch with the large dilatation rate in the relatively deep layer is for small-dispersed objects. (3) To help the S^3OD converge well in the train-from-scratch process, the BathchNorm strategy is integrated in each convolutional layer. (4) A Remoting Sensing Small Object (RSSO) dataset is built, and extensive experiments conducted on it demonstrated that our proposed S^3OD achieves the state-of-the-art accuracy for small objects detection and even performs better than several one-stage pretrained methods.

2   Proposed Method

The overview framework of our proposed Single Stage Small Object Detector (S^3OD) is illustrated in Fig. 2. As the figure shown, our S^3OD is built on the structure of classic one-stage detection network-YOLOv3. The fine-gained feature map for small-scale objects is extracted by the designed backbone with the down-sampling factor of 16, instead of 32 in standard darknet53 network. Meanwhile the backbone employs several dilated residual blocks to enlarge the receptive filed with the high spatial resolution. The two-branch feature attention module is introduced for small-dense and small-dispersed objects detection in remote sensing images. Finally, BatchNorm is adopted to the whole designed network to train from scratch in a good convergence performance.

2.1   Small Down-Sampling Factor in S^3OD Backbone

Most of remote sensing object detection methods usually rely on backbone networks like VGGNet [13], ResNet [14], which are used to classification task. The task of classification is different from the object detection which not only needs to recognize the classes of objects but also needs to get the accurate bounding-boxes. Notice that the down-sampling operations (e.g. max-pooling and convolution with stride 2) are one keys of things for translation invariance. In contrast, the local texture information is more critical for object detection especially for complex remote sensing images. In this case, we analyze the performance of VGGNet, ResNet and Darknet53 with various

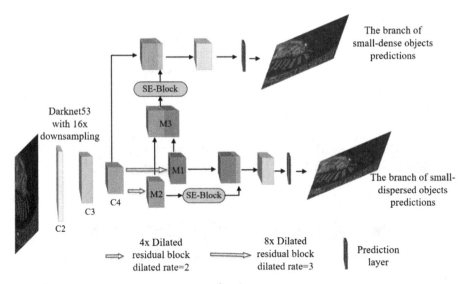

Fig. 2. The overview framework of our S³OD method for small object detection in remote sensing images. The backbone is darknet53 with 16x down-sampling factor and the two-branch dilated feature attention module is designed for small-dense objects and small-dispersed objects.

configurations, and discover that the down-sampling factor has a great impact on detection performance. Based on this point, we redesign the architecture of detector by adopting the down-sampling factor of 16. As Fig. 2 shown, the feature map C4, M1 and M2 have the same size of width and height in different layer with 16x down-sampling factor, which keeps the abundant information for detection feature maps and substantially improves the detection accuracy for small objects in remote sensing images.

2.2 The Two-Branch Dilated Feature Attention Module

Reducing the down-sampling factor equals to reducing the valid receptive field, which will be harmful for vision tasks. To efficiently enlarge the receptive field, a new dilated residual block structure, which consists of a 1×1 convolution and a 3×3 dilated convolution, is adopted to S³OD. Notice that, a dilated 3×3 convolution with d_s dilation could have the same receptive field as the convolution with kernel size of $3 + 2$ $(d_s - 1)$. In additions, Shallow layers usually only have low semantic information which may be not enough to recognize the category of the object instances. Therefore, the 8x dilated residual blocks with dilated rate of 3 and the 4x dilated residual blocks with dilated rate of 2 are constructed to get different receptive field and different depth-level feature map. It is illustrated in Fig. 3.

As Fig. 3 shown, the feature map passed through the 8x dilated residual block from C4 is denoted as M1, the feature map passed through the 4x dilated residual blocks from C4 is denoted as M2. M1 can bring large valid receptive field and high-level representations with a deeper layer, which is mainly designed for the dispersed objects

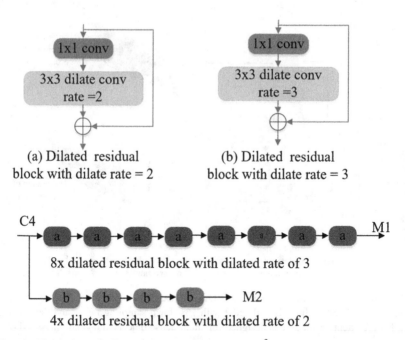

Fig. 3. The illustration of different dilated residual block in S³OD in a and b. C4 passes through 8x dilated residual block to get M1, and passes through 4x dilated residual block to get M2 in the two-branch dilated feature attention module.

in remote sensing images. Compared with M1, M2 brings a smaller valid receptive field from a shallower layer, which can make up the loss of information of M1 owing to convolution operation with a lager dilate rate. For small-dense objects detection, we concatenate M1 with M2 to get a high-representation feature map M3 with different depth and different receptive field. C4 feature map keeps the abundant texture information. In order to get the fine-gained feature map, we concatenate C4 with the M3 to detect small-dense objects in remote sensing images. In this two-branch module, we use SE block [20]. SE block can enhance informative features according to attention mechanism and suppress features that are of little use of the current task. Especially for remote sensing images, SE block can weaken the noise and relatively enhance the object attention information. The overview pipeline is shown in Fig. 2.

2.3 Training S³OD from Scratch with BatchNorm

BatchNorm can reparameterize the optimization problem to make its landscape significantly smoother instead of reducing the internal covariate shift. We add BatchNorm in each convolution layer in both the backbone and detection head subnetworks, which introduces a more predictable and stable behavior of the great gradients to allow for larger searching space and faster convergence (see Fig. 4). Our proposed train-from-scratch S³OD performs better than several one-stage pretrained models.

3 Experiments

In this section, we conduct experiments on our built small dataset of remote sensing images to demonstrate the effectiveness of our proposed S^{3}OD method. The dataset description, implementation details, evaluation metrics, and experimental results will be introduced in detail.

3.1 Dataset Description

The proposed method is evaluated over the small object images which are collected from two publicly available datasets including NWPU-VHR10 [21] and AIIA2018_2nd [22]. NWPU-VHR10 has 800 high-resolution remote sensing images in total with 10 classes of objects including plane, ship, storage tank, baseball diamond, tennis court, basketball court, ground track field, harbor, bridge and vehicle. The AIIA2018_2nd dataset of remote sensing images is provided from the second stage of AIIA[1] Cup Competition of Typical Object Recognition for Satellite Imagery, which covers six classes: airport, airplane, harbor, boat, oilcan, bridge. The dataset includes 2421 images whose size varies from 512 × 512 pixels to 5120 × 3584.

We select the small objects from the two publicly available datasets above to build a new Remoting Sensing Small Object (RSSO) dataset. RSSO dataset has 1369 images for train and 307 images for test and includes three classes like airplane, ship/boat and storage tank/oilcan which are the common categories in both NWPU-VHR10 and AIIA2018_2nd. Evaluating the images in RSSO, it can be seen that mainly objects are small-dense and small-dispersed and the size of remote sensing object is so small to 5x4, which is a great challenge for small object detection. Some examples of RSSO are given in Fig. 1.

3.2 Implementation Details and Evaluation Metrics

The proposed S^{3}OD is trained with Stochastic Gradient Descent (SGD), where momentum is 0.9, the learning rate is 0.01 on a single NVIDIA GeForce GTX 1080Ti GPU with 11 GB memory, along with the deep learning framework PyTorch. Batch size is set to 4. Total training iterations for RSSO dataset are 400 epochs, i.e. 136800 steps. Mean Average Precision is used as the evaluation metric followed by the standard PASCAL VOC criteria, i.e. IoU > 0.5 between ground truths and predicted boxes [23].

3.3 Experimental Results

In our experiments, we trained the state-of-the-art algorithms, like YOLOV3, TridentNet, YOLT models with hyper parameter architecture for the purpose of comparison. Our proposed S^{3}OD uses BatchNorm on every convolution layer and train it from scratch. In addition, YOLT and TridentNet are both trained by the way of

---

[1] AIIA is China Artificial Intelligence Industry Development Alliance.

fine-tuning from the pretrained backbone models. YOLT is trained by the Darknet19 baseline and TridentNet is trained by the Darknet53 baseline. Experimental results on the test set of RSSO dataset are shown in the Table 1. As Table 1 shown, our proposed S^{3}OD outperforms YOLT, YOLOv3 fine-tuned with the pretrained model and TridentNet by 6.8%, 4.5% and 4.1% respectively which demonstrates its effectiveness for small object detection from remote sensing images. Especially for small-dense objects mainly including boat and oilcan, our S^{3}OD has a large improvement because of our introduced two-branch attention module.

Table 1. Detection results of YOLOv3, YOLT, TridentNet and our proposed S^{3}OD on mAP over the RSSO test set.

Method	mAP	Airplane	Boat	Oilcan
YOLOv3 without pretrained model	0.531	0.7261	0.3055	0.5614
YOLT	0.595	0.8903	0.3080	0.5881
YOLOv3 fine-tuned with pretrained model	0.618	0.8700	0.4007	0.5840
TridentNet	0.622	0.8644	0.4102	0.5901
S^{3}OD (ours)	0.663	0.8965	0.4667	0.6246

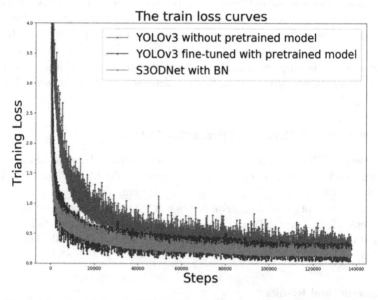

Fig. 4. The training loss value is illustrated in this figure. The total loss including x + y coordinates loss, w + h coordinates loss, confidence loss and class score loss are shown. Green and blue curves present YOLOv3 without pretrained model and YOLOv3 fine-tuned with pretrained model respectively, red curve is the train-from-scratch S^{3}OD with BatchNorm. (Color figure online)

Fig. 5. Visual detection results on test dataset of our proposed S³OD method. Small objects including airplane, oilcan, boat detection results are shown from top to bottom respectively. S³OD has better performance in detection of dense and dispersed objects.

In order to illustrate the performance of the proposed train-from-scratch S^{3}OD in convergence, we train YOLOv3 in two ways including training without pretrained model and training with pretrained model to make a comparison. The Fig. 4 shows the training total loss value including x + y coordinates loss, w + h coordinates loss, confidence loss and class score loss. As Fig. 4 shown, green and blue curves present YOLOv3 without pretrained model and YOLOv3 fine-tuned with pretrained model respectively, red curve is our train-from-scratch S3OD with BatchNorm. Our trained S^{3}OD by BatchNorm from scratch has a better and stably convergence performance. And the mAP performance is better than two YOLOv3 models. These results indicate that using BatchNorm on each convolution layers is critical to train from scratch.

Figure 5 shows a few sample results from the RSSO test dataset and the corresponding detection is airplane, oilcan and boat which are small-densely or small-dispersedly distribution in remoting sensing images. The proposed S^{3}OD is capable of correctly detecting those small objects under various scenarios which are in low contrast, sparse texture and complex background. Besides, S^{3}OD is still prone to detection failure objects that are heavily overlapped with each other and will miss detecting objects which are too small to get the efficient feature. For this issue, we believe a better dilated convolutional network with a proper down-sampling factor and a better Non-Maximum-Suppression (NMS) can be adopted to address, which we will do in our feature work.

4   Conclusions

Aiming to improve the detection performance of small objects in remote sensing images, this paper presents an effective S^{3}OD method. A detection backbone with the small down-sampling factor is designed to keep high spatial resolution, two-branch dilated feature attention module is presented for small-dense and small-dispersed purposefully. Furthermore, BatchNorm is introduced to get a better training process for a robust detector. The experimental results on RSSO dataset demonstrate the effectiveness of the proposed method. Our proposed S^{3}OD pipeline exhibits strong competency in handling small object detection tasks. For future work, we will focus on the further tasks of small object detection and multi-scale object detection for remote sensing images.

Acknowledgments. The work was supported by National Natural Science Foundation of China (No. 91748131, No. 61771471, No. 61374159), the Youth Innovation Promotion Association Chinese Academy of Sciences (No. 2015112), the Foundation of CETC Key Laboratory of Data Link Technology (CLDL-20182316, CLDL-20182203), Natural Science Foundation of Shaanxi province (No. 2018MJ6048), and the Seed Foundation of Innovation and Creation for Graduate Students in Northwestern Polytechnical University (No. ZZ2019178).

References

1. Wu, Y., Zhang, R., Li, Y.: The detection of built-up areas in high-resolution SAR images based on deep neural networks. In: Zhao, Y., Kong, X., Taubman, D. (eds.) ICIG 2017. LNCS, vol. 10668, pp. 646–655. Springer, Cham (2017). https://doi.org/10.1007/978-3-319-71598-8_57
2. Zhang, W., Wang, S., Thachan, S., Chen, J., Qian, Y.: Deconv R-CNN for small object detection on remote sensing images. In: IEEE International Geoscience and Remote Sensing Symposium (IGARSS), pp. 2483–2486. IEEE, Valencia (2018)
3. Redmon, J., Farhadi, A.: Yolo9000: better, faster, stronger. In: IEEE Conference on Computer Vision and Pattern Recognition (CVPR), pp. 6517–6525. IEEE, Honolulu (2017)
4. Liu, W., et al.: SSD: single shot multibox detector. In: Leibe, B., Matas, J., Sebe, N., Welling, M. (eds.) ECCV 2016. LNCS, vol. 9905, pp. 21–37. Springer, Cham (2016). https://doi.org/10.1007/978-3-319-46448-0_2
5. Ren, S., He, K., Grishick, R., Sun, J.: Faster R-CNN: towards real-time object detection with region proposal networks. In: Advances in Neural Information Processing Systems (NIPS), Canada, pp. 91–99 (2015)
6. Dai, J., Li, Y., He, K., Sun, J.: R-FCN: object detection via region-based fully convolutional networks. In: Advances in Neural Information Processing Systems (NIPS), pp. 379–387 (2016)
7. Lin, T.Y., Dollar, P., Girshick, R., He, K., Hariharan, B., Belongie, S.: Feature pyramid networks for object detection. In: IEEE Conference on Computer Vision and Pattern Recognition (CVPR), pp. 936–944. IEEE, Honolulu (2017)
8. Lin, T.Y., Goyal, P, Girshick, R., He, K., Dollar, P.: Focal loss for dense object detection. In: IEEE International Conference on Computer Vision (ICCV), pp. 2999–3007. IEEE, Venice (2017)
9. Redmon, J., Farhadi, A.: Yolov3: an incremental improvement. arXiv Preprint. arXiv:1804.02767 (2018)
10. Li, Y.H., Chen, Y.T., Wang, N.Y., Zhang, Z.X.: Scale-aware trident networks for object detection. arXiv Preprint. arXiv:1901.01892 (2019)
11. Pang, J., Li, C., Shi, J. Xu, Z., Feng, H.: R2-CNN: fast tiny object detection in large-scale remote sensing images. arXiv Preprint. arXiv:1902.06042 (2019)
12. Van Etten, A.: Satellite imagery multiscale rapid detection with windowed networks. In: IEEE Winter Conference on Applications of Computer Vision (WACV), pp. 735–743. IEEE, Hilton Waikoloa Village (2019)
13. Simonyan, K., Zisserman, A.: Very deep convolutional networks for large-scale image recognition. arXiv Preprint. arXiv:1409.1556 (2014)
14. He, K., Zhang, X., Ren, S., Sun, J.: Deep residual learning for images recognition. In: Proceedings of the IEEE Conference on Computer Vision and Pattern Recognition (ICCV), pp. 770–778. IEEE, Amsterdam (2016)
15. Shen, Z., Liu, Z., Li, J., Jiang, Y.G., Chen, Y., Xue X.: DSOD: learning deeply supervised object detectors from scratch. In: IEEE International Conference on Computer Vision (ICCV), pp. 1937–1945. IEEE, Venice (2017)
16. Huang, G., Liu, Z.: Densely connected convolutional networks. In: IEEE Conference on Computer Vision and Pattern Recognition (CVPR), pp. 2261–2269. IEEE, Honolulu (2017)
17. Li, Z., Peng, C., Yu, G., Zhang, X., Deng, Y., Sun, J.: DetNet: a backbone network for object detection. arXiv Preprint. arXiv:1804.06215 (2018)

18. Zhu, R., et al.: ScratchDet: training single-shot object detectors from scratch. In: IEEE Conference on Computer Vision and Pattern Recognition (CVPR), accepted. IEEE, Long Beach (2019)
19. Santurkar, S., Tsipras. D., Ilyas, A., Madry, A.: How does batch normalization help optimization? In: Conference on Neural Information Processing Systems (NeurIPS), Montréal, pp. 2483–2493 (2018)
20. Hu, J., Shen, L., Sun, G.: Squeeze-and-excitation networks. In: IEEE Conference on Computer Vision and Pattern Recognition (CVPR), pp. 7132–7141. IEEE, Utah (2018)
21. Cheng, G., Han, J., Zhou, P., Guo, L.: Multi-class geospatial object detection and geographic image classification based on collection of part detectors. ISPRS J. Photogrammetry Remote Sens. 98(98), 119–132 (2014)
22. AIIA2018 Dataset Homepage. https://www.datafountain.cn/competitions/288/datasets
23. Everingham, M., Eslami, S.M., Gool, L., Williams, C.K., Winn, J., Zisserman, A.: The pascal visual object classes challenge: a retrospective. Int. J. Comput. Vision 111(1), 98–136 (2015)

Virtual Reality

Super Multi-view 3D Display with 170 Viewpoints Based on Rotating OLED Display Columns

Qirui Tan, Haiming Lu[⊠], and Zengxiang Lu

Research Institute of Information Technology, Tsinghua University, Beijing, China
luhm@tsinghua.edu.cn

Abstract. A super multi-view three-dimensional display is a kind of glasses-free auto-stereoscopic display which has a large number of views to provide smooth motion parallax. Current super multi-view display technology has some limitations, such as small display area, lack of immersion sense. In this study, we developed a super multi-view 3D display with 170 viewpoints based on rotating OLED display columns. The optical lenses of super wide viewing angle were optimized using optical software Zemax. The light intensity distributions of 170 viewpoints in the viewing zone were simulated using non-sequential ray tracing software LightTools. Each viewpoint width varied from 50 mm to 55 mm, which was less than a normal adults' pupillary distance. Finally, the simulation results were verified experimentally. The results show that super multi-view 3D display based on rotating OLED display columns has large display area and deep immersion sense.

Keywords: Optical design · Optical lenses · Super multi-view · OLED display columns · Uniform rotation

1 Introduction

A super multi-view three-dimensional display, which has a large number of views, is a kind of glassesless-type and natural 3D display. Its display theory is based on binocular vision, through which a human with two eyes is able to perceive a 3-D image of their surroundings [1, 2]. A normal adults' pupillary distance is from 6 to 7 cm. Owing to the eyes' different positions on the head, binocular viewing of a scene creates two slightly different images in each of the two eyes. These differences provide information that the brain can use to synthesize stereoscopic images of the visual scene [3–5]. When the number of views is increased, the super multi-view display can provide smooth motion parallax and reduce accommodation-vergence conflict [6]. Recently, super multi-view display attracts extensive research interests all over the world. Different approaches were investigated to realize the super multi-view display. In this study, we develop a super multi-view 3D display with 170 viewpoints based on rotating OLED display columns.

© Springer Nature Switzerland AG 2019
Y. Zhao et al. (Eds.): ICIG 2019, LNCS 11903, pp. 361–371, 2019.
https://doi.org/10.1007/978-3-030-34113-8_30

The conventional super multi-view 3D display has some problems, such as small display area, lack of immersion sense. Yasuhiro [7] developed a super multi-view display with 256 viewpoints, as illustrated in Fig. 1. Sixteen flat-panel 3D displays having 16 views were used to construct a super multi-view display having 256 views. However, the screen size is only 10.3 inches and the display area is rather small. Yao et al. [8, 9] realized an omnidirectional 3D display with the scanning LED and cylindrical parallax barrier, as shown in Fig. 2. The images have a resolution of 1380 circumferential pixels and 480 vertical pixels, achieving a single-view-angle resolution of 233 pixels × 480 pixel within a cylindrical space of ϕ 383 mm × 480 mm. A viewer can watch 360-degree images around the display device. However, the immersion sense is weak. Hidefumi et al. [10] disclosed a three dimensional video display device with rotating LED array in their patent, as shown in Fig. 3. In the display device, a rotating LED unit has a left-eye LED array and a right-eye LED array. The left-eye LED array displays a left-eye image and the right-eye LED array displays a right-eye image. The viewer recognizes a three dimensional image in a range of 360-degree based on binocular parallax. However, the number of viewpoints is small and the stereoscopic perception is weak. As is shown in Fig. 4, we realized a large-screen display system with rotating LED arrays, and planned to realize a super multi-view 3D display based on the large-screen display system.

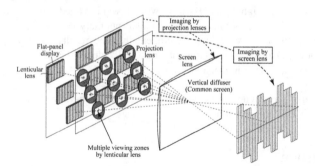

Fig. 1. Super multi-view display with 256 viewpoints.

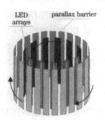

Fig. 2. Omnidirectional 3D display system based on scanning LED.

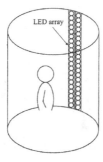

Fig. 3. Three dimensional video display device with rotating LED array.

Fig. 4. Large-screen display system with rotating LED arrays.

In this study, we proposed a super multi-view 3D display with 170 viewpoints based on rotating OLED display columns. Each of the OLED display columns is composed of OLED display units and optical lenses, which generate 170 viewpoints. This technique provides 3D images to the viewers with smooth motion parallax and deep immersion sense.

2 Principle and Design

A super multi-view three-dimensional display device is schematically described in Fig. 5. The display device includes several OLED display columns which are on a circumference with an equal distance. Each of the OLED display columns has several vertically aligned units, each of which is composed of OLED display unit and optical lenses. When the OLED display columns rotate in a circumferential direction around the central axis, a viewer who is in the center is surrounded by three-dimensional image. This gives the viewer an illusory sensation as if the viewer is in the real world of the displayed image. Therefore, the viewer can obtain the realistic sensation and the deep immersion.

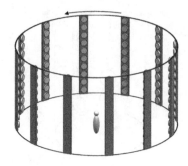

Fig. 5. Super multi-view 3D display device based on rotating OLED display columns.

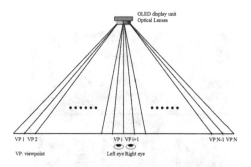

Fig. 6. Super multi-view formation for left eye and right eye.

Figure 6 illustrates the super multi-view formation in the proposed display device. The collimated input light, which is from the pixel of the OLED display unit, can propagate in a particular direction when it passes through the optical lenses. Therefore, the optical lenses allow a viewer to see only one pixel from the position of their left eye and another pixel from their right eye. When the OLED display columns rotate in a circumferential direction, based on the persistence of vision, one viewpoint image is incident to the left eye of the viewer and another viewpoint image is incident to the right eye of the viewer. As the viewer changes his viewing position, different viewpoint images are individually incident to the left eye and right eye. Thus, the super multi-view 3D display images can be viewed from all directions around the viewer.

The optical lenses composed of 7 elements are from the patent of super wide-angle lens [11], as shown in Fig. 7. 7 elements of the optical lenses are made from materials with different refractive indices and different dispersions. Five elements are made from crown glass and two elements are made from flint glass. Crown glass is an optical glass that has a low refractive index and high Abbe number. Flint glass is an optical glass that has a relatively high refractive index and low Abbe number. This combination can effectively correct optical aberrations [12, 13]. Meanwhile, the curved surface of each lens is further optimized to be an even aspherical surface in order to reduce optical aberrations. The even asphere's more complex surface profile can reduce or eliminate

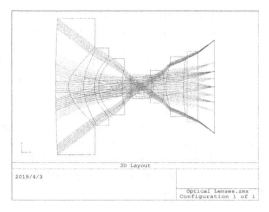

Fig. 7. Optical lenses composed of 7 elements.

spherical aberrations and can also reduce other optical aberrations [14]. And the equation of the even asphere is as follow.

$$z = \frac{cr^2}{1 + \sqrt{1 - (1+k)c^2 r^2}} + \sum a_i r^{2i} \tag{1}$$

The optical lenses are optimized according to the viewing requirements of super multi-view 3D display. For realizing super wide viewing angle, the full field angle of the optical lenses is 130°. In order to make the display unit compact and lightweight, the total length of the optical lenses is less than 5 mm. The central thickness of the lens is more than 0.3 mm, thus it's convenient to produce in the production process. According to the Nyquist sampling frequency [15], the pixel size of OLED display unit is 15 μm and the resolution of the optical lenses is 34 lp/mm. For all field angles, MTF should be more than 0.3. In the process of optimization, nine typical field angles are defined as −1, −0.7, −0.5, −0.3, 0, 0.3, 0.5, 0.7, and 1 times the half maximum field angle. These field angles are symmetrical with respect to the central axis of the optical lenses. In the optical design process, human eyes are most sensitive to the green light, so the wavelength is 550 nm. A converse light path is adopted for the convenience of optical design using the optical software Zemax. The parameters of the optimized optical lenses are listed in Table 1.

Table 1. Parameters of the optimized optical lenses.

Lens no.	Radius (mm)	Thickness (mm)	Material	Conic
1	35	0.357	SK5	0
2	1.226	0.3	KZFSN2	0
3	0.88	0.64	SF15	−0.207
4	1.489	0.571	KZFSN2	2.181
5	−0.671	0.3	SF15	−0.016
6	0.989	0.487	KZFSN2	−9.093
7	Infinity	0.3	BK7	0

The total length of the optical lenses is 4.4 mm, and the effective focal length is 0.69 mm. The structure of the optical lenses is compact, thus the optical lenses and the OLED display units are convenient to be fixed to the display columns. Figure 8(a) illustrates the geometric radii of nine field angles. The geometrical radius of each light spot is almost equal to the pixel size of OLED display unit. The distribution of the central light spot is uniform; however, the distribution of the non-central light spots are asymmetrical, especially the marginal light spots. This is the reason that the optical lenses composed of 7 elements can't completely correct the optical aberrations, and the optical aberrations still exist especially for the marginal light. Modulation transfer function (MTF) of the optical lenses is shown in Fig. 8(b). MTF of each field angle is more than 0.5 which meets the design requirement. The resolution of the optical lenses is suitable for the resolution of the OLED display unit.

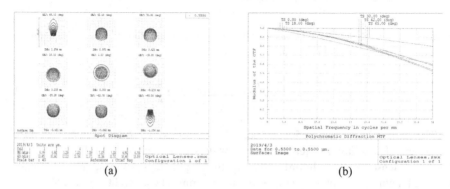

(a)   (b)

Fig. 8. Spot diagram (a) and MTF (b).

3 Simulation and Analysis

Based on the previous design of the optical lenses, the distribution of super multi-view is simulated in this part. The diameter of the super multi-view 3D display device is 4 m, thus the viewing distance is 2 m. The forward light path of the optical lenses is adopted and non-sequential ray tracing is simulated with the non-sequential ray tracing software LightTools. Non-sequential ray tracing implies that there is no predefined sequence of curved surfaces that traced rays must hit. The curved surfaces that the rays hit are determined solely by the physical positions and directions of the rays. Rays may hit any curved surface, and may hit the same curved surface multiple times, or not at all [16]. Non-sequential ray tracing is a complete simulation of the propagation path of true light. OLED is an optical source that obeys Lambert's cosine law, which states that the intensity of reflected light is directly proportional to the cosine of the angle from which it is viewed. The luminous flux of the pixel is assumed to be 1 lm. The receiving surface is located at a viewing distance of 2 m to obtain illuminance values for 170 viewpoints at different positions, as shown in Fig. 9. Because nine typical field angles are symmetrical with respect to the central axis of the optical lenses, the five field angles of 0, 0.3, 0.5, 0.7, and 1 times the half maximum field angle are adopted. And the light intensity distributions of five field angles are shown in Fig. 10.

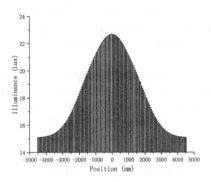

Fig. 9. Illuminance values of 170 viewpoints at different positions.

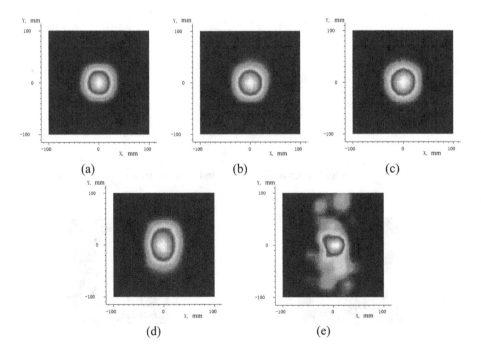

Fig. 10. Light intensity distributions of five field angles. (a) 0°; (b) 18°; (c) 30°; (d) 42°; (e) 65°.

The illuminance values of 170 viewpoints are symmetrical with respect to the central viewpoint. The peak illuminance value of the central viewpoint is 22.68 lx, and the illuminance values show a declining trend as the position of the viewpoint is gradually moved away from the position of the central viewpoint. Thus, the brightness of the marginal pixels should be increased in order to make the illuminance value of each viewpoint uniform. Over 90% of the illuminance of each viewpoint concentrated in the range of 50 mm. The width of the viewpoint is less than a normal adults' pupillary distance, which is from 58 to 64 mm. The light intensity distribution of the central viewpoint is better than that of the marginal viewpoint, and this is the reason that the optical lenses of 7 elements have the limited ability of correcting optical aberrations.

In order to illustrate the crosstalk of the viewpoints, Fig. 11 shows the illuminance values of five central viewpoints which are taken as an example. A normal adults' pupillary distance is from 58 to 64 mm, thus the crosstalk exists in the adjacent viewpoints, as shown in Fig. 12(a). In order to make left eye and right eye distinguish the different viewpoints, pixel 1 and 3 will work together, as shown in Fig. 12(b). When a viewer moves from the current two viewpoints to the next two viewpoints, the odd number pixels and the even number pixels will work alternatively.

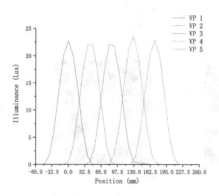

Fig. 11. Crosstalk of 5 central viewpoints.

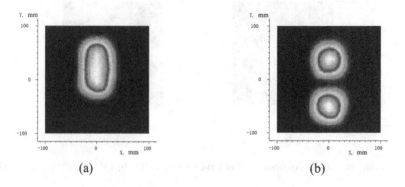

Fig. 12. Light intensity distributions of (a) VP 1 and VP 2; (b) VP 1 and VP 3.

4   Experimental Results

Based on the theoretical design and simulation results, the experimental verification is performed in this part. The super multi-view 3D display unit is composed of OLED display unit and optical lenses. The horizontal resolution of the OLED display unit is 170 pixels, and the pixel pitch is 15 μm. The green light, which human eyes are most sensitive to, is adopted in the experiment. The optical lenses are composed of 7 elements, as shown in Fig. 13(a). Figure 13(b) illustrates the side view of super multi-view 3D display unit. This unit is a prototype and we will make it compact and lightweight in our future work. A digital camera is used to capture the images of the viewpoints, which is equivalent to monocular viewing at a viewing distance of 2 m. 170 viewpoints are symmetrical with respect to the central axis of the OLED display

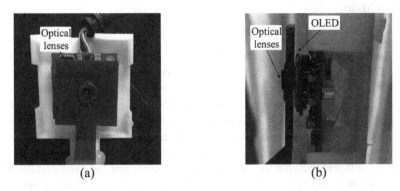

Fig. 13. Front view (a) and side view (b) of super multi-view 3D display unit.

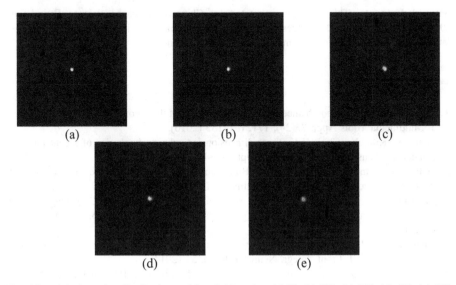

Fig. 14. Light intensity distributions of five field angles. (a) 0°; (b) 18°; (c) 30°; (d) 42°; (e) 65°.

unit, and therefore five typical field angles of 0°, 18°, 30°, 42°, and 65° are chosen. The images of five viewpoints are captured, as shown in Fig. 14.

In all field angles of 130°, each pixel can be seen clearly. Each viewpoint width varies from 50 mm to 55 mm, which is less than a normal adults' pupillary distance. With an increase in the field angle, the brightness and contrast of the images decreased, which is consistent with our simulation results. The distribution of the central viewpoint is relatively concentrated. However, the distribution of the marginal viewpoint is relatively dispersed. In order to make the display unit compact, the optical lenses of 7 elements are adopted. But 7 elements have the limited ability of correcting optical aberrations, especially for the marginal field angle. The illuminance of the marginal viewpoint is lower than that of the central viewpoint, so the brightness of the marginal pixels should be increased to make the brightness of each viewpoint uniform.

5   Conclusions

In this study, a super multi-view 3D display with 170 viewpoints is proposed. The optical lenses of super wide-angle 130° were designed with the optical software Zemax. The parameters of the optical lenses were optimized according to the field angle, the pixel size, and MTF. The light intensity distributions of 170 viewpoints in the viewing zone were simulated using Non-sequential ray tracing software LightTools. Super multi-view 3D display unit, which was composed of OLED display unit and optical lenses, was used to verify the simulation results. 170 viewpoints can be seen clearly at the viewing distance of 2 m. In order to make left eye and right eye distinguish the different viewpoints, the odd number pixels and the even number pixels will work alternatively. The display unit meets the requirements of super multi-view 3D display based on rotating OLED units.

Acknowledgements. This work is supported by China Postdoctoral Science Foundation (2018M631472), Technical Services of Large Screen Display Field (20173000130), Beijing National Research Center for Information Science and Technology.

References

1. Lin, Y., Haiwei, D., Abdulhameed, A.: See in 3D: state of the art of 3D display technologies. J. Multimedia Tools Appl. **75**(24), 17121–17155 (2016)
2. Hong, J., Kim, Y., Choi, H.J.: Three-dimensional display technologies of recent interest: principles, status, and issues. J. Appl. Opt. **50**(34), 87–115 (2011)
3. Gangyi, J., Junming, Z., Mei, Y., et al.: Binocular vision based objective quality assessment method for stereoscopic images. J. Multimedia Tools Appl. **74**(18), 8197–8218 (2015)
4. Mizushina, H., Nakamura, J., Takaki, Y., et al.: Super multi-view 3D displays reduce conflict between accommodative and vergence responses. J. Soc. Inf. Disp. **24**(12), 747–756 (2016)
5. Otero-Millan, J., Macknik, S.L., Martinez-Conde, S.: Fixational eye movements and binocular vision. J. Front. Integr. Neurosci. **8**(52), 52 (2014)
6. Geng, J.: Three-dimensional display technologies. J. Adv. Opt. Photonics **5**(4), 456–535 (2013)

7. Takaki, Y., Nichiyo, N.: Multi-projection of lenticular display to construct a 256-view super multi-view display. J. Opt. Exp. **18**(9), 8824–8835 (2010)
8. Zhenning, Y., Haifeng, L., Di, L., et al.: An aanlysis of omnidirectional 3D display system based on scanning LED. J. Acta. Opt. Sinica **31**(12), 1233003-1–1233003-5 (2006)
9. Haifeng, H., Xu, L., Di, L., et al.: Panoramic view field three-dimensional display device based on pitch multi viewing angle. CN101762881A (2010)
10. Hidefumi, Y., Tsuyoshi, M., Satoshi, S.: Three dimensional video display device. US9047792B2 (2015)
11. Fujian, D., Jianke, W.R.: Super wide-angle lens. WO2017/020587A1 (2017)
12. Yan, Y., Sasian, J.M.: Miniature camera lens design with a freeform surface. In: Society of Photo-Optical Instrumentation Engineers (SPIE) Conference Series (2017)
13. Hou, G., Lyu, L.: Design of ultra wide-angle photographic objective based on ZEMAX. J. Appl. Opt. **37**(3), 441–445 (2016)
14. Chuen Lin, T.: Ultra-wide angle lens design with relative illumination analysis. J. Eur. Opt. Soc. Rapid Publ. **11**, 16001-1-5 (2016)
15. Li, H., Yan, C.: Design of wide-angle lens for 8 mega-pixel mobile phone camera. J. Chin. Opt. **7**(3), 456–461 (2014)
16. Pravdivtsev, A.V., Akram, M.N.: Simulation and assessment of stray light effects in infrared cameras using non-sequential ray tracing. J. Infrared Phys. Technol. **60**(5), 306–311 (2013)

The Study and Application of Adaptive Learning Method Based on Virtual Reality for Engineering Education

Yi Lin$^{(\boxtimes)}$ ⓘ and Shunbo Wang ⓘ

College of Physics and Information Engineering,
Fuzhou University, Fuzhou, China
linyi@fzu.edu.cn, 1319048401@qq.com

Abstract. As educational reform efforts continue, a challenge for most adaptive learning software is how to integrate theoretical knowledge with practice, especially in the field of engineering education. Developing an understanding of how to incorporate virtual reality in education to enhance the quality of learning has become a research hotspot in the e-learning field. For this purpose, a novel adaptive virtual reality learning method based on learning styles model is proposed in this paper, then a virtual reality learning system for engineering education is constructed based on the proposed approach. In this method, learning style are categorized via learning style index to predict learning preferences, then differentiated virtual learning environment of engineering education are provided to students according to their individual learning preferences. During the learning process, various types of learning data are recorded and analyzed automatically. Then the prejudged learning preferences are continually adjusted by the learning data when the immersive learning experience is offered to students by the customization of learning scene and teaching material in virtual environment. To adapt to differentiated individuals, the structure and content of virtual learning environment are gradually optimized, with the ultimate goal of equipping the environment to meet an unlimited array of actual student learning needs. Compared with the traditional adaptive learning method based on learning style, a comparison of experimental results shows that the proposed method is more effective in stimulating learner enthusiasm and can greatly improve student academic performance.

Keywords: Engineering education · Learning styles model · Virtual reality

1 Introduction

In the field of engineering education in China, a second classroom is usually chosen to supplement the learning accomplished in the first classroom. With the continuous advancement of technology, the style of second-classroom learning has gone through many changes. Adaptive learning [1–4] which is currently the most widely applied learning method, is driven by data to meet student needs and improve learning efficiency. Initially, adaptive learning adjusts the learning content and mode based on a student's academic performance. However, by neglecting the subjective initiatives of

© Springer Nature Switzerland AG 2019
Y. Zhao et al. (Eds.): ICIG 2019, LNCS 11903, pp. 372–383, 2019.
https://doi.org/10.1007/978-3-030-34113-8_31

students, enthusiasm for learning often declines rather than increases, which results in a negative learning outcome.

To solve these above problems, Thalmann [5] suggested that learning styles models are the most useful frameworks for adaptive system development among other sources. Learning outcomes can be improved by adopting the correct learning style, i.e. the learning approach with which each student will best learn. Students with different learning styles have diverse preferred way to learn [6]. Consequently, the learning styles model has been integrated into adaptive learning [7] and the most widely used is the Felder & Silverman learning styles model [8] proposed by Felder and Silverman in 1988. The learning style framework for students in engineering education has the following four dimensions: sensing and intuitive, visual and verbal, active and reflective and sequential and global. Using the Index of Learning Style [8] (ILS) to determine the type of learning style the student belongs to, a learning strategy is then designed by teacher. In addition to determining learning styles based on answers to the ILS questionnaire, other researchers have developed methods based on this model [6, 9, 10]. One mainstream method is to convert different learning styles into a range of statistical rules and to infer the learning style by determining whether student operations conform to these rules. According to the Felder & Silverman model of learning styles, Graf [11] labels student behaviors with respect to a certain learning style as: "strong indication", "average" and "in disagreement", then determines the learning style by the information acquired. That is, if a student often exercises, he/she is more likely to have an active learning style. Other methods speculate about the learning style to which a user belongs using Bayesian networks [12], hidden Markov models [13, 14] or decision trees [15]. Cha [13] designed a learning system that uses a specific interface based on the Felder & Silverman model, in which operation data is recorded while the students are interacting with the system. Eventually, learning style can be predicted automatically by Decision Tree and Hidden Markov Chain once the system has obtained the students' operation preferences.

However, there are a number of problems with the adaptive learning system when using the learning styles model in reality. On one hand, since the data is one-sided, it is not sufficiently comprehensive to optimize the learning environment based only on the human-computer interactive data obtained by a keyboard and mouse. On the other hand, it is impossible for students to consolidate and expand the knowledge learned without the opportunity to experiment. In addition, an adaptive learning environment that emphasizes theory alone can lead to a decrease in student interest. A virtual-learning environment constructed using virtual reality technology can address these limitations. First, a variety of real-time interactive technologies can be used to provide multimodal feedback data generated during the learning process. Secondly, virtual reality provides a multi-dimensional and vivid display environment that can enrich the presentation of knowledge. Finally, the immersive classroom simulated by virtual reality technology can greatly enhance student enthusiasm for autonomous learning [16–18].

In summary, in this paper, a novel adaptive virtual reality learning method based on learning styles model is proposed, then a virtual reality learning system for engineering education (VRLS) is constructed based on the proposed approach. In this method, learning preferences are first predicted by the learning style classified by ILS, and an initial virtual learning environment is built on the basis of the identified learning preferences. Next, operation data are recorded and analyzed during the learning process to obtain preference hints for guiding adjustments to the learning preferences. Lastly, the user experience, teaching materials and learning mode are continually optimized with respect to the learning preferences. Compared with the traditional adaptive learning method based on learning style, the proposed method in this paper has the following three advantages via virtual reality technology. Frist, the learning is more personalized. There are abundant ways of human-computer interaction in virtual reality. The adaptive system is driven by more data and can more accurately adapt to each student to fully stimulate their learning enthusiasm. Secondly, there are more opportunities for experimentation. In engineering education, the mastery of both theoretical knowledge and practical ability are indispensable. By learning in a virtual environment, the need for teaching experiments can be satisfied and practical skills can be strengthened. The third advantage is the more immersive learning experience. A first classroom environment simulated by virtual reality can enable students to experience and learn naturally.

2 Methodology and Implement

The core concept of the proposed learning method is that each construction of the virtual learning environment is based on learning preferences. Figure 1 shows the workflow of the adaptive virtual reality learning method. The preliminary construction of virtual learning environment is shown in the real wireframe, with the dotted wireframe showing the optimization of virtual learning environment. Initially, learning preferences are predetermined based on learning style, and a preliminary virtual learning environment is constructed by the obtained learning preferences. Then, learning data is collected and analyzed as students experience the environment, during which preference hints are acquired with which to adjust the previous learning preferences. The virtual learning environment is then optimized based on the adjusted learning preferences. The above procedure is repeated until the environment is most compatible with the student's learning preferences.

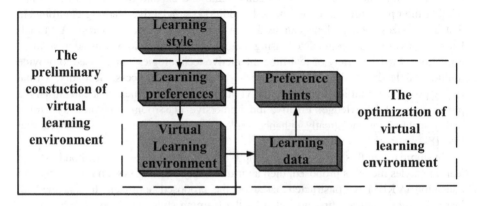

Fig. 1. The workflow of adaptive virtual reality learning method

2.1   Learning Style

Learning style refers to the way that a student prefers to learn, with each student having their own learning style. As such, it is necessary to classify student learning styles. The classification method used in this paper based on the ILS proposed by Felder and Silverman [8]. Figure 2 shows the result of the ILS [8]. Student learning styles in engineering education can be categorized into the following four dimensions, as outlined in the Felder & Silverman learning styles model: sensing and intuitive, visual and verbal, active and reflective and sequential and global. In the ILS, students must complete 44 questions, with each dimension having 11 questions. The answers to these questions are scored by adding or subtracting 1. Finally, the student's tendency toward each learning style is quantified as a ranging from −11 to 11, and the student's learning style is then derived from that score.

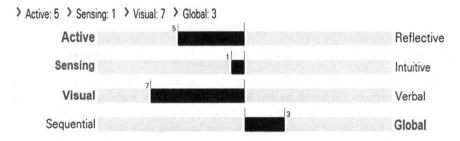

Fig. 2. The result of the ILS [8]

2.2   Learning Preferences

After prejudging a students' learning style, it is possible to determine that students' preference regarding teaching materials and learning mode, which are generally referred to as learning preferences. Learning preferences indicate the optimal learning strategy of a student, and a virtual learning environment built based on the learning preferences is most suitable for student. Table 1 lists the learning preferences with respect to the four learning-style dimensions described in the Felder & Silverman learning styles model [8], in which it can be found that each learning style has different learning preferences.

Table 1. Table of the preferences with respect to the four learning-style dimensions

Learning style	Preferences of teaching materials	Preferences of learning mode
Sensing	Emphasis on fact, data and practical problem-solving method	Memory, experiment and observation
Intuitive	Emphasis on theory, theorem and basic understanding	Imagination, derivation and innovation
Visual	Emphasis on chart, picture and graphic	Observation
Verbal	Emphasis on words and symbol	Listen, read and discussion
Sequential	Emphasis on logic and sequencing	Derivation and analysis
Global	Emphasis on synthesis and relevance	Divergent thinking and synthesis
Active	Emphasis on fact, data and practical problem-solving method	Experiment, discussion and testing
Reflective	Emphasis on theory, theorem and basic understanding	Observation and reflection

2.3   The Preliminary Construction of Virtual Learning Environment

The preliminary construction of virtual learning environment mainly depends on the learning preferences predicted by the learning style. Since learning preferences are divided into teaching materials and learning modes, the major focus of the preliminary construction of the virtual learning environment involves their selection.

To provide an immersive experience to students, the virtual learning environment is split into learning and testing scenes. According to the learning preferences shown in Table 1 and a real first-classroom situation, the virtual learning environment is composed of six learning modes, including test, video, transparencies, pen and paper, experiment and discussion. These learning modes are selected to establish a virtual learning environment based on the learning preferences. For example, the learning-mode preferences relevant to an active learning style are experiment, discussion and testing. Therefore, the preliminary learning scene for an active learning style includes video, transparencies, pen and paper, experiment and discussion and this scene can be freely switched to the testing scene. The testing scene for an active learning style simulates real testing and students can evaluate their own knowledge mastery in this scene. Based on the virtual learning environment described above, the preliminary learning and testing scene for an active learning style can be built in VRLS, as shown in Figs. 3 and 4, respectively.

Teaching materials are divided into six types, depending on the learning preferences listed in Table 1 and are assigned to the students with respect to their learning styles. For example, the video and transparencies in the learning scene shown in Fig. 3 are teaching materials that emphasis on fact, data and practical problem-solving method.

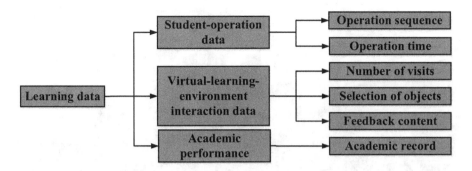

Fig. 5. Learning data

Fig. 4. The preliminary testing scene for an active learning style

2.4 Learning Data

The learning data generated by students during the learning process can directly or indirectly reveal their preferences, which means the learning preferences can be adjusted accordingly. This is an indispensable aspect of optimizing the virtual learning environment. The data sources used in traditional data-driven systems are mainly user operation data, system-interaction data and student-background data [6]. Figure 5 shows the learning data focused and collected in this study, including student-operation data, virtual-learning-environment interaction data and academic performance. The student-operation data includes the operation sequence and operation time. The virtual-learning-environment interaction data consists of number of visits, selection of objects and feedback content. The academic performance contains academic record.

The VRLS in this paper is realized by UNITY 3D combined with HTC VIVE. As such, the student operation and interaction data are chiefly obtained by recording the interaction between virtual learning environment and the HTC VIVE handles, such as touch, click and vibration. Compared with the simple mouse-keyboard interaction of tradition adaptive systems, virtual reality with real-time and abundant interactive technology offers more learning data that can drive system optimization and thus more accurately meet student requirements.

Fig. 3. The preliminary learning scene for an active learning style

2.5   Preference Hints

Figure 6 shows the formation and function of preference hints derived from the analysis of learning data. First, a threshold determined by the specific teaching content is set for objective data such as the operation sequence, operation time, number of visits, selection of objects and academic record. By defining data by thresholds, the data can be translated into preference hints for learning. For example, if operation-time data reveals that the total time spent by a student in experimentation is longer than the time suggested in the teaching content, then the experiment learning mode can be identified as one of the student's learning preferences. Secondly, useful information about optimization can be acquired by analyzing subjective data on feedback content. Finally, all the information obtained is aggregated to adjust the learning preferences that were predetermined based on learning style.

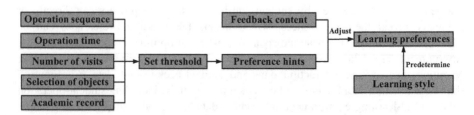

Fig. 6. The formation and function of preference hints

2.6   The Optimization of Virtual Learning Environment

The learning preferences predicted by learning style determine the selection of teaching materials and learning modes for the preliminary construction of the virtual learning environment. The virtual learning environment is then optimized by adjusting the learning preferences based on learning data generated during the learning process. Figure 7 shows the optimization of the virtual learning environment, which includes optimization of the learning mode, teaching material and user experience. Based on learning preferences, optimization of the learning mode is accomplished by adjusting the learning-mode components in the learning scene, optimization of the teaching material is realized by selecting the teaching-material content and optimization of the user experience is achieved by improving the system settings of the virtual learning environment. Finally, new learning data is generated throughout the learning process and the learning preferences are continually adjusted even after the virtual learning environment is optimized, thereby achieving the goal of continuously optimizing the virtual learning environment with respect to learning preferences.

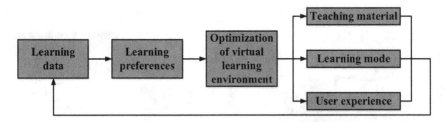

Fig. 7. The optimization of virtual learning environment

Depending on the description of the optimization of the virtual learning environment, the preliminary construction of the VRLS can be optimized. Figure 8 shows the comparison of the VRLS for an active learning style before and after optimization. According to the learning data, it is found that the number of visits to the next-page button of transparencies is less than half the total number of pages, whereas the operation time of discussion is longer than that of the other learning modes. In addition, student feedback indicates that they find the components of the learning scene to be too complicated. Therefore, to better adapt to the students, the transparencies learning mode is deleted and the discussion learning mode is expanded when the VRLS is optimized.

Fig. 8. The comparison of the VRLS for an active learning style before and after optimization

3   Experiment and Results

"kuxuexi" is an adaptive learning system used in China based on learning styles model [19]. Figure 9(a) shows a learning scene used in "kuxuexi", where the student is learning from a teaching video provided by this system. Figure 9(b) shows a learning scene used in VRLS, where the student is learning in a virtual environment with handles and a helmet. In the experiment, for the learning content, we selected a physical circuit course that emphasizes both practical ability and theoretical knowledge in engineering education. We then compared the student performances when using VRLS and "kuxuexi" to evaluate whether the virtual-reality-based method can improve learning performance.

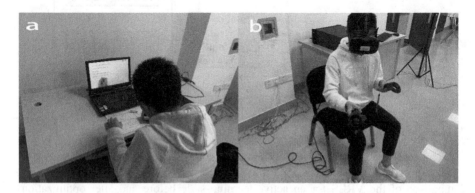

Fig. 9. The learning scene used in (a) "kuxuexi" and (b) VRLS

3.1   The Experimental Method

In the experiment, 30 students with an active learning style are selected as participants in an evaluation study. The students were randomly divided into two groups, A and B, each of which consisted of ten males and five females.

Figure 10 shows the experimental evaluation process, which was divided into three stages: assessment of prior knowledge, learning process and evaluation of learning outcome. The assessment of prior knowledge involved a pre-test to assess the degree of understanding of the students regarding the circuit curriculum. In the learning process, students from the two groups experienced different learning environments. The students in Group A learned by "kuxuexi" and the students in Group B learned by VRLS, but the two groups were provided with the same teaching materials and completed the same exercises. The evaluation of the learning outcome involved the use of a post-test to assess the students' performances in the different environments. The difficulty level and content of the pre-test and post-test were similar, the total score for the two tests was 40 points and the duration was 20 min. The results were recorded as scores.

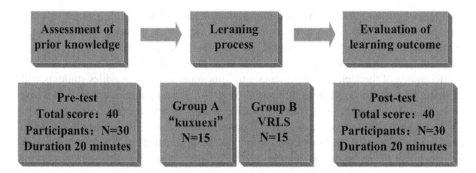

Fig. 10. The experimental evaluation process

3.2 Experimental Results and Discussion

Table 2 shows the results of the pre-test and post-test. The mean pre-test score in Group A is 24.6 (SD = 3.3) and the mean post-test score in Group B is 25.8 (SD = 2.8). The results of pre-test of the two groups are analyzed by one-way analysis of variance (ANOVA) and found no significant initial difference between the two groups.

The mean post-test scores are 32.4 (SD = 3.4) for Group A and 37.2 (SD = 2.3) for Group B. An Analysis of Covariance (ANCOVA) is conducted to extract the difference between the groups, using the pre-test scores as the covariate and the post-test scores as dependent variables. The results indicate that the differences in post-test means are statistically significant. The effect size (Cohen's d) is 0.637, which means that the learning outcome was greatly enhanced by learning in the VRLS. Furthermore, in the experiment, it is found that the students in Group B to be more active and less distracted during the learning process than those in Group A.

Table 2. The results of pre-test and post-test

Group	N	Pre-test		Post-test	
		Mean	SD	Mean	SD
Group A	15	24.6	3.3	32.4	3.4
Group B	15	25.8	2.8	37.2	2.3

4 Conclusion

To take advantage of virtual reality technology in the skillful application of both theoretical knowledge and practice, then achieve the goal of improving the learning quality. A novel adaptive virtual reality learning method based on learning styles model is proposed in this paper, then a virtual reality learning system for engineering education was constructed based on the proposed approach. In this method, a student's learning style is obtained by his/her Index of Learning Style score, from which the learning preferences are predicted. Next, based on the learning preferences, a preliminary virtual learning environment is constructed and the learning preferences are then adjusted based on learning data. Finally, the virtual learning environment is continually and iteratively optimized by the learning preferences. The proposed learning method not only solves the problem of one-sided data but also addresses the shortcomings of the lack of experimentation. This approach also provides students with more abundant knowledge presentations, a variety of learning modes and an immersive virtual-learning environment. Thus, the enthusiasm of student for autonomous learning can be improved from many aspects by adopting this method. The experimental results confirmed that the enthusiasm of students can be stimulated and their learning performance can be improved by learning in the adaptive virtual reality learning system based on learning styles model.

Although the method proposed in this paper can be used to enhance student learning enthusiasm, there are many other possibilities for improving learning efficiency via virtual reality technology, which merit further investigation. Our next step is to study the problems associated with adaptive learning in the virtual reality environment and to identify possible approaches to solve them.

Acknowledgement. Thanks to the funding of China Scholarship Council and their constant supports. Furthermore, I would like to express my gratitude to the consistent and instruction of researchers from Key Laboratory of Digital Fujian IoT Engineering and Applications.

References

1. Tavangarian, D., Leypold, M.E., Nölting, K., Röser, M.: Is e-Learning the solution for individual learning. Electron. J. e-Learn. **2**(2), 273–280 (2004)
2. Dos Santos, C.T., Osorio, F.S.: An intelligent and adaptive virtual environment and its application in distance learning. In: Proceedings of the Working Conference on Advanced Visual Interfaces, Gallipoli, Italy, pp. 362–365. Association for Computing Machinery (2004)
3. Ovesleová, H.: E-learning platforms and lacking motivation in students: concept of adaptable UI for online courses. In: Marcus, A. (ed.) DUXU 2015. LNCS, vol. 9188, pp. 218–227. Springer, Cham (2015). https://doi.org/10.1007/978-3-319-20889-3_21
4. Vaughan, N., Gabrys, B., Dubey, V.N.: An overview of self-adaptive technologies within virtual reality training. J. Comput. Sci. Rev. **22**, 65–87 (2016)
5. Thalmann, S.: Adaptation criteria for the personalized delivery of learning materials: a multi-stage empirical investigation. Australas. J. Educ. Technol. **30**(1), 45–60 (2014)
6. Truong, H.M.: Integrating learning styles and adaptive e-learning system: current developments, problems and opportunities. J. Comput. Hum. Behav. **55**, 1185–1193 (2016)
7. El-Bishouty, M.M., Aldraiweesh, A.: Use of Felder and Silverman learning style model for online course design. J. Educ. Technol. Res. Dev. **67**(1), 161–177 (2019)
8. Felder, R.M., Silverman, L.K.: Learning and teaching styles in engineering education. J. Eng. Educ. **78**(7), 674–681 (1988)
9. Botsios, S., Georgiou, D., Safouris, N.: Contributions to adaptive educational hypermedia systems via on-line learning style estimation. J. Educ. Technol. Soc. **11**(2), 322–339 (2008)
10. Scott, E., Rodriguez, G., Soria, A., Campo, M.: Are learning styles useful indicators to discover how students use Scrum for the first time? J. Comput. Hum. Behav. **36**, 56–64 (2014)

11. Graf, S., Kinshuk, Liu, T.-C.: Supporting teachers in identifying students' learning styles in learning management systems: an automatic student modelling approach. J. Educ. Technol. Soc. **12**(4), 3–14 (2009)
12. Alkhuraiji, S., Cheetham, B., Bamasak, O.: Dynamic adaptive mechanism in learning management system based on learning styles. In: Proceedings of the 2011 11th IEEE International Conference on Advanced Learning Technologies, pp. 215–217. IEEE Computer Society (2011)
13. Cha, H.J., Kim, Y.S., Park, S.H., Yoon, T.B., Jung, Y.M., Lee, J.-H.: Learning styles diagnosis based on user interface behaviors for the customization of learning interfaces in an intelligent tutoring system. In: Ikeda, M., Ashley, K.D., Chan, T.-W. (eds.) ITS 2006. LNCS, vol. 4053, pp. 513–524. Springer, Heidelberg (2006). https://doi.org/10.1007/11774303_51
14. Dorca, F.A., Lima, L.V., Fernandes, M.A., Lopes, C.R.: Automatic student modeling in adaptive educational systems through probabilistic learning style combinations: a qualitative comparison between two innovative stochastic approaches. J. Braz. Comput. Soc. **19**(1), 43–58 (2013)
15. Özpolat, E., Akar, G.B.: Automatic detection of learning styles for an e-learning system. J. Comput. Educ. **53**(2), 355–367 (2009)
16. Bian, H.-X.: Application of virtual reality in music teaching system. Int. Emerg. Technol. Learn. **11**(11), 21–25 (2016)
17. Smith, S., Ericson, E.: Using immersive game-based virtual reality to teach fire-safety skills to children. J. Virtual Reality **13**(2), 87–99 (2009)
18. Xie, Y., Ryder, L., Chen, Y.: Using interactive virtual reality tools in an advanced Chinese language class: a case study. J. TechTrends **63**(3), 251–259 (2019)
19. Kuxuexi. http://kuxuexi.com/. Accessed 09 May 2019

Implementation and Evaluation of Touch and Gesture Interaction Modalities for In-vehicle Infotainment Systems

Dan Zhao[1], Cong Wang[1,2], Yue Liu[1,2,3(✉)], and Tong Liu[1]

[1] Beijing Institute of Technology, Beijing 100081, China
liuyue@bit.edu.cn
[2] China Electronics Standardization Institute, Beijing 100007, China
[3] AICFVE of Beijing Film Academy, 4, Xitucheng Road, Haidian, Beijing 100088, China

Abstract. The arrival of the Internet of Vehicles has promoted the transformation of in-vehicle human-computer interaction. As a new way of human-computer interaction, gesture interaction plays an important role in such interaction and technology update. This paper proposes the implementation of an in-vehicle driving simulator that allows infotainment system to be controlled by dynamic hand gestures and touch screen. Thirty participants were asked to interact with the infotainment system in two ways separately and randomly while performing the driving test. Moreover, three kinds of data related to the degradation of the driver's performance, including driving efficacy, visual attention and subjective workload were collected. In addition, the fuzzy comprehensive evaluation method is used to evaluate the usability of interactive gestures. The experimental results show that compared with the touch screen interaction, gesture control significantly reduces the driver's distraction and improves safety during driving.

Keywords: Driving simulation · Gestures · Touch · Driving distraction · Gesture usability

1 Introduction

With the development of intelligent automobile industry, vehicle products gradually developed from traditional means of transportation into a multi-functional, informational and intelligent human-machine interaction system. The introduction of information systems allows drivers to handle other events while driving the car, such as answering calls, turning on navigation devices, adjusting music and so on. However, the enrichment of functions increases the driving risk while providing convenience to the driver. To find an interactive modality that not only satisfies the driver's interaction demand but also minimize the driving risk is of great significance.

Commonly used in-vehicle interaction methods mainly include the button and knob control, which are the most widely used interaction method at present. Touch screen interaction is an interactive way developed with the promotion of a new generation of mobile smart devices. Due to the high penetration rate of mobile design, users are more

Y. Zhao et al. (Eds.): ICIG 2019, LNCS 11903, pp. 384–394, 2019.
https://doi.org/10.1007/978-3-030-34113-8_32

likely to accept such interaction [1]. However, the two interaction modes mentioned above may distract the driver and increase the driving risk. Speech is a more acceptable way of interaction with hand-free and eye-free, thus is one of the most popular modalities in use. However, the speech semantic recognition accuracy needs to be improved. At the same time, speech is susceptible to the environment, especially when the environment is noisy, the command understanding ability will be reduced [2]. In recent years, gesture acquisition devices such as Kinect and Leap Motion have been widely used in the field of human-computer interaction with the advantages of high precision and small size, which laid a technical foundation for the application of gesture control in the car [3, 4].

In this paper, we conducted an experimental evaluation of gesture interaction in a driving simulator and compared it to the direct touch interaction. The influence of the two interaction modalities on driving performance is summarized by analyzing the completion of driving tasks and eye tracking data. The driving behavior under different road conditions is analyzed by comparing to the existing works [5–7]. The driver's acceptance of gesture control in the vehicle is also studied.

2   Experiment Design

2.1   Driving Environment Simulation

In the driving environment, we usually refer to other human-vehicle interaction behavior except driving tasks as sub-tasks. When studying the completion of sub-tasks and the influence on the driver's attention under different interaction modalities, the simulated driving cockpit is usually used, so that the subjects can complete the driving task in the simulated environment.

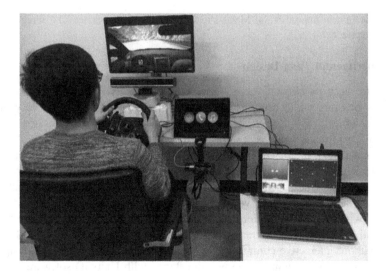

Fig. 1. Simulated driving environment.

Our simulated driving platform (Fig. 1) allows the driver to manipulate infotainment functions via gestures and touch screen. The drivers complete the driving task through LG29 device. A Surface Pro mounted on the right side of the steering wheel serves as the center console and runs an application with typical infotainment scenarios like phone and music. Figure 2 shows the phone and music interfaces of the infotainment system. A Leap Motion controller is placed at the front of the Surface Pro to capture and recognize the user's gestures. In order to quantitatively evaluate the influence of touch and mid-air gestures on the performance of the driver, the SMI eye tracker placed in front of the display is used to measure the driver's gaze diversion data.

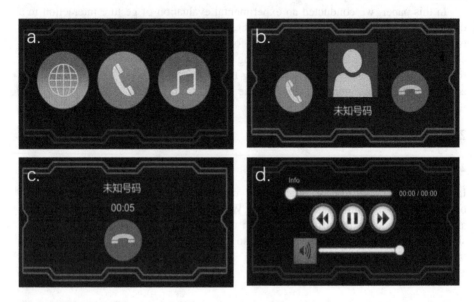

Fig. 2. Infotainment interfaces. (a) Menu interface. (b) Incoming phone. (c) Calling interface. (d) Music interface.

2.2 Experimental Task Design

The task for each participant was to complete the interactive task as efficiently and quickly as possible while driving the vehicle. Since the driving skills vary greatly among the subjects, a within-subject design was used, which compensated for fluctuations in performance between subjects. Inspired by the Lane Change Test (ISO 26022 standard) [7], the driving task is designed to include four separate tracks with two different road conditions (RD). For road condition 1, almost no road barriers are set in Track 1 and Track 2, but for road condition 2, a variety of different continuous road barriers as shown in Fig. 3 was set in Track 3 and Track 4. Each participant can familiarize with the road conditions in Track 1 and 3 and perform interactive tasks in Track 2 and 4 (For the convenience of description, we will simply refer to Track 1 and Track 3 without interactive commands as Track 1-N and Track 3-N). The design and implementation of the driving scene was developed with Unity3D software.

Four gestures (as shown in Fig. 4) were used in the experiment to complete the interactive task, i.e. answer/hang up the phone, turn up/down the volume and switch to the next/previous song. In order to reduce the user's memory demands, the gestures 'Swipe Right' and 'Swipe Left' were multiplexed, when the system has a telephone access, the user can complete the operation of answering/hanging up the call by Swipe Right/Left, and when the system is in the music playing mode, the Swipe Right/Left gesture can help the user to complete the operation of switching to the next/previous song. Since the system would pause the music being played while the phone was connected, the multiplexing of gestures does not cause any conflict. Each gesture was identified with the help of the Leap Motion SDK.

(a) Road Condition 1.   (b) Road Condition 2.

Fig. 3. Different road conditions.

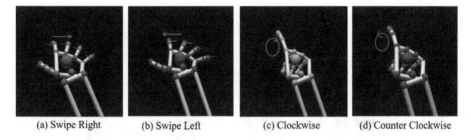

(a) Swipe Right   (b) Swipe Left   (c) Clockwise   (d) Counter Clockwise

Fig. 4. Four hand gestures used in gesture interaction. (a) Swipe Right: answer the phone or switch to the next song. (b) Swipe Left: hang up the phone or switch to the previous song. (c) Clockwise: turn up the volume. (d) Counter Clockwise: turn down the volume.

2.3 Experiment Procedure

30 participants (17 males, 13 females) between 21 and 30 years (M = 24, SD = 1.94) were recruited for the experiment. Each subject would complete an experiment consisting of four parts with a total time span of one hour under the guidance of the experimental assistant. A pre-test exercise to ensure that the subject is familiar with the simulated driving environment and operation should be completed first. Then participants performed two test trials with touch and gesture interaction in random order. During the driving part, they were instructed to perform gestures through text-to-speech

output. The instructions were 'Answer/hang up the call' (occurred four times during each road condition), 'Switch to the next song' (three times each), 'Switch to the previous song' (two times each) and 'Adjust the volume' (three times each). During the gesture interaction, the gesture was executed once and the corresponding interactive task was completed once toon. In particular, the volume changes range from 0-1, the gesture was completed once and the volume changes by 0.1. The order of instructions was the same over all participants. After each trail, all participants were asked to evaluate the task load using NASA task load index (NASA-TLX). Finally, participants gave an overall rating for the usability of gesture interaction.

3   Results and Discussion

3.1   Driving Efficacy

Driving efficacy indexes are mainly reflected in experiment completion time, interactive task completion rate and autonomous interaction. Regarding all the tasks, the experiment completion time for the touch was larger than that for the gesture as shown in Fig. 5. However, the significance test results showed that both interaction modalities had no significant difference in the experimental completion time under various road conditions This is caused by the fact that the difference in driving habits between participants leads to the variation of driving speed and time.

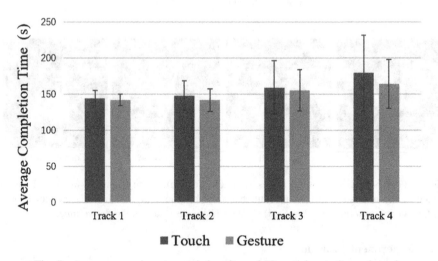

Fig. 5. Average experiment completion time of 30 participants for each track.

Another phenomenon that we found is that some participants chose not to execute interactive instructions when road conditions are complex to ensure driving safety. To account for this situation, the interactive task completion rate index was defined. As can be seen in Fig. 6, for road condition 1, the average task completion rate of the touch interaction was almost the same as that of gesture interaction (Track 2: Touch Mean,

M = 97.50%, Standard Deviation, SD = 6.97%; Gesture M = 99.17%, SD = 2.54%, F-value, F = 1.513, p-value, p = 0.224), however, for road condition 2, the average task completion rate of gesture interaction is significantly higher than that of the touch (Track 4: Touch M = 93.06%, SD = 8.21%; Gesture M = 98.61%, SD = 3.84%, F = 11.262, p < 0.01). The difference implies that the touch screen interaction has a high visual occupancy rate. For gesture interaction, an experienced driver can control the steering wheel with one hand while performing the driving task with the other hand.

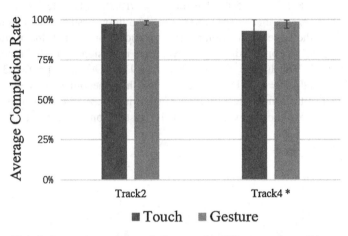

Fig. 6. Interactive task completion rate for different road conditions.

Other parameters, such as the number of accidents that occurred while performing interactive tasks and the frequency of autonomous interactions (Autonomous operation means the user's active interaction with the infotainment system without any interactive instructions.) are also counted as auxiliary indicators for experimental evaluation. The statistical results are shown in Table 1. It can be seen from the table that the accidents (over all 30 participants) caused by gesture interaction is lower than that of the touch under the simple road condition. For the complicated road conditions, although the number of accidents of the two interactions is similar, the task completion rate of touch is lower.

Table 1. Statistical results of auxiliary indexes (over all 30 participants).

Interactive modalities	Road conditions	Accidents	Autonomous operation
Touch	Track 2	12	21
	Track 4	12	3
Gesture	Track 2	6	22
	Track 4	14	8

3.2   Visual Attention

In order to analyze the driver's visual attention, SMI eye tracker is used to collect the subjects' gaze diversion data during the experiment. Through the eye tracker, we obtained the dwell time of primary visual attention lobe (PVAL), which refers to the road area that the driver pays attention to when there is no interactive task. Figure 7 shows the average dwell time for four tracks in two interaction modalities. The significant difference in dwell time occurs on track 2 for road condition 1 (Track2: Touch M = 54.64%, SD = 13.50%; Gesture M = 61.93%, SD = 13.39%; F = 4.407, p < 0.05), which means that under simple road condition gesture interactions reduce the distraction of the driver's attention relative to touch. For Track 4, the average dwell time for gesture interactions is higher, however there is no significant difference relative to touch. (Track4: Touch M = 57.13%, SD = 13.91%; Gesture M = 60.63%, SD = 14.29%; F = 0.920, p = 0.341) The reason for this phenomenon is that the task completion rate of the touch interaction on Track 4 is low. As mentioned in Sect. 3.1, the participant chooses not to execute interactive instructions to ensure driving safety.

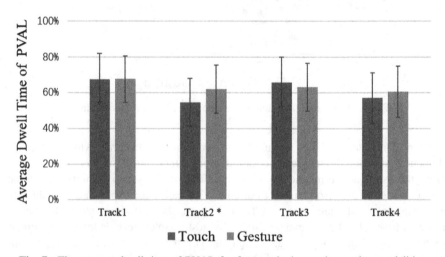

Fig. 7. The average dwell time of PVAL for four tracks in two interaction modalities.

The effects of sub-tasks on visual attention under different road conditions are illustrated in Fig. 8. It can be seen from Fig. 8 that for the touch screen interaction, the interactive task has a significant distraction of the driver's attention under both road conditions (Touch: Road Condition 1 F = 12.690, p < 0.01; Road Condition 2 F = 5.512, p < 0.05). However, for gesture interactions, results are completely oppo-site (Gesture: Road Condition 1 F = 2.810, p = 0.099; Road Condition 2 F = 0.529, p = 0.470). This result indicates that gesture interaction is superior in maintaining attention and is less affected by road conditions.

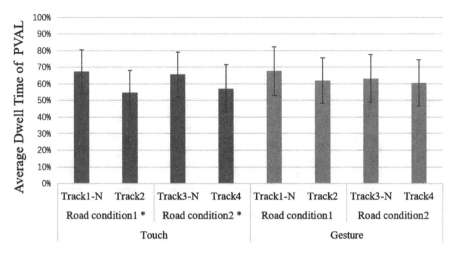

Fig. 8. Visual attention under different road conditions.

3.3 Subjective Task Load

In our experiments, the NASA-TLX is used to evaluate the interaction load. The NASA-TLX is a multi-dimensional rating procedure that provides an overall workload score based on a weighted average of ratings on six subscales: Mental Demand (MD), Physical Demand (PD), Temporal Demand (TD), Own Performance, Effort and Frustration [8]. The magnitude ratings on each subscale were set to 0 to 20 in our experiments. The overall task load score of touch interaction is higher than that of the gesture (Touch: M = 9.72, SD = 2.96, Max Load = 14.47, Min Load = 3.60; Gesture: M = 8.17, SD = 3.16, Max Load = 13.87, Min Load = 3.33). More details are shown in Fig. 9, which show that the two interaction methods only have significant differences in TD and Effort (TD: Touch M = 2.009; Gesture M = 1.236; $p < 0.05$. Effort: Touch M = 2.680; Gesture M = 1.856; $p < 0.05$). Regarding the TD, the participants indicated that they wanted to complete the instructions as soon as possible during the touch screen interaction, so that they could refocus their attentions on the driving task to prevent security problems, but they did not have such concerns for gesture interaction. For the effort difference, the participants explained that they need to pay more effort into the touch interaction.

3.4 Gesture Usability

In order to evaluate the usability of gesture control, we chose the usability principle proposed in [9], which evaluates each gesture from the following four dimensions: easy to learn and remember, effective, intuitive and comfortable and natural. We also added a 5th dimension indicator of the overall rating for the gesture interaction. The score for each dimension was set to 0 to 10. After counting all the participants' scores on gesture interaction, we found that the average overall rating was 7.73 (SD = 1.62), which means that gesture control can help the subject to complete the interaction

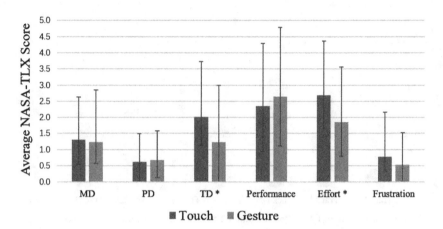

Fig. 9. The average task load of each subscale in two interaction modalities.

requirements. Figure 10 illustrates the average score of each gesture in each dimension. Based on the results, we can find that in terms of comfortable and natural, the scores of each gesture are relatively lower than other dimensions. We believe that this phenomenon is caused by the fact that participants use gesture interactions less frequently in their daily lives. In addition, for the Swipe Left gesture, in order to avoid misrecognition of the Leap Motion, the user needs to wrap the hand to the left side of the device and then perform the gesture, which increases the user's discomfort. For the volume adjustment gesture, the user needs to perform the gesture multiple times to get the expected volume level.

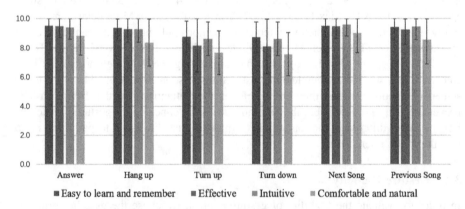

Fig. 10. The average score of each gesture in each dimension.

To make the evaluation results more significant, we use the fuzzy comprehensive evaluation method to quantify gesture preference degree. The evaluation results are shown in Table 2. Through these, we found that the quantified result of the gesture preference degree is consistent with the usability rating results, similar to the phenomenon that the volume adjustment gesture has a relatively low score, and the user's preference for the gesture no longer tends to be excellent.

Table 2. Fuzzy comprehensive evaluation results.

	Excellent	Good	Medium	Bad	Low
Answer: Swipe right	85.27%	13.15%	1.58%	0.00%	0.00%
Hang up: Swipe left	77.39%	20.31%	0.77%	1.53%	0.00%
Turn up: Clockwise	47.20%	44.79%	6.41%	0.78%	0.82%
Turn down: Counter-clockwise	46.48%	44.73%	7.20%	0.77%	0.82%
Next song: Swipe right	86.00%	12.40%	1.60%	0.00%	0.00%
Previous song: Swipe left	78.83%	18.84%	0.78%	1.55%	0.00%

4 Conclusions

This paper presents a user study that compared the differences between gestures interaction with infotainment system and touch screen interaction in a simulated in-vehicle environment. The experimental results show that gesture interaction benefits from touch which has a better overall impression and better interaction efficiency. The efficacy index shows that although there is no significant difference in the completion time between the two interaction modalities, in terms of task completion rate, gesture interaction shows obvious advantages in complex road conditions, which means that gesture interaction can help drivers reduce distraction. Further proof of such conclusion is reflected in the result of visual attention analysis. By counting the average dwell time, we first conclude that under simple road conditions, gesture interactions can help drivers maintain their attentions on the road. Then we calculate the influence of the sub-task on the dwell time under different road conditions, and get the opposite result of the two interactions, that is, for touch interaction, the interactive task has a significant distraction of the driver's attention under both road conditions, but no significant difference with gesture. Evaluation of another indicator shows that the overall task load rating of touch interaction is higher than that of gesture, especially in the dimensions of time demand and effort. Finally, the usability of gestures is also considered, and different gesture solutions for each secondary task were comparatively analyzed based on the fuzzy comprehensive evaluation method.

In future work, simpler gestures should be explored to support gesture interactions for more control without increasing task load. At the same time, the gesture interaction system also needs to provide more gestures to users, for users to select a gesture that conforms to their interaction habits.

Acknowledgements. This work was supported by the National Key Research and Development Program of China (No. 2018YFB1005002) and the National Natural Science Foundation of China (No. 61661146002) and the 111 Project (B18005).

References

1. Kim, H., Song, H.: Evaluation of the safety and usability of touch gestures in operating in-vehicle information systems with visual occlusion. J. Appl. Ergon. **45**(3), 789–798 (2014)
2. Neßelrath, R., Moniri, M.M., Feld, M.: Combining speech, gaze, and micro-gestures for the multimodal control of in-car functions. In: International Conference on Intelligent Environments, London (2016)
3. Manawadu, U.E., Kamezaki, M., Ishikawa, M., et al.: A hand gesture based driver-vehicle interface to control lateral and longitudinal motions of an autonomous vehicle. In: IEEE International Conference on Systems, Budapest. IEEE (2017)
4. May, K.R., Gable, T.M., Walker, B.N.: A multimodal air gesture interface for in vehicle menu navigation. In: Proceedings of the 6th International Conference on Automotive User Interfaces and Interactive Vehicular Applications – AutomotiveUI (2014)
5. Angelini, L., Baumgartner, J., Carrino, F., et al.: Comparing gesture, speech and touch interaction modalities for in-vehicle infotainment systems. In: Actes de la 28ième conférence francophone sur l'Interaction Homme-Machine on - IHM 2016 (2016)
6. Häuslschmid, R., Menrad, B., Butz, A.: Freehand vs. micro gestures in the car: driving performance and user experience. In: 3d User Interfaces, Arles (2015)
7. Kopinski, T., Eberwein, J., Geisler, S., et al.: Touch versus mid-air gesture interfaces in road scenarios - measuring driver performance degradation. In: IEEE International Conference on Intelligent Transportation Systems, Rio de Janeiro (2016)
8. Hart, S.G.: NASA-task load index (NASA-TLX); 20 years later. In: Proceedings of the Human Factors & Ergonomics Society Annual Meeting, vol. 50, no. 4661, pp. 904–908 (2006)
9. Ma, J., Du, Y.: Study on the evaluation method of in-vehicle gesture control. In: IEEE International Conference on Control Science & Systems Engineering, Beijing. IEEE (2017)

Mixed Reality Medical First Aid Training System Based on Body Identification

Jiayu Wang[1], Ruoxiu Xiao[1], Lijing Jia[2], and Xianmei Wang[1(✉)]

[1] School of Computer and Communication Engineering, University of Science and Technology Beijing, Beijing 100083, China
xmwang@ustb.edu.cn
[2] Emergency Department, Chinese PLA General Hospital, Beijing 100853, China

Abstract. Effective first aid training is helpful to improve the survival rate of the wounded in the face of natural disasters, emergencies and wars. While, traditional first aid training relies on the explanation and demonstration of experts, which has certain limitations. In this paper, we propose a novel type of first aid training system. The implementation of the system mainly includes three steps. First, medical body model images are collected to construct data sets. Second, key parts of the human body are identified and located based on a designed lightweight YOLO_v2 network. Finally, according to the results of the human identification, virtual guidance will be merged in the real environment by HoloLens glasses, and be uploaded to the server. With the Mixed Reality technology, we superimpose the corresponding virtual emergency instructions of cardiopulmonary resuscitation and artificial respiration in key parts of the body, and pass back to HoloLens glasses to realize first aid training. Experimental results show that the proposed medical first aid training system can make learners have a real touch and improve learning efficiency.

Keywords: Body identification · You Only Look Once (YOLO) · Mixed Reality · Medical first aid · Training system

1 Introduction

With the development of society, improving first aid awareness and skills as well as training the self and mutual rescue capability of emergency has become a sensitive issue. The number of traumatic injuries caused by natural disasters, emergencies and wars accounts for about 50% of the deaths in one hour, nearly 50% of deaths within 5 min, and more than 90% within 30 min. In the first 10 min, whether the injured person can get effective dressing, hemostasis, fixation and prevention of asphyxia is a decisive period of time [1]. Therefore, in the early stage of rescue, whether the rescue skill can be used usefully, whether the first aid equipment can be operated quickly and accurately, and whether we can organize the treatment scientifically and rationally are the keys to improve the survival rate of the wounded and reducing the disability rate.

In recent years, with the development of artificial intelligence technology, smart wearable devices represented by Virtual Reality (VR) are gradually favored by more

© Springer Nature Switzerland AG 2019
Y. Zhao et al. (Eds.): ICIG 2019, LNCS 11903, pp. 395–406, 2019.
https://doi.org/10.1007/978-3-030-34113-8_33

and more professionals in medical fields, which is also increasingly widespread [2]. By using VR technology and various types of first aid training simulator, it is better to help students learn relevant trauma treatment methods and skills, make an early assessment of the symptoms of the wounded correctly, and improve the clinical judgment ability of emergency. For example, the US Naval Medical Center and Texas A&M University have jointly developed the virtual clinical learning project "Pulse!!" [3] since 2005. The project is based on a three-dimensional virtual learning platform that allows learners to integrate into a virtual clinical environment, diagnose and operate patients, as well as provide users with unlimited, repeatable and immersive clinical experience. But students are still in a completely virtual scene in the "Pulse!!" system, without any touch at all. Laerdal Corporation in the United States has produced a portable SimMan training simulator [4]. The simulator has been preset simulated programs, and users can set up and store them. Teachers can use computers to display the curve of various physiological parameters within a certain time range. The simulated cases can be run automatically, so that teachers have more time to supervise the trainees. And the control of the simulator can be switched to the manual mode at any time. The simulator also can perform real-time recording, storage, printing, and make a fair and objective assessment. Thoman [5] developed a computer model of intracranial dynamics and integrated into a full-scale patient simulator, which can display the brain metabolism speed, blood flow, blood volume, perfusion pressure, and intracranial pressure with the corresponding changes in lung and cardiovascular physiological parameters. Donnelly [6] designed a simulator with a liquid circulation system. The power supply, water pump and control system are installed in the simulator to make the liquid circulate in head, trunk, upper limbs and lower limbs. And the parameter of body temperature can change in a certain situation. However, students are unable to accurately locate the injury location due to lack of experience in the process of using the simulator, which reduces the learning efficiency of first aid skills.

In view of the above deficiencies, we propose a Mixed Reality (MR) [7] medical first aid training system based on body identification, which allows students to locate the body parts of the medical model automatically at any time by wearing a MR glasses [8] and superimpose the virtual first aid instruction on the located parts. However, it was found that the traditional recognition algorithm has a slow detection speed, which does not meet the real-time requirements, and is prone to recognition errors, which does not meet the accuracy requirements. So, we improve the network structure model based on the YOLO_v2 algorithm and optimize the key parameters of the model so that it can quickly and accurately identify the body parts. Then, we use MR technology to superimpose the pre-designed virtual emergency operation at the corresponding parts of the model. Therefore, students can have a sense of touch, which enhances the quality of learning while the initiative and enthusiasm.

2   Method

In this section, we focus on how to use the camera mounted on HoloLens to identify and locate the key parts of the medical body model online and in real time to obtain the exact position of body parts. At the same time, we will study MR and Simultaneous

Localization and Mapping (SLAM) technology to construct the spatial information of the scene, so that the virtual emergency animation can be accurately and stably superimposed on the medical body model. Thereby we can provide virtual guidance to the emergency personnel. The steps of the proposed method can be described as Fig. 1.

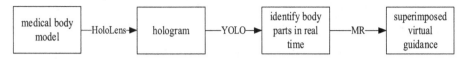

Fig. 1. Flow chart of medical first aid training system.

2.1 Identify and Locate the Key Parts of the Medical Body Model

Identification and location the key parts of the medical body model are basic and vital to fuse virtual instructional animation. If the recognition is wrong, it will not be superimposed on the correct position, which will mislead the rescuer to perform the correct first aid. Traditional target detection methods run complexly and slowly [9]. The deep learning target detection You Only Look Once (YOLO) algorithm [10] which is based on regression thought has greatly improved the detection speed, but it still leads to inaccurate locating. The YOLO_v2 [11] algorithm bases on YOLO algorithm, which further improves the detection accuracy. In addition, due to the simple scenario and the inability to obtain a rich set of images, the model assumptions may be so complicated and the training data is so small that it may produce a problem of over-fitting [12]. Therefore, we will lighten the YOLO_v2 network structure, that is, reduce the number of convolution layers to achieve faster and more accurate identification and prevent overfitting.

In order to ensure the effect of the training and the accuracy of the recognition, pictures of medical body model should be collected with various angles and various positions. And the annotation is completed according to the Pascal VOC labeling rules [13] to realize the identification of face and left hand, right hand, left leg, and right leg.

Under the condition of uniform learning rate and training times, the influence of convolutional layers on the recognition results is studied. Five convolutional layer structures are shown in Fig. 2.

When lightening the YOLO_v2 network, the input picture is normalized to a standard picture with the length and width of 416 pixels and 3 channels at first. And then the picture is converted into the feature map 1 by different layer of convolution and pool. Then, the feature map 1 is treated in two directions. The first direction is to recombine the feature map 1 into the feature map 2 according to a certain rule. And the second direction is to convert the feature map 1 through different layer of convolution and pool again into the feature map 3. The results of the two directions are merged to obtain the feature map 4. Finally, the feature map is obtained by convolution again.

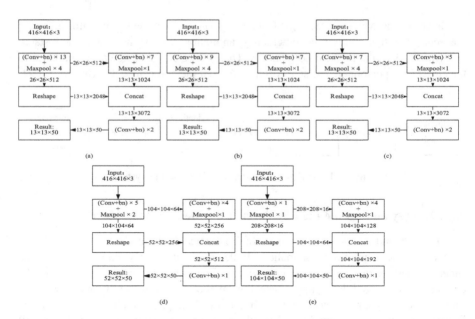

Fig. 2. Five sets of convolutional layer structures. (a) Original YOLO_v2 network structure, containing 22 convolutional layers. (b) Lightweight YOLO_v2 network structure, containing 18 convolutional layers. (c) Lightweight YOLO_v2 network structure, containing 14 convolution layers. (d) Lightweight YOLO_v2 network structure, containing 10 convolution layers. (e) Lightweight YOLO_v2 network structure, containing 6 convolution layers.

2.2 Superimposed Virtual First Aid Instruction

We study the joint development of Microsoft HoloLens and Unity3D, which realizes the integration of virtual objects into real scenes. MR technology is currently focused on superimposing computer-generated virtual scenes onto real-world scenes [7]. It allows virtual objects to be superimposed on a real scene through an optical see-through head-mounted display which is attached to a computer. So that they can appear together in the user's viewing scene. We use Microsoft HoloLens glasses to generate multi-dimensional hologram that can be viewed in all directions in the real world [8]. Then we use SLAM technology to construct the spatial information of the scene [14], so that the rescue virtual animation can be accurately and stably superimposed on the medical body model, which can play a virtual guidance role for first aid training. The process of superimposing virtual guidance using MR technology is shown in Fig. 3.

SLAM is critical to making the virtual first aid guidance model stably shown in the real world. In order to superimpose virtual models in an ever-changing environment, we need to constantly create an environment map and then locate and track the person's movement [15]. The role of SLAM is to let the device acquire the surrounding environment information in real time and accurately, and place the virtual object in the correct position. So, no matter how the user's position changes, the position of the virtual object can be fixed in the same position. First, we extract the FAST feature points [16] from the first keyframe. In each subsequent frame image, we use the 2D-2D

recognition result   HoloLens   superimposed first
                                                                    aid guidance

Fig. 3. Flow chart of superimposed virtual guidance of first aid using MR technology.

data association method [17] to track until the user inserts the second keyframe. Second, according to the ORB algorithm [18], we match the feature of the adjacent frame image. In order to minimize the matching error, the feature needs to be symmetrically searched between two frames. If the matching in the two directions is inconsistent, the feature will be discarded. After the second key frame is successfully added, the MLESAC28 method [19] is utilized to calculate the homography matrix H between two key frames. Third, the method in the literature [20] is used to decompose H to restore the camera relative pose. Finally, initial map points are generated by triangulation. The flow of the proposed method can be described as Fig. 4.

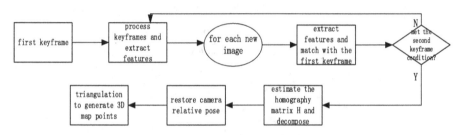

Fig. 4. Flow chart of SLAM system.

Therefore, when the user is in a state of no movement, only the head moves, the scene in the current view can be drawn, that is, the objects in the scene are invariant to the user's body. According to SLAM, the map and the current perspective are used to render the superimposed virtual objects, so they will look more realistic and users will have no sense of violation.

3   Experiments and Discussion

To achieve the Mixed Reality medical first aid training system based on body parts identification proposed in this study, we randomly choose 1,200 pieces of medical body model images with resolution of 3,024 * 4,032 to construct a dataset (1,000 images as a training set and 200 images as a testing set). In the Linux OS, with a NVIDIA GeForce GTX 745 graphics card and Darknet framework, the body parts identification based on the lightweight YOLO_v2 network structure is realized. Then, in Windows 10 OS, the virtual first aid guidance model is made by Maya 2018. Finally, based on 2017.4.13f1 (64-bit) version of Unity3D, the virtual first aid guidance model is superimposed on the right parts of the medical body model and can be seen in HoloLens glasses.

3.1   Analysis the Accuracy and Real-Time of Identification

The calculation formula of the filter in the last convolution layer is based on the number of categories of data, as shown in Eq. (1).

$$filter = num \times (classes + coords + 1) \tag{1}$$

In this system, the number of the filter in the last convolution layer is 50, the number of categories is 5, the momentum is 0.9, the decay is 0.0005, the learning rate is 10^{-4}, and the max batches is 20,000.

Accuracy (ACC), Recall, Mean Average Precision (mAP), and Intersection-over-Union (IoU) are used to quantify the accuracy of the algorithm, and are calculated in accordance with the literature [21] as follows:

$$ACC = \frac{TP + TN}{TP + TN + FP + FN} \tag{2}$$

$$Recall = \frac{TP}{TP + FN} \tag{3}$$

$$\begin{cases} Precision = \dfrac{TP}{TP + FP} \\ AP_A = \dfrac{\sum Precision_A}{N(\text{Images})_A} \\ mAP = \dfrac{\sum AP_A}{N_{classes}} \end{cases} \tag{4}$$

$$IoU = \frac{Detection\text{Result} \cap GroundTruth}{Detection\text{Result} \cup GroundTruth} \tag{5}$$

Table 1 gives the quantitative results of identification for the five convolutional layer structures corresponding with Fig. 2.

Table 1. reveals that as the number of convolutional layers decreases, both training time and prediction time are shortened (reduced 8-layer convolution, shortened training time by 90 h, and shortened prediction time by 0.031 s). Comparing the results of experiments (a), (b), and (c), as the number of convolution layers decreases, the accuracy of the prediction model is improved (reduced the 8-layer convolution, and the accuracy rate is increased by 2.52%). That is, because the training standard is too high, over-fitting occurs, and it is suppressed by lowering the training standard. However, ACC has not reached 100%, indicating that there is still a situation in which the part that is not the body is recognized as a body part, or the recognition results are incorrect,

Table 1. Identification results of the five convolutional layer structures.

Type	Training Time/h	ACC/%	Recall/%	mAP/%	IoU/%	Prediction Time/s
(a)	152	94.64	100.00	85.52	88.92	0.147
(b)	134	95.54	100.00	89.38	91.89	0.132
(c)	62	97.16	100.00	95.38	95.39	0.116
(d)	36	78.95	82.00	60.39	80.01	0.033
(e)	25	74.22	80.11	37.44	76.30	0.018

or the correct body part is not recognized. And Recall is 100%, that is FN = 0, indicating that the three groups of network structures (a), (b), and (c) must be able to locate key parts of the medical body model. At the same time, in the experiments (a), (b), and (c), the mAP and IoU values show an upward trend. As the number of convolution layers decreases, the prediction frame and the real detection frame overlap increases, as same as the recognition accuracy (reduced the 8-layer convolution, mAP is increased by 9.86%, and IoU increased by 6.47%). In general, in the network structures of (a), (b), and (c), there is a case where not a body part is recognized as a body part, or the recognition results are incorrect. The error probability is the smallest and the recognition accuracy is the highest in the group of (c).

Comparing the results of the five groups of experiments, although the training time and prediction time of the (d) and (e) groups are significantly shortened, the prediction results have a large number of recognition errors. The training time of group (e) (25 h) is 40.32% shorter than that of group (c) (62 h), but the mAP of group (e) (37.44%) is 39.25% lower than that of group (c) (95.38%). That is, there is a situation in which the part that is not the body is recognized as the body part, or the recognition results are incorrect, or the correct body part is not recognized. And the detection frame and the real frame have a lower degree of coincidence in group (e). In general, due to the considerable reduction in the number of convolution layers, the number of picture channels is reduced, training standards are too low, and recognition is awful.

3.2 Display of the Recognition Results

The recognition results and predicted values corresponding to the five convolutional layer structures are shown in Fig. 5.

Figure 5 gives qualitatively results of the identification. In groups (a), (b), and (c), it can be observed that the prediction value is improved, and the prediction box is more and more accurate. Among them, group (c) has the best recognition result (all the parts to be determined are all correctly marked, and the predicted values are higher than 80%). Group (d) cannot accurately identify the left hand and left leg. The predicted value is lower (both right hand and right leg are below 75%), and the prediction frame is too large. Group (e) cannot accurately identify left hand and right hand, and the predicted value is the lowest (face, right hand and right leg are lower than 70%).

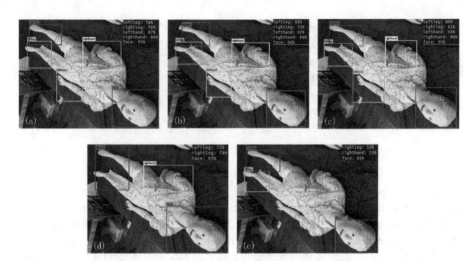

Fig. 5. Five sets of convolutional layer structures. (a) Original YOLO_v2 network structure, containing 22 convolutional layers. (b) Lightweight YOLO_v2 network structure, containing 18 convolutional layers. (c) Lightweight YOLO_v2 network structure, containing 14 convolution layers. (d) Lightweight YOLO_v2 network structure, containing 10 convolution layers. (e) Lightweight YOLO_v2 network structure, containing 6 convolution layers.

3.3   Deviation Between Predicted and True Values

According to the literature [22], we use the loss function to estimate the degree of inconsistency between the predicted and true values of the model. The loss function is as follows:

$$loss = \sum_{i=0}^{s^2} coordError + iouError + classError \tag{6}$$

According to the literature [23], YOLO network model supplements the loss function, where *coordError*, *iouError* and *classError* are calculated as follows:

$$coordError = 5\sum_{i=0}^{s^2}\sum_{j=0}^{B}\prod_{ij}^{obj}[(x_i - \hat{x}_i)^2 + [(y_i - \hat{y}_i)^2] + 5\sum_{i=0}^{s^2}\sum_{j=0}^{B}\prod_{ij}^{obj}[(\sqrt{\omega_i} - \sqrt{\hat{\omega}_i})^2 + [(\sqrt{h_i} - \sqrt{\hat{h}_i})^2] \tag{7}$$

$$iouError = \sum_{i=0}^{s^2}\sum_{j=0}^{B}\prod_{ij}^{obj}(C_i - \hat{C}_i)^2 + 0.5\sum_{i=0}^{s^2}\sum_{j=0}^{B}\prod_{ij}^{noobj}(C_i - \hat{C}_i)^2 \tag{8}$$

$$classError = \sum_{i=0}^{s^2}\prod_{ij}^{noobj}\sum_{c\in classes}(p_i(c) - \hat{p}_i(c))^2 \tag{9}$$

where x, y, ω, C and p are values of network prediction. $\hat{x}$, $\hat{y}$, $\hat{\omega}$, $\hat{C}$ and $\hat{p}$ are labeled values. $\prod_{ij}^{obj}$ and $\prod_{ij}^{noobj}$ respectively indicate that the object falls into the j bounding box in lattice i and does not falls into the j bounding box in lattice i.

The loss function corresponding to the five convolutional layer structures is shown in Fig. 6.

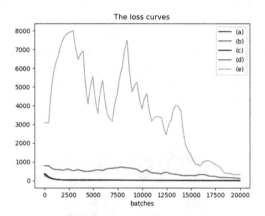

Fig. 6. Loss function image corresponding to five sets of convolutional layers

By observing Fig. 6, it is found that after 20,000 iterations, the loss function curves of groups (a), (b), and (c) almost coincide, and converge to 0, that is, the predicted value of the model is close to the true one. The loss function curve of group (d) is slightly higher than (a), (b), and (c). And after 20,000 iterations, the loss function curve does not converge to 0, that is, the predicted value of the model is different from the true one. The loss function curve of group (e) has a large jitter, and is higher than others. After 20,000 iterations, it still does not converge, indicating that the predicted value of the model differs greatly from the true one because the training requirements are too low.

Based on a comprehensive analysis of Figs. 5, 6 and Table 1, we consider that groups (a) and (b) have long training time due to high standards, and the predicted values are rather low. At the same time, the prediction time is too long to meet the real-time requirements. The experimental training standards of the groups (d) and (e) are too low, resulting in incorrect recognition, which cannot meet the accuracy requirements. If we want better recognition results, we need more training times and long training time. While the training time of group (c) is moderate (62 h), and the correct rate of identified body parts is the highest (ACC is 97.16%, Recall is 100%, mAP is 95.38%). Detection frame and the real frame have high coincidence (IoU is 95.39%). Last but not least, the prediction time is the shortest (0.116 s), and the predicted value is almost the same as the real one (the loss function curve approaches to 0). It meets the demand of real-time and accurate recognition. Therefore, we select the network structure of the group (c) to realize the identification of key parts of the medical body model, in order to achieve the location of virtual guidance based on MR technology.

3.4   Display of Superimposed Virtual First Aid Guidance

The system uploads the real environment seen by HoloLens glasses to the server in real time, and uses the network structure of group (c) to identify the face, left hand, right hand, left leg and right leg of the medical body model. Then we use SLAM technology to render the superimposed virtual guidance and transmit them back to HoloLens glasses, so that they can appear in the user's observation scene, which realizes the integration of the virtual object into the real scene, as shown in Fig. 7. The system can realize the first aid operation of cardiopulmonary resuscitation and artificial respiration. The model has high observability, but there are still bad phenomena such as stuttering and flickering. It is necessary to study how to improve hardware and optimize system structure in further work.

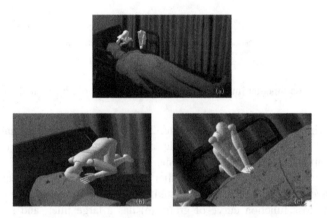

Fig. 7. Integrate virtual first aid instructions into the real scene. (a) Overall renderings. (b) First aid instruction for cardiopulmonary resuscitation. (c) First aid instruction for artificial respiration.

Above all, in order to quickly and accurately obtain the face, left hand, right hand, left leg and right leg position information of the medical body model, we lightweight the YOLO_v2 network structure. So, the system can realize the real-time recognition and localization of them through the camera assembled on HoloLens glasses. At the same time, we make virtual first aid guidance models. Through MR and SLAM technology, we construct the spatial information of the scene, so that the virtual first aid instruction animation of cardiopulmonary resuscitation and artificial respiration can be accurately and stably superimposed on the medical body model. Thus, the system acts as a virtual guidance to emergency personnel.

4 Conclusion

With the development of society and the progress of civilization, improving first aid awareness and skills as well as training the self and mutual rescue capability of emergency has become a sensitive issue. Therefore, we propose a new approach of medical first aid training based on body identification. The implementation of the system mainly includes following steps. First, collect medical body model images and construct data sets. Second, using the Darknet framework, we identify and locate the key parts of the medical body model based on the lightweight YOLO_v2 network structure. Finally, the real environment seen by the HoloLens glasses is uploaded to the server in real time. Virtual emergency instruction is superimposed on the appropriate parts of the body by SLAM technology, and transmitted back to HoloLens glasses to realize first aid teaching. The system can be used to learn the first aid operation of cardiopulmonary resuscitation and artificial respiration. Models have high observability. Students can have a real touch and improve learning efficiency.

The system also has a few shortcomings. The recognition algorithm of the body can still be improved. The superimposed model can still have bad phenomena such as stuttering and flickering. There are only two kinds of teaching guidance realized, which are relatively simple. The system lacks an interactive interface. Students are required to follow some instructions to run the program.

In view of the deficiencies, we can carry out further research from the following directions. For the detection of the medical body model and system stuttering, parameters such as momentum, decay, learning rate, and max batches can be improved in the algorithm. In addition, more teaching guidance models and evaluation systems can be produced to test the learning effects and make the system more complete.

Acknowledgements. This work was supported in part by grants from National Natural Science Foundation of China (61701022), Beijing Science & Technology Program (Z181100001018017) and Beijing Natural Science Foundation (7182158).

References

1. Kureckova, V., Gabrhel, V., Zamecnik, P., et al.: First aid as an important traffic safety factor–evaluation of the experience–based training. Eur. Transp. Res. Rev. **9**(1), 5 (2017)
2. Gavish, N., Gutiérrez, T., Webel, S., et al.: Evaluating virtual reality and augmented reality training for industrial maintenance and assembly tasks. Interact. Learn. Environ. **23**(6), 778–798 (2015)
3. Dunne, J.R., McDonald, C.L.: Pulse!!: a model for research and development of virtual-reality learning in military medical education and training. Mil. Med. **175**(suppl_7), 25–27 (2010)
4. McLellan, B.: A medical simulation model for teaching trauma skills. J. Emerg. Med. **14**(3), 393 (1996)
5. Thoman, W.J., Lampotang, S., Gravenstein, D., et al.: A computer model of intracranial dynamics integrated to a full-scale patient simulator. Comput. Biomed. Res. **31**(1), 32–46 (1998)

6. Donnelly, M.M., Olson, W.A.: Mechanical simulator for modeling thermal properties of a premature infant: U.S. Patent 5,409,382[P], 25 April 1995
7. Ohta, Y., Tamura, H.: Mixed Reality: Merging Real and Virtual Worlds. Springer, Heidelberg (2014)
8. Maimone, A., Georgiou, A., Kollin, J.S.: Holographic near-eye displays for virtual and augmented reality. ACM Trans. Graph. (TOG) 36(4), 85 (2017)
9. Krizhevsky, A., Sutskever, I., Hinton, G.E.: ImageNet classification with deep convolutional neural networks. In: Advances in Neural Information Processing Systems, pp. 1097–1105 (2012)
10. Redmon, J., Divvala, S., Girshick, R., et al.: You only look once: unified, real-time object detection. In: Proceedings of the IEEE Conference on Computer Vision and Pattern Recognition, pp. 779–788 (2016)
11. Redmon, J., Farhadi, A.: YOLO9000: better, faster, stronger. In: Proceedings of the IEEE Conference on Computer Vision and Pattern Recognition, pp. 7263–7271 (2017)
12. Srivastava, N., Hinton, G., Krizhevsky, A., et al.: Dropout: a simple way to prevent neural networks from overfitting. J. Mach. Learn. Res. 15(1), 1929–1958 (2014)
13. Everingham, M., Van Gool, L., Williams, C.K.I., et al.: The pascal visual object classes (voc) challenge. Int. J. Comput. Vision 88(2), 303–338 (2010)
14. Kim, A., Eustice, R.M.: Active visual SLAM for robotic area coverage: theory and experiment. Int. J. Rob. Res. 34(4–5), 457–475 (2015)
15. Lindgren, R., Tscholl, M., Wang, S., et al.: Enhancing learning and engagement through embodied interaction within a mixed reality simulation. Comput. Educ. 95, 174–187 (2016)
16. Chen, T., Tian, G.Y., Sophian, A., et al.: Feature extraction and selection for defect classification of pulsed eddy current NDT. NDT E Int. 41(6), 467–476 (2008)
17. Genc, Y., Riedel, S., Souvannavong, F., et al.: Marker-less tracking for AR: a learning-based approach. In: Proceedings, International Symposium on Mixed and Augmented Reality, pp. 295–304. IEEE (2002)
18. Rublee, E., Rabaud, V., Konolige, K., et al.: ORB: an efficient alternative to SIFT or SURF. In: ICCV, vol. 11, no. 1, p. 2 (2011)
19. Torr, P.H.S., Zisserman, A.: MLESAC: a new robust estimator with application to estimating image geometry. Comput. Vis. Image Underst. 78(1), 138–156 (2000)
20. Faugeras, O.D., Lustman, F.: Motion and structure from motion in a piecewise planar environment. Int. J. Pattern Recognit. Artif Intell. 2(03), 485–508 (1988)
21. Ren, S., He, K., Girshick, R., et al.: Faster R-CNN: towards real-time object detection with region proposal networks. In: Advances in Neural Information Processing Systems, pp. 91–99 (2015)
22. Janowczyk, A., Madabhushi, A.: Deep learning for digital pathology image analysis: a comprehensive tutorial with selected use cases. J. Pathol. Inf. 7 (2016)
23. Lin, T.Y., Goyal, P., Girshick, R., et al.: Focal loss for dense object detection. In: Proceedings of the IEEE International Conference on Computer Vision, pp. 2980–2988 (2017)

Feature Learning for Cross-Domain Problems

Attention-Aware Invertible Hashing Network

Shanshan Li[1], Qiang Cai[1], Zhuangzi Li[1(✉)], Haisheng Li[1], Naiguang Zhang[2], and Jian Cao[1]

[1] School of Computer and Information Engineering, Beijing Technology and Business University, Beijing, China
shanshanli233@126.com, caiq@th.btbu.edu.cn, lizhuangzii@163.com
{lihsh,caojian}@th.btbu.edu.cn
[2] Information Technology Institute, Academy of Broadcasting Science, NRTA, Beijing, China
zhangnaiguang@abs.ac.cn

Abstract. In large-scale image retrieval tasks, hashing methods based on deep convolutional neural networks (CNNs) play an important role due to elaborate semantic feature representation. However, they usually progressively discard information during feature transformation, thus leading to incomplete and unsatisfactory hashing codes for image retrieval. This study tries to design an invertible architecture to maintain image information, meanwhile focus on necessary parts of image features. Consequently, in this paper, we propose a novel attention-aware invertible hashing network (AIHN) for image retrieval. By invertible feature representations, the final hash codes can be completely obtained from input images without any information loss. For highlighting informative regions, we present a novel attention-aware invertible block as the basic module of AIHN, which can promote generalization ability by spatial attention mechanism. Extensive experiments conducted on benchmark datasets demonstrate the effectiveness of our invertible feature representation on hash code generation, and show the promising performance on image retrieval of our methods against the state-of-the-arts.

Keywords: Image retrieval · Deep hashing · Attention mechanism

1 Introduction

With the explosive growth of data in practical applications such as image retrieval, approximate nearest neighbor (ANN) search has become a hot topic in recent years. In the existing ANN technology, hashing method has become one of the most popular and effective technologies because of its fast query speed and low memory cost. Amounts of studies have shown that hashing has improved

---

S. Li, Q. Cai and Z. Li—These authors contributed equally to this paper and share the first authorship.

© Springer Nature Switzerland AG 2019
Y. Zhao et al. (Eds.): ICIG 2019, LNCS 11903, pp. 409–420, 2019.
https://doi.org/10.1007/978-3-030-34113-8_34

the performance on image retrieval tasks [7,23]. However, these methods are defective in feature representation and can not be trained end-to-end.

Recently, convolutional neural networks (CNNs) are gradually applied to image hashing retrieval, and have achieved promising performance. Xia et al. [22] firstly adopt the CNN architecture in the hash algorithm. Later, series of deep hashing methods based on CNN [16,17] are proposed in an end-to-end manner, showing the effectiveness of deep feature representation. The performance of these deep learning hash methods has been greatly improved compared with the traditional hash method in many benchmarks. Moreover, it proves crucial to jointly learn similarity-preserving representations and control quantization error of converting continuous representation into binary codes [3]. However, existing deep feature representation are generated with gradually discarding image information. It may result in discarding of representative feature variability in the process of feature transformation, which can not guarantee obtaining complete image information. In addition, informative regions of image are not highlighted well in existing algorithm, causing poor generalization ability.

To effectively solve the above-mentioned problems, we propose a novel image retrieval framework based on invertible network with spatial attention mechanism. Firstly, a reversible network is proposed, which guarantee the lossless representative features transformed from original image. In such a way, all the information of the image will be forwarded through the network. Then, we adopt spatial attention architecture to tell where to focus, which also improves the representation of interests. Spatial attention effectively learns which information to emphasize or suppress in the process of information transmission. As shown in Fig. 1, our method yield most of state-of-the-art retrieval performance. To summarize, the main contributions of this paper are three-fold:

- We propose an effective invertible network with lossless image information for image retrieval, where the whole framework can be trained end-to-end;
- To excavate informative regions of features, we adopt spatial attention module in our invertible block to learn how to focus on objective information and suppress unnecessary ones.
- Extensive experiments on benchmark datasets show that our architecture is effective and achieves promising performance.

The rest of the paper is organized as follows: in Sect. 2, we introduce some related work about our algorithm. The proposed method is illustrated in Sect. 3, followed by the experimental results in Sect. 4. In Sect. 5, we conclude our work.

2   Related Work

2.1   Hashing Methods

Existing hashing methods [1,25] can be roughly divided into two categories, namely unsupervised hashing and supervised hashing. Unsupervised hashing exploit unlabeled data to learn a set of functions, which encode data to binary codes [5,21]. Locality-Sensitive Hashing (LSH) [5] is the most representative unsupervised hashing algorithm, achieving promising performance compared with previous approaches. LSH guarantees similar data points preserve similar binary codes after the same hash mapping, vice versa. Supervised hashing [18,20] further exploit label information during learning to generate compact hash code. Supervised Hashing with Kernels (KSH) utilizes the pair-wised labels to generate effective hash functions, which guarantees minimizing the Hamming distances for similar pair-wise data and meanwhile maximizing the dissimilar ones.

In recent years, CNN have shown significant success in computer vision [13–15,19,26–31,34–37]. In the domain of hashing retrieval, [22] was the first deep neural network, achieving promising performance compared with conventional approaches. Deep Hashing Network (DHN) [33] not only preserves pairwise similarity but also controls the quantization error. For improving DHN, HashNet balances training data consisting of positive pairs and negative pairs, and reduces quantization error by continuation technology, thus gaining the most advanced performance on several benchmark datasets. But the high-dimensional features obtained in these methods are accompanied with gradual loss of image information, and we can not ensure whether the discarded information variability is significant.

2.2 Attention Mechanism

The attention mechanism can be viewed as a strategy to bias the allocation of available processing resources towards the most informative components of an input [10]. Attention module has been widely applied in the Natural Language Processing (NLP) field like machine translation, sentence generation etc. And these performance is surprisingly remarkable. Meanwhile, in the image vision field, attention mechanism also demonstrates powerful capabilities. For example, Hu et al. [9] utilize attention to propose an object relation module, which models the relationship among a set of objects and improves object recognition. In this work [24], a self-attention module is introduced in order to better generate images. A channel-wise attention was proposed for image super-resolution task [32]. In our work, the attention-aware invertible hashing network aims at utilizing spatial attention to enhance informative features from the spatial domain, which can accurately tell which information to emphasize or suppress.

3 Our Method

3.1 Overview

The architecture of AIHN is shown in Fig. 1. The pair-wise images are firstly fed into an invertible downsample layer to increase the number of output channels, while decreasing the spatial resolution. Then, the output is split into two sublayers (x_1, y_1) of equal channel dimension. Next, sublayers (x_1, y_1) are put into the invertible block. It is worth noting that spatial attention and invertible downsampling module are introduced in the invertible block. Spatial attention module is to notice the most informative components of an input, and invertible downsampling module is adopted to reduce the number of computations while maintaining good performance. More details about these two will be introduced in Sects. 3.2 and 3.3 below. After totally 100 similar blocks, invertible high-dimensional features are obtained through followed concatenation operation. The invertible features are send to average pooling and linear layer after a ReLU non-linearity. The results are quantized by Sgn function to get pair-wise binary hash codes. The pairwise similarity loss is adopted for similarity-preserving learning in the Hamming space, and quantization loss is to control both the binarization error and the hash code quality. The invertible downsampling, spatial attention module, as well as invertible block will be introduced in next sections in detail.

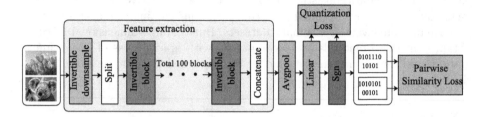

Fig. 1. The framework of the proposed invertible spatial-attention hashing network.

3.2   Invertible Downsampling

In order to facilitate calculation and avoid the use of irreversible module at the same time, we introduce invertible downsampling module to our architecture instead of Maxpooling used in [6]. It not only reduce the spatial resolution of the input for the sake of simplicity but also potentially increase the number of channel for lossless information. As shown in Fig. 2, downsampled by a factor of θ 4, the output's channel is 4 times the original, and the size of each feature map is reduced by 4 times. And also invertible downsampling preserves roughly the spatial ordering, thus avoiding mixing different neighborhoods via the next convolution. Invertible downsampling operation can be written as below:

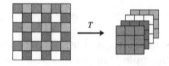

Fig. 2. The illustration of invertible downsampling.

$$T(\theta, Fe(c, w, h)) = Fe(\theta \times c, w/(\theta/2), h/(\theta/2)) \tag{1}$$

where θ represents scaling factor which determines the downsampled size directly, T is the function of downsampling operation, and $Fe(c, w, h)$ denotes feature maps with channel c, width w, and height h.

For reducing computational costs, invertible downsampling is designed tightly for our architecture. It will correspond to an invertible downsampling operator respectively at the begin of our network and depth $d = 6, 22, 94$.

3.3   Invertible Block

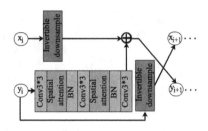

Fig. 3. The structure of invertible block.

The invertible block is an important component for our invertible hashing network. It not only determines the reversibility of information flow, but also generates attentioned features with lossless information. Spatial attention module and invertible downsampling module introduced in Sects. 3.2 and 3.4 are adopted in the invertible block. In particular, spatial attention module mining the objective information and invertible downsampling module allows us to reduce the number of computations while maintaining good performance. The details of the invertible block are illustrated as Fig. 4.

Detailedly, sublayers (x_i, y_i) obtained through splitting operation are doing different two operations. x_i is feed to a invertible downsampling layer with scaling factor θ 4 directly, so we can get $T(4, x_i)$. y_i is sent to a bottleneck block F, mainly consisting of a succession of 3 convolutional operators. The second convolutional layer has four times fewer channels than the other two, while their corresponding filter sizes are respectively 1×1, 3×3, 1×1. The first and the second are preceded by spatial attention module, Batch normalization (BN) and ReLU non-linearity. What needs to be emphasized is that the last convolution layer are followed by batch normalization and ReLU non-linearity only. Obtained $F(y_i)$ plus $T(4, x_i)$, then Y_{i+1} is got. Meanwhile, y_i is also feed to an invertible downsampling layer for convenient calculation, and x_{i+1} is equal to output $T(4, y_i)$. In summary, the detailed operation is described as below:

$$x_{i+1} = T(4, y_i) \tag{2}$$

$$y_{i+1} = F(y_i) + T(4, x_i) \tag{3}$$

and reverse propagation can be computed by the following:

$$y_i = T^{-1}(4, x_{i+1}) \tag{4}$$

$$x_i = T^{-1}(4, (y_{i+1} - F(y_i))) \tag{5}$$

where T^{-1} represents reverse calculation of T function.

3.4   Spatial Attention

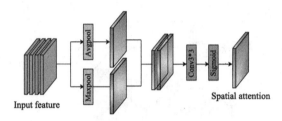

Fig. 4. Diagram of spatial attention module.

The spatial attention module aims to highlight the expressions of key objects for image retrieval. Firstly, it learns a set of weight maps from the feature maps, and provides a larger weight for the informative region in each feature map, while providing a smaller weight for the background region. Then, the learned weight maps is multiplied by the feature map, so feature maps focusing on key objects and suppressing background regions is obtained. More specifically, the spatial attention tell which information to emphasize or suppress in the process of feature transmission. As shown in Fig. 3, feature maps are send to a Max-pooling and average pooling operation respectively, both which demonstrate effective in highlighting informative regions. Then concatenating the both outputs to generate a concentrated feature descriptor. Next, we apply a convolution layer followed by sigmoid operation on the attentioned feature descriptor to get a spatial attention map $SA(Fe) \in R^{H \times W}$, which tell information flow which part to emphasize or suppress. In short, the detailed operation is described as below:

$$SA(Fe) = \sigma(g^{7 \times 7}(Cat(Ap(Fe), Mp(Fe)))) \tag{6}$$

where σ presents the sigmoid operation, $g^{7 \times 7}$ denotes a convolution operation with kernel size of 7×7, cat is concatenation operation along the channel axis, $Ap(Fe)$ and $Mp(Fe)$ respectively represent average pooling and Max-pooling operation, and Fe is a brief expression of feature map.

3.5   Loss Function

In our paper, we focus on the supervised setting utilizing label information. We can easily obtain a set of image pairs, where each pair (a_i, a_j) consists of an image a_i and $a_j(j \neq i)$. Using both category information, we can get the similarity s_{ij} of image pair (a_i, a_j). Following [3,33], the similarity information is constructed directly by image labels:if two images a_i and a_j share at least one label, they are similar and $s_{ij} = 1$; otherwise, they are dissimilar and $s_{ij} = 0$.

Intuitively, the desired hash codes should be able to preserve the relative similarities in the image pairs. Corresponding optimization goal is to make the Hamming distance between two similar points as small as possible, and simultaneously make the Hamming distance between two dissimilar points as large as possible. In this way, we can define a pairwise loss that has also been successfully applied in prior research [16], which is defined over the output binary codes (b_i, b_j) corresponding to the training image pair (a_i, a_j):

$$l_1 = min(-(s_{ij}\beta_{ij} - log(1 + e^{\beta_{ij}}))) \tag{7}$$

where $\beta_{ij} = \frac{1}{2}b_i^T b_j$, s_{ij} presents the similarity of image pair (a_i, a_j). To pursue representative hash codes, we learn our Invertible Hashing Network by minimizing the pairwise loss. This can drive our network to process strong capability of distinguishing the images. Since the hash codes are discrete, we additionally adopt the following quantization loss for each image a_i:

$$l_2 = ||b_i - u_i||_2^2 \tag{8}$$

where $u_i \in \mathbb{R}^{c \times 1}$, $b_i \in (-1, 1)^c$, and c represent the hash code length. Based on the two type of loss, we can train our Invertible Hashing Network through the following function:

$$l = l_1 + l_2 = -\sum_{s_{ij} \in S}(s_{ij}\beta_{ij} - log(1 + e^{\beta_{ij}})) + \lambda \sum_{i=1}^{n}||b_i - u_i||_2^2 \tag{9}$$

where λ is the hyper-parameter; $||.||_2$ denotes the l_2 norm.

4   Experiments

4.1   Dataset and Evaluation

We evaluate the effect of the proposed AIHN with several state-of-the-art hashing methods on two benchmark datasets.

- CIFAR-10 is a single-label dataset with 60000 images divided into 10 categories (6000 images per class). We follow [2,33] to randomly select 100 images per class for training, 500 images per class for testing, and the rest 54000 images used as database.

– NUS-WIDE81 is a multi-label dataset, which contains 269648 images consisting of 81 categories. We follow similar experimental protocols in [3,33], and
randomly sample 5000 images as test images, 10000 images for training, and
the remaining images used as database. To evaluate our method, the mean
average precision (MAP) is used to measure the accuracy of our proposed
method and other baselines (Fig. 5).

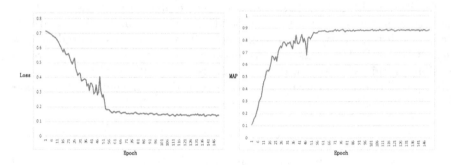

Fig. 5. The curve convergence of our network on CIFAR-10 with 16 bits code.

4.2   Implementation Detail

Network Detail. The proposed network is trained specifically for image hashing retrieval. The input image size of our network is $3 \times 224 \times 224$. After the
invertible downsampling with $\theta = 4$, the size of features becomes $12 \times 112 \times 112$.
Then, the spliting operation guarantees two sublayers with equal channel. Next,
both sublayers pass through totally 100 similar invertible blocks. It will correspond to an invertible downsampling operator respectively at the block = 6,
22, 94. The spatial resolution of these layers is reduced by a factor 4 while
increasing the number of channels respectively to 48, 192, 768 and 3072. Furthermore, it means that the corresponding spatial resolutions are respectively
56×56, 28×28, 14×14, 7×7. Last, the obtained representation is spatially
averaged and projected onto one-dimensional vector after a ReLU nonlinearity.
Binary hashing code can be obtained through Sgn computation conducted on
the one-dimensional vector.

Training Detail. We randomly crop a set of 224×224 patches for training.
The training batch size is set to 64 in each back-propagation. This network is
trained via an end-to-end manner. Pairwise similarity loss and quantilization
loss are concurrently adopted in CIFAR-10 and NUS-WIDE81, where the data
augmentation with random horizontal flip is adopted. The SGD is adopted for
optimizing our network, and the initial learning rate is set to 0.05. For each 50
epochs, the learning rate will decrease by the scale of 0.1. The hyper-parameter

λ in our network is chosen by a validation set, which is 10 for CIFAR-10 and 100 for NUS-WIDE81. At test time, we rescale the image size to 256×256 and perform a center crop of size 224×224. The curve convergence of our network on CIFAR-10 with 16 bits code are shown below. Experiments are performed on two NVIDIA Titan XP GPUs for training and testing.

4.3   Compare with State-of-the-Arts

We use MAP evaluation metrics to compare retrieval performance of AIHN with classical or state-of-the-art methods: supervised shallow methods ITQ-CCA [8], BRE [11], KSH [18], SDH [20] and supervised deep methods CNNH [22], DNNH [12], DHN [33], HashNet [3]. For fair comparison, all methods use identical training and test sets. We adopt MAP@5000 for evaluation in NUS-WIDES. For shallow hashing methods, we use as image features the 4096-dimensional $DeCAF_7$ feature [4]. For deep hashing methods, we use raw images as the input. We adopt the AlexNet architecture for all deep hashing methods.

Table 1. The best MAPs for each category are shown in boldface. Here, the MAP value is calculated based on the top 5000 returned neighbors for NUS-WIDE dataset.

Method	CIFAR-10 (MAP)				NUS-WIDES (MAP)			
	16-bits	32-bits	48-bits	64-bits	16-bits	32-bits	48-bits	64-bits
ITQ-CCA [8]	0.4258	0.4652	0.4774	0.4932	0.5706	0.4397	0.0825	0.0051
BRE [11]	0.4216	0.4519	0.4002	0.3438	0.5502	0.5422	0.4128	0.2202
KSH [18]	0.4368	0.4585	0.4012	0.3819	0.5185	0.5659	0.4102	0.0608
SDH [20]	0.5620	0.6428	0.6069	0.5012	0.6681	0.6824	0.5979	0.4679
CNNH [22]	0.5512	0.5468	0.5454	0.5364	0.5843	0.5989	0.5734	0.5729
DNNH [12]	0.5703	0.5985	0.6421	0.6118	0.6191	0.6216	0.5902	0.5626
DHN [33]	0.6929	0.6445	0.5835	0.5883	0.6901	0.7021	0.6685	0.5664
HashNet [3]	0.7476	0.7776	0.6399	0.6259	0.6944	0.7147	0.6736	0.6190
AIHN	**0.7897**	**0.7967**	**0.8054**	**0.8076**	**0.7434**	**0.7555**	**0.7599**	**0.7590**

Experimental results are as shown in Table 1. It can be seen that our method AIHN achieves the best performance among all the methods. Specifically, compared to the best shallow hashing method using deep features as input, ITQ-CCA, we achieve absolute boosts of 33.45%, 48% in average MAP for different bits on CIFAR-10 and NUS-WIDE dataset respectively. Compared to the state-of-the-art deep hashing method, HashNet, we achieve absolute boosts of 10.21%, 7.9% in average MAP for different bits on the two datasets, respectively. An interesting phenomenon is that the performance boost of AIHN over HashNet is significantly different across the two datasets. Specifically, the performance boost on NUS-WIDES is much larger than that on CIFAR-10 generally. But with the code length increasing, MAP has an exciting increase in CIFAR10 dataset.

4.4   Ablation Experiment

For investigating the effectiveness of proposed two different components, we research two AIHN variants: (1) AIHN-AI is a AIHN variant without using spatial attention module, and replace invertible network with Alexnet which may cause gradually information lost. (2) AIHN-A is a AIHN variant using invertible network for feature extraction. But in each invertible block, there is no spatial attention module adopted.

AIHN-A outperforms AIHN-AI by very large margins of 10.58%, 8.69%, 10.71% and 9% in MAP with corresponding 16, 32, 48, 64 code lengths on CIFAR-10. The invertible Network guarantees that the final hash codes can be completely obtained from input images without any information loss. AIHN outperforms AIHN-A by 0.75%, 1.48%, 0.03%, 1.77% in MAP with different 16, 32, 48, 64 code lengths on CIFAR-10 respectively. These results validate that the spatial attention module can enhance efficiency and improve MAP results. That is because the spatial attention module can better capture the objective information. As shown in Table 2, our proposed AIHN achieves the highest result in terms of the MAP evaluation metrics in CIFAR-10 dataset. Further analysis, we can find that Invertible Network which guarantees the lossless generated features contributes to our network largely. This can be explained as the following: when learning image features, progressively discarding variability about the input image may cause effective information to be discarded.

Table 2. Results of ablation study on CIFAR-10

Method	CIFAR-10(MAP)			
	16-bits	32-bits	48-bits	64-bits
AIHN-AI	0.6764	0.6950	0.6980	0.6999
AIHN-A	0.7822	0.7819	0.8051	0.7899
AIHN	**0.7897**	**0.7967**	**0.8054**	**0.8076**

5   Conclusion

In this paper, we propose a novel attention-aware invertible hashing network for image retrieval. By invertible feature representations, the final hash codes can be completely obtained from input images without any information loss, so as to produce accurate hash codes with complete image information. For highlighting informative regions, we present a novel attention-aware invertible block as the basic module of AIHN, which can promote generalization ability by spatial attention mechanism. Extensive experiments conducted on benchmark datasets have demonstrated the state-of-the-art performance of our method.

Acknowledgement. This work was supported by National Key R&D Program of China (2018YFB0803700) and National Natural Science Foundation of China (61602517, 61877002).

References

1. Cao, Y., Long, M., Wang, J., Liu, S.: Collective deep quantization for efficient cross-modal retrieval. In: Thirty-First AAAI Conference on Artificial Intelligence (2017)
2. Cao, Y., Long, M., Wang, J., Zhu, H., Wen, Q.: Deep quantization network for efficient image retrieval. In: Thirtieth AAAI Conference on Artificial Intelligence (2016)
3. Cao, Z., Long, M., Wang, J., Yu, P.S.: Hashnet: deep learning to hash by continuation. In: Proceedings of the IEEE International Conference on Computer Vision, pp. 5608–5617 (2017)
4. Donahue, J., et al.: Decaf: a deep convolutional activation feature for generic visual recognition. In: International Conference on Machine Learning, pp. 647–655 (2014)
5. Gionis, A., Indyk, P., Motwani, R., et al.: Similarity search in high dimensions via hashing. In: VLDB, vol. 99, pp. 518–529 (1999)
6. Gomez, A.N., Ren, M., Urtasun, R., Grosse, R.B.: The reversible residual network: backpropagation without storing activations. In: Advances in Neural Information Processing Systems, pp. 2214–2224 (2017)
7. Gong, Y., Kumar, S., Rowley, H.A., Lazebnik, S.: Learning binary codes for high-dimensional data using bilinear projections. In: Proceedings of the IEEE Conference on Computer Vision and Pattern Recognition, pp. 484–491 (2013)
8. Gong, Y., Lazebnik, S., Gordo, A., Perronnin, F.: Iterative quantization: a procrustean approach to learning binary codes for large-scale image retrieval. IEEE Trans. Pattern Anal. Mach. Intell. **35**(12), 2916–2929 (2013)
9. Hu, H., Gu, J., Zhang, Z., Dai, J., Wei, Y.: Relation networks for object detection. In: Proceedings of the IEEE Conference on Computer Vision and Pattern Recognition, pp. 3588–3597 (2018)
10. Hu, J., Shen, L., Sun, G.: Squeeze-and-excitation networks. In: Proceedings of the IEEE Conference on Computer Vision and Pattern Recognition, pp. 7132–7141 (2018)
11. Kulis, B., Darrell, T.: Learning to hash with binary reconstructive embeddings. In: Advances in Neural Information Processing Systems, pp. 1042–1050 (2009)
12. Lai, H., Pan, Y., Liu, Y., Yan, S.: Simultaneous feature learning and hash coding with deep neural networks. In: Proceedings of the IEEE Conference on Computer Vision and Pattern Recognition, pp. 3270–3278 (2015)
13. Li, C., Liu, Q., Liu, J., Lu, H.: Ordinal distance metric learning for image ranking. IEEE Trans. Neural Netw. Learn. Syst. **26**(7), 1551–1559 (2014)
14. Li, C., Wang, X., Dong, W., Yan, J., Liu, Q., Zha, H.: Joint active learning with feature selection via cur matrix decomposition. IEEE Trans. Pattern Anal. Mach. Intell. **41**(6), 1382–1396 (2018)
15. Li, C., Wei, F., Dong, W., Wang, X., Liu, Q., Zhang, X.: Dynamic structure embedded online multiple-output regression for streaming data. IEEE Trans. Pattern Anal. Mach. Intell. **41**(2), 323–336 (2018)
16. Li, W.J., Wang, S., Kang, W.C.: Feature learning based deep supervised hashing with pairwise labels. arXiv preprint arXiv:1511.03855 (2015)
17. Liu, H., Wang, R., Shan, S., Chen, X.: Deep supervised hashing for fast image retrieval. In: Proceedings of the IEEE Conference on Computer Vision and Pattern Recognition, pp. 2064–2072 (2016)
18. Liu, W., Wang, J., Ji, R., Jiang, Y.G., Chang, S.F.: Supervised hashing with kernels. In: 2012 IEEE Conference on Computer Vision and Pattern Recognition, pp. 2074–2081. IEEE (2012)

19. Liu, Y., Zhu, X., Zhao, X., Cao, Y.: Adversarial learning for constrained image splicing detection and localization based on atrous convolution. IEEE Trans. Inf. Forensics Secur. (2019)
20. Shen, F., Shen, C., Liu, W., Tao Shen, H.: Supervised discrete hashing. In: Proceedings of the IEEE Conference on Computer Vision and Pattern Recognition, pp. 37–45 (2015)
21. Weiss, Y., Torralba, A., Fergus, R.: Spectral hashing. In: Advances in Neural Information Processing Systems, pp. 1753–1760 (2009)
22. Xia, R., Pan, Y., Lai, H., Liu, C., Yan, S.: Supervised hashing for image retrieval via image representation learning. In: Twenty-Eighth AAAI Conference on Artificial Intelligence (2014)
23. Yu, F., Kumar, S., Gong, Y., Chang, S.F.: Circulant binary embedding. In: International Conference on Machine Learning, pp. 946–954 (2014)
24. Zhang, H., Goodfellow, I., Metaxas, D., Odena, A.: Self-attention generative adversarial networks. arXiv preprint arXiv:1805.08318 (2018)
25. Zhang, P., Zhang, W., Li, W.J., Guo, M.: Supervised hashing with latent factor models. In: Proceedings of the 37th International ACM SIGIR Conference on Research & Development in Information Retrieval, pp. 173–182. ACM (2014)
26. Zhang, X.Y.: Simultaneous optimization for robust correlation estimation in partially observed social network. Neurocomputing **205**, 455–462 (2016)
27. Zhang, X.Y., Shi, H., Li, C., Zheng, K., Zhu, X., Duan, L.: Learning transferable self-attentive representations for action recognition in untrimmed videos with weak supervision. arXiv preprint arXiv:1902.07370 (2019)
28. Zhang, X.Y., Shi, H., Zhu, X., Li, P.: Active semi-supervised learning based onself-expressive correlation with generative adversarial networks. Neurocomputing **345**, 103–113 (2019)
29. Zhang, X.Y., Wang, S., Yun, X.: Bidirectional active learning: a two-way exploration into unlabeled and labeled data set. IEEE Trans. Neural Netw. Learn. Syst. **26**(12), 3034–3044 (2015)
30. Zhang, X.Y., Wang, S., Zhu, X., Yun, X., Wu, G., Wang, Y.: Update vs. upgrade: modeling with indeterminate multi-class active learning. Neurocomputing **162**, 163–170 (2015)
31. Zhang, X.: Interactive patent classification based on multi-classifier fusion and active learning. Neurocomputing **127**, 200–205 (2014)
32. Zhang, Y., Li, K., Li, K., Wang, L., Zhong, B., Fu, Y.: Image super-resolution using very deep residual channel attention networks. In: Ferrari, V., Hebert, M., Sminchisescu, C., Weiss, Y. (eds.) ECCV 2018. LNCS, vol. 11211, pp. 294–310. Springer, Cham (2018). https://doi.org/10.1007/978-3-030-01234-2_18
33. Zhu, H., Long, M., Wang, J., Cao, Y.: Deep hashing network for efficient similarity retrieval. In: Thirtieth AAAI Conference on Artificial Intelligence (2016)
34. Zhu, X., Li, Z., Zhang, X.Y., Li, C., Liu, Y., Xue, Z.: Residual invertible spatio-temporal network for video super-resolution. In: AAAI Conference on Artificial Intelligence (2019)
35. Zhu, X., Li, Z., Zhang, X., Li, H., Xue, Z., Wang, L.: Generative adversarial image super-resolution through deep dense skip connections. In: Computer Graphics Forum, vol. 37, pp. 289–300. Wiley Online Library (2018)
36. Zhu, X., Liu, J., Wang, J., Li, C., Lu, H.: Sparse representation for robust abnormality detection in crowded scenes. Pattern Recogn. **47**(5), 1791–1799 (2014)
37. Zhu, X., Zhang, X., Zhang, X.Y., Xue, Z., Wang, L.: A novel framework for semantic segmentation with generative adversarial network. J. Vis. Commun. Image Represent. **58**, 532–543 (2019)

Dynamic Multi-label Learning
with Multiple New Labels

Lun Wang, Wentao Xiao, and Shan Ye$^{(\boxtimes)}$

College of Computer Science and Technology, Donghua University,
Shanghai, China
lifeng@dhu.edu.cn

Abstract. In a traditional multi-label learning task, an instance or object often has multiple labels. Previous works assume that the class labels are always fixed, i.e, the class labels in the test set are the same as that in the training set. Different from previous methods, we study a new problem setting where multiple new labels emerge in a dynamic environment. In this paper, we decompose the multiple labels pool to adjust the dynamic environment. The proposed method has several functions: classify instances on currently known labels, detect the emergence of several new labels then separate them using clustering, and construct a new classifier for each new label that works collaboratively with the classifier for known labels. Experimental results on publicly available data sets demonstrate that our method achieves superior performance, compared with the state-of-the-arts.

Keywords: Multi-label learning · Clustering · Emerging new labels · Incremental learning

1 Introduction

In the traditional supervised learning, only one label is often to be predicted for each instance [10,13]. However, in many practical application, one instance might be associated with multiple labels simultaneously. For example, an image may be complicated and contain multiple topics [1,18]; in the document classification tasks, an article may be related to several semantic labels [14]; in the gene function prediction and classification tasks, a gene may have multiple isolated functions [3,16].

In recent years, some methods have been proposed to process such data and achieve great performance [2,5,7,18]. For example, multi-instance multi-label learning (MIML) [2] is a recent proposed framework for training multiple labels model for already known labels and has some variant adopting algorithms based on that [4,6]. The algorithms mentioned above ignore a fact that data stream might emerge some unseen new labels. To solve this problem with the situation of streaming data, there exist some experimental methods being proposed to revise a pre-trained model as the new labels emerging by multiple iterations, such as

© Springer Nature Switzerland AG 2019
Y. Zhao et al. (Eds.): ICIG 2019, LNCS 11903, pp. 421–431, 2019.
https://doi.org/10.1007/978-3-030-34113-8_35

Multi-Label Learning with Emerging New Labels (MuENL) [8]. However, this kind of method is only able to deal with one single new label in one iteration. In other words, when the test data contain multiple new labels in one iteration, this method will take the multiple new labels as just one new label. This will lead to degenerating performance.

To meet the above challenge, we propose a novel multi-label learning method which can handle multiple new labels emerging in one iteration. In order to make the proposed method better adopt to the complicated environment, we integrate some features into the algorithm [8], which can achieve significant improvement. With the dynamic multi-label learning setting, we assume that objects arrive in a data stream, and no ground truths for class labels are available in the test data stream at all times, except for the initial training data set. Our method consists of four components: (1) A linear classifier is constructed to optimize both the pairwise label ranking loss and the classification loss on the known labels; (2) a new outlier detector based on both initial and test data stream are constructed; (3) the cluster for the emerging new labels are found based on the Density-based spatial clustering of applications with noise (DBSCAN) [9]; (4) a classifier updating procedure can incorporate new labels to produce a robust classifier. This can tolerate detection errors for the future data stream which contains the same new label, and then remodel the detector for each new label identified.

The rest of the paper is organized as follows: The Sect. 2 describes some related work about the multi-label learning, incremental learning, and outlier detection. Section 3 introduces the problem formation and the details of our algorithm. Section 4 describe the experiments, followed by the conclusion in Sect. 5.

2   Related Work

In this section we review some related works of our proposed method, which mainly include multi-label learning, incremental learning and outlier detection, successively.

Multi-label classification is a special case of the typical classification problem where one instance may be associated with multiple labels. The multi-label classification problem has been a question of great interest in a wide range of real-world applications in recent years, such as image annotation [15], text classification [17,18], and so on. Formally, multi-label classification can be thought as a generalization of multi-class classification. For given input space $\mathbf{X} = \{x_1, x_2, \cdots, x_n\}$, the classification is aim to predict $\hat{y} \in 2^{\mathbf{L}}$ where $2^{\mathbf{L}}$ is a powerset of label set $\mathbf{L}$, so that each predicted output is a subset to the label set. The common techniques to perform multi-label learning are problem transformation methods and adapted algorithms [20]. The problem transformation methods try to transform the origin problem into multiple traditional single-label classification problems (including binary-class and multi-class), then apply off-the-shelf algorithms to the transformed equivalent problem set. For example, *Binary Relevance* (BR) [19] is the most common technique which simply decomposes multi-label task into multiple binary classification independently, each of which is to predict single label in label set. Due to the neglect of labels correlations, BR has been criticized for poor performance [20,21]. There are many researches that take the label correlation into account [22,23].

Furthermore, the methods mentioned above all assume that class label numbers are in a fixed count, thus, they cannot not be applied to our problem setting. To fit with the dynamic multi-label learning setting, one may use *incremental learning* to cope with potential infinite data stream. The goal of *incremental learning* is for the learning model to learn new data without forgetting its existing knowledge, i.e., without re-training from scratch. One common approach to perform incremental learning is batch-incremental learning [12,24]. When new arrived data filled up a batch with enough amount of data, the system will sufficient to train/update a good performing classifier by exploited such batch of data. Moreover, in real-world dynamic scenario, new unknown labels may emerge with the stream of data. Learning new labels from data stream is a kind of incremental learning is called *class-incremental learning* (C-IL) [25]. Here our multi-label learning setting with emerging new labels is the combination of batch-incremental learning and class incremental learning.

In multi-instance multi-label learning case, a new label may co-occur with known labels which makes it difficult to separate instances with new labels only from instances with known labels only. Besides, to train new effective classifiers for new labels, one need filter out the uninformative data whose labels are all known. The straightforward strategy to handle such data selection problem is design a detection to determine whether observed instance has new unknown labels. Zhu et al. proposed *MuENL* [8] approach to address above challenges by taking both feature and label spaces into account. As for the detection solution for new unknown label, *MuENL* regards it as an outlier detection problem. The batch to train classifiers for new unknown labels in *MuENL* only select from the data whose features deviate from the general data sets as the new label data samples. It is worth mentioned that *MuENL* only constructs one classifier for one batch of observed instance to predict one new label or one meta-label [26] that encapsulates a subset of labels.

3   The MuPND Approach

The challenge here is to study a robust classifier for multi-labels containing both new and old labels. Furthermore, we also integrate the DBSCAN algorithm to address the awkward problems when there are multi-new labels erupting concurrently in just one iteration. We call our method proposed in this paper MuPND.

3.1   Problem Formulation

Our approach and experiment are based on a open dynamic multi-learning setting, we have an initial labeled training data set, and then the unlabeled test data come successively in a data stream fashion. Suppose the $\mathcal{X}$ denote the input feature space, and we define the $X_0 = [\boldsymbol{x}_{-n+1}, \cdots, \boldsymbol{x}_{-1}, \boldsymbol{x}_0]^\top \subseteq \mathcal{X}$ as the observed initial data set in the training process. Then the unlabeled test data stream contains an instance x_t which probably has a new label at the time t. Let $X_t, t \in \{1, 2, \cdots, T\}$ be the accessible data trunk at time t.

We denote $c_0 = \{1, 2, \cdots, \ell\}$ as the already known labels in the initial training data set. And the number in the vector c represents the index of the labels set. At the time t, the original c_0 is being updated to c_t and initial ℓ is being updated to ℓ', the ℓ' represents the maximum numbers of labels set. That is, at the time t, supposing we have detected $n(n \geq 0)$ new labels, the label collection will be enlarged with n new labels, $\ell' = \ell + n : c_t = c_{t-1} \cup \{\ell'\}$. Let $Y_0 = [y_{-n+1}, \cdots, y_{-1}, y_0] \in \{-1, 1\}^{\ell \times n}$ be the initial label matrix of X_0, and $y_t = [y_{t,1}, \cdots, y_{t,\ell}]$ represents the label vector of the test data x_t at the time t. The $y_{t,j}$ has two opposite values:$\{-1, 1\}$. If x_t contains the j-th label, the $y_{t,j}$ should be 1, otherwise $y_{t,j}$ should be -1.

Theorem 1. *Given the initial X_0 and Y_0, our goal is to find a function set $\mathcal{H}_t = [h_{t,1}, h_{t,2}, \cdots, h_{t,\ell}]$, where $h_{i,j}$ has two opposite values $\{-1, 1\}^\ell$ represents whether owns j-th class label, $j \in \{1, 2, \cdots, \ell\}$, at time $t \in \{1, 2, \cdots, T\}$. And for each x_t, we output $\hat{y}_t = \mathcal{H}_t(x_t)$ as the predicted label vector.*

3.2 The Algorithm

We assume that the ground truth is not available throughout the entire test data stream. The problems needed to be solved in new multi-labels learning mainly lie in two aspects. The first one is to construct a detector to identify new labels. The Second one is to take multiple new labels apart if they erupt in one iteration, that is, when we might need to update the model for multiple labels concurrently. Otherwise, there is a considerably great chance that we might mistakenly train one weight vector for multiple new labels.

And we approach this problems mentioned above by using the following two core technologies. (i) Firstly, we use a extended isolation forest called MuENL-Forest [8] which will generate a outlier detector $\mathcal{D}_t(x_t)$ based on the previous training data and label attributes. If the output of $\mathcal{D}_t(x_t) = 1$, then it indicates that the current x_t contains a new label. Otherwise, if the output is -1, it indicates there is no new label in x_t. (ii) Secondly, we adopt the Density-based spatial clustering of applications with noise (DBSCAN) to the buffer container when it reaches the pre-set maximum. That is, for the data with new labels in the container, we cluster them into several groups, and each group maps to one new label. Finally, when the cluster procedure finishes, we execute the classifier model updating process step by step, and each step depended on the previous step in order to get a more robust model: $\mathcal{H}_t = [h_{t,1}, h_{t,2}, \cdots, h_{t,\ell}] \rightarrow \mathcal{H}_t' = [h_{t,1}, h_{t,2}, \cdots, h_{t,\ell}, \mathcal{D}_t]$.

Algorithm 1 summarizes the MuPND method. It has four components: (i) the multi-label classifier for $\mathcal{H}_0$. (ii) MuENLForest detector $\mathcal{D}_t$. (iii) DBSCAN explicitly decomposes the multiple new labels lying in the buffer pool into n new labels. (iv) update the model $\mathcal{H}_t \rightarrow \mathcal{H}_{t+n}$. One point we need to declare is that the weight sampling vector are used to reduce the probability of previous instances being selected during the construction of MuENLForest, and give a preference to recent instances. Therefore we let the s being multiplied by a decay factor 0.8.

Algorithm 1. The overview of MuPND

Input: Initial training data: X_0, Y_0, C_0
Output: Function set $\mathcal{H}_t$ for each $\boldsymbol{x}_t$
1: Get an initial $\mathcal{H}_0$ by training X_0, Y_0;
2: Construct an initial new label detector $\mathcal{D}_0$ based on X_0;
3: Initialize sampling weight vector $\boldsymbol{s}_0 = \mathbf{1}_{|X_0|}$
4: $\mathcal{H}_1 = [\mathcal{H}_0, \mathcal{D}_0]; \mathcal{D}_1 = \mathcal{D}_0$;
5: **repeat**
6:    Receive a new instance (never seen before) $\boldsymbol{x}_t, X_t = [X_{t-1}; \boldsymbol{x}_t^\top]$;
7:    Enlarge the sampling weight vector $\boldsymbol{s}_t = [\boldsymbol{s}_{t-1}; 1]$ simultaneously;
8:    **if** $\mathcal{D}_t(\boldsymbol{x}_t) \geq 1$ **then**
9:       Add $\boldsymbol{x}_t$ to Buffer;
10:      **if** $|Buffer| \geq$ MAX_BUFFER_SIZE **then**
11:         Execute DBSCAN to decompose Buffer container;
12:         Get n clusters for n new labels;
13:         **repeat**
14:            Create $\mathcal{D}_{t+i}$ and $\mathcal{H}_{t+i}$ from $i = 0$, and each $\mathcal{D}_{t+i}$ depends on $\mathcal{D}_{t+i-1}$ iteratively;
15:         **until** $i > n$
16:         Empty Buffer ;
17:         $\ell \leftarrow \ell + n; \boldsymbol{v}_t = \boldsymbol{v}_{t-n} \cup \{\ell\}$;
18:         Update the $\boldsymbol{s}_t \leftarrow 0.8\boldsymbol{s}_t$;
19:      **end if**
20:   **end if**
21:   $c_t = c_{t-n}; \mathcal{D}_t = \mathcal{D}_{t-n}; \mathcal{H}_t = \mathcal{H}_{t-n}$
22: **until**
23: **return** $\mathcal{H}_t$

The Linear Multi-label Classifier. Formally, given an instance $\boldsymbol{x}$, we define the linear classifier on label i as

$$h_i(\boldsymbol{x}) = \text{sign}\left(\boldsymbol{w}_i^\top \boldsymbol{x} + b_i\right) \tag{1}$$

While we minimize the misclassification loss and the pairwise label ranking loss in order to obtain the overall performance. The convex optimization for each $\boldsymbol{w}_i$ can be written as

$$\min_{w_i, b_i, \xi, \zeta} \frac{1}{2}\|\boldsymbol{w}_i\|^2 + C_1 \sum_{k=1}^n \xi_k + C_2 \sum_{j=1}^\ell \sum_{k=1}^n \zeta_{j,k}$$
$$\text{s.t.} \quad y_{i,k} f_{i,k} \geq 1 - \xi_k$$
$$\Delta_{j,k}\left(f_{i,k} - f_{j,k}\right) \geq 1 - \zeta_{j,k} \tag{2}$$
$$\xi_k \geq 0, \zeta_{j,k} \geq 0$$
$$j \in \{1, 2, \cdots, \ell\}, k \in \{1, 2, \cdots, n\}$$

In details, $\Delta_{j,k} = y_{i,k} - y_{j,k}, f_{i,k} = \boldsymbol{w}_i^\top \boldsymbol{x}_k + b_i$, and C_1, C_2 are two parameters to trade off. To simplify the calculative process, we replace the b_i by adding an attribute value 1 at the end of $\boldsymbol{x}_k$, then $f_{i,k} = \boldsymbol{w}_i^\top [\boldsymbol{x}_k; 1]$. Equation (2) can be rewritten as

$$
\min_{\boldsymbol{w}_i} \sum_{j=1}^{\ell} \sum_{k=1}^{n} \left[1 - (y_{i,k} - y_{j,k}) (f_{i,k} - f_{j,k})\right]_+ \\
+ \lambda_1 \sum_{k=1}^{n} \left[1 - y_{i,k} f_{i,k}\right]_+ + \frac{\lambda_2}{2} \|\boldsymbol{w}_i\|^2
\tag{3}
$$

MuENLForest for New Label Detection. Here, we suppose the new label appears when an instance has an unseen co-occurrence feature or label. There are some previous work that have already done a nice job, such as the isolation forest (iForest) [11]. However, the traditional iForest only considers the input feature space, and employs the average path length calculated by the test instance traverses over all trees as the anomaly score. And whether the instance contains a new label depends on whether it locates in a spare region. Since instances with new labels may share the same dense region of instances with some common known labels. Therefore, we adopt an extended iForest called MuENLForest [8] as our new label detector, which captures the characteristics in both the feature space and the label patterns.

We can briefly describe the construction of MuENLForest in following procedures: MuENLForest consists of g MuENLTree; and each MuENLTree is built using a random subset of $(X_t, \mathcal{H}_t(X_t))$ of size ψ (pre-set constant value) using sampling weight $\boldsymbol{s}_t$. And the novel part of the MuENLForest is that a covering ball is being attached at each leaf node of the tree. The following part gives a detail about how the covering ball functions in the outlier detection.

Theorem 2. *MuENLTree is a binary tree consists of internal nodes and leaf nodes. Let $\boldsymbol{a} = [\boldsymbol{x}, \mathcal{H}_t(\boldsymbol{x})]$ denote the training sample with predictive values. Each internal node is being split into two son nodes by the test: $\|\boldsymbol{a}^q - \boldsymbol{p}_1\| \leq \|\boldsymbol{a}^q - \boldsymbol{p}_2\|$, where $\boldsymbol{p}_1$ and $\boldsymbol{p}_2$ are two cluster center both having q attributes and $\boldsymbol{a}^q$ is the q projection of $\boldsymbol{a}$. Each leaf node has a ball covering S satisfying radius $r = \max_{x \in S} \|\boldsymbol{a} - \boldsymbol{m}\|$, where $\boldsymbol{m} = \text{mean}(S)$.*

As a result, for those instances which contain the similar features and attributes, they will locate on the same leaf node. After we have constructed the MuENLForest, that is $\mathcal{D}_t(\cdot)$, we are ready to predict the new label. If $\mathcal{D}_t(\boldsymbol{x}_t) = 1$, it indicates the instance $\boldsymbol{x}_t$ contains a new label. Otherwise, if $\mathcal{D}_t(\boldsymbol{x}_t) = -1$, it does not have a new label. More specifically, if the instance falls on the same leaf node but outside the covering ball, it suggests that the instance has some attributes different from others. Therefore, the instance holds a new label in a considerably high probability.

DBSCAN to Decompose the Buffer Pool. Every time, when the new labels Buffer pool reaches the BUFFER_MAX_SIZE, the traditional approaches will regard all the instances in the Buffer Pool have a common new label. Under the real circumstance, we might meet the situation that the instances in one Buffer Pool will contain multiple labels in one iteration. That is, for example, Buffer pool contains BUFFER_MAX_SIZE instances emerging with $n(n > 1)$ new labels. Such behaviors that mistakenly training one model for multiple new labels can be avoided by applying the DBSCAN algorithms. Generally, the DBSCAN decomposes the Buffer container into n central clusters, which can improve the robust of the classifier for multiple new labels. The following part gives details how the DBSCAN functions and being integrated with the decomposition process.

The DBSCAN is a density-based clustering non-parametric algorithm, which can describe the closeness of sample distribution. In this paper, we assume that instances with the same new label will locate in the same cluster. Therefore, different clusters will represent the different labels. It makes sense, because we have already illustrated that among the MuENLForest leaf nodes, those instances with new labels are determined by their distance away from the normal instances as mentioned in the above section.

There is one other thing worth noting is that we need to update the classifier of new label located in each cluster dependently. That is, supposing we have trained the classifier for the i-th label, the next step for us to train the classifier for the $i + 1$-th label are based on the i-th label classifier.

Multi-label Classifier Update. Finally, once the DBSCAN has completed the decomposition process for multiple new labels, we can update the multi-label classifier. The update process includes the construction for new labels, and update of the existing model for known labels. Here we adopt a previous method [9], that is to introduce a latent variable which estimates the true label assignment of each instance in $\mathcal{X}_t$, where a predicted label by the detector is the initial value of the latent variable. Then the optimization process simultaneously learns this latent label assignment and the classifier which best fits the data. In this way, the learned classifier is more tolerant to the errors of the detector. The solution can be formulated as the following:

Suppose there are n clusters collected in the buffer pool, and $X_{B,i}$ represents collection of instances containing i-th new labels. X_U is the set of instances with (predicted) known labels only, where $X_U = X_t \backslash X_B$ and $X_B = [X_{B,1}, X_{B,2}, \ldots, X_{B,n}]$. Let $\boldsymbol{p} = [p_1, p_2, \cdots, p_m]^\top$ be the unknown assignment of the new label of the $X_{t,i} = [X_{B,i}; X_U]$ where m is the number of instances in $[X_{B,i}; X_U]$; and $p_k = 1$ if $\boldsymbol{x}_k \in [X_{B,i}; X_U]$; $p_k = 0$ otherwise.

Different from Eq. (3), we replace $y_{i,k}$ with $2p_k - 1$. As a result, the optimization problem of building classifier $\boldsymbol{w}_a$ and learning $\boldsymbol{p}$ for the new label ℓ is cast as follows:

$$\min_{\boldsymbol{w}_a, \boldsymbol{p}} \sum_{j=1}^{\ell} \sum_{k=1}^{m} [1 - (2p_k - 1 - y_{j,k})(f_{\ell,k} - f_{j,k})]_+$$

$$+ \lambda_1 \sum_{k=1}^{m} [1 - (2p_k - 1) f_{\ell,k}]_+ + \frac{\lambda_2}{2} \|\boldsymbol{w}_a\|^2 + \frac{\lambda_3}{2} \|\boldsymbol{p}\|^2 \tag{4}$$

$$\text{s.t. } p_k \in \{0,1\}, k \in \{1,2,\cdots,m\}$$

Since above equation is a NP-hard problem. Therefore, we relax the constraint from $p_k \in \{0,1\}$ to $p_k \in [0,1]$, then optimize $\boldsymbol{p}$ and $\boldsymbol{w}_a$ alternately. That is, we can do the optimization in Eqs. (5) and (6).

$$\min_{\boldsymbol{p}} \sum_{j=1}^{\ell} \sum_{k=1}^{m} [1 - (2p_k - 1 - y_{j,k})(f_{\ell,k} - f_{j,k})]_+$$

$$+ \lambda_1 \sum_{k=1}^{m} [1 - (2p_k - 1) f_{\ell,k}]_+ + \frac{\lambda_3}{2} \|\boldsymbol{p}\|^2 \tag{5}$$

$$\text{s.t. } p_k \in [0,1], k \in \{1,2,\cdots,m\}$$

After we have solve the Eqs. (5) and (6) using the subgradient of the objective function. Then we project $\boldsymbol{p}$ to $[0,1]$: $\boldsymbol{p} \leftarrow \min(1, [\boldsymbol{p}]_+)$ to satisfy the box constraint.

$$\min_{\boldsymbol{w}_a} \sum_{j=1}^{\ell} \sum_{k=1}^{m} [1 - (2p_k - 1 - y_{j,k})(f_{\ell,k} - f_{j,k})]_+$$

$$+ \lambda_1 \sum_{k=1}^{m} [1 - (2p_k - 1) f_{\ell,k}]_+ + \frac{\lambda_2}{2} \|\boldsymbol{w}_a\|^2 \tag{6}$$

4   Experiments

4.1   Experiment on Yeast Data Set

To evaluate the performance of MuPND approach, we use the yeast data set. We divide the data set into two parts, the first one is initial training data set with already known class labels, and the second one is unlabeled instances. To ensure that the emerging order of the test data in second part has no effects on the result, we shuffle the data stream randomly. Table 1 shows the details about our experiment data information. As shown in the Table 1, there are 1313 instances with known labels in the initial training data set and 402 unlabeled instances as test data stream.

Firstly, as illustrated above in the Algorithm section, we get a initial classifier and outlier detection forest by training the fist part of data. After the training process has already completed, we adjust the BUFFER_MAX_SIZE to a enough big integer to simulate the situation that we might meet multiple new labels in one iteration. In our experiment using yeast data set, 3 new labels (A to C) are

Table 1. Yeast data set information

	Instances	Dimensions	Labels
Initial training data	1313	103	11
Unlabeled data stream	402	103	14

emerging in one buffer pool, that is one iteration. Then we apply the DBSCAN to split the buffer pool into three groups which represent 3 new labels. Table 2 shows the parameters used in the MuPND, including the MinPts and radius parameter of DBSCAN used in the experiment.

Table 2. Parameters used in MuPND

Parameter	Model	Description
$|\text{Buffer}| = 127$		BUFFER_MAX_SIZE
$\lambda_1, \lambda_2 \in \{0.001, 0.01, 0.1, 1\}$	Multi-label classifier	Trade-off parameter
$|q| = 5$ $g = 100$ $\psi = 256$	MuENLForest	New label detection Forest construction
$\text{MinPts} = 5$ $\varepsilon = 1.325$	DBSCAN	Two pre-set parameters
$\lambda_3 = 1$	Multi-label classifier update	Trade-off parameter

4.2 Experiment Result

When DBSCAN finishes the cluster tasks, we update the classifier separately and dependently for each new label. To be more specifically, firstly we train a new classifier for new label, supposedly A, and then append the weight vector w_a to the previous Model. Once we get a new Model for new label A, then we need to retrain the detection forest using the predicted values by new Model. That is, every time we update Model, we will use the Model from previous step. After each updating the label classifier for one new label, we evaluate the performance of the classifier. The experiment results are shown in the Table 3. We evaluate the average precision.

On the same data set, we conducted experiments with the method proposed in this paper and the MuENL method respectively. The experiment data are shown below. Through this comparative experiment, we can see that in general, the algorithm in this paper can achieve better performance in Average Precision.

Table 3. Average precision

	P1	P2	P3
Our method	0.7092	0.6841	0.84079
MuEND	0.69512	0.73955	0.69363

5   Conclusions

The paper proposes a dynamic multi-label learning method for handling with multiple new labels. The core idea of decomposing the new label pool into multiple new labels separately has enabled the whole problem to be solved satisfactorily. The public data set demonstrate that the performance, especially average precision, get improved by our method. In the future, we will try to optimize other loss functions, such as ranking loss and hamming loss.

References

1. Boutell, M.R., Luo, J., Shen, X., Brown, C.M.: Learning multilabel scene classification. Pattern Recogn. **37**(9), 1757–1771 (2004)
2. Zhou, Z.-H., Zhang, M.-L., Huang, S.-J., Li, Y.-F.: Multi-instance multi-label learning. Artif. Intell. **176**(1), 2291–2320 (2012)
3. Li, Y., Ji, S., Kumar, S., Ye, J., Zhou, Z.: Drosophila gene expression pattern annotation through multi-instance multi-label learning. In: Proceedings of the 21st International Joint Conference on Artificial Intelligence, Pasadena, CA, pp. 1445–1450 (2009)
4. Zhou, Z.-H., Zhang, M.-L.: Multi-instance multi-label learning with application to scene classification. In: Advances in Neural Information Processing Systems 19, pp. 1609–1616. MIT Press, Cambridge (2007)
5. Li, C., Wei, F., Dong, W., Liu, Q., Wang, X., Zhang, X.: Dynamic structure embedded online multiple-output regression for streaming data. IEEE Trans. Pattern Anal. Mach. Intell. (T-PAMI) **41**(2), 323–336 (2019)
6. Nguyen, N.: A new SVM approach to multi-instance multi-label learning. In: Proceedings of the 10th IEEE International Conference on Data Mining, Sydney, Australia, pp. 384–392 (2010)
7. Li, C., Wei, F., Yan, J., Dong, W., Liu, Q., Zha, H.: Self-paced multi-task learning. In: AAAI (2016)
8. Zhu, Y., Ting, K.M., Zhou, Z.-H.: Multi-label learning with emerging new labels. IEEE Trans. Knowl. Data Eng. **30**(10), 1901–1914 (2018)
9. Ester, M., Kriegel, H.P., Sander, J., Xu, X.: A density-based algorithm for discovering clusters in large spatial databases with noise. In: KDD (1996)
10. Li, C., Liu, Q., Dong, W., Zhu, X., Liu, J., Lu, H.: Human age estimation based on locality and ordinal information. IEEE Trans. Cybern. **45**(11), 2522–2534 (2014)
11. Liu, F.T., Ting, K.M., Zhou, Z.H.: Isolation forest. In: Proceeding ICDM 2008 Proceedings of the 8th IEEE International Conference on Data Mining, pp. 413–422 (2008)
12. Ruping, S.: Incremental learning with support vector machines. In: Proceedings of the 1st IEEE International Conference on Data Mining, pp. 641–642 (2001)

13. Li, C., Liu, Q., Liu, J., Lu, H.: Learning ordinal discriminative features for age estimation. In: IEEE Computer Vision and Pattern Recognition (2012)
14. Gao, S., Wu, W., Lee, C., Chua, T.: A MFoM learning approach to robust multiclass multi-label text categorization. In: ICML (2004)
15. Song, L., et al.: A deep multi-modal CNN for multi-instance multi-label image classification. IEEE Trans. Image Process. **27**(12), 6025–6038 (2018)
16. Li, C., Liu, Q., Liu, J., Lu, H.: Ordinal distance metric learning for image ranking. IEEE Trans. Neural Netw. Learn. Syst. **26**(7), 1551–1559 (2015)
17. Burkhardt, S., Kramer, S.: Online multi-label dependency topic models for text classification. Mach. Learn. **107**(5), 859–886 (2018)
18. Li, C., Wei, F., Yan, J., Zhang, X., Liu, Q., Zha, H.: A self-paced regularization framework for multilabel learning. IEEE Trans. Neural Netw. Learn. Syst. **29**(6), 2660–2666 (2018)
19. Boutell, M.R., Luo, J., Shen, X., Brown, C.M.: Learning multi-label scene classification. Pattern Recogn. **37**(9), 1757–1771 (2004)
20. Zhang, M., Zhou, Z.: A review on multi-label learning algorithms. IEEE Trans. Knowl. Data Eng. **26**(8), 1819–1837 (2014)
21. Zhang, M.L., Li, Y.K., Liu, X.Y., et al.: Binary relevance for multi-label learning: an overview. Front. Comput. Sci. **12**(2), 191–202 (2018)
22. Fürnkranz, J., Hüllermeier, E., Mencía, E.L., Brinker, K.: Multilabel classification via calibrated label ranking. Mach. Learn. **73**(2), 133–153 (2008)
23. Read, J., Pfahringer, B., Holmes, G., Frank, E.: Classifier chains for multi-label classification. Mach. Learn. **85**(3), 333–359 (2011)
24. Read, J., Bifet, A., Pfahringer, B., Holmes, G.: Batch-incremental versus instance-incremental learning in dynamic and evolving data. In: Hollmén, J., Klawonn, F., Tucker, A. (eds.) IDA 2012. LNCS, vol. 7619, pp. 313–323. Springer, Heidelberg (2012). https://doi.org/10.1007/978-3-642-34156-4_29
25. Zhang, B., Su, J., Xu, X.: A class-incremental learning method for multi-class support vector machines in text classification. In: 2006 International Conference on Machine Learning and Cybernetics, Dalian, China, pp. 2581–2585 (2006)
26. Read, J., Puurula, A., Bifet, A.: Multi-label classification with meta-labels. In: 2014 IEEE International Conference on Data Mining, Shenzhen, pp. 941–946 (2014)

Density Map Estimation for Crowded Chicken

Dong Cheng, Tianze Rong, and Guitao Cao[✉]

East China Normal University, Shanghai, China
dong_cheng0525@foxmail.com, 51174500119@stu.ecnu.edu.cn,
gtcao@sei.ecnu.edu.cn

Abstract. Intensive breeding is the trend of the breeding industry. In order to make it more convenient to manage and reduce labor costs, sometimes we need to estimate the number of individuals in the poultry farm and discriminate the density distribution to help scientific management. At the same time, crowd density estimation is a developing research direction in deep learning. There are both similarities and differences between crowd counting task and chicken counting task. Aimed at the characteristics of poultry farm images, this paper presents a solution to density estimation and counting of poultry individuals in poultry farm by deep network method. We designed an end to end model and transform the problem into a pixel-level classification problem to get the density map.

Keywords: Density estimation · Flock counting · Pixel level classification

1 Introduction

Computer vision detection is playing a more and more important role in whether production or daily life. In this case, it's of imperative to estimate the density distribution of poultry in the breeding area so that makes it possible to analyze the growth of poultry. Object detection and crowd counting are two of the most relevant research directions. The method is supposed to be specialized while its requirements are also different from the ordinary detection since density counting in the chicken house is distinctive. Lack of detection of the results is not of particular concern, but the overall distribution of the flock is the focus. Specialists can infer the status of the chickens through changes in the distribution of the flock. We find in the image that it is restricted by the situation of uncertain-view, uncertain-brightness, and position-indeterminate. Usually, some chickens are incomplete within the camera lens range. Moreover, images sometimes need to be split and processed separately because of image resolution and interfering objects. It may split one chicken into two or three parts such as Fig. 1. So most

National Natural Science Foundation of China under Grant.

Fig. 1. As shown in the figure, some chickens are divided into multiple parts when one image is split, and the same situation exists at the edge of the image.

of the previous methods mentioned e.g. object detection does not take it into account. To effectively achieve the goal, a certain number of pictures were collected and analyzed, including daytime and night illumination. While the clarity of the images obtained is limited by the environment inside the chicken house. At the same time, it is hard to point out the head of the chicken so accurate such as crowd counting dataset. Considering that the aim of the task is not the location of a particular target, but the aggregation of the entire flock, we transfer the problem into a pixel-level problem, i.e. discriminate all pixels in the image into two classes, chicken or not. After that, we try to get the result density map by some other operations.

The paper is organized as follows. Section 2 discusses the related work. Section 3 shows the proposed technical approach followed with a description of dataset used in this paper in Sect. 4. Experiments are presented in Sects. 5 and 6 concludes this paper.

2   Related Work

Active learning is a good way to reduce the cost of manual labeling. [1] proposed a novel bidirectional active learning algorithm that explores into both unlabeled and labeled data sets simultaneously in a two-way process. [2] aimed to address the issues and develop a novel framework for effective and efficient model learning. [3] took this idea to video detection and proposed a novel weakly supervised framework. [5] used active learning to select the most informative patents for labeling.

Image segmentation is an important field in computer vision. The classic method is to use Sobel or other operators on the image. Since there are some deep learning method has come out recently, at present, the best performance at present is semantic-based image segmentation. [14] applied an up-sampling structure on image segmentation first. [21] developed the up-sampling structure before and increased the accuracy in medical image segmentation. [4] proposed a novel post-processing method based on Generative Adversarial Network is explored to reinforce spatial contiguity in the output label maps. Of course, [22] can not be ignored, it used a ROIAlign layer and mask branch to improve the accuracy of both detection and segmentation, whats more [23] is the latest development of the Mask-RCNN.

Crowd counting is the most similar task before. Most of the previous works used a multi-column architecture. [9] combined two different convolution kernels for feature extraction and obtained a good result. [10] trained a custom network with three CNN columns, each of which with a different receptive filed could capture a specific range of head sizes. However, it's high time-consuming to run three CNN columns. [12] proposed to predict which column to run for each input image patch. But the models above are all difficult to implement and they are slow at inference. To overcome the limitation, Li et al. replaced some pooling layers in the CNN with dilated convolutional filters [11,13]. Walker detect [18] in the street also combined a task of density estimation. Otherwise, [19] noticed the impact of human body structure on density estimation. [8] propose a novel feature selection based method for facial age estimation. A pre-trained model was designed to detect all kinds of parts of the human body. Whats more, [24] presented an end-to-end differentiable optical flow network for unsupervised optical flow learning. And [25] purposed a novel tube-and-droplet framework to effectively capture the rich information in 3D tube representation.

We also considered the efficiency and accuracy of the method from some other works before. [7] introduced a good method for steaming data to regress and [6] combined simultaneous sample and feature selection tasks to improve the result.

In this paper, we concluded the model structures and ideas before. It is convinced that the direction of density estimation is multi-scale image information acquisition and expansion of the receptive field. Dilated convolution [11] and multi-column [10,12] both aim at enlarging the receptive field and reducing missing pixel information, thus we considered Fully Convolutional Networks(FCN) [14], replacing the last few fully connected layers by convolutional layers to make efficient end-to-end learning and inference that can take arbitrary input size. Its up-sampling operation is a useful way to expanse the receptive field. We combined the advantage of FCN and designed our own model to finish this work, and then get the density map by a density estimation with the feature map that Network output.

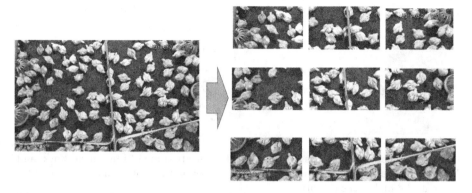

Fig. 2. The images we collected are shown. And when we split the source images, we may take the object apart, which influence the result a lot.

3   The Proposed Approach

3.1   Pixel Level Classification

Compared to general target detection, the process of density estimation needs to expand the receptive field in the process of extracting features. Like the dilate convolution in [13] and so on. Instead of traditional object counting work, we try to point each pixel of the object to avoid complex conditional constraints on detection. So we choose FCN [14] structure to achieve this goal. This net is convenient and converts our work into a binary classification problem. Of course, we also regress some other parameters in a pixel-level classification to finish the estimation task. We named it ChickenNet, which is an end to end model and the size of the input image is arbitrary.

3.2   Net Design

Fully connected network is widely used in image segmentation. Unlike other density estimation tasks, we have some particular difficulties. First of all, there is no such amount of images to train, and the crowd counting datasets are also invalid in this task. Whatsmore, the training set of the flock is difficult to calibrate. So we try another way that regardless of the object as a point for density estimation. We designed a network based on FCN to discriminate all pixels on the graph into two categories. And then use the output feature map to get the result. Figure 3 is the main architecture of the network. We choose VGG16 [15] to extract image features, imitate the FCN, remove the last fully connected layer and then perform the up-sampling operation. We can get the result of pixels' classification, which likes a mask of the source image. Then calculate a Gaussian kernel to do Gaussian blur operation, and obtain the final density map. In order to regress the size of the chicken, we add a new parameter S, and then change the loss function for it.

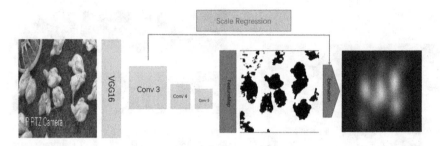

Fig. 3. The image data flow is shown. We get the feature map from our network, and then a special estimation module is designed to generate the Density map. The brighter the area, the higher the density.

3.3   Chicken Scale Estimation

Chicken scale estimation is a very important part in our work. We don't regard the objection as a point differs from other estimation methods, which means we need some different methods to generate the density map. Through a convolutional neural network, we can get the feature map of the images, it helps to determine if there is a target at the pixel location. Of course, we are supposed to have another way to transform it to a density map. In order to estimate the distribution of the chicken, it's essential to know the size of the chicken from the collected images. Therefore, in our ChickenNet model, before up-sampling, we add a fully connected layer to regress the average number of the pixels of each chicken, and the loss function is also changed. For decreasing the influence of the classification task, we define the loss function as following. M is a constant, we set M is 200 to get the best density map.

$$loss = BCEloss + \|S - PS\|_2 / M \tag{1}$$

3.4   Density Map Generating

According to the output feature map, we need to generate a density map quickly and accurately. Kernel density estimation [16] is applied in many other methods of density estimation to get the final heatmap. We first used this method. But, the density of the entire image needs to be updated when calculating the Gaussian kernel for each point, but our output image has too many points to calculate. So it costs too much to generate the density map. However, to some extent, our method has got a mask of all object chickens, which reflected a certain distribution. By calculating a Gaussian kernel and execute Gaussian blur operation, the results are remarkable in our data set. As is shown in Fig. 3.

Gaussian blur is a very simple and common image processing method. Sometimes it may surprise you. This is the process of resetting each pixel value in the image by setting each pixel to the average of the surrounding pixels. And normal distribution is obviously a weight distribution model. Two-dimensional Gaussian function is shown.

Fig. 4. The idea of segmentation while generating a density map is shown. It can be used to improve detection results.

$$G(x, y) = \frac{1}{2\pi\delta^2} e^{(-x^2+y^2)/2\delta^2} \tag{2}$$

And then we need to set the value of δ to calculate the weight matrix. Each point is multiplied by its own weight value, and after accumulating, the Gaussian blur result of the center point is obtained. And in our work, this simple method can help to transform the mask of the source image to a density heat map. The only one should be considered is the size of the Gaussian kernel. To some extent, the size of the object chicken.

4   Dataset

We collected about 100 images from different view angles in some chicken houses. And for these images, it's difficult to point out the chicken head. So we choose other ideas instead of head counting estimation. Before importing the images to the purposed approach, we need to preprocess the collected pictures to improve the accuracy of the estimation. We choose about half of the collected images to make our train set. A mask image for each image in the training set and estimate the average size of the target. For convenience, we assume that the value of the target size is represented by a square box, so one parameter S is enough. As is shown in Fig. 5.

4.1   Image Splitting

The images that we collected are too big to detect and to estimate. In order to reduce noise pixels and the number of pixels that need to be processed. We divide one image into nine parts, just like Fig. 2, then detect chickens in each part. Thanks to the idea of segmentation, it's unnecessary to care if one chicken has been divided into several parts. Because we deal with the problem at pixel-level, and each pixel will only be divided into two classes. Finally, we contact the nine output feature map in order and transform them into a big density map. As is shown in Fig. 4.

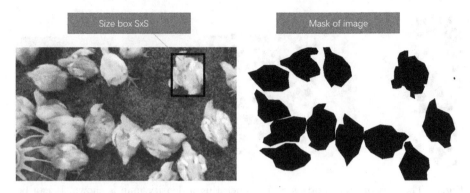

Fig. 5. The train dataset that we made for the model. Including source images, mask images, and their average object size S.

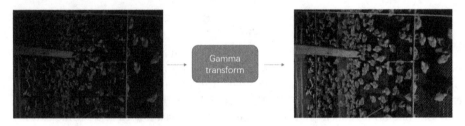

Fig. 6. Use gamma transform to process lower brightness pictures.

4.2 Gamma Luminance Transformation

In the dataset, some images are in a dark situation. So gamma transform is considered. It is shown in Fig. 6. Gamma transform can enhance the contrast of the image, and the basic form of gamma transformation is

$$s = cr^{\gamma} \tag{3}$$

r is the gray value of the input image, s is the gray value of the output image, and c is just a constant. γ is the variable needs to adjust. After some trials, we choose a parameter γ for our collected images.

4.3 Ground Truth

We identified all the locations of the pixels that contain the target, and get a pixel point set as ground truth(GT). In other words, we define some areas of the source image as ground truth. In order to compare this method to others. We count the number of missing and misclassified pixels as an evaluation indicator for the model. We set ChickenNet to predict pixel set as PT. Considering our model outputs more points, we decide to calculate two values as follows. The smaller the values are, the better the effect of the model.

$$P1 = count(PT \setminus GT)/count(GT) \tag{4}$$

Table 1. Comparing two methods

Methods	YoloV3	ChickenNet
P1	16%	1.3%
P2	9%	2.5%

$$P2 = count(GT \setminus PT)/count(GT) \tag{5}$$

5 Experiments

The experiment involves an object detect method (yolov3) [17] and our purposed model. In order to reduce the probability of missed detection, the source images are split into nine parts. And then we compare these two methods by P1 and P2. The scenes of the captured images have similarities, so about ten images is enough to train the detection model. We use about 50 images to test these two methods, and their P1, P2 are shown in Table 1.

5.1 Object Detect Method

We train a yolov3 object detection model to deal with the data. The yolov3 model is one of the best object detection models. And we have also tried other models like yolov2 and faster-RCNN [20], but they all do not work. While training the model, only several train images are required. We make the train set and doesn't box the location of the target where the edge portion is cut. But after detection, still some 'chicken parts' are detected as a complete target. This may influence the final density map result. For example, the edge of the image being cut will have more of the detected object, making it brighter in the density map. After detection, kernel density estimation is considered to generate the density map. The detection output is replaced with a two-dimensional Gaussian kernel at each coordinate point, then superimpose all the Gaussian kernel to get the heat map. As is shown in Fig. 7, all detected locations are identified. And according to the detection result, there are still some missed chickens. Meanwhile, it takes about 3 min for one image to generate its density map, it is too long if we want real-time monitoring.

5.2 ChickenNet Method

The train set has 30 images. Including source images, mask images, and their average object size S. Although the output may result in a little more disturbing pixels, it does not influence the whole distribution; On the other hand, the output density map is still accurate. And the model can be trained quickly. So we can get the conclusion that our method has a higher fault tolerance rate, and can truly reflect the aggregation of chickens for this situation. Meanwhile, our model is easier to train. So it can update itself quicker and easier than other models.

Fig. 7. Yolo v3 detection result and the density map generated by kernel density estimation.

6   Conclusion

In this paper, we present a new approach based on a fully connected network for crowded chicken density estimation and name the new model ChickenNet. We transform the problem into a pixel level problem, and aiming to our image set, we find Gaussian blur idea can simply generate the density map. An end to end model is completed at last. However, we do the other experiment to compare. Use yolo detection model and kernel density estimation to do chicken density estimation task. The result is acceptable but not as good as our proposed model.

References

1. Zhang, X.Y., Wang, S., Yun, X.: Bidirectional active learning: a two-way exploration into unlabeled and labeled data set. IEEE Trans. Neural Netw. Learn. Syst. **26**(12), 3034–3044 (2015)
2. Zhang, X.Y., Shi, H., Zhu, X., et al.: Active semi-supervised learning based on self-expressive correlation with generative adversarial networks. Neurocomputing **345**, 103–113 (2019)
3. Zhang, X.Y., Shi, H., Li, C., et al.: Learning transferable self-attentive representations for action recognition in untrimmed videos with weak supervision. arXiv preprint arXiv:1902.07370 (2019)
4. Zhu, X., Zhang, X., Zhang, X.Y., et al.: A novel framework for semantic segmentation with generative adversarial network. J. Vis. Commun. Image Represent. **58**, 532–543 (2019)
5. Zhang, X.: Interactive patent classification based on multi-classifier fusion and active learning. Neurocomputing **127**, 200–205 (2014)
6. Li, C., Wang, X., Dong, W., et al.: Joint active learning with feature selection via CUR matrix decomposition. IEEE Trans. Pattern Anal. Mach. Intell. **41**(6), 1382–1396 (2018)
7. Li, C., Wei, F., Dong, W., et al.: Dynamic structure embedded online multiple-output regression for streaming data. IEEE Trans. Pattern Anal. Mach. Intell. **41**(2), 323–336 (2018)
8. Li, C., Liu, Q., Dong, W., et al.: Human age estimation based on locality and ordinal information. IEEE Trans. Cybern. **45**(11), 2522–2534 (2014)

9. Boominathan, L., Kruthiventi, S.S.S., Babu, R.V.: CrowdNet: A Deep Convolutional Network for Dense Crowd Counting (2016)
10. Zhang, Y., Zhou, D., Chen, S., et al.: Single-image crowd counting via multi-column convolutional neural network. In: Computer Vision & Pattern Recognition (2016)
11. Chen, L.C., Papandreou, G., Kokkinos, I., et al.: DeepLab: semantic image segmentation with deep convolutional nets, atrous convolution, and fully connected CRFs. IEEE Trans. Pattern Anal. Mach. Intell. 40(4), 834–848 (2018)
12. Sam, D.B., Surya, S., Babu, R.V.: Switching Convolutional Neural Network for Crowd Counting (2017)
13. Li, Y., Zhang, X., Chen, D.: CSRNet: Dilated Convolutional Neural Networks for Understanding the Highly Congested Scenes (2018)
14. Long, J., Shelhamer, E., Darrell, T.: Fully convolutional networks for semantic segmentation. IEEE Trans. Pattern Anal. Mach. Intell. 39(4), 640–651 (2014)
15. Simonyan, K., Zisserman, A.: Very deep convolutional networks for large-scale image recognition. Computer Science (2014)
16. Härdle, W.: Kernel Density Estimation. Smoothing Techniques. Springer, New York (1991)
17. Redmon, J., Farhadi, A.: Yolov3: an incremental improvement. arXiv preprint arXiv:1804.02767 (2018)
18. Zhang, N.C., Li, N.H., Wang, X., et al.: Cross-scene crowd counting via deep convolutional neural networks. In: 2015 IEEE Conference on Computer Vision and Pattern Recognition (CVPR). IEEE Computer Society (2015)
19. Huang, S., Li, X., Zhang, Z., et al.: Body structure aware deep crowd counting. IEEE Trans. Image Process. 27(3), 1049–1059 (2017)
20. Ren, S., He, K., Girshick, R., et al.: Faster R-CNN: towards real-time object detection with region proposal networks. In: International Conference on Neural Information Processing Systems (2015)
21. Ronneberger, O., Fischer, P., Brox, T.: U-net: convolutional networks for biomedical image segmentation. In: Navab, N., Hornegger, J., Wells, W.M., Frangi, A.F. (eds.) MICCAI 2015. LNCS, vol. 9351, pp. 234–241. Springer, Cham (2015). https://doi.org/10.1007/978-3-319-24574-4_28
22. He, K., Gkioxari, G., Dollár, P., et al.: Mask r-cnn. In: Proceedings of the IEEE International Conference on Computer Vision, pp. 2961–2969 (2017)
23. Liu, S., Qi, L., Qin, H., et al.: Path Aggregation Network for Instance Segmentation (2018)
24. Ren, Z., Yan, J., Ni, B., et al.: Unsupervised deep learning for optical flow estimation. In: Thirty-First AAAI Conference on Artificial Intelligence (2017)
25. Lin, W., Zhou, Y., Xu, H., et al.: A tube-and-droplet-based approach for representing and analyzing motion trajectories. IEEE Trans. Pattern Anal. Mach. Intell. 39(8), 1489–1503 (2017)

Vessel Segmentation of Liver CT Images by Hessian-Based Enhancement

Jie Li, Mengda Zhang, and Yongpeng Gao[(⊠)]

Yan Shan University, Qinhuangdao 066004, China
83928386@qq.com

Abstract. The structure and morphology of hepatic vessels play an important role in the discovery and diagnosis of liver lesions. In this paper, a vascular segmentation method for liver ct image based on Hessian enhancement algorithm is proposed, and the hepatic vessels in CT image are segmented and extracted more accurately. Firstly, the improved Hessian filtering algorithm is used to enhance the structure of vascular branch. The other two classical algorithms are compared in the aspects of algorithm running efficiency, signal-to-noise ratio and image quality, and it is proved that the improved Hessian filtering algorithm in scripture is preprocessed. High image quality. Then the level set method based on threshold velocity function is used to remove the non-vascular region with low gray value by adding threshold constraints on the basis of the velocity function of the general level set method, which can effectively reduce the phenomenon of over-segmentation. The experimental results show that compared with the other three classical algorithms, the proposed method has better results in segmentation accuracy, over-segmentation rate, under-segmentation rate, sensitivity and specificity.

Keywords: Vessel segmentation · Liver CT image · Image enhancement

1 Introduction

As the digestive and metabolic center of the human being, the liver is related closely to the endocrine and immune defense system, the incidence of liver lesions is generally higher than most other visceral organs. Liver diseases are seriously harmful to human health, and liver tumors will even threaten the lives of patients. In the statistical report of global cancer incidence and death in 2018 [1], the number of deaths due to liver tumors was 781,631. Liver tumors are one of the most common cancer diseases.

The structure and shape of the hepatic vessels provide important information for the planning and outcome evaluation of liver surgery. For example, in liver transplantation and tumor resection, it is very important to determine the three-dimensional structure of the liver and its vascular system and the location of the lesion. Therefore, accurate localization of intrahepatic vessels is essential in clinical practice, and small dimension of numerous vascular structures in the liver brings great difficulties in early clinical examination [2].

Hepatic vascular segmentation consists of three parts: pretreatment, vascular enhancement and vascular segmentation. The preprocessing is to get the interested liver

Y. Zhao et al. (Eds.): ICIG 2019, LNCS 11903, pp. 442–455, 2019.
https://doi.org/10.1007/978-3-030-34113-8_37

region from the image. Vascular enhancement aims to increase the contrast between vascular structure and background, which is beneficial to subsequent vascular.

Multi-scale Hessian matrix based filters [3] for vascular enhancement are the most commonly used methods to obtain vascular geometric information. These filters use the eigenvalues of the Hessian matrix to enhance contrast and can distinguish between block structures. Tubular and discoid structures. Filtering methods proposed by Frangi [4], Sato [5], Li [6], Erdt's [7] and Zhou [8] have been widely used in image segmentation preprocessing. Luu [9] uses Frangi filter based on Hessian matrix to segment abdominal CTA liver blood vessels. The accuracy of liver vascular segmentation using filter is significantly higher than that without filter. Ourselin [10] improved multi-scale Hessian filter enhances CTA brain images and produces a nearly uniform response in all vascular structures. The boundary between vascular structure and background is accurately enhanced. Ajam [11] combines bilateral filter with Hessian filter, which can smooth the image well and enhance the edge and geometric structure.

The simplest and intuitive methods for vascular segmentation are threshold segmentation, morphological operation, and regional growth method. Compared with other advanced technologies, these methods have higher efficiency, but it is difficult to set the best parameters. Active contour model (ACM) method was first introduced from [12], and many researchers have carried out extensive research. Level set method uses partial derivative equation to evolve formula, embeds contour into higher dimension (level set) space, and uses implicit active contour for image segmentation. Wang [13] et al. proposed an automatic liver segmentation algorithm based on level set, in which the probability Atlas method with maximum posterior classification was used to obtain the initial liver segmentation, and then the level set method based on shape and intensity prior was used to refine the segmentation.

Based on the above research background, this paper achieves the extraction of liver region and enhancement of local contrast by preprocessing, proposes the method of liver vascular enhancement and chooses the appropriate algorithm for vascular segmentation. The main contents of this paper are as follows: the second part is image preprocessing; the third part uses the improved Hessian matrix operator to enhance the liver image; the forth part uses threshold level set method to segment blood vessel.

2 Preprocessing

The 3dircadb dataset was selected to carry out the vascular method experiment. In the abdominal ct image, the liver is the largest area. In order to enhance the blood vessels of the liver, it is necessary to preprocess the original data image. With regard to methods and steps of proposed image processing in this paper, the liver CT images with image numbers 1–105, 4–62, 18–50, 10–75, respectively, will be taken as examples, as shown in Fig. 1.

The complete abdominal image and the liver mask image are used for template matching, and the liver parts in each abdominal image are extracted separately. After template matching, the black area of the background of the image is too large, and the boundary needs to be removed by row and column scanning method to get the minimum area containing the liver. The results are shown in Fig. 2.

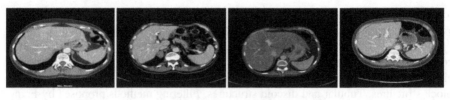

a. Patient No.1-105   b. Patient No.4-62   c. Patient No.18-50   d. Patient No.10-75

Fig. 1. Liver CT images of 4 patients in this paper

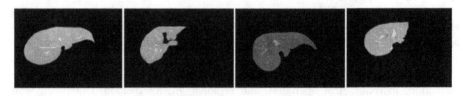

a. Liver Region Images of 4 Patients

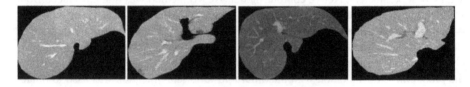

b. Boundary-removed Images of 4 Patients

Fig. 2. Boundary-removed liver images

In order to make the vascular structure and the background region easy to distinguish, the image after removing the boundary also needs to carry on the image contrast enhancement processing. In this paper, adaptive contrast enhancement processing is used. The specific formulas for image enhancement are as follows:

$$I(x, y) = M(x, y) + H(f(x, y) - M(x, y)) \tag{1}$$

$$H = \alpha \frac{M}{\sigma(x, y)}, \ 0 < \alpha < 1 \tag{2}$$

Here, $I(x, y)$ is pixel value after enhancement, M is the global average (it can also be set as a reasonable value), α is a coefficient parameter, whose value falls generally between 0 from 1. The adaptive contrast enhancement effect is shown in Fig. 3.

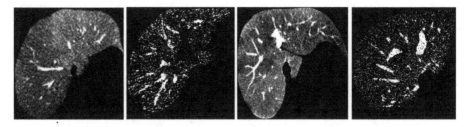

Fig. 3. Contrast enhancement processing of 4 patients

3   CT Hepatic Vascular Enhancement

Enhanced filter based on the analysis of eigenvalues of Hessian matrix applied to d-dimensional images [14] selectively amplifies the specific local intensity distribution or structure in the image. The image intensity function g near point x can be approximated by second-order Taylor expansion:

$$G(m+f, \alpha) \approx G(m) + f^T \nabla I(m, \alpha) + \frac{1}{2} f^T J(m, \alpha) f \tag{3}$$

Where f is a perturbed vector, according to the scale space theory, the Hessian matrix g (m, α), calculated by proportional α, is obtained by convolution:

$$\frac{\partial}{\partial m} J(m, \alpha) = G(x) * \frac{\partial}{\partial m} G(m, \alpha) \tag{4}$$

Then the dimensional Hessian matrix in the current scale space is represented as the following formula:

$$J_{a,b}(m, \alpha) = \frac{\alpha^2 G(m) * \alpha^2}{\partial m_a \partial n_b} G(m, \alpha) \quad a, b = 1, \dots, D \tag{5}$$

Here, $G(m, \alpha) = (2\pi\alpha^2)^{-D/2} exp(-m^T m / 2\alpha^2)$ stands for Gaussian function of D-dimension, * is convolution symbol. Then the two-dimensional Hessian matrix in this scale can be expressed as the following formula:

$$J_\alpha(m, n) = \alpha^2 \begin{bmatrix} \frac{\partial^2 G_\alpha(m,n)}{\partial m^2} & \frac{\partial^2 G_\alpha(m,n)}{\partial m \partial n} \\ \frac{\partial^2 G_\alpha(m,n)}{\partial n \partial m} & \frac{\partial^2 G_\alpha(m,n)}{\partial n^2} \end{bmatrix} \tag{6}$$

For the second-order and third-order Hessian matrices, by analyzing the sign and size relationship of the Hessian eigenvalues, the shape (tubular, massive and discoid) of the position of the blood vessel of the pixel can be roughly deduced or the pixel belongs to the background region. By using the feature analysis of Hessian, the local second-order structure of the image can be decomposed to reduce the amount of computation, which is given by Hessian feature vector. Let λ_1, λ_2, λ_3 be the eigenvalues of the third-order Hessian matrix, and the corresponding curvature is shown in Fig. 4.

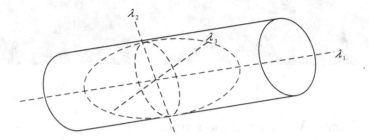

Fig. 4. The curvatures corresponding to Hessian matrix eigenvalues

In ideal situation, Hessian-based vascular enhancement is a process of image structure enhancement using corresponding enhancement functions when a set of eigenvalues satisfy a specific relationship [3]. In two-dimensional images, the symbols of the eigenvalues and the corresponding gray values of the vascular structure and background region are shown in Table 1.

Table 1. Hessian matrix eigenvalue pattern in 2D images

λ_1	λ_2	Mode
Noise	Noise	None
Low	High–	Bright pipe structure
Low	High+	Dark pipe structure
High–	High–	Bright block structure
High+	High+	Dark block structure

Among them, high refers to the large absolute value of eigenvalues, low means that the absolute value of eigenvalues is small, noise is noise, /-represents the positive and negative eigenvalues.

The more common Hessian filter can only enhance the tube structure in the vascular structure, such as Frangi method. However, in medical images, the branches of many blood vessels can not be enhanced only as tubular structures. It is more suitable to treat the branch structure as the block structure in the table. We propose an improved method based on Hessian matrix and apply it to hepatic vascular images. The tubular structure and block structure in the image can be enhanced at the same time to achieve better enhancement effect.

According to experience, the gray value of vascular structure in two-dimensional CT image is higher than that in non-vascular structure region, so λ_1, λ_2 are all negative values, and the subsequent calculation is facilitated by the $\lambda_i = -\lambda_i$ method. In order to enhance the tiny blood vessels and blood vessel targets in the lower contrast region, we integrate the corresponding feature values at different scales into λ_ρ as follows.

$$\lambda_\rho = \begin{cases} \lambda_2, & \lambda_2 > \tau \max_x \lambda_2(x,s) \\ \tau \max_x \lambda_2(x,s), & 0 < \lambda_2 \leq \tau \max_x \lambda_2(x,s) \\ 0, & \text{others} \end{cases} \tag{7}$$

Different enhanced responses are required for pixel points at different locations (vascular structure and branch). In order to enhance the structure of the branch, the vascular enhancement function $\lambda_2^2(\lambda_\rho - \lambda_2)(3/(2\lambda_2 + \lambda_\rho))^3$ is introduced [15]. In order to enhance the vessel structure, the vascular enhancement function $e^{-\lambda_2/\lambda_\rho}$ with tubular structure is introduced. In the case of other λ_1, λ_2 not related, it is generally considered that this pixel is located in the background region, where the enhancement function is 0. Therefore, the enhancement function of the Hessian matrix of the three-dimensional image is as follows:

$$V = \begin{cases} \lambda_2^2(\lambda_\rho - \lambda_2)(\frac{3}{2\lambda_2 + \lambda_\rho}), & \text{others} \\ e^{-\frac{\lambda_2}{\lambda_\rho}}, & \lambda_2 \geq \lambda_\rho/2 > 0 \\ 0, & \lambda_2 \leq 0 \vee \lambda_\rho \leq 0 \end{cases} \tag{8}$$

In order to reduce the error enhancement of liver parenchyma, liver contour edge and noise, the noise suppression function $\left(1 - e^{-S^2/2\gamma}\right)$ [4] in the Frangi algorithm is introduced to obtain the final functional response:

$$V_P = V \cdot (1 - e^{-S^2/2\gamma}) \tag{9}$$

Where $S = \sqrt{\lambda_1^2 + \lambda_2^2 + \lambda_\rho^2}$, γ is the noise function suppression term. Integrate the response of the filter into different scales:

$$V_0 = \max_{s_{min} \leq s \leq s_{max}} V(s) \tag{10}$$

The results are shown in Fig. 5.

Parameters in the above three algorithms are shown in Table 2.

It is shown in Fig. 5 that the improved Hessian filtering algorithm can achieve better enhancement effect and enhance the structure of vascular branches. Compared with Frangi algorithm, the enhancement method in this paper can enhance the branches of blood vessels better, and the intersection of blood vessels is more effective. When edge diffusion EED algorithm is used for vascular enhancement, some small vascular structures will be lost, the other two algorithms are obviously better than it.

In this paper, the three vascular enhancement methods are evaluated by the efficiency of the algorithm and the peak signal-to-noise ratio (PSNR) in the resulting image. Five groups of data with best results are selected from results, and the running time results of the three algorithms are shown in Table 3.

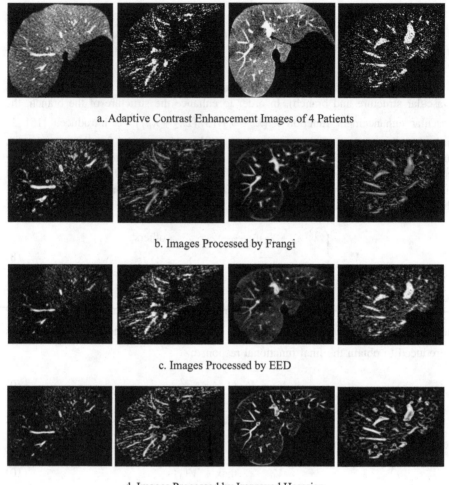

a. Adaptive Contrast Enhancement Images of 4 Patients

b. Images Processed by Frangi

c. Images Processed by EED

d. Images Processed by Improved Hesssian

Fig. 5. Vascular enhancement images

Table 2. The parameters of Frangi, EED and improved Hessian

Algorithm	Parameter
Frangi	$\alpha = 0.5$, $\beta = 0.5$, $\gamma = 15$, $\sigma_{min} = 1$, $\sigma_{max} = 4$, $v = 5$
EED	$a = 2$, $\varepsilon = 1$, $k_{min} = 0.1$, $k_{max} = 3$
Improved Hessian	$\gamma = 30$, $\tau = 0.6$

In addition to the comparison of the running efficiency of each algorithm, an evaluation criterion is needed to explain the quality of the running result image. In this paper, the contrast noise ratio is introduced to analyze the experimental results.

Table 3. Time of three vascular enhancement methods

Time(s)	Frangi	EED	Improved Hessian
1	16.79	20.10	14.18
2	20.12	21.27	18.73
3	27.88	24.33	16.11
4	26.45	32.25	21.47
5	22.13	27.39	20.34

The formula for calculating the contrast noise ratio of (psnr) is as follows:

$$C = \frac{|S_a - S_b|}{\sigma} \tag{11}$$

Where, S_a is the average grayscale of vascular structures, S_b is gray mean of vascular background, σ is standard deviation of image noise. The contrast between vascular structure and background can be obtained by calculating the contrast noise ratio. The contrast noise ratios of the respective images obtained from the above five groups of data are calculated and compared, as shown in Table 4.

Table 4. PSNR of three enhancement methods

PSNR(dB)	Frangi	EED	Improved Hessain
1	13.72	10.22	18.73
2	18.21	11.38	20.31
3	14.11	15.33	18.91
4	16.87	9.19	19.44
5	16.23	7.27	17.24

It can be seen intuitively that the signal-to-noise ratio of the improved Hessian filter is higher than that of the Frangi algorithm and the edge diffusion EED algorithm, and the image quality is higher. Therefore, the vascular image enhanced by the improved Hessian filtering method is used in the liver vascular segmentation below.

4   Hepatic Vascular Segmentation

The level set method is realized on the idea of the curve evolution process. The movement of pixel points on the curve is always along the vertical direction of the tangent vector of its point, and the continuous change of the line is explained by implicit form [16]. The process of curve evolution to the boundary of vascular structure region is transformed into the mathematical process of finding zero level set even if the "force" of curve motion is assumed that $\varphi(x, t), x \in R^2$ is a scalar function. During the time t, the zero-level set function evolved into a curve C is ϕ (x, t). At this point, curve C evolves into a zero level set φ, as shown in Fig. 6.

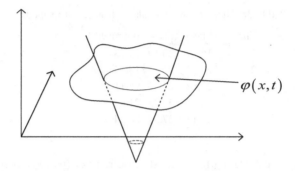

Fig. 6. Zero-level set image

In this paper, the level set model with gray threshold term is added to the velocity function to reduce the above over-segmentation and improve the segmentation accuracy. The principle is as follows. Let p be a point on the curve. According to the above evolution principle, the evolution at point p is only related to the property of the velocity function at point p. Therefore, the mathematical expression of the motion of point p with time t is given.

$$\frac{\partial C(p,t)}{\partial t} = vN(p,t) \tag{12}$$

In this equation, v refers to the velocity function at the p point of the curve, which determines the stopping position of the p point, that is, the evolution result. The relationship between the velocity function at a certain point on the curve and the curvature of that point is as follows:

$$v = P(I)(1 - \varepsilon k) \tag{13}$$

Where ε refers to the smoothness of the curve, I refers to the gray value, $P(I)$ refers to the function term. The level set equation can evolve into:

$$\frac{\partial C(p,t)}{\partial t} = N(p,t)[P(I)(1 - \varepsilon k)] \tag{14}$$

It is converted into:

$$\frac{\partial C(p,t)}{\partial t} = N(p,t)[\alpha D(I) + (1 - \alpha)k] \tag{15}$$

Where, $D(I)$ is the limiting term of the velocity function, which refers to the feature of controlling the curve stop. $\alpha \in [0, 1]$, is a parameter controlling the curve smoothness. To introduce the threshold limit condition into $D(I)$:

$$D(I) = \frac{U - L}{2} - \left| I - \frac{U + L}{2} \right| \tag{16}$$

In the formula, U and L refer to the maximum and minimum values of the gray value interval. When the gray value of the axis pixel point of the curve is inside the interval $[L, U]$, the curve will expand outward; otherwise, the curve will shrink inward. By setting the appropriate U and L, the curve evolution can achieve a good segmentation effect. In this paper, the interval is set to $[61, 241]$ according to the effect of many tests. The experimental results are shown in Fig. 7. In the figure, the blue part represents the mark made by the expert, and the red part represents the segmentation result obtained in this paper.

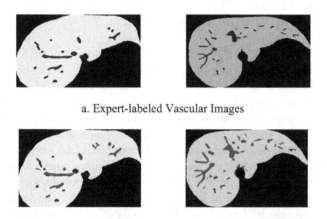

a. Expert-labeled Vascular Images

b. Vascular Images Processed by Region Growth Bsaed On Morphological

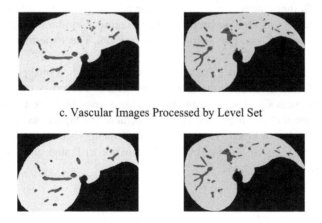

c. Vascular Images Processed by Level Set

d. Vascular Images Processed by Method of this paper

Fig. 7. Vascular images of three segmentation methods (Color figure online)

In order to better compare the influence of segmentation methods on segmentation effect, this paper selects segmentation accuracy, over-segmentation rate and under-segmentation rate to analyze based on expert mark. The average over-segmentation rate and average under-segmentation rate are shown in Table 5.

Table 5. The average value comparison of SA, OR and UR(%)

	SA			OR			UR		
	RG	LS	TLS	RG	LS	TLS	RG	LS	TLS
1	79.66	82.83	87.43	2.52	6.85	1.80	13.47	9.44	6.28
2	77.66	78.37	82.93	0.65	9.23	0.72	17.85	11.73	5.13
3	72.37	85.42	86.66	1.34	6.44	0.99	16.65	8.58	5.81
4	78.13	80.88	83.39	1.72	5.17	0.53	18.18	13.32	8.47
5	76.41	83.33	95.74	1.58	8.29	1.27	12.23	7.33	3.53

From the broken line diagram of segmentation accuracy, it can be seen that the level set method based on threshold velocity function is obviously better than the region growth and common level set method based on morphology, and the accuracy of segmentation is higher. From the point of view of excessive cutting rate broken line diagram, the common level set method is prone to wrong segmentation under normal circumstances, and the non-vascular structure is regarded as the vascular structure, so that the segmentation effect is not good. From the broken line diagram of under-segmentation rate, the region growth method based on morphology is easy to cause missing segmentation of effective structure of blood vessels. The level set method based on threshold velocity function is superior to the other two methods in the case of over-segmentation and under-segmentation.

In order to further quantitatively compare the advantages and disadvantages of the vascular enhancement method we propose, three filtering algorithms are combined with the threshold level set vascular segmentation method. The experimental results in Fig. 8.

Taking the above 5 groups of data as an example, 10 slice images were selected from each set of data to calculate the average segmentation accuracy of the 5 groups of data using three methods of vessel enhancement, as shown in Table 6.

It can be seen that the improved Hessian method has higher accuracy and more accurate segmentation of blood vessels after enhancement, which quantitatively proves that the improved Hessian filtering method is superior to Frangi and edge enhanced EED algorithm.

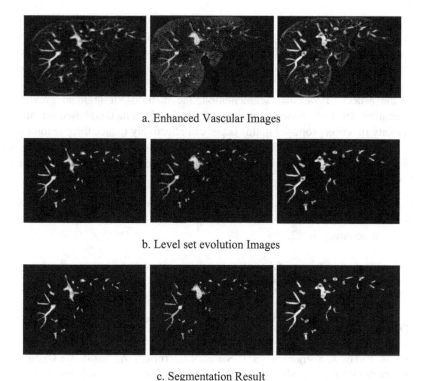

a. Enhanced Vascular Images

b. Level set evolution Images

c. Segmentation Result

Fig. 8. Segmentation results used different vessel enhancement methods

Table 6. The average of segmentation accuracy (unit: %)

	Frangi	EED	Improved Hessian
1	84.27	85.37	85.96
2	81.33	80.66	83.37
3	82.54	82.83	84.75
4	73.38	70.32	78.24
5	80.23	78.54	82.76

5   Conclusion

A vascular segmentation model for liver CT images based on Hessian enhancement algorithm is proposed in this paper. The method includes image preprocessing, vascular enhancement, vascular segmentation and so on. It can be used for liver CT image vascular segmentation with high accuracy and automation. The experimental results show that the method proposed in this paper has great advantages in vascular enhancement and vascular segmentation.

(1) In the aspect of vascular enhancement, compared with Frangi, EED vascular enhancement method, the improved Hessian filtering method proposed in this paper can better enhance the structure of vascular branches, which is beneficial to the subsequent vascular segmentation treatment and improve the accuracy of vascular segmentation.

(2) In the aspect of vascular segmentation, the methods of regional growth segmentation, level set model are compared. The level set method based on threshold velocity function proposed in this paper can effectively reduce the phenomenon of over-segmentation by adding threshold constraints on the basis of the velocity function of the general level set method to remove the non-vascular region with low gray value.

In this paper, the level set method based on threshold velocity function and the improved Hessian method are combined to segment the blood vessels, and the average segmentation accuracy is 82.73%.

Acknowlegement. We are grateful to all the reviewers for valuable comments. This work is supported by Natural Science Foundation of Hebei Province (No. F2019203569).

References

1. Bray, F., Ferlay, J., Soerjomataram, I., Siegel, R.L., Torre, L.A., Jemal, A..: Global cancer statistics 2018: GLOBOCAN estimates of incidence and mortality worldwide for 36 cancers in 185 countries. CA Cancer J. Clin. **68**, 394–424 (2018)
2. Chung, M., Lee, J.: Accurate liver vessel segmentation via active contour model with dense vessel candidates. Comput. Methods Programs Biomed **166**, 311–328 (2018)
3. Tankyevych, O., Talbot, H., Dokladal, P.: Curvilinear morpho-Hessian filter. In: IEEE International Symposium on Biomedical Imaging: from Nano to Macro, pp. 490–517 (2008)
4. Frangi, A.F., Niessen, W.J., Vincken, K.L., Viergever, M.A.: Multiscale vessel enhancement filtering. In: Wells, W.M., Colchester, A., Delp, S. (eds.) MICCAI 1998. LNCS, vol. 1496, pp. 130–137. Springer, Heidelberg (1998). https://doi.org/10.1007/BFb0056195
5. Sato, Y., Westin, C.F., Bhalerao, A., et al.: Tissue classification based on 3D local intensity structures for volume rendering. IEEE Trans. Vis. Comput. Graph. **6**(2), 160–180 (2000)
6. Li, Q., Sone, S., Doi, K.: Selective enhancement filters for nodules, vessels, and airway walls in two- and three-dimensional CT scans. Med. Phys. **30**(8), 20–40 (2003)
7. Erdt, M., Raspe, M., Suehling, M.: Automatic hepatic vessel segmentation using graphics hardware. In: Dohi, T., Sakuma, I., Liao, H. (eds.) Medical Imaging and Augmented Reality. MIAR 2008. LNCS, vol. 5128. Springer, Heidelberg (2008). https://doi.org/10.1007/978-3-540-79982-5_44
8. Zhou, C., Heang, P.C., Sahiner, B., et al.: Automatic multiscale enhancement and segmentation of pulmonary vessels in CT pulmonary angiography images for CAD applications. Med. Phys. **34**(12), 34–42 (2007)
9. Luu, H.M., Klink, C., Moelker, A., et al.: Quantitative evaluation of noise reduction and vesselness filters for liver vessel segmentation on abdominal CTA images. Phys. Med. Biol. **60**(10), 3905–3926 (2015)

10. Ourselin, S., Styner, M.A., Jerman, T., et al.: SPIE Proceedings [SPIE SPIE Medical Imaging - Orlando, Florida, United States] Medical Imaging 2015: Image Processing - Beyond Frangi: an improved multiscale vesselness filter, p. 94132A, 21 February 2015

11. Ajam, A., Aziz, A.A., Asirvadam, V.S., et al.: Cerebral vessel enhancement using bilateral and Hessian-based filter. In: 6th International Conference on Intelligent and Advanced Systems (ICIAS). IEEE (2016)

12. Kass, M., Witkin, A., Terzopoulos, D.: Snakes: active contour models. Int. J. Comput. Vis. **1**(4), 321–331 (1998)

13. Wang, J., Cheng, Y., Guo, C., et al.: Shape–intensity prior level set combining probabilistic atlas and probability map constrains for automatic liver segmentation from abdominal CT images. Int. J. Comput. Assist. Radiol. Surg. **11**(5), 817–826 (2016)

14. Orlowski, P., Orkisz, M.: Efficient computation of Hessian-based enhancement filters for tubular structures in 3D images. IRBM **30**(3), 128–132 (2009)

15. Jerman, T., Pernus, F., Likar, B., et al.: Enhancement of vascular structures in 3D and 2D angiographic images. IEEE Trans. Med. Imaging **35**(9), 2107–2118 (2016)

16. Adalsteinsson, D., Sethian, J.A.: A Fast Level Set Method for Propagating Interfaces (1995)

An Industrial Defect Detection Platform Based on Rapid Iteration

Jianchao Zhu[1(✉)], Dong Cheng[1], and Qingjie Kong[2]

[1] East China Normal University, Shanghai, China
51174500068@stu.ecnu.edu.cn, dong_cheng0525@foxmail.com
[2] Riseye Intelligent Technology Co., Ltd., Shenzhen, China
qjkong@riseye.ai

Abstract. With the improvement of the precision of industrial cameras and the popularity of applications, the visual inspection model method of deep learning is more and more widely used in the field of industrial inspection. According to the analysis of the basic needs of the current industrial inspection field, we found that many need to carry out rapid detection and iteration of small data sets. We propose a platform model that is more in line with current industrial inspection production. And the model is based on many convolutional neural network architectures, including spatial transformer network, Faster-RCNN, YOLO, etc.

Keywords: Industrial detection · Deep learning · Rapid iteration

1   Introduction

In recent years, more and more deep learning visual inspection methods have been applied to industrial production. But in fact, there are many difficulties. The purpose of using deep learning method is to replace traditional manual testing to improve production efficiency. According to the different products to be detected, and the difference between imaging and lighting, generally, before the application, it is necessary to test the effect of the detection on the small data set. So the platform is supposed to quickly determine whether such products can be tested for deep learning detection model. The detection of traditional computer graphics accounts for a large proportion. However, it has the disadvantages of high lighting requirements and a single detection environment.

According to the real cases we have obtained, many times merchants only allow a small number of images to be tested, even single digits. So at least, we should prove that the model is useful and the evaluation should be finished as soon as possible.

In order to overcome the difficulties above, we combine the previous technical methods, select the appropriate ones, and propose our own platform. Spatial transform network [11] is considered to put the object in the right place, and several object detection methods and data augmentation algorithms are combined together.

ⓒ Springer Nature Switzerland AG 2019
Y. Zhao et al. (Eds.): ICIG 2019, LNCS 11903, pp. 456–466, 2019.
https://doi.org/10.1007/978-3-030-34113-8_38

Regarding the general detection with high-precision requirements, the industry uses traditional fixed detection methods to pursue accuracy rather than the versatility of the task, such as feature extraction and location with traditional visual algorithms. However, in many cases, lighting and cameras do not fully meet the requirements. Therefore, in the case where the detection algorithm is difficult to meet the standard, it can only be replaced by humans. Our platform can play a better role in this situation. For a single simple industrial product, only 100 to 200 images are required to accurately locate and detect such serious defects as scratches, creases, etc. Besides, due to the characteristics of convolutional neural networks, our method has a higher fault tolerance for the changes of detecting environment, e.g. the detection results will not be easily affected just by a slight change in brightness.

The contribution of this paper can be summarized as follows:

(i) We first adopt the existing STN to our classification and object detection tasks in industrial field, which can be seen as a way of data augmentation and solve the problem of too little industrial data. Besides, this method has a fast iteration speed and has a good application prospect in industrial detection.

(ii) We then propose our industrial defect detection platform which has a friendly user interface and a wealth of detection capabilities, including image classification and object detection tasks. Anyone can easily train the model and judge the pros and cons of the model by the built-in evaluation metrics so that the best model can be applied to the actual industrial detection task. The advantages of our platform are simple operations, fast iteration speed and robustness to the lighting environment.

2 Related Work

Generally, there are four major tasks about image recognition in computer vision, i.e. classification, localization, detection and segmentation. We only discuss image classification and object detection in this paper, which are both supervised learning tasks learning a function that maps an input to an output based on example input-output pairs. However, in many cases, the labeled data is scarce, and the unlabeled data is quite rich. The cost of manually labeling data is very large, so active learning has emerged. Active learning queries the most useful unlabeled samples through a certain algorithm, and then label them by experts. Next, the labeled samples are used to train the classifier to improve the accuracy of the model. Many active learning methods [18,28,30–32] have been proposed recently.

For image classification, the amount of the samples plays a critically important role in achieving higher performance. Thus, data augmentation, applying some transformation to the original dataset, is proposed and widely used to generate more synthetic samples. There has been a variety of data augmentation methods so far, e.g. random cropping, horizontal flipping [13] and some generative models [6,26,33]. In other words, it is used to avoid overfitting problem, or called weak generalization ability, caused by too little data, which is also a focus in industrial detection. Besides, SPMTL [17] attempts to jointly learn the tasks by taking into consideration the complexities of both tasks and instances to improve the generalization ability of the model.

Object detection is another important topic in computer vision. It has a great development in recent years and can be summarized as two-stage and one-stage object detection methods. Two-stage object detection methods like R-CNN [5] is well known for its breakthrough progress in object detection. R-CNN was originally proposed to apply large convolutional neural networks to bottom-up proposal regions to locate and segment objects. This method first creates some pre-selected areas called bounding boxes, and then score the boxes to obtain the most possible position of the detected target. After a series of developments, Fast R-CNN [4] and Faster R-CNN [24] have been successively proposed. Various image detection methods based on CNN have emerged in an endless stream. Mask R-CNN [8] integrates image detection and segmentation, and also achieves good performance.

On the other hand, one-stage detection is a better choice if the real-time and feedback speed need to be taken into account. YOLO [21–23] and SSD [19] are the representatives. They can quickly detect and locate the target in the image through regression and feature processing, which is the main algorithm for video detection [29]. A further application of object detection is face recognition [16]. Person re-identification is one of the research directions, and [27] combined the structure of human and proposed a novel framework for addressing the problem of cross-view spatial misalignments in person Re-ID.

However, when applied to the industrial field, the methods mentioned above seem to be cumbersome. For VOC [3], CIFAR-10 [12], ImageNet [14] and other large datasets with high-quality images, there are enough number of samples to facilitate the training of models. If the project needs to land in the industrial field, the first problem needed to overcome is how to obtain acceptable detection results with small number of samples, and the tolerance of the manufacturers for the results. As a consequence, we combine the characteristics of the previous models and integrate them to overcome the problems faced by industrial detection to some extent, i.e., less training samples and quick iteration requirements. STN [11] is a tiny and well-designed network. It has been applied to natural environment text detection [2] in many studies before and is placed before the detection network, so as to make it lightweight and fast to detect tile and distortion targets. Here we use this idea to help overcome some of the difficulties in industrial detection, i.e. we can insert STN before the classification network or the detection network so that the target can be reshaped and be good for recognition. Finally, the results are displayed clearly by our platform.

3   Proposed Platform

The overall architecture of our platform can be illustrated in Fig. 1. The platform is divided into two major sections, namely image classification and object detection. Each section includes at least three phases of training, testing and detection, while the object detection section has an additional phase to create data sets called image annotation. The platform runs on a Ubuntu system.

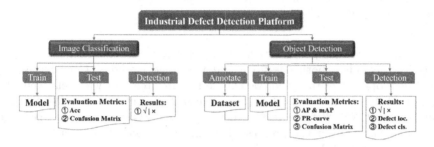

Fig. 1. The overall architecture of our industrial defect detection platform, where the green graphics denotes the model learnt from data set and the orange graphics denotes the output of testing and detection phase. (Color figure online)

3.1 Image Classification

Training. In training phase, we embed a spatial transformer network before a simple CNN to let the network learn how to transformer the input image so that the model can be better trained and the accuracy of classification can be further improved, which can be seen as a data augmentation method. We offer a variety of CNN backends to choose from, including the simple LeNet [15], AlexNet [13], VGG [25], and popular ResNet [9], DenseNet [10], ResNeXt, etc. We record the loss and accuracy values during training and draw a curve to dynamically monitor the progress.

Testing. In testing phase, we evaluate the trained model by two metrics, namely overall accuracy and confusion matrix. Regarding the confusion matrix, it is used to describe the performance of a classifier, including the precision and recall of each category. Each column of it represents the category to predict, with the total number of each column representing the number of samples predicted for that category. Similarly, each row of the matrix represents the ground truth category and the total number of each row represents the number of samples for that category. The number in each column indicates how many samples are predicted as this category.

Detection. In detection phase of image classification, we directly feed the image to the model to output the probability for each category and take the highest as the final result of the classification.

3.2 Object Detection

Annotation. Training data for object detection requires images and the corresponding ground truth annotation result. So this phase is designed to create datasets. The labeling results are stored as separated XML files according to the rules of VOC2007 [3].

Training. In training phase, we support several network architectures for object detection, including both one-stage and two-stage methods. Considering the rapid development of this field, we choose the architectures with relatively the highest efficiency and the best performance so far, namely Faster R-CNN [24] and Mask R-CNN [8] for two-stage detection and YOLOv3 [23] for one-stage detection. We monitor the progress of training by epoch-loss&accuracy curve mentioned in Sect. 3.1.

Testing. In testing phase of object detection, we choose AP (Average Precision), mAP (mean Average Precision), PR-curve (Precision-Recall curve) and confusion matrix as evaluation metrics. Note that AP and PR-curve are used to evaluate each category, while mAP and confusion matrix evaluate the overall performance of the model.

Detection. In detection phase, we feed the raw image into the trained model and the output is the annotated image with targets detected, including the bounding box indicating location and the category of each target.

The details will be displayed in the case study in Sect. 4.

4   Case Study

In this section, we present a case study on gear detection that demonstrates our platform's ability to solve such problems. Here we compare with traditional visual algorithms to highlight the advantages of our platform.

4.1 Traditional Visual Algorithm

We use OpenCV to process and detect defects, whose full name is open source computer vision library. As the name suggests, it mainly provides graphics processing and implementation methods for different applications. The core module that we mainly use to process images is the Imgroc module, which includes linear or nonlinear filtering operations, morphological operations, thresholding operations, etc. In addition, image matrix transformation operations, line detection, edge detection and other derivative detection methods are also the key point.

The image of the gear that needs to be processed is shown in Fig. 2(a). Since the gear we selected is centrally symmetric, the universality is not so high, but the advantage is that the features are clear. Symmetry defects or image

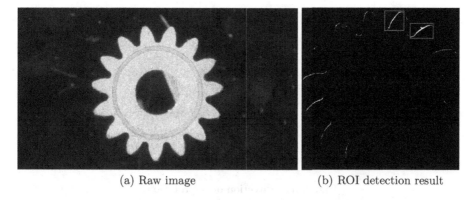

(a) Raw image   (b) ROI detection result

Fig. 2. Input raw image and output result image.

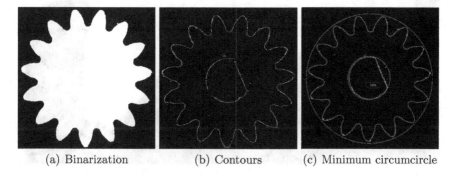

(a) Binarization   (b) Contours   (c) Minimum circumcircle

Fig. 3. Preprocess for the gear image.

changes caused by shooting can be quickly detected. Here we take the surface of the part as the research object. The main idea of our gear defect detection is that, considering the gear is a central symmetrical figure, we calculate the gear template and then calculate the difference between the template and the original image to locate the defect.

Observing the contrast of the image, the noises are not so obvious that we can directly select a fixed threshold [20] to binarize the image and the result can be seen in Fig. 3(a). We can find that the noises have been eliminated and the contours can then be extracted as Fig. 3(b). The inner contour is relatively stable compared to the rough outer contour, so we can select the center of circumcircle of the inner contour as the center of rotation. All we need to do is find the smallest circumcircle of the contours in the center of the gear in Fig. 3(b). We can use the method proposed by [7], which is quite common in the task of gesture recognition. The result is illustrated in Fig. 3(c). Now we get two main circles. We record the center of the inner circle as p_1 and the radius as r_1. We record the center of the outer circle as p_2 and the radius as r_2. Then we can extract ROI area from these data, namely $Rect(p_1.x - r_2, p_1.y - r_2, r_2 * x, r_2 * x)$. After

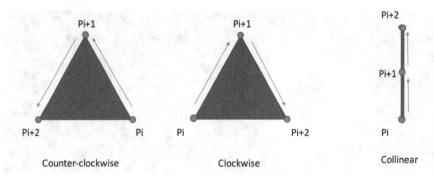

Fig. 4. The direction of the rotation

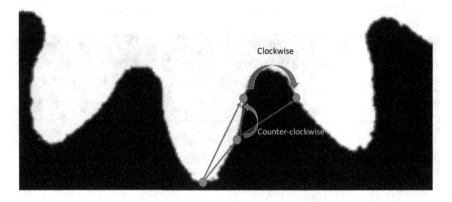

Fig. 5. The situation in a raw image.

the ROI area is extracted, the pixel points that need to be operated are greatly reduced, which is more convenient.

Next, we need to count the number of teeth of the gear. The premise is to determine the relative characteristics of the sawtooth relative to other shapes and to count according to the uniquely determinable feature. We can think of the gears that need to be counted as convex hull, and then use the method of convex hull detection [1] to judge the convex part of the gear. This method is convenient and clear. We find the lowest point in the image set to P_0. Then, the other points and the cosine values of the vector and the X-axis are calculated. Based on this value, all the points on the permutation graph are arranged from large to small P_1, P_2... P_i. After that we should judge the the direction of vector rotation from vector $P_iP_i + 1$ to vector $P_iP_i + 1$. If the rotation is counterclockwise, then this point is the constituent point of the convex hull. And in Fig. 4, we show the direction of the rotation. It can be judged by their cross product. $C.z = P_i.x * P_i.y - P_i.x * P_i.y$. And the positive and negative values of $C.z$ correspond to clockwise and counterclockwise, respectively. The situation is shown in Fig. 5.

Finally, we rotate the gear at some specific angles based on the number of teeth to find the average value, which we take as a template for the gear. We then calculate the difference between the template and the original raw image and binary the result to filter out the interference. We judge the area of the connected area beyond a certain threshold as a defect and mark it with the bounding box, and the result is shown in Fig. 2. Of course, this is only the result of the ROI, so we also need to mark the defects in the original raw image according to the coordinates of the bounding box obtained.

4.2 Deep Learning Algorithm

Now we present our deep learning method on solving this kind of problem. Note that this is an object detection task, taking into account the requirements of detection speed and accuracy, we choose to use YOLOv3 under the trade-off.

With our platform, what we need to do is to annotate the target for each gear image, namely marking the bounding boxes on the image and set the category for each box. Next, we only need to input the images and their corresponding annotation data into the network. After a few hours' training, computer has automatically extracted and learned the features through the deep neural network formed by the convolutional layer. Finally, we can get a model output by our platform that stores important information for solving gear defect detection tasks.

The model can be evaluated in the testing phase mentioned in Sect. 3.2. AP and overall performance of the model is shown in Fig. 6. As can be seen from the figure, there are a total of 100 test images and all of them are detected with a threshold of 0.8. The number of missed and false detection are both 0,

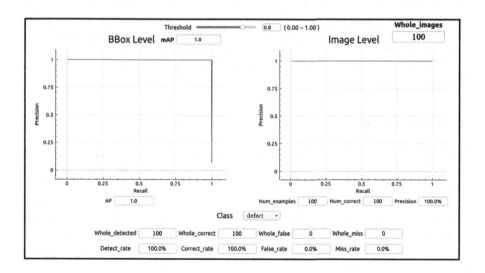

Fig. 6. Evaluation metrics by our platform.

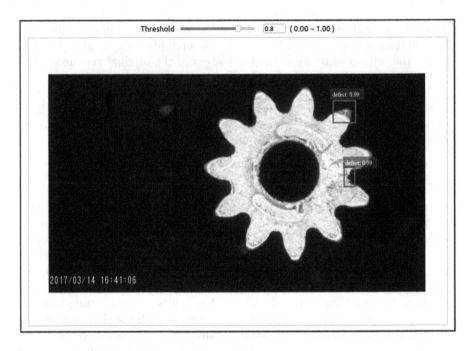

Fig. 7. An example of detection result by our platform.

and the detection accuracy reaches 100%. The data for this batch of gear defect detection has only one category, namely 'defect', whose AP (Average Precision) also reaches 100%, indicating that all the bounding boxes exist in the testing data are detected. The result is a good example of how our model (our platform) can handle this task.

An example of detection result is illustrated in Fig. 7. It can be found that when the threshold is set to 0.8, a total of two defects are detected, and the scores are both 0.99, which indicates that our model has high confidence in the judgment it makes.

5   Conclusion

Comparing the traditional method with the platform we proposed, it can be clearly seen that deep learning can effectively reduce the difficulty of industrial appearance defect detection and greatly improve the efficiency of algorithm development, because we do not have to spend a lot of time on researching and testing algorithms. In addition, the detection efficiency of our framework is also superior to traditional algorithms, reaching 20 fps. Another point is that our platform is more robust to different environmental conditions, such as not having a big impact on the results due to changes in the lighting configuration.

References

1. Barber, C.B., Dobkin, D.P., Huhdanpaa, H.: The quickhull algorithm for convex hulls. ACM Trans. Math. Softw. **22**(4), 469–483 (1996)
2. Bartz, C., Yang, H., Meinel, C.: STN-OCR: a single neural network for text detection and text recognition (2017)
3. Everingham, M., Van Gool, L., Williams, C.K.I., Winn, J., Zisserman, A.: The PASCAL visual object classes (VOC) challenge. Int. J. Comput. Vision **88**(2), 303–338 (2010)
4. Girshick, R.B.: Fast R-CNN. CoRR (2015)
5. Girshick, R.B., Donahue, J., Darrell, T., Malik, J.: Rich feature hierarchies for accurate object detection and semantic segmentation (2013)
6. Goodfellow, I.J., et al.: Generative adversarial nets. In: International Conference on Neural Information Processing Systems (2014)
7. Har-Peled S, M.S.: Fast algorithms for computing the smallest k -enclosing circle (2005)
8. He, K., Gkioxari, G., Dollár, P., Girshick, R.B.: Mask R-CNN (2017)
9. He, K., Zhang, X., Ren, S., Sun, J.: Deep residual learning for image recognition. CoRR (2015)
10. Huang, G., Liu, Z., Weinberger, K.Q.: Densely connected convolutional networks. CoRR (2016)
11. Jaderberg, M., Simonyan, K., Zisserman, A., Kavukcuoglu, K.: Spatial transformer networks (2015)
12. Krizhevsky, A.: Learning multiple layers of features from tiny images (2009)
13. Krizhevsky, A., Sutskever, I., Hinton, G.E.: Imagenet classification with deep convolutional neural networks. In: International Conference on Neural Information Processing Systems (2012)
14. Deng, J., Dong, W., Socher, R., Li, L.J., Li, K., Fei-Fei, L.: Imagenet: a large-scale hierarchical image database. In: IEEE Conference on Computer Vision and Pattern Recognition (2009)
15. LeCun, Y., Bottou, L., Bengio, Y., Haffner, P.: Gradient-based learning applied to document recognition. In: Proceedings of the IEEE (1998)
16. Li, C., Liu, Q., Dong, W., Zhu, X., Liu, J., Lu, H.: Human age estimation based on locality and ordinal information. IEEE Trans. Cybern. **45**(11), 2522–2534 (2017)
17. Li, C., Fan, W., Yan, J., Dong, W., Liu, Q., Zha, H.: Self-paced multi-task learning (2016)
18. Li, C., Wang, X., Dong, W., Yan, J., Liu, Q., Zha, H.: Joint active learning with feature selection via cur matrix decomposition. IEEE Trans. Pattern Anal. Mach. Intell. **41**(99), 1382–1396 (2018)
19. Liu, W., et al.: SSD: single shot MultiBox detector. In: Leibe, B., Matas, J., Sebe, N., Welling, M. (eds.) ECCV 2016. LNCS, vol. 9905, pp. 21–37. Springer, Cham (2016). https://doi.org/10.1007/978-3-319-46448-0_2
20. Ohtsu, N.: A threshold selection method from gray-level histograms. IEEE Trans. Syst. Man Cybern. **9**(1), 62–66 (2007)
21. Redmon, J., Divvala, S.K., Girshick, R.B., Farhadi, A.: You only look once: unified, real-time object detection (2015)
22. Redmon, J., Farhadi, A.: Yolo9000: better, faster, stronger. arXiv preprint arXiv:1612.08242 (2016)
23. Redmon, J., Farhadi, A.: Yolov3: an incremental improvement. arXiv (2018)

24. Ren, S., He, K., Girshick, R.B., Sun, J.: Faster R-CNN: towards real-time object detection with region proposal networks (2015)
25. Simonyan, K., Zisserman, A.: Very deep convolutional networks for large-scale image recognition. Computer Science (2014)
26. Yang, X., Deng, C., Zheng, F., Yan, J., Liu, W.: Deep spectral clustering using dual autoencoder network (2019)
27. Yang, S., Lin, W., Yan, J., Xu, M., Wu, J., Wang, J.: Person re-identification with correspondence structure learning (2015)
28. Zhang, X.Y., Wang, S., Yun, X.: Bidirectional active learning: a two-way exploration into unlabeled and labeled data set. IEEE Trans. Neural Networks Learn. Syst. **26**(12), 3034–3044 (2017)
29. Zhang, X.Y., Shi, H., Li, C., Zheng, K., Duan, L.: Learning transferable self-attentive representations for action recognition in untrimmed videos with weak supervision (2019)
30. Zhang, X.Y., Shi, H., Zhu, X., Li, P.: Active semi-supervised learning based on self-expressive correlation with generative adversarial networks. Neurocomputing **345** (2019). https://doi.org/10.1016/j.neucom.2019.01.083
31. Zhang, X.Y., Wang, S.P., Zhu, X.B., Wu, G.J., Wang, Y.P.: Update vs. upgrade: modeling with indeterminate multi-class active learning. Neurocomputing **162**, 163–170 (2015)
32. Zhang, X.Y.: Interactive patent classification based on multi-classifier fusion and active learning. Neurocomputing **127**, 200–205 (2014)
33. Zhu, X., Zhang, X., Zhang, X.Y., Xue, Z., Wang, L.: A novel framework for semantic segmentation with generative adversarial network. J. Vis. Commun. Image Represent. **58** (2018). https://doi.org/10.1016/j.jvcir.2018.11.020

Deep Super-Resolution Hashing Network for Low-Resolution Image Retrieval

Feng Dai[1], Zhuangzi Li[1(✉)], Naiguang Zhang[2(✉)], Qian Wang[3], Xiaobin Zhu[4], and Peng Li[5]

[1] School of Computer and Information Engineering,
Beijing Technology and Business University, Beijing, China
daifeng1994@163.com, lizhuangzii@163.com
[2] Information Technology Institute, Academy of Broadcasting Science,
NRTA, Beijing, China
zhangnaiguang@abs.ac.cn
[3] Beijing Goldwind Science & Creation Windpower Equipment Co., Ltd.,
Beijing, China
wangqian36084@goldwind.com.cn
[4] School of Computer and Communication Engineering,
University of Science and Technology Beijing, Beijing, China
zhuxiaobin@ustb.edu.cn
[5] College of Information and Control Engineering,
China University of Petroleum, Beijing, China
lipeng@upc.edu.cn

Abstract. In image retrieval, deep learning based hashing approaches have achieved promising performance in recent years. However, they are usually trained on a specific resolution, so it will cause unpleasant retrieval results with low-resolution input. In this paper, we propose a novel end-to-end deep super-resolution hashing network (DSRHN) for low-resolution image retrieval. It aims to adopt super-resolution techniques to promote semantic information of low-resolution images, so that benefits hashing code generation in a more representative fashion. The proposed network consists of two major components, which are trained alternatively, named super-resolution network and hashing network. The super-resolution network is not only optimized by MSE loss for pixel-wise image reconstruction, but also optimized by perceptual loss extracted by the hashing network for semantic learning. As for the hashing network, we adopt hashing semantic loss to optimize it for accurate hash code generation, and utilize a discriminative loss to improve the discriminative ability for the super-resolved images and high-resolution images. Extensive experiments show that our method achieve state-of-the-art performance on low-resolution images retrieval.

Keywords: Image retrieval · Deep hashing · Image super-resolution

F. Dai and Z. Li—These authors contributed equally to this paper and share the first authorship.

© Springer Nature Switzerland AG 2019
Y. Zhao et al. (Eds.): ICIG 2019, LNCS 11903, pp. 467–478, 2019.
https://doi.org/10.1007/978-3-030-34113-8_39

1   Introduction

Image similarity search in the era of big data has attracted wide attention in different applications such as information retrieval, data mining and pattern recognition. In order to efficiently store and real-time match millions of images, images discriminative representation in huge datasets has become an important research direction. Many existing methods represent images as binary hash codes by hashing function, so that the similarity search of high-dimensional images is replaced by calculating Hamming distance [18]. In addition, hashing functions are robust to various image transformations such as rotation, translation, scale and lightning, since they are carefully designed to extract distinctive patterns from images.

Many methods of learning to hash [8,22] have been proposed to achieve efficient image retrieval. But the traditional learning-based approach can not effectively represent images feature [16,17,30,32]. Recently, deep learning based hashing methods [13,27,34] have shown that deep neural networks can enable end-to-end representation learning and hash coding with nonlinear hash functions. And it achieve advanced performance. However, in the real world, the retrieval images is not necessarily the same quality as the image of the training model, and the images resolution often decreases due to some factors. Existing deep hashing approaches cannot effectively represent LR images with binary hash codes, which may result in poor hash retrieval. In order to solve the abovementioned problems, this paper presents an end-to-end deep hash model (DSRHN) to generate efficient binary hash codes directly from LR images. To the best of our knowledge, our approach is the first attempt to use an end-to-end multitask framework [19] for LR images hashing tasks. We not only learn the intensity similarity mapping between HR images and LR images, but also explore the mapping of images in Hamming space. DSRHN consists of two parts: a super-resolution network (SRNet) and a hash encoding network (HashNet). SRNet are trained to produce SR images from LR images. And the HashNet is trained to generate binary hash code from images, which is also used to constrain the SR images generated by SRNet and the corresponding HR images to be consistent on hash semantics. Because of this limitation, the retrieval result of LR images are close to that of HR images.

In short, we make contributions of our work. (1) We propose a novel end-to-end learning [28,29,38] framework for LR images retrieval. This method allows LR images to get more semantic information via high-efficiency repair ability of super-resolution network. Thus achieving efficient LR images retrieval. (2) We conduct extensive experiments on two benchmark datasets and achieve state-of-the-art performance. The rest of the paper is organized as follows: Sect. 2 describes the related work. Sections 3 and 4 introduce the proposed method and experimental results respectively. Section 5 concludes the paper.

2 Related Work

2.1 Image Hashing Method

In general, hashing methods can be divided into data-independent and data-dependent methods. Locality Sensitive Hash (LSH) [7] was one of the data-independent method of early research. LSH uses random linear projections to map the original data to a low-dimensional feature space, and then obtains binary hash codes. LSH and its several variants (e.g., kernel LSH [12] and p-norm LSH [4]) are widely used for large-scale image retrieval. However, data-independent methods are affected by some factors such as low efficiency and the need for longer hash codes, so it cannot be effectively used in practical applications. Due to the limitations of data-independent methods, the current research on hash function mainly uses various machine learning techniques for given datasets. Data-independent methods can be further divided into supervised, semi-supervised, and unsupervised methods. The unsupervised hash method directly learns the hash function from unlabeled data points and represents the data points as binary codes. Typical learning criteria methods include reconstruction error minimization [1,33,37] and graph structure learning [23,26]. Iterative Quantization (ITQ) [8] is an unsupervised method of generating binary codes by achieving better quantization rather than random projection. The semi-supervised hashing method improves the quality of the hash code by leveraging the supervisory information into learning process. Semi-Supervised Hashing (SSH) [25] is one of the semi-supervised methods that uses pairwise information on labeled samples to preserve semantic similarity. Compared to unsupervised and semi-supervised methods, supervised methods use semantic labels to improve performance. One of the representatives is Kernel-based Supervised Hashing (KSH) [22] to generate high quality hash codes by using pairwise relationships between data points.

Recently, the deep learning hashing methods [23,31,37] have achieved breakthrough results in images retrieval datasets due to the powerful learning ability of deep networks. The first deep hash model (CNNH) [27] decomposes hash learning into approximate hash code learning and subsequent hash functions and image feature learning. DNNH [13] improved CNNH to learn feature representation [15] and hash code simultaneously via triple loss optimization model. DHN [34] preserving pairwise semantic similarity and controlling the quantization error by simultaneously optimizing the pairwise cross-entropy loss and quantization loss improved DNNH. DPSH [20] learns feature representation and hash codes simultaneously with pairwise data points via an end-to-end approach. Deep cauchy hashing (DCH) [2] utilize a pairwise cross-entropy loss based on Cauchy distribution to learn binary hash code. However, existing learning-based hashing methods are only for a given dataset of the same resolution. This is an ideal situation in the real world and many images are low-resolution. When reduced-resolution images is processed with a trained hash model, the search results will be poor. This paper proposes a high quality binary hash code generation method for LR images. We apply images super-resolution technology to images hashing, and use multi-task framework to deal with hashing problem.

2.2   Image Super Resolution Method

Image Super Resolution technology (ISR) is to estimate HR images from LR images. With the rapid development of deep learning, the ISR method based on Convolutional Neural Network (CNN) [6,35,36] shows excellent performance. Dong et al. [5] first proposed the image super-resolution framework SRCNN based on deep learning, and achieved excellent performance compared with the previous method. A faster network framework FSRCNN [6] was proposed to accelerate the training and testing of SRCNN. Ledig et al. [14] introduced the deep network ResNet [10] into the super-resolution task and used the perceptual loss and generative adversarial network (GAN) [9] for photo-realistic SR. Since the image super-resolution technology can make the LR images get more semantic information, we combine the images super-resolution task to deal with the hash retrieval problem of the LR images.

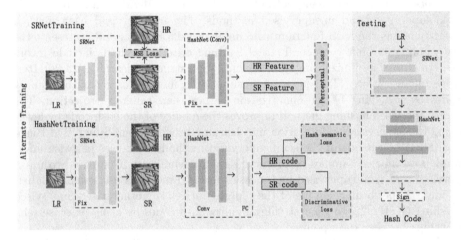

Fig. 1. The framework of the proposed deep super-resolution hashing network (DSRHN).

3   Our Method

3.1   Overview

In order to solve the LR images hashing problem in an end-to-end learning framework, this paper proposes an advanced end-to-end multi-task deep learning framework (DSRHN), as shown in Fig. 1. DSRHN mainly consists of two parts: a super-resolution network (SRNet) and a hash encoding network (HashNet). Our framework is an alternating learning process. First, we fix HashNet to train super-resolution networks via two loss functions: the last convolutional layer features of HashNet for x_i and x_i^{SR} produce perceptual loss, the output of SRNet and HR images produce pixel-wise mean square error (MSE) loss. Second, we fix SRNet to train hash network utilizes two losses: a hash semantic loss that preserves the hash semantic similarity and a discriminant loss that maintains the robustness of the HashNet. For test process, we directly input the LR images into SRNet, then input the SR images of SRNets' output into HashNet, and finally represent the output of HashNet as a hash code through the sign function. The sign function is defined as:

$$sign(x) = \begin{cases} 1, & if \ x \geq 0 \\ -1. & otherwise \end{cases} \tag{1}$$

3.2   SRNet

The top half of Fig. 1 shows our super-resolution network SRNet. The main purpose of SRNet is to learn a mapping function of LR images to HR images. The input and output of SRNet are LR images $\{x_i^{LR}, x_j^{LR}\}$ and SR images $\{x_i^{SR}, x_j^{SR}\}$. This process can be defined as:

$$X^{SR} = F_{SR}(X^{LR}) \tag{2}$$

where $F_{SR}(\cdot)$ denotes the super-resolution function. The main part of SRNet is 16 residual blocks. For the residual blocks we use two convolutional layers with small 3×3 kernels and 64 feature maps combined batch-normalization layers and ParametricReLU activation function. In order to improve the resolution of the input images, we adopt two trained sub-pixel convolution layers proposed by Shi et al. [24]. In particular, unlike traditional image super-resolution methods, we super-resolution LR images on hash semantics. We make content loss for the features of SR and HR images in the final convolution layer of HashNet. This method can ensure that the SR images have the similar binary hash codes to the HR images.

Considering the feature preservation of SR and HR images, the following loss functions are used to learn HR images:

$$L_{mse} = \left\| X^{HR} - X^{SR} \right\|_2^2 \tag{3}$$

where the X_{LR} denotes the input LR images, and X_{SR} is ground truth HR images. $\|\cdot\|_2$ denotes the L2 norm. Considering the SR images and corresponding HR images should keep similarity on hash semantics, we adopt perceptual loss based on the feature of the last convolutional layer of the HashNet:

$$\begin{aligned} L_{per} &= \left\| F_{cov}(X^{HR}) - F_{cov}(X^{SR}) \right\|_2^2 \\ &= \left\| F_{cov}(X^{HR}) - F_{cov}(F_{SR}(X^{LR})) \right\|_2^2 \end{aligned} \tag{4}$$

where $F_{cov}(\cdot)$ denotes the HashNet convolutional layer. Overall, combining Eqs. (3) and (4), the loss of the SRNet can be written as:

$$L_{SR} = L_{per} + \lambda L_{mse} \tag{5}$$

where λ is the hyper-parameter.

3.3   HashNet

The bottom half of Fig. 1 is our hash encoding network denoted as HashNet. The purpose of HashNet is to learn nonlinear hash function $f : x \mapsto h \in \{-1, 1\}^K$ from an input space R^D to Hamming space $\{1, 1\}^K$ via deep neural networks. Alexnet [11] is adopted as the basic network of HashNet. HashNet consists of five convolution layers (c1-c5) and two fully connected layers (fc6,fc7), which are pre-trained on the ImageNet dataset. In order to obtain hash codes, we add a K-node hash layer called fch, each node of fch layer corresponds to a target hash code. Using fch layer, the previous representation is converted to k-dimensional representation. HashNet can encode each data point into a K-bit binary hash code with similar information S preserved. For HashNet, the input is SR images pairs, HR images pairs, and pairwise similarity relation $\{x_i, x_i^{SR}, x_j, x_j^{SR}, S_{ij}\}$. $S = \{s_{ij}\}$ is defined as:

$$S_{ij} = \begin{cases} 0, & if\ images\ x_i\ and\ x_j\ share\ same\ class\ label \\ 1. & otherwise \end{cases} \tag{6}$$

After the HashNet is trained, the binary hash code B is calculated through the trained hashing network:

$$b_i = sign(F_{hash}(x_i|\theta)) \tag{7}$$

where b_i is hash code, $F_{hash}(\cdot)$ denotes the hash function, θ denotes the parameters of the HashNet, x_i represents the input images. In addition, the hash function we learned has the ability to distinguish SR from HR images. It is contrary to SRNet's expectation that SR and HR images remain hash semantically identical. This learning method enables SRNet and HashNet to learn better.

Usually calculate the distance between binary hash codes using Hamming distance, it can be calculated as:

$$dist_H = \frac{1}{2}(K - \langle b_i, b_j \rangle) \tag{8}$$

where K is the length of the hash code, $\langle \cdot \rangle$ denotes the inner product between hash codes. From Eq. (8) we know that Hamming distance is related to inner product. The larger the inner product of the two hash codes, the smaller the Hamming distance and vice versa. Therefore, we can learn the discriminative hash code by replacing the similarity of semantic labels with the inner product between hash codes. Based on this fact, we use the following loss function as DPSH [20] does. Firstly, it is hoped that pairwise label can be fitted by similarity (inner product) between sample binary codes.

$$p(s_{ij}|b_i, b_j) = \begin{cases} \sigma(\langle b_i, b_j \rangle), & s_{ij} = 1 \\ 1 - \sigma(\langle b_i, b_j \rangle). & s_{ij} = 0 \end{cases} \tag{9}$$

where $\sigma(x) = 1/(1 + e^{-x})$ is the sigmoid activation function, $\langle b_i, b_j \rangle = \frac{1}{2}b_i^T b_j$. $p(\cdot)$ is the conditional probability of s_{ij} given the pair of corresponding hash codes $[b_i, b_j]$. Based on the above, the following loss function is used to preserves the similarity of hash semantics:

$$
\begin{aligned}
L_{hs} &= -\log p(S|B) = -\sum_{s_{ij} \in S} \log p(s_{ij}| \langle b_i, b_j \rangle) \\
&= -\sum_{s_{ij} \in S}(s_{ij} \langle b_i, b_j \rangle - \log(1 + e^{\langle b_i, b_j \rangle}))
\end{aligned}
\tag{10}
$$

Equation (10) is negative log likelihood loss function, which represents the Hamming distance of two similar images as small as possible and the Hamming distance of two different images as large as possible. However, the hash code $b_i \in \{-1, +1\}$ is discrete. This is hard to optimize. To solve this problem, equality constraints can be optimized by moving them to regularization terms. So use the following loss function to optimize:

$$
L_{hs} = -\sum_{s_{ij} \in S}(s_{ij} \langle v_i, v_j \rangle - \log(1 + e^{\langle v_i, v_j \rangle})) + \gamma \sum_1^n \|b_i - v_i\|
\tag{11}
$$

where v is the binary code after relaxation. The last part $(\gamma \sum_1^n \|b_i - v_i\|)$ of the equation is the regularization term, γ is the hyper-parameter.

In order to ensure that the hash codes learned by the hash function can distinguish SR and HR images and make the HashNet robust, we design a discriminative loss for optimizing the hashing network:

$$
L_{dis} = \max(m - \left\|F_{hash}(x_i^{HR}) - F_{hash}(x_i^{SR})\right\|_2^2, 0)
\tag{12}
$$

where $F_{hash}(\cdot)$ denotes hash network (HashNet), and $m > 0$ is a margin threshold parameter. Overall, combining Eqs. (11) and (12), the loss of the hash network can be written as:

$$
L_{hash} = L_{hs} + \alpha L_{dis}
\tag{13}
$$

where α is the hyper-parameter.

4   Experiments

To validate the performance of our proposed method, we conducted extensive experiments on two widely used benchmark datasets (i.e. NUS-WIDE and MS-COCO) to verify the effectiveness of our approach. We start with introducing the datasets and then present our experimental results.

4.1   Datasets and Evaluation Metrics

In the experiments, we conduct hashing on two experiments widely-used datasets: NUS-WIDE [3] and MS-COCO [21].

- **NUS-WIDE** dataset consists of 269,648 web images associated with the tag. It is a multi-label dataset where each image can be annotated with multiple tags. Following DPSH [20], we selected only 195,834 images belonging to the 21 most common concepts. For NUS-WIDE datasets, if two images share at least one public tag, they will be defined as similar. We randomly sampled 100 images per class (i.e., a total of 2,100 images) as a test set, with 500 images per class (i.e., a total of 10,500 images) as a training set. The rest of the image is considered a gallery during the testing phase.

- **MS-COCO** datasets we used consists 82,783 training images and 40,504 validation images, each of which is labeled by some of the 80 semantic concepts. Following DCH [2], we randomly extracted 5,000 images as query points, the rest as databases, and 10,000 images are randomly sampled from the database for training. For MS-COCO dataset, two images will be defined as a ground-truth neighbor (similar pair) if they share at least one common label.

Evaluation Metrics: We use mean average precision (mAP), precision, and recall to evaluate the performance of DSRHN compared to the aforementioned unsupervised hashing functions for low-resolution image retrieval. In particular, our low-resolution images are obtained from experimental datasets by interpolation, that is, the original dataset images are high-quality images and interpolated to obtain low-resolution images. We report the results of image retrieval with map@5000, mAP@5000 is mAP calculated over the top 5000 ranked images from the gallery set.

4.2   Ablation Study

We perform an ablation experiment to examine the true validity of our framework for low-resolution images hashing. We evaluated this experiment with DSRHN, HashNet-LR, HashNet-HR, and HashNet-SRGAN. The HashNet-LR approach is to directly use the low resolution images as input to our hash network without using a super resolution network; The HashNet-HR method inputs high resolution images into our hash network; The HashNet-SRGAN approach uses SRGAN work instead of our super-resolution network for a non-end-to-end LR images hashing.

As shown in Table 2. First of all, we can see from HashNet-SRGAN and HashNet-LR that super-resolution network does have effect on LR images hash retrieval. In particular, our DSRHN works best. Secondly, we can see that the result of HashNet-HR directly retrieving HR images and DSRHN retrieving LR images is very close, which shows that our framework is very good at learning the mapping of LR images to HR images on hash semantics. A comparison of DSRHN and HashNet-SRGAN shows that our end-to-end framework can better enhance the semantics of LR images on hash retrieval tasks.

4.3   Comparisons

For image retrieval, we compare our method with the previous deep supervised hash functions including deep pairwise-supervised hashing (DPSH) [20], deep hashing network (DHN) [34], and deep cauchy hashing (DCH) [2].

Table 1. LR images retrieval results (mAP@5000) of DSRHN and Its Variants, HashNet-LR, HashNet-HR, HashNet-SRGAN on two Datasets.

Method	NUS-WIDE				MS-COCO			
	12bits	24bits	32bits	48bits	12bits	24bits	32bits	48bits
HashNet-LR	71.32	72.29	72.97	73.01	55.73	56.61	57.86	56.61
HashNet-SRGAN	71.31	72.84	72.88	73.21	57.67	61.27	61.10	61.27
DSRHN	**77.07**	**79.40**	**80.02**	**80.23**	**63.94**	**68.34**	**69.21**	**69.63**
HashNet-HR	77.42	79.87	80.56	80.78	64.43	69.40	69.92	70.38

Table 2. LR images retrieval results (mAP@5000) of DSRHN on NUS-WIDE and MS-COCO datasets, when the number of hash bits are 12, 24, 32 and 48.

Method	NUS-WIDE				MS-COCO			
	12bits	24bits	32bits	48bits	12bits	24bits	32bits	48bits
DCH	63.92	66.22	66.98	67.21	47.82	48.21	46.18	48.95
DHN	67.91	69.75	69.39	71.30	49.89	51.66	52.44	53.47
DPSH	69.54	72.10	71.61	72.56	55.09	55.73	57.86	56.61
DSRHN(Ours)	**77.07**	**79.40**	**80.02**	**80.23**	**63.94**	**68.34**	**69.21**	**69.63**

Table 1 shows the DSRHN and other optional models' mAP@5000 results on different hash bits. The results show that our model is always superior to other models with significant effects in terms of different bit numbers, datasets and metrics. The main reason is our framework directly enhances the hash semantics of low resolution images. Figure 2 show the results of precision-recall curves with 12 bits, and mAP@5000 with 48 bits w.r.t. different numbers of top returned images. It can be seen that our method not only works best, but also has excellent retrieval stability.

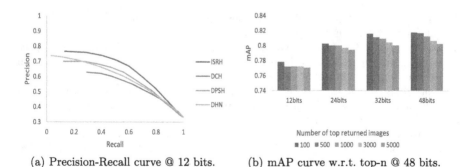

(a) Precision-Recall curve @ 12 bits.   (b) mAP curve w.r.t. top-n @ 48 bits.

Fig. 2. The results of DSRHN and comparison methods on the NUS-WIDE dataset.

4.4   Implementation Details

The proposed network consists of two parts: SRNet and HashNet. The SRNet is trained specially for 4× scale factor super-resolution. We randomly crop the 224× 224 patch in each images as the ground truth, and downsample it to 56×56 as the input LR patch for training. We use 16 residual blocks with two convolutional layers with small 3×3 kernels and 64 feature maps combined batch-normalization layers and ParametricReLU activation function. SRNet is optimized by Adam with the learning rate 0.001. For the HashNet, we use AlexNet network directly. And it is optimized by SGD with the learning rate 0.01. The λ of L_{SR} is set as 0.1, and the α of L_{hash} is set as 0.01. The training process is stopped when the training reaches 150 epochs and we select the best model for comparison. Experiments are performed on a NVIDIA TitanXp GPU.

5   Conclusion

This paper proposes a novel images hash retrieval framework (DSRHN) based on deep super-resolution. The framework consists of two main components: a super-resolution network and a hash encoding network. Super-resolution networks trained on large-scale image retrieval datasets can recover low-resolution images to high-resolution images while providing more abundant semantic information. The hash encoding network can represent the recovered images as a binary code. We use binary code for image retrieval experiments. Experimental results show that the proposed DSRHN algorithm has achieved the state-of-the-art performance.

Acknowledgements. This work was supported by National Key R&D Program of China (2018YFB0803700) and National Natural Science Foundation of China (61602517).

References

1. Cao, Y., et al.: Binary hashing for approximate nearest neighbor search on big data: a survey. IEEE Access **6**, 2039–2054 (2018)
2. Cao, Y., Long, M., Liu, B., Wang, J.: Deep cauchy hashing for hamming space retrieval. In: Proceedings of the IEEE Conference on Computer Vision and Pattern Recognition, pp. 1229–1237 (2018)
3. Chua, T.-S., Tang, J., Hong, R., Li, H., Luo, Z., Zheng, Y.: NUS-wide: a real-world web image database from national university of Singapore. In: Proceedings of the ACM International Conference on Image and Video Retrieval, p. 48. ACM (2009)
4. Datar, M., Immorlica, N., Indyk, P., Mirrokni, V.S.: Locality-sensitive hashing scheme based on p-stable distributions. In: Proceedings of the Twentieth Annual Symposium on Computational Geometry, pp. 253–262. ACM (2004)
5. Dong, C., Loy, C.C., He, K., Tang, X.: Learning a deep convolutional network for image super-resolution. In: Fleet, D., Pajdla, T., Schiele, B., Tuytelaars, T. (eds.) ECCV 2014. LNCS, vol. 8692, pp. 184–199. Springer, Cham (2014). https://doi.org/10.1007/978-3-319-10593-2_13

6. Dong, C., Loy, C.C., Tang, X.: Accelerating the super-resolution convolutional neural network. In: Leibe, B., Matas, J., Sebe, N., Welling, M. (eds.) ECCV 2016. LNCS, vol. 9906, pp. 391–407. Springer, Cham (2016). https://doi.org/10.1007/978-3-319-46475-6_25
7. Gionis, A., Indyk, P., Motwani, R., et al.: Similarity search in high dimensions via hashing. In: VLDB, vol. 99, pp. 518–529 (1999)
8. Gong, Y., Lazebnik, S., Gordo, A., Perronnin, F.: Iterative quantization: a procrustean approach to learning binary codes for large-scale image retrieval. IEEE Trans. Pattern Anal. Mach. Intell. 35(12), 2916–2929 (2013)
9. Goodfellow, I., et al.: Generative adversarial nets. In: Advances in Neural Information Processing Systems, pp. 2672–2680 (2014)
10. He, K., Zhang, X., Ren, S., Sun, J.: Deep residual learning for image recognition. In: Proceedings of the IEEE Conference on Computer Vision and Pattern Recognition, pp. 770–778 (2016)
11. Krizhevsky, A., Sutskever, I., Hinton, G.E.: Imagenet classification with deep convolutional neural networks. In: Advances in Neural Information Processing Systems, pp. 1097–1105 (2012)
12. Kulis, B., Grauman, K.: Kernelized locality-sensitive hashing. IEEE Trans. Pattern Anal. Mach. Intell. 34(6), 1092–1104 (2012)
13. Lai, H., Pan, Y., Liu, Y., Yan, S.: Simultaneous feature learning and hash coding with deep neural networks. In: Proceedings of the IEEE Conference on Computer Vision and Pattern Recognition, pp. 3270–3278 (2015)
14. Ledig, C., et al.: Photo-realistic single image super-resolution using a generative adversarial network. In: Proceedings of the IEEE Conference on Computer Vision and Pattern Recognition, pp. 4681–4690 (2017)
15. Li, C., Liu, Q., Dong, W., Zhu, X., Liu, J., Hanqing, L.: Human age estimation based on locality and ordinal information. IEEE Trans. Cybern. 45(11), 2522–2534 (2014)
16. Li, C., Liu, Q., Liu, J., Lu, H.: Ordinal distance metric learning for image ranking. IEEE Trans. Neural Netw. Learn. Syst. 26(7), 1551–1559 (2014)
17. Li, C., Wang, X., Dong, W., Yan, J., Liu, Q., Zha, H.: Joint active learning with feature selection via cur matrix decomposition. IEEE Trans. Pattern Anal. Mach. Intell. 41(6), 1382–1396 (2018)
18. Li, C., Wei, F., Dong, W., Wang, X., Liu, Q., Zhang, X.: Dynamic structure embedded online multiple-output regression for streaming data. IEEE Trans. Pattern Anal. Mach. Intell. 41(2), 323–336 (2018)
19. Li, C., Yan, J., Wei, F., Dong, W., Liu, Q., Zha, H.: Self-paced multi-task learning. In: Thirty-First AAAI Conference on Artificial Intelligence (2017)
20. Li, W.-J., Wang, S., Kang, W.-C.: Feature learning based deep supervised hashing with pairwise labels. arXiv preprint arXiv:1511.03855 (2015)
21. Lin, T.-Y., et al.: Microsoft COCO: common objects in context. In: Fleet, D., Pajdla, T., Schiele, B., Tuytelaars, T. (eds.) ECCV 2014. LNCS, vol. 8693, pp. 740–755. Springer, Cham (2014). https://doi.org/10.1007/978-3-319-10602-1_48
22. Liu, W., Wang, J., Ji, R., Jiang, Y.-G., Chang, S.-F.: Supervised hashing with kernels. In: 2012 IEEE Conference on Computer Vision and Pattern Recognition, pp. 2074–2081. IEEE (2012)
23. Liu, Y., Zhu, X., Zhao, X., Cao, Y.: Adversarial learning for constrained image splicing detection and localization based on atrous convolution. IEEE Trans. Inf. Forensics Secur. 14, 2551–2566 (2019)

24. Shi, W., et al.: Real-time single image and video super-resolution using an efficient sub-pixel convolutional neural network. In: Proceedings of the IEEE Conference on Computer Vision and Pattern Recognition, pp. 1874–1883 (2016)
25. Wang, J., Kumar, S., Chang, S.-F.: Semi-supervised hashing for large-scale search. IEEE Trans. Pattern Anal. Mach. Intell. **34**(12), 2393–2406 (2012)
26. Weiss, Y., Torralba, A., Fergus, R.: Spectral hashing. In: Advances in Neural Information Processing Systems, pp. 1753–1760 (2009)
27. Xia, R., Pan, Y., Lai, H., Liu, C., Yan, S.: Supervised hashing for image retrieval via image representation learning. In: Twenty-Eighth AAAI Conference on Artificial Intelligence (2014)
28. Zhang, X.-Y.: Simultaneous optimization for robust correlation estimation in partially observed social network. Neurocomputing **205**, 455–462 (2016)
29. Zhang, X.-Y., Shi, H., Li, C., Zheng, K., Zhu, X., Duan, L.: Learning transferable self-attentive representations for action recognition in untrimmed videos with weak supervision. arXiv preprint arXiv:1902.07370 (2019)
30. Zhang, X.-Y., Shi, H., Zhu, X., Li, P.: Active semi-supervised learning based on self-expressive correlation with generative adversarial networks. Neurocomputing **345**, 103–113 (2019)
31. Zhang, X.-Y., Wang, S., Yun, X.: Bidirectional active learning: a two-way exploration into unlabeled and labeled data set. IEEE Trans. Neural Netw. Learn. Syst. **26**(12), 3034–3044 (2015)
32. Zhang, X.-Y., Wang, S., Zhu, X., Yun, X., Wu, G., Wang, Y.: Update vs. upgrade: modeling with indeterminate multi-class active learning. Neurocomputing **162**, 163–170 (2015)
33. Zhang, X.: Interactive patent classification based on multi-classifier fusion and active learning. Neurocomputing **127**, 200–205 (2014)
34. Zhu, H., Long, M., Wang, J., Cao, Y.: Deep hashing network for efficient similarity retrieval. In: Thirtieth AAAI Conference on Artificial Intelligence (2016)
35. Zhu, X., Li, Z., Zhang, X., Li, C., Liu, Y., Xue, Z.: Residual invertible spatio-temporal network for video super-resolution. In: Thirtieth AAAI Conference on Artificial Intelligence (2019)
36. Zhu, X., Li, Z., Zhang, X., Li, H., Xue, Z., Wang, L.: Generative adversarial image super-resolution through deep dense skip connections. In: Computer Graphics Forum, vol. 37, pp. 289–300. Wiley Online Library (2018)
37. Zhu, X., Liu, J., Wang, J., Li, C., Hanqing, L.: Sparse representation for robust abnormality detection in crowded scenes. Pattern Recogn. **47**(5), 1791–1799 (2014)
38. Zhu, X., Zhang, X., Zhang, X.-Y., Xue, Z., Wang, L.: A novel framework for semantic segmentation with generative adversarial network. J. Vis. Commun. Image Represent. **58**, 532–543 (2019)

Incomplete-Data Oriented Dimension Reduction via Instance Factoring PCA Framework

Ernest Domanaanmwi Ganaa[1,3], Timothy Apasiba Abeo[1,4], Sumet Mehta[1], Heping Song[1], and Xiang-Jun Shen[1,2(✉)]

[1] School of Computer Science and Communication Engineering,
JiangSu University, Zhenjiang 212013, Jiangsu, China
xjshen@ujs.edu.cn
[2] Jingkou New-Generation Information Technology Industry Institute,
JiangSu University, Zhenjiang, China
[3] School of Applied Science and Technology, Wa Polytechnic, 553, Wa, Ghana
[4] School of Applied Science, Tamale Technical University, 3ER, Tamale, Ghana

Abstract. In this paper, we propose an instance factoring PCA (IFPCA) framework for dimension reduction in incomplete datasets. The advantage of IFPCA over the traditional PCA is that, a penalty is imposed on the instance space via a scaling-factor to suppress the effect of outliers in pursuing projections. We geometrically use two scaling-factor strategies, total distance and cosine similarity metrics. Both strategies can learn the relationship between each data point and the principal projection in the feature space. In this way, better low-rank projections are obtained through scaling the data iteratively to suppress the impact of noise in the training set. Extensive experiments on COIL-20, ORL and USPS datasets prove the superiority of the proposed framework over state-of-the-art dimensionality reduction methods such as LSDA, gLPCA, RPCA-OM, PCA, LPP and RCDA.

Keywords: Principal component analysis · Instance factoring · Incomplete-data · Dimensionality reduction · Manifold learning

1 Introduction

Massive data is generated daily such as through city-installations of high speed cameras for public safety. These data are mostly incomplete due to sensor failures or environmental obstructions in recordings. This poses a great challenge to algorithms of video surveillance in processing such missing, noisy and high dimensional datasets.

Many manifold learning methods have been proposed for dimensionality reduction (DR). These methods can broadly be divided into global structure and local structure learning. Local structure learning methods such as, Locality Sensitive Discriminant Analysis (LSDA) [1] finds a projection that maximizes the margin between data points from different classes at each local area. Neighborhood Preserving Embedding (NPE) [2] is an unsupervised linear dimensionality reduction technique which solves the out of sample problem in Locally Linear Embedding (LLE). Locality Preserving

© Springer Nature Switzerland AG 2019
Y. Zhao et al. (Eds.): ICIG 2019, LNCS 11903, pp. 479–490, 2019.
https://doi.org/10.1007/978-3-030-34113-8_40

Projections (LPP) [3] finds a good linear embedding that preserves local structure information. And global structure learning methods, such as Linear Discriminant Analysis (LDA) [4] captures the global geometric structure of data by maximizing the between class distance and minimizing the within class distance. Isomap [5] is another global learning method which estimates the geodesic distance between samples and uses multidimensional scaling to induce a low dimensional manifold.

Among the global DR methods, PCA is the most popular, simplest and efficient technique [6]. But, it is sensitive to outliers or noisy data points [7–10]. Thus, several adaptations of PCA have been developed in the past few years to improve its performance. Representatives such as graph-Laplacian PCA (gLPCA) [11] learns a low dimensional representation of data that incorporates graph structures. Optimal mean robust principal component analysis (RPCA-OM) [12] removes the mean in a given dataset automatically by integrating the mean into the dimensionality reduction objective function. Abeo et al. [13] also extended the minimizing least squares idea of PCA to consider both data distribution and penalty weights in dealing with outliers. Yang et al. [14] estimated corrupt instances by making full use of both intra-view and interview correlations between samples, considering samples in the same view to be linearly correlated. Li et al. [15] proposed ordinal preserving projection (OPP) for learning to rank by using two matrices which work in the row and column directions respectively to leverage the global structure of the dataset and ordinal information of the observations. Most existing adaptations of the standard PCA learn how to select suitable features instead of suitable samples; because of this, corrupt instances have not be efficiently handled in the past. Research in DR is still being vigorously pursued by researchers to either improve the performance of existing techniques or develop new ones.

We propose a novel framework called incomplete-data oriented dimension reduction via instance factoring PCA framework (IFPCA) to address the sensitivity of PCA to corrupt instances. In this framework, a scaling-factor that imposes a penalty on the instance space is introduced to suppress the impact of outliers or corrupt instances in pursuing projections. Two strategies: total distance and cosine similarity metrics are used geometrically to iteratively learn the relationship between each instance and the principal projection in the feature space. Through this, the two strategies are able to distinguish between authentic and corrupt instances. Thus, low-rank projections are achieved through enhanced discrimination between relevant and noisy instances. The main contributions of this paper are summarized as follows:

1. We propose a novel framework by introducing a scaling-factor into the traditional PCA model to impose a penalty on the instance space in pursuing projections. The goal here is to significantly suppress the impact of outliers.
2. We further propose two scaling-factor strategies: total distance and cosine similarity metrics. These metrics iteratively evaluate the importance of each instance by learning the relationship between each instance and the principal projection in the feature space.
3. Finally, with the iterative discrimination ability, IFPCA can obtain better low-rank projections in incomplete datasets.

Extensive experiments on COIL-20, ORL and USPS datasets demonstrate the superiority of our method over state-of-the-art methods. The rest of the paper is organized as follows: Sect. 2 presents formulation of the propose framework, experiments, results and complexity analysis are presented in Sect. 3, and conclusions and recommendations are made in Sect. 4.

2   The Proposed IFPCA Method

To illustrate our idea, we start by observing the objective function of PCA:

$$\min_{w^T w=1} \sum_{i=1}^{n} (x_i - ww^T x_i)^2 = min \left\| X - ww^T X \right\|_2^2 \tag{1}$$

where $\{\mathbf{w}\}_{j=1}^{d}$ is a subset of orthogonal projection vectors in $\Re^m$ and the set of data points $\{\mathbf{x}_i\}_{i=1}^{n}$ is zero-mean m-dimensional data points. It can be seen that, PCA uses a least square framework to minimize the sum distance between the original dataset X and the reconstructed dataset $ww^T X$. This geometrically will force the projection vector w to pass through the densest data points to minimize the sum distance. This can be seen in Fig. 1, where u_1 is the first principal projection vector. From this intuition, we evaluate the importance of instances by considering the relationship between each instance and the principal projection u_1. That is, the closer an instance to the projection vector u_1, the more important the instance in pursuing projections.

Therefore, we extend formula (1) to include a scaling-factor. This factor imposes a penalty on the instance space to suppress the impact of noise in incomplete datasets. The following is our propose function:

$$\min_{D,p} \left\| X - XDpp^T D \right\|_F^2 = \max_{D,p} p^T DX^T XDp \tag{2}$$

$$s.t. \; p^T D^2 p = 1$$

where p is a vector of sample space and $D = diag(d_1, d_2, \cdots, d_n)$ is a diagonal matrix that evaluates the importance of each instance in X. With this penalty, we are actually pursuing a projection $Z = Dp$ with $Z^T Z = I$ that considers the effect of instances. For example, if a lower scaling-factor d_i is assigned to the projection Z, the component of sample space Z_i is suppressed, which means the corresponding sample x_i contributes little to the projection Z.

To enforce the constraint in formula (2), we introduce the Lagrange multiplier (λ) and take partial derivatives w.r.t. p to obtain:

$$X^T XDp = \lambda Dp \tag{3}$$

It can be observed that Eq. (3) is a standard eigenvalue problem.

Mathematically, there is a direct relationship [16] between PCA and SVD when PCA components are calculated from the covariance matrix. The equation for singular value decomposition (SVD) of X is as follows:

$$X = u\Sigma v^T \quad s.t. \; u^T u = I_r, v^T v = I_r \tag{4}$$

In our proposed model, $v = DP$, where P is the set of r projections of p. Thus, the projection u in feature space can be obtained as follows:

$$u = XDP\Sigma^{-1} \qquad (5)$$

where the low dimension feature space u is obtained with an injection of sample factors different from the traditional PCA. In this way, IFPCA can learn a low dimensional subspace from both sample and feature spaces of a dataset for improved performance.

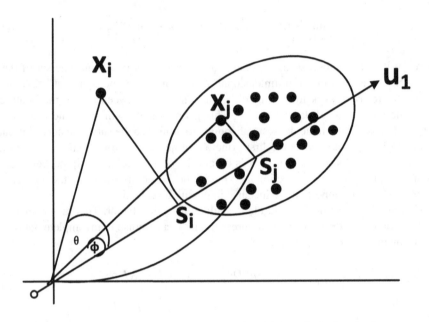

Fig. 1. Illustration of an instance relationship with the principal projection

2.1   Strategies of Building Matrix D

In this subsection, we model the relationship between scaling-factor D and the principal projection u_1 using two strategies: total distance and cosine similarity metrics. Both can be obtained geometrically as shown in Fig. 1.

The first strategy uses total distance metric to iteratively learn the relationship between each instance and the principal projection u_1. The total distance of an instance is defined as the square sum of the distances between the coordinate of each instance and the coordinates of every other instance in the training set to the projection u_1. The total distance of an instance is a natural way to evaluate its importance within the set. From Fig. 1, we can observe that the total distance of instance x_i which is outside the cluster will be relatively bigger than that of instance x_j within the cluster. Therefore, instance x_i is more likely to be an outlier or corrupt instance than x_j. From Fig. 1, the coordinate of instance x_i to the projection u_1 is computed through:

$$s_i = u_1^T x_i \qquad (6)$$

Algorithm 1. The proposed IFPCA method

1: **Input:** Training set X
2: **Output:** The projection vector p
3: **Parameters:** ε
4: **Initialize:** Initialize D as an identity matrix
5: **while** not converged **do**
6:     obtain p based on eqn. (3).
7:     obtain u based on eqn. (5)
8:     Update D based on eqn. (7) or (9)
9:     Compute loss from formula (2).
10: **end while**

We then compute d_i through total distance metric as follows:

$$d_i = \sum_{i,j=1}^{n} (s_i - s_j)^2 \tag{7}$$

Thus, the bigger the d_i, the more likely x_i is a noisy or corrupt instance and hence its relevance will be scaled accordingly to suppress its effect on the projection.

The second strategy uses cosine similarity metric to build the scaling-factor D. This also iteratively learns the angle relationship between each instance in the training set and the principal projection u_1. Thus, by normalizing formula (6), the angle between each instance and the principal projection u_1 is defined as follows:

$$\cos \theta_i = \frac{u_1^T x_i}{\|u_1\| \cdot \|x_i\|} \tag{8}$$

From formula (8), a bigger $\cos \theta_i$ implies a smaller angle θ_i between instance x_i and the principal projection u_1 and vice versa. We illustrate the relationship between an instance and the principal projection in Fig. 1. From Fig. 1, it can be seen that, angle ϕ of instance x_j is relatively smaller than angle θ of instance x_i. Thus, x_j will be considered probably more important in finding best projections than x_i which might be noisy. Recall that d_i is a negative factor, we compute d_i through the similarity metric as follows:

$$d_i = \frac{1}{abs(\cos \theta_i) + \varepsilon} \tag{9}$$

where, $\varepsilon = 0.0001$ is a parameter to avoid d_i approaching infinity.

By iteratively scaling the data using these two strategies, the effect of corrupt instances in the training set will considerably minimize leading to better low-rank projections. The algorithm of the proposed IFPCA method is as shown in algorithm 1.

3 Experiments and Complexity Analysis

To demonstrate the effectiveness of the proposed IFPCA algorithm, we conduct experiments on COIL-20, ORL and USPS datasets using the proposed IFPCA and six state-of-the-art DR methods such as LSDA [1], gLPCA [11], RPCA-OM [12], PCA [17], LPP [3] and RCDA [18].

3.1   Parameter Settings

For each dataset, we randomly sampled 60%, 70% of the instances for training and 40 and 30% respectively for testing in our experiments. The parameters of LSDA [1], gLPCA [11], RPCA-OM [12], PCA [17], LPP [3] and RCDA [18] were set according to their literature. We set the k-nearest-neighbors parameter K to 5 in IFPCA, and all other relevant comparative methods, in order to make a very fair comparison. We finally make use of the K-nearest neighbor (KNN) classifier for classifications. We record results for our framework as IFPCA-1 and IFPCA-2, where IFPCA-1 and IFPCA-2 represent cosine similarity and total distance metrics respectively. The experiments are repeated 15 times and we record the average classification accuracies, corresponding optimal dimensions and standard deviations for the various methods.

3.2   Results Discussions and Analysis

We discuss and analyze the results obtained for each method on the three datasets used for our experiments in this section.

Object Recognition. We validate the proposed methods on object recognition using COIL-20 dataset. This dataset [19] contains 1440 observations of 20 objects with 72 poses each. The objects were placed on a motorized turntable against a black background and rotated through 360° to vary the object pose with respect to a fix camera. Images of the 20 objects were taken at pose intervals of 5°. The results for the various methods are shown in Table 1 with best results in bold. From Table 1, we can see that IFPCA-1 and IFPCA-2 both have superior performances than all the comparative methods. For optimal dimensions, IFPCA-1 and IFPCA-2 obtain phenomenal optimal dimensions in both samples as compare to the other six comparative methods. For the 60% sample, IFPCA-1 outperforms IFPCA-2 by a small margin of 0.16%, gLPCA by an impressive margin of 2.69%, RPCA-OM by 1.61%, PCA by 3.44%, LPP by 11.86%, LSDA by 11.25% and RCDA by 2.19%. Again, IFPCA-1 and IFPCA-2 obtain the lowest variances in both cases which prove their consistency in performance.

Thus, the proposed methods have superior performances than all other comparative methods in object recognition and optimal dimensions. This is because the two proposed methods can detect and sufficiently suppress the impact of noisy data points in the training set than the other comparative methods. Figure 2 shows the trend of classification accuracies of each method against the variation of dimensions. It is evident from Fig. 2 that IFPCA-1, IFPCA-2, RPCA-OM, PCA and RCDA attain stable performances in higher dimensions above 10. While the performances of gLPCA, LPP and LSDA decline considerably as the dimensions increase.

Face Recognition. We further validate the effectiveness of the proposed method on face recognition using the ORL face dataset. This dataset [20] has 40 subjects, each with 10 faces at different poses making a total of 400 images of size 112×92. However, the images were resized to 32×32 for our experiments. These images were taken at different times, lighting and facial expressions. The faces are in an upright position in

Table 1. Mean classification accuracies ± standard deviation (%) and (optimal dimensions) of the various methods on the COIL-20 dataset.

Sample	60%	70%
IFPCA-1	**97.84 ± 0.05(21)**	**98.89 ± 0.001(23)**
IFPCA-2	97.68 ± 0.009(36)	98.77 ± 0.003(37)
RCDA	95.65 ± 0.40(57)	97.21 ± 0.31(58)
PCA	94.40 ± 0.39(92)	95.50 ± 0.28(95)
RPCA-OM	96.23 ± 0.11(57)	98.46 ± 0.20(60)
gLPCA	95.15 ± 0.18(214)	96.31 ± 0.23(217)
LPP	85.98 ± 1.42(155)	87.49 ± 1.25(163)
LSDA	86.59 ± 1.48(142)	88.41 ± 1.39(144)

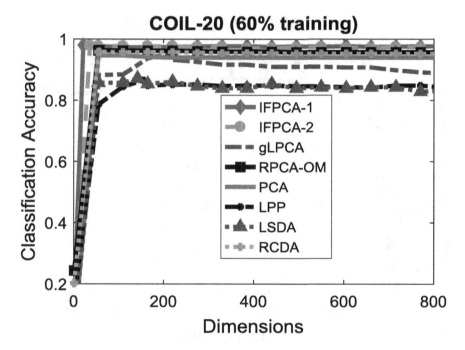

Fig. 2. Classification accuracies against the variation of dimensions on the COIL-20 dataset by the various methods

frontal view with a slight left-right rotation. The results for the various methods are shown in Table 2 with best results in bold.

The results as shown in Table 2, clearly indicate that IFPCA-1 and IFPCA-2 both have exceptional performances compared to all the comparative methods in face recognition in both the 60 and 70% training samples. For the 70% training sample, IFPCA-1 achieves a remarkable face recognition accuracy of 98.67% and the best optimal dimension of 25 with gLPCA and LPP achieving the worst dimensions of 279 each. Thus, for

Table 2. Mean classification accuracies ± standard deviation (%) and (optimal dimensions) of the various methods on the ORL dataset.

Sample	60%	70%
IFPCA-1	**97.41 ± 0.09(24)**	**98.67 ± 0.21(25)**
IFPCA-2	96.57 ± 0.14(34)	98.29 ± 0.11(36)
RCDA	95.51 ± 0.28(58)	96.47 ± 0.23(59)
PCA	92.90 ± 0.68(158)	94.32 ± 0.45(160)
RPCA-OM	94.32 ± 0.85(126)	95.83 ± 0.37(127)
gLPCA	94.02 ± 0.20(279)	95.61 ± 0.33(279)
LPP	91.01 ± 1.07(279)	92.12 ± 0.83(279)
LSDA	88.24 ± 0.90(155)	90.54 ± 0.85(195)

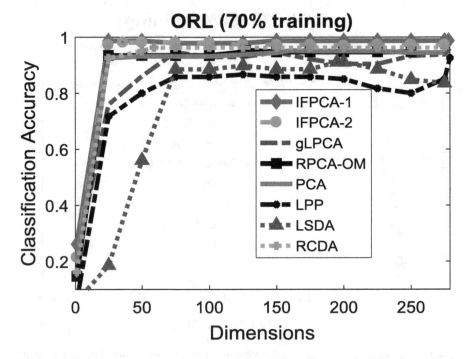

Fig. 3. Classification accuracies against the variation of dimensions on the ORL dataset by the various methods

face recognition accuracy, IFPCA-1 outperforms IFPCA-2 by a little margin of 0.38%, gLPCA by 3.06%, RPCA-OM by 2.84%, PCA by 4.35%, LPP by 6.55%, LSDA by 8.13% and RCDA by 2.20%. Figure 3 shows the trend of classification accuracies of each method against the variation of dimensions. It is clear from Fig. 3 that the performances of IFPCA-1, IFPCA-2, RPCA-OM, PCA and RCDA have once again been stable irrespective of increases in dimensions. While that of gLPCA, LPP and LSDA are considerably unstable. The results further show that IFPCA-1 and IFPCA-2 have the most consistent performances in the 60 and 70% samples respectively.

Handwritten Digit Recognition. In our quest to further demonstrate the effectiveness of our framework, we run experiments on the USPS dataset. This dataset [21] consists of handwritten digits from 0 to 9. The training and testing sets consist of 7291 examples and 2007 examples respectively. Each example has 256 attributes or pixels that describe each digit. The results for the various methods are shown in Table 3 with best results in bold.

From Table 3, IFPCA-1 and IFPCA-2 once again out perform all the comparative methods in handwritten digit recognition for both training samples of the USPS dataset. For the 60% sample, IFPCA-1 has a digit recognition accuracy of 0.55% more than IFPCA-2, 1.87% more than gLPCA, 1.69% more than RPCA-OM, 3.06% more than PCA, 3.09% more than LPP, 3.73% more than LSDA and 1.75% more than RCDA. IFPCA-1 further obtains the best optimal dimensions of 27 and 29 in the 60 and 70% training samples respectively.

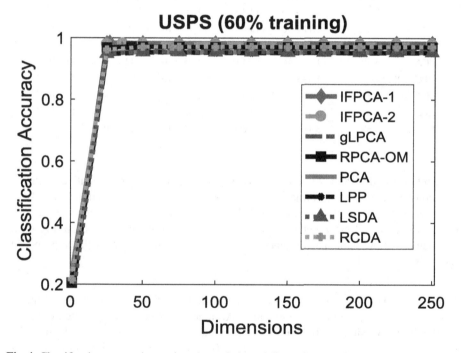

Fig. 4. Classification accuracies against the variation of dimensions on the USPS dataset by the various methods

Table 3. Mean classification accuracies $\pm$ standard deviation (%) and (optimal dimensions) of the various methods on USPS dataset.

Sample	60%	70%
IFPCA-1	**98.40 ± 0.03(27)**	**98.87 ± 0.002(29)**
IFPCA-2	97.85 ± 0.011(36)	98.56 ± 0.014(37)
RCDA	96.65 ± 0.33(70)	97.51 ± 0.25(71)
PCA	95.34 ± 0.18(55)	96.40 ± 0.15(60)
RPCA-OM	96.71 ± 0.17(42)	97.52 ± 0.22(44)
gLPCA	96.53 ± 0.27(53)	97.03 ± 0.36(55)
LPP	95.31 ± 0.18(71)	96.29 ± 0.31(73)
LSDA	95.67 ± 0.21(74)	96.50 ± 0.19(80)

Table 4. Computation time in seconds for training and testing for each method

Dataset	COIL20		ORL		USPS	
	Training	Testing	Training	Testing	Training	Testing
IFPCA-1	3.26	4.62×10^{-3}	1.93×10^{-1}	1.18×10^{-3}	1.69	2.20×10^{-3}
IFPCA-2	2.12	2.71×10^{-3}	1.68×10^{-1}	1.13×10^{-3}	3.82	5.40×10^{-3}
RCDA	3.51	$2.24 \times 10-2$	2.05	1.95×10^{-2}	4.02	5.13×10^{-2}
PCA	5.29×10^{-1}	1.95×10^{-2}	8.44×10^{-2}	1.95×10^{-2}	4.42×10^{-1}	2.80×10^{-2}
RPCA-OM	1.12	1.48×10^{-2}	1.33×10^{-1}	4.24×10^{-3}	1.78	1.01×10^{-1}
gLPCA	6.10×10^{-1}	5.93×10^{-3}	5.81×10^{-2}	2.46×10^{-3}	5.33×10^{-1}	6.50×10^{-3}
LPP	6.08×10^{-1}	$1.43x10^{-2}$	8.00×10^{-2}	5.32×10^{-3}	5.44×10^{-1}	7.48×10^{-3}
LSDA	5.62×10^{-1}	3.18×10^{-2}	1.16×10^{-1}	2.05×10^{-2}	4.24×10^{-1}	1.28×10^{-2}

IFPCA-1 and IFPCA-2 obtain the lowest variances than the comparative methods. The consistency in the performances of IFPCA-1 and IFPCA-2 proved their ability to discover better intrinsic structure of the dataset. Figure 4 shows the trend of classification accuracies of each method against the variation of dimensions. From Fig. 4 all the methods show stable performances in dimensions above 20, but with the proposed methods in the lead.

Complexity Analysis. We compare the computational times of the proposed methods to the other six comparative methods. All algorithms were implemented in MAT-LAB R2016b version 9.1.0.441655 64-bit using a personal computer with Intel (R) Core(TM) i5-7500 CPU @ 3.40 GHz with 8.00 GB memory and Windows 7 operating system environment. The convergence of the proposed framework depends on the importance evaluation diagonal matrix D. The computation time of an eigenvalue problem on a training set X of size $m \times n$ is $O(m^3)$. This means that a complexity of $O(m^3)$ is required by the proposed framework to compute the projection vector p since our framework is an eigenvalue problem. For the inner loop, if it takes k number of iterations in pursuing D for convergence to be attained, the complexity is $O(kmn)$. Hence, the total complexity of the framework becomes $O(t(m^3 + kmn))$, where t is the number of iterations of the outer loop. Table 4 shows the computation time for each method on all three datasets.

4 Conclusions and Recommendation

We proposed in this paper a novel incomplete-data oriented dimension reduction via instance factoring PCA framework. Different from other variants of PCA, a scaling-factor that imposes a penalty on the instance space is introduced to suppress the impact of noise in pursuing projections. Two strategies, cosine similarity and total distance metrics are used geometrically to iteratively learn the relationship between each instance and the principal projection.

Comprehensive experiments on COIL-20, ORL and USPS datasets demonstrate the effectiveness of the proposed framework in both dimension reduction and classification tasks. This is because it is able to obtain low-rank projections in incomplete datasets by suppressing the effect of noisy or corrupt instances. This shows that our framework is more noise tolerant than the other comparative methods. We will extend this framework to low rank representation in the near future.

Acknowledgments. This work was funded in part by the National Natural Science Foundation of China(No. 61572240) and Natural Science Foundation of Jiangsu Province (No. BK20170558).

References

1. Deng, C., He, X., Zhou, K., Han, J., Bao, H.: Locality sensitive discriminant analysis (2007)
2. Teoh, A.B.J., Han, P.Y.: Face recognition based on neighbourhood discriminant preserving embedding. In: International Conference on Control, Automation, Robotics and Vision, pp. 428–433 (2009)
3. Feng, G., Hu, D., Zhou, Z.: A direct locality preserving projections (DLPP) algorithm for image recognition. Neural Process. Lett. **27**(3), 247–255 (2008)
4. Chen, J., Ye, J., Li, Q.: Integrating global and local structures: a least squares framework for dimensionality reduction. In: IEEE Conference on Computer Vision and Pattern Recognition, pp. 1–8 (2007)
5. Yang, M.H.: Face recognition using extended isomap. In: International Conference on Image Processing (2002)
6. Wiriyathammabhum, P., Kijsirikul, B.: Robust principal component analysis using statistical estimators. arXiv preprint arXiv:1207.0403 (2012)
7. Jolliffe, I.T., Cadima, J.: Principal component analysis: a review and recent developments. Philos. Trans. Roy. Soc. A Math. Phys. Eng. Sci. **374**(2065), 20150202 (2016)
8. Roweis, S.T.: EM algorithms for PCA and SPCA. In: Advances in Neural Information Processing Systems, pp. 626–632 (1998)
9. Kriegel, H.-P., Kröger, P., Schubert, E., Zimek, A.: A general framework for increasing the robustness of PCA-based correlation clustering algorithms. In: Ludäscher, B., Mamoulis, N. (eds.) SSDBM 2008. LNCS, vol. 5069, pp. 418–435. Springer, Heidelberg (2008). https://doi.org/10.1007/978-3-540-69497-7_27
10. Vaswani, N., Bouwmans, T., Javed, S., Narayanamurthy, P.: Robust PCA, subspace learning, and tracking. IEEE Signal Process. Mag. **35**, 32–55 (2018)

11. Jiang, B., Ding, C., Luo, B., Tang, J.: Graph-Laplacian PCA: closed-form solution and robustness. In: Proceedings of the IEEE Conference on Computer Vision and Pattern Recognition, pp. 3492–3498 (2013)
12. Nie, F., Yuan, J., Huang, H.: Optimal mean robust principal component analysis. In: International Conference on Machine Learning, pp. 1062–1070 (2014)
13. Abeo, T.A., Shen, X.J., Gou, J.P., Mao, Q.R., Bao, B.K., Li, S.: Dictionary-induced least squares framework for multi-view dimensionality reduction with multi-manifold embeddings. IET Comput. Vision **13**(2), 97–108 (2019)
14. Yang, W., Shi, Y., Gao, Y., Wang, L., Yang, M.: Incomplete-data oriented multiview dimension reduction via sparse low-rank representation. IEEE Trans. Neural Netw. Learn. Syst. **29**, 6276–6291 (2018)
15. Li, C., Liu, J., Liu, Y., Xu, C., Liu, Q., Lu, H.: Ordinal preserving projection: a novel dimensionality reduction method for image ranking. In: Proceedings of the 2nd ACM International Conference on Multimedia Retrieval, p. 17. ACM (2012)
16. Wall, M.E., Rechtsteiner, A., Rocha, L.M.: Singular value decomposition and principal component analysis. In: Berrar, D.P., Dubitzky, W., Granzow, M. (eds.) A Practical Approach to Microarray Data Analysis, vol. 5, pp. 91–109. Springer, Boston (2003). https://doi.org/10.1007/0-306-47815-3_5
17. Vidal, R., Ma, Y., Sastry, S.S.: Generalized Principal Component Analysis. IAM, vol. 40. Springer, New York (2016). https://doi.org/10.1007/978-0-387-87811-9
18. Huang, K.K., Dai, D.Q., Ren, C.X.: Regularized coplanar discriminant analysis for dimensionality reduction. Pattern Recogn. **62**(Complete), 87–98 (2017)
19. Alom, M.Z., Josue, T., Rahman, M.N., Mitchell, W., Yakopcic, C., Taha, T.M.: Deep versus wide convolutional neural networks for object recognition on neuromorphic system. arXiv preprint arXiv:1802.02608 (2018)
20. Jiang, R., Al-Maadeed, S., Bouridane, A., Crookes, D., Celebi, M.E.: Face recognition in the scrambled domain via salience-aware ensembles of many kernels. IEEE Trans. Inf. Forensics Secur. **11**(8), 1807–1817 (2016)
21. Proedrou, K., Nouretdinov, I., Vovk, V., Gammerman, A.: Transductive confidence machines for pattern recognition. In: Elomaa, T., Mannila, H., Toivonen, H. (eds.) ECML 2002. LNCS (LNAI), vol. 2430, pp. 381–390. Springer, Heidelberg (2002). https://doi.org/10.1007/3-540-36755-1_32

Pose-Invariant Facial Expression Recognition Based on 3D Face Morphable Model and Domain Adversarial Learning

Xiao Ma[1], Kaige Zhang[2($\boxtimes$)], and Xuan Yang[3]

[1] School of Computer Science and Engineering,
South China University of Technology, Guangzhou 510641, China
201630610632@mail.scut.edu.cn
[2] Department of Computer Science, Utah State University, Logan 84322, USA
kg.zhang@aggiemail.usu.edu
[3] College of Software, Taiyuan University of Technology, Taiyuan 030600, China

Abstract. Pose is one of the most important factors affecting performance of face related recognition algorithms including facial expression recognition (FER). Traditionally, non-frontal FER is conducted by either performing face formalization or designing separate models for different poses. Different from those methods, we propose a one-stage FER approach by training a pose invariant deep convolutional network (DCNN) with the following novelties: First, we introduce the 3D face morphable model to reconstruct high fidelity 3D faces for data augmentation which increases the pose variety without losing expression information. Second, we employ domain adversarial learning to eliminate the influence of domain difference between real 2D face images and 3D synthetic face images at feature level, which realizes a one-stage deep FER approach that is robust to different face poses. Third, the proposed approach provides a solution for cross-domain problems involving data from different sources, which can be applied to other face related recognition problems. The method is validated using three FER datasets FER2013, multi-PIE and BU-3DFE; and it outperforms the current state-of-the-art methods.

Keywords: Facial expression recognition · Deep learning · 3D morphable model · Domain adaptation

1 Introduction

Computer vision based facial expression recognition (FER) has been a research topic for many years. In the early time, Ekman et al. [1] defined six basic facial expressions shared among human beings to express their emotions (i.e., anger, disgust, fear, happiness, sadness and surprise). With the fast development of artificial intelligence, FER has gained increasing attentions because of its valuable applications such as driver fatigue monitoring, human-computer interaction, medical care, digital entertainment, etc. In general, FER is conducted by

© Springer Nature Switzerland AG 2019
Y. Zhao et al. (Eds.): ICIG 2019, LNCS 11903, pp. 491–502, 2019.
https://doi.org/10.1007/978-3-030-34113-8_41

feature extraction and machine classification. Traditionally, feature extraction is conducted by using hand-crafted feature extractors such as local binary patterns (LBPs) [2], histogram of gradients (HOG) [3], and histogram of optical flow (HOF) [11]; and for machine classification, it can be support vector machine, Bayesian classifiers, random forest, etc. These methods achieved some success on FER; however, in-the-wild facial expression recognition task is still a challenge due to the high appearance changes.

Over the last several years, deep learning has achieved great success and dominated the state-of-the-arts in many challenging problems [4], in which an artificial neural network (ANN) with multiple hidden layers is used; and it has been viewed as the most promising means for solving in-the-wild FER problem. However, deep learning based approach is a data-driven strategy which relies on large amount of relevant training data; in practice, the available datasets mainly consist of frontal face images, that makes the FER with large pose face images remain a challenge.

There has been methods addressing non-frontal face expression recognition problems, which involves 3D and 2D methods [5–7]. Traditionally, the 3D method was suffering from the computation efficiency and hard-to-converge problems [5]; and the 2D based methods are usually designed as view-specific and they required a similar amount of data in different poses for the training, which limits the performance of the methods because that there exists a disproportion in the availability of frontal and non-frontal view facial expression data [6]. Such problem is more distinct in deep learning based method because of the inherent data-hungry and data-dependence. During the past several years, the 3D face morphable model has achieved impressive progress and the model has been used to reconstruct high fidelity tridimensional faces which can not only construct the 3D face shape from a 2D face image but can also reserve the other attributes such as face expressions [7,8]. With the fact that 3D model is able to produce 2D face images from arbitrary views, it can be used to improve the face related recognition algorithms.

In this paper, we propose a one-stage pose-invariant FER approach by training a DCNN. First, the 68-landmarks are located accurately from a 2D face image. Then, the state-of-the-art 3D morphable model (3DDFA) [8] is used to reconstruct the 3D face model from the 2D image without losing the original facial expression information; and the reconstructed 3D face is used to produce high fidelity 2D face images with the same emotion as the original face at multiple poses. At last, the augmented facial image data, including original and 3D generated face images, are utilized to perform a joint, alternative training for FER where feature-level domain adversarial learning is utilized for network training to eliminate the influence of domain difference between 3D-generated face images and the real 2D face images. The experimental results demonstrate the effectiveness of the proposed method.

The rest of the paper is organized as follows. In Sect. 2, it introduces the works related to the proposed method. In Sect. 3, it discusses the proposed method. In Sect. 4, it presents the experimental settings and the results. In Sect. 5, it concludes the paper.

2   Related Works

Systematic FER has been discussed in some survey papers [9–11]. Here, we first review some FER works related to this work. Then, we give a brief introduction to other related works including 3D face morphable model and generative adversarial learning.

2.1   Facial Expression Recognition

Deep learning based methods have been used for FER with the availability of large amount training data. Mollahossein et al. [12,13] introduced deep neural networks for automatic feature extraction which outperformed the hand-crafted feature extraction methods. Jung et al. [14] fine-tuned a deep neural network for FER. Hasani et al. [15] proposed a spatio-temporal FER method using DCNN and conditional random field. Based on local facial action units, Liu et al. [16,17] extract facial features on several key points for FER. These works achieved very good performances for frontal face expression recognition; however, they are suffering from performance degradation with large pose face images. Pose-invariant FER has been studies for many years of which the traditional pattern classification methods were employed [18–20]. Recently, deep learning based methods have also been utilized to address this issue. Zhang et al. [21] combined traditional feature extraction method (SIFT) with deep neural network for multi-view FER. Liu et al. [22] proposed a multi-channel pose-aware CNN for multi-view FER. Lai et al. [23] employed generative adversarial networks (GANs) to perform face frontalization before expression recognition of non-frontal faces. A common issue in deep learning based methods is the lacking of sufficient labeled face data which results a network either biased to the frontal face recognition or with poor performance.

2.2   3D Face Morphable Model

Blanz et al. [24] proposed the 3D face morphable model which can be directly matched to a 2D image, where the head pose, expression, illumination and other parameters are free variables subject to be optimized. Based on accurate landmark detection, it can be used to reconstruct photo-realistic face from a 2D face image [7]. Recently, by introducing deep neural networks, the state-of-the-art of 3D face alignment has been pushed to a new level. For example, Zhu et al. [8] utilized deep neural network to regress the 3DMM parameters from 2D face images to reconstruct high fidelity 3D faces where the landmark information is used. Chang et al. [25] proposed ExpNet which regress the 3D expression parameters directly from the face images without using landmark detection. In this work, we used the 68-landmark detection as a proxy step and reconstruct 3D face from a 2D face image with expression label to generate face images at multiple poses for data augmentation.

2.3   Domain Adversarial Learning

Goodfellow et al. [26] proposed the generative adversarial network (GAN) which can be trained to generate real-like images by minimizing the distribution difference of the data generated from random noise or from real-world by playing a max-min game. While GAN provided a strategy to generate real-like data at the image level, Ganin et al. [27] proposed deep domain adaptation which can transfer two or multiple domains to a common domain at feature level. The com-mon thing is that they both used the adversarial loss to make the generated images/features indistinguishable by the discriminator (i.e., eliminate the domain difference between two datasets at image/feature level). In this work, we introduced the domain adversarial learning for a joint training to eliminate the domain difference between 3D-generated face images and the real face image which reserves the facial expression information in the meanwhile.

3   Proposed Method

3.1   Overview

This approach employs the 3DMM for data augmentation and proposes a novel learning strategy to overcome the domain problem that has troubled the network training. Figure 1 is an overview of the proposed method. Given a 2D face image, it first performs 68-landmark detection with a well-trained deep convolutional neural network. Then the landmarks and the original 2D face image is sent to 3DDFA to fit the 3D morphable model (3DMM) and reconstruct a 3D face with high fidelity where the expression parameters are also well regressed. The 3D model is then used to produce 2D face images with different poses for non-frontal-face data augmentation. Ideally with sufficient data, the deep classification network can be trained to recognition different facial expressions; however, it is found that the network can well classify the 3D generated face images but suffered performance degradation when dealing with the real 2D data. In order to eliminate the influence of domain difference between the generated face images and the original 2D face image, it introduces feature-level domain adaptation to perform a joint training which updates the network parameters with original 2D face image and generated 2D face image alternatively, following the training of a generative adversarial network (GAN).

3.2   2D Facial Landmark Detection

Landmark detection has been a proxy step for 3DMM fitting of which a 2D image and the corresponding key points are necessary to construct a high fidelity 3D face. Comparing to regressing a complicated 3D face morphable model (some recent work has tried to regress 3D face model directly from 2D image [25]), the landmarks detection using a DCNN is relatively easy and the effectiveness has been studied and verified by many references [28]. In this work, we start from performing the 68-facial landmarks detection from 2D face images (i.e.,

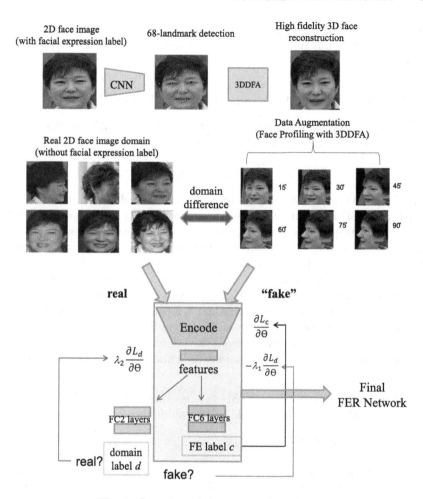

Fig. 1. Overview of the proposed method.

performing a 2D face alignment) with a deep convolutional network. Then the landmark information and the original 2D image are used to reconstruct the corresponding 3D face with 3D face morphable model.

For landmark alignment, the most widely used dataset 300-W-LP [29] is introduced; it is obtained by expanding the 300-W dataset where the landmark annotation is available. Following [30], we directly train a deep convolutional network to regress the landmark coordinates with the normalized mean error loss:

$$NME = \frac{1}{N} \sum_{k=1}^{N} \frac{\|x_k - y_k\|_2}{d} \tag{1}$$

where x is the ground truth (GT) landmarks of a 2D face image, y is the estimated landmark coordinates obtained by the deep network, and d is the square-root of the GT bounding box. VGG-16 is used as the base network for the training and the network is fine-tuned based on the state-of-the-art face recognition network [31].

3.3   Multi-pose Data Augmentation with 3D Model

3D Face Reconstruction. Blanz et al. [24] developed the 3D morphable model for human-face description with the following formulation:

$$S = \bar{S} + A_{id}\alpha_{id} + A_{exp}\alpha_{exp} \tag{2}$$

where S is a 3D face model, $\bar{S}$ is a mean face model, A_{id} is the principle axes trained on the 3D face scans with neutral expression, α_{id} is the shape parameter, A_{exp} is the principle axes trained on the offsets between expression scans and neutral scans and α_{exp} is the expression parameter. It has been studied in many works [7,8] that with the accurate 68-landmarks and the original face image, the 2D image can be mapped to the 3D model to obtain a 3D face. In this paper, it employs the state-of-the-art 3D face alignment method [8] where a deep convolutional network is trained for parameter optimization via minimizing the difference of the generated 2D face and the real 2D face. By this way, a high fidelity 3D face can be constructed from the related real 2D face image with the same facial emotion. Refer [8] for more details about the face reconstruction.

Data Augmentation. After the 3D face is constructed, it can be projected onto specific 2D plane with the scale orthographic projection:

$$V(p) = f * Pr * R * (\bar{s} + A_{id}\alpha_{id} + A_{exp}\alpha_{id}) + t_{2d} \tag{3}$$

where $V(p)$ is the model construction and projection function, leading to the 2D positions of model vertices, f is the scale factor, Pr is the orthographic projection matrix, R is the rotation matrix and t_{2d} is the translation vector.

Based on the 3D-2D geometric mapping described above, it can generate 2D face images of arbitrary poses with the same expression label as the original image which can be used to augment the image data of non-frontal face. In our experiments, yaw angles of 15°, 30°, 45°, 60°, 75°, 90° are produced for each face; and they are used to train a deep neural network for FER.

3.4   Joint Training with Domain Adaptation

Ideally, if the related data is sufficient (i.e., non-frontal face images with different poses), the network could be trained to recognize facial expressions under different poses with a classic 6-class Sofmax loss. However, in our initial attempts, it was found that the network achieved very bad performance on the testing set for both frontal and non-frontal face images, even worse than the network trained without using data augmentation [refer Sect. 4.3]. After further exploration, it was found that the network did well on the 3D generated face images. That indicates: (1) the 2D images generated from the 3D model is facial expression distinguishable; (2) the 3D model was well aligned which reserved the expression information; (3) the generated 2D images are not totally the same as the images captured directly using a camera.

In conclusion, there is a domain difference between the generated 2D images from the 3D model and the real 2D images which has failed the network training. That is, the "well-trained" network is a biased one which tends to deal with the generated images well; however, the true target, FER from real 2D face images, was not achieved. While the network can be used for the FER task by first fitting a 2D image to a 3D model and then generates a face image for FER, it is time consuming and tedious.

To develop a straight-forward FER deep network from 2D face images, we introduce the domain adaptation where the domain adversarial loss is utilized:

$$L_{adv} = -E_{x \in I}[log D(x)] \tag{4}$$

where x is the input face image, I is the 3D generated image dataset. It is combined with the regular softmax loss to perform a joint training which eliminates the domain difference between the generated face images and the real 2D face images. Different from other joint learning approaches which combined the losses as whole for the training, we treated them separately and updated the parameters alternatively using the images from the two domains. Thus, when the input image is a real 2D face image, it updates the network with the gradient computed from the domain loss $\frac{\partial L_d^r}{\partial \theta}$; however, when the input image is a 3D generated image, it updates the network using both the domain loss and the expression class loss, of which the negative gradient of the domain loss is used which aims at eliminating the domain difference between generated face images and real face images. Finally, the full objective is

$$L_{final} = 1\{x \in I\} * (L_{adv} + \lambda_1 L_d) + 1\{x \in R\} * \lambda_2 L_d \tag{5}$$

where I is the 3D generated dataset, R is the real dataset, and λ_1 and λ_2 are experimental results 0.30 and 0.65, respectively.

3.5   Implementation

As illustrated in Fig. 1, the network architecture is detailed as follows:
C_96_7_2 - ReLU - C_128_3_2 - ReLU - C_128_3_1 - ReLU - C_256_3_2 - ReLU - C_256_3_1 - ReLU - C_256_3_2 - ReLU - C_512_3_1 - ReLU - C_512_3_2 - ReLU - C_512_3_1 - ReLU - C_512_3_2 - ReLU - FC_512 - ReLU - FC_6/FC_2- SF_6/SF_2
The naming rule follows the format: "layer type_channel number_kernel size_stride"; "C" denotes convolution; "FC" is fully connected layer; and SF is the softmax layer. For instance, "C_64_7_2" means that the first layer is a convolutional layer and the number of channels is 64, the kernel size is 7 and the stride is 2. Note that the FC_6 is designed for the classification of 6 expressions; FC_2 is designed for the adversarial learning where the 2 channels represent for the two domains.

For training, different from other joint learning approaches which combined the losses as whole for the training, we adopt the training strategy of GAN and treated the two losses separately and update the network parameters by alternatively backpropogating the domain loss and the 6-class classification loss where the adversarial loss with negative gradients is back-propagated when the input sample is from 3DMM model.

4   Experiments

4.1   Dataset and Settings

To evaluate the proposed method, we compare with different methods including the traditional handcrafted-feature extraction and deep learning based methods. The confusion matrix and overall accuracy on the multi-view FER datasets Multi-PIE [32] and BU-3DFE [33] are computed quantitatively to verify the effectiveness of the propose method.

Multi-PIE database [32] contains the face images of 337 subjects, 235 male instances and 107 female instances; there are more than 750000 images captured with fifteen cameras on different illuminations and viewpoints. Each subject was asked to give six different kinds of expressions: neutral (NE), smile (SM), squint (SQ), surprise (SU), disgust (DI), and scream (SC). Finally, the data of 100 subjects were selected which includes complete six emotions with good quality, and 13 poses are used in the experiments which includes $0°$, $±15°$, $±30°$, $±45°$, $±60°$, $±75°$, $90°$ face views. The training testing split is 80:20.

BU-3DFE database [33] is a 3D facial emotion dataset which contains face images of 100 subjects, 56 female instances and 44 male instances. Slightly different form the Multi-PIE data, there are seven different facial expressions including anger (AN), disgust (DI), fear (FE), happiness (HA), sadness (SA), surprise (SU), and neutral (NE) in four levels. In the experiments, the models are used to generate 2D face images under different views including $0°$, $±30°$, $±45°$, $±60°$, $90°$. The 100 subjects are randomly divided into 80 training subjects and 20 testing subjects.

4.2   Experimental Results

To provide an objective evaluation of the proposed method, we compare the proposed method with nine existing methods including kNN, LDA, LPP, D-GPLVM, GPLRF, GMLDA, GMLPP, MvDA, and DS-GPLVM as reported in [34]. As shown in Table 1, the proposed method achieves new state-of-the-art in average accuracy; and it also outperforms the other methods at different poses including the recognition from frontal faces. Moreover, different from most previous methods, the proposed method achieves close results (around 93%) on different poses which demonstrates the pose robustness of the propose method.

Table 1. Overall accuracy of different methods on Multi-PIE

Method	Pose					Avg.
	−30	−15	0	15	30	
KNN	80.88	81.74	68.36	75.03	74.78	76.15
LDA	92.52	94.37	77.21	87.07	87.47	87.72
LPP	92.42	94.56	77.33	87.06	87.68	87.81
D-GPLVM	91.65	93.51	78.70	85.96	86.04	87.17
GMLDA	90.47	94.18	76.60	86.64	85.72	86.72
GMLPP	91.86	94.13	78.16	87.22	87.36	87.74
MvDA	92.49	94.22	77.51	87.10	87.89	87.84
Zhang [35]	90.97	94.72	89.11	93.09	91.30	91.80
Proposed	93.10	94.96	92.80	94.60	92.20	93.53

From Table 2, the proposed method achieves very good recognition performance for different expressions. But the recognition accuracies of DI and SQ are lower than the other expressions; it is similar as the results reported in some references [36] which indicates that the recognition of the emotions is inherently difficult. For the results on BU-3DFE, since it is 3D data, the proposed method achieves very good result because the method itself is based on 3D model.

Table 2. Confusion matrix on Multi-PIE and BU-3DFE

Dataset	Multi-PIE							BU-3DFE					
DI	91.92	0	1.90	5.60	0	2.80	AN	95.30	2.70	0	1.30	0	1.07
SC	0.38	98.00	0	0	2.48	0	DI	0.27	85.48	0.20	4.36	2.10	5.93
SM	3.40	0	94.25	2.00	1.05	0	FE	0.50	0	92.82	5.44	0.17	0.20
SQ	4.20	0	1.80	91.9	0	5.70	HA	1.53	2.20	5.25	82.50	5.53	3.40
SU	0	2.00	0.45	0	95.42	1.20	SA	2.40	1.08	1.19	3.22	89.00	3.90
SE	0.10	0	1.60	0.50	1.05	90.3	SU	0	8.54	0.54	3.18	3.20	85.50
	DI	SC	SM	SQ	SU	NE		SU	SA	HA	FE	DI	AN

4.3   Ablation Study

The advantage of the proposed method is effective data augmentation which introduced 3D generated data to train the network. Here, we perform the ablation studies with the following settings: (1) directly training a CNN; (2) directly introduce extra data to train the CNN; (3) introduce the 3D model to augment the data at different poses and train the CNN; (4) train the CNN with 3D augmentation and domain adversarial learning. They are used to demonstrate the effectiveness of 3D model and the necessary of the proposed domain adversarial learning.

Table 3. Ablation study

Method	Pose					Avg.
	−30	−15	0	15	30	
CNN	90.67	94.53	89.01	93.01	91.10	91.66
CNN + FER2013	90.01	94.21	93.21	92.57	90.47	92.09
CNN + FER + 3D	70.10	71.10	72.32	71.20	70.13	70.97
CNN + 3D + DA (Proposed)	93.10	94.96	92.80	94.60	92.20	93.53

In Table 3, it shows that directly training a CNN achieved similar results as the deep learning method in [35], in which the recognition of large yaw angle faces are better than those frontal faces. By introducing the extra data FER2013, the CNN are trained to achieve better results on frontal faces (pose with 0°); however, there is performance degradation on the non-frontal faces. The results indicate that the deep network is data-dependence and the network was trained biased to the frontal faces since the FER2013 contains more frontal faces. For the approach that directly training the CNN with 3D augmented data, as discussed in the method part, the method achieved very bad results on all different poses due to the domain difference. Finally, the proposed method with domain adversarial learning overcomes the problem and achieves new state-of-the-art performance.

5   Conclusion

In this paper, we have proposed a novel deep learning strategy for pose-invariant facial expression recognition. It introduced 3DMM for data augmentation which has first shown that there exists a domain difference between the real 2D images and the generated images with 3DMM and such difference can fail the training. More important, it proposed a solution for this problem by introducing the feature-level domain adversarial learning to train the network which eliminated the influence of the domain difference without losing the expression information. The experimental results demonstrated the effectiveness of the proposed method and it achieved new state-of-the-art on two multi-view FER datasets. In the future, we will apply the proposed method to other face related recognition tasks.

References

1. Ekman, P., Friesen, W.: Constants across cultures in the face and emotion. J. Pers. Soc. Psychol. **172**, 124–129 (1971)
2. Zhong, L., Liu, Q., Yang, P., Metaxas, D.: Learning active facial patches for expression analysis. In: CVPR, pp. 2562–2569. IEEE (2012)
3. Dalal, N., Triggs, B.: Histograms of oriented gradients for human detection. In: Proceedings of IEEE CVPR, San Diego (2005)

4. LeCun, Y., Bengio, Y., Hinton, G.: Deep learning. Nature **521**, 436–444 (2015)
5. Sandbach, G., Zafeiriou, S., Pantic, M., Yin, L.: Static and dynamic 3D facial expression recognition: a comprehensive survey. Image Vis. Comput. **30**(10), 683–697 (2012)
6. Hassner, T., Harel, S., Paz, E., Enbar, R.: Effective face frontalization in unconstrained images. In: IEEE Conference on Computer Vision and Pattern Recognition, pp. 4295–4304 (2015)
7. Zhu, X., Lei, Z., Yan, J., Yi, D., Li, S.: High-fidelity pose and expression normalization for face recognition in the wild. In: IEEE Conference on Computer Vision and Pattern Recognition, pp. 787–796 (2015)
8. Zhu, X., Lei, Z., Liu, X., Shi, H., Li, S.: Face alignment across large poses: a 3D solution. In: Proceedings of Conference Computation Vision Pattern Recognition, Las Vegas (2016)
9. Zeng, Z., Pantic, M., Roisman, G.I., Huang, T.S.: A survey of affect recognition methods: audio, visual, and spontaneous expressions. IEEE Trans. Pattern Anal. Mach. Intell. **31**(1), 39–58 (2009)
10. Sariyanidi, E., Gunes, H., Cavallaro, A.: Automatic analysis of facial affect: a survey of registration, representation, and recognition. IEEE Trans. Pattern Anal. Mach. Intell. **37**(6), 1113–1133 (2015)
11. Li, S., Deng, W.: Deep facial expression recognition: a survey. arXiv preprint arXiv:1804.08348v2 (2018)
12. Mollahosseini, A., Chan, D., Mahoor, M.: Going deeper in facial expression recognition using deep neural networks. In: Applications of Computer Vision (WACV), pp. 1–10 (2016)
13. Mollahosseini, A., Hasani, B., Mahoor, M.: AffectNet: a database for facial expression, valence, and arousal computing in the wild. IEEE Trans. Affect. Comput. **10**(99), 1010–1022 (2017)
14. Jung, H., Lee, S., Yim, J., Park, S., Kim, J.: Joint fine-tuning in deep neural networks for facial expression recognition. In: IEEE ICCV, pp. 2983–2991 (2015)
15. Hasani, B., Mahoor, M.: Spatio-temporal facial expression recognition using convolutional neural networks and conditional random fields. In: Automatic Face & Gesture Recognition, pp. 790–795 (2017)
16. Liu, M., Li, S., Shan, S., Chen, X.: AU-aware deep networks for facial expression recognition. In: IEEE Automatic Face and Gesture Recognition (FG), pp. 1–6 (2013)
17. Liu, M., Li, S., Shan, S., Wang, R., Chen, X.: Deeply learning deformable facial action parts model for dynamic expression analysis. In: Cremers, D., Reid, I., Saito, H., Yang, M.-H. (eds.) ACCV 2014. LNCS, vol. 9006, pp. 143–157. Springer, Cham (2015). https://doi.org/10.1007/978-3-319-16817-3_10
18. Pantic, M., Rothkrantz, M.: Automatic analysis of facial expressions: the state of the art. IEEE Trans. Pattern Anal. Mach. Intell. **22**(12), 1424–1445 (2000)
19. Rudovic, O., Pantic, M., Patras, I.: Coupled Gaussian processes for pose-invariant facial expression recognition. TPA- MI **35**(6), 1357–1369 (2013)
20. Zheng, W., Tang, H., Lin, Z., Huang, T. S.: A novel approach to expression recognition from non-frontal face images. In: IEEE ICCV, pp. 1901–1908 (2009)
21. Zhang, Z., Luo, P., Chen, C.L., Tang, X.: From facial expression recognition to interpersonal relation prediction. Int. J. Comput. Vision **126**(5), 1–20 (2018)
22. Liu, Y., Zeng, J., Shan, S., Zheng, Z.: Multi-channel pose-aware convolution neural net-works for multi-view facial expression recognition. In: Automatic Face & Gesture Recognition, pp. 458–465 (2018)

23. Lai, Y., Lai, S: Emotion-preserving representation learning via generative adversarial network for multi-view facial expression recognition. In: Automatic Face & Gesture Recognition, pp. 263–270 (2018)

24. Blanz, V., Romdhani, S., Vetter, T.: Face identification across different poses and illuminations with a 3D morphable model. In: IEEE International Conference on Automatic Face and Gesture Recognition, pp. 192–197 (2002)

25. Chang, F., Tran, A., Hassner, T., Masi, I., Nevatia1, R., Medioni, G.: ExpNet: landmark-free, deep, 3D facial expressions. arXiv preprint arXiv:1802.00542v1 (2018)

26. Goodfellow, I.J., Pouget-Abadie, J., Mirza, M., Xu, B., Warde-Farley, D., Bengio, Y.: Generative adversarial nets. In: NIPS (2014)

27. Ganin, Y., Lempitsky, V.: Unsupervised domain adaptation by backpropagation. arXiv preprint arXiv:1409.7495 (2014)

28. Bulat, A. and Tzimiropoulos, G.: How far are we from solving the 2D & 3D Face Alignment problem? In: IEEE ICCV (2018)

29. Sagonas, C., Tzimiropoulos, G., Zafeiriou, S., Pantic, M.: 300 faces in-the-wild challenge: the first facial landmark localization challenge. In: IEEE CVPR (2013)

30. Parkhi, O. M., Vedaldi, A., Zisserman, A.: Deep face recognition. In: British Machine Vision Conference (2015)

31. Goodfellow, I.J., et al.: Challenges in representation learning: a report on three machine learning contests. In: Lee, M., Hirose, A., Hou, Z.-G., Kil, R.M. (eds.) ICONIP 2013. LNCS, vol. 8228, pp. 117–124. Springer, Heidelberg (2013). https://doi.org/10.1007/978-3-642-42051-1_16

32. Gross, R., Matthews, I., Cohn, J., Kanade, T., Baker, S.: Multi-pie. Image Vis. Comput. **28**(5), 807–813 (2010)

33. Yin, L., Wei, X., Sun, Y., Wang, J., Rosato, M.: A 3D facial expression database for facial behavior research. In: 7th International Conference on Automatic Face and Gesture Recognition, pp. 211–216 (2006)

34. Eleftheriadis, S., Rudovic, O., Pantic, M.: Discriminative shared Gaussian processes for multiview and view-invariant facial expression recognition. IEEE TIP **24**(1), 189–204 (2015)

35. Zhang, F., Zhang, T, Mao, Q., Xu, C.: Joint pose and expression modeling for facial expression recognition. In: IEEE CVPR (2018)

36. Zhang, T., et al.: A deep neural network-driven feature learning method for multiview facial expression recognition. IEEE Trans. Multimedia **18**(12), 2528–2536 (2016)

Multimodal and Multiclass Semi-supervised Image-to-Image Translation

Jing Bai[1,2(✉)], Ran Chen[1,2], Hui Ji[1,2], and Saisai Li[1,2]

[1] North Minzu University, Yinchuan 750021, China
baijing@nun.edu.cn
[2] Ningxia Provice Key Laboratory of Intelligent Information and Data Processing, Yinchuan 750021, China

Abstract. In this paper, we propose a multimodal and multiclass semi-supervised image-to-image translation (MM-SSIT) framework to address the dilemma between expensive labeled work and diversity requirement of image translation. A cross-domain adversarial autoencoder is proposed to learn disentangled latent domain-invariant content codes and domain-specific style codes. The style codes are matched with a prior distribution so that we can generate a series of meaningful samples from the prior space. The content codes are embedded into a multiclass joint data distribution by an adversarial learning between a domain classifier and a category classifier so that we can generate multiclass images at one time. Consequently, multimodal and multiclass cross-domain images are generated by joint decoding the latent content codes and sampled style codes. Finally, the networks for MM-SSIT framework are designed and tested. Semi-supervised experiments with comparisons to state-of-art approach show that the proposed framework has the ability to generate high-quality and diversiform images in case of fewer labeled samples. Further experiments in the unsupervised setting demonstrate that MM-SSIT is superior in learning disentangled representation and domain adaption.

Keywords: Image-to-image translation · Semi-supervised · Adversarial auto encoder · Adversarial learning

1 Introduction

Owing to the quick development in AI technology, image-to-image translation has become a compelling topic in recent years [1–3]. Existing approaches usually simplify this problem as a deterministic one-to-one image mapping. However, the cross-domain image translation is multimodal in many scenarios [2, 3]. In this paper, we focus on the multimodal image-to-image translation.

Currently, there are mainly two kinds of image-to-image translation. One of them is supervised [4, 5], which needs paired examples in different domains. Because the requirement is harsh and impractical in many cases, unsupervised image-to-image translation has emerged [2, 3, 6–8]. In order to generate cross-domain images, these methods always assume that the images of two domains share domain-invariant content codes [2], and the content codes share the same data distribution. Unfortunately, this

Y. Zhao et al. (Eds.): ICIG 2019, LNCS 11903, pp. 503–514, 2019.
https://doi.org/10.1007/978-3-030-34113-8_42

assumption is equivalent to the requirement that the cross-domain data must be of single or similar categories. As a result, they fail to generate images between two domains including multiple categories, even the domains containing 0–9.

In this paper, we propose a semi-supervised framework for image-to-image translation, which can achieve multimodal and multiclass image translation with a small number of labeled samples in the absence of paired examples. First of all, we make the same assumptions as MUNIT [2] that the latent space of images can be decomposed into a content space and a style space, and the images in different domains share a common content space but not the style space. Furthermore, we make a different assumption that the images of same categories share the same content distribution. Accordingly, as Fig. 1 shown, we instantiate our semi-supervised translation idea based on the semi-supervised representation learning by introducing the following models:

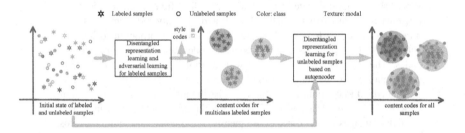

Fig. 1. The multimodal and multiclass semi-supervised representation learning.

Autoencoder (AE). It is used to disentangle the latent codes of style and content, and generate a series of cross-domain images by recombining its content code and the style samples of the target domain.

Adversarial AutoEncoder (AAE). It is added to encoder so as to make the style code of each domain satisfy a particular distribution. Thus, we can generate various style of a domain by sampling from its style distribution.

Adversarial Learning. It is added to encoder so as to embed the domain invariant content attributes into a joint data distribution by an adversarial learning between a domain classifier and a category classifier [9].

This paper makes the following contributions. (1) A Multimodal and Multiclass Semi-supervised Image-to-Image Translation (MM-SSIT) framework is proposed to achieve diversiform image-to-image translation in case of semi-supervised; (2) A novel cross-domain joint data distribution is constructed through the proposed cross-domain adversarial autoencoder, which not only extracts domain invariant content attributes but also captures semantic attributes and makes the content codes of same categories be a cluster; (3) A set of networks for MM-SSIT are designed, which can support semi-supervised image-to-image translation effectively. (4) The experiments on different datasets demonstrate the diversity and superior image quality compared with the state-of-the-art approach.

2 Related Work

2.1 GAN

Generative Adversarial Networks (GANs) have been successfully applied to various computer vision tasks, such as image generation [10–12], image translation [2–8] and semantic segmentation [13]. The work Pix2pix [4] presents conditional adversarial networks as a general solution to image-to-image translation problems, which has achieved remarkable results. However, the work relies on paired examples and only can complete one-to-one mapping. Since then, CycleGAN [6] and DualGAN [7] are proposed to translate an image from a source domain to a target domain in the absence of paired examples by constructing cycle consistency loss. Liu et al. [8] propose an unsupervised image-to-image translation framework based on Coupled GANs [14]. These works have produced good results for image translation, but they can only accomplish one-to-one mapping.

2.2 Multimodal Image Translation

One of these methods can generate a discrete number of outputs by explicitly constructing multimodal codes [15, 16]. The model BicycleGAN [5] can generate continuous and multimodal images. However, the above methods need aligned image pairs for training, which is not available in many tasks. Subsequently, two unsupervised learning works InfoGAN [12] and MUNIT [2] are proposed to generate continuous one-to-more image translation. The only drawback is that these methods require high purity of training data, i.e. implicitly adding a single category restriction to data. This undoubtedly increases its training cost and limits its application scope. Accordingly, Hou et al. propose an image translation framework CDAAE [3], which can generate various samples with a certain input by training in supervised or unsupervised settings. This work provides a useful inspiration for our study.

3 MM-SSIT Framework

3.1 Formulation

Let $x_1 \in \chi_1$ and $x_2 \in \chi_2$ be images from two different domains. Our goal is to learn a more effective joint data distribution from two independent edge data distributions $p(x_1)$ and $p(x_2)$ with fewer labeled samples, then generate multimodal and multiclass cross-domain images for the input image. To solve this problem, we assume that data $x_i \in \chi_i$ can be decoupled independently into a content code $z_i^c \in C_i$ and a style code $z_i^s \in S_i$. Here, for images from a domain i, the content code z_i^c follow the data distribution $q(z_i^c)$, denoting as $z_i^c \sim q(z_i^c)$, and the style code z_i^s follow the data distribution $q(z_i^s)$, denoting as $z_i^s \sim q(z_i^s)$. Then a multiclass joint data distribution of content codes is constructed through an adversarial learning between a domain classifier and a category classifier. Finally, various cross-domain images are generated by joint decoding of the latent content codes and sampled style codes.

3.2   Overall Framework

To address the above issues, Fig. 2 shows the overall framework of MM-SSIT. As shown in the figure, MM-SSIT consists of two parts: an encoder module and a decoder module, which will be described separately below.

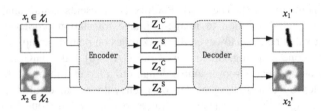

Fig. 2. The overall framework of MM-SSIT.

3.3   Encoder Module

As shown in Fig. 3, inputting an image from a source domain, firstly a disentangled representation learning module is used to decouple its content code and style code, then AAE is used to make the style code satisfy a given distribution, and adversarial learning between a domain classifier and a category classifier is used to make the content features of the same category share the same content distribution.

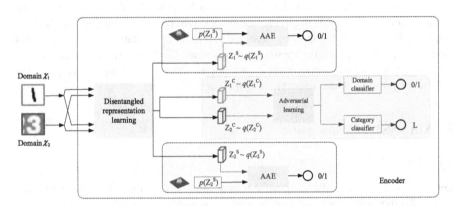

Fig. 3. The encoder framework of MM-SSIT.

Style Encoding Based on AAE. This module is designed to make the style code $z_i^s \sim q(z_i^s)$ satisfy a given distribution $p(z_i^s)$. Therefore, the adversarial loss $L_i^{adv}(i \in \{1,2\})$ between $q(z_i^s)$ and $p(z_i^s)$ can be defined as follows:

$$L_i^{adv} = \log(p(z_i^s)) + \log(1 - q(z_i^s)) \tag{1}$$

Content Encoding Based on Adversarial Learning. With the objective of achieving multiclass cross-domain data generation, this module is designed to construct a multiclass joint data distribution where data from different domains with the same semantic label are in the same cluster. Therefore, the adversarial learning between a domain classifier and a category classifier is introduced into content encoding. Here, the domain classifier is used to determine which domain the received content code is from, thus defining a domain discriminant loss L_{Domain} as formula (2). Furthermore, the category classifier is used to judge category labels of the given images, thus defining a category classifier discriminant loss L_{label} as formula (3). When the training is finished, the joint data distribution can be obtained. In order to ensure a good effect of domain smoothing, the loss functions $L_{cc}^{semi-su}$ and L_{cc}^{un} are defined for the training with fewer labeled data and unlabeled data, respectively.

$$L_{Domain} = \log(q(z_1^c)) + \log(1 - q(z_2^c)) \tag{2}$$

$$L_{label} = F_{CE}(L_1, E_1^c(x_1)) + F_{CE}(L_2, E_2^c(x_2)) \tag{3}$$

$$L_{cc}^{semi-su} = F_{CE}(L_1, E_1^c(x_{1->2})) + F_{CE}(L_2, E_2^c(x_{2->1})) \tag{4}$$

$$L_{cc}^{un} = F_{CE}(E_1^c(x_1), E_1^c(x_{1->2})) + F_{CE}(E_2^c(x_2), E_2^c(x_{2->1})) \tag{5}$$

Where L_i and E_i^c represent the label and the content code of an image $x_i \in \chi_i$, respectively, and F_{CE} (*1,*2) represents the cross-entropy loss between *1 and *2.

3.4 Decoder Module

As shown in Fig. 4, having obtained their content codes and style codes (z_i^c, z_i^s), $i \in \{1, 2\}$ for any images $x_i \in \chi_i$, we can reconstruct the original images or generate cross-domain images. In order to achieve generation ability, a pixel-level reconstruction loss between the generated image and the input image is required. Especially, inputting an image $x_i \in \chi_i$, its reconstruction loss L_i^{rec}, $i \in \{1, 2\}$, can be defined as follows:

$$L_i^{rec} = ||D_i(z_i^c, z_i^s) - x_i||_2 \tag{6}$$

Where, D_i (*1,*2) is the output image by decoding the content code and style code (*1, *2) of the image $x_i \in \chi_i$, $||^*||_2$ represents the L2 regularization norm.

By synthesizing the loss functions of the above stages, the overall loss of the model with fewer labeled samples $L^{semi-su}$ is defined as follows:

$$L^{semi-su} = L_1^{adv} + L_2^{adv} + L_{Domain} + L_{label} + L_{cc}^{semi-su} + L_1^{rec} + L_2^{rec} \tag{7}$$

While the overall loss of the model without any labeled samples L^{un} is defined as follows:

$$L^{un} = L_1^{adv} + L_2^{adv} + L_{Domain} + L_{label} + L_{cc}^{un} + L_1^{rec} + L_2^{rec} \tag{8}$$

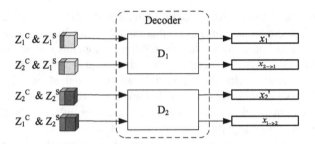

Fig. 4. The decoder framework of MM-SSIT.

4 Network Design

For the proposed framework MM-SSIT, we design a set of networks to achieve semi-supervised multimodal and multiclass image-to-image translation.

4.1 Network for Disentangled Representation Learning Module

Figure 5 shows the designed network for the disentangled representation learning module of MM-SSIT. In this network, the sub-networks for content coding and style coding are composed of 5 layers and 4 layers, while their output are a 8-dimensional style code and a 128-dimensional initial content code, respectively. Because the content code and the style code of an image have the same shallow features, the sub-networks between content coding and style coding share their first two convolution layers. Furthermore, in order to alleviate the gradient disappearance and gradient explosion which aggravate by multilayer neural networks, a batch normalized BN layer (except the last convolution layer of style coding) is added after each convolution layer. More detailed information about every convolution layer is illustrated in Fig. 5.

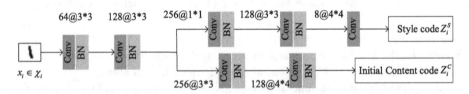

Fig. 5. The network of the disentangled representation learning module.

4.2 Network for Style AAE Module

Figure 6 shows the designed adversarial autoencoder network for the style coding module of MM-SSIT. With a real image code as the negative sample and a random sampling of Normal Distribution as the positive sample, the network is trained to discriminate an input code is true or false through four successive Mlp(256, 64, 16, 1). Finally, the style code disentangled from an image $x_i \in \chi_i$ follows the given Normal Distribution of corresponding domain after training.

Fig. 6. The network of style AAE module.

4.3   Network for Content Adversarial Learning Module

Figure 7 shows the designed adversarial learning network for the content coding module of MM-SSIT. This network consists of two sub-networks: a category classifier, composing of one Mlp(k) layer and one softmax layer, where k is the number of categories; and a domain classifier, composing of a series of Mlp(256, 128, 64, 64, 2). With initial content codes of two different domains as input, the category classifier is used to classify the images according to their semantic labels, while the domain classifier is designed to discriminate the images' domain, and its output 01 represents domain χ_1 and the output 10 represents domain χ_2. After training, a domain-invariant joint data distribution is constructed, on which the data points from the same classes clustered together while data points from different classes far from each other.

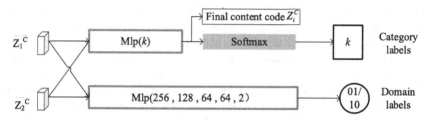

Fig. 7. The network of the content adversarial learning module.

4.4   Network for Decoder Module

As the decoder framework shown in Fig. 8, there are two decoders for MM-SSIT. They share the same network architectures but different training data. The detailed network for each decoder is shown in Fig. 8. Firstly, content codes and style codes are recombined and fed into the decoder. Then one 4 * 4 deconvolution layer with three consecutive 3 * 3 deconvolution layers is recombined to decode images from inputting codes. Finally, the images of data reconstruction or cross-domain generation can be achieved after training is complete. It is noted that a batch normalized BN layer is also added after each deconvolution layer.

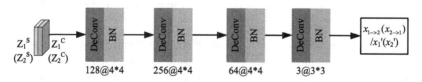

Fig. 8. The network of the decoder module.

5 Experiments

5.1 Semi-supervised Image-to-Image Translation Experiment

Datasets. We conduct semi-supervised experiments on the dataset MNIST-SVHN. MNIST [17] is composed of 60000 handwritten digit images, while SVHN [18] is composed of 99289 street number image from Street View House Numbers dataset. Both of them are divided into ten categories of 0–9. The digit images from MNIST are gray images of 1 * 28 * 28, while the street number images from SVHN are colored images of 3 * 32 * 32. Therefore, we adjust the digit images to 3 * 32 * 32 three-channel images by data completion and channel expansion before training. In the experiment, 50000 images from MNIST and 73257 images from SVHN are randomly selected for training, and the remaining images are used for testing.

In semi-supervised experiments, there is no need to provide any paired examples, only need to label fewer samples. In this paper, 100 training samples per class are randomly selected for labeling, and the remaining samples are completely unlabeled.

Semi-supervised Experiment on SVHN-MNIST. SVHN (denoting as source domain, s) and MNIST (denoting as target domain, t) are two different domains in this experiment. Figure 9(a)–(d) shows part of the experimental results of s2s, t2t, t2s and s2t, respectively. Here, s2s means the input is an image of source domain SVHN while the outputs are a series of images from the same class but target domain MNIST, the same as t2t, t2s and s2t. The multimodal same-domain translation results in Fig. 9(a) and (b) show that the generated images not only maintain the same content attributes as the input image but also are various and very natural. In addition, the multimodal cross-domain translation results in Fig. 9(c) and (d) are also various, and they show that generated images successfully captures style attributes of the target domain and maintain semantic attributes of the input image. It is noted all the experimental results are achieved in case of nearly 1/62 training data with labels, which demonstrate the effectiveness for semi-supervised image-to-image translation of the proposed framework and designed networks.

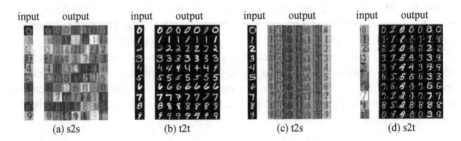

(a) s2s   (b) t2t   (c) t2s   (d) s2t

Fig. 9. Semi-supervised image-to-image translation results on SVHN-MNIST.

A good image generator should ensure that the generated image and the input image have the same content attributes, i.e. semantic labels. Therefore, the classification accuracy of generated images is calculated and compared with the state-of-art method CDAAE [3] in the same semi-supervised setting. Table 1 shows all results on MNIST-SVHN, which indicate that the proposed method has an evident advantage over CDAAE for all kinds of image-to-image translations. In addition, whether it is the algorithm in this paper or the CDAAE, the classification accuracies of generated images from the same domain are high, while from different domains are low. This phenomenon illustrates the difficulty of image-to-image translation.

Table 1. Classification accuracy comparisons of four kinds of translations on the MNIST-SVHN. The best performance indicators are marked as bold. (%)

Method	s2s	t2t	t2s	s2t
CDAAE	83.77	72.83	31.06	34.84
MM-SSIT (Ours)	**91.47**	**76.39**	**38.23**	**40.37**

Discussion of Different Partial Weight Sharing Schemes in Decoder. For the two decoders in MM-SSIT, they can share no weights or partial weights. This experiment is designed to evaluate the influence of different weights sharing schemes on the semi-supervised image-to-image translation by comparing classification accuracies. Figure 10 shows the comparison results of our model under the same semi-supervised conditions but different weights sharing schemes between two decoders. In Fig. 10, for s2s and t2t, except for the method with 1st&2nd&3rd layers weights sharing, all methods achieve similar accuracies; while for s2t and t2s, the method with 1st&2nd layers weights sharing outperforms the other methods. On average, the method only sharing the 1st layer achieves the best performance, which is 2.4%, 0.9%, 67.0% and 4.0% higher than it of the schemes of share-0, share-1st&2nd, share-1st&2nd&3rd and share-4th, respectively. The translation results of s2t and t2s for five kinds of weight sharing schemes in Fig. 11 also verify these findings.

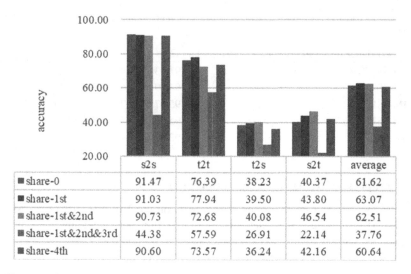

Fig. 10. Classification accuracy comparisons of four kinds of translations using five kinds of weights sharing schemes of decoders on the MNIST-SVHN.

Discussion of Different Number of Sample Labels. In this section, we will compare the effects of the proposed method using different numbers of labeled samples. Table 2 shows the results of our method by adding labels to 1/62, 1/6, 1/3 and all training data as well as the result of CDAAE [3] with all training data labeled, respectively. Obviously, the classification accuracies increase as the number of labeled samples increases. When labeled samples are 1/62, 1/6 and 1/3, their classification accuracies are 73%, 91% and 96% of the classification accuracy using 100% labeled samples. Furthermore, on average, the performance of our method only using 1/3 labeled samples is comparable to that of CDAAE using 100% labeled samples. These results fully illustrate that the proposed method can achieve high-quality image-to-image translation using fewer labeled samples.

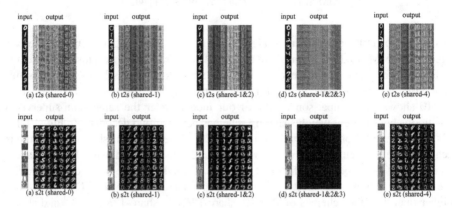

Fig. 11. Semi-supervised image-to-image translation results of s2t and t2s for five kinds of weight sharing schemes on the MNIST-SVHN.

Table 2. Classification accuracy comparisons of different numbers of labeled samples on the MNIST-SVHN. (%)

Method (labeled samples ration in training sets)	s2s	t2t	t2s	s2t	Average
MM-SSIT(1/62)	91.03	77.94	39.5	48.8	64.32
MM-SSIT(1/6)	94.99	88.36	65.91	70.48	79.94
MM-SSIT(1/3)	95.87	90.52	74.38	78.61	84.85
MM-SSIT(1/1)	95.96	90.45	80.78	85.42	85.42
CD-AAE(1/1)	92.03	90.34	78.05	78.81	84.81

5.2   Unsupervised Image-to-Image Translation Experiment

Datasets. We conduct unsupervised experiments on the NIR-VIS and Edges-Shoes. *NIR-VIS* [19]. A face image datasets with two domains including near infrared (NIR) and visible light (VIS) images. This dataset is divided into 724 classes, we select 582 classes with more than five images for both VIS and NIR in our experiment.

In each class, we further select 3 images for training and other 2 images for testing. Here, all images are of 3 * 128 * 128.

Edges-Shoes. A dataset from the pix2pix [4]. For each domain, we randomly select 1000 images for training and 100 images for testing, and resize them into 3 * 128 * 128. In the experiment, we directly use the paired examples provide by pix2pix.

Figure 12(a)–(b) and (c)–(d) show a part of unsupervised image-to-image translation results on VIS-NIR and Edges-Shoes, respectively. In the experiment, the generated image's content code is obtained from the input image, while its style code is sampled from a prior distribution of target domain. It can be seen that for both complex face datasets and shoe datasets with more texture information, the proposed model can achieve good translation results based on the good disentangled representation of contents and styles.

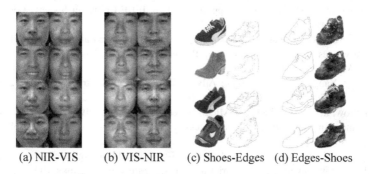

(a) NIR-VIS   (b) VIS-NIR   (c) Shoes-Edges   (d) Edges-Shoes

Fig. 12. Unsupervised image-to-image translation results on VIS-NIR and Edges-Shoes.

6 Conclusion

We present a general framework for semi-supervised image-to-image translation. Our model achieves diversiform and high-quality cross-domain translation results with fewer labeled samples. Future research will further extend the proposed framework to better deal with high-resolution image-to-image translation.

Acknowledgments. This work is supported by National Natural Science Foundation of China (61762003), Natural Science Foundation of Ningxia (2018AAC03124), and Key R&D Program Projects of Ningxia 2019 (Research on Intelligent Assembly Technology Based on Multi-source Information Fusion).

References

1. Zhu, X., Li, Z., et al.: Generative adversarial image super-resolution through deep dense skip connections. In: Computer Graphics Forum (CGF), vol. 37, no. 7, pp. 289–300 (2018)

2. Huang, X., Liu, M.-Y., Belongie, S., Kautz, J.: Multimodal unsupervised image-to-image translation. In: Ferrari, V., Hebert, M., Sminchisescu, C., Weiss, Y. (eds.) ECCV 2018. LNCS, vol. 11207, pp. 179–196. Springer, Cham (2018). https://doi.org/10.1007/978-3-030-01219-9_11

3. Hou, H., Huo, J., Gao, Y.: Cross-Domain Adversarial Auto-Encoder (2018). https://arxiv.org/abs/1804.06078. Accessed 17 Apr 2018

4. Isola, P., Zhu, J.Y., Zhou, T., et al.: Image-to-image translation with conditional adversarial networks. In: CVPR 2016, vol. 1, pp. 5967–5976. IEEE Computer Society, Los Alamitos (2017)

5. Zhu, J.Y., Zhang, R., Pathak, D., et al.: Toward multimodal image-to-image translation. In: The 30th Advances in Neural Information Processing Systems, Long Beach, pp. 465–476. Curran Associates (2017)

6. Zhu, J.Y., Park, T., Isola, P., et al.: Unpaired image-to-image translation using cycle-consistent adversarial networks. In: ICCV 2017, vol. 1, pp. 2242–4421. IEEE Computer Society, Los Alamitos (2017)

7. Yi, Z., Zhang, H., Gong, P.T.M.: DualGAN: unsupervised dual learning for image-to-image translation. In: ICCV 2017, vol. 1, pp. 2868–2876. IEEE Computer Society, Los Alamitos (2017)

8. Liu, M.Y., Breuel, T., Kautz, J.: Unsupervised image-to-image translation networks. In: The 30th Advances in Neural Information Processing Systems, Long Beach, pp. 700–708. Curran Associates (2017)

9. Wang, B., Yang, Y., Xu, X., et al.: Adversarial cross-modal retrieval. In: The 25th ACM International Conference on Multimedia, New York, pp. 157–162 (2017)

10. Goodfellow, I., Pouget-Abadie, J., Mirza, M., et al.: Generative adversarial nets. In: The 27th of Advances in Neural Information Processing Systems, Montreal, pp. 2672–2680. Curran Associates (2014)

11. Zhang, X., Shi, H., Zhu, X., Li, P.: Active semi-supervised learning based on self-expressive correlation with generative adversarial networks. Neurocomputing 345, 103–113 (2019)

12. Chen, X., Duan, Y., Houthooft, R., et al.: InfoGAN: interpretable representation learning by information maximizing generative adversarial nets. In: The 29th Advances in Neural Information Processing Systems, Barcelona, pp. 2172–2180. Curran Associates (2016)

13. Cai, Q., Xue, Z., Zhang, X., Zhu, X.: A novel framework for semantic segmentation with generative adversarial network. J. Vis. Commun. Image Represent. (JVCI) 58, 532–543 (2019)

14. Liu, M.Y., Tuzel, O.: Coupled generative adversarial networks. In: The 29th Advances in Neural Information Processing Systems, Barcelona, pp. 469–477. Curran Associates (2016)

15. Chen, Q., Koltun, V.: Photographic image synthesis with cascaded refinement networks. In: ICCV 2017, vol. 1, pp. 1520–1529. IEEE Computer Society, Los Alamitos (2017)

16. Ghosh, A., Kulharia, V., Namboodiri, V., et al.: Multi-agent diverse generative adversarial networks. In: CVPR 2018, vol. 1, pp. 8513–8521. IEEE Computer Society, Los Alamitos (2018)

17. Yann, L., Corinna, C., Christopher, J.B.: MNIST Handwritten Digit Database. AT&T Labs (2010). http://yann.lecun.com/exdb/mnist

18. Yuval, N., Tao, W., Adam, C., et al.: Reading digits in natural images with unsupervised feature learning. In: NIPS Workshop on Deep Learning and Unsupervised Feature Learning, vol. 2011, p. 5 (2011)

19. Li, S., Yi, D., Lei, Z., Liao, S.: The CASIA NIR-VIS 2.0 face database. In: Proceedings of the IEEE Conference on Computer Vision and Pattern Recognition Workshops, Los Alamitos, pp. 348–353 (2013)

Advanced Signal Processing Methods in Spectral Imaging

Unsupervised Person Re-identification Based on Clustering and Domain-Invariant Network

Yangru Huang[1], Yi Jin[1(✉)], Peixi Peng[2], Congyan Lang[1], and Yidong Li[1]

[1] School of Computer and Information Technology, Beijing Jiaotong University, Beijing, China
{yrhuang,yjin,cylang,ydli}@bjtu.edu.cn
[2] Institute of Automation, Chinese Academy of Sciences, Beijing, China
peixi.peng@ia.ac.cn

Abstract. Person re-identification (Re-ID) is a task which aims to determine whether a pedestrian in a camera has emerged in other cameras. Earlier works stress importance of the supervised learning methods, however, creating labels by hand is too slow and expensive. Hence, supervised methods are always limited in real-world applications. To address the problem, we propose a novel domain adaptation framework for unsupervised person Re-ID. First, target data are clustered and selected to add relative reliable supervised information for target domain. Second, a novel domain adaptive network is designed to decompose the representations to person-related and domain-related part. The former aims at learning domain-invariant and discriminative representation by a adversarial loss and a Re-ID loss with the label smoothing regularization. And the latter further improve a model's ability of extracting domain-invariant features by separating the domain unique features. What's more, during learning representation for target domain, a labeled source data not only is utilized to initialize the model but also participate in the training as a beneficial supervision information to generalize the Re-ID model. Experimental results on Market-1501 and DukeMTMC-reID evidence the superior performance of the proposed model over state-of-the-art methods.

Keywords: Person Re-ID · Domain adaptation · Clustering

1 Introduction

Person re-identification (Re-ID) is a retrieval task of identifying the same person image captured from distinctively non-overlapping camera views. It has become an increasingly popular task in video surveillance due to its application and research significance. Despite the best efforts from many computer vision researchers, it remains an unsolved problem. It is difficult that the person image often undergoes dramatically changes in appearance and background due to changes in view angle, background clutter, illumination conditions and so on.

© Springer Nature Switzerland AG 2019
Y. Zhao et al. (Eds.): ICIG 2019, LNCS 11903, pp. 517–528, 2019.
https://doi.org/10.1007/978-3-030-34113-8_43

Recently, as the deep learning based technologies are developed, the performance of person Re-ID has been improved significantly by learning robust representations with invariance property [5,9,23] or learn an effective distance metric [7,20,21]. All of those approaches focus on the supervised way which requires a plenty of large-scale, high-quality annotated data. However, collecting and annotating data for every new task are extremely expensive and time-consuming. Therefore, the supervised methods may be limited in real-world scenarios.

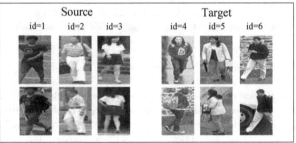

(a) open set domain adaptation

(b) closed set domain adaptation

Fig. 1. The difference of open set domain adaptation and closed set domain adaptation. For the former, target dataset contains absolutely different categories compared with the source dataset. For the latter, target dataset contains only images of the categories of the source dataset.

To address the aforementioned challenge, a common solution is the unsupervised domain adaptation [2,14] which attempts to transfer knowledge from labeled source data to unlabeled target data. However, the source dataset and the target dataset are drawn from two different distributions. Hence, if the model trained on the source dataset is directly used on the target dataset, the accuracy will decline dramatically. In addition, standard unsupervised domain adaptation method is denoted as the closed set problem which assume that the source and target domains contain the same set of classes. This assumption is not appropriate for domain adaptive person Re-ID which is an open set task. As shown in Fig. 1, open set domain adaptation includes images of unknown classes which are not present in source domains. Therefore, most domain adaptation methods cannot be directly applied to person Re-ID task.

To make a person Re-ID model practical, existing methods solve the problem from two aspects. One way is to generate cross-domain source data which have similar style with target data [3,17]. Another way is to design a domain-shared model to learn the domain-invariant features from both source data and target data [10]. Different with previous works, in this paper, a novel method is designed to effectively transfer discriminative representation from a large number of labeled source dataset to unlabeled target dataset.

First, the model pre-trained on labeled source dataset is deployed to extract features for target unlabeled dataset. And then the clustering method is performed on the target features. However, it is obvious that the assigned pseudo labels may not be correct, so only relative reliable samples are selected to train model in a supervised way. The rest samples with unreliable labels in target data still are unlabeled but also take part in the training afterwards in an unsupervised way.

Second, to address the domain shift between datasets, a novel domain adaptive model is designed by decomposing the representations to person-related discriminative representations and domain-related representations, as shown in Fig. 2. For person-related discriminative representations, the domain-adversarial loss is performed on the source and the target data with relative reliable labels to match the feature space distributions of different datasets. Meanwhile, considering the confidence of target labels, the Re-ID loss with label smooth regularization is designed to recognize the identity of pedestrians. What's more, to reduce information loss, a decoder is designed to reconstruct feature maps from the person-related and domain-related features on source dataset and all target dataset.

To sum up, the contributions of our work are:

(1) Different from existing unsupervised Re-ID models, we propose to solve the Re-ID task by adapting the representation learning from the auxiliary labeled datasets.
(2) We are the first to integrate the cluster method with the domain-invariant model. The learning strategy facilitates the model to pay more attention to the domain-invariant and discriminative features at the same time effectively reduce the loss of information.
(3) Extensive experiments and ablation study on Market-1501 and DukeMTMC-reID demonstrate the proposed method is effective and can be applicable to unsupervised cross-dataset transfer learning problem.

2   Related Works

Supervised Person Re-ID Methods. Most of the existing works focus on the supervised method [7,11,15,26] which train a model based on a sufficient number of labeled images across cameras. Main stream works can be categorized into two ways. One way is representation learning [11] which explores to design the discriminative features. Metric learning [7, 15] is another powerful way to address the problem of person re-identification and it aims at learning the similarity of two images. However, directly deploying these trained methods to the real-world environment always leads to poor performance due to domain shift and the lack of label information.

Deep Domain Adaption. With the popularity of deep learning methods, more and more researchers use deep neural networks to enhance the performance of domain adaption. Yosinski *et al.* [18] demonstrate the generalizability of layers and find the first 3 layers of neural network learn mostly general features and higher layers learn higher levels of representations. Tzeng *et al.* [13] first propose the DDC method which fixed the first seven layers of AlexNet and add adaptive metrics to the previous layer of the classifier to solve the adaptive problem of deep network. Then Long [8] propose the DAN method to extend the DDC method. In contrast to the DDC method which only has one adaptive layer and a single kernel MMD, the DAN method add three adaptive layers at the same time and adopt a multi-kernel MMD measurement (mk-mmd) with better representation ability. Bousmalis *et al.* [2] propose a novel method, the Domain Separation Networks (DSN), for learning domain-invariant representations. However, in person Re-ID datasets, the source dataset and the target dataset have totally different identities, so traditional domain adaptation methods is not suitable to our task.

Domain Adaption in Person Re-ID. Although we have made a great progress in the field of supervised learning methods, it is inevitable to label these images manually, and the work is really expensive. Hence, it is necessary for us to further study unsupervised methods. Peng *et al.* [10] propose a multi-task dictionary learning model to transfer a learn a view-invariant representation from the labeled source dataset to the unlabeled target dataset. However, hand-craft methods always have a poor performance on large-scale dataset. Fan *et al.* [4] propose a method by clustering the unlabeled training set and using CNN fine tuning for iterative training. However, the method only use a labeled source data to initialize the model but ignore the labeled source data during the training of target domain. Recently, Generative Adversarial Networks (GAN) become more and more popular. In order to achieve cross-dataset classification tasks, there are many methods utilize GAN to transfer the style of different domain person images [3, 17, 26]. For example, Deng *et al.* are inspired by CycleGAN and apply it to generate images with similar target domain style. In [25], Zhong *et al.* introduce a Hetero-Homogeneous Learning (HHL) to learn camera-invariant network for target domain. However, the methods based on GAN is difficult to keep person identities during the progress of generating images.

3   Methodology

3.1   Problem Definition

In this section, we introduce some notations and definitions that are used in this paper. Assume the labeled source dataset $D_s = \{(I_i^s, y_i^s)\}_{i=1}^{N_s}$ including N_s

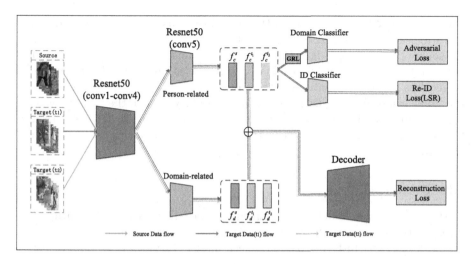

Fig. 2. Illustration of the proposed model. During training, the source data and all target data is input Resnet-50 (conv1-conv4) to extract features. And then, the model is decomposed to the person-related part and the domain-related part. For person-related part, only source and target (t_1) data is input to domain and ID classifier to learn domain-invariant discriminative features. For domain-related part, on the one hand, explicitly modeling what is unique to each domain is able to improve the ability of the model to extract domain-invariant features. On the other hand, for source, target (t_1) and target (t_2), domain-related part is combined with person-invariant part to reconstruct image for reducing information loss.

image samples and the unlabeled target dataset $D_t = \{I_i^t\}_{i=1}^{N_t}$ including N_t image samples, where I_i^s and I_i^t collected from different domains. The goal of the proposed domain-adaptive model is to make use of labeled source samples D_s to learn a model $M : I_i^t \mapsto y_i^t$ and make it equally effectual on the target samples D_s by learning the domain-invariant discriminative representations.

To minimize the discrepancy of the source dataset and target dataset effectively, a novel domain adaptation framework is designed. First, a model pretrained on source labeled data is utilized to extract features of target data. And the cluster method is adopted to generate weak labels for target samples and only those samples $D_{t_1} = \{I_i^{t_1}, y_i^{t_1}\}_{i=1}^{N_{t_1}}$ with more reliable labels are selected. It is a good way to supply the supervised information for the target dataset. The rest target data $D_{t_2} = \{I_i^{t_2}\}_{i=1}^{N_{t_2}}$ still are unlabeled. Second, source data, target data with weak labels D_{t_1}, target data without labels D_{t_2} are input the proposed domain-adaptive model (DAM). As shown in Fig. 2, Resnet-50 [6] is adopted as the backbone of the feature extraction module. As is known, in the neural network, the features extracted by the first several layers are general features. And with the deepening of network layers, the latter layers emphasise more on the specific features of learning tasks. To perform cross-dataset person Re-ID and further improve Re-ID performance, we keep the first several layers and introduce 2 branches to learn the person-related and domain-related representations after Conv4 respectively. For the first branch, the features $(f_c^s, f_c^{t_1})$ of the source D_s and target data D_{t_1} are input to domain classifier and ID classifier to learn domain-invariant discriminative representations. Specially, the labels of target data D_{t_1} may deviate from the ground truth, thus, the cross entropy with the label smoothing regularization(LSR) is deployed. For the second branch, the domain-related features $(f_d^s, f_d^{t_1}$ and $f_d^{t_2})$ is combined with person-related features $(f_c^s, f_c^{t_1}$ and $f_c^{t_2})$ to reconstructed image for reducing the information loss.

3.2 Clustering

Firstly, the original model $\phi(\cdot; \theta)$ trained on labeled source dataset is utilised to initialize the parameters of target model. And then generating weak labels for target dataset by clustering based on such model. The idea is formulated as:

$$\min_{y, C_1, \dots, C_J} \sum_{k=1}^{K} \sum_{y_i=k} \|\phi(x_i; \theta) - C_j\|^2 \tag{1}$$

where C_J is the cluster center of samples and y_i is the sample label. But not all generated weak labels are correct, in order to avoid erroneous labels making the model get stuck in a bad local optimum or oscillating, we merely select these more reliable samples which are more closer to the each ID class center C_j. To achieve this, a threshold is set, if the distance between sample and the corresponding cluster center is lower than the threshold, then x_i is selected as a reliable sample and is placed into target data D_{t_1} for supervised training; otherwise, x_i is placed into target dataset D_{t_2} for unsupervised training.

3.3 Learning

To alleviate domain shift for cross-dataset person Re-ID, a novel domain-adaptive model is designed. All data is input to Resnet-50 (conv1-conv4) to extract general features, and 2 branches (conv5) to learn person-related and domain-related parts respectively. For person-related part, the goal is to learn domain-shared and discriminative features related to person Re-ID by adversarial loss and Re-ID loss. Domain-related part is combined with person-related part to reconstruct image by reconstruction loss.

Adversarial Loss. Early methods for domain adaptation always try to find a common feature space. However, inspired by generative adversarial nets (GAN), more and more adversarial learning approaches have showed state-of-the-art performance for cross-dataset transfer learning. Hence, in the paper, adversarial learning [8] is adopted to make the features' distributions become more similar during training by confusing domain classification.

The adversarial loss trains the adversarial discriminator using a standard classification loss. During the forward propagation, the model leaves the input unchanged, but during the backpropagation, the gradient is reversed by multi-plying a negative scalar. Mathematically, the adversarial layer can be treated as a function $g(\cdot)$:

$$forward : g(x) = x$$
$$backward : g(x) = -x \tag{2}$$

The objective function of adversarial loss optimized by the stochastic gradient descent can be expressed as:

$$\mathcal{L}_{adv} = -\sum_{i=0}^{N_s+N_{t1}} d_i \log \hat{d}_i + (1-d_i) \log(1-\hat{d}_i) \tag{3}$$

where d_i denotes one hot encoding of domain labels, and $\hat{d}_i$ denotes the domain category prediction. Under the effect of adversarial loss, even if there are differences between the two domains, the outputs of feature extractor still are domain-invariant features.

Re-ID Loss. In order to make the model discriminative and preserve identity information, the Re-ID loss is designed to predict the output labels of source dataset and target data D_{t_1}. This part mainly focuses on learning the discriminative representations of pedestrians. Re-ID loss can be denoted as minimizing the negative log-likelihood of the ground truth class:

$$\mathcal{L}_{id} = -\sum_{i=0}^{N_s+N_{t_1}} q(i) \log p(i) \tag{4}$$

where $q(i)$ denotes the ground truth distribution and $p(i)$ is the predicted probability prediction.

However, considering the noise caused by weak labels or existing mislabeled samples in real data, we apply the label smoothing regularization (LSR) [12] to alleviate the influence of noisy samples by re-weighting the samples with weak labels. The LSR function can be written as:

$$q_{LSR}(i) = \begin{cases} \frac{\varepsilon}{N_s+N_{t_1}} & i \neq y \\ 1 - \varepsilon + \frac{\varepsilon}{N_s+N_{t_1}} & i = y \end{cases} \tag{5}$$

where $\varepsilon \in [0,1]$ is a hyper-parameter denoting the confident of the ground truth. And the cross-entropy loss with $q_{LSR}(i)$ is expressed as:

$$\mathcal{L}_{id_{LSR}} = -(1-\varepsilon) \log(p(y)) - \frac{\varepsilon}{N_s+N_{t_1}} \sum_{i=1}^{N_s+N_{t_1}} log(p(i)) \tag{6}$$

Reconstruction Loss. In order to reduce information loss in above procedure, a shared decoder is introduced to reconstruct the input sample by concatenating the person-related and domain-related representations. The reconstruction loss is defined as:

$$\mathcal{L}_{rec} = \sum_{i=1}^{N_s} \|Decoder(f_c^s + f_d^s)\|_2^2 +$$

$$\sum_{i=1}^{N_{t_1}} \|Decoder(f_c^{t_1} + f_d^{t_1})\|_2^2 + \sum_{i=1}^{N_{t_2}} \|Decoder(f_c^{t_2} + f_d^{t_2})\|_2^2 \qquad (7)$$

where $f_c^s, f_c^{t_1}, f_c^{t_2}$ denote the person-related representations of source, target D_{t_1} and target D_{t_2} respectively. And $f_d^s, f_d^{t_1}, f_d^{t_2}$ denote the domain-related representations of source, target D_{t_1} and target D_{t_2} respectively.

In short, the final integrated training objective can be written as follows:

$$\mathcal{L}_{total} = \mathcal{L}_{id} + \alpha\mathcal{L}_{adv} + \beta\mathcal{L}_{rec} \qquad (8)$$

where α and β are hyper-parameters and control the relative importance of each item. The model is trained by minimizing $\mathcal{L}_{total}$. The experiments is a iteration progress until the model is stable. In general, the number of iterations is typically < 5 in our experiment.

4   Experiment

4.1   Datasets

Table 1. Comparison with State-of-the-art Methods.

Methods	Duke → Market				Market → Duke			
	Rank-1	Rank-5	Rank-10	mAP	Rank-1	Rank-5	Rank-10	mAP
UMDL [10]	34.5	52.6	59.6	12.4	18.5	31.4	37.6	7.3
PUL [4]	45.5	60.7	66.7	20.5	30.0	43.4	48.5	16.4
CAMEL [19]	54.5	–	–	26.3	–	–	–	–
TJ-AIDL [16]	58.2	74.8	81.1	26.5	44.3	59.6	65.0	23.0
SPGAN+LMP [3]	57.7	75.8	82.4	26.7	46.4	62.3	68.0	26.2
CamStyle [26]	58.8	78.2	84.3	27.4	48.4	62.5	68.9	25.1
HHL [25]	62.2	78.8	84.0	31.4	46.9	61.0	66.7	27.2
Ours	**68.0**	**82.3**	**87.7**	**39.5**	**58.1**	**74.5**	**79.7**	**29.6**

For experiments, two widely used benchmark datasets Market-1501 [22] and DukeMTMC-reID [24] are chosen. The details are described as follows:

Market-1501 consists of 32,668 annotated bounding boxes of 1,501 identities which is collected in front of a supermarket at Tsinghua University. Images of each identity are captured by at most six cameras and each annotated identity is present in at least two cameras. There are 19,732 images with 751 identities used for testing and 12,936 images with 750 identities used for training. Market-1501 dataset adopts Deformable Part Model (DPM) as pedestrian detector.

DukeMTMC-reID is sampled from video at 120 frames per image, resulting in 36,411 images. There are 1,404 people under more than two cameras, and 408 people under only one. It is composed of 16,522 training images of 702 identities, 2,228 query images of the other 702 identities and 17,661 gallery images.

A single-shot experiment setting is adopted. In each experiment, the source dataset is supposed to be labeled, and target dataset is supposed to be unlabeled. What's more, both rank-1 accuracy and mean Average Precision (mAP) are employed for person Re-ID evaluation.

4.2 Implementation Details

The model is implemented by using Pytorch. ResNet-50 [6] model is adopted with weights pre-trained on ImageNet as basic model. If Market is viewed as the source dataset with labels, Duke will be considered as the target datset without labels, and vice versa. During the progress of training, stochastic gradient descent with a momentum of 0.9 is adopted. And the learning rate is set to 0.001 and decay to 1×10^{-4} and 1×10^{-5} after 20 epochs and 120 epochs respectively. The maximum number of iterations is set to 200. For the label smoothing regularization(LSR), $\varepsilon = 0.1$. For the clustering step, standard kmeans clustering is adopted and k-means++ [1] is used to select initial cluster centers.

4.3 Comparison with State-of-the-Art Methods

We compare our approach with state-of-the-art methods when tested on Market and Duke, as shown in Table 1. From the results, it is evident that our model with the performance in Rank-1 accuracy = 68.0% (58.1%) and mAP = 39.5% (29.6%) is able to get better performance on Market (Duke) when compared with existing unsupervised methods including hand-craft method UMDL [10], based on weak labels method PUL [4], based on attribute-identity method TJ-AIDL [16], and based on GAN methods SPGAN [3], CamStyle [26] and HHL [25]. Specially, when the method is compared with PUL [4] which also use a labeled source data to initialize the model but ignore the labeled source data during training, our method leads to +22.5% (+38.0%) and +19.0% (+13.2%) improvement on Market (Duke) in Rank-1 and mAP, respectively. And when compared with current best results HHL [25], our model is 5.8% (11.2%) higher than HHL [25] on Market (Duke).

4.4 Ablation Studies

The Effectiveness of Adversarial Loss. As shown in Tables 2 and 3, when our method is compared to the direct transfer method, the loss gains 25.7%

Table 2. Methods comparison when tested on Market.

Methods	Duke → Market			
	Rank-1	Rank-5	Rank-10	mAP
Direct transfer	42.3	59.5	67.1	17.5
Ours w/o $\mathcal{L}_{adv}$	66.3	80.8	86.9	37.6
Ours w/o $\mathcal{L}_{id}(LSR)$	67.1	81.6	87.5	38.7
Ours w/o $\mathcal{L}_{rec}$	66.9	81.2	87.1	38.1
Ours	**68.0**	**82.3**	**87.7**	**39.5**

Table 3. Methods comparison when tested on Duke.

Methods	Market → Duke			
	Rank-1	Rank-5	Rank-10	mAP
Direct transfer	29.3	45.4	52.0	14.5
Ours w/o $\mathcal{L}_{adv}$	56.3	72.8	77.9	27.8
Ours w/o $\mathcal{L}_{id}(LSR)$	57.2	73.6	78.1	28.7
Ours w/o $\mathcal{L}_{rec}$	56.9	73.8	78.5	28.5
Ours	**58.1**	**74.5**	**79.7**	**29.6**

(28.8%) improvements in Rank-1 accuracy on Market (Duke). This indicates that adversarial loss is effective by confusion the domain classification, and the abundant unlabeled data have been well utilized by learning domain-invariant features.

The Effectiveness of Re-ID Loss with LSR. As Table 2 (Table 3) shown, when we introduce Re-ID loss with LSR, the result can improve by +0.9% (+1.8%) in Rank-1 on Market (Duke) respectively. This shows that Re-ID loss with LSR indeed helps for unsupervised Re-ID by re-weighting the samples with generated weak labels.

The Effectiveness of Reconstruction Loss. We observe that reconstruction loss is able to improve the Rank-1 by +1.1% (+1.2%) on Market (Duke). The experiment demonstrates that reconstruction loss is an effective way to reduce the loss of information.

4.5   The Impact of the Cluster Number

We evaluate the impact of the cluster number which is set to 300, 500, 700, 900, 1100. As shown in Fig. 3, our method is robust for the number of cluster. Even if the number of cluster is different from the actual situation, our method can still exceed many methods. Specially, when the cluster is close to the actual number of categories, our method have the best effect.

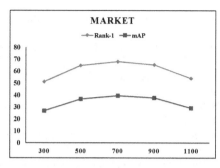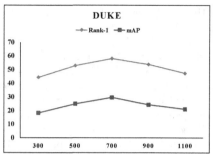

Fig. 3. The impact of cluster number on Market and Duke.

5 Conclusion

This paper proposes a novel unsupervised cross-dataset transfer learning method for Re-ID task. The proposed model aims to learn discriminative representation by leveraging the labeled dataset. To achieve that, we design a special domain adaptation framework for person Re-ID. In contrast to most existing approaches, our method combine cluster method and domain-invariant model to train the target model in an iterative way. We also show the importance of making full use of the relative reliable weak labels information on the target dataset. Extensive experiments demonstrate the effectiveness and robustness of the proposed model.

Acknowledgments. I am thankful to and fortunate enough to get constant support from the Fundamental Research Funds for the Central Universities (No. 2018JBM017), the Joint Fund for the Ministry of Education of China and China mobile Communications Corp. (MCM20170201) and the Natural Science Foundation of China (NSFC) under Grants 61702515. Also, I would like to extend our sincere esteems to all staff in laboratory for their timely support.

References

1. Arthur, D., Vassilvitskii, S.: k-means++: the advantages of careful seeding. In: ACM-SIAM Symposium on Discrete Algorithms, pp. 1027–1035. Society for Industrial and Applied Mathematics (2007)
2. Bousmalis, K., Trigeorgis, G., Silberman, N., Krishnan, D., Erhan, D.: Domain separation networks. In: NIPS, pp. 343–351 (2016)
3. Deng, W., Zheng, L., Kang, G., Yang, Y., Ye, Q., Jiao, J.: Image-image domain adaptation with preserved self-similarity and domain-dissimilarity for person reidentification. In: CVPR, vol. 1, p. 6 (2018)
4. Fan, H., Zheng, L., Yan, C., Yang, Y.: Unsupervised person re-identification: clustering and fine-tuning. ACM Trans. Multimedia Comput. Commun. Appl. **14**(4), 83 (2018)
5. Geng, M., Wang, Y., Xiang, T., Tian, Y.: Deep transfer learning for person reidentification. arXiv preprint arXiv:1611.05244 (2016)

6. He, K., Zhang, X., Ren, S., Sun, J.: Deep residual learning for image recognition. In: CVPR, pp. 770–778 (2016)
7. Hermans, A., Beyer, L., Leibe, B.: In defense of the triplet loss for person re-identification. arXiv preprint arXiv:1703.07737 (2017)
8. Long, M., Cao, Y., Wang, J., Jordan, M.I.: Learning transferable features with deep adaptation networks. arXiv preprint arXiv:1502.02791 (2015)
9. Matsukawa, T., Okabe, T., Suzuki, E., Sato, Y.: Hierarchical Gaussian descriptor for person re-identification. In: CVPR, pp. 1363–1372 (2016)
10. Peng, P., et al.: Unsupervised cross-dataset transfer learning for person re-identification. In: CVPR, pp. 1306–1315 (2016)
11. Sun, Y., Zheng, L., Yang, Y., Tian, Q., Wang, S.: Beyond part models: person retrieval with refined part pooling. arXiv preprint arXiv:1711.09349 (2017)
12. Szegedy, C., Vanhoucke, V., Ioffe, S., Shlens, J., Wojna, Z.: Rethinking the inception architecture for computer vision. In: CVPR, pp. 2818–2826 (2016)
13. Tzeng, E., Hoffman, J., Darrell, T., Saenko, K.: Simultaneous deep transfer across domains and tasks. In: ICCV, pp. 4068–4076 (2015)
14. Tzeng, E., Hoffman, J., Saenko, K., Darrell, T.: Adversarial discriminative domain adaptation. In: CVPR, vol. 1, p. 4 (2017)
15. Varior, R.R., Haloi, M., Wang, G.: Gated siamese convolutional neural network architecture for human re-identification. In: Leibe, B., Matas, J., Sebe, N., Welling, M. (eds.) ECCV 2016. LNCS, vol. 9912, pp. 791–808. Springer, Cham (2016). https://doi.org/10.1007/978-3-319-46484-8_48
16. Wang, J., Zhu, X., Gong, S., Li, W.: Transferable joint attribute-identity deep learning for unsupervised person re-identification. In: CVPR (2018)
17. Wei, L., Zhang, S., Gao, W., Tian, Q.: Person transfer GAN to bridge domain gap for person re-identification. In: CVPR (2018)
18. Yosinski, J., Clune, J., Bengio, Y., Lipson, H.: How transferable are features in deep neural networks? In: NIPS, pp. 3320–3328 (2014)
19. Yu, H.-X., Wu, A., Zheng, W.-S.: Cross-view asymmetric metric learning for unsupervised person re-identification. In: ICCV (2017)
20. Zhang, L., Xiang, T., Gong, S.: Learning a discriminative null space for person re-identification. In: CVPR, pp. 1239–1248 (2016)
21. Zhang, Y., Li, B., Lu, H., Irie, A., Ruan, X.: Sample-specific SVM learning for person re-identification. In: CVPR, pp. 1278–1287 (2016)
22. Zheng, L., Shen, L., Tian, L., Wang, S., Wang, J., Tian, Q.: Scalable person re-identification: a benchmark. In: ICCV, pp. 1116–1124 (2015)
23. Zheng, L., Yang, Y., Hauptmann, A.G.: Person re-identification: past, present and future. arXiv preprint arXiv:1610.02984 (2016)
24. Zheng, Z., Zheng, L., Yang, Y.: Unlabeled samples generated by GAN improve the person re-identification baseline in vitro. In: ICCV, vol. 3 (2017)
25. Zhong, Z., Zheng, L., Li, S., Yang, Y.: Generalizing a person retrieval model hetero- and homogeneously. In: Ferrari, V., Hebert, M., Sminchisescu, C., Weiss, Y. (eds.) ECCV 2018. LNCS, vol. 11217, pp. 176–192. Springer, Cham (2018). https://doi.org/10.1007/978-3-030-01261-8_11
26. Zhong, Z., Zheng, L., Zheng, Z., Li, S., Yang, Y.: Camera style adaptation for person re-identification. In: CVPR, pp. 5157–5166 (2018)

Bilinear Factorization via Recursive Sample Factoring for Low-Rank Hyperspectral Image Recovery

Yuxuan Wang, Timothy Apasiba Abeo, Liangjun Wang,
Dickson Keddy Wornyo, and Xiang-Jun Shen[✉]

School of Computer Science and Telecommunication Engineering,
Jiangsu University, Zhenjiang, China
xjshen@ujs.edu.cn

Abstract. Low-rank hyperspectral image recovery (LRHSIR) is a very challenging task in various computer vision applications for its inherent complexity. Hyperspectral image (HSI) contains much more information than a regular image due to significant number of spectra bands and the spectral information can be considered as multiview. In this paper, a method of bilinear factorization via recursive sample factoring (BF-RSF) is proposed. Different from traditional low rank models with each data point being treated equally, the importance of each data point is measured by the sample factoring that imposes a penalty on each sample in our BF-RSF model. The sample factoring is a cosine similarity metric learnt from the angle between each data point and the principal component of the low-rank matrix in the feature space. That is, the closer a data point to the principal component vector, the more likely it is a clean data point. By imposing the sample factoring onto the training dataset, the outliers or noise will be detected and their effect will be suppressed. Therefore, a better low-rank structure of clean data can be obtained especially in a heavy noisy scenario, with the effect of noisy data points in modeling being suppressed. Extensive experimental results on SalinasA, demonstrate that BF-RSF outperforms state-of-the-art low-rank matrix recovery methods in image clustering tasks with various levels of corruptions.

Keywords: Hyperspectral image (HSI) · Bilinear factorization · Sample factoring · Cosine similarity metric

1 Introduction

Hyperspectral image (HSI) contains much more information than a regular image due to significant number of spectra bands and the spectral information can be considered as multiview. Therefore, HSI has been widely applied in remote sensing monitoring and its high spectral resolution can help distinguish different materials. Low rank hyperspectral image recovery (LRHSIR) [1] is one of

© Springer Nature Switzerland AG 2019
Y. Zhao et al. (Eds.): ICIG 2019, LNCS 11903, pp. 529–540, 2019.
https://doi.org/10.1007/978-3-030-34113-8_44

popular techniques in image processing which can discover the underlying structure of the given observations. The inspiration of which is that, in real case, even very high-dimensional observations are from a low-dimensional subspace. As a theoretical foundation in computer vision, the effectiveness of LRHSIR has been proven by several fundamental tasks [2]. Therefore, recovering low-rank and sparse matrices from corrupted observations has obtained greatly attention in computer vision, machine learning and statistics. And, many computer vision tasks can be formulated as low dimensional linear models. Typical examples are Robust Principal Component Analysis (RPCA) [3] and Low Rank Representation (LRR) [4]. These two models are widely used for representation of images in computer vision tasks, such as subspace segmentation [5], image classification [6] and subspace clustering [7]. The advantage of these low rank algorithms is that the data points from different categories are treated as samples from a union of multiple low-rank subspaces. Thereby, it can provide a good representation of the data [8].

Among state-of-the-art models, RPCA is one of the most widely used algorithms. Candes et al. [3] proposed RPCA, which recovers a subspace structure from noisy data by decomposing the data matrix into two components of a low rank matrix and a sparse matrix through introducing the nuclear norm. It can be seen that singular value decomposition (SVD) is the most widely used technique when all components of the data matrix are observed. To avoid this expensive singular value decomposition, fixed-rank strategies have been proposed to obtain the low-rank representation. For example, Liu et al. [9] proposed the fixed-rank representation (FRR) as a unified framework for unsupervised visual learning which can reveal the structure of multiple subspaces in closed-form when the data is noiseless. Moreover, Wen et al. [10] constructed a nonlinear successive over-relaxation (SOR) algorithm and showed that its speed is several times faster than many other methods.

Recently, some researchers proposed another strategy which introduced bilinear factorization to accelerate the computation process. This approach benefits from fast numerical methods for optimization. Therefore, the calculation of a bilinear factorization of a matrix becomes a fundamental operation in many computer vision applications [11]. We can see that factorization approach to low-rank subspace estimation is a method to minimize a loss function between an observed measurement matrix and a bilinear factorization. Unfortunately, in the presence of missing data, the bilinear factorization problem becomes NP-Hard [12]. Thus, the problem of low-rank matrix factorization in the presence of missing data has seen significant attention in computer vision research. Many researchers focused on initialization strategies or algorithms that are robust to initialization. For example, Aguiar et al. [13] proposed an optimal algorithm in the absence of noise when the missing data follows a Young diagram. To solve those scenarios which exhibit band patterns, Buchanan et al. [14] showed that alternated minimization algorithms are subject to flattening and proposed a Newton method to optimize bilinear factor jointly.

However, the performance of RPCA could be depressed if observations are insufficient. Unfortunately, the presence of missing data is often the situation in practice. Hence, besides properly modeling the low-rank structure, it is the core to the performance of recovery when handling the problem of missing data. Thus, some researchers [15,16] explored the idea of adding an indicator matrix or a weight matrix to measure the entries of the data matrix. Aside from that, Cabral et al. [17] proposed a unified approach to bilinear factorization and nuclear norm regularization that inherits the benefits of both. Moreover, Lin et al. [18] proposed a new algorithm for robust matrix factorization (RMF) which is based on the Majorization Minimization (MM) technique. These methods have also been extended to handle outliers, in which case, the L2 norm is only optimal to Gaussian noise and is fragile to outliers. For robustness, Ke and Kanade [19] suggested replacing the LS loss with the L1 norm, minimized by alternated linear programming. Guo et al. [20] proposed a method for recovering the low rank matrix with robust outlier estimation, termed as ROUTE, in a unified manner.

In this paper, we present a new method of utilizing bilinear factorization via recursive sample factoring. Inspired by the theoretical results in [21], it can be shown that many nuclear norm regularized problems can be optimized with a bilinear factorization by using the variational definition of the nuclear norm. Furthermore, data points are selected by introducing sample scaling factor in BF-RSF. The sample scaling factor is a cosine similarity metric accounting for the angle between each data point and the principal component vector of low-rank matrix in feature space. In our model, sample scaling factor is used to not only measure the significance of data points, but also to impose restriction onto the training dataset iteratively to reduce the noise effect. By this modeling, BF-RSF can learn better low-rank structure of clean data especially in a heavy noisy scenario, with noisy data being suppressed.

We summarize our key contributions in the following:

(1) The advantage of bilinear factorization lies in that it is a fast numerical method for optimization. Meanwhile, the significance of each data point is measured by the sample scaling factor, which is learnt from the relationship between the data point and the principal component vector of the low-rank matrix. Therefore, noisy data points can be detected and suppressed from the dataset.
(2) A better low-rank structure of clean data can be learnt through BF-RSF, by imposing sample scaling factor onto the training dataset iteratively.
(3) Extensive experimental results demonstrate that our BF-RSF method significantly improves the performance of image clustering especially in a heavy noisy scenario.

The remainder of this paper is structured as follows. We present our proposed method of bilinear factorization via recursive sample factoring (BF-RSF) in Sect. 2. Experimental results are presented in Sect. 3. Finally, we draw conclusions in Sect. 4.

2   Methodology

2.1   Problem Formulation

In this subsection, we present a brief review of the formulation of our BF-RSF model. Formally, low-rank matrix recovery with missing data can be directly or indirectly formulated as

$$\min_{Z} f\left(\mathbf{X} - \mathbf{Z}\right) + \lambda \|\mathbf{Z}\|_*$$
$$s.t. \text{rank}\left(\mathbf{Z}\right) = r \tag{1}$$

where $f\left(\cdot\right)$ denotes a loss function and $\mathbf{X} = [\mathbf{x}_1, \mathbf{x}_2, \ldots \mathbf{x}_n] \in \Re^{d \times n}$ is the data matrix. $\mathbf{Z}$ is the low rank matrix. λ is a trade-off parameter between the loss function and the low rank regularization induced by the nuclear norm.

According to [22], $\mathbf{Z}$ can be decomposed as $\mathbf{Z} = \mathbf{U}_{d \times r}\mathbf{V}_{n \times r}^{\mathbf{T}}$ in which r is the rank of $\mathbf{Z}$. In [23], the nuclear norm can be alternated as $\min_{Z=UV^T} \frac{1}{2}\left(\|\mathbf{U}\|_F^2 + \|\mathbf{V}\|_F^2\right)$ by using the variational definition of nuclear norm. And it has been shown that the loss function can be written as $\|\cdot\|_{l_p}$. Therefore, Cabral et al. [17] unified bilinear factorization and nuclear norm and then Eq. 1 can be rewritten as follows:

$$\min_{Z,U,V} \|\mathbf{W} \odot \left(\mathbf{X} - \mathbf{Z}\right)\|_{l_p} + \frac{\lambda}{2}\left(\|\mathbf{U}\|_F^2 + \|\mathbf{V}\|_F^2\right)$$
$$s.t. \mathbf{Z} = \mathbf{UV^T} \tag{2}$$

where $\mathbf{X} \in \Re^{d \times n}$ is the data matrix and $\mathbf{Z} \in \Re^{d \times n}$ is the low rank matrix. $\|\cdot\|$ is a matrix norm. $\mathbf{W}$ is a weight matrix with the same size as $\mathbf{X}$. The entry value of $\mathbf{W}$ being 0 means that the component at the same position in $\mathbf{X}$ is missing, and 1 otherwise. The operator $\odot$ is the Hadamard element-wise product. We can choose different types of l_p according to different kinds of noise. For instance, it is reasonable to choose l_2 norm for the assumption of Gaussian noise, or more exactly, the Frobenius norm $\|\cdot\|_F$ in matrix form as the measurement. However, l_2 norm is not appropriate any longer for the presence of outliers and l_1 norm has long been recommended [24].

Different from traditional method which imposed a weight matrix directly, efforts are made to seek another reasonable solution to measure the significance of each data point in our BF-RSF model. We expect that clean data points have high weights while the noisy ones possess low weights. To this end, a cosine similarity metric is developed. As shown in Fig. 1, U_1 is the principal component vector, and x_i and x_j are two data points. One can be seen that, the angle between x_j and U_1 is much larger than that of x_i. Evidently, x_i is a clean data point, while x_j is an outlier. This indicates that we can exploit $d_i = |\cos\theta_i|$ to measure the significance of the data points. And the choice of U_1 mentioned above will be discussed as follows. As claimed in [25], any $\mathbf{Z}$ can be decomposed as $\mathbf{U\Sigma V^T}$, where $\mathbf{U}$ and $\mathbf{V}$ are left and right singular vectors. In our model, we choose U_1 which is the column vectors of $\mathbf{U}$ corresponding to the maximum

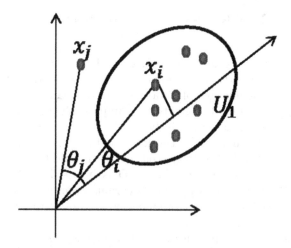

Fig. 1. Illustration of our model.

eigenvalue of σ. This principal component vector is also illustrated in Fig. 1 from a geometrical view.

In summary, d_i can be computed through

$$d_i = |\cos \theta_i| + \varepsilon = \left| \frac{x_i^T U_1}{\|x_i\| \, \|U_1\|} \right| + \varepsilon \tag{3}$$

where ε is a small constant to prevent d_i from 0.

With the factor d, we can impose this penalty factor onto the data to alleviate the noise effect before inputting them in the low-rank model. Let

$$\mathbf{D} = \begin{bmatrix} d_1 & & \\ & \ddots \, d_i & \\ & & \ddots \, d_n \end{bmatrix},$$ and the low rank matrix is achieved by solving the

following optimization:

$$\min_{Z,U,V} \|(\mathbf{X} - \mathbf{Z}) \, \mathbf{D}\|_1 + \frac{\lambda}{2} \left(\|\mathbf{U}\|_F^2 + \|\mathbf{V}\|_F^2 \right)$$
$$s.t. \mathbf{ZD} = \mathbf{UV^T}, \ \hat{\mathbf{X}} = \mathbf{XD}, \ \hat{\mathbf{Z}} = \mathbf{ZD} \tag{4}$$

where $\mathbf{X} \in \Re^{d \times n}$ is the data matrix, $\mathbf{Z}$ is a low-rank structure matrix, and $\mathbf{U} \in \Re^{d \times r}$, $\mathbf{V} \in \Re^{n \times r}$.

It can be seen that the factor d is suitable for our goal. As shown in Fig. 1, the angle is to $\pi/2$, the higher probability that the data point is a noisy point, and a lower factor is assigned to the data.

Therefore, the effect of noisy data points will be suppressed. By contrast, the effect of those data points that are close to the principal component vector will be enhanced.

The characteristics of BF-RSF are summarized as follows:

(1) In our BF-RSF model, the scaling factor is learnt from relationship between the principal component vector and each data point by introducing the cosine similarity metric. The sample scaling factor matrix $\mathbf{D}$ is introduced to measure the significance of data points and it can reduce the impact of noisy data points in modeling with the sample scaling factor being imposed onto the training dataset iteratively.

(2) With this model, our BF-RSF can learn better low-rank structure of clean data especially in a heavy noisy scenario, as the effect of noisy data points in modeling being suppressed. When $\mathbf{D}$ is imposed on $\mathbf{X}$, the low rank solution of $\mathbf{Z}$ will tend to keep more low-rank structure of data points with bigger cosine similarity. Therefore a better low-rank structure of clean data is achieved in our model.

(3) $\mathbf{Z}$ in Eq. 4 is used for representing the low-dimensional structure of the new dataset $\hat{\mathbf{X}}$. In this way, we propose a low-rank matrix recovery framework with sample scaling factor. Compared to other algorithms, the performance of our method is the best.

2.2   Optimization

In this subsection, we introduce an optimization algorithm to solve the problem defined in Eq. 4. The augmented Lagrangian function of the problem in Eq. 4 is

$$
\begin{aligned}
L = \min_{Z,U,V,Y,\mu} \ & \|(\mathbf{X} - \mathbf{Z})\,\mathbf{D}\|_1 + \tfrac{\lambda}{2}\left(\|\mathbf{U}\|_F^2 + \|\mathbf{V}\|_F^2\right) \\
& + \left\langle \mathbf{Y}, \hat{\mathbf{Z}} - \mathbf{U}\mathbf{V}^{\mathbf{T}} \right\rangle + \tfrac{\mu}{2}\left\|\hat{\mathbf{Z}} - \mathbf{U}\mathbf{V}^{\mathbf{T}}\right\|_F^2
\end{aligned}
\tag{5}
$$

where $\mathbf{Y}$ is a Lagrange multiplier, $\mu > 0$ is a penalty parameter, and $\|\cdot\|_F$ denotes the Frobenious norm of a matrix.

For $\mathbf{U} \in \Re^{d \times r}$ and $\mathbf{V} \in \Re^{n \times r}$, the solution is obtained by equating the derivatives of Eq. 5 with respect to $\mathbf{U}$ and $\mathbf{V}$ to 0. Then, $\mathbf{U}$ and $\mathbf{V}$ are obtained as follows:

$$
\mathbf{U} = \left(\mathbf{Y} + \mu\hat{\mathbf{Z}}\right)\mathbf{V}\left(\lambda\mathbf{I}_{\mathbf{r}} + \mu\left(\mathbf{V}^{\mathbf{T}}\mathbf{V}\right)\right)^{-1}
\tag{6}
$$

$$
\mathbf{V} = \left(\mathbf{Y} + \mu\hat{\mathbf{Z}}\right)^{T}\mathbf{U}\left(\lambda\mathbf{I}_{\mathbf{r}} + \mu\left(\mathbf{U}^{\mathbf{T}}\mathbf{U}\right)\right)^{-1}
\tag{7}
$$

For known $\mathbf{U}$ and $\mathbf{V}$, and introducing a relaxation variable $\mathbf{J}$ to denote $\left(\hat{\mathbf{X}} - \hat{\mathbf{Z}}\right)$, $\mathbf{J}$ can be updated as follows:

$$
\mathbf{J} = \operatorname*{argmin}_{\mathbf{J}} \tfrac{1}{\mu}\|\mathbf{J}\|_1 + \tfrac{1}{2}\left\|\mathbf{J} - \left(\hat{\mathbf{X}} - \mathbf{U}\mathbf{V}^{\mathbf{T}} + \tfrac{\mathbf{Y}}{\mu}\right)\right\|_F^2
\tag{8}
$$

Finally, $\mathbf{Z}$ can be obtained via $\mathbf{Z} = \mathbf{U}\mathbf{V}^{\mathbf{T}}\mathbf{D}^{-1}$ and the whole algorithm is presented in Algorithm 1.

Algorithm 1. Algorithm of our BF-RSF method.

1: Input: training dataset $\mathbf{X}$, regulation parameter λ.

2: Initialize: t = 0, k = 0, $\mathbf{J}_{k=0} = 0$, $\mathbf{Z}_{k=0} = 0$, $\varepsilon_1 = 10^{-6}$, $\varepsilon_2 = 10^{-6}$, $\varepsilon = 10^{-4}$, $\mathbf{D} = diag(ones(n,1))$

3: **while** not converged **do**

4:    Update $\hat{\mathbf{X}}$ and $\hat{\mathbf{Z}}$ by $\hat{\mathbf{X}} = \mathbf{XD}$, $\hat{\mathbf{Z}} = \mathbf{ZD}$.

5:    Initialize: $\mathbf{Y} = 0$, $\mu > 0$, $\rho > 0$.

6:    Set: $\mathbf{J}_k = \mathbf{J}_{k-1}$, $\mathbf{Z}_k = \mathbf{Z}_{k-1}$.

7:    **while** not converged **do do**

8:        Update $\mathbf{U}$ while fixing others by Eq. (6).
$$\mathbf{U} = \left(\mathbf{Y} + \mu\hat{\mathbf{Z}}\right)\mathbf{V}\left(\lambda\mathbf{I_r} + \mu\left(\mathbf{V^TV}\right)\right)^{-1}$$

9:        Update $\mathbf{V}$ while fixing others by Eq. (7).
$$\mathbf{V} = \left(\mathbf{Y} + \mu\hat{\mathbf{Z}}\right)^T\mathbf{U}\left(\lambda\mathbf{I_r} + \mu\left(\mathbf{U^TU}\right)\right)^{-1}$$

10:        Update $\mathbf{J}$ while fixing others by Eq. (8).
$$\mathbf{J} = \underset{J}{argmin}\, \tfrac{1}{\mu}\|\mathbf{J}\|_1 + \tfrac{1}{2}\left\|\mathbf{J} - \left(\hat{\mathbf{X}} - \mathbf{UV^T} + \tfrac{\mathbf{Y}}{\mu}\right)\right\|_F^2$$

11:        $\hat{\mathbf{Z}} = \hat{\mathbf{X}} - \mathbf{J}$

12:        Update the multipliers.
$$\mathbf{Y} = \mathbf{Y} + \mu\left(\hat{\mathbf{Z}} - \mathbf{UV^T}\right)$$

13:        Update μ by $\mu = \min\left(\rho\mu, \max\left(\mu\right)\right)$

14:        $t_k = t_k + 1$

15:        Check convergence conditions
$$\left\|\hat{Z} - UV^T\right\|_\infty < \varepsilon_1$$

16:    **end while**

17:    Update $\mathbf{Z}$ by $\mathbf{Z} = \mathbf{UV}^T D^{-1}$

18:    Update $[U, S, V] = svd(\mathbf{Z})$, $U_1 = U(:, 1)$

19:    Update $\hat{\mathbf{D}}$ by $d_i = |\cos\theta_i| + \varepsilon$

20:    $k = k + 1$

21:    Check convergence conditions
$$\left\|\hat{Z} - UV^T\right\|_\infty < \varepsilon_2$$

22: **end while**

23: Output:$\mathbf{Z}$, $\mathbf{U}$, $\mathbf{V}$

---

3   Experiments

In this section, we evaluate the performance of our proposed BF-RSF method in comparison with several state-of-the-art methods including Unifying [17], Practical [16], MoG [24] and ROUTE-LRMR [20]in image clustering [7].

We perform the experiments on the hyperspectral image dataset, SalinasA-scene. Salinas was collected by the 224-band AVIRIS sensor over Salinas Valley, California, and is characterized by high spatial resolution (3.7-m pixels). The area covered comprises 512 lines by 217 samples. We discarded the 20 water absorption bands, in this case bands: [108–112], [154–167], 224. This image was available only as at sensor radiance data. It includes vegetables, bare soils and vineyard fields. Salinas groundtruth contains 16 classes. In our experiment,

(a)   (b)

Fig. 2. The 2D images of SalinasA. (Color figure online)

we choose SalinasA which is a small sub-scene of Salinas image and is usually used too. It comprises 86 * 83 pixels located within the same scene at [samples, lines]=[591–676, 158–240] and includes 6 classes.

Visualized Analysis on SalinasA. In order to show the advantage of our proposed method, we visualized the feature representation of SalinasA in 2D space. Figure 2 shows the two-dimensional representations obtained from the dataset. Different classes are denoted as different colors and there are 6 clusters in this SalinasA dataset.

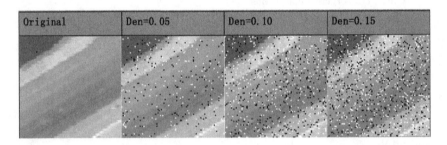

Fig. 3. The examples of the original and corrupted images under different densities (Den.) from SalinasA dataset.

Data Preparation. The SalinasA image is reshaped to a resolution of 7138 × 204. for our experiment. In our experiment, we gradually increase the level of noise and the levels are divided into three grades: 5%, 10% and 15%. Fig. 3 shows some images of the original and corrupted images under the above grades of noise on this dataset.

Parameter Settings. The parameters of each algorithm are tuned with a boot-strapped grid search under a level of 5% corruption rate. For Unifying and Practical methods, the parameter λ is set as 0.001. In MoG, the parameter λ is set as 0.1. α, β and γ are set as 50, 1 and 0.01 respectively in ROUTE-LRMR provided by [20]. The parameter λ in our proposed method is set as 0.1.

Table 1. The clustering accuracies obtained from our proposed method and other comparative methods on SalinasA dataset

	0%	5%	10%	15%
Unifying	0.6716	0.6556	0.6326	0.6261
Practical	0.6653	0.6403	0.6365	0.6241
ROUTE-LRMR	0.6762	0.6628	0.6441	0.6317
MoG	0.6687	0.6535	0.6335	0.6287
BF-RSF	**0.6857**	**0.6654**	**0.6543**	**0.6441**

After parameters being selected, the spectral clustering algorithms are used to segment the data into clusters and 6 clusters are obtained in SalinasA. To estimate the clustering effectiveness of each algorithm, the clustering process is repeated 5 times on SalinasA dataset, the clustering accuracies are recorded in Table 1. In Table 1, the mean of the clustering accuracies of each algorithm are recorded under degrees of 0%, 5%, 10%, 15% samples per pixel corrupted.

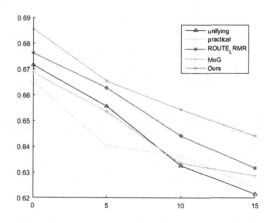

Fig. 4. Variation of clustering accuracies in different corruption rates on SalinasA dataset.

Results. From Table 1, the clustering accuracies of our proposed BF-RSF are seen higher than other comparative methods when no corruption is added. By gradually increasing the corruption rate, the clustering robustness in both algorithms is seen in a decrease. For example, the clustering results in our BF-RSF are seen decreasing from 0.6857 to 0.6441 and from 0.6716 to 0.6261 in Unifying. However, it can be seen that our BF-RSF shows its robustness in clustering performance and the clustering accuracies are always higher than others under the various levels of corruptions. This demonstrates that the introduced sample scaling factor can suppress the effect of noisy data and improves the clustering performance in a heavy noisy scenario.

Moreover, Fig. 4 illustrates the variation of clustering results in different corruption rates on SalinasA dataset. It can be seen that the accuracies are not much differences between ours and ROUTE-LRMR under the levels of 0% and 5%. With the increasing of corruption rate, the accuracies of ours become higher than others. This indicates that the robustness of our proposed BF-RSF in clustering is enhanced by introducing the sample scaling factor.

From the above discussion, one can be seen that the performance of BF-RSF is better than others, especially in a high level of corruptions. In our proposed method, the sample scaling factor is imposed onto the training dataset iteratively which can suppress the effect of noise. Therefore, our BF-RSF can learn better low-rank structure of clean data especially in a heavy noisy scenario.

4 Conclusions

In this paper, we proposed the bilinear factorization via recursive sample factoring for low-rank hyperspectral image recovery, which is named as BF-RSF. In the presence of missing data or outliers, the robustness of L1-norm measurement is preferable over L2-norm. At the same time, different from traditional methods which directly imposed a weight matrix, we introduce a sample scaling factor to measure the significance of each data point. The sample scaling factor is a cosine similarity metric which is learnt through the relationship between the principal component vector of the low-rank matrix and each data point. By imposing the sample scaling factor onto the dataset iteratively, the noisy data will be detected and their impact will be suppressed. On the other hand, our BF-RSF model can learn better low-rank structure of clean data especially in a heavy noisy scenario, with the effect of noisy data points in modeling being suppressed. Extensive experimental results on SalinasA hyperspectral image dataset show that BF-RSF outperforms state-of-the-art low-rank matrix recovery methods in subspace clustering, especially in the experiments with heavy noisy data injected.

Acknowledgements. This work was funded in part by the National Natural Science Foundation of China (No. 61572240, 61601202, 61572503, 61872424).

References

1. Tian, L., Du, Q., Kopriva, I., Younan, N.: Spatial-spectral based multi-view low-rank sparsesubspace clustering for hyperspectral imagery. In: IEEE International Geoscience and Remote Sensing Symposium, pp. 8488–8491 (2018)
2. Bao, B.K., Zhu, G., Shen, J., Yan, S.: Robust image analysis with sparse representation on quantized visual features. IEEE Trans. Image Process. **22**(3), 860–871 (2013)
3. Candès, E.J., Li, X., Ma, Y., Wright, J.: Robust principal component analysis? J. ACM **58**(3), 1–37 (2011)

4. Liu, G., Lin, Z., Yan, S., Sun, J., Yu, Y., Ma, Y.: Robust recovery of subspace structures by low-rank representation. IEEE Trans. Pattern Anal. Mach. Intell. **35**(1), 171–184 (2013)
5. Liu, G., Lin, Z., Yu, Y.: Robust subspace segmentation by low-rank representation. In: Proceedings of the 27th International Conference on Machine Learning, pp. 663–670 (2010)
6. Wang, J., Yang, J., Yu, K., Lv, F., Huang, T., Gong, Y.: Locality-constrained linear coding for image classification. In: IEEE Conference on Computer Vision and Pattern Recognition, pp. 3360–3367 (2010)
7. Elhamifar, E., Vidal, R.: Sparse subspace clustering: algorithm, theory, and applications. IEEE Trans. Pattern Anal. Mach. Intell. **35**(11), 2765–2781 (2012)
8. Bao, B.K., Liu, G., Xu, C., Yan, S.: Inductive robust principal component analysis. IEEE Trans. Image Process. **21**(8), 3794–3800 (2012)
9. Liu, R.S., Lin, Z.C., De la Torre, F., Su, Z.X.: Fixed-rank representation for unsupervised visual learning. In: IEEE Conference on Computer Vision and Pattern Recognition, pp. 598–605 (2012)
10. Wen, Z., Yin, W., Zhang, Y.: Solving a low-rank factorization model for matrix completion by a nonlinear successive over-relaxation algorithm. Math. Program. Comput. **4**(4), 333–361 (2012)
11. Bao, B.K., Xu, C., Min, W., Hossain, M.S.: Cross-platform emerging topic detection and elaboration from multimedia streams. ACM Trans. Multimedia Comput. Commun. Appl. **11**(4), 1–21 (2015)
12. Gillis, N., Glineur, F.: Low-rank matrix approximation with weights or missing data is NP-hard. SIAM J. Matrix Anal. Appl. **32**(4), 1149–1165 (2011)
13. Aguiar, P., Xavier, J., Stosic, M.: Spectrally optimal factorization of incomplete matrices. In: IEEE Conference on Computer Vision and Pattern Recognition (2008)
14. Buchanan, A.M., Fitzgibbon, A.W.: Damped Newton algorithms for matrix factorization with missing data. In: IEEE Conference on Computer Vision and Pattern Recognition, pp. 316–322 (2005)
15. Okatani, T., Yoshida, T., Deguchi, K.: Efficient algorithm for low-rank matrix factorization with missing components and performance comparison of latest algorithms. In: IEEE International Conference on Computer Vision, vol. 1, pp. 842–849 (2011)
16. Zheng, Y.Q., Liu, G.C., Sugimoto, S., Yan, S., Okutomi, M.: Practical low-rank matrix approximation under robust L1-norm. IEEE Conference on Computer Vision and Pattern Recognition, vol. 1, pp. 1410–1417 (2012)
17. Cabral, R., Torre, F.D.L., Costeira, J.P., Bernardino, A.: Unifying nuclear norm and bilinear factorization approaches for low-rank matrix decomposition. IEEE International Conference on Computer Vision, vol. 1, pp. 2488–2495 (2013)
18. Lin, Z., Xu, C., Zha, H.: Robust matrix factorization by majorization minimization. IEEE Trans. Pattern Anal. Mach. Intell. **40**(1), 208–220 (2017)
19. Ke, Q., Kanade, T.: Robust L1 norm factorization in the presence of outliers and missing data by alternative convex programming. In: IEEE Conference on Computer Vision and Pattern Recognition (2005)
20. Guo, X., Lin, Z.: ROUTE: robust outlier estimation for low rank matrix recovery. In: Proceedings of the Twenty-Sixth International Joint Conference on Artificial Intelligence, pp. 1746–1752 (2017)
21. Burer, S., Monteiro, R.: Local minima and convergence in low-rank semidefinite programming. Math. Program. **103**(3), 427–444 (2005)
22. Mazumder, R., Hastie, T., Tibshirani, R.: Spectral regularization algorithms for learning large incomplete matrices. J. Mach. Learn. Res. **11**(11), 2287–2322 (2010)

23. Recht, B., Fazel, M., Parrilo, P.A.: Guaranteed minimum-rank solutions of linear matrix equations via nuclear norm minimization. SIAM Rev. **52**(3), 471–501 (2010)
24. Meng, D., Torre, F.D.L.: Robust matrix factorization with unknown noise. In: IEEE International Conference on Computer Vision, pp. 1337–1344 (2013)
25. Gerbrands, J.J.: On the relationships between SVD, KLT and PCA. Pattern Recogn. **14**(1), 375–381 (1981)

A Hybrid Convolutional Neural Network with Anisotropic Diffusion for Hyperspectral Image Classification

Feng Lu, Qichao Liu, Mohsen Molaei, and Liang Xiao[✉]

School of Computer Science and Engineering,
Nanjing University of Science and Technology, Nanjing, China
xiaoliang@mail.njust.edu.cn

Abstract. Recent research has shown that methods based on deep convolutional neural networks (DCNN) can achieve high accuracy in the classification of hyperspectral image (HSI). However, convolution operations with different dimensions in deep neural networks usually perform in an isotropic structure, resulting in the loss of extracting deep feature of anisotropic neighborhood. Thus how to improve the ability of discriminative features learning is the key issue in DCNN. In this paper, we propose an anisotropic diffusion partial differential equation (PDE) driven hybrid CNN framework, named PM-HCNN. The proposed framework uses 2D convolution and 3D convolution layers to extract of spectral and spatial contexts in HSI. And a PDE based diffusion layer is cascaded as feature propagation layers after hybrid convolution layers to propagate the intrinsical discriminative features of various classes. Due to the anisotropic diffusion on the feature space, the classification mistakes of traditional CNNs with a small number of training data can be further eliminated while object boundaries can be preserved. Experimental results on several popular datasets show that the proposed PM-HCNN achieved state-of-the-art performance compared with the existing deep learning-based methods.

Keywords: Convolutional neural networks · Hyperspectral image classification · Anisotropic diffusion model · Feature propagation

1 Introduction

Hyperspectral remote sensors provide an effective method for human to observe the Earth's surface. Hyperspectral imagery (HSI) with high resolution in both spectral and spatial domains (i.e. derived from sensor systems) can be used in a wide range of specific applications, such as agriculture, physics, and surveillance. In this case, the acquired hyperspectral images can provide an almost continuous spectral curve for each pixel in the image. Capturing rich spectral information while acquiring spatial information, facilitates the generation of complex models to identify and classify different types of materials or plants in the images. However, the increase of the amount of hyperspectral image data and the redundancy in spectral information bring great challenges to the classification of hyperspectral images.

© Springer Nature Switzerland AG 2019
Y. Zhao et al. (Eds.): ICIG 2019, LNCS 11903, pp. 541–552, 2019.
https://doi.org/10.1007/978-3-030-34113-8_45

In past decades, many effective methods have been proposed for the classification of HSIs. For example, k-nearest neighbor (KNN) [1] has been used to construct a distance function to analyze the similarity between testing samples and training samples. In [2], support vector machine (SVM) has more potential to determine the decision boundary between classes by kernel methods. Also inspired by hybrid huberized SVM (HHSVMs), a random HHSVM algorithm [3] for HSI was proposed. Meanwhile, low-dimensional sparse representation-based classification (SRC) [4] and random forest-based classifiers [5] have also been proved to be effective in HSI classification. Nevertheless, the existing methods mentioned above paid less attention to the spatial relationship of the neighboring pixels, and the feature vectors fed into the classifier are represented only by the spectral features of the pixels.

In recent years, spatial features have been considered in the classification process to resolve the issues raised by some pixels of different categories with similar spectrums. Consequently, some works have been conducted to introduce spatial information of HSI into classification, such as Markov Random Field (MRF) [6] and wavelet transform [7]. In the meantime, several traditional filters have also been adopted in the classification, such as bilateral filter, mean filter and Gabor filter. Furthermore, with considering spatial domains of HSI, for the first time in the [8], an edge retention filter [8] was proposed to construct the spectral and spatial information of HSIs. In [9], the Gabor filter was combined with the nearest regular subspace (RMS), and then the spatial features extracted by the filter were fed to the RMS classifier.

Recently, the deep learning models have been introduced into the field of computer vision as a powerful tool. Due to the powerful feature representation ability of deep networks, many typical deep learning methods have been applied into the HSI classification, such as deep belief networks (DBNs) [10] and convolutional neural networks (CNNs) [11, 12]. In order to enhance the utilization of HSI spectral-spatial structures, Li et al. [13] proposed a new hyperspectral classification framework based on a fully CNN, and integrated the optimized extreme learning machines (ELM). Cao et al. [14] combines Markov random fields and convolutional neural networks to classify images by formulating the problem from Bayesian. Additionally, Zhang et al. [15] uses a multi-scale summation approach based on regions, and then feeds all spectral and spatial information into a fully connected network.

Despite the significant improvements by deep networks in spectral-spatial joint classification, the standard convolution operations in deep networks usually perform in an isotropic structure, therefore, which fails to extract the features of anisotropic neighborhood of HSIs, a phenomenon which additionally challenges the accurate classification of pixels near the object boundaries. In order to eliminate the drawback of deep networks with isotropic convolution, we propose an anisotropic diffusion-driven hybrid CNN framework, named PM-HCNN. In this work, first we use 2D and 3D hybrid convolution layers to extract spectral-spatial features from original HSI, and then a diffusion layer is added after the hybrid convolution layers to propagate the intrinsical discriminative features of various classes. Lastly, to enable feature extraction layer and the diffusion layer work collaboratively, we integrated the diffusion layer into the whole network and trained together. The experimental results on two popular HSI datasets demonstrate that the proposed PM-HCNN achieved state-of-the-art performance compared with the existing deep learning-based methods.

2 Anisotropic Diffusion Driven Hybrid CNN

Figure 1 shows the whole deep learning framework of HSI classification with aniso-tropic diffusion. The whole deep learning framework is divided into two parts: a feature extraction layer based on 2D and 3D convolution operations and a feature propagation layer based on anisotropic diffusion. Since the network is an end-to-end framework, the input is $X \in \mathbb{R}^{H \times W \times B}$, i.e., indicates the original HSI, and the output is $\tilde{F} \in \mathbb{R}^{H \times W \times L}$, i.e., indicates the probabilities that the pixel belongs to each class.

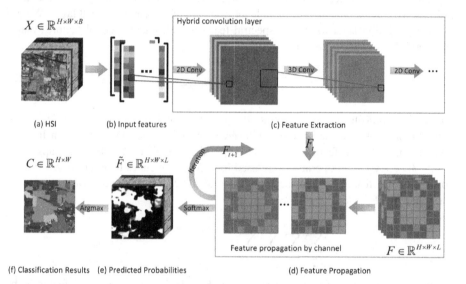

Fig. 1. The hybrid CNN with anisotropic diffusion (PM-HCNN) for hyperspectral image (HSI) classification. H, W, B, L denote the height, width, bands, and categories.

2.1 Hybrid 2D and 3D Convolution Layers

CNN automatically learns the features of images at various levels through convolution operations, which is consistence with our common sense of understanding images. Therefore, once CNN was proposed, its hierarchical design was gradually recognized as the most effective and successful technique in the field of computer vision.

2D-CNN can extract context representation features efficiently during the feature extraction. The value at position (x, y) on the ith feature map in the lth layer is given by Eq. (1):

$$F_{l,i}^{x,y} = \sigma\left(\sum_{m}\sum_{h=0}^{H_l-1}\sum_{w=0}^{W_l-1} K_{l,i,m}^{h,w} F_{(l-1),m}^{(x+h),(y+w)} + b_{l,i}\right) \qquad (1)$$

where $F_{(l-1),m}^{(x+h),(y+w)}$ is the value at position $(x+h, y+w)$ on the mth feature map in the $(l-1)$th layer, m indexes over the set of the feature maps in the $(l-1)$th layer which is connected to the current feature map, $b_{l,i}$ is the bias of the ith feature map in the lth layer, H_l and W_l are the height and width of the kernels, $K_{l,i,m}^{h,w}$ stands for the value of the kernel connected to the ith feature map in the lth layer at the position (h, w), and $\sigma(\cdot)$ is the activation function.

Due to the large number of bands in the hyperspectral image, the 2D convolution operation will generate a large number of parameters, which leads to over-fitting. The 1×1 2D convolution kernel used in the experiment can not only solve the above problem, but also realize the cross-channel information combination and increase the nonlinear characteristics. What is more, in this experiment, we combine a 2D convolutional layer and a 3D convolutional layer into one hybrid convolutional layer. We use a 2D convolution layer to extract spectral features and obtain spectral features maps. The formula is changed as follows:

$$F_{l,i}^{x,y} = \sigma(\sum_m K_{l,i,m} F_{(l-1),m}^{x,y} + b_{l,i}) \tag{2}$$

where $K_{l,i,m}$ indicates the value of the ith spectral convolution kernel of the lth hybrid convolutional layer at the position m. Thereafter we use the 3D convolution layer to convolve the spectral feature maps and output the spatial-spectral feature maps. Normally, 3D convolution operations are used for 3D feature cubes in an effort to compute spatiotemporal features when the input data is 3D. The 3D convolution operation is formulated as follows:

$$F_{l,i}^{x,y,z} = \sigma(\sum_m \sum_{h=0}^{H_l-1} \sum_{w=0}^{W_l-1} \sum_{r=0}^{R_l-1} K_{l,i,m}^{h,w,r} F_{(l-1),m}^{(x+h),(y+w),(z+r)} + b_{l,i}) \tag{3}$$

where i is the number of kernels in this layer, $F_{l,i}^{x,y,z}$ is the value on the ith feature cube in the lth layer at position (x, y, z), R_l indicates the spectral depth of 3D kernel, $K_{l,i,m}^{h,w,r}$ is the (h, w, r)th value of the kernel linked to the mth feature cube in the previous layer. In our model, each feature cube is processed independently. So m in Eq. (3) need to be set 1, and the transformed formula for 3D convolution operation is as follows:

$$F_{l,i,j}^{x,y,z} = \sigma(\sum_{h=0}^{H_l-1} \sum_{w=0}^{W_l-1} \sum_{r=0}^{R_l-1} K_{l,i}^{h,w,r} F_{(l-1),j}^{(x+h),(y+w),(z+r)} + b_{l,i}) \tag{4}$$

where j is the number of feature cubes in the preceding layer, $K_{l,i}^{h,w,r}$ is the (h, w, r)th value of the kernel linked to the jth feature cube of the preceding layer, $F_{l,i,j}^{x,y,z}$ is the output that is calculated by convolving the jth feature cube of the preceding layer with the ith kernel of the lth layer at the position (x, y, z).

In summary, we use a 2D convolution, of which size is 1×1, to reduce the dimension of the channel without changing height and width of the input data, and then extract the spectral and space information by 3D convolution. In addition, a plurality of the above hybrid convolution layers are used to construct a deep network, and the characteristics of both 2D and 3D convolution can be fully utilized to facilitate the purpose of extracting deep spectral-spatial features.

2.2 Feature Propagation Layers with Anisotropic Diffusion

A hyperspectral image with B channels and $H \times W$ size will be put into the neural network as a whole. Take the Indian Pines dataset as an example, BN is added before each 2D convolution layer to speed up the convergence of gradients, save computational resources and shorten the training time in the experiment.

In the stage of feature extraction, the spectral dimension of the data is transformed into 128 when passing through the 2D convolution layer containing 128 $1 \times 1 \times B$ kernels. Moreover, for the 3D convolution layers, the kernel size is set to $(3, 3, 7)$, the kernel number is set to 2, the method of padding is set to "same", and the stride is set to $(1, 1, 1)$, so the output of this hybrid layer becomes 2 channel feature maps. The input of the second hybrid convolution layer is the output of the last hybrid convolution layer, and the output of this layer is the same type of feature maps after the same convolution operations. Finally, we use $1 \times 1 \times 256$ 2D convolution layer to perform a pixel-by-pixel convolution operation on the feature maps.

For the following detailed explanation, after passing through the last 2D convolution layer, the output is F, then the calculation formula of F is:

$$F_{x,y,m} = \sum_m O_{i,m} F'_{x,y,m} + b_i \tag{5}$$

where $F'_{x,y,m}$ is the value at the position (x, y) on the mth feature map which output by the last hybrid convolution layer, $O_{i,m}$ is the ith convolution kernel and b_i indicates bias.

In order to enhance the quality of the feature maps and propagate the intrinsical discriminative features of various classes, after the hybrid convolution layers, we cascade a feature propagation (FP) layers with anisotropic diffusion. The idea is borrowed from the nonlinear PDE which was proposed by Perona and Malik (also known as PM diffusion) in [16].

Let $F_t^{x,y}$ denotes the value at the position (x, y) on the final pth feature map ($p = 1, \ldots, L$) in the tth iteration, the resulted anisotropic diffusion feature map can be defined as follows:

$$
\begin{aligned}
F_{t+1}^{x,y} = F_t^{x,y} + \lambda(\alpha_N \cdot \nabla_N(F_t^{x,y}) + \alpha_S \cdot \nabla_S(F_t^{x,y}) \\
+ \alpha_E \cdot \nabla_E(F_t^{x,y}) + \alpha_W \cdot \nabla_W(F_t^{x,y}))
\end{aligned} \tag{6}
$$

where t represents the number of iterations, E, S, W, and N represent East, South, West, and North, respectively, and $\lambda \in [0, 1/4]$ is used for the stability of the numerical scheme. α_N represents the diffusion coefficient in the north which controls the rate of diffusion. $\nabla_N(F_t^{x,y})$ indicates the derivative in the north. They can be expressed in detail as follows:

$$
\begin{aligned}
\alpha_N &= \exp(-\|\nabla_N F\|^2/k^2) & \alpha_S &= \exp(-\|\nabla_S F\|^2/k^2) \\
\alpha_E &= \exp(-\|\nabla_E F\|^2/k^2) & \alpha_W &= \exp(-\|\nabla_W F\|^2/k^2)
\end{aligned} \tag{7}
$$

$$\nabla_N(F_t^{x,y}) = F_t^{x,y-1} - F_t^{x,y} \quad \nabla_S(F_t^{x,y}) = F_t^{x,y+1} - F_t^{x,y}$$
$$\nabla_E(F_t^{x,y}) = F_t^{x-1,y} - F_t^{x,y} \quad \nabla_W(F_t^{x,y}) = F_t^{x+1,y} - F_t^{x,y}$$

(8)

In Eqs. (7) and (8), the constant term k is used to control the sensitivity to the edge. And the symbol ∇ needs more attention and should not be confused with the gradient operator ∇, as it is used to represent the nearest-neighbor differences. The entire formula requires three parameters to be set beforehand: the number of iterations t, parameter λ and thermal conductivity parameter k. Larger values of k and λ, corresponds to the smoother image, and makes it more difficult to preserve the marginal features of the image.

After the FP layer, the formula for converting F into the classification probability $\tilde{F}$ is defined as:

$$\tilde{F}_k = \frac{e^{F_k}}{\sum_{i=1}^{L} e^{F_i}}$$

(9)

where $\tilde{F}_k$ is the probability that a pixel at a certain position belonging to category $k(1 \leq k \leq L)$ in the hyperspectral image.

Finally, the classification results $C \in \mathbb{R}^{h \times w}$ is computed as follows:

$$C = \text{Argmax}(\tilde{F})$$

(10)

In deep learning, the loss function can evaluate the quality of the model and provide the direction of optimization. PM-HCNN adopts cross entropy as the loss function. In the network, the training set consists of pixels with corresponding class labels in the hyperspectral image. If the pixel $X^{x,y}$ of the hyperspectral image at the position (x, y) is a training sample, then $X^{x,y} \in D_{train}$. $Q^{x,y}$ indicates the probability vectors at the position (x, y). When $X^{x,y}$ belongs to category $k(1 \leq k \leq L)$, the corresponding vector $Q^{x,y}$ at the kth position is 1, and the rest is 0. Let $V_{train} \in \mathbb{R}^{H \times W \times L}$ be the probability labels of the network output $\tilde{F}$. It is converted from the labels corresponding to the training sample. Then the element in V_{train} satisfies the following formula:

$$V_{train}^{x,y} = \begin{cases} Q^{x,y} & X^{x,y} \in D_{train} \\ 0 & otherwise \end{cases}$$

(11)

where 0 is a vector whose elements are all 0, $V_{train}^{x,y}$ indicates the probability vector at the (x, y) position. So the loss function of the network in the training phase is:

$$Loss(\tilde{F}, V_{train}) = -\sum_{x=1}^{H} \sum_{y=1}^{W} \sum_{k=1}^{L} V_{train}^{x,y,k} \log(\tilde{F}^{x,y,k})$$

(12)

where $\tilde{F}^{x,y,k}$ and $V_{train}^{x,y,k}$ represent the specific value of $\tilde{F}$ and V_{train} at the position (x, y, k). The loss function of the verification set can also be obtained by the same reasoning.

3 Experimental Analysis

In order to verify the validity of the proposed model in the classification, this paper uses two different hyperspectral datasets for experiments: The Indian Pines (IN) and Kennedy Space Center (KSC) dataset. In addition, five methods based on deep learning are selected for the comparative experiments: 2D-CNN [17], DC-CNN [18], 3D-CNN [19], MC-CNN [20] and SSRN [21]. Meanwhile, the paper uses the overall accuracy (OA), average accuracy (AA) and kappa statistic to measure the classification result of each model. OA is the ratio of the number of class pixels of the correct classification to the total number of categories. AA is the average of the ratio between each type of prediction and the total number of each category. Kappa coefficient is a method based on confusion matrix to measure classification accuracy.

3.1 Experimental Environment and Parameters

In the experiment, the training and testing process were conducted on a same computer with the following configuration: CPU: i7-8700K, GPU: NVIDIA GeForce GTX 1080Ti and Memory: 32 GB.

For the IN dataset, in the training process, the optimizer is Adam, initial learning rate is 0.001, and the number of iterations is set to 500. The network consists of 4 hybrid convolution layers, and the number of output channels is set to 128. For the 3D convolution kernel, the kernel size is set to (3, 3, 7), the method of padding is set to "same", the stride is set to (1, 1, 1) and the activation function is Sigmoid. In addition, the parameters of the FP layer are set as follows: the number of iterations t is 7, the k of the thermal conductivity is 5 and λ is 1/7.

For the KSC dataset, in the training process, the optimizer is Adam, the initial learning rate is 0.0005, and the number of iterations is set to 300. The network consists of 4 hybrid convolution layers, and the number of output channels is set to 64. For the 3D convolution kernel, the kernel size is set to (5, 5, 7), the method of padding is set to "same", the stride is set to (1, 1, 1) and the activation function is Sigmoid. In addition, the parameters of the FP layer are set as follows: the number of iterations t is 3, the k of the thermal conductivity is 3 and λ is 1/8.

3.2 Datasets

The Indian Pine dataset was gathered by airborne Visible/Infrared Imaging Spectrometer (AVIRIS) sensor in 1992 over the Indian Pines test site in Indiana, USA. It was the first benchmark dataset to be used for the study of hyperspectral image classification techniques with a cut size of 145 × 145. The Indian Pines scene consists of 21025 pixels and 224 spectral reflectance bands in the wavelength range 0.4–2.5 μm, but 24 bands that cannot be reflected by water need to be removed for this study. Because of the tremendous unbalanced number of samples among different classes and mixed pixels in the image, so the Indian Pines dataset has been widely used to evaluate the performance of classification methods. The dataset covers sixteen categories. And the numbers of training, verification, and test samples which belong to different classes are shown in Table 1.

The KSC dataset was acquired by the NASA AVIRIS (Airborne Visible/Infrared Imaging Spectrometer) instrument over the Kennedy Space Center (KSC), Florida, on March 23, 1996. The spatial resolution of The KSC data is about 18 m. And after removing water absorption and low SNR bands, 176 bands remain. Due to the similarity of spectral signatures for certain vegetation types, it is difficult to distinguish the land cover for the environment. For classification purposes, 13 classes were defined for the site. The numbers of training, verification, and test samples which belong to different classes are shown in Table 2.

3.3   Experimental Results

In our experiment, we randomly selected 10 sets of training samples for each data set for repeated experiments. The final classification result is presented as "mean". We use the same proportion of training, validation, and test data for the same dataset.

For IN dataset, the split percentage of training, validation, and testing data is 10%, 1%, 89%, respectively. Figure 2 shows the classification maps for IN dataset obtained by different methods. Table 1 shows the exact value of OA, AA, Kappa for each class by different methods. Under the same conditions, PM-HCNN has improved on OA and Kappa when comparing to other methods. And it is only slightly lower than MC-CNN by 0.14% in AA. Compared with SSRN, the three indicators increased by 0.46%, 6.77% and 0.53% respectively.

For KSC dataset, we use 5% of the labeled pixels as the training set, 1% for validation and 94% for test datasets, respectively. The classification maps of different methods are shown in Fig. 3. And from Table 2, we can get the exact value of OA, AA, Kappa for each class by different methods. It is obvious that PM-HCNN achieves the best result with an overall accuracy of 98.57%, which is 0.69% higher than the second best (97.88%) obtained by SSRN, and is 5.55% higher than the result of 93.02% by DC-CNN. Also for AA and KAPPA, the proposed method achieves the best result.

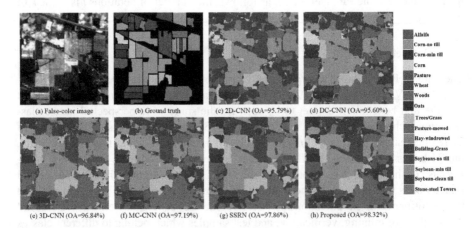

Fig. 2. The classification maps for IN dataset by different methods.

Table 1. Individual class, overall, average accuracy (%) and Kappa statistics of all methods on the Indian Pines dataset using 10% training samples and 1% validation samples.

Class	Samples			2D-CNN	DC-CNN	3D-CNN	MC-CNN	SSRN	Proposed
	Train	Val	Test						
Alfalfa	5	1	48	100	95.48	99.41	98.18	99.42	99.38
Corn-notill	143	14	1277	94.11	93.90	96.07	96.25	98.40	98.40
Corn-mintill	83	8	743	93.69	94.33	94.65	96.84	97.13	97.91
Corn	23	2	209	95.40	94.99	97.65	97.16	96.71	99.50
Pasture	49	4	444	96.87	98.17	98.76	99.03	97.20	99.80
Trees/Grass	74	7	666	98.35	98.54	98.00	98.61	99.01	99.05
Pasture-mowed	2	1	23	100	100	98.82	98.03	80	96.63
Hay-windrowed	48	4	437	96.58	98.19	99.09	99.45	99.45	99.86
Oats	2	1	17	100	93.84	95.00	97.64	0	93.86
Soybeans-notill	96	9	863	94.27	92.18	96.18	95.21	96.38	91.82
Soybean-mintill	246	24	2198	95.81	95.90	96.08	96.68	98.02	98.98
Soybean-cleantill	61	6	547	93.74	94.51	97.02	96.04	95.42	88.64
Wheat	21	2	189	99.68	99.37	99.78	99.58	98.95	98.27
Woods	129	12	1153	98.39	98.16	98.82	99.30	99.48	98.99
Building-Grass	38	3	339	95.67	92.18	94.72	95.71	96.76	98.02
Stone-steelTowers	9	1	85	94.48	93.15	95.48	95.48	97.05	99.35
OA				95.79	95.60	96.84	97.19	97.86	98.32
AA				96.69	95.81	97.22	97.45	90.59	97.36
Kappa				95.20	94.99	96.40	96.80	97.56	98.09

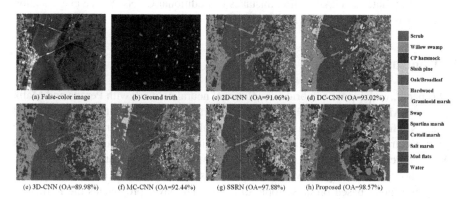

(a) False-color image   (b) Ground truth   (c) 2D-CNN (OA=91.06%)   (d) DC-CNN (OA=93.02%)

Scrub
Willow swamp
CP hammock
Slash pine
Oak/Broadleaf
Hardwood
Graminoid marsh
Swap
Spartina marsh
Cattail marsh
Salt marsh
Mud flats
Water

(e) 3D-CNN (OA=89.98%)   (f) MC-CNN (OA=92.44%)   (g) SSRN (OA=97.88%)   (h) Proposed (OA=98.57%)

Fig. 3. The classification maps for KSC dataset by different methods

Table 2. Individual class, overall, average accuracy (%) and Kappa statistics of all methods on the Kennedy Space Center dataset using 5% training samples and 1% validation samples.

Class	Samples			2D-CNN	DC-CNN	3D-CNN	MC-CNN	SSRN	Proposed
	Train	Val	Test						
Scrub	18	4	325	97.65	98.54	98.58	98.97	98.84	99.23
Willow swamp	13	3	227	88.78	90.17	82.31	89.13	97.07	98.93
CP hammock	13	3	240	64.38	74.71	73.55	78.51	97.13	98.85
Slash pine	13	3	236	67.29	78.33	60.33	76.57	89.77	95.57
Oak/broadleaf	9	2	150	65.42	63.94	64.64	61.00	87.78	89.33
Hardwood	12	3	214	79.15	89.88	79.29	86.72	99.32	95.67
Swamp	6	2	97	80.14	87.94	77.98	82.79	93.55	84.91
Graminoid marsh	20	4	366	88.49	92.59	93.37	92.93	98.59	99.37
Spartina marsh	26	6	488	90.87	94.10	88.06	88.86	98.50	98.86
Cattail marsh	21	5	378	99.52	95.57	98.36	99.15	99.32	99.67
Salt marsh	21	5	393	99.64	99.00	99.69	99.84	99.74	100
Mud flats	26	6	471	97.98	96.34	89.44	95.47	98.16	97.96
Water	47	10	870	98.98	100	98.56	99.21	100	100
OA				91.06	93.02	89.98	92.44	97.88	98.57
AA				86.02	89.32	84.93	88.40	96.75	96.80
Kappa				90.04	92.23	88.84	91.58	97.64	98.41

In summary, for the two datasets, what is clear is that PM-HCNN can retain the little features at the boundary of regions belonging to different categories and make some different categories of features more visible. Furthermore, the proposed method can also eliminate the classification mistakes of traditional CNNs. So the classification accuracy has been improved when comparing to other methods.

4 Conclusion

In this paper, we propose a hybrid convolutional neural network with Perona and Malik diffusion (PM-HCNN) and apply it to hyperspectral image classification. The proposed PM-HCNN framework uses an end-to-end convolutional architecture to automatically extract spectral and spatial features through hybrid convolution layers which contains 2D and 3D convolution layers. For the loss of extracting deep feature of anisotropic neighborhood after using convolution operations, the framework contains a feature propagation layer based on anisotropic diffusion. The layer propagates the intrinsical discriminative features of various classes and makes each class more distinguishable from every other classes. These improvements result in preserving object boundaries and eliminate the classification mistakes of traditional CNNs with a small number of training data. Equipped with the analysis of experimental results, PM-HCNN framework can be used to get better classification accuracy than other methods. The future direction of our work is to established a unified diffusion driven CNN architecture, in which all the hyper-parameters both in the diffusion unit and CNN can be learnt from the training sets.

Acknowledgments. This work has been supported by the Jiangsu Provincial Social Developing Project (BE2018727), the Fundamental Research Funds for the Central Universities (Grant No.30918011104), the National Major Research Plan of China (Grant No. 2016YFF0103604), the Jiangsu Provincial Natural Science Foundation of China (Grant No. BK20161500).

References

1. Blanzieri, E., Melgani, F.: Nearest neighbor classification of remote sensing images with the maximal margin principle. IEEE Trans. Geosci. Remote Sens. **46**(6), 1804–1811 (2008)
2. Melgani, F., Bruzzone, L.: Classification of hyperspectral remote sensing images with support vector machines. IEEE Trans. Geosci. Remote Sens. **42**(8), 1778–1790 (2004)
3. Liu, W., Shen, X., Du, B., Tsang, I.W., Zhang, W., Lin, X.: Hyperspectral imagery classification via stochastic HHSVMs. IEEE Trans. Image Process. **28**(2), 577–588 (2019)
4. Liu, J., Wu, Z., Wei, Z., Xiao, L., Sun, L.: Spatial-spectral kernel sparse representation for hyperspectral image classification. IEEE J. Sel. Top. Appl. Earth Obs. Remote Sens. **6**(6), 2462–2471 (2013)
5. Ham, J., Chen, Y., Crawford, M.M., Ghosh, J.: Investigation of the random forest framework for classification of hyperspectral data. IEEE Trans. Geosci. Remote Sens. **43**(3), 492–501 (2008)
6. Zhang, B., Li, S., Jia, X., Gao, L., Peng, M.: Adaptive Markov random field approach for classification of hyperspectral imagery. IEEE Geosci. Remote Sens. Lett. **8**(5), 973–977 (2011)
7. Tang, Y., Lu, Y., Yuan, H.: Hyperspectral image classification based on three-dimensional scattering wavelet transform. IEEE Trans. Geosci. Remote Sens. **53**(5), 2467–2480 (2015)
8. Kang, X., Li, S., Benediktsson, J.A.: Spectral-spatial hyperspectral image classification with edge-preserving filtering. IEEE Trans. Geosci. Remote Sens. **52**(5), 2666–2677 (2014)
9. Li, W., Du, Q.: Gabor-filtering-based nearest regularized subspace for hyperspectral image classification. IEEE J. Sel. Top. Appl. Earth Obs. Remote Sens. **7**(4), 1012–1022 (2014)
10. Chen, Y., Zhao, X., Jia, X.: Spectral-spatial classification of hyperspectral data based on deep belief network. IEEE J. Sel. Top. Appl. Earth Obs. Remote Sens. **8**(6), 2381–2392 (2015)
11. Hu, W., Huang, Y., Wei, L., Zhang, F., Li, H.: Deep convolutional neural networks for hyperspectral image classification. J. Sens. **2015**(2), 1–12 (2015)
12. Lee, H., Kwon, H.: Going deeper with contextual CNN for hyperspectral image classification. IEEE Trans. Image Process. **26**(10), 4843–4855 (2017)
13. Li, J., Zhao, X., Li, Y., Du, Q., Xi, B., Hu, J.: Classification of hyperspectral imagery using a new fully convolutional neural network. IEEE Geosci. Remote Sens. Lett. **26**(10), 4843–4855 (2017)
14. Cao, X., Zhou, F., Xu, L., Meng, D., Xu, Z., Paisley, J.: Hyperspectral image classification with Markov random fields and a convolutional neural network. IEEE Trans. Image Process. **27**(5), 2354–2367 (2018)
15. Zhang, M., Li, W., Du, Q.: Diverse region-based CNN for hyperspectral image classification. IEEE Trans. Image Process. **27**(6), 2623–2634 (2018)

16. Perona, P., Malik, J.: Scale-space and edge detection using anisotropic diffusion. IEEE Trans. Pattern Anal. Mach. Intell. **12**(7), 629–639 (1990)
17. Makantasis, K., Karantzalos, K., Doulamis, A., Doulamis, N.: Deep supervised learning for hyperspectral data classification through convolutional neural networks. In: IEEE International Geoscience and Remote Sensing Symposium (IGARSS), pp. 4959–4962 (2015)
18. Zhang, H., Li, Y., Zhang, Y., Shen, Q.: Spectral-spatial classification of hyperspectral imagery using a dual-channel convolutional neural network. Remote Sens. Lett. **8**(5), 438–447 (2017)
19. Li, Y., Zhang, H., Shen, Q.: Spectral–spatial classification of hyperspectral imagery with 3D convolutional neural network. Remote Sens. **9**(1), 67 (2017)
20. Chen, C., Zhang, J.-J., Zheng, C.-H., Yan, Q., Xun, L.-N.: Classification of hyperspectral data using a multi-channel convolutional neural network. In: Huang, D.-S., Gromiha, M., Han, K., Hussain, A. (eds.) ICIC 2018. LNCS (LNAI), vol. 10956, pp. 81–92. Springer, Cham (2018). https://doi.org/10.1007/978-3-319-95957-3_10
21. Zhong, Z., Li, J., Luo, Z., Michael, C.: Spectral-spatial residual network for hyperspectral image classification: a 3-D deep learning framework. IEEE Trans. Geosci. Remote Sens. **56**(2), 847–858 (2018)

Computer Vision for Autonomous Driving

Online Multi-object Tracking Using Single Object Tracker and Markov Clustering

Jiao Zhu, Shanshan Zhang$^{(\boxtimes)}$, and Jian Yang

PCA Lab, Key Lab of Intelligent Perception and Systems for High-Dimensional Information of Ministry of Education, and Jiangsu Key Lab of Image and Video Understanding for Social Security, School of Computer Science and Engineering, Nanjing University of Science and Technology, Nanjing, China
{jiaozhu,shanshan.zhang,csjyang}@njust.edu.cn

Abstract. In this paper, we address the challenging problem of online Multi-Object Tracking (MOT). We find for those targets that are occluded or too small, the detectors usually fail to locate them. But an SOT tracker always provides a prediction for each target in the next frame. Therefore, we propose to use Single Object Tracking (SOT) predictions as complementary to detections. Also, we solve the data association problem via a new clustering method based on the Markov Clustering Algorithm (MCL). We first build a graph based on the targets, detections and SOT predictions, and then separate different identities by clustering. Experimental results on the MOT17 benchmark shows that our proposed method outperforms previous state-of-the-art methods w.r.t. MOTA and also reduces the number of false negatives and fragments significantly.

Keywords: Multi-object Tracking · Single Object Tracking · Markov Clustering

1 Introduction

Multiple object tracking (MOT) in videos serves as a fundamental and important task for many vision applications, such as video surveillance and autonomous driving. The purpose of this task is to locate multiple objects in each frame and obtain the trajectory for each identity. Most recently proposed approaches for MOT adopt the tracking-by-detection framework, which formulates the tracking problem as data association and solves it by linking detections frame by frame [3, 25, 30–32, 38]. According to different requirements of application systems, MOT can be handled in either offline or online mode. The offline mode makes full use of all frames across the entire sequences to generate trajectories; in contrast, the online mode only has access to previous frames and the current frame. In this paper, we focus on the online mode, which is more challenging and is required by most online systems.

As we all know, the association algorithm is critical for the multiple object tracking task. For online MOT, a conventional way is to perform matching among

© Springer Nature Switzerland AG 2019
Y. Zhao et al. (Eds.): ICIG 2019, LNCS 11903, pp. 555–567, 2019.
https://doi.org/10.1007/978-3-030-34113-8_46

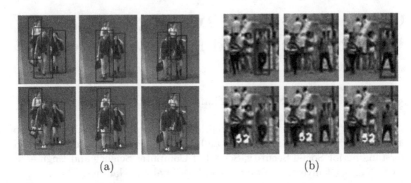

(a)   (b)

Fig. 1. Illustration of missing detections and recovered MOT results from our proposed method. Two major factors that cause missing detections are (a) occlusion and (b) small scale. Top row: detections. Bottom row: our MOT results. The two sequences are from MOT17-04 and MOT17-02 sets, respectively.

detections in neighboring frames. Concurrent methods have made great efforts on learning effective feature representations for matching [32,37]. A big disadvantage of those methods is that they rely on the provided detections, which are sometimes noisy and they are not able to recover from missing detections. We show two examples in the upper row of Fig. 1, where the missing detections are caused by occlusion and small scale. Several works [43–45] have a great progress for pedestrian detection, but it is quite time consuming for these detectors to make efficient work for recognizing and understanding video sequences with complex scenes.

In order to overcome the above problems, some methods propose to use single object tracking (SOT) predictions as compensation [7,47]. The SOT method predicts the location of an identity in the next frame given the location in the current frame. Previous methods rely too much on the SOT predictions, resulting in frequent drifts towards other identities in complex scenes. As of now, it still remains an open question how to integrate the detections and SOT predictions, which are independent to each other.

Therefore, in this paper we investigate how to integrate pre-generated detections and single object tracking predictions in a unified framework. We propose a new graph clustering algorithm to locally cluster three groups of bounding boxes on two neighboring frames: the MOT targets on frame $t-1$; the SOT predictions on frame t; and the detections on frame t. After clustering, the target location of each identity on frame t will be estimated by all the bounding boxes belonging to its cluster. The MOT results on frame t are then used as targets when processing frame t and $t+1$.

In summary, our contributions are as follows:

– In order to compensate for noisy and missing detections, we propose to consider SOT predictions and integrate two sources of bounding boxes in a more balanced manner for online MOT.

– We propose a new graph clustering procedure using the Markov Cluster Algorithm (MCL) algorithm to locally cluster MOT targets, SOT predictions and detections into different identities according to similarities represented by deep features.
– From the experimental results on the challenging MOT17 benchmark, we demonstrate that our method achieves state-of-the-art results among online methods. As shown in Fig. 1b, our approach is able to recover missing detections so as to obtain more complete trajectories.

2   Related Work

Multi-object Tracking Using SOT Tracking. Some previous works [7,40, 47] have attempted to use single object tracking approaches to solve the MOT problem. Zhu *et al.* [47] design a cost-sensitive tracking loss based on ECO [9] tracker and propose Dual Matching Attention Networks with spatial and temporal attention mechanisms. It relies too much on the single object tracking predictions without making full use of detections. Chu *et al.* [7] use CNN-based single object tracker with spatial-temporal attention mechanism to handle the drift caused by occlusion and interaction among targets, but it does not consider how to deal with missing targets. Different from previous works, we integrate detections and single object tracking predictions in a more balanced way to estimate the targets' final locations. The single object tracker runs independently to track targets even when they are occluded.

Multi-object Tracking by Data Association. Data association is important for the MOT task. Most online processing methods [3,13,38] adopt Hungarian Algorithm [26] to match detections and targets. Wojke *et al.* [38] propose a simple online and real-time tracking method with a deep association metric, but it depends too much on the quality of detections and features based on the appearance and position. On the other hand, offline methods consider MOT task as a global optimization problem by using the multi-cut model [30–32] or network flow [10,36,42]. For detection based graph models, it is effective to fix noisy detections, but is hard to find the global optimal solution. In this paper, we borrow the idea of graph clustering from offline MOT, but reduce the scale of the graph from global to local by a large margin. In this way, our method is able to fix noisy detections but it makes the optimization problem much easier to solve.

3   Online MOT Framework

The framework of the proposed online MOT algorithm is shown in Fig. 2. First, an SOT tracker is used to make prediction for each target at frame t (see Sect. 3.1). All bounding boxes of targets, SOT predictions and detections are cropped into image patches for further processing. Second, an affinity graph

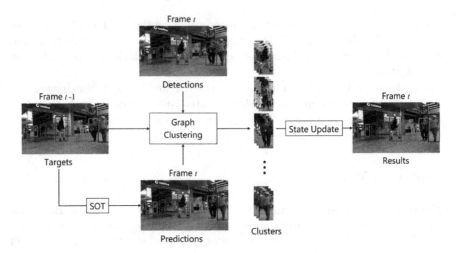

Fig. 2. The proposed online MOT framework. The graph clustering is performed on top of the targets, predictions and detections. Each cluster consists of a group of image patches from the same identity. After clustering, we update the location of each target in frame t by taking into account both SOT predictions and detections.

model is built based on the whole set of image patches. After that, we utilize a new clustering procedure to partition all image patches into groups, one for an identity (see Sect. 3.2). Finally, we update location of each target at frame t according to the predictions and detections inside the cluster (see Sect. 3.3).

In the following, we will describe each component of our framework in more detail.

3.1 SOT Algorithm

For a tracking-by-detection framework, the MOT performance very much rely on the quality of detections. When the detector fails to find a tiny or occluded object, the trajectory becomes broken and a wrong ID switch may happen in this frame. Fortunately, the SOT method can be used to recover missing detections.

In this paper, we choose the Discriminative Correlation Filter Tracker with Channel and Spatial Reliability (DCF-CSR) [23] for tracking each single object. The spatial reliability map adapts the correlation filters to support to the part of the object during tracking. This strategy enlarges the search region when the target happens to be occluded. The channel reliability scores which reflect channel-wise quality of the learned filters, are used for weighting the per-channel filter responses. The DCF-CSR tracker obtains state-of-the-art results on several standard object tracking benchmarks, including OTB100 [39], VOT2015 [18] and VOT2016 [17]. It also runs in real-time on a single CPU as it uses computationally efficient features, i.e. HoG [8] and Colornames [33].

Given a set of D-channel features $F = \{f_1, ..., f_D\}$ and correlation filters $H = \{h_1, ..., h_D\}$, the location corresponding to the maximum value in the correlation response indicates the new position of the target. Additionally, the DCF-CSR tracker introduces channel reliability weights $W = \{w_1, ..., w_D\}$ that considered as scaling factors based on the discriminative power of each feature channel.

$$\tilde{Y} = \sum_{l=1}^{D} f_l \star h_l \cdot w_l. \tag{1}$$

Here, the symbol $\star$ represents circular correlation computation between features f_l and filters h_l. The optimal correlation filters H are estimated by minimizing the following cost function:

$$\varepsilon(H) = \sum_{l=1}^{D} \|f_l \star h_l - Y\|^2 + \lambda \|h_l\|^2, \tag{2}$$

where the variable Y is the desired output, which is a 2-D Gaussian function centred at the target location, and λ is a regularization parameter that controls overfitting.

3.2   Graph Clustering

We solve the data association problem via a graph clustering method. Different from previous works, our graph is constructed based on two adjacent frames with local information. Since the number of clusters is unknown, we use the Markov Cluster Algorithm (MCL) [34] to partition the graph into multiple sub-graphs.

Graph Definition. For every two adjacent frames $t - 1$ and t, we first define a finite set V, which consists of a series of bounding boxes: the targets at frame $t - 1$, the predictions by SOT tracker and the provided detections at frame t. Another finite set E is composed of edges. Each element $e \in E$ represents an edge between two nodes $v, w \in V$. Every edge $e \in E$ has a cost, represented by the similarity $c \in (0, 1)$ computed based on deep feature of two nodes. A weighted and undirected graph $G = (V, E)$ shown in Fig. 3a is then defined with the following two constraints:

- For $v, w \in V$, if both of them come from the same category among the targets, SOT predictions and detections, they should not be connected, the edge $\{v, w\} \notin E$.
- For $v, w \in V$, if they are too far way in either the spatial domain or the feature domain, they should not be connected, the edge $\{v, w\} \notin E$.

Clustering. Given an affinity graph, we apply our proposed clustering algorithm to partition it into clusters, each of which consists of bounding boxes of one single identity. We show an illustration in Fig. 3b.

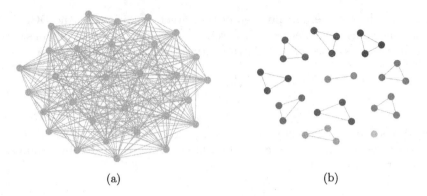

(a)   (b)

Fig. 3. Illustration of our graph clustering method. (a) In the graph, each node indicates one bounding box; each edge represents affinity between a pair of nodes. We measure similarity with CNNs features. (b) Nodes are grouped into different clusters, each of which consists of bounding boxes of one identity.

To partition the graph thoroughly, we develop a new graph clustering method by running the Markov Cluster Algorithm (MCL) for multiple rounds. The MCL algorithm finds cluster structure in a graph by a mathematical bootstrapping procedure. It simulates random walks through the graph by alternation of two operators called expansion and inflation. Expansion coincides with taking the power of the graph matrix using the normal matrix product (i.e. matrix squaring), and allows flow to connect different regions of the graph. Inflation corresponds with taking the Hadamard power of the graph matrix, and changes the probabilities associated with the collection of random walks. Shortening the expansion parameter and increasing the inflation parameter are able to improve the granularity or tightness of clusters.

In our method, we run the MCL algorithm for multiple times to reach reasonable numbers of predictions and detections in each cluster. The detail of our graph clustering is illustrated in Algorithm 1. First, The MCL process is applied on the whole graph and obtains coarse clusters where sometimes one node is contained in multiple clusters or alone in a cluster. Then, we adapt the inflation parameter step by step and perform a loop graph clustering (Algorithm 2) on overlapping clusters where multiple targets are connected. After that, we adopt the loop graph clustering again on a sub-graph consisting of all incomplete clusters so as to make sure each detection node connect to its target. Here, incomplete clusters indicate those ones missing SOT predictions or detections.

3.3   State Update

After clustering, we classify all clusters into four different types according to the number of prediction and detection boxes in each cluster. We show an illustration in Fig. 4.

Algorithm 1. Graph Clustering

Input: Affinity Graph $G = (V, E)$.
Output: Confirmed Clusters Set M.
 1: $M \leftarrow \varnothing$, incomplete clusters set $D \leftarrow \varnothing$;
 2: Apply MCL algorithm to cluster on Graph G to discover clusters set C;
 3: **for** $c \in C$ **do**
 4:　$n1$, $n2$, $n3 \leftarrow$ the numbers about target, prediction and detection in c;
 5:　**if** $n1 = 0$ **or** $n2 = 0$ **or** $n3 \geq 0$ **then**
 6:　　$D = D \cup c$;
 7:　**else if** $n1 = 1$ **and** $n2 = 1$ **and** $n3 \geq 1$ **then**
 8:　　$M = M \cup c$;
 9:　**else**
10:　　Get a sub-graph g by a overlapping cluster c;
11:　　Loop graph clustering (Algorithm 2) on g to get clusters set S;
12:　　**for** $s \in S$ **do**
13:　　　$k1$, $k2$, $k3 \leftarrow$ the numbers about target, prediction and detection in s;
14:　　　**if** $k1 = 1$ **and** $k2 = 1$ **and** $k3 \geq 1$ **then**
15:　　　　$M = M \cup s$;
16:　　　**else**
17:　　　　$D = D \cup s$;
18:　　　**end if**
19:　　**end for**
20:　**end if**
21: **end for**
22: Get a sub-graph g by D;
23: Loop graph clustering (Algorithm 2) on g to get clusters set S;
24: **for** $s \in S$ **do**
25:　$M = M \cup s$;
26: **end for**

For each type of cluster, we design a corresponding state update strategy, and explain different strategies in the following:

(a) The state is estimated by merging the SOT prediction and detection(s).
(b) The state is first estimated by Kalman filter prediction and then refined by merging the prediction and detection(s).
(c) The state is estimated by the SOT prediction.
(d) The target is seen as out of view, so we remove it from the MOT list.

4 Experiments

Dataset. We evaluate our proposed online MOT method on the MOT17 benchmark dataset [24]. The dataset consists of 7 videos for train and 7 videos for test. Each video sequence is provided with 3 sets of detections, i.e. DPM [12], Faster-RCNN [27] and SDP [41].

Algorithm 2. Loop Graph Clustering

Input: Sub-graph $G = (V, E)$, Initial inflation parameter r, Increment Δr.
Output: Clusters Set C.
 1: $NOT\_OK \leftarrow true$;
 2: **while** NOT_OK **do**
 3:     Cluster on Graph G with inflation parameter r to discover clusters set C;
 4:     **for** $c \in C$ **do**
 5:         $n1, n2, n3 \leftarrow$ the numbers about target, prediction and detection in c;
 6:         **if** $n1 = 0$ **or** $n2 = 0$ **or** $n3 = 0$ **then**
 7:             $NOT\_OK \leftarrow false$;
 8:         **else if** $n1 = 1$ **and** $n2 = 1$ **and** $n3 >= 1$ **then**
 9:             $NOT\_OK \leftarrow false$;
10:         **else**
11:             $NOT\_OK \leftarrow true$;
12:             $break$;
13:         **end if**
14:         $r \leftarrow r + \Delta r$;
15:     **end for**
16: **end while**

(a)   (b)   (c)   (d)

Fig. 4. Illustration of four cluster types. We classify clusters into four types only for target including (a) One target, one prediction and one or more detections; (b) One target and one or more detections; (c) One target and one prediction; (d) One target. The circle, triangle, square indicate targets, SOT predictions and detections, respectively.

Evaluation Metrics. We adopt the evaluation metrics defined in [2, 19, 22, 24, 28]: Multiple Object Tracking Accuracy (MOTA) [2], Multiple Object Tracking Precision (MOTP) [2], ID F1 score (IDF1) [28], the ratio of Mostly Tracked targets (MT), the ratio of Mostly Lost targets (ML), the number of False Positives (FP), the number of False Negatives (FN), the number of Identity Switches (IDS) [22] and the number of fragments (Frag). In these metrics, we mainly force on MOTA which can intuitively measure the performance of tracker. As illustrated in Eq. (3), MOTA combines three error sources: false positives (FP), missed targets (FN) and identity switches (IDS).

$$MOTA = 1 - \frac{\sum_t (FN_t + FP_t + IDS_t)}{\sum_t GT_t} \tag{3}$$

Implementation Details. We call the DCF-CSR tracker by OpenCV tracking API which contains implementations of many single object tracking algorithms. To reduce drifts, the tracker always serves the final updated location as template.

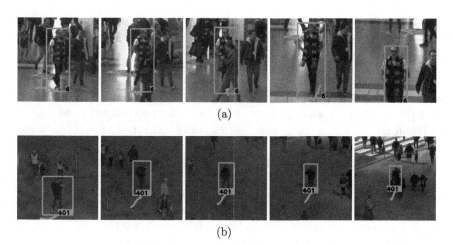

Fig. 5. Tracking examples from the MOT-CVPR19 challenge. The top tracklet of ID 6 and the bottom tracklet of ID 401 in our results are from CVPR19-01 set and CVPR19-03 set respectively.

Table 1. Tracking performance on the test set of the MOT17 benchmark dataset.

Mode	Method	MOTA↑	MOTP↑	IDF1↑	MT↑	ML↓	FP↓	FN↓	IDS↓	Frag↓
Online	GMPHD_N1Tr [1]	42.1	77.7	33.9	11.9%	42.7%	18,214	297,646	10,698	10,864
	EAMTT [29]	42.6	76.0	41.8	12.7%	42.7%	30,711	288,474	4,488	5,720
	FPSN [20]	44.9	76.6	48.4	16.5%	35.8%	33,757	269,952	7,136	14,491
	PHD_GSDL [14]	48.0	77.2	49.6	17.1%	35.6%	23,199	265,954	3,998	8,886
	AM_ADM [21]	48.1	76.7	52.1	13.4%	39.7%	25,061	265,495	2,214	5,027
	DMAN [47]	48.2	75.9	55.7	19.3%	38.3%	26,218	263,608	2,194	5,378
	Ours	48.4	76.3	45.5	19.4%	35.9%	33,525	255,091	2,531	4,944
Offline	MHT_bLSTM [16]	47.5	77.5	51.9	18.2%	41.7%	25,981	268,042	2,069	3,124
	IOU [4]	45.5	75.9	39.4	15.7%	40.5%	19,993	281,643	5,988	7,404
	EDMT [6]	50.0	77.3	51.3	21.6%	36.3%	32,279	247,297	2,264	3,260

If the target is only tracked by single object tracker over a period of time $t_{max} = 30$, it will be seen as out of view and be removed from MOT list. We employ a pre-trained CNN model [37] trained on a large-scale person re-id dataset [46] to extract deep feature with 128 dimensionality. The affinity graph is based on the cosine distance of pair-wise deep feature with thresholds about the feature domain and the space domain: $\tau_f = 0.2$ and $\tau_s = 9.4877$.

4.1   Results on the MOT Benchmark Datasets

We evaluate our proposed method on the test sets of the MOT17 benchmark and compare it with the state-of-the-art MOT trackers in Table 1. The symbol "↑" means that higher is better and the symbol "↓" means that lower is better.

Compared to other online methods, our MOT method achieves the best performance in terms of MOTA, MT, FN and Frag metrics. Especially, our method

Table 2. Comparison performance with different SOT trackers on the train set of the MOT17 benchmark dataset.

SOT	MOTA↑	MOTP↑	IDF1↑	MT↑	ML↓	FP↓	FN↓	IDS↓	Frag↓
MOSSE [5]	27.5	81.2	20.7	1.9%	81.5%	3,374	236,840	3,178	6,643
KCF [15]	49.8	81.5	48.8	12.2%	64.8%	11,457	155,130	2,601	2,436
UDT [35]	50.4	81.1	50.4	13.1%	63.7%	14,201	151,360	1,683	2,062
DCF-CSR [23]	50.6	81.5	50.0	13.0%	63.9%	14,214	150,660	1,719	2,085

Table 3. Contributions of SOT and clustering.

Method	MOTA↑	FP↓	FN↓	IDS↓	(FP + FN + IDS) ↑
Baseline	47.7	7,802	165,041	3,354	176,197
+ clustering	48.2	7,463	165,050	2,044	174,557
+ SOT	49.1	21,523	147,783	2,140	171,446
+ SOT, clustering	50.6	14,214	150,660	1,719	166,593

has far achievements than other online methods in terms of FN and Frag. The scores of FN and Frag precisely explain that our method can fix the problems caused by missing detections. Besides, the performance of our method in MOTA is also near with state-of-art offline methods performance. Also we show some instances of our results in Fig. 5. Those tracklets are from MOT CVPR 2019 challenge [11], which was released not long ago and is hiding other results now. Therefore, we are not able to compare our method with other ones, but we can visualize tracking results, that will be helpful to find success and failure cases.

4.2   Ablation Study

SOT Algorithm Selection. In terms of performance of single object tracking, we compare MOT results with different state-of-the-art SOT methods on the train sets of the MOT17 benchmark dataset. We use MOSSE [5], KCF [15], DCF-CSR [23] and UDT [35] respectively to get different results. Among these SOT methods, MOSSE, KCF and DCF-CSR are all correlation filter trackers based on different hand-crafted features, while UDT tracker is an unsupervised correlation filter tracking method with deep features. As illustrated in Table 2, DCF-CSR and UDT have pretty performance in terms of all metrics. But considering about running speed and the value of MOTA, we finally choose DCF-CSR as the single object tracker in our MOT method.

Impact of SOT and Clustering. We set up different experiments to demonstrate the contributions of SOT algorithm and graph clustering. First, we associate only targets and detections by building an assignment problem that can be solved by the Hungarian Algorithm [26]. Second, we consider the data association as a local optimization by adopting the MCL algorithm. Last, we add single object tracking module to previous experiments. As illustrated in Table 3, clustering works better than assignment, and the method with single object tracking performs better than one without single object tracking. In general, SOT and clustering modules have positive effects on the performance of MOT.

5 Conclusions

In this paper, we introduce a unified online multi-object tracking framework which integrates single object tracking predictions and pre-generated detections, and applies graph clustering to solve local optimization. For single object tracking, we use DCF-CSR tracker to track each target location. For graph clustering, we take the MCL algorithm repeatedly to reach reasonable cluster results. In the end, we evaluate our proposed method on the MOT benchmark dataset and obtain better performance than other state-of-the-art trackers.

Acknowledgments. The authors would like to thank the editor and the anonymous reviewers for their critical and constructive comments and suggestions. This work was supported by the National Natural Science Foundation of China (Grant No. 61702262, U1713208), Program for Changjiang Scholars, Funds for International Cooperation and Exchange of the National Natural Science Foundation of China (Grant No. 61861136011), Natural Science Foundation of Jiangsu Province, China (Grant No. BK20181299), CCF-Tencent Open Fund (RAGR20180113), "the Fundamental Research Funds for the Central Universities" No.30918011322, and Young Elite Scientists Sponsorship Program by CAST (2018QNRC001).

References

1. Baisa, N.L., Wallace, A.: Development of a N-type GM-PHD filter for multiple target, multiple type visual tracking. J. Vis. Commun. Image Represent. **59**, 257–271 (2019)
2. Bernardin, K., Stiefelhagen, R.: Evaluating multiple object tracking performance: the clear mot metrics. J. Image Video Process **2008**, 1–10 (2008)
3. Bewley, A., Ge, Z., Ott, L., Ramos, F., Upcroft, B.: Simple online and realtime tracking. In: ICIP (2016)
4. Bochinski, E., Eiselein, V., Sikora, T.: High-speed tracking-by-detection without using image information. In: AVSS (2017)
5. Bolme, D.S., Beveridge, J.R., Draper, B.A., Lui, Y.M.: Visual object tracking using adaptive correlation filters. In: CVPR (2010)
6. Chen, J., Sheng, H., Zhang, Y., Xiong, Z.: Enhancing detection model for multiple hypothesis tracking. In: CVPR Workshop (2017)
7. Chu, Q., Ouyang, W., Li, H., Wang, X., Liu, B., Yu, N.: Online multi-object tracking using CNN-based single object tracker with spatial-temporal attention mechanism. In: ICCV (2017)
8. Dalal, N., Triggs, B.: Histograms of oriented gradients for human detection. In: CVPR (2005)

9. Danelljan, M., Bhat, G., Shahbaz Khan, F., Felsberg, M.: Eco: efficient convolution operators for tracking. In: CVPR (2017)
10. Dehghan, A., Tian, Y., Torr, P.H., Shah, M.: Target identity-aware network flow for online multiple target tracking. In: CVPR (2015)
11. Dendorfer, P., et al.: CVPR19 tracking and detection challenge: how crowded can it get? arXiv preprint arXiv:1906.04567 (2019)
12. Felzenszwalb, P.F., Girshick, R.B., McAllester, D., Ramanan, D.: Object detection with discriminatively trained part-based models. IEEE Trans. Pattern Anal. Mach. Intell. **32**(9), 1627–1645 (2010)
13. Feng, W., Hu, Z., Wu, W., Yan, J., Ouyang, W.: Multi-object tracking with multiple cues and switcher-aware classification. arXiv preprint arXiv:1901.06129 (2019)
14. Fu, Z., Feng, P., Angelini, F., Chambers, J., Naqvi, S.M.: Particle PHD filter based multiple human tracking using online group-structured dictionary learning. IEEE Access **6**, 14764–14778 (2018)
15. Henriques, J.F., Caseiro, R., Martins, P., Batista, J.: High-speed tracking with kernelized correlation filters. IEEE Trans. Pattern Anal. Mach. Intell. **37**(3), 583–596 (2015)
16. Kim, C., Li, F., Rehg, J.M.: Multi-object tracking with neural gating using bilinear LSTM. In: Ferrari, V., Hebert, M., Sminchisescu, C., Weiss, Y. (eds.) ECCV 2018. LNCS, vol. 11212, pp. 208–224. Springer, Cham (2018). https://doi.org/10.1007/978-3-030-01237-3_13
17. Kristan, M., et al.: The visual object tracking vot2016 challenge results. In: ICCV Workshop (2016)
18. Kristan, M., et al.: The visual object tracking vot2015 challenge results. In: ICCV Workshop (2015)
19. Leal-Taixé, L., Milan, A., Reid, I., Roth, S., Schindler, K.: Motchallenge 2015: towards a benchmark for multi-target tracking. arXiv preprint arXiv:1504.01942 (2015)
20. Lee, S., Kim, E.: Multiple object tracking via feature pyramid siamese networks. IEEE Access **7**, 8181–8194 (2019)
21. Lee, S.H., Kim, M.Y., Bae, S.H.: Learning discriminative appearance models for online multi-object tracking with appearance discriminability measures. IEEE Access **6**, 67316–67328 (2018)
22. Li, Y., Huang, C., Nevatia, R.: Learning to associate: hybridboosted multi-target tracker for crowded scene. In: CVPR (2009)
23. Lukežič, A., Vojíř, T., Čehovin Zajc, L., Matas, J., Kristan, M.: Discriminative correlation filter with channel and spatial reliability. In: CVPR (2017)
24. Milan, A., Leal-Taixé, L., Reid, I., Roth, S., Schindler, K.: Mot16: a benchmark for multi-object tracking. arXiv preprint arXiv:1603.00831 (2016)
25. Milan, A., Schindler, K., Roth, S.: Multi-target tracking by discrete-continuous energy minimization. IEEE Trans. Pattern Anal. Mach. Intell. **38**(10), 2054–2068 (2016)
26. Munkres, J.: Algorithms for the assignment and transportation problems. SIAM **5**(1), 32–38 (1957)
27. Ren, S., He, K., Girshick, R., Sun, J.: Faster R-CNN: towards real-time object detection with region proposal networks. In: NIPS (2015)
28. Ristani, E., Solera, F., Zou, R., Cucchiara, R., Tomasi, C.: Performance measures and a data set for multi-target, multi-camera tracking. In: Hua, G., Jégou, H. (eds.) ECCV 2016. LNCS, vol. 9914, pp. 17–35. Springer, Cham (2016). https://doi.org/10.1007/978-3-319-48881-3_2

29. Sanchez-Matilla, R., Poiesi, F., Cavallaro, A.: Online multi-target tracking with strong and weak detections. In: Hua, G., Jégou, H. (eds.) ECCV 2016. LNCS, vol. 9914, pp. 84–99. Springer, Cham (2016). https://doi.org/10.1007/978-3-319-48881-3_7

30. Tang, S., Andres, B., Andriluka, M., Schiele, B.: Subgraph decomposition for multi-target tracking. In: CVPR (2015)

31. Tang, S., Andres, B., Andriluka, M., Schiele, B.: Multi-person tracking by multicut and deep matching. In: Hua, G., Jégou, H. (eds.) ECCV 2016. LNCS, vol. 9914, pp. 100–111. Springer, Cham (2016). https://doi.org/10.1007/978-3-319-48881-3_8

32. Tang, S., Andriluka, M., Andres, B., Schiele, B.: Multiple people tracking by lifted multicut and person re-identification. In: CVPR (2017)

33. Van De Weijer, J., Schmid, C., Verbeek, J., Larlus, D.: Learning color names for real-world applications. IEEE Trans. Image Process. 18(7), 1512–1523 (2009)

34. Van Dongen, S.M.: Graph clustering by flow simulation. Ph.D. thesis (2000)

35. Wang, N., Song, Y., Ma, C., Zhou, W., Liu, W., Li, H.: Unsupervised deep tracking. In: CVPR (2019)

36. Wang, X., Türetken, E., Fleuret, F., Fua, P.: Tracking interacting objects using intertwined flows. IEEE Trans. Pattern Anal. Mach. Intell. 38(11), 2312–2326 (2016)

37. Wojke, N., Bewley, A.: Deep cosine metric learning for person re-identification. In: WACV (2018)

38. Wojke, N., Bewley, A., Paulus, D.: Simple online and realtime tracking with a deep association metric. In: ICIP (2017)

39. Wu, Y., Lim, J., Yang, M.H.: Object tracking benchmark. IEEE Trans. Pattern Anal. Mach. Intell. 37(9), 1834–1848 (2015)

40. Xiang, Y., Alahi, A., Savarese, S.: Learning to track: online multi-object tracking by decision making. In: ICCV (2015)

41. Yang, F., Choi, W., Lin, Y.: Exploit all the layers: fast and accurate CNN object detector with scale dependent pooling and cascaded rejection classifiers. In: CVPR (2016)

42. Zhang, L., Li, Y., Nevatia, R.: Global data association for multi-object tracking using network flows. In: CVPR (2008)

43. Zhang, S., Benenson, R., Omran, M., Hosang, J., Schiele, B.: How far are we from solving pedestrian detection? In: CVPR (2016)

44. Zhang, S., Benenson, R., Omran, M., Hosang, J., Schiele, B.: Towards reaching human performance in pedestrian detection. IEEE Trans. Pattern Anal. Mach. Intell. 40(4), 973–986 (2017)

45. Zhang, S., Yang, J., Schiele, B.: Occluded pedestrian detection through guided attention in CNNs. In: CVPR (2018)

46. Zheng, L., et al.: MARS: a video benchmark for large-scale person re-identification. In: Leibe, B., Matas, J., Sebe, N., Welling, M. (eds.) ECCV 2016. LNCS, vol. 9910, pp. 868–884. Springer, Cham (2016). https://doi.org/10.1007/978-3-319-46466-4_52

47. Zhu, J., Yang, H., Liu, N., Kim, M., Zhang, W., Yang, M.-H.: Online multi-object tracking with dual matching attention networks. In: Ferrari, V., Hebert, M., Sminchisescu, C., Weiss, Y. (eds.) ECCV 2018. LNCS, vol. 11209, pp. 379–396. Springer, Cham (2018). https://doi.org/10.1007/978-3-030-01228-1_23

Neighborhood Encoding Network for Semantic Segmentation

Xiaotian Lou, Xiaoyu Chen, Lianfa Bai, and Jing Han[✉]

Jiangsu Key Laboratory of Spectral Imaging and Intelligent Sense, Nanjing
University of Science and Technology, Nanjing 210094, China
eohj@njust.edu.cn

Abstract. With recent advances of deep neural networks, semantic segmentation algorithms are in rapid development. However, as pixel-level semantic segmentation is often treated as pixel-wise classification task where the neighbor correlation is ignored during inference, the entirety of results is inevitably impaired. In order to increase the correlation ship among the pixels in neural networks, we propose neighborhood encoding network (NENet) to extract the semantics and encode the pixel-level correlation of inputs in a backbone network. In NENet, we use neighborhood prediction module (NPM) to decode the pixel-level correlation and get the result. The NPM can also help the backbone network encode the correlation during training phase. We also design a stage-wise training strategy with NPM for correlation transmission, which eases the training process and increases the performance effectively. The structure of NENet can be expanded to other encoder-decoder network. We evaluate the proposed NENet on CamVid and Cityscpaes datasets, and the NENet achieves impressive results.

Keywords: Semantic segmentation · Neural network · Neighborhood encoding · Neighborhood prediction

1 Introduction

The semantic segmentation can be described as a classification task, and each pixel of input is recognized by analyzing its global and local data. Traditional methods [17, 20] extract features based on texture and color information, cluster pixels to blobs and then analyze the semantics of blobs.

With the success of deep learning, the deep neural network is widely adopted in semantic segmentation task [18, 19]. In neural networks, the task of semantic segmentation is considered as a pixel-level classification, where a feature map is often computed for classification pixel by pixel. In other words, pixels in the feature map are recognized individually ignoring the clustering process in traditional methods. However, the neural nodes in high-level layers of deep neural network have wide receptive field along with rich local semantics, training the pixels individually causes the output lose the correlation of neighboring pixels within its pixel features. So the methods based on deep learning often have a poor performance on edges or details, while the results of traditional segmentation methods often have clear edges.

Y. Zhao et al. (Eds.): ICIG 2019, LNCS 11903, pp. 568–578, 2019.
https://doi.org/10.1007/978-3-030-34113-8_47

One remedy for segmentation networks is to add a post-process to adjust results based on texture and color of inputs, such as Conditional Random Fields (CRF) [2]. CRF is one of graph models which helps approximate the posterior distribution of results based on network inputs and outputs. However, CRF involves much computation and adds computation latency.

In order to obtain fine features for semantic segmentation in neural networks, input data goes through a backbone network to encode its high-level semantics and then passed by a upsample network to recover spatial details. This encoder-decoder structure helps the feature map extract both high-level semantics and low-level details. Each pixel in the feature map is computed from a number of neighboring neural nodes in previous layers. So the feature of each pixel contains not only the semantics but also the neighboring correlation. Through the encoder network, the spatial resolution of feature map gets smaller but the channel number become more, which means the local context information or neighboring correlation is encoded to pixel feature in feature maps.

As semantic segmentation is considered as a classification task, the loss function in segmentation networks is often designed as pixel-wise cross entropy loss [15]. Though the pixel feature has the ability to extract neighboring correlation, the pixel-wise loss function does not guide the network to learn the neighboring correlation. So if we consider the neighboring correlation in loss function, the potentials of networks will be further explored.

The methods based on encoder-decoder structure have an encoder network and a decoder network. The training difficulty and the optimizing state are affected by the complexity of network, such as depth of the network and number of convolution kernels. ResNet [1] is proposed to ease the training process by accumulating residuals to approximate. The training target is also converted to sparse residuals with skip layers which helps us train up to 1000 layers ResNet. ResNet improves the network degradation and gradient vanishing, and now skip layer has become one of most commonly used layers. Optimizing training strategy can also help network convergence. The relay backpropagation is proposed for effective learning of deep convolutional neural networks. By training sub-networks separately, the relay backpropagation helps the network converge to better state.

This paper proposes neighborhood encoding network (NENet) to extract more neighboring correlation for semantic segmentation by training the network to encode neighboring correlation to pixel feature in feature map. A new relay loss is also designed for level-wise training. The proposed NENet is evaluated on CamVid [3] and Cityscapes [4] dataset and achieves impressive results.

2 Related Work

Semantic segmentation is widely used in various fields, the segmentation results are also used as masks in other tasks, such as pedestrian detection and Landmark Localization. Affords have been made to increase the performance and enhance the training efficiency.

2.1 Context Encoding for Semantic Segmentation

In order to enhance the strength to classify, different types of layers are proposed to generate a fine feature map. In addition to adopt more powerful backbone networks, recent methods also enhance the context encoding ability by combining features with different encoded semantics.

In order to enhance the perception of convolution layer, DeepLab propose Atrous convolution [5], which has larger receptive field with the same number of parameters compared with conventional convolution.

Spatial Pyramid Pooling (SPP) [8] is first proposed to deal with multi-scale problem in object detection. SPP uses pooling operator to compute spatial pyramid of sample feature, then combine them to obtain features containing multi-scale semantics for multi-scale detection.

Combining Atrous convolution and SPP to enhance context encoding has been popular practice. DeepLab V2 and V3 are devoted to construct Atrous Spatial Pyramid Pooling module (ASPP) to enhance the feature semantics by combining features computed by convolution with various Atrous rates. Dense ASPP [6] takes the advantages of DenseNet [7] and further enhance ASPP module. PSPNet [9] design PSP module to combine different scale feature for segmentation and achieves state-of-art results.

2.2 Pixel Level Correlation Extraction in Pixel Level Tasks

As encoder networks have extract feature maps with rich global and local context, some methods attempt to obtain pixel level correlation within networks.

The concept of Adaptive Affinity Fields (AAF) [10] is proposed to analyze and match the neighboring pixels' correlation in semantic segmentation, and adds an extra affinity field matching loss function to learn optimal affinity fields and enhance the performance of spatial structures and small details.

EncNet [11] studies the impact of global context in semantic segmentation by capturing the semantic context of scenes and selectively highlights class-dependent feature maps. With the semantic context, EncNet significantly improves the performance.

2.3 Training Strategy in Segmentation Networks

In pixel-level tasks, the methods based on deep neural network often adopt an upsample network appended to backbone encoder network to recover the resolution. The extra network inevitably increases the depth of network and increases the difficulty of training. In order to ease the training process of network, converge to optimal state, different methods are proposed.

Skip layer [21] is proposed in ResNet, which adds the identity of the input to output in one Resblock. This practice converts the training target of the layer to residuals of labels and then makes the network easier for training.

Batch Normalization [16] is proposed to improve internal covariate shift problem by normalizing layer inputs. Batch Normalization allows us to use higher learning rates and downplay the importance of weights initialization.

Auxiliary loss function is also used for network training in many methods. PSPNet [9] and BiSeNet [12] use add extra auxiliary loss function appended to hidden layer and train the network with weighted loss. Relay propagation strategy divides the network into several subnetworks and trains them separately with their loss functions.

3 Proposed Method

Neighborhood encoding network (NENet) attempts to encode the pixel level correlation in the network and utilizes the correlation for better segmentation. The following sections are organized according to the parts of network structure, NPM blocks and training strategy.

3.1 Neighborhood Encoding Network

We design our neighborhood encoding network (NENet) based on encoder-decoder structure. The overall structure design refers to the lightweight semantic segmentation network ENet [13]. The NENet is set up with an encoder network and a decoder network as shown in Fig. 1. The encoder network consists of an initialize block, two downsampling blocks and 20 Resblocks implemented among initializing and downsampling blocks, the decoder network consists of two upsampling blocks, a neighborhood prediction module (NPM) and 3 Resblocks implemented among upsampling blocks and NPM. Compared with original ENet, we add skip layers in NENet and replace the last deconvolution layer with our NPM. We train our NENet with our level-wise relay strategy.

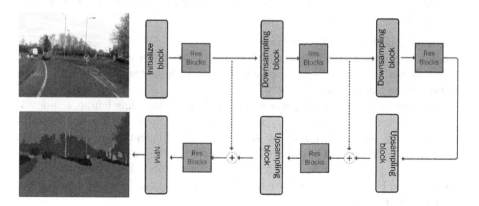

Fig. 1. Structure of NENet.

3.2   Neighborhood Prediction Module

Review of Deconvolution

In order to decoder the spatial semantics from high level feature map with low resolution, common practice is to interpolate the feature map and approximate the target with convolution or use deconvolution directly. As interpolation operator is one of specific states of deconvolution, so the two practice are actually the same way to approximate each pixel target with the same convolution kernel in the final layer at testing phase, as illustrated in Fig. 2.

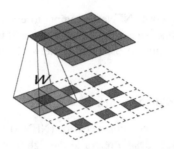

Fig. 2. Illustration of deconvolution operators. (Color figure online)

The lower blue graph is the input with dash line fillers, while the upper green graph is the output. The actual operation of deconvolution is just convolution after upsampling. So the each pixels in output is computed with weight W, despite the position or relationship in neighborhood. Although the feature map has big receptive field and rich neighboring correlation, the predictor of deconvolution only computes the result with individual feature of pixels. In order to utilize the neighboring correlation for semantic segmentation, we put forward neighborhood prediction module in the following subsection.

Design of Neighborhood Prediction Module

In order to extract neighboring correlation, we design the neighborhood prediction module to predict neighboring four pixels of target with the feature at corresponding position of the feature map.

As shown in Fig. 3, The neighboring pixels of target (including left-up, left-down, right-up, right-down pixels) are approximated by four convolution kernels W_1, W_2, W_3, W_4 separately based on the feature. So different from deconvolution operator, the NPM use four directional kernels to predict four neighboring target maps, which makes a good use of the neighboring correlation extracted by the encoder. After approximation by the four kernel, the four directional map can be used to recover the complete result of target.

At the training phase, because the output is computed by the NPM, the layers before NPM is trained to extract more neighboring correlation information to ensure the NPM to recover better results close to labels. So NPM can help extract more

Fig. 3. Illustration of NPM in NENet.

neighboring correlation at training phase and makes a better use of neighboring correlation at testing phase.

3.3 Level-Wise Relay Training for NENet

The encoder-decoder network has two subnetworks, an encoder network and a decoder network. Although the skip layer is used in ResBlocks, the gradient vanishing problem still exists to some degree. From this respect, the gradient values in lower layers are smaller and then the lower layers cannot make the information, including neighboring correlation, better for propagating to top.

In order to help the network extract more semantics and neighboring correlation, we propose the level-wise relay training. We append neighborhood prediction module (NPM) to each ResBlock before Upsampling block to approximate the target at different level, and compare them with the ground truth, as shown in Fig. 1. The scaled ground truths are nearest interpolated with original ground truth. The different levels of loss are computed the different levels of outputs and corresponding scaled ground truths (Fig. 4).

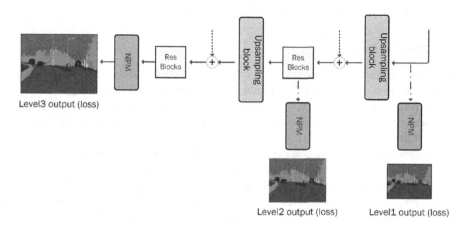

Fig. 4. Level-wise relay training for NENet.

The training process is from Level1 loss to Level3 loss. Because the information stream is propagating from down to top, and the details of input are on the decrease along with the propagation, we insert relay training process is to help the network maintain and extract more semantics. The NPM is further helps extract the neighboring correlation information.

By adding the relay NPM, the approximation of target is computed step by step, from coarse to fine.

4 Experiment

We set up the experiments with the CamVid and Cityscapes dataset to evaluate our NENet. The computing platform is NVIDIA GTX 2080Ti and our NENet is implemented on PyTorch toolkit.

CamVid. The Cambridge-driving Labeled Video Database (CamVid) a street scene dataset from the perspective of driving automobile. The CamVid consists of 367 images for training and 233 images for testing, including 11 classes, with the resolution of 480 * 360.

Cityscapes. The Cityscapes is also a street scene dataset which consists of 2975 images for training, 500 for validation and 1525 for testing, at the resolution of 2048 * 1024. In order to speed up the training and inference process, we downsample the images and ground truth to the resolution of 1024 * 512.

PASCAL VOC intersection-over-union metric (IoU) [14] is used to evaluate the methods on CamVid and Cityscapes, and Mean IoU is used to describe the performance on the whole dataset. The definition of IoU is

$$IoU = \frac{TP}{(TP + FP + FN)}. \tag{1}$$

where *TP*, *FP* and *FN* are the numbers of true positive, false positive, and false negative pixels, respectively, determined over the whole test set.

4.1 Ablation Study

In order to evaluate the different part of our NENet, we design two comparison experiments to testify the validity of network structure and training strategy.

We first evaluate our baseline method ENet, and add skip decoder and neighborhood prediction module (NPM) separately, and construct NENet gradually. The result is shown in Table 1.

We also set up a comparison experiment to evaluate our level-wise relay loss [21]. The Level1 loss only means the training process only contain one step with Level1 loss. In weighted loss, we set weight values for each level of loss and train the network in one step. The weight values are 8, 4, 2, 1 from level1 to level8. Summed loss is also a one-step training but the final loss is the sum of the for level loss (Table 2).

Table 1. Comparison of different settings of network.

Method	Mean IoU
ENet	54.37
ENet with skip decoder	60.25
ENet with NPM	59.89
NENet	64.01

Table 2. Comparison of different types of training strategy based on NENet.

Training strategy	Mean IoU
Level1 loss only	60.25
Weighted loss	59.92
Summed loss	61.84
Level-wise relay loss	64.01

4.2 Result on CamVid Dataset

In order to compare our NENet with the benchmark network ENet and some other popular lightweight segmentation networks like FCN, SegNet, we did experiments on the Camvid dataset and got the segmentation results for each class. As shown in the Table 3, due to the NPM and the new training methods, NENet performs better in small targets and details. For example, mIoU is much better in sigh, fence and cyclist. At the same time, in the comparison of the overall mIoU, our NENet also performed better, mIoU reached 64.01, which was 9.61 higher than the original ENet, Fig. 5 shows the results of NENet.

Table 3. Results on CamVid.

Methods	Building	Tree	Sky	Car	Sign	Road	Pedestrian	Fence	Pole	Sidewalk	Cyclist	Mean IoU
Bayesian SegNet	n/a											63.1
ENet	71.1	63.5	90.3	69.9	22.4	91.1	35.2	19.3	23.3	72.2	39.5	54.4
FCN8	77.8	71.0	88.7	76.1	32.7	91.2	41.7	24.4	19.9	72.7	31.0	57.0
DeepLab LFOV	81.5	74.6	89.0	82.2	42.3	92.2	48.4	27.2	14.3	75.4	50.1	61.6
FC-DenseNet56	77.6	72.0	92.4	73.2	31.8	92.8	37.9	26.2	32.6	79.9	31.1	58.9
NENet	80.3	73.7	91.8	75.5	39.8	92.7	50.7	36.1	34.2	78.0	51.4	64.01

4.3 Result on Cityscapes Dataset

We also conducted a comparative experiment on Cityscapes. In order to speed up the training, and in order to decrease the computational pressure, we resize the training data so that the size of the training image is 1024 * 512. As shown in the Table 4, compared

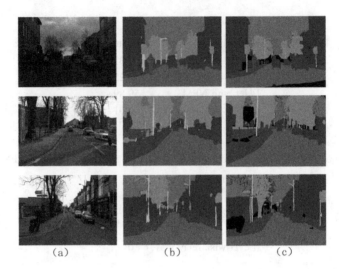

(a)   (b)   (c)

Fig. 5. Result samples of CamVid. From left to right: (a) Input, (b) NENet, (c) Ground truth.

with SegNet, ENet and ESPNet, NENet has achieved better results. And Fig. 6 shows the segmentation result of NEnet.

Table 4. Results on Cityscapes dataset.

Methods	Input size	Mean IoU
SegNet	1024×512	56.1
ENet	1024×512	58.3
ESPNet	1024×512	60.3
NENet	1024×512	61.55

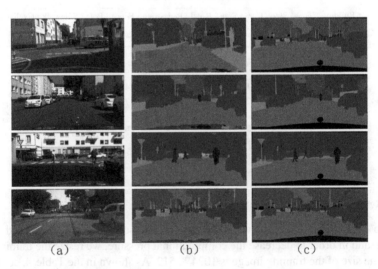

(a)   (b)   (c)

Fig. 6. Result samples on Cityscapes. From left to right: (a) Input, (b) NENet, (c) Ground truth.

5 Conclusion

This paper proposes a NENet for semantic segmentation. We use neighborhood prediction module (NPM) encoding in the encoder part and extract more neighboring correlation in the decoder part to enhance the performance of segmentation. Level-wise relay training strategy is designed to ensure the training efficiency with (NPM). The NENet achieves impressive result on CamVid and Cityscapes datasets, and has a bright prospect.

Acknowledgement. This work is supported by The Natural Science Foundations of China 61727802, Key Research & Development programs in Jiangsu China, BE2018126.

References

1. He, K., Zhang, X., Ren, S., et al.: Deep residual learning for image recognition. In: Proceedings of the IEEE Conference on Computer Vision and Pattern Recognition, pp. 770–778 (2016)
2. Krähenbühl, P., Koltun, V.: Efficient inference in fully connected CRFs with gaussian edge potentials. In: Advances in Neural Information Processing Systems, pp. 109–117 (2011)
3. Brostow, G.J., Fauqueur, J., Cipolla, R.: Semantic object classes in video: a high-definition ground truth database. Pattern Recogn. Lett. **30**(2), 88–97 (2009)
4. Cordts, M., Omran, M., Ramos, S., et al.: The cityscapes dataset for semantic urban scene understanding. In: Proceedings of the IEEE Conference on Computer Vision and Pattern Recognition, pp. 3213–3223 (2016)
5. Chen, L.C., Papandreou, G., Schroff, F., et al.: Rethinking atrous convolution for semantic image segmentation. arXiv preprint arXiv:1706.05587 (2017)
6. Yang, M., Yu, K., Zhang, C., et al.: Denseaspp for semantic segmentation in street scenes. In: Proceedings of the IEEE Conference on Computer Vision and Pattern Recognition, pp. 3684–3692 (2018)
7. Huang, G., Liu, Z., Van Der Maaten, L., et al.: Densely connected convolutional networks. In: Proceedings of the IEEE Conference on Computer Vision and Pattern Recognition, pp. 4700–4708 (2017)
8. He, K., Zhang, X., Ren, S., et al.: Spatial pyramid pooling in deep convolutional networks for visual recognition. IEEE Trans. Pattern Anal. Mach. Intell. **37**(9), 1904–1916 (2015)
9. Zhao, H., Shi, J., Qi, X., et al.: Pyramid scene parsing network. In: Proceedings of the IEEE Conference on Computer Vision and Pattern Recognition, pp. 2881–2890 (2017)
10. Ke, T.-W., Hwang, J.-J., Liu, Z., Yu, S.X.: Adaptive affinity fields for semantic segmentation. In: Ferrari, V., Hebert, M., Sminchisescu, C., Weiss, Y. (eds.) ECCV 2018. LNCS, vol. 11205, pp. 605–621. Springer, Cham (2018). https://doi.org/10.1007/978-3-030-01246-5_36
11. Zhang, H., Dana, K., Shi, J., et al.: Context encoding for semantic segmentation. In: Proceedings of the IEEE Conference on Computer Vision and Pattern Recognition, pp. 7151–7160 (2018)
12. Yu, C., Wang, J., Peng, C., Gao, C., Yu, G., Sang, N.: BiSeNet: bilateral segmentation network for real-time semantic segmentation. In: Ferrari, V., Hebert, M., Sminchisescu, C., Weiss, Y. (eds.) ECCV 2018. LNCS, vol. 11217, pp. 334–349. Springer, Cham (2018). https://doi.org/10.1007/978-3-030-01261-8_20

13. Paszke, A., Chaurasia, A., Kim, S., et al.: Enet: a deep neural network architecture for real-time semantic segmentation. arXiv preprint arXiv:1606.02147 (2016)
14. Everingham, M., Van Gool, L., Williams, C.K.I., et al.: The pascal visual object classes (VOC) challenge. Int. J. Comput. Vision **88**(2), 303–338 (2010)
15. Rubinstein, R.Y., Kroese, D.P.: The Cross-Entropy Method: a Unified Approach to Combinatorial Optimization. Monte-Carlo Simulation and Machine Learning. Springer Science & Business Media, New York (2013)
16. Ioffe, S., Szegedy, C.: Batch normalization: accelerating deep network training by reducing internal covariate shift. arXiv preprint arXiv:1502.03167 (2015)
17. Kim, J., Kwon Lee, J., Mu Lee, K.: Accurate image super-resolution using very deep convolutional networks. In: Proceedings of the IEEE Conference on Computer Vision and Pattern Recognition, pp. 1646–1654 (2016)
18. Badrinarayanan, V., Kendall, A., Cipolla, R.: SegNet: a deep convolutional encoder-decoder architecture for image segmentation. IEEE Trans. Pattern Anal. Mach. Intell. **39**(12), 2481–2495 (2017)
19. Lin, G., Milan, A., Shen, C., et al.: RefineNet: multi-path refinement networks for high-resolution semantic segmentation. In: Proceedings of the IEEE Conference on Computer Vision and Pattern Recognition, pp. 1925–1934 (2017)
20. Kato, Z., Pong, T.C.: A Markov random field image segmentation model for color textured images. Image Vis. Comput. **24**(10), 1103–1114 (2006)
21. Shen, L., Lin, Z., Huang, Q.: Relay backpropagation for effective learning of deep convolutional neural networks. In: Leibe, B., Matas, J., Sebe, N., Welling, M. (eds.) ECCV 2016. LNCS, vol. 9911, pp. 467–482. Springer, Cham (2016). https://doi.org/10.1007/978-3-319-46478-7_29

Coarse-to-Fine 3D Human Pose Estimation

Yu Guo, Lin Zhao, Shanshan Zhang$^{(\boxtimes)}$, and Jian Yang$^{(\boxtimes)}$

PCA Lab, Key Lab of Intelligent Perception and Systems for High-Dimensional Information of Ministry of Education, and Jiangsu Key Lab of Image and Video Understanding for Social Security, School of Computer Science and Engineering, Nanjing University of Science and Technology, Nanjing, China
{csyguo,linzhao,shanshan.zhang,csjyang}@njust.edu.cn

Abstract. Leveraging powerful deep convolutional networks, 2d human pose estimation has achieved great success. On the other hand, 3d human pose estimation is still a challenging task that attracts great attention. Due to the inherent depth ambiguity in 2d to 3d mapping, conventional methods are typically not able to predict 3d locations precisely, especially for the joints far from the torso. In this paper, we propose a coarse-to-fine model to predict 3d joint locations progressively. We observe that some joints like shoulders and hips are relatively easy to get precise 3d locations, which can be utilized to facilitate the prediction of hard joints that are far from the torso. To make this happen, a set of constraints based on human limb length ratio prior is proposed to guide the model to generate reasonable predictions. We conduct experiments on the Human3.6M dataset. Comparison of experimental results on the benchmark dataset turns out that our approach outperforms the baseline method.

Keywords: 3D human pose estimation · Human limb length ratio prior · Deep learning

1 Introduction

Human pose estimation, also called as human keypoints detection, has received extensive attention in recent years. The primary purpose of human pose estimation is to predict human joint locations from monocular RGB information. Human pose estimation is a classical middle-level computer vision task and can greatly facilitate other related high-level tasks such as pedestrian detection [28] and action recognition [7].

Following the success of deep convolutional networks, current 2d human pose estimation methods perform well even in complex outdoor environments. Figure 1 shows typical 2d human pose estimation results predicted by stacked hourglass [18] on Human3.6M dataset [11]. However, unlike on Human3.6M dataset [11]. However, unlike 2d human pose estimation, it is challenging to obtain annotated data for 3d human pose estimation tasks. Most 3d human

© Springer Nature Switzerland AG 2019
Y. Zhao et al. (Eds.): ICIG 2019, LNCS 11903, pp. 579–592, 2019.
https://doi.org/10.1007/978-3-030-34113-8_48

Fig. 1. Typical 2d human pose estimation results produced by stacked hourglass model [18]. Images are from Human3.6M dataset. We can see that stacked hourglass model performs well on Human3.6M dataset.

pose datasets only contain indoor data collected in a laboratory environment, which leads to lack of diversity. Thus, models tend to overfit when training on such datasets. Besides, ambiguity is a widespread problem when mapping 2d to 3d, which also results in unreasonable predictions.

In this paper, we propose a novel coarse-to-fine method for 3d human pose estimation. From our analysis, we find that current models usually produce large errors when predicting keypoints located at the end of limbs, such as wrists and ankles. In contrast, joints like shoulders and hips are relatively easy to predict. Table 1 shows detailed statistics about errors of each joint by [14]. We assume that *easy* joints can be helpful to guide the prediction of *hard* joints. Therefore we propose a coarse-to-fine method to predict different joints in a progressive way. An intuitive way to deal with ambiguity in 3d human pose estimation is to leverage the prior of human structure. For instance, Dabral *et al.* [5] use legal angular constraints in their model. Here, we propose a set of limb length ratio (LLR) constraints to reduce the shifts of joints from the true locations.

Our contributions can be summarized as follows:

- We propose a specific coarse-to-fine method for 3d human pose estimation task to enhance precision of the joints far from the torso. Based on the statistical analysis of predictions produced by the previous state-of-the-art method, we divide joints into three groups according to different difficulty levels. *Easy* joints are predicted first, and then they are used to facilitate the prediction of harder joints.
- A set of human limb length ratio (LLR) constraints based on the statistics of physical human body structure are used to avoid unreasonable predictions, allowing the model to perform more robust on *hard* joints.
- By combining the coarse-to-fine model and LLR constraints, our method outperforms the baseline on the Human 3.6M dataset. Especially the improvement is more significant for those joints far from the torso.

Table 1. Detailed statistics on the error of each joint produced by [14]. Numbers denote the error of each joint in millimeters. Under protocol 2, the model predictions are post-processed with rigid alignments.

Joint	Hip	RHip	RKnee	RFoot	LHip	LKnee	LFoot	Spine	Thorax	Neck
Protocol 1	0.00	23.28	67.74	92.72	23.28	67.76	102.5	44.94	50.58	62.89
Protocol 2	33.48	43.67	53.09	71.12	38.56	54.23	77.06	34.03	27.55	37.37

Joint	Head	LShoulder	LElbow	LWrist	RShoulder	RElbow	RWrist
Protocol 1	73.32	64.15	88.17	120.38	66.35	94.69	120.95
Protocol 2	44.21	43.82	58.10	90.76	37.08	63.12	90.14

2   Related Work

Since our method is specifically designed for the 3d human pose estimation task, we will first review recent works on it. Moreover, we will review recent works on the usage of human structure prior to the task for human pose estimation.

2.1   3D Human Pose Estimation

The topic of 3d human pose estimation attracts increasing attention in recent years due to its potentially broad application prospects. The purpose of 3d human pose estimation task is to estimate accurate spatial position coordinates of human keypoints from RGB images. It is proven that positions of human keypoints are beneficial for generic action recognition tasks in previous works [13,22]. In the current stage, it is almost impossible to predict 3d coordinates in the world coordinate system, as is declared in [14]. Thus most of the current methods predict coordinates in the camera coordinate system [5,9,25]. In this paper, our model predicts 3d human keypoint locations in the camera coordinate system as well.

Various types of methods, as well as diverse representations are proposed for 3d human pose estimation. A typical way of 3d human pose estimation is to use 3d coordinates to represent human keypoint locations and to regress coordinates from a single RGB image directly, as is proposed in [21]. However, the mapping from RGB images to 3d coordinates is so complex that it is challenging to learn the potential knowledge between images and coordinates. In order to overcome this problem, volumetric representation is used as supervision [21,27], which contains richer information than coordinates. Volumetric representation, however, leads to a huge number of model parameters and increasing computational complexity. A compromise solution is to use 3d coordinates as supervision, leveraging 2d human pose predictions at the same time. With the help of powerful convolutional neural networks (CNN), the performance of 2d human pose estimation has great improvements in recent years. A simple yet effective method is to use 2d human pose predictions as input to regress 3d coordinates of human keypoints [14]. Based on this work, [9] combines temporal information with 2d to 3d pose regression, which allows the model to perform well. However, temporal information puts high demands on the data, and also such a model costs too much computation, making it hard to be used in practical applications.

These works make good progress, but it is worth mentioning that the points far from torso flutter heavily in their predictions. This phenomenon is consistent with the problem in 2d pose estimation, as proposed in [24]. In this paper, we propose a coarse-to-fine method, which takes 2d human pose prediction from a single image as input and predicts the 3d coordinates of human keypoints. We divide human keypoints to three groups according to different difficulty levels. The further the keypoints are from the human torso, the harder they are for a model to predict. Our model predicts *easy* keypoints first and then predicts *medium* and *hard* keypoints in turn, leveraging former prediction results.

2.2   Human Structure Prior in Pose Estimation

In previous works, models often generate unreasonable predictions, which makes human structure prior indispensable in human pose estimation tasks. In 2d human pose estimation, [4] leverages generative adversarial networks to guide a model to learn human structure prior implicitly. [5] proposes angular constraints based on the human prior that the range of motions of human joints is limited and symmetry. These constraints are reasonable while the limb length ratio can be another useful constraint, whose distribution is proven to obey specific rules [6]. In this paper, we propose a set of constraints based on the human limb length ratio, and experiments demonstrate it is helpful for a model to get better performance in the task of 3d human pose estimation.

3   Method

In this section, we will discuss the method proposed for 3d human pose estimation. We start with the coarse-to-fine method and introduce the limb length ratio (LLR) constraint to solve the problem better.

3.1   Coarse-to-Fine Model

In previous works, models usually perform worse when predicting keypoints far from the torso such as wrists and ankles. In order to overcome this problem, we propose a coarse-to-fine method. In our method, we first divide keypoints into three groups according to the prediction difficulty. From Table 1, we can observe that the closer the keypoints are to the body torso, the more accurate the model prediction is. For instance, the model performs better when predicting the location of the head than elbows; and performs worse when predicting ankles than knees. Thus we can divide keypoints, according to their distance to the torso, into three groups: *easy*, *medium*, and *hard*. A detailed demonstration is shown in Fig. 2. According to Table 1, we classify head, spine, thorax, hip and shoulder as *easy* joints, elbow and knee as *medium* joints, wrists and ankles as *hard* joints, as shown in Fig. 2.

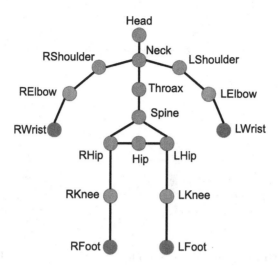

Fig. 2. Keypoints grouped by prediction difficulties. Circles colored in blue, orange and red denote *easy*, *medium* and *hard* joints respectively. The position of hip is the midpoint of left hip and right hip. (Color figure online)

Based on the characteristic of different difficulty levels of joints, we design a specific coarse-to-fine model. The network structure of our model is shown in Fig. 3. The input of our model is 2d keypoints predictions produced by a 2d human pose estimator, and the output is predictions of 3d human keypoints coordinates. As we can see in Fig. 3, our model contains three stages. In the first stage, we predict *easy* joints by using a simple fully-connected network, which is effective in a regression task mapping 2d coordinates to 3d coordinates [14]. In the second and third stage, we predict *medium* and *hard* keypoints, taking both 2d keypoints and 3d coordinates predictions produced in the previous stage(s) as input. Therefore we can leverage predicted 3d joint coordinates as auxiliary information to guide the model to produce more accurate predictions for challenging keypoints. In order to merge 2d keypoints and 3d keypoint predictions produced in previous stages, we adopt channel wise self-attention blocks, as is proposed in [10], to guide the model to assign appropriate weights for predicted 3d keypoint coordinates in the second and third stages. We compute Euclidean distance between 3d keypoints prediction and groundtruth as the keypoints loss L_K,

$$L_K(x, y) = \frac{1}{m} \sum_{i=1}^{m} \|x_i - y_i\|, \tag{1}$$

where x, y stands for the model prediction and groundtruth respectively, m stands for the number of keypoints. Considering that our model produces predictions in three stages, the loss function is written as

$$L_{CTF}(x, y) = \theta_1 L_K(x_e, y_e) + \theta_2 L_K(x_m, y_m) + \theta_3 L_K(x_h, y_h), \tag{2}$$

where subscript e, m, h denotes *easy*, *medium*, and *hard* keypoints respectively.

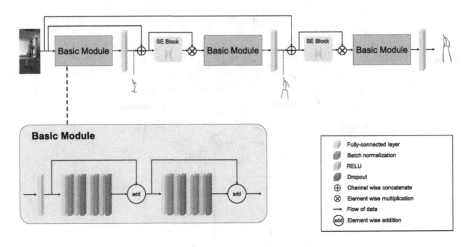

Fig. 3. Network structure of our coarse-to-fine model. For a given RGB image, we first obtain 2d keypoint locations via a 2d human pose estimator. Then we design the coarse-to-fine model in order to predict 3d keypoint coordinates from 2d keypoints. Our method can be divided into 3 stages and we predict positions of *easy*, *medium* and *hard* joints in order. During the second and the third stages, the model leverages predictions from previous stage(s).

3.2   LLR Constraint

Human pose prior knowledge is helpful in the 3d human pose estimation task; and human limb length ratio (LLR) is an important prior, which is studied in [6]. Within the best of our knowledge, few researches focus on LLR prior, which helps predict accurate 3d coordinates. In this paper, we propose a set of LLR constraints based on the LLR prior. According to the research of *De Leva* [6], we can assume that the distribution of adult limb length ratio obeys normalization distribution. Therefore we can census the dataset to get the mean value and stand deviation of the limb length ratio of the dataset.

The length of a limb can be computed as follows,

$$l(x_1, x_2) = \|x_1 - x_2\|, \tag{3}$$

where x_1, x_2 stands for 3d coordinates of corresponding keypoints lying at the ends of limbs. The limb length ratio between limb p and limb q can be computed as follows,

$$r(p, q) = \frac{l(p_{x_1}, p_{x_2})}{l(q_{x_1}, q_{x_2})}, \tag{4}$$

where p_{x_1}, p_{x_2}, q_{x_1} and q_{x_2} stand for 3d keypoint coordinates lying at the ends of limb p and limb q respectively. Then the LLR loss can be written as

$$L_{LLR}(X) = \frac{1}{m} \sum_{i=1}^{m} \left(1 - \frac{1}{\sqrt{2\pi} s} exp(-\frac{1}{2} \frac{\left(r(X_{i_p}, X_{i_q}) - \overline{R}\right)^2}{s} \right), \tag{5}$$

Table 2. Comparison to current state-of-the-art methods on the Human3.6M validation set under protocol 1. Bold indicates the best results.

Protocol 1	Direct	Discuss	Eating	Greet	Phone	Photo	Pose	Purch	Sitting	SitingD	Smoke	Wait	WalkD	Walk	WalkT	Avg
LinKDE [11]	132.7	183.6	132.3	164.4	162.1	205.9	150.6	171.3	151.6	243.0	162.1	170.7	177.1	96.6	127.9	162.1
Tekin et al. [26]	102.4	147.2	88.8	125.3	118.0	182.7	112.4	129.2	138.9	224.9	118.4	138.8	126.3	55.1	65.8	125.0
Zhou et al. [30]	87.4	109.3	87.1	103.2	116.2	143.3	106.9	99.8	124.5	199.2	107.4	118.1	114.2	79.4	97.7	113.0
Du et al. [8]	85.1	112.7	104.9	122.1	139.1	135.9	105.9	166.2	117.5	226.9	120.0	117.7	137.4	99.3	106.5	126.5
Park et al. [20]	100.3	116.2	90.0	116.5	115.3	149.5	117.6	106.9	137.2	190.8	105.8	125.1	131.9	62.6	96.2	117.3
Zhou et al. [31]	91.8	102.4	96.7	98.8	113.4	125.2	90.0	93.8	132.2	159.0	107.0	94.4	126.0	79.0	99.0	107.3
Nie et al. [19]	90.1	88.2	85.7	95.6	103.9	103.0	92.4	90.4	117.9	136.4	98.5	94.4	90.6	86.0	89.5	97.5
Mehta et al. [15]	57.5	68.6	59.6	67.3	78.1	82.4	56.9	69.1	100.0	117.5	69.4	68.0	76.5	55.2	61.4	72.9
Mehta et al. [16]	62.6	78.1	63.84	72.5	88.3	93.8	63.1	74.8	106.6	138.7	78.8	73.9	82.0	55.8	59.6	80.5
Martinez et al. [14]	51.8	56.2	58.1	59.0	69.5	78.4	55.2	58.1	74.0	94.6	62.3	59.1	65.1	49.5	52.4	62.9
CTF (ours)	49.9	55.3	56.7	57.4	66.7	77.1	53.2	55.5	71.9	89.4	60.2	58.2	62.9	48.8	51.2	61.2
CTF+LLR (ours)	**49.4**	**54.3**	**55.7**	**56.9**	**66.4**	**74.5**	**53.2**	**55.4**	**71.7**	**89.0**	**60.0**	**57.0**	**62.7**	**48.0**	**50.7**	**60.6**

Table 3. Comparison to current state-of-the-art methods on the Human3.6M validation set under protocol 2. Bold indicates the best results.

Protocol 2	Direct	Discuss	Eating	Greet	Phone	Photo	Pose	Purch	Sitting	SitingD	Smoke	Wait	WalkD	Walk	WalkT	Avg
Akhter and Black [1]	199.2	177.6	161.8	197.8	176.2	186.5	195.4	167.3	160.7	173.7	177.8	181.9	176.2	198.6	192.7	181.1
Ramakrishna et al. [23]	137.4	149.3	141.6	154.3	157.7	158.9	141.8	158.1	168.6	175.6	160.4	161.7	150.0	174.8	150.2	157.3
Zhou et al. [29]	99.7	95.8	87.9	116.8	108.3	107.3	93.5	95.3	109.1	137.5	106.0	102.2	106.5	110.4	115.2	106.7
Bogo et al. [3]	62.0	60.2	67.8	76.5	92.1	77.0	73.0	75.3	100.3	137.3	83.4	77.3	86.8	79.7	87.7	82.3
Moreno-Noguer [17]	66.1	61.7	84.5	73.7	65.2	67.2	60.9	67.3	103.5	74.6	92.6	69.6	71.5	78.0	73.2	74.0
Martinez et al. [14]	39.5	43.2	46.4	47.0	51.0	56.0	41.4	40.6	56.5	69.4	49.2	45.0	49.5	38.0	43.1	47.7
CTF+LLR (ours)	**38.8**	**42.1**	**44.4**	**46.0**	**49.8**	**53.4**	**40.5**	**39.3**	**54.5**	**63.5**	**47.6**	**43.2**	48.6	**36.6**	**41.5**	**46.5**

where X_{i_p} and X_{i_q} denote the limb in the ratio pair respectively, $\overline{R}$ and s denote the mean value and standard deviation of the limb length ratio of a chosen pair $r(X_{i_p}, X_{i_q})$ that computed on the training set respectively. In addition, we use the Gaussian function to punish the ratio offset. Then the final loss function is

$$Loss = \alpha L_{CTF} + \beta L_{LLR}, \tag{6}$$

where α and β are hyper-parameters and denote scale coefficients of the corresponding loss items.

4 Experiments

In this section, we will first describe the implementation details, followed by experimental results on the Human3.6M dataset [11]. In addition, intuitive comparisons between our model and benchmark methods are present.

Table 4. Comparison of the baseline and our method w.r.t the prediction errors of *medium* and *hard* keypoints.

Joints		Protocol 1			Protocol 2		
		Baseline [18]	Ours	Δ	Baseline [18]	Ours	Δ
Medium	LKnee	67.8	59.2	−8.6	54.2	48.3	−5.9
	RKnee	67.7	60.4	−7.3	53.1	48.5	−4.6
	LElbow	88.2	79.2	−9.0	58.1	52.2	−5.9
	RElbow	94.7	83.9	−10.8	63.1	55.6	−7.5
Hard	LFoot	102.5	89.9	−12.6	77.1	65.6	−11.5
	RFoot	92.7	81.9	−10.8	71.1	61.4	−9.8
	LWrist	120.4	105.1	−15.3	90.8	79.0	−11.8
	RWrist	121.0	102.7	−18.2	90.1	75.7	−14.4

4.1 Dataset

We conduct experiments on the Human3.6M dataset to demonstrate the performance of our method. Human3.6M is a widely used dataset in the field of 3d human pose estimation, which contains comprehensive annotations. The data of Human3.6M dataset are collected in a laboratory environment, including 11 professional actors and 17 scenarios. 3d human keypoint position annotations are obtained from a high-speed motion capture system with 4 calibrated cameras. In this paper, we choose 5 actors as the training set and 2 actors as the validation set, which is consistent with widely used protocols [12,14,27]. It is worth mentioning that we do not leverage the temporal information considering real-time performance.

4.2   Implementation Details

In our coarse-to-fine method, we use the predictions of stacked hourglass [18], a state-of-the-art 2d human pose estimation method, as the input of our coarse-to-fine method. A prediction of stacked hourglass includes 16 keypoints. We reshape each 2d human pose prediction to a vector with shape 1×32 and reshape corresponding 3d human pose ground truth to a vector with shape 1×48 during data preprocessing. The 3d human pose ground truth coordinate is transformed to the camera coordinate system. In order to facilitate comparisons with other methods, we set the keypoint *Hip* as the coordinate system origin, which is the midpoint of the left hip and right hip, following [9,14]. In order to make the model easier to convergence, we normalize 2d pose predictions and 3d pose ground truth with mean and variance calculated in the training set. In order to avoid the gradient explosion problem, we clip the maximum L2 norm of gradient every time backpropagation is operated. The model is trained with 128 batch size and 1.22 million iterations in total; the initial learning rate is set to 1×10^{-3}, which is decreased by 0.96 every 10k iterations.

All experiments are conducted on one Nvidia Tesla K80 GPU with 12 Gigabyte memory.

Fig. 4. Qualitative results of our method on the Human3.6M dataset. Each row of the figure contains 2 samples and each sample contains 4 columns. In each sample, each column represents RGB image, 2d human pose prediction produced by stacked hourglass model [18], 3d human pose prediction of our method and the ground truth of 3d human pose in turn. In order to more clearly present the 3d predictions, we rotate the figures in the third and forth columns slightly around the y axis.

4.3   Comparison with State-of-the-Art Methods

In Table 2, we present the results of our methods and make a comparison with the state-of-the-art methods under protocol 1. We can see clearly that our coarse-to-fine method performs well on Human3.6M dataset. When combined with LLR loss, the performance of our method is further improved and decreases the average error to 60.6 mm. Under protocol 2, rigid alignment is applied to the predictions and our method outperforms comparison methods on every action, as shown in Table 3. In Table 4, we can clearly see that our method, which combines LLR loss and coarse-to-fine method, outperforms the baseline method when predicting *medium* and *hard* keypoints. Figure 4 presents some examples of our predicted 3d human poses on the Human3.6M dataset.

In order to explore the generalization performance of our method, we conduct qualitative experiments on MPII dataset [2] and make a comparison between our method and [14], as is shown in Fig. 5. We can see that in most situations, our method produces more reasonable predictions compared with [14] even in wild scenes. While it is worth mentioning that the occlusion of 2d joints has a huge negative impact on 3d prediction.

Fig. 5. Qualitative results on the MPII dataset [2]. Each row contains two samples and each sample includes three columns. In each sample, each column represents the RGB image with corresponding 2d human pose prediction, 3d predictions of [14] and 3d predictions of our method in turn.

5 Conclusion

In this paper, we propose a coarse-to-fine method for 3d human pose estimation and a set of human structure based limb length ratio constraints. Experimental results indicate that our method is useful, mainly when predicting challenging keypoints that are far from the torso. Encouraged by the current results, we will investigate how to explore context information to improve the performance further.

Acknowledgements. The authors would like to thank the anonymous reviewers for their critical and constructive comments and suggestions. This work was supported by the National Natural Science Foundation of China under Grant No. U1713208, 61702262 and 61802189, Funds for International Cooperation and Exchange of the National Natural Science Foundation of China under Grant No. 61861136011, Natural Science Foundation of Jiangsu Province, China under Grant No. BK20181299 and BK20180464, the Fundamental Research Funds for the Central Universities under Grant No. 30918011322 and 30918014107, Program for Changjiang Scholars, CCF-Tencent Open Fund No. RAGR20180113, and Young Elite Scientists Sponsorship Program by CAST No. 2018QNRC001.

References

1. Akhter, I., Black, M.J.: Pose-conditioned joint angle limits for 3D human pose reconstruction. In: CVPR, pp. 1446–1455 (2015)
2. Andriluka, M., Pishchulin, L., Gehler, P., Schiele, B.: 2D human pose estimation: new benchmark and state of the art analysis. In: CVPR (2014)
3. Bogo, F., Kanazawa, A., Lassner, C., Gehler, P., Romero, J., Black, M.J.: Keep it SMPL: automatic estimation of 3D human pose and shape from a single image. In: Leibe, B., Matas, J., Sebe, N., Welling, M. (eds.) ECCV 2016. LNCS, vol. 9909, pp. 561–578. Springer, Cham (2016). https://doi.org/10.1007/978-3-319-46454-1_34
4. Chen, Y., Shen, C., Wei, X.S., Liu, L., Yang, J.: Adversarial PoseNet: a structure-aware convolutional network for human pose estimation. In: ICCV, pp. 1212–1221 (2017)
5. Dabral, R., Mundhada, A., Kusupati, U., Afaque, S., Sharma, A., Jain, A.: Learning 3D human pose from structure and motion. In: Ferrari, V., Hebert, M., Sminchisescu, C., Weiss, Y. (eds.) ECCV 2018. LNCS, vol. 11213, pp. 679–696. Springer, Cham (2018). https://doi.org/10.1007/978-3-030-01240-3_41
6. De Leva, P.: Adjustments to Zatsiorsky-Seluyanov's segment inertia parameters. J. Biomech. **29**(9), 1223–1230 (1996)
7. Du, Y., Wang, W., Wang, L.: Hierarchical recurrent neural network for skeleton based action recognition. In: CVPR, pp. 1110–1118 (2015)
8. Du, Y., et al.: Marker-less 3D human motion capture with monocular image sequence and height-maps. In: Leibe, B., Matas, J., Sebe, N., Welling, M. (eds.) ECCV 2016. LNCS, vol. 9908, pp. 20–36. Springer, Cham (2016). https://doi.org/10.1007/978-3-319-46493-0_2
9. Hossain, M.R.I., Little, J.J.: Exploiting temporal information for 3D human pose estimation. In: Ferrari, V., Hebert, M., Sminchisescu, C., Weiss, Y. (eds.) ECCV 2018. LNCS, vol. 11214, pp. 69–86. Springer, Cham (2018). https://doi.org/10.1007/978-3-030-01249-6_5

10. Hu, J., Shen, L., Sun, G.: Squeeze-and-excitation networks. In: CVPR, pp. 7132–7141 (2018)
11. Ionescu, C., Papava, D., Olaru, V., Sminchisescu, C.: Human3.6M: large scale datasets and predictive methods for 3D human sensing in natural environments. IEEE Trans. Pattern Anal. Mach. Intell. **36**(7), 1325–1339 (2014)
12. Kanazawa, A., Black, M.J., Jacobs, D.W., Malik, J.: End-to-end recovery of human shape and pose. In: CVPR, pp. 7122–7131 (2018)
13. Luvizon, D.C., Picard, D., Tabia, H.: 2D/3D pose estimation and action recognition using multitask deep learning. In: CVPR, pp. 5137–5146 (2018)
14. Martinez, J., Hossain, R., Romero, J., Little, J.J.: A simple yet effective baseline for 3D human pose estimation. In: ICCV, pp. 2640–2649 (2017)
15. Mehta, D., et al.: Monocular 3D human pose estimation in the wild using improved CNN supervision. In: 3DV, pp. 506–516 (2017)
16. Mehta, D., et al.: VNect: Real-time 3D human pose estimation with a single RGB camera. ACM Trans. Graph. **36**(4), 44 (2017)
17. Moreno-Noguer, F.: 3D human pose estimation from a single image via distance matrix regression. In: CVPR, pp. 2823–2832 (2017)
18. Newell, A., Yang, K., Deng, J.: Stacked hourglass networks for human pose estimation. In: Leibe, B., Matas, J., Sebe, N., Welling, M. (eds.) ECCV 2016. LNCS, vol. 9912, pp. 483–499. Springer, Cham (2016). https://doi.org/10.1007/978-3-319-46484-8_29
19. Nie, B.X., Wei, P., Zhu, S.C.: Monocular 3D human pose estimation by predicting depth on joints. In: 2017 IEEE International Conference on Computer Vision (ICCV), pp. 3467–3475. IEEE (2017)
20. Park, S., Hwang, J., Kwak, N.: 3D human pose estimation using convolutional neural networks with 2D pose information. In: Hua, G., Jégou, H. (eds.) ECCV 2016. LNCS, vol. 9915, pp. 156–169. Springer, Cham (2016). https://doi.org/10.1007/978-3-319-49409-8_15
21. Pavlakos, G., Zhou, X., Derpanis, K.G., Daniilidis, K.: Coarse-to-fine volumetric prediction for single-image 3D human pose. In: CVPR, pp. 7025–7034 (2017)
22. Popa, A.I., Zanfir, M., Sminchisescu, C.: Deep multitask architecture for integrated 2D and 3D human sensing. In: CVPR, pp. 6289–6298 (2017)
23. Ramakrishna, V., Kanade, T., Sheikh, Y.: Reconstructing 3D human pose from 2D image landmarks. In: Fitzgibbon, A., Lazebnik, S., Perona, P., Sato, Y., Schmid, C. (eds.) ECCV 2012. LNCS, vol. 7575, pp. 573–586. Springer, Heidelberg (2012). https://doi.org/10.1007/978-3-642-33765-9_41
24. Ronchi, M.R., Perona, P.: Benchmarking and error diagnosis in multi-instance pose estimation. In: ICCV, pp. 369–378 (2017)
25. Sun, X., Xiao, B., Wei, F., Liang, S., Wei, Y.: Integral human pose regression. In: Ferrari, V., Hebert, M., Sminchisescu, C., Weiss, Y. (eds.) ECCV 2018. LNCS, vol. 11210, pp. 536–553. Springer, Cham (2018). https://doi.org/10.1007/978-3-030-01231-1_33
26. Tekin, B., Rozantsev, A., Lepetit, V., Fua, P.: Direct prediction of 3D body poses from motion compensated sequences. In: CVPR, pp. 991–1000 (2016)
27. Trumble, M., Gilbert, A., Hilton, A., Collomosse, J.: Deep autoencoder for combined human pose estimation and body model upscaling. In: Ferrari, V., Hebert, M., Sminchisescu, C., Weiss, Y. (eds.) ECCV 2018. LNCS, vol. 11214, pp. 800–816. Springer, Cham (2018). https://doi.org/10.1007/978-3-030-01249-6_48
28. Zhang, S., Yang, J., Schiele, B.: Occluded pedestrian detection through guided attention in CNNS. In: CVPR, pp. 6995–7003 (2018)

29. Zhou, X., Zhu, M., Leonardos, S., Daniilidis, K.: Sparse representation for 3D shape estimation: a convex relaxation approach. IEEE Trans. Pattern Anal. Mach. Intell. **39**(8), 1648–1661 (2017)
30. Zhou, X., Zhu, M., Leonardos, S., Derpanis, K.G., Daniilidis, K.: Sparseness meets deepness: 3D human pose estimation from monocular video. In: CVPR, pp. 4966–4975 (2016)
31. Zhou, X., Sun, X., Zhang, W., Liang, S., Wei, Y.: Deep kinematic pose regression. In: Hua, G., Jégou, H. (eds.) ECCV 2016. LNCS, vol. 9915, pp. 186–201. Springer, Cham (2016). https://doi.org/10.1007/978-3-319-49409-8_17

Monocular SLAM System in Dynamic Scenes Based on Semantic Segmentation

Chao Sheng, Shuguo Pan$^{(\boxtimes)}$, Pan Zeng, Lixiao Huang, and Tao Zhao

School of Instrument Science and Engineering, Southeast University,
Nanjing 210096, China
{seushengchao, psg}@seu.edu.cn

Abstract. The traditional feature-based visual SLAM algorithm is based on the static environment assumption when recovering scene information and camera motion. The dynamic objects in the scene will affect the positioning accuracy. In this paper, we propose to combine the image semantic segmentation based on deep learning method with the traditional visual SLAM framework to reduce the interference of dynamic objects on the positioning results. Firstly, a supervised Convolutional Neural Network (CNN) is used to segment objects in the input image to obtain the semantic image. Secondly, the feature points are extracted from the original image, and the feature points of the dynamic objects (cars and pedestrians) are eliminated according to the semantic image. Finally, the traditional monocular SLAM method is used to track the camera motion based on the eliminated feature points. The experiments on the Apolloscape datasets show that compared with the traditional method, the proposed method improves the positioning accuracy in dynamic scenes by about 17%.

Keywords: Monocular SLAM · Dynamic objects · Deep learning · Semantic segmentation · CNN

1 Introduction

SLAM (simultaneous localization and mapping) is the key technology of robot autonomous operation in unknown environment. Based on the environment data detected by robot external sensors, SLAM constructs the surrounding environment map for the robot and provides the position of the robot in the environment map at the same time. Compared with ranging instruments such as radar and sonar, the visual sensor has the characteristics of small size, low power consumption and abundant information acquisition, it can provide rich texture information in the external environment. Therefore, visual SLAM has become the focus of current research, and been applied on autonomous navigation, VR/AR and other fields.

In recent years, many visual SLAM systems have been invented and show the impressive performance on localization and mapping. In 2007, Davision et al. [1] proposed MonoSLAM, which establishes the framework of a probabilistic visual SLAM system, and proposes a method for the initialization of monocular features and the estimation of feature direction. The algorithm is the pioneering work of monocular real-time visual SLAM. In 2007, David Murray et al. [2] proposed PTAM, the system uses two threads to separate feature tracking and map building, and adopts bundle adjustment based on keyframes for global optimization. Engel et al. [3] proposed LSD-SLA in 2014. It is a direct method using pixel information as much as possible instead of feature points to estimate camera motion, and the optimization is achieved by minimizing photometric error. The team published DSO [4] in 2016, which is one of the most effective visual odometries based on direct method. In 2015, Mur-Artal et al. [5] proposed the ORB- SLAM based on the PTAM framework. It uses ORB features to track and match, and adds automatic initialization, loop closing detection, relocalization based on bag of word and back-end optimization method. ORB-SLAM is one of the most effective visual SLAM algorithms. The team has proposed ORB-SLAM2 [6] later, which is not only suitable for monocular cameras, but also for stereo and RGB-D cameras.

However, all above SLAM systems are based on the static environment assumption meaning the target scene must keep stationary during processing. Dynamic objects in the scene have negative effect on positioning accuracy.

At present, the traditional visual SLAM algorithm based on feature points deals with simple dynamic scene problems by detecting dynamic points and marking them as outliers. ORB-SLAM reduces the effect of dynamic objects on positioning and mapping accuracy by RANSAC, chi-square test, keyframe method, and local map. The direct method deals with occlusion problem caused by dynamic objects by optimizing cost function. In 2013, Zhang et al. [7] proposed a novel representation and updating method for keyfame to adaptively model the dynamic environments, where the appearance or structure changes can be effectively detected and handled. In the same year, Zou et al. [8] introduced intercamera pose estimation and intercamera mapping to deal with dynamic objects by using multiple cameras in the localization and mapping process. With the development of deep learning technology, semantic information of the image has been explored to improving the performance of SLAM. Chen et al. [9] integrated CNN-based multiple object detection and traditional monocular SLAM to detect moving objects in the scene.

In this paper, we propose a novel method to improve localization accuracy of the feature-based visual SLAM algorithm in dynamic scenes: We firstly introduce semantic segmentation method based on deep learning to obtain the semantic image. Then a ORB detector is used for extracting feature points and dynamic features are eliminated according to the semantic image. Finally, we adapted traditional features-based SLAM framework to track the camera motion by using the eliminated feature points.

2   Approach

2.1   Image Semantic Segmentation

We adapt the ICNet [10] (Image Cascade Network) for segmenting dynamic objects. The system achieves the real-time image inference with decent result on a single GPU card, so it meets the requirement of SLAM for real-time performance. The overall structure of the network is shown in Fig. 1.

Three novel components of the network are as follows:

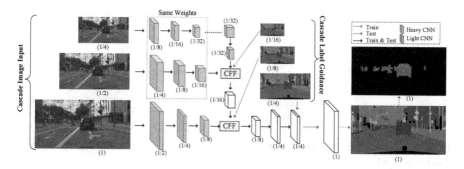

Fig. 1. Network structure of ICNet. Numbers in parentheses are size ratios to the original input image. 'CFF' is the cascade feature fusion unit. There are three branches. The first three layers of the top and middle branches share the same weights. Layers in green of the last two branches is light for high efficiency. Only the process pointed to by the black arrow is used for both training and testing. (Color figure online)

(1) **Cascade Image Input.** Classical image semantic segmentation network like FCN is very time consuming for high-resolution images. ICNet takes cascade image input to overcome the shortcoming. In the top branch of ICNet, the original image is firstly downsampled to a 1/4 sized image, then fed into the PSPNet to obtain a 1/32 sized feature map which is a coarse prediction and misses a lot of details and boundaries. In the middle and bottom branches, a 1/2 sized image and the original image are used for recovering and refining the coarse prediction. Although the prediction of the top branch is coarse, it contains the most semantic parts. Therefore, the CNNs of the last two branches used for refining segmentation boundaries and details are light. The output feature maps of different branch are fused by 'CFF' unit (cascade feature fusion), and the cascade label guidance enhances the learning procedure in different branch.

(2) **Cascade Feature Fusion.** 'CFF' unit is used for combining the output feature map of different branch, the structure of the unit is shown in Fig. 2. The input of the unit consists of two feature maps and a label, where F1 has the size $H_1 \times W_1 \times C_1$, F2 has the size $H_2 \times W_2 \times C_2$, and the label size is $H_1 \times W_1 \times 1$. The up-sampling with rate 2 is applied on F1 to obtain the same size as F2. Then a dilated convolution layer with kernel size $3 \times 3 \times C_3$ and dilation 2 is used for refining, so the output size of F1 becomes $H_2 \times W_2 \times C_3$. For F2, in order to get the same size as the output of F1, a convolution with kernel size $1 \times 1 \times C_3$ is applied. Through two batch normalization layers and a 'sum' layers, the fused feature map F2 with size $H_2 \times W_2 \times C_3$ is obtained. The label guidance is used for getting the auxiliary loss.

(3) **Cascade Label Guidance.** As shown in Fig. 1, three ground truth labels in different resolution (1/16, 1/8, 1/4 of the original image resolution) are adopted to get three independent loss items in different branch, the strategy can enhance the learning procedure. The total loss function can be expressed as:

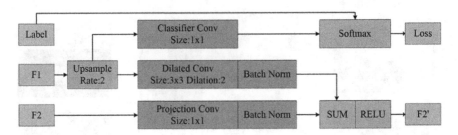

Fig. 2. Structure of 'CFF' unit. F1 and F2 are feature maps of different branch, the spatial size of F2 is twice of F1.

$$L_{total} = -\sum_{t=1}^{3} \omega_t \frac{1}{Y_t X_t} \sum_{y=1}^{Y_t} \sum_{x=1}^{X_t} \log \frac{e^{F_{\tilde{n},y,x}^t}}{\sum_{n=1}^{N} e^{F_{n,y,x}^t}} \tag{1}$$

ω_t is the loss weight in each branch. The feature map of each branch F^t has the spatial size $Y_t \times X_t$. N is objects category. The value at position (n, y, x) is $F_{n,y,x}^t$, the corresponding ground truth label for 2D position (y, x) is $\tilde{n}$.

In summary, compared to other segmentation networks which bring accurate segmentation results but take long runtime, ICNet can achieve the real-time image semantic segmentation with decent result, it is practical for SLAM system which operates in real time.

2.2　Feature Points Extraction and Elimination

Traditional featured-based visual SLAM method such as ORB-SLAM firstly extracts feature points from original image, then the sparse or dense 3D structure of the scene and the camera motion are restored by using the corresponding relation of the image feature points at different frames, and the scene is assumed to be static. In the back-end optimization, RANSAC iterations method or chi-square test is used for eliminating the outliers, However, if the scene is too complex, RANSAC or chi-square test will not be so reliable [9].

We directly eliminate the feature points of dynamic objects by the semantic image in the extraction stage. Firstly, we extract ORB feature points from the input image. Then the elimination unit is applied on culling feature points of dynamic objects (cars and pedestrians) based on the segmented image we already get from semantic section. The framework is shown in Fig. 3.

2.3　Camera Motion Tracking

After getting the eliminated feature points, we track the camera motion to get the positioning result based on the monocular ORB-SLAM framework which is a representative system at feature points category. The overall framework is shown in Fig. 4.

The brief introduction of the framework are as follows:

Semantic Segmentation

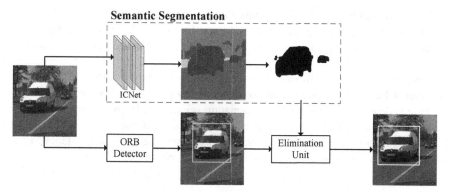

Fig. 3. Framework of feature points extraction and elimination. Green marks in the picture are ORB feature points. The car is driving. Yellow box: before processing. White box: after processing. We can see that feature points of the dynamic car are successfully eliminated. (Color figure online)

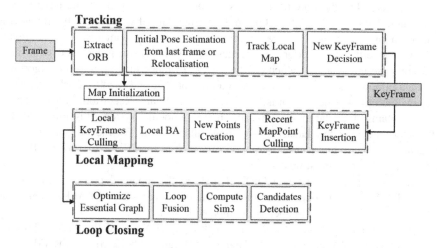

Fig. 4. Overall framework of ORB-SLAM. There are three parallel threads: Tracking, local mapping and loop closing. BA means bundle adjustment.

(1) **Tracking.** The tracking thread is used for estimating the camera motion with every frame, and deciding the occasion of inserting a new keyframe. The initial pose is obtained by the feature matching between the current frame and last frame, then optimized by motion-only bundle adjustment. Note that chi-square test is used here for removing mismatches, it has a certain effect on removing feature matches of dynamic objects, but may failed when facing many dynamic objects. The relocalization is applied when the tracking is lost. After getting the initial pose, matches between feature points of current frame and local map are searched by projection, and the pose will be optimized again. In the end, the thread decides whether inserting a new keyframe or not.

(2) **Local Mapping.** The local mapping thread is in charge of processing keyframes and achieving optimal sparse reconstruction by the local bundle adjustment. The unmatched ORB features in current keyframe are matched with the connected keyframes to triangulate new map points. In order to select high quality points and remove redundant keyframes, an exigent culling strategy is adapted.

(3) **Loop Closing.** The loop closing searches for loops with each new keyframe. If a loop is detected, a similarity transformation is calculated, which informs about the accumulated drift in the loop. Then the two sides of the loop are aligned and duplicated points are fused. Finally, in order to achieve global consistency, a pose graph optimization over similarity constraints is performed.

3   Experiment and Analysis

In this paper, the feasibility and stability of the proposed algorithm in dynamic scenarios are verified by the scene analysis part of the public Apolloscape [11] automatic driving dataset. For the traditional SLAM algorithm based on the static environment assumption, the dynamic car traveling in the former dataset will destroy the robustness and positioning accuracy of the algorithm. The dataset contains multiple image sequences in different outdoor road scenes, and each picture is matched with high-precision pose information, which can be used to evaluate the output of the algorithm. The dataset contains three road scenes: road01, road02, and road03. Each road scene contains multiple segment records, such as Record001 and Record002. Each segment record contains binocular images. Because it is a monocular system, it is only used. The left camera image in the dataset for the monocular system. For the sake of simplicity, the data sequence of the data set is abbreviated, such as road01\Record067 as r01R067, and other sequences are similar.

This paper adopts monocular ORB-SLAM2 as the monocular SLAM framework. Since ORB-SLAM2 is one of the most outstanding and stable SLAM systems, the experimental results of this paper are compared with it.

All experiments are on a workstation with an Intel Xeon E5-2690V4 at 2.6 GHz with 128 GB of RAM and a Nvidia TitanV GPU card with 12 GB of VRAM.

3.1   Results of Semantic Segmentation

Results of segmentation is shown in Fig. 5.

3.2   Results of Feature Points Elimination

We extract ORB feature points from the input image, then eliminate feature points of dynamic objects based on the segmented image. Results of elimination is shown in Fig. 6.

Input image	Semantic image	Binary image

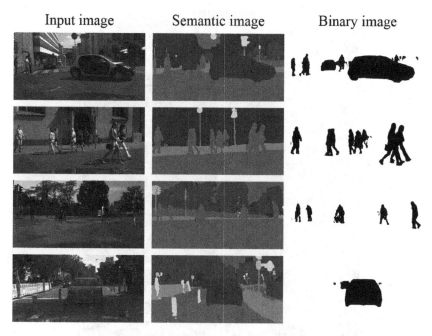

Fig. 5. Results of semantic segmentation. The middle column shows that trees, building, road, traffic signs and other objects in the scene are decently segmented. Right side only preserves the segmentation results of the dynamic objects (cars and pedestrians). Although the boundaries are not perfectly accurate, the result is enough for feature points elimination.

3.3 Results of Positioning

Figure 7 is the plan views of the positioning trajectories of the r01R067 and r02R019 sequences in ORB-SLAM2 and our algorithm respectively. It can be seen from the figure that the estimated results of the two systems are basically coincident with the actual trajectory, but the deviation from the ground truth of our algorithm is smaller than that of ORB-SLAM2, and our positioning result is more accurate.

Figure 8 shows the error of the two algorithms in the X, Y, and Z directions and the absolute trajectory error (ATE) with time in r01R067 and r02R019 sequences. It can be seen that compared with ORB-SLAM2, both the trajectory error in the X, Y, and Z directions and the absolute trajectory error (ATE) of our algorithm are smaller. In about 82 s of r01R067 sequences, due to the large proportion of dynamic cars in the scene, the trajectory error of ORB-SLAM2 rises sharply, and the absolute trajectory error reaches 17.7 m.

Table 1 gives the absolute trajectory error statistics of the eight ApolloScape image sequences in our algorithm and ORB-SLAM2. It can be seen from the table that the positioning result of this paper is better than ORB-SLAM2, and the positioning accuracy is improved by about 17%.

Fig. 6. Results of feature points elimination. The white car is a dynamic object which is moving on the road. The four images in the left column show the result before elimination process, there are many feature points (green masks) that belong to the dynamic car. The right column shows the result after eliminating, we can see that the car's feature points have been completely culled. The images have been clipped for a clearer display. (Color figure online)

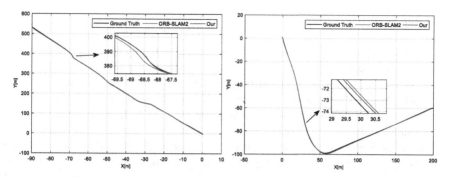

Fig. 7. Positioning trajectories of r01R067 and r02R019 sequences in our algorithm and ORB-SLAM2. The left one is the positioning trajectories of r01R067 sequence, and the right one shows positioning trajectories r02R019 sequence.

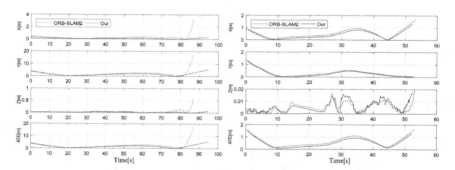

Fig. 8. Errors of the two algorithms in the X, Y, and Z directions and the absolute trajectory error (ATE) with time in r01R067 and r02R019 sequences. The left and right show the errors of r01R067 sequence and r02R019 sequence respectively.

Table 1. Comparison of positioning results of two algorithms on ApolloScape dataset.

Sequence	ORB-SLAM2			Our			Improvement
	rmse	max	std	rmse	max	std	rmse
r01R036	0.28	0.61	0.13	**0.23**	0.55	0.11	**17.86%**
r01R067	3.46	17.7	2.55	**1.93**	5.52	1.08	**24.14%**
r01R069	0.89	2.13	0.4	**0.84**	2.17	0.4	**5.62%**
r02R006	0.58	1.37	0.29	**0.44**	1.27	0.24	**24.14%**
r02R019	0.9	1.69	0.39	**0.75**	1.54	0.33	**16.67%**
r03R001	0.18	0.44	0.1	**0.16**	0.39	0.08	**11.11%**
r03R004	0.07	0.18	0.04	**0.06**	0.17	0.04	**14.30%**
r03R030	0.09	0.27	0.05	**0.07**	0.19	0.04	**22.22%**

4 Conclusion

In this paper, aiming to reduce the negative influence caused by dynamic objects on the traditional feature-based SLAM algorithm, we introduce a novel method that combining the image semantic segmentation method based on deep learning with the traditional visual SLAM framework. Experiments on Apolloscape datasets shows that compared with full ORB-SLAM and incomplete ORB-SLAM, our method improves the positioning accuracy in dynamic scenes by about 13% and 31% respectively. The method of this paper still needs to be improved. We treat all cars and pedestrians in the scene as dynamic objects when doing feature points elimination, it is a waste for static objects if the condition of the car is switching between driving and stopping. We will focus on how to track the motion of not only the camera itself but also objects in the scene, then perform the features elimination policy by judging if objects are moving or not.

Acknowledgments. This research was supported by Jiangsu Surveying and Mapping Geographic Information Scientific Research Project (JSCHKY201808), National Key Research and Development Project (2016YFB0502101) and National Natural Science Foundation of China (41574026, 41774027).

References

1. Davison, A.J., Reid, I.D., Molton, N.D., et al.: MonoSLAM: real-time single camera SLAM. IEEE Trans. Pattern Anal. Mach. Intell. **29**(6), 1052–1067 (2007)
2. Klein, G., Murray, D.: Parallel tracking and mapping for small AR workspaces. In: Proceedings of the Sixth IEEE and ACM International Symposium on Mixed and Augmented Reality (ISMAR 2007), Nara, Japan. IEEE, November 2007
3. Engel, J., Schöps, T., Cremers, D.: LSD-SLAM: large-scale direct monocular SLAM. In: Fleet, D., Pajdla, T., Schiele, B., Tuytelaars, T. (eds.) ECCV 2014. LNCS, vol. 8690, pp. 834–849. Springer, Cham (2014). https://doi.org/10.1007/978-3-319-10605-2_54
4. Engel, J., Koltun, V., Cremers, D.: Direct sparse odometry. IEEE Trans. Pattern Anal. Mach. Intell. **40**(3), 611–625 (2016)
5. Mur-Artal, R., Montiel, J.M.M., Tardos, J.D.: ORB-SLAM: a versatile and accurate monocular SLAM system. IEEE Trans. Rob. **31**(5), 1147–1163 (2015)
6. Mur-Artal, R., Tardos, J.D.: ORB-SLAM2: an open-source SLAM system for monocular, stereo, and RGB-D cameras. IEEE Trans. Rob. **33**(5), 1255–1262 (2017)
7. Tan, N.W., Liu, N.H., Dong, Z., et al.: Robust monocular SLAM in dynamic environments. In: 2013 IEEE International Symposium on Mixed and Augmented Reality (ISMAR). IEEE Computer Society (2013)
8. Zou, D., Tan, P.: CoSLAM: collaborative visual SLAM in dynamic environments. IEEE Trans. Pattern Anal. Mach. Intell. **35**(2), 354–366 (2012)
9. Chen, W., Fang, M., Liu, Y.H., et al.: Monocular semantic SLAM in dynamic street scene based on multiple object tracking. In: IEEE International Conference on Cybernetics and Intelligent Systems (CIS) and IEEE Conference on Robotics, Automation and Mechatronics (RAM), pp. 599–604. IEEE (2017)

10. Zhao, H., Qi, X., Shen, X., Shi, J., Jia, J.: ICNet for real-time semantic segmentation on high-resolution images. In: Ferrari, V., Hebert, M., Sminchisescu, C., Weiss, Y. (eds.) ECCV 2018. LNCS, vol. 11207, pp. 418–434. Springer, Cham (2018). https://doi.org/10.1007/978-3-030-01219-9_25

11. Huang, X., Cheng, X., Geng, Q., et al.: The apolloscape dataset for autonomous driving. In: Proceedings of the IEEE Conference on Computer Vision and Pattern Recognition Workshops, pp. 954–960 (2018)

DeLTR: A Deep Learning Based Approach to Traffic Light Recognition

Yiyang Cai[✉], Chenghua Li, Sujuan Wang, and Jian Cheng

Institute of Automation, Chinese Academy of Sciences, Beijing, China
16231148@buaa.edu.cn

Abstract. Traffic light recognition is crucial for the intelligent driving system. In the application scenarios, the environment of traffic lights is very complicated, due to different weather, distance and distortion conditions. In this paper, we proposed a Deep-learning based Traffic Light Recognition method, named DeTLR, which can achieve a reliable recognition precision and real-time running speed. Our DeTLR system consists of four parts: a skip sampling system, a traffic light detector (TLD), preprocessing, and a traffic light classifier (TLC). Our TLD combines MobileNetV2 and the Single Stage Detector (SSD) framework, and we design a small convolutional neural network for the TLC. To run our system in real-time, we develop a skip-frames technique and make up the delay of the time in the final response system. Our method could run well in complex natural situations safely, which benefits from both the algorithm and the diversity of the training dataset. Our model reaches a precision of 96.7% on green lights and 94.6% on red lights. The comparison to the one-step method indicates that our two-step method is better both in recall and precision, and running time's difference is only about 0.7 ms. Furthermore, the experiments on other datasets (LISA, LaRA and WPI) show a good generalization ability of our model.

Keywords: Traffic light recognition · Deep learning · Convolutional neural network

1 Introduction

The traffic light recognition (TLR) is an important task in advanced driving assistant systems (ADAS) or autonomous driving systems. The real application scenarios of the traffic lights are complicated due to various distances, illumination, and distortion conditions. In addition, real-time recognition is important to ensure the system's reliability. To achieve traffic light recognition, there are two main streams: methods based on traditional features and methods based on deep learning.

Some related work that used the traditional methods of traffic light recognition suffered from two main drawbacks: poor adaptation and heavy time consumption. For instance, in [6], the color segmentation was applied to detect traffic lights.

© Springer Nature Switzerland AG 2019
Y. Zhao et al. (Eds.): ICIG 2019, LNCS 11903, pp. 604–615, 2019.
https://doi.org/10.1007/978-3-030-34113-8_50

However, due to different illumination conditions, the lights' color varied, making its performance not very good. In [8], the model used the morphology feature to detect urban traffic light. However, the complicated background in the urban area made it difficult to extract morphology features. Time consumption is also a problem for traditional methods. For instance, [5] and [6] applied traditional feature extraction such as HOG feature extraction but it was time-consuming, making it difficult to achieve real-time performance. There were also deep-learning methods. For example, in [3], YOLO was applied to detect the traffic light, and in [4], a network named PCANet was introduced. However, these networks' structures were kind of complex, weakening their ability of real-time application. To conclude, while the deep learning method is better than traditional methods to deal with complicated scenarios, the structure of the deep learning model should be simple to achieve real-time performance.

Fig. 1. Pipeline of the proposed deep-learning-based traffic light recognition system (DeTLR). It includes four steps: skip sampling, traffic light detector (TLD), preprocessing, and traffic light classifier (TLC)

Therefore, in this paper, we propose a deep-learning based traffic light recognition (DeTLR) model with four main modules (see Fig. 1): skip sampling system, traffic light detector (TLD), preprocessing, and traffic light classifier (TLC). The TLD module applies MobileNetV2-SSDLite, and TLC is based on a self-designed small convolutional neural network (CNN) structure, named small-Net. Both the MobileNetV2 and SSD are very light, adopting methods such as deep-wise convolution, which ensures the real-time running speed of our TLD module. Plus, our TLC based on smallNet is efficient, taking only 1.6 ms on the RK3399 platform. By training on a large dataset, our DeTLR system can deal with various application scenarios and have a good performance of generalization. Furthermore, to ensure real-time recognition on slower devices, we devise a skip sampling technique, which can make up the time delay in the final decision-making process. To verify the model's performance, we conduct several experiments related to the model's running speed and generalization.

2 Method

2.1 Skip Sampling Module

Boosting the TLR's efficiency is crucial for the ADAS's reliability and real-time recognition. For some systems, due to the restriction of their devices' calculation ability, they require some practical method to make up loss caused by the

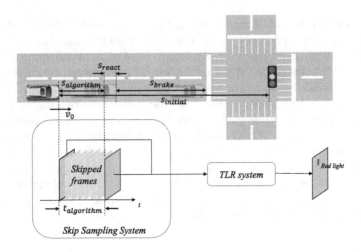

Fig. 2. A demonstration of the skipping sampling system.

hardware. Therefore, we propose an algorithm in the system's input module (see Fig. 2).

Generally speaking, the system's real-time recognition and reliability performance are related to two factors: the vehicle's speed and its distance to the traffic light. For instance, when a red light is detected and classified, the current distance should be longer than the car's braking distance (see Fig. 2). Some variables used in the analysis are shown in Table 1.

Table 1. Variables table of establishing real-time and reliability criterion

Variables	Definition
$s_{initial}$	Distance of the light and car when detectable light is firstly received
s_{brake}	Distance for car to brake safely
t_{react}	Time for the manipulator to react. In ADAS system, it refers to the driver's reacting time, while in automatic driving, it can be ignored
v_0	Initial velocity of the car
$t_{algorithm}$	Time the system take to recognize and classify traffic lights
μ	Dynamic friction factor of the road
g	Gravitational acceleration constant

According to the description, we can establish the criterion of judging the system's real-time recognition and reliability. Once a red light appears, if $s_{initial}$ ensures that the car can brake within the distance of s_{brake}, then the system is reliable and safe. From a practical perspective, we can establish a set of more specific relations among these variables. Let the initial velocity to be v_0, by physical knowledge the relationship between braking distance and velocity is as following:

$$s_{brake} = \frac{v_0^2}{2g\mu} \qquad (1)$$

We can obtain criterion of real-time detection and reliability as follows:

$$s_{initial} > v_0 \times (t_{algorithm} + t_{react}) + \frac{v_0^2}{2g\mu} \qquad (2)$$

In practice, however, the braking system is not locked entirely in the normal driving process. Therefore, we decided to add a modifying coefficient of η in the Eq. (2). Since our system can ensure safety during normal driving, emergency situations are sufficiently under control. Thus, Eq. (2) can be modified into (3):

$$s_{initial} > v_0 \times (t_{algorithm} + t_{react}) + \eta \times \frac{v_0^2}{2g\mu} \qquad (3)$$

Analyze these variables, only $s_{initial}$ and $t_{algorithm}$ are closely related to our TLR system's performance, and the rest are related to external conditions or the vehicle itself. With better detection performance, vehicle can gain further $s_{initial}$ and shorter $t_{algorithm}$. The method of depth estimation in a single frame can be applied to work out $s_{initial}$, and we can use different devices (both CPU and GPU) to measure $t_{algorithm}$.

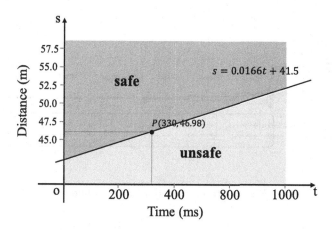

Fig. 3. The relationship between $s_{initial}$ and $t_{algorithm}$, when $s_{initial}$ is above the line, the skip sampling system's real-time performance is ensured

Here is an example of determining the number of frames to omit. Supposing that the velocity of the car is 60 km/h, equal to 16.7 m/s, and the t_{react} is about 0.8 s. Additionally, for the normal road surface, μ is 0.75, the modifying coefficient μ is 1.5. According to the relation above, we can obtain that the quantitative relationship between $s_{initial}$ and $t_{algorithm}$ is:

$$s_{initial} > 0.0166 \times t_{algorithm} + 41.5 \tag{4}$$

$t_{algorithm}$ is in the millisecond and $s_{initial}$ is in the meter, and the relationship is shown in Fig. 3. Suppose that the video is 30 FPS. We can get the result of $s_{initial}$ from $t_{algorithm}$. This result means that in the condition of skip sampling recognition, the detectable frame must be obtained at $s_{initial}$ or further. Otherwise, the vehicle is unsafe, such as the sample point in Fig. 3.

2.2   Traffic Light Detector (TLD)

In our TLD model, the main network derives from MobileNetV2 (see Fig. 4), connected to SSDLite. From stage 3 to stage 8, every stage uses a 1×1 kernel to get complete object detection. The classification part judges the box's category, and *cls* refers to the number of objection's states (in our DeTLR system, it equals to 2, light and no-traffic lights.). The position part determines the object's position. After this process, a non maximum suppression (NMS) is provided to confirm the result of object detection. According to [2], the network is memory-efficient, with a max number of channels/memory 200K, comparing to other networks such as ShuffleNet (600K) and MobileNetV1 (800K). Calculation of MobileNetV2 also indicates that it has fewer parameters (3.4M in [2]), leading to less time of objecting detection.

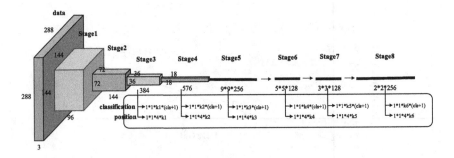

Fig. 4. Structure of our TLD module

The SSDLite is a friendly variant of regular SSD. It is a model based on traditional convolutional neural networks, such as VGG. Regular convolutions in the structure are replaced by separable convolutions (depthwise followed by 1 * 1 projection) in SSDLite prediction layers. SSDLite has the parameter number of 4.3M, much less than traditional object detection structure such as YOLO (50.7M)

The input of TLD is resized into 288×288, and the output is the traffic light's bounding boxes.

2.3   Preprocessing

Shapes and further morphological characteristics of traffic lights can be different in different scenarios. The input of the TLC is quadrate, but the bounding boxes obtained by TLD is often long and narrow. To solve this problem, Therefore, we introduce an intermediate preprocessing method. Initially, we select the maximum value of width and height as criteria of scaling and scale the box with the proportion of criteria to the expected size. Since the shape of boxes is not altered, there will be a gap of blank in the expected size of an input template. To deal with these blank pixels, we choose to fill them with color detect at the edge of boxes (see Fig. 5).

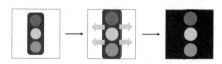

Fig. 5. Our preprocessing method (Color figure online)

After preprocessing, the input of our TLC can be satisfied. In our paper, the preprocessing resizes all bounding boxes into 32×32 crops.

2.4   Traffic Light Classifier (TLC)

As mentioned in the introduction, our TLC is a convolutional neural network named smallNet. Our TLC's structure is shown in Table 2. The smallNet consists of three main layers, making the structure simple. The input is a 32×32 crop, and the output is one of the four traffic light categories, green, red, yellow, and none type.

Table 2. The structure of smallNet

Input	$3 \times 32 \times 32$
Convolution	filters:16, kernel:(3,3), padding:1, ReLU
Max-pooling	kernel:(2,2)
Convolution	filters:64, kernel:(3,3), padding:1, ReLU
Max-pooling	kernel:(2,2)
Convolution	filters:64, kernel:(3,3), padding:1, ReLU
Max-pooling	kernel:(2,2)
Fully connected	units:128, ReLU
Fully connected	units:4, softmax

From Table 2, we can give a theoretical analysis of its efficiency, by calculating its the number of parameters and FLOPs (refer to floating point operations per second). The classifier's total amount of parameters is about 55K. The FLOPs of our TLC model is about 5.2M. The two theoretical results indicate that our TLC model is light and efficient.

3   Experiments

3.1   Datasets

Our DeTLR model is trained and validated on the Berkeley Driving Dataset (BDD). The dataset contains 100,000 videos, and each of them is about 40 s long, sized of 1280 × 720, and 30 fps. The dataset has two advantages. Firstly, the dataset covers different weather conditions, time and regions, meaning that it contains various scenarios with different illumination conditions, distances, and distortion degrees (see Fig. 6). Another advantage is its great capacity of images with precise labels, which makes it suitable to be training set for a model based on deep learning methods.

Table 3. Information of datasets

Dataset	Sequence	Image numbers	Image size	Labels
BDD	100,000	120 million	1280 × 960	BB positions[a] green/red/yellow/none
WPI	28[b]	10,000	1980 × 1080	BB positions green/red/yellow
LaRA	1	11,000	640 × 480	BB positions green/red/yellow
LISA	4[c]	16,000	1280 × 960	BB positions green/red/yellow

[a]Bounding boxes.
[b]11 sequences for training, and 17 sequences for testing.
[c]2 sequences for daytime, and 2 sequences for night-time.

Besides the BDD dataset, other datasets are also used in this paper, including WPI [4], LaRA [5], and LISA [10,11]. From their comparison (see Table 3), the BDD's advantages mentioned above are reasonable, and different scenarios and great capacity make the BDD suitable for training a deep-learning model.

3.2   Experiment Setup

In the experiment, we train our model on NVIDIA's GPUs and evaluate the running time on TITAN Black GPU and RK3399 platforms. To gain the best performance, our TLD and TLC modules use a different setup.

Fig. 6. Frames of different scenarios in the BDD dataset.

In the process of TLD training, the input is normalized into 288×288. We train our TLD on two GPUs, the batch size of each GPU is 16. The learning rate is initialized to 0.0001, and the SGD learning algorithm is based on the multistep method, and the weight decay is 0.00001.

In the process of TLC training, the input is normalized into 32×32 crops. We train the model with a batch size of 16. Our learning algorithm is based on Adam method, with the learning parameter initialized to 0.01 and the weight decay set to 0.9. The iteration number is 15. The testing batch size is also 16.

Due to the precise ground truth provided by the BDD dataset, we initially extract the boxes from original images to train our TLC. We have extracted more than 100,000 boxes with the label of bounding boxes and their categories (see Table 4). The distribution of each type is not balanced, with a relatively more example of green light and red light, and fewer yellow light. However, from the samples shown in Fig. 7, the yellow lights are similar to red ones. Classifying yellow to red ones can actually increase the DeTLR's reliability. Furthermore, in reality, the chance of meeting yellow lights is much lower than the green and red lights. Therefore, the dataset's unbalanced distribution can have a little negative effect.

Table 4. Distribution of training and testing sets

	Green	Red	Yellow	None	Total
Training set	53,305	31,917	1,994	35,251	120,239
Testing set	13,026	7,979	498	8,813	30,052
Total	66,331	39,896	2,492	44,064	150,291

3.3 TLC Performance

Firstly, we test the performance of TLC. Our TLC initially works to ground truth boxes extracted from the BDD dataset. We collect the results of recall, precision as well as running time (see Table 5). The running time of TLC is about 0.7 ms on Nvidia's Titan Black GPU.

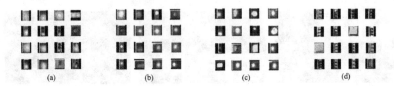

Fig. 7. Traffic light samples: (a) green, (b) red, (c) yellow, (d) none (Color figure online)

Table 5. Our TLC's performance

Type	Recall (%)					Precision (%)				
	Green	Red	Yellow	None	Total	Green	Red	Yellow	None	Total
Performance	96.6	96.5	50.8	93.7	95.3	96.8	95.1	45.9	95.8	95.2

The result shows that green, red, and none type of traffic lights' recognition reaches a high recall and precision rate. Although the performance on yellow lights is not really good, our TLC result shows that about 73% of false classification is a red type. Since classifying a yellow light into red one does no harm for practical driving, this minor error can be ignored.

3.4 Comparison to the One-Step Detection Framework

In this experiment, we compare our DeTLR model (two-step) to a one-step variant, which combines the detection and classification steps into one single step. When using our DeTLR model, the parameter cls in our TLD model remains the value 2 (judge if the box is the traffic light or not). When using one-step traffic light detection, it not only judges the box is the traffic light or not, but also provides its color category, so the parameter cls is modified to the value 5. Both two methods are tested on Nvidia's Titan Black GPU (see Table 6).

We also compare two methods' mean average precision (MAP), which is an important criterion for the performance. The one-step method's MAP is 26.27%, while the two-step's method gains 33.84%. This also indicates that when our TLD has better performance than the one-step method.

Table 6. The comparison of DeTLR (two-step) to the one-step method

	Recall (%)					Precision (%)				
	Green	Red	Yellow	None	Total	Green	Red	Yellow	None	Total
DeTLR	96.3	**96.8**	**49.6**	**92.2**	**94.8**	**96.7**	**94.6**	**44.8**	95.1	**94.1**
One-step	**96.4**	96.5	47.5	92.1	94.3	96.2	93.9	44.6	**95.2**	93.7

The one-step model is 100 ms on average, and the two-step method is 100 ms (TLD) plus 0.7 ms (TLC). The result in the table shows that the average performance of our two-step DeTLR model is better than the one-step model, and the average running time's difference is small enough to be ignored. This is because the identification's precision of two categories is much easier than five categories, and our TLC model can be trained to a high precision independently. In conclusion, our DeTLR model can have a better performance than the one-step model. Figure 8 shows some examples of our model's result.

Fig. 8. Our DeLTR's achievement of TLR in the BDD dataset.

3.5 Generalization

Generalization is an important property of the traffic light recognition model because scenarios, in reality, are various. To verify this property, we fine-tune the model on different datasets and analyze its performance. These datasets include WPI, LaRA, and LISA. Firstly, we fine-tune our model on the WPI dataset and obtain the performance on every sequence (see Fig. 9).

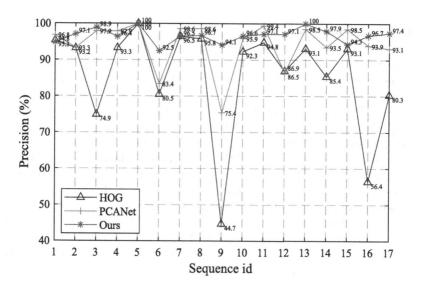

Fig. 9. Our DeTLR model's generalization on WPI dataset, HOG and PCANet's result can refer to [4]

Our DeTLR model has a better average performance than both HOG and PCANet. Our performance is more stable and remains at a relatively high level. The average precision of our model is 96.7%, and PCANet's precision is 93.1%, and the HOG feature is 80.5%.

Table 7. Our DeTLR model's generalization on the LaRA and LISA dataset.

Dataset	Precision of different methods (%)				
LaRA	Algorithm[a]	SVM	LDA	KNN	Our DeTLR
	Performance	92.8	89.7	90.3	94.9
LISA	Algorithm[b]	RGB.Seg SVM	Multilayer perceptron	Naive Bayes	Our DeTLR
	Performance	84.0	83.0	73.0	94.2

[a]SVM, KNN, LDA are in the reference [5]
[b]RGB-Seg.+SVM, Multilayer perceptron are in the reference [6]

We then apply the similar method to LaRA and LISA datasets (see Table 7). As the Table 3 shows, the LISA dataset is separated by the condition of illumination (day and night), and the result of this test verifies that our model has reliable TLR performance in different illumination conditions. To conclude our DeTLR model has a stable performance on different datasets, indicating our model's generalization performance is good.

4   Conclusion

In this paper, we propose a deep-learning based traffic light recognition (DeTLR) model. The model can achieve reliable recognition and real-time running speed. The model consists of three main modules: a skip sampling system, a traffic light detector (TLD), and a traffic light classifier (TLC). We use MoblieNetV2 and the Single Stage Detector (SSD) framework to construct the TLD, and design a small convolutional neural network for the TLC. The skip sampling system is developed to make up the delay of the time in the response system. We train our models on the BDD dataset, which includes plenty of real scenarios. We get a precision of 96.7% for green lights and 94.6% on red lights. Our TLD and TLC module are separate, and make our model a two-step model. A comparison of the one-step model and two-step model shows that the two-step model has better performance than the one-step model, because it has better precision. The experiments on other datasets for traffic light recognition also shows that our model has a good generalization performance.

References

1. Yu, F., et al.: BDD100K: a diverse driving video database with scalable annotation tooling. arXiv (2018)
2. Sandler, M., Howard, A., Zhu, M., Zhmoginov, A., Chen, L.: MobileNetV2: inverted residual and linear bottlenecks. In: IEEE/CVF Conference on Computer Vision and Pattern Recognition (CVPR), pp. 4510–4520. IEEE (2017)
3. Behrendt, K., Novak, L., Botros, R.: A deep learning approach to traffic lights: detection, tracking and classification. In: IEEE International Conference on Robotics and Automation (ICRA), pp. 1370–1377. IEEE (2017)
4. Chen, Z., Huang, X.: Accurate. In: IEEE Intelligent Transportation Systems Magazine, pp. 28–42. IEEE (2016)
5. Michael, M., Schlipsing, M.: Extending traffic light recognition: efficient classification of phase and pictogram. In: IEEE International Joint Conference on Neural Network (IJCNN), pp. 1–8. IEEE (2015)
6. Binangkit, J.L., Widyantoro, D.H.: Increasing accuracy of traffic light color detection and recognition using machine learning. In: IEEE International Conference on Telecommunication Systems Services and Applications (TSSA), pp. 1–5. IEEE (2016)
7. Haltakov, V., Mayr, J., Unger, C., Ilic, S.: Semantic segmentation based traffic light detection at day and at night. In: Gall, J., Gehler, P., Leibe, B. (eds.) GCPR 2015. LNCS, vol. 9358, pp. 446–457. Springer, Cham (2015). https://doi.org/10.1007/978-3-319-24947-6_37
8. Charette, R., Nashashibi, F.: Real time visual traffic lights recognition based on spot light detection and adaptive traffic lights templates. In: IEEE Intelligent Vehicles Symposium, pp. 358–363. IEEE (2009)
9. Cai, Z., Li, Y., Gu, M.: Real-time recognition system of traffic light in urban environment. In: IEEE Symposium on Computational Intelligence for Security and Defence Applications, pp. 1–6. IEEE (2012)
10. Sooksatra, S., Kondo, T.: Red traffic light detection using fast radial symmetry transform. In: IEEE International Conference on Electrical Engineering/Electronics, Computer, Telecommunications and Information Technology (ECTI-CON), pp. 1–6. IEEE (2014)
11. Jensen, M.B., Philipsen, M.P., Møgelmose, A., Moeslund, T.B. Trivedi, T.M.: Red traffic light detection using fast radial symmetry transform. In: IEEE Transactions on Intelligent Transportation Systems, pp. 1800–1815. IEEE (2016)
12. Philipsen, M.P., Jensen, M.B., Møgelmose, A., Moeslund, T.B., Trivedi, T.M.: Traffic light detection: a learning algorithm and evaluations on challenging dataset. In: IEEE International Conference on Intelligent Transportation Systems, pp. 2341–2345. IEEE (2015)
13. Fairfield, N., Urmson, C.: Traffic light mapping and detection. In: IEEE International Conference on Robotics and Automation (ICRA), pp. 5421–5426. IEEE (2011)

Learning Toward Visual Recognition in the Wild

Second-Order Pooling Deep Hashing for Image Retrieval

Yongchao Yang[1], Jingdong Cheng[1], Chao Che[1], Jianxin Zhang[1(✉)], and Lin Shan[2(✉)]

[1] Key Lab of Advanced Design and Intelligent Computing
(Ministry of Education), Dalian University, Dalian, China
jxzhang0411@163.com
[2] School of Economic and Management, Dalian University of Science
and Technology, Dalian, China
linshan_dl@163.com

Abstract. Recently, due to advantages of high computational efficiency, small storage cost as well as high discriminability, deep hash methods have been widely studied in a number of large-scale visual applications. To achieve more compact hash representation, we propose a novel supervised deep hash method for image retrieval task in this work, which successfully embeds second-order pooling operation into existing deep hash model in an end-to-end manner, namely second-order pooling deep hashing (SoPDH). Our SoPDH mainly consists of four parts, i.e., a basic deep feature extraction module, a second-order pooling operation based on matrix decomposition, a hash encoding module and a semantic classification layer. The embedded second-order pooling operation not only guarantees the local prominence of deep features, but also introduces the global statistic feature information, which could lead to a more robust hash coding result. We extensively evaluate the proposed SoPDH on two commonly-used datasets, and experimental results demonstrate its effectiveness for image retrieval task.

Keywords: SoPDH · Deep hashing · Second-order pooling · Image retrieval

1 Introduction

Approximate Nearest Neighbor (ANN) search algorithms provide a crucial and practical role in large-scale image retrieval. Among them, hashing methods, which effectively reduce storage space and time requirements, become one of the most important image retrieval techniques, attracting more and more attention in recent years. Current hashing methods mainly can be divided into two categories, i.e., unsupervised hashing and supervised hashing. The unsupervised hashing does not employ label information to learn the hash coding. Representative unsupervised hashing methods include Iterative Quantization (ITQ) [1] and

© Springer Nature Switzerland AG 2019
Y. Zhao et al. (Eds.): ICIG 2019, LNCS 11903, pp. 619–629, 2019.
https://doi.org/10.1007/978-3-030-34113-8_51

Spectral Hashing [2]. In contrast, supervised hashing methods aim to fully consider the label information of given samples during the learning process of hash encoding, resulting in superior retrieval accuracy compared with unsupervised. Generally, supervised information can be embedded in three different forms: point-wise labels [3], pair-wise labels [4] and ranking labels [5]. Additionally, due to the brilliant success of deep networks in a variety of computer vision tasks [9,11,13], hashing based on deep learning has also become the mainstream of hash algorithms. Hashing based on deep network originates from the convolutional neural network hash (CNNH) learning method proposed by Xia et al [6]. After that, some representative deep hashing research works, such as DNNH [7], DLBHC [8] and HashGAN [9], are gradually put forward. Most of the existing deep hashing methods utilize classical deep model of VGG [21] based on convolution and pooling operations, in which the extracted local details of input images can be effectively applied to hash learning.

The design of deep neural network models focuses on versatility and scalability, and shallow computer vision architectures are usually designed with global computing and visual structure modeling. Recently, Ionescu et al. combined the deep network with the shallow visual architecture and proposed a back propagation algorithm based on matrix decomposition [12], which achieved significant results in image classification. Then, more and more research results illuminate that matrix decomposition can well preserve global information which can provide more discriminant feature representation result [18–20]. Inspired by the binary learning method of binary hash coding and the back propagation algorithm of matrix decomposition, it will be an interesting work that whether matrix decomposition in deep hash learning could bring a more compact encoding result for image retrieval. Therefore, in this work, we try to embed global pooling operator into existing deep hash model based on matrix decomposition, and then a novel deep hash method called second-order pooling deep hashing (SoPDH) is proposed. The embedded global pooling operation not only guarantees the local presentation of deep features, but also introduces global statistic information, which results in a more compact hash coding. We evaluate the proposed SoPDH on two commonly-used benchmarks, and experimental results also illuminate that SoPDH is effective for image retrieval task.

The reminder of this work is organized as follows. Section 2 describes the details of second-order pooling deep hashing method. Experimental evaluation and results are givens in Sect. 3. Finally, conclusions are drawn in Sect. 4.

2   Methods

2.1   Network Architecture

The proposed second-order pooling deep hashing (SoPDH) mainly consists of four parts, a basic convolutional network to extract the first-order deep feature, a second-order pooling operation based on matrix singular value decomposition to explore global statistics information, a hash encoding module and a classification layer to preserve image semantic supervision information. Figure 1 illustrates the general architecture of the proposed SoPDH method.

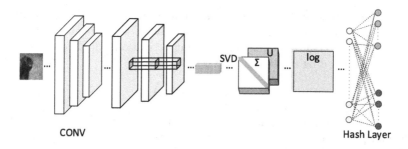

Fig. 1. Architecture of the second-order pooling deep hashing

In this work, CNN-F [16] network is adopted as the basic convolutional network to extract the first-order deep feature, and it can be replaced by other more powerful deep networks such as VGG-VD16 [16] and ResNet [17]. The basic part of CNN-F is composed of five convolutional layers, and the size of input image is 224×224. As the original image is propagated layer by layer, deeper convolutional features are obtained to replace the previous shallow features. Assume that the output of the final convolutional layer is recorded by

$$X = \{x_i | x_i = \phi(I_i; \theta)\}_{i=1}^{N} \tag{1}$$

where I_i indicates the i-th image, ϕ represents the basic network structure, and θ is the parameters of the network. x_i represents the first-order feature statistics of the i-th image, and N is the number of images.

After acquiring above first-order convolutional features, second-order pooling operation is added to achieve more robust deep feature representation. The second-order pooling is realized by using the matrix singular value decomposition as given in reference [12], and it vigorously assigns local feature descriptors to global high-order statistics. This second-order process mainly includes two steps. Firstly, the x_i can be rewritten as

$$x_i = U\Sigma V^T \tag{2}$$

where U, V are the positive definite matrices, i.e., $U^T U = I$, $V^T V = I$, and Σ represents diagonal matrix. Then, second-order pooling presentation m_i can be computed by

$$m_i = \log(x_i^T x_i + \varepsilon I) = \log(V\Sigma^T \Sigma V^T + \varepsilon I) \tag{3}$$

In Eq. (3), parameter ε is a small real value whose role is to avoid the singular value problem because of the non-full rank covariance matrix. εI represents the operation of normalization.

Because of that Matrix function of the diagonalizable matrix $A = U\Sigma U^T$ can be represented as $f(A) = Uf(\Sigma)U^T$. Similarly, Eq. (3) can be expressed as:

$$m_i = V\log(\Sigma^T \Sigma + \varepsilon I)V^T \tag{4}$$

The hash coding module adds a hash hidden layer after the global matrix operation layer, maps to the specified encoding bit K, and then cooperates with the activation function to implement encoding activation [13]. The specific function of the hash coding module is shown in Eq. (5):

$$h_i = \sigma(W_h^T m_i + v_i) \tag{5}$$

where $\sigma(x) = \frac{1}{1+e^{-x}}$ is the sigmoid activation function, W_h, v_h represent the weight and parameters of the hash layer, respectively.

Consequently, the hash code from hash encoding module is applied as the input of classification unit. Similar to the deep learning method of binary hash coding, this unit can generate predicted image class information as

$$\tilde{y}_i = W_f^T h_i + v_f \tag{6}$$

where W_f, v_f respectively represent the weights and parameters of the classification module.

2.2   Loss Function and Optimization

The classification error is determined by measuring the difference between the predicted value and the actual label by cross entropy. This loss function can be expressed in detail as follows:

$$L = -\frac{1}{N} \sum_{i=1}^{N} \sum_{k=1}^{K} y_{ik} \log \tilde{y}_{ik} \tag{7}$$

where $y_{ik} = 1$ indicates that the i-th image belongs to the k-th class. $\tilde{y}_{ik}$ indicates that the i-th image is predicted to be the k-th value, and K represents the total number of categories of the image.

We use the stochastic gradient descent method (SGD) combined with the chain rule to solve the partial derivatives for each parameter. The gradient between the loss function and the coding feature approximating hash code can be written as:

$$\frac{\partial L_i}{\partial h_i} = \sum_{k=1}^{K} \frac{\partial L}{\partial \tilde{y}_{ik}} \cdot \frac{\partial \tilde{y}_{ik}}{\partial h_i} = -\sum_{k=1}^{K} \frac{y_{ik}}{\tilde{y}_{ik}} \cdot \frac{\partial \tilde{y}_{ik}}{\partial h_i} \tag{8}$$

On the basis of the nonlinear layer gradients described in [12], gradient from the hash code reverse back to higher-order pooling characteristics associated with the middle of the complex variables (V, Σ), specifically expressed as:

$$\begin{cases} \frac{\partial h_i}{\partial V} = 2(\frac{\partial h_i}{\partial m_i})_{sym} V \log\left(\Sigma^T \Sigma + \varepsilon I\right) \\[4mm] \frac{\partial h_i}{\partial \Sigma} = 2\Sigma(\Sigma^T \Sigma + \varepsilon I)^{-1} V^T \left(\frac{\partial h_i}{\partial m_i}\right)_{sym} V \end{cases} \tag{9}$$

where A_{sym} can be expressed by $A_{sym} = \frac{1}{2}\left(A^T + A\right)$.

According to the principle of backpropagation of SVD proposed in [12], the back propagation of concrete elaboration update can take advantage of the global matrix operation in forward propagation, which can ensure the structural integrity and numerical stability during the training. The back propagation to the hash code x_i is as follows:

$$\frac{\partial h_i}{\partial x_i} = U \left\{ 2\Sigma \left(K^T \circ \left(V^T \frac{\partial h_i}{\partial V} \right) \right)_{sym} + \left(\frac{\partial h_i}{\partial \Sigma} \right)_{diag} \right\} V^T \tag{10}$$

where A_{diag} represents a diagonal matrix, $\circ$ indicates Kronecker product, and $K_{ij} = \begin{cases} \frac{1}{\delta_i^2 - \delta_j^2}, i \neq j \\ 0, i = j \end{cases}$ δ_i, δ_j denotes the singular value.

Finally, the gradient gradually propagates back to the initial layer according to the propagation of BP algorithm. The parameters of our deep hashing model with second-order pooling operation can be updated iteratively in an end-to-end manner, taking the reduction of quantization error as a criterion.

3 Experiments and Results

This section aims to evaluate the proposed second-order pooling deep hashing (SoPDH) for image retrieval task, which mainly consists of four sub-sections, i.e., datasets and settings, evaluation metrics, experimental results on CIFAR-10 dataset and experimental results on MINIST dataset. All experiments are performed on a PC with 3.30 GHz CPU, 64 GB RAM and NVIDIA GTX 1080 GPU using MATLAB R2018a.

3.1 Datasets and Settings

CIFAR-10 and MINIST datasets are utilized to evaluate the given SoPDH method. The CIFAR-10 includes 10 classes images, and each class consists of 6,000 colored images with the size of 32×32 pixels. This dataset supplies 50,000 training images and 10,000 mutually exclusive test images. MNIST dataset is composed of approximately 70,000 grayscale images, in which contains 60,000 training images and 10,000 test images, respectively. All of the images in this dataset are 0 to 9 handwritten digits with the size of 28×28 pixels. In this work, we employ the same experimental protocol as [7] to provide a fair comparison. According this protocol, 5000 training images are averagely selected from 10 classes for training, and 1000 test images are averagely chosen as the test samples.

3.2   Evaluation Metrics

Mean average precision (mAP) and P@K evaluation metrics are adopted to measure the performance of SoPDH. Precision@K: This metric corresponds to the percentage of relevant images among the top K retrieved images:

$$P@K = \frac{\#\{relevant\ images\ in\ top\ K\ result\}}{K} \tag{11}$$

where $\#\{\cdot\}$ represents set cardinality and K denotes the number of returning images. Based on the Hamming distances between test set and database, mAP metric ranks all the test images and then calculate the area below the recall-precision curve. The mAP metric can be computed as:

$$AP = \frac{\Sigma_k P@K \times 1\{image\ k\ is\ relevant\}}{\#\{retreived\ relevant\ image\}} \tag{12}$$

$$mAP = \frac{1}{q} \sum\nolimits_i AP_i \tag{13}$$

where $1\{\cdot\} \in 0, 1$ is an indicator function and q is the number of query samples.

3.3   Experimental Results on CIFAR-10 Dataset

Table 1 reports compared mAP results with various hash code bits on CIFAR-10 dataset. We compare SoPDH with typical deep hashing methods of CNNH [6], DNNH [7] and DLBHC [8]. Additionally, results of several traditional hashing methods in [7], such as ITQ, MLH and CCA-ITQ, are also included. As shown in Table 1, our SoPDH achieves the optimal retrieval performance among these methods, and it gains the best mAP accuracy of 0.752 at 48-bit code. Moreover, SoPDH outperforms three traditional hashing methods by a large margin. Compared with its baseline of DLBHC, though SoPDH obtains the similar performance at 12-bit code, it obtains 2.4%, 4.2% and 4.5% performance improvement over DLBHC at code length of 24-bit, 32-bit and 48-bit, respectively. The compared mAP results illuminate that embedding second-order pooling operation into deep hashing is effective for image retrieval.

Then, P@K results achieved by SoPDH with four different code bits on CIFAR-10 dataset are given in Fig. 2. Here, we only report the results with K value ranging from 100 to 1000. As shown in Fig. 2, the higher precision can be achieved with the increasing of top retrieved image number and code bits. Note that the overall precision may decrease when the top retrieved image number is larger than 1000. To compare SoPDH with other hashing methods, we further show the compared P@K results at code length of 48-bit on CIFAR-10 dataset in Fig. 3. As shown in Fig. 3, our SoPDH achieves the optimal retrieval precision compared with other hashing methods. when K value is larger than 400, SoPDH can gain the precision over 0.8, and better precision can be obtained

Table 1. Compared mAP results on CIFAR-10 dataset

Methods	12-bit	24-bit	32-bit	48-bit
ITQ [1]	0.162	0.169	0.172	0.175
MLH [10]	0.182	0.195	0.207	0.211
CCA-ITQ [15]	0.264	0.282	0.288	0.295
CNNH [6]	0.439	0.511	0.509	0.522
DNNH [7]	0.552	0.566	0.558	0.581
DLBHC [8]	0.674	0.704	0.701	0.707
SoPDH (Ours)	**0.673**	**0.728**	**0.743**	**0.752**

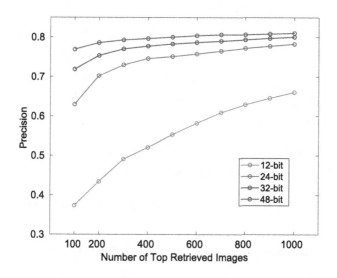

Fig. 2. P@K results of SoPDH on CIFAR-10 dataset

with increasing K value. In contrast, retrieval accuracy decrease with the larger K value for three non-deep hashing methods and DLBHC. Specially, SoPDH gains almost 10% accuracy improvement over its baseline (DLBHC) under the max K value of 1000. Therefore, compared P@K results well demonstrate the effectiveness of the proposed SoPDH method.

3.4   Experimental Results on MNIST Dataset

Table 2 lists the compared mAP results on the MNIST dataset. Consistent with the CIFAR-10 dataset, experimental results of non-deep hash methods are from the literature [7]. Meanwhile, our experimental protocol is the same with [7] to give a fair comparison. As can be seen from Table 2, SoPDH gains 1.1% accuracy improvement over its baseline DLBHC at the code length of 12-bit. For the remaining 24-bit, 32-bit and 48-bit hashing codes, SoPDH outperforms DLBHC with retrieval accuracy of 3.5%, 3.5%, and 3.7%, respectively. Therefore, compared to DLBHC, our SoPDH achieves average mAP performance improvement of 2.95% compared to DLBHC. Moreover, SoPDH is significantly superior to other compared hash methods. Therefore, the compared results demonstrate that our SoPDH is effective on the MNIST dataset.

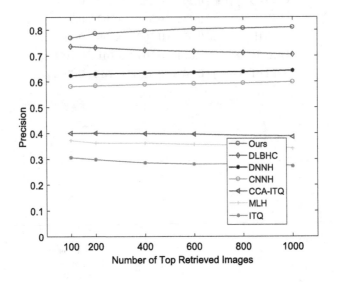

Fig. 3. Compared K-sample accuracy curves on CIFAR-10 dataset (48-bit)

Table 2. Compared mAP results on MNIST dataset

Methods	12-bit	24-bit	32-bit	48-bit
ITQ [1]	0.388	0.436	0.422	0.429
MLH [10]	0.472	0.666	0.652	0.654
CCA-ITQ [15]	0.659	0.694	0.714	0.726
CNNH [6]	0.957	0.963	0.956	0.960
DLBHC [8]	0.932	0.931	0.937	0.935
Ours	**0.943**	**0.966**	**0.972**	**0.972**

To compare SoPDH with other hashing methods, we further show compared P@K results of several typical hashing methods at code length of 48-bit in Fig. 4. Our SoPDH has significantly P@K accuracy improvement over each compared method. By comparing the P@K precision curves on the MNIST dataset, we can further demonstrate that our proposed second-order pooling deep hashing model is effective in deep hash learning.

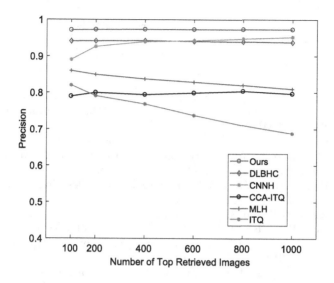

Fig. 4. Compared K-sample accuracy curves on MNIST dataset (48-bit)

4   Conclusions

In this work, we propose a novel second-order pooling deep hashing, i.e., SoPDH, for image retrieval. SoPDH successfully embeds the second-order global statistic information into existing deep hashing model by employing singular value decomposition of local feature matrix in an end-to-end manner, which leads to a more compact hashing code. Experiment results on two benchmarks also show that SoPDH is significantly superior to its baseline, which illuminates its effectiveness for image retrieval task. In the future, we will perform SoPDH on some large-scale image datasets or for other visual tasks to make a further evaluation. Additionally, our feature work will try to mine more powerful high-level statistics for deep hashing network.

Acknowledgements. This work is supported by the National Natural Science Foundation of China (Nos. 61972062, 61603066), the National Key R&D Program of China (No. 2018YFC0910506), the Liaoning Provincial Natural Science Foundation (No. 2019-MS-011) and the Liaoning BaiQianWan Talents Program.

References

1. Gong, Y., Lazebnik, S., Gordo, A., et al.: Iterative quantization: a Procrustean approach to learning binary codes. In: IEEE Conference on Computer Vision and Pattern Recognition (CVPR), pp. 817–824 (2011)
2. Weiss, Y., Torralba, A., Fergus, R.: Spectral hashing. In: Advances in Neural Information Processing Systems (NIPS), pp. 1753–1760 (2009)

3. Shen, F., Shen, C., Liu, W., et al.: Supervised discrete hashing. In: IEEE Conference on Computer Vision and Pattern Recognition (CVPR), pp. 37–45 (2015)

4. Wang, J., Kumar, S., Chang, S.F.: Sequential projection learning for hashing with compact codes. In: International Conference on Machine Learning (ICML), pp. 1127–1134 (2010)

5. Wang, J., Wang, J., Yu, N., et al.: Order preserving hashing for approximate nearest neighbor search. In: Proceedings of the 21st ACM International Conference on Multimedia (ACM MM), pp. 133–142 (2013)

6. Xia, R., Pan, Y., Lai, H., et al.: Supervised hashing for image retrieval via image representation learning. In: Twenty-Eighth AAAI Conference on Artificial Intelligence (AAAI), pp. 2156–2162 (2014)

7. Lai, H., Pan, Y., Liu, Y., et al.: Simultaneous feature learning and hash coding with deep neural networks. In: IEEE Conference on Computer Vision and Pattern Recognition (CVPR), pp. 3270–3278 (2015)

8. Lin, K., Yang, H.F., Hsiao, J.H., et al.: Deep learning of binary hash codes for fast image retrieval. In: IEEE Conference on Computer Vision and Pattern Recognition Workshops (CVPRW), pp. 27–35 (2015)

9. Cao, Y., Liu, B., Long, M., et al.: HashGAN: deep learning to hash with pair conditional Wasserstein GAN. In: IEEE Conference on Computer Vision and Pattern Recognition (CVPR), pp. 1287–1296 (2018)

10. Norouzi, M., Fleet, D.J.: Minimal loss hashing for compact binary codes. In: International Conference on Machine Learning (ICML), pp. 353–360 (2011)

11. Li, C., Deng, C., Li, N., et al.: Self-supervised adversarial hashing networks for cross-modal retrieval. In: IEEE Conference on Computer Vision and Pattern Recognition (CVPR), pp. 4242–4251 (2018)

12. Ionescu, C., Vantzos, O., Sminchisescu, C.: Matrix backpropagation for deep networks with structured layers. In: IEEE International Conference on Computer Vision (CVPR), pp. 2965–2973 (2015)

13. Yang, H.F., Lin, K., Chen, C.S.: Supervised learning of semantics-preserving hash via deep convolutional neural networks. IEEE Trans. Pattern Anal. Mach. Intell. **40**(2), 437–451 (2018)

14. Krizhevsky, A., Sutskever, I., Hinton, G.E.: ImageNet classification with deep convolutional neural networks. In: Advances in Neural Information Processing Systems (NIPS), pp. 1097–1105 (2012)

15. Gong, Y., Lazebnik, S., Gordo, A., et al.: Iterative quantization: a procrustean approach to learning binary codes for large-scale image retrieval. IEEE Trans. Pattern Anal. Mach. Intell. **35**(12), 2916–2929 (2013)

16. Chatfield, K., Simonyan, K., Vedaldi, A., Zisserman, A.: Return of the devil in the details: delving deep into convolutional nets. In: Proceedings of the British Machine Vision Conference (BMVC) (2014)

17. He, K.M., Zhang, X.Y., Ren, Q.S., Sun, J.: Deep residual learning for image recognition. In: IEEE Conference on Computer Vision and Pattern Recognition (CVPR), pp. 770–778 (2016)

18. Valmadre, J., Bertinetto, L., Henriques, J., et al.: End-to-end representation learning for correlation filter based tracking. In: Proceedings of the IEEE Conference on Computer Vision and Pattern Recognition (CVPR), pp. 2805–2813 (2017)

19. Arnab, A., Jayasumana, S., Zheng, S., Torr, P.H.S.: Higher order conditional random fields in deep neural networks. In: Leibe, B., Matas, J., Sebe, N., Welling, M. (eds.) ECCV 2016. LNCS, vol. 9906, pp. 524–540. Springer, Cham (2016). https://doi.org/10.1007/978-3-319-46475-6_33

20. Jampani, V., Kiefel, M., Gehler, P.V.: Learning sparse high dimensional filters: image filtering, dense CRFs and bilateral neural networks. In: Proceedings of the IEEE Conference on Computer Vision and Pattern Recognition (CVPR), pp. 4452–4461 (2016)

21. Simonyan, K., Zisserman, A.: Very deep convolutional networks for large-scale image recognition. arXiv preprint arXiv:1409.1556 (2014)

Scene Recognition with Comprehensive Regions Graph Modeling

Haitao Zeng[1,2(✉)] and Gongwei Chen[2]

[1] China University of Mining and Technology, Beijing 100083, China
[2] Key Laboratory of Intelligent Information Processing, Institute of Computing Technology, Chinese Academy of Sciences, Beijing 100190, China
{haitao.zeng,gongwei.chen}@vipl.ict.ac.cn

Abstract. Learning the regional contents of scenes comprehensively is key to scene recognition. Due to semantic diversity and spatial complexity in scene images, modeling based on these regional contents is challenging. The current works mainly focus on some small and partial regions of the scene, while ignoring the majority region of the scene. In contrast, we propose the Semantic Regional Graph modeling framework for the comprehensive selection of discriminative semantic regions in scenes. To explore the relations of these regions, we propose to model these regions in geometric aspect based on the graph model, and generate the discriminative representations for scene recognition. Experimental results demonstrate the effectiveness of our method, which achieves state-of-the-art performances on MIT67 and SUN397 datasets.

Keywords: Scene recognition · Graph Neural Network

1 Introduction

The goal of scene recognition is to predict scene labels for images. Scene recognition is a challenging task of computer vision since the scene images are composed of various regional contents (e.g. foreground and background) with highly flexible spatial layouts. This characteristic determines that extracting the discriminative information of scenes requires the comprehensively learning of regional contents. Therefore, how to model these regional contents to obtain consistent visual representations is becoming the main challenge in the filed of scene recognition.

Some earlier methods [7,27,30] propose to model the local regional representations with BOW (Bag of Words) encoding for scene recognition. With the developments of Convolution Neural Networks (CNNs) [1,9,14], some scene recognition methods [11,24,26,32,34,37] propose to learn regional features with the CNN models. These methods can be divided into two branches: some methods [24,26,32] propose to extract CNN features on local patches, which are annotated with the image-level label, and trained in weak supervision, leading to the ambiguity and noise in training. While, some other methods [34,37] attempt to generate region proposal to locate the object regions for feature extraction,

© Springer Nature Switzerland AG 2019
Y. Zhao et al. (Eds.): ICIG 2019, LNCS 11903, pp. 630–641, 2019.
https://doi.org/10.1007/978-3-030-34113-8_52

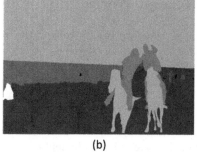

(a)   (b)

Fig. 1. (a) An example image, (b) its annotations in COCO-Stuff dataset

which are then fed to the followed networks for classification. However, considering the characteristics of scene image, the object based methods still have the limitation, since the object regions can only cover the relatively small and partial area of the scene, while the majority area of the scene is ignored, which may decrease the performance of scene recognition. In contrast, our motivation is to obtain more comprehensive information in the scenes.

Obtaining more comprehensive information in the scenes requires that the extracted region information have diversity. In addition to objects, the scenes usually consist of a much larger area of "stuff" (amorphous background regions, e.g. *sea, sand,* and *sky*), which also contain discrimination to different scenes. In our work, we propose to obtain discriminative regional information based on the stuff, since stuff covers a wider area, and it is essential to determine the scene category (e.g. as shown in Fig. 1 *sky, sand* and *sea* are the imperative elements in the beach category). Moreover, the object based works [34,37] also inspire us that the object regions can also provide discriminative information. Therefore, in our work, we take both object and stuff into account as the discriminative semantic regions, and learn the relation of these semantic regions to generate discriminative representations.

In this paper, we propose a semantic regional graph modeling (SRG) framework for scene recognition. To perform scene recognition, we first feed an image into the pre-trained semantic segmentation network (e.g. DeeplabV2 [4] pre-trained on COCO-Stuff [3]) to generate the label map that has the same resolution as the input image. To obtain the information of scenes comprehensively, we implement three region selection methods on the label map to select the discriminative semantic regions, including the region of stuff and object. We extract these regional representations based on a pre-trained CNN through *RoIAlign* [13]. These regional features are concatenated together as the node representations of graph convolution network [15] (GCN). And we propose to learn the relations between these regions on the geometric aspects through GCN, which is used to optimize the corresponding node representations. Finally, we feed these optimized representations into classifier to predict scene labels. We conduct several experiments on MIT67 [20] and SUN397 [36], the experimental results illustrate the effectiveness of the proposed method.

2   Related Works

In this section, we briefly review the works that related to our topic in several aspects. The differences and connections of these works with ours are also being argued.

2.1   Scene Recognition

Scene recognition is an essential domain in computer vision. In some early works [23,28], the basic visual elements (e.g. color, shape, and texture) play an important role in learning the global features of images. However, since scenes are relatively abstract, scene images are generally composed of multiple semantic regions. Thus, some works [7,8,12,25,27,30] propose to perform scene recognition based on local region features. Lazebnik et al. [27] present the Spatial Pyramid Matching (SPM) which divides the image into several local sub-regions, extracts the feature on each region, and then concatenates the features of all sub-regions to predict the image label. Additionally, Perronnin et al. [7] propose to use Fisher Vector (FV) to encode local handcrafted features (e.g. SIFT [17]) for scene recognition. Alternatively, Song et al. [25] propose to exploit multiple local features with context modeling, and also propose to embed multi-feature in semantic manifold.

Recently, the deep learning methods have made great impacts in some fields of computer vision, such as image recognition [1], object detection [21] and semantic segmentation [4]. Hence, some recent scene recognition works propose their methods based on the convolution neural networks (CNNs), and sharply improve the performances. Zhou et al. [2] present a massive scene-centric dataset Places that generate better generalization than object-centric dataset (e.g. ImageNet [22]). However, due to the structure of CNNs, some discriminative regional contents might be discarded during training. To deal with this problem, some methods propose to learn regional features. Wang et al. [32] propose PatchNets which is trained in weak supervision. During the training process, images are cropped into several patches and annotated with their image-level label. Song et al. [25] propose to embed multi-scale regional features with a hierarchical context modeling method. Wu et al. [34] propose to use the region proposal method to detect the discriminative object regions in the image to guide the scene recognition. In contrast to the current methods, we extract both object and stuff features as the discriminative semantic regions, and model the relations of these semantic regions in the geometric aspect through the graph network.

2.2   Graph Neural Network

Inspired by the impact of Graph Neural Network (GNN) in processing the non-Euclidean data, some recent works [5,15,18,35,39] in the computer vision have also employed the GNN to improve the performance, such as multi-label prediction [18], zero-shot recognition [35], fine-grained image recognition [5] and 3D human pose regression [16]. Yang et al. [39] develop an attentional graph convolutional network to implement scene graph generation by upgrading the nodes in both visual and semantic features. While we also employ GCN [15] to upgrade the node representations, the graph we constructed is for each image, and with geometric information, thus, the relation between regions can be better captured, and the discriminative information can be preserved.

3   Semantic Regional Graph Model

The semantic regional graph modeling framework (SRG) including a semantic region selection module, a graph modeling network module, and a scene classification module. The architecture of our framework is illustrated in Fig. 2.

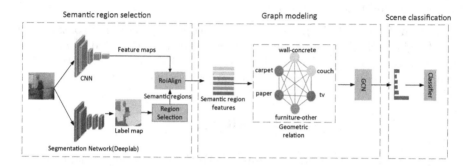

Fig. 2. The framework of SRG, which includes a semantic region selection module to determine the discriminative semantic regions, and a graph modeling module to learn the relation of semantic regions in geometric aspect, and a scene classification module to conduct classification. (*couch, tv* and *paper* are the object semantic regions, *wall-concrete, furniture-other* and *carpet* are the stuff semantic regions)

3.1   Semantic Region Selection Module

Generally, both stuff and object regions can provide discriminative information. To obtain these semantic regions comprehensively, abundant annotation is required. In our work, we adopt the COCO-Stuff [3] dataset, which contains 91 stuff categories and 80 object categories. Since the COCO-Stuff [3] dataset is a semantic segmentation dataset, we propose to implement our method based on the semantic segmentation network.

Given an image I, we feed it into a pre-trained semantic segmentation model (e.g. DeeplabV2 pre-trained on the COCO-Stuff), and obtain a label map $S \in R^{H \times W}$ as output. The label map S has the same resolution of input image I. The value S_{ij} of the pixel (i, j) in S represents the predicted category of its counterpart in I. For each category c, we can define a category binary map S^c based on S, which can be formalized as:

$$S_{ij}^c = \begin{cases} 1, & S_{ij} = c \\ 0 & S_{ij} \neq c \end{cases}$$

In practice, some category-wise binary maps will have no or few positive pixel (the value of the pixel is 1). These maps bring useless or noise information about desired semantic regions. So we set a threshold T to filter them. First, we count the number P^c of positive pixels in each category map S^c. Then, we select a new subset $\{\bar{c} \mid P^{\bar{c}} > T\}$ of categories.

Based on the binary map $S^{\bar{c}}$, we generate the connected components as semantic regions by applying the algorithm in [33]. By performing the same operation on all selected category-wise binary maps, we can obtain the set $\mathbf{R}$ of semantic regions. Each item r in $\mathbf{R}$ corresponds to a semantic region, and contains two elements $r = [r^1, r^2]$, where $r^1 = \{x, y, w, h\}$ contains the coordinate of central point and width and height of this region and r^2 denotes the predicted category of this region. To determine the discriminative semantic regions, we design several region selection methods:

Maximum Region (MR): The simplest selection method only consider the area of regions. Given region r, the area of region can be computed by r^1. Then, we choose top N regions which are listed in descending order by area. We define the operator $\mathcal{S}(\cdot)$ to represent this selection process. The selected region set V is obtained by,

$$V = \mathcal{S}(\mathbf{R}, N)$$

Category guided Maximum region (CM): Considering the semantic diversity, we propose another selection method by considering the category information r^2 of region. To address the issue that many large regions in $\mathbf{R}$ belong to a few categories, we choose the maximum region of each category in $\mathbf{R}$ to form a new region set $\mathbf{R}^{cm}$. Then the operator $\mathcal{S}(\cdot)$ is performed on $\mathbf{R}^{cm}$ to obtain the selected region set V.

Category guided Union (CU): To bring abundant and useful information, another selection operation is based on the union of regions within same predicted category. We compute the union of regions of every category $\bar{c}$, and use the union as the element to form a new region set $\mathbf{R}^{cu}$. Then the operator $\mathcal{S}(\cdot)$ is performed on $\mathbf{R}^{cu}$ to obtain the selected region set V.

After obtaining the discriminative semantic region set V, we extract the local representations of regions through a pre-trained CNN. For each region v_i in V, we can use the coordinate of central point and width and height with *RoIAlign* [13] operation to generate the representation $x_i \in R^d$ of this region. To make use of global information, we regard the image as a global region with the geometry information $\{x = W/2, y = H/2, W, H\}$ and add it into the region set V. Finally, the region representation matrix $X \in R^{(N+1) \times d}$ is obtained.

3.2   Graph Modeling Module

In order to model these regions, we reorganize them in form of graph and perform GCN [15] to capture the discriminative relation between regions. Unlike the conventional convolutions, the GCN is operated on the non-Euclidean data, which requires to learn a specific function $f_{gcn(,)}$

$$X^{(t+1)} = f_{gcn}(X^{(t)}, A) \tag{1}$$

where $X \in R^{N \times d}$(N indicates the number of regions, and d denotes the dimension of region representation) is the region representation matrix and $A \in R^{N \times N}$ is the corresponding adjacency matrix (we will discuss the construction process of A later). When applying the convolution operation [15], the function f_{gcn} can be formalized as:

$$\bar{X}^{(t+1)} = \eta(\widetilde{\theta}^{-\frac{1}{2}} \widetilde{A} \widetilde{\theta}^{-\frac{1}{2}} \bar{X}^{(t)} W^{(t)}) \tag{2}$$

where $X^{(t+1)} \in R^{N \times d}$ denotes the optimized representations of regions, and $\widetilde{A} = A + I_N$, $\theta_{ii} = \sum_j \widetilde{A}_{ij}$ is the degree matrix of $\widetilde{A}$, $W^{(t)}$ denotes the trainable weight matrix. $\eta(\cdot)$ is the non-linear activation function ReLU.

To optimize the node representations on the graph. We need to extract the local representation set $X = \{X_1, ...X_i, ...X_N\}$, and construct the adjacency matrix A. Since we have extracted the node representations that based on the *RoIAlign* [13]. Therefore, we only discuss the way of constructing the adjacency matrix A.

Geometric Relation: To understand the connection of each node representation on the graph, we construct the adjacency matrix A. Since the impact of geometric relation in scenes is heavily. Thus, in order to model the relation of semantic regions, we define the geometric representation based on each region, and construct the corresponding geometric adjacency matrix. For a pair of regions v_i and v_j in region set V, a 4-dimensional relative geometric feature is produced, as

$$\left(\log\left(\frac{|x_i - x_j|}{w_i} \right), \log\left(\frac{|y_i - y_j|}{h_i} \right), \log\left(\frac{w_j}{w_i} \right), \log\left(\frac{h_j}{h_i} \right) \right)$$

Then, this feature is embedded into a high-dimensional (d_s-dim) representation O_{ij} by performing method in [29]. The embedded feature is projected by $W_o \in R^{d_s \times 1}$ into a scalar, which can be represented as:

$$\alpha_{ij} = O_{ij} W_o,$$
$$A^{gr} = softmax(\alpha) \tag{3}$$

After constructing the adjacency matrix, we can apply the graph convolution network in $Eq.(6)$ to update the regional representation $X^{(t)}$, and generate the updated $X^{(t+1)}$.

3.3   Scene Classification Module

To prevent over-fitting, we only adopt one-layer GCN. After the operation of graph modeling, we obtain the final region representations X^1, then use the global region representation X_1^1 as image representation. Finally, the image representation is fed into an one-layer fully connected network for classification.

4 Experiments

In this section, we introduce the experimental details of our SRG. And we design several experiments, to evaluate the performance of SRG on two widely used scene recognition benchmarks, MIT67 [20] and SUN397 [36].

4.1 Experimental Datasets

MIT67: There are 67 indoor scene categories and 15,620 images. Each category contains at least 100 images. For evaluation experiments, each category contains 80 images for training and 20 images for test following the original protocol.

SUN397: There are 397 categories and 108,754 images in this dataset. Following the original paper, we divide 50 images for training and 50 images for test. Due to this dataset is relatively large, evaluating on this dataset is challenging.

4.2 Implementation Details

In the semantic region selection module, we adopt the DeeplabV2 [4] pre-trained on the COCO-Stuff [3] as our basic segmentation model. The resolution of the input image is fixed as 448×448, which leads to 448×448 label map. Based on this map, we select the discriminative regions of the image by our region selection methods, in which the threshold T is 0.01, and the selected number N of selected discriminative regions is determined on the statistics of the distribution of the number of regions, which are shown in Fig. 3. The mean values of the two benchmarks are *15.61* and *10.46*, respectively. Thus, the number of regions we selected in MIT67 and SUN397 are *16* and *10* respectively (if the number of semantic regions in some images is lower than N, we fill the selected region set with fake regions, whose representations are denoted by zeros, and geometric information is $\{x = 0, y = 0, W = 1, H = 1\}$). Then, we extract these representations based on Res50-PL model (ResNet50 [14] model pre-trained on the Places365). The initial region representation matrix is $(N + 1) \times 2048$.

In the graph modeling module, we adopt one layer GCN to upgrade the node representations. The initial node representations are regularized with the L2 regularization factor, then fed into our graph model. In the training phase, we train our models for 20 epochs with the batch size of 32 and Adam optimizer, and the initial learning rate is set to 0.001, and is divided by 10 at 10/15/18th epoch. On the two benchmarks, the hidden layer units in graph convolution are 4096, and 8192, for MIT67 and SUN397 datasets respectively. We use omit regularization (dropout) in our final classifier with a rate of 0.5.

After graph modeling, we obtain the final region representations. We only adopt one layer GCN to upgrade, and use the global region representation as image representation to conduct scene classification, which can prevent the impact of the fake region representations upgrade.

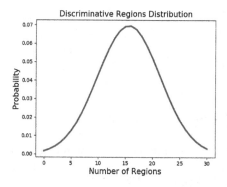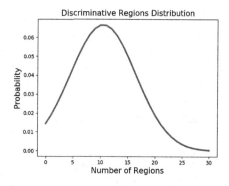

Fig. 3. The distribution of discriminative regions in MIT67 and SUN397.

4.3   Results

In this subsection, we conduct several experiments to evaluate the performance of our approach. The classification results of the linear SVM are set as the **baselines,** whose inputs are initial global region representations.

Effectiveness of Different Region Selections. In the semantic region selection module, we set three region selection methods, such as Maximum Region (MR), Category guided Maximum region (CM) and Category guided Union (CU). We conduct some detailed experiments in Table 1, and analyze the effectiveness of three selection methods. In Table 1, it can be noticed that three region selection methods have achieved higher results than the baselines, which demonstrates the effectiveness of our region selection method. In addition, we can observe that CM performs better than MR, which indicates when selecting regions based on the semantic meanings, more discriminative information of the image can be learned. Moreover, the slightly lower performance of CU demonstrates that selecting the union of regions may result in redundancy. Therefore, it's essential to ensure the diversity of semantics and avoid redundant information when selecting discriminative semantic regions.

Table 1. Comparisons of different region selection methods

Baseline	Region selection			MIT67(%)	SUN397(%)
	MR	CM	CU		
✓	–	–	–	86.87	71.53
–	✓	–	–	87.99	74.03
–	–	✓	–	**88.13**	**74.06**
–	–	–	✓	87.69	73.89

Moreover, three region selection methods are based on the same graph modeling. In Table 1, it can be noted that our best results are 1.26% and 2.53% over baselines. This confirms that the effectiveness of modeling the geometric relation between discriminative semantic regions, which can boost the performance of scene recognition.

The Effectiveness of Different Kinds of Semantic Regions. To determine the effectiveness of different kinds of semantic regions, we construct the following experiments. We divide the semantic regions into different sets, including stuff and object sets. According to the statistics, the number N of selected regions is *4/12* (object/stuff) in MIT67, *2/8* (object/stuff) in SUN397. We select these regions based on the CM region selection method. In Table 2, we can observe that the stuff and object are both over the baselines when the number of regions is equal, which indicates that we can obtain discriminative information from both stuff and object regions. When enlarging the number of stuff regions, there are still improvements. Furthermore, when considering both stuff and object regions, the improvement of performances are also obvious, which demonstrates that object and stuff regions can provide complementary information. Thus, obtaining comprehensive information of scene images can improve the performances of scene recognition.

Table 2. Comparisons of different semantic regions.

Regions	Object	Stuff	Object & Stuff	MIT67(%)	SUN397(%)
2	✓	–	–	–	71.92
2	–	✓	–	–	72.41
8	–	✓	–	–	73.4
10	–	–	✓	–	74.06
4	✓	–	–	87.01	–
4	–	✓	–	87.09	–
12	–	✓	–	87.46	–
16	–	–	✓	88.13	–
Baseline	–	–	–	86.87	71.53

4.4 Comparison with State-of-the-Art Methods

We compare our SRG with state-of-the-art methods. The results are shown in Table 3. It can be observed that our SRG outperforms the current state-of-the-art methods, confirming the effectiveness of our method. Compared with the region based works [24,32,34,37], our SRG achieves the best performance, which demonstrates the effectiveness of our method. To the best of our knowledge, our SRG obtains state-of-the-art performance in the domain of scene recognition.

Table 3. Comparisons of our method with state-of-the-art methods

Approaches	MIT67(%)	SUN397(%)
Places365+VGGNet16 [2]	76.5	63.2
MetaObject-CNN [34]	78.9	58.11
MLR+CFV+FCR1-w [37]	82.24	64.53
LS-DHM [10]	83.75	67.56
VSAD+FV+Places205-VGGNet-16 [32]	86.2	73.0
PowerNorm [19]	86.3	–
Places401-Deeper-BN-Inception (B2)[31]	86.7	72.0
SDO [6]	86.72	73.41
MP [24]	86.9	72.6
MFAFVNet+Places [38]	87.97	72.01
Adi-Red [40]	–	73.59
Our SRG	**88.13**	**74.06**

5   Conclusion

In this paper, we propose our semantic regional graph modeling framework for scene recognition. To select the discriminative semantic regions in the scene comprehensively, we conduct several region selection methods, effectively capturing the discriminative semantic regions, ensuring the semantic diversity and avoiding redundancy. In the graph learning module, we optimize the region representations in the relation of geometric aspects, and generate the discriminative scene representations. The exploration of stuff and object regions also demonstrates the complementarity of them. Based on the comprehensive semantic regions, our method can obtain state-of-the-art performances on MIT67 and SUN397 datasets.

References

1. Sutskever, I., Krizhevsky, A., Hinton, G.E.: ImageNet classification with deep convolutional neural networks. In: NIPS, pp. 1106–1114 (2012)
2. Bolei, Z., Aditya, K., Agata, L., Antonio, T., Aude, P.: Places: an image database for deep scene understanding. arXiv preprint arXiv:1610.02055 (2016)
3. Caesar, H., Uijlings, J., Ferrari, V.: COCO-Stuff: thing and stuff classes in context. In: CVPR (2018)
4. Chen, L.C., Papandreou, G., Kokkinos, I., Murphy, K., Yuille, A.L.: DeepLab: semantic image segmentation with deep convolutional nets, atrous convolution, and fully connected CRFs. IEEE Trans. Pattern Anal. Mach. Intell. **40**(4), 834–848 (2018)
5. Chen, T., Lin, L., Chen, R., Wu, Y., Luo, X.: Knowledge-embedded representation learning for fine-grained image recognition. In: IJCAI (2018)

6. Cheng, X., Lu, J., Feng, J., Yuan, B., Zhou, J.: Scene recognition with objectness. Pattern Recogn. **74**, 474–487 (2018)
7. Perronnin, F., Sánchez, J., Mensink, T.: Improving the Fisher Kernel for large-scale image classification. In: Daniilidis, K., Maragos, P., Paragios, N. (eds.) ECCV 2010. LNCS, vol. 6314, pp. 143–156. Springer, Heidelberg (2010). https://doi.org/10.1007/978-3-642-15561-1_11
8. Fredembach, C., Schroder, M., Susstrunk, S.: Eigenregions for image classification. IEEE Trans. Pattern Anal. Mach. Intell. **26**(12), 1645–1649 (2004)
9. Maaten, L., Huang, G., Liu, Z., Weinberger, K.Q.: Densely connected convolutional networks. In: CVPR (2017)
10. Guo, S., Huang, W., Wang, L., Qiao, Y.: Locally supervised deep hybrid model for scene recognition. IEEE Trans. Image Process. **26**(2), 808–820 (2017)
11. Heranz, L., Jiang, S., Li, X.: Scene recognition with CNNs: objects, scales and dataset bias. In: CVPR (2016)
12. Jiang, S., Chen, G., Song, X., Liu, L.: Deep patch representations with shared codebook for scene classification. ACM Trans. Multimedia Comput. Commun. Appl. **15**, 1–17 (2019)
13. Gkioxari, G., He, K., Dollar, P., Girshick, R.: Mask R-CNN. In: ICCV, pp. 2980–2988 (2017)
14. Ren, S., He, K., Zhang, X., Sun, J.: Deep residual learning for image recognition. In: CVPR, pp. 770–778 (2016)
15. Kipf, T.N., Welling, M.: Semi-supervised classification with graph convolutional networks. In: ICLR (2017)
16. Peng, X., Zhao, L., Tian, Y., Kapadia, M., Metaxas, D.N.: Semantic graph convolutional networks for 3D human pose regression. In: CVPR (2019)
17. Lowe, D.G.: Distinctive image features from scale-invariant keypoints. Int. J. Comput. Vision **60**, 91–110 (2004)
18. Min, Z., Wei, C.X.S., Wang, P., Guo, Y.: Multi-label image recognition with graph convolutional networks. In: CVPR (2019)
19. Koniusz, P., Zhang, H.: A deeper look at power normalizations. In: CVPR (2018)
20. Quattoni, A., Torralba, A.: Recognizing indoor scenes. In: CVPR, pp. 413–420 (2009)
21. Ren, S., He, K., Girshick, R., Sun, J.: Beyond bags of features: spatial pyramid matching for recognizing natural scene categories. In: NIPS (2015)
22. Russakovsky, O., et al.: ImageNet large scale visual recognition challenge. Int. J. Comput. Vision **115**, 211–252 (2015)
23. Shen, J., Shepherd, J., Ngu, A.H.H.: Semantic-sensitive classification for large image libraries. In: International Multimedia Modelling Conference, pp. 340–345 (2005)
24. Song, X., Jiang, S., Herranz, L.: Multi-scale multi-feature context modeling for scene recognition in the semantic manifold. IEEE Trans. Image Process. **26**(8), 2721–2735 (2017)
25. Song, X., Jiang, S., Herranz, L.: Joint multi-feature spatial context for scene recognition on the semantic manifold. In: CVPR (2015)
26. Song, X., Jiang, S., Herranz, L., Kong, Y., Zheng, K.: Category co-occurrence modeling for large scale scene recognition. Pattern Recogn. **59**, 98–111 (2016)
27. Schmid, C., Lazebnik, S., Ponce, J.: Beyond bags of features: spatial pyramid matching for recognizing natural scene categories. In: CVPR (2006)
28. Vailaya, A., Jain, A., Figueiredo, M., Zhang, H.: Content-based hierarchical classification of vacation images. In: IEEE International Conference on Multimedia Computing and Systems, pp. 518–523 (1999)

29. Vaswani, A., et al: Attention is all you need. In: NIPS (2017)
30. Wang, J., Yang, J., Yu, K., Lv, F., Huang, T., Gong, Y.: Locality-constrained linear coding for image classification. In: CVPR (2010)
31. Wang, L., Guo, S., Huang, W., Xiong, Y., Qiao, Y.: Knowledge guided disambiguation for large-scale scene classification with multi-resolution CNNs. IEEE Trans. Image Process. **26**(4), 2055–2068 (2017)
32. Wang, Z., Wang, L., Wang, Y., Zhang, B., Qiao, Y.: Weakly supervised patchnets: describing and aggregating local patches for scene recognition. IEEE Trans. Image Process. **26**(4), 2028–2041 (2017)
33. Mark, J.B., Wilhelm, B.: Principles of Digital Image Processing: Core Algorithms. UTICS. Springer, London (2009). https://doi.org/10.1007/978-1-84800-195-4
34. Wu, R., Wang, B., Wang, W., Yu, Y.: Harvesting discriminative meta objects with deep CNN features for scene classification. In: ICCV (2015)
35. Ye, Y., Wang, X., Gupta, A.: Zero-shot recognition via semantic embeddings and knowledge graphs. In: CVPR (2018)
36. Xiao, J., Hays, J., Ehinger, K.A., Oliva, A., Torralba, A.: SUN Database: large-scale scene recognition from abbey to zoo. In: CVPR, pp. 3485–3492 (2010)
37. Xie, G.-S., Zhang, X.-Y., Yan, S., Liu, C.-L.: Hybrid CNN and dictionary-based models for scene recognition and domain adaptation. IEEE Trans. Circuits Syst. Video Technol. **27**, 1263–1274 (2017)
38. Vasconcelos, N., Li, Y., Dixit, M.: Deep scene image classification with the MFAFVNet. In: ICCV (2017)
39. Yang, J., Lee, S., Lu, J., Batra, D., Parikh, D.: Graph R-CNN for scene graph generation. In: ECCV (2018)
40. Zhao, Z., Larson, M.: From volcano to toyshop: adaptive discriminative region discovery for scene recognition. In: ACM MM (2018)

MaaFace: Multiplicative and Additive Angular Margin Loss for Deep Face Recognition

Weilun Liu, Jichao Jiao$^{(\boxtimes)}$, Yaokai Mo, Jian Jiao,
and Zhongliang Deng

Beijing University of Posts and Telecommunications, Peking, China
{liuweilun,jiaojichao,moyaokai,jiaojian}@bupt.edu.cn,
dengzhl902@gmail.com

Abstract. Because convolutional neural networks can extract discriminative features, they are widely used in face recognition and significantly improve the performance in face recognition. In order to improve the accuracy of the face recognition, in addition to improving the structures of convolutional neural networks, many new loss functions have been proposed to enhance the distinguishing ability to extract features, such as SphereFace and ArcFace. Inspired by SphereFace and ArcFace, we propose a new loss function called MaaFace, in which the angular multiplier and the angular addition are introduced into the loss function simultaneously. We give a detailed derivation of MaaFace and conduct extensive experiments on different networks and different data sets. Experiments show that our proposed loss function can achieve an out performance than the latest face recognition loss functions in face recognition accuracy. Finally, we explain why MaaFace can achieve better performance through statistical analysis of the experimental data.

Keywords: Face recognition · Convolutional neural networks · Loss function

1 Introduction

Convolutional neural networks are widely used in computer vision [1] and greatly promote the development of it. As face recognition is a representative classification task in computer vision, convolutional neural networks are widely used in it and improve the face recognition effect. There are four main factors affecting face recognition accuracy, including dataset, neural network architecture, initialization, loss function.

1.1 Dataset

A good dataset should be sufficient, complete and noise-free. A sufficient amount of data for training can reduce overfitting. Completeness requires the dataset covers various situations that may occur in practice, such as changes in illumination, pose, age, etc. Noise-free means that the data is labeled correctly, available and in the same form. MS-Celeb-1M [2], VGGFace2 [3], LFW [4], CFP [5], AgeDB [6] and MegaFace [7] are some datasets commonly used.

© Springer Nature Switzerland AG 2019
Y. Zhao et al. (Eds.): ICIG 2019, LNCS 11903, pp. 642–653, 2019.
https://doi.org/10.1007/978-3-030-34113-8_53

1.2   Neural Network Architecture

The neural network architecture not only affects the face recognition accuracy but also affects the time required for training and actual use. In general, the deeper the network, the better the effect of face recognition. However, it will need a larger training dataset to avoid overfitting, longer time to train and take more time in actual use. VGG network [8], Google Inception V1 network [9], ResNet [10] and Inception-ResNet [11] are some basic network structures commonly used.

1.3   Initialization

The method of neural network parameter initialization has a direct impact on the final recognition effect. Good parameter initialization can make the neural network more convergent and optimize the performance of the neural network. Commonly used initialization methods are Msra initialization [12], Xavier initialization [13], Random initialization [14] and so on.

1.4   Loss Function

The loss function can be roughly divided into two categories. One is the Euclidean margin-based loss measured by Euclidean distance, another is the Angular and Co-sine margin-based loss measured by angular distance and the cosine distance.

In [15], the softmax loss was introduced into the neural network of face recognition. A lot of loss functions are variants of it. Based on softmax loss, Center loss [16] adds constraints on the deviation between features and their corresponding intra-class center, so that the feature space of the same person is compressed. Considering the distance between the most different individuals in intra-class and the distance between the nearest inter-class centers, Range loss [17] reduces the feature distance of the same person and enlarges the distance between different people. In addition to adding the constraints of intra-class and inter-class distances, Marginal loss [18] sets an empirical minimum threshold for intra-class distance and inter-class distance.

Different from the Euclidean margin-based loss function, SphereFace [19] sets the bias of the fully connected layer of the loss function to 0 and takes L2 normalization on the weights of the fully connected layer. In addition, SphereFace introduces an angular multiplier, which makes the classification boundary $\cos(u\theta)$. CosFace [20] normalizes the features and turns the training classification boundaries into $\cos\theta - v$, converting the face classification to a measure based on the cosine distance, further enhancing the effect of face recognition. ArcFace [21] turns the training classification boundaries into $\cos(\theta + v)$.

Although ArcFace is currently the best loss function in the field of face recognition, we found that when using ArcFace as the loss function, all the class feature centers of training dataset are approximately evenly distributed in the feature space, which is an over-fitting of the training dataset and limits the effect of face recognition.

SphereFace is mainly to compress the feature space of the intra-class, as ArcFace aims to make the feature distance of inter-class to be larger. Inspired by SphereFace and ArcFace, combine the advantages of them, we propose a new loss function called

MaaFace, whose classification boundary is $\cos(u\theta + v)$. Our main contributions are as follows:

(1) Compared with ArcFace, besides the angular addition v, we introduce the angular multiplier u into the loss function simultaneously. This can alleviate the over-fitting problem caused by the angular addition.
(2) MaaFace advances the state-of-the-art performance over most of the benchmarks on popular face databases including LFW, CFP, AgeDB.

An overview of the rest of the paper is as follows: The derivation process of the MaaFace are introduced in Sect. 2. The experimental results are shown in Sect. 3. Finally, the conclusion is indicated in Sect. 4.

2 Proposed Approach

In this chapter, we introduce several variants of the softmax loss and present how to derive the expression of MaaFace in detail.

2.1 Softmax Loss

As one of the basic classification loss functions of the convolutional neural network, the softmax loss is as follows:

$$L_1 = -\frac{1}{m}\sum_{i=1}^{m}\log\frac{e^{W_{y_i}^T x_i + b_{y_i}}}{\sum_{j=1}^{n}e^{W_j^T x_i + b_j}} \tag{1}$$

where m is the batch size. n is the number of face categories of the training dataset. $x_i \in \mathbf{R}^d$ is the feature extracted from the i-th image, where d represents the dimension of the features. y_i is the real category of the i-th image. $W \in \mathbf{R}^{d \times n}$ and $b \in \mathbf{R}^n$ respectively refer to the weights and bias of the last fully connected layer of the convolutional neural network.

The classification boundary of softmax loss is $(W_1 - W_2)x + b_1 - b_2 = 0$, as shown in Fig. 1. It does not explicitly write the intra-class distance and the inter-class distance as penalty terms into the formula. Although softmax loss is widely used in convolutional neural networks for face recognition, the performance is not satisfied.

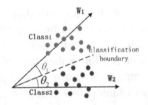

Fig. 1. Geometric interpretation of softmax loss

2.2   SphereFace

Assume the angle between the vectors W_j^T and x_i is θ_j, let the absolute value of b_j be 0, we can get $W_j^T x_i + b_j = ||W_j|| \, ||x_i|| \cos \theta_j$. It is noted that normalizing the weights of the fully connected layer can accelerate the convergence speed of the training [29]. Fixing $||W_j|| = 1$ by $L2$ normalization, Eq. 1 can be rewritten as:

$$L_2 = -\frac{1}{m} \sum_{i=1}^{m} \log \frac{e^{||x_i|| \cos \theta_{y_i}}}{e^{||x_i|| \cos \theta_{y_i}} + \sum_{j=1, j \neq y_i}^{n} e^{||x_i|| \cos \theta_j}} \tag{2}$$

An Angular multiplier u is introduced by SphereFace [19]:

$$L_3 = -\frac{1}{m} \sum_{i=1}^{m} \log \frac{e^{||x_i|| \cos(u\theta_{y_i})}}{e^{||x_i|| \cos(u\theta_{y_i})} + \sum_{j=1, j \neq y_i}^{n} e^{||x_i|| \cos \theta_j}} \tag{3}$$

where $\theta_{y_i} \in [0, \pi/u]$.

The classification boundary of SphereFace is $||x||(\cos(u\theta_1) - \cos \theta_2) = 0$. Making that the angle between the vectors of two inter-class feature centers is θ, we can get $\theta_1 = \frac{1}{u+1}\theta$, as shown as Fig. 2(a). The introduction of the angular multiplier u in SphereFace has a very obvious geometric interpretation, which compresses the feature space of each class and improves the accuracy of face recognition.

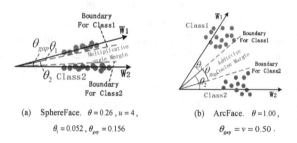

(a)   SphereFace. $\theta = 0.26$, $u = 4$,   (b)   ArcFace. $\theta = 1.00$,

$\theta_1 = 0.052$, $\theta_{gap} = 0.156$ $\theta_{gap} = v = 0.50$.

Fig. 2.   Geometric interpretation examples of SphereFace and ArcFace

To eliminate the constraint $\theta_{y_i} \in [0, \pi/u]$, SphereFace replaces $\cos(u\theta_{y_i})$ with $\varphi(\theta_{y_i})$:

$$L_4 = -\frac{1}{m} \sum_{i=1}^{m} \log \frac{e^{||x_i||\varphi(\theta_{y_i})}}{e^{||x_i||\varphi(\theta_{y_i})} + \sum_{j=1, j \neq y_i}^{n} e^{||x_i|| \cos \theta_j}} \tag{4}$$

where $\varphi(\theta_{y_i}) = (-1)^k \cos(u\theta_{y_i}) - 2k$, $\theta_{y_i} \in [\frac{k\pi}{u}, \frac{(k+1)\pi}{u}]$, $k \in [0, u-1]$ and k is an integer. The parameter u is an integer greater than 0, controlling the degree of compression of each intra-class angle in the feature space. A dynamic super parameter λ is introduced to ensure training convergence, $\varphi(\theta_{y_i})$ is rewritten as follows:

$$\varphi(\theta_{y_i}) = \frac{(-1)^k \cos(u\theta_{y_i}) - 2k + \lambda \cos(\theta_{y_i})}{1 + \lambda} \qquad (5)$$

where λ is set to 1000 at the beginning and gradually reduced to 5 when training, so that the angular range of each intra-class is gradually compressed.

2.3   ArcFace

In [22], it is proved that the normalization of the output features can accelerate the training convergence. Fixing $||x_i|| = 1$ by L2 normalization and scales it to s, Eq. 2 can be written as:

$$L_5 = -\frac{1}{m} \sum_{i=1}^{m} \log \frac{e^{s \cdot \cos \theta_{y_i}}}{e^{s \cdot \cos \theta_{y_i}} + \sum_{j=1, j \neq y_i}^{n} e^{s \cdot \cos \theta_j}} \qquad (6)$$

ArcFace improved the loss function by introducing an angular addition v [21]:

$$L_6 = -\frac{1}{m} \sum_{i=1}^{m} \log \frac{e^{s \cdot \cos(\theta_{y_i} + v)}}{e^{s \cdot \cos(\theta_{y_i} + v)} + \sum_{j=1, j \neq y_i}^{n} e^{s \cdot \cos \theta_j}} \qquad (7)$$

where $\theta_{y_i} \in [0, \pi - v]$.

The classification boundary is $||x||(\cos(\theta_1 + v) - \cos \theta_2) = 0$. Making the angular distance between two classes centers is θ, the maximum distance between the individual and its corresponding class center is $\theta_1 = \frac{\theta - v}{2}$.

The angular addition v of ArcFace specifies the minimum distance between the most similar individuals between inter-class, as SphereFace doesn't explicitly write the minimum inter-class distance as penalty terms into the formula. The distance between the nearest inter-class features of SphereFace is smaller than ArcFace's. Therefore, SphereFace is easier to confuse individuals between inter-classes and ArcFace gets a better effect, as shown in Fig. 2.

2.4   MaaFace

SphereFace loss function compresses the angular space of intra-class, making the intra-class features more compact. However, SphereFace does not optimize the distance of inter-class, which tends to cause the distance between the class centers to be too small and limits the effect of face recognition. ArcFace is the opposite of SphereFace, which is just mainly to optimize the distance between classes. When the distance between the class centers is close, ArcFace has a better control effect on the distance of the intra-class. However, as the distance between the class centers increases, this control effect becomes weaker and the distribution of features within the class becomes much looser, as shown in Fig. 3.

Increasing the angular addition v can compress the feature space of the intra-class. However, in the initial stage of increasing v, the distance between inter-class centers tends to increase while the feature space of the intra-class remains almost unchanged.

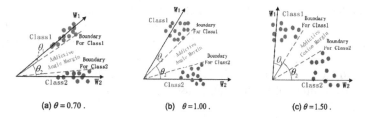

(a) $\theta = 0.70$.   (b) $\theta = 1.00$.   (c) $\theta = 1.50$.

Fig. 3. Feature space of intra-class (θ_1) changes with inter-class centers distance (θ) when using ArcFace as the loss function ($v = 0.5$)

This will make the inter-class centers of the training dataset tend to be evenly distributed in the feature space, as shown in Fig. 4. At this time, the minimum distance between a class center and its nearest inter-class center is the same as others', which does not meet the actual situation that the training data inter-class centers are randomly distributed in the feature space. This is overfitting of the training dataset. Then as v continues to increase, the feature space of the intra-class begins to be compressed while the inter-class centers remain evenly distributed.

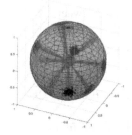

Fig. 4. Features distribution of Fashion-MNIST [25] using ArcFace as the loss function ($v = 0.5$)

Inspired by SphereFace and ArcFace, we propose a new loss function called MaaFace by combing with the advantages of both of them. We introduce the angular multiplier u and the angular addition v into the loss function simultaneously. The loss function is:

$$L_7 = -\frac{1}{m}\sum_{i=1}^{m}\log\frac{e^{s\cdot\cos(u\theta_{y_i}+v)}}{e^{s\cdot\cos(u\theta_{y_i}+v)}+\sum_{j=1,j\neq y_i}^{n}e^{s\cdot\cos\theta_j}} \tag{8}$$

Where u is an integer larger than 1 and $v \in [0, \pi]$.

The classification boundary becomes $||x||(\cos(u\theta_1 + v) - \cos\theta_2) = 0$. Let the angular distance between the inter-class centers is θ, so that $\theta_1 = \frac{\theta-v}{u+1}$. As shown in Fig. 5, MaaFace keeps a certain minimum angular distance between inter-class by introducing the angular addition v. By introducing the angular multiplier u, MaaFace compresses the feature space of the intra-class. Let v be a value that is not very large. When the distance between the inter-class centers increases, the angular multiplier can still keep the feature space of the intra-class compact. On the one hand, the angular multiplier can compress the feature space of the intra-class. On the other hand, the angular multiplier maintains the flexible distribution of the inter-class centers and reduces the over-fitting of the training dataset.

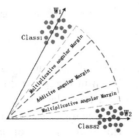

Fig. 5. Geometric interpretation of MaaFace

To eliminate the constraint $\theta_{y_i} \in [0, \frac{\pi-v}{u}]$, we further replace $\varphi(\theta_{y_i}) = \cos(u\theta_{y_i} + v)$ with $\varphi(\theta_{y_i}) = (-1)^k \cos(u\theta_{y_i} + v) - 2k$, where $u\theta_{y_i} + v \in [k\pi, (k+1)\pi]$, $k \in [0, u]$ and k is an integer, $\theta_{y_i} \in [0, \pi]$.

Considering the training convergence problem, referring to the training process of SphereFace, we introduce the hyper parameter α:

$$\varphi(\theta_{y_i}) = \alpha((-1)^k \cos(u\theta_{y_i} + v) - 2k) + (1-\alpha)\cos(\theta_{y_i} + v) \qquad (9)$$

It is noted that α gradually increased from 0 to 0.2 during training.

3 Experiments

In this section, we will describe our experiment from three aspects, including datasets, network structure, experimental results.

3.1 Dataset

3.1.1 Training Dataset
MS-Celeb-1M. MS-Celeb-1M contains approximately 10M images. It contains 100k celebrities and each person has 100 photos on average. In order to reduce noise and get a higher quality data set, the features of all images are firstly extracted in [23]. After that, the portion, whose distance between themselves and their intra-class feature center is greater than a given threshold, is removed. Finally, the image with the distance near the threshold is checked manually. The refined dataset is published available within a binary file by [21]. We use MS-Celeb-1M as the training dataset. The refinement dataset contains 85,164 people with a total of 3.8M images.

3.1.2   Testing Dataset

LFW: LFW is a dataset in the unconstrained natural scene where the photos vary greatly in orientation, expression, and lighting environment [4]. It contains 13,233 photos of 5,749 people. The database randomly selected 6000 pairs of faces to form face recognition image pairs, in which 3000 pairs of photos belong to the same person, and 3000 pairs of photos belong to different people.

CFP: The CFP is a 500-person dataset with 10 front images and 4 contour images per person [5]. CFP has two sub-dataset, namely frontal-frontal (FF) and frontal-profile (FP). The FF contains 3500 pairs of random image pairs belonging to the same person and 3500 pairs of random image pairs belonging to different people, in which the images of each pair are frontal images. The FP contains 3500 pairs of random image pairs belonging to the same person and 3500 pairs of random image pairs belonging to different people, in which each pair of images contains a front image and a profile image. We only use the most challenging subset CFP-FP as the vilification dataset.

AgeDB: The AgeDB dataset contains 12,240 images of 440 people, whose images vary greatly in poses, lighting, and age [6]. This dataset contains four sub-datasets for different age spans, namely 5 years, 10 years, 20 years, 30 years. Each sub-dataset contains 3,000 image pairs of the same person and 3000 image pairs of different people. Here, we only test on AgeDB-30, which is the most difficult one.

3.2   Network Structure

All models, implemented by MxNet proposed by [24] in this paper, are trained on four NVIDIA Titan X Pascal (12 GB) GPUs. Momentum is set at 0.9 while weight decay is set at $5e-4$. The batch size is 512. The learning rate is started at 0.1. As for ArcFace, following [21], the learning rate is divided by 10 at the 100k, 140k, 160k, 180k iterations. Total iteration step is set as 200k. As for MaaFace, we first train with hyper parameter $\alpha = 0.0$ and the learning rate is divided by 10 at the 50k, 80k, 100k, 120k iterations. Then at the 130k iterations, the learning rate is reset as 0.1. At each iteration later, α adds $5e-6$ until α equals 0.2. The learning rate is divided by 10 at the 160k, 170k, 175k, 178k iterations. Total iteration step is set as 185k.

We use SE-LResNetE-IR as the base network and just replace loss function with ours. The dimension of the features extracted by SE-LResNetE-IR is 512. Before training, we use MTCNN [25] to perform face detection and alignment on images. The faces will then be cropped and resized to 112×112 pixels. Then, we normalize each pixel in RGB images by subtracting 127.5 and dividing it by 128.

In order to illustrate the universality of the loss function, we performed experiments on the models of 34, 50, and 100 layers respectively.

3.3   Analysis of Experimental Results

We firstly train on the 50 layers models with different angular multiplier u and different angular addition v. The result is shown in Table 1. When $u = 2$ and $v = 0.3$, we get the best performance in combination. So, we fix the angular multiplier u as 2 and the angular addition v as 0.3. In [21], ArcFace gets the best performance when the angular addition v as 0.5. We train the models with 34 layers, 50 layers, 100 layers respectively, and get the results as Table 2.

Table 1. Test performance (%) of MaaFace with different angular multiplier u and different angular addition v (50 layers).

v	u	LFW	CFP-FP	AgeDB-30
0.2	2	99.53	92.84	97.22
0.2	3	99.60	92.63	97.50
0.2	4	99.70	**93.09**	97.47
0.2	5	99.70	92.86	97.48
0.3	2	**99.68**	**93.01**	**97.68**
0.3	3	**99.78**	92.19	97.73
0.3	4	99.72	92.50	97.62
0.3	5	99.73	92.43	96.87
0.4	2	99.77	92.57	97.53
0.4	3	99.77	92.30	97.43
0.4	4	99.75	92.57	97.62
0.4	5	**99.78**	92.49	97.62
0.5	2	99.72	91.93	97.53
0.5	3	99.77	91.64	97.53

Table 2. Test performance (%) of MaaFace and ArcFace with models of different layers

Loss	LFW	CFP-FP	AgeDB-30
MaaFace-34($u = 2$, $v = 0.3$)	**99.67**	**91.33**	**97.28**
ArcFace-34($v = 0.5$)	99.60	90.36	97.13
MaaFace-50($u = 2$, $v = 0.3$)	**99.68**	**93.01**	**97.68**
ArcFace-50($v = 0.5$)	99.65	92.50	97.30
MaaFace-100($u = 2$, $v = 0.3$)	99.73	**93.91**	**97.77**
ArcFace-100($v = 0.5$)	**99.80**	93.53	97.72

Although the result on LFW dataset of MaaFace-100 is a little smaller than that of ArcFace-100, the other results of MaaFace are better than ArcFace's. It proves that introduced the angular multiplier u and the angular addition v into the loss function simultaneously can improve the performance of the face recognition. In order to explain why this can get a better result, we have statistics on the distribution of the shortest distance between feature centers of inter-class. As shown in Fig. 6, compared to ArcFace, the distribution of MaaFace is more random, which reduces over-fitting to some extent. Therefore, MaaFace can get better performance.

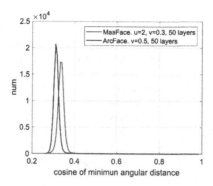

Fig. 6. Distribution statistics of the nearest feature centers

4 Conclusion

In this paper, we propose a new loss function, called MaaFace. Through extensive experiments, we can prove that the loss function can effectively improve the face recognition effect compared with the most advanced loss functions on the same convolutional neural network. Besides, we explain why MaaFace can get better performance through theoretical derivation and mathematical statistics.

Acknowledgements. The project sponsored by the National Key Research and Development Program (No. 2016YFB0502002).

References

1. Voulodimos, A., Doulamis, N., Doulamis, A., Protopapadakis, E.: Deep learning for computer vision: a brief review. In: Computational Intelligence and Neuroscience (2018)
2. Guo, Y., Zhang, L., Hu, Y., He, X., Gao, J.: MS-Celeb-1M: a dataset and benchmark for large-scale face recognition. In: Leibe, B., Matas, J., Sebe, N., Welling, M. (eds.) ECCV 2016. LNCS, vol. 9907, pp. 87–102. Springer, Cham (2016). https://doi.org/10.1007/978-3-319-46487-9_6
3. Cao, Q., Shen, L., Xie, W., Parkhi, O.M., Zisserman, A.: VGGFace2: a dataset for recognising faces across pose and age. In: 13th IEEE International Conference on Automatic Face & Gesture Recognition (FG 2018), pp. 67–74. IEEE (2018)
4. Huang, G.B., Mattar, M., Berg, T., Learned-Miller, E.: Labeled faces in the wild: a database for studying face recognition in unconstrained environments. In: Workshop on Faces in 'Real-Life' Images: Detection, Alignment, and Recognition (2008)
5. Sengupta, S., Chen, J.-C., Castillo, C., Patel, V.M., Chellappa, R., Jacobs, D.W.: Frontal to profile face verification in the wild. In: IEEE Winter Conference on Applications of Computer Vision (WACV), pp. 1–9. IEEE (2016)
6. Moschoglou, S., Papaioannou, A., Sagonas, C., Deng, J., Kotsia, I., Zafeiriou, S.: AgeDB: the first manually collected, in-the-wild age database. In: Proceedings of the IEEE Conference on Computer Vision and Pattern Recognition Workshops, pp. 51–59 (2017)

7. Kemelmacher-Shlizerman, I., Seitz, S.M., Miller, D., Brossard, E.: The MegaFace benchmark: 1 million faces for recognition at scale. In: Proceedings of the IEEE Conference on Computer Vision and Pattern Recognition, pp. 4873–4882 (2016)

8. Parkhi, O.M., Vedaldi, A., Zisserman, A.: Deep face recognition. In: BMVC, vol. 3, p. 6 (2015)

9. Szegedy, C., et al.: Going deeper with convolutions. In: Proceedings of the IEEE Conference on Computer Vision and Pattern Recognition, pp. 1–9 (2015)

10. He, K., Zhang, X., Ren, S., Sun, J.: Identity mappings in deep residual networks. In: Leibe, B., Matas, J., Sebe, N., Welling, M. (eds.) ECCV 2016. LNCS, vol. 9908, pp. 630–645. Springer, Cham (2016). https://doi.org/10.1007/978-3-319-46493-0_38

11. Szegedy, C., Ioffe, S., Vanhoucke, V., Alemi, A.A.: Inception-v4, inception-ResNet and the impact of residual connections on learning. In: Thirty-First AAAI Conference on Artificial Intelligence (2017)

12. He, K., Zhang, X., Ren, S., Sun, J.: Delving deep into rectifiers: surpassing human-level performance on imagenet classification. In: Proceedings of the IEEE International Conference on Computer Vision, pp. 1026–1034 (2015)

13. Glorot, X., Bengio, Y.: Understanding the difficulty of training deep feedforward neural networks. In: Proceedings of the Thirteenth International Conference on Artificial Intelligence and Statistics, pp. 249–256 (2010)

14. Thimm, G., Fiesler, E.: Neural network initialization. In: Mira, J., Sandoval, F. (eds.) IWANN 1995. LNCS, vol. 930, pp. 535–542. Springer, Heidelberg (1995). https://doi.org/10.1007/3-540-59497-3_220

15. Taigman, Y., Yang, M., Ranzato, M.A., Wolf, L.: DeepFace: closing the gap to human-level performance in face verification. In: Proceedings of the IEEE Conference on Computer Vision and Pattern Recognition, pp. 1701–1708 (2014)

16. Wen, Y., Zhang, K., Li, Z., Qiao, Y.: A discriminative feature learning approach for deep face recognition. In: Leibe, B., Matas, J., Sebe, N., Welling, M. (eds.) ECCV 2016. LNCS, vol. 9911, pp. 499–515. Springer, Cham (2016). https://doi.org/10.1007/978-3-319-46478-7_31

17. Zhang, X., Fang, Z., Wen, Y., Li, Z., Qiao, Y.: Range loss for deep face recognition with long-tailed training data. In: Proceedings of the IEEE International Conference on Computer Vision, pp. 5409–5418 (2017)

18. Deng, J., Zhou, Y., Zafeiriou, S.: Marginal loss for deep face recognition. In: Proceedings of the IEEE Conference on Computer Vision and Pattern Recognition Workshops, pp. 60–68 (2017)

19. Liu, W., Wen, Y., Yu, Z., Li, M., Raj, B., Song, L.: SphereFace: deep hypersphere embedding for face recognition. In: Proceedings of the IEEE Conference on Computer Vision and Pattern Recognition, pp. 212–220 (2017)

20. Wang, H., et al.: CosFace: large margin cosine loss for deep face recognition. In: Proceedings of the IEEE Conference on Computer Vision and Pattern Recognition, pp. 5265–5274 (2018)

21. Deng, J., Guo, J., Xue, N., Zafeiriou, S.: ArcFace: additive angular margin loss for deep face recognition (2018)

22. Wang, F., Xiang, X., Cheng, J., Yuille, A.L.: NormFace: L2 hypersphere embedding for face verification. In: Proceedings of the 25th ACM International Conference on Multimedia, pp. 1041–1049. ACM (2017)

23. Xiao, H., Rasul, K., Vollgraf, R: Fashion-MNIST: a novel image dataset for benchmarking machine learning algorithms (2017)

24. Chen, T., et al.: MXNet: a flexible and efficient machine learning library for heterogeneous distributed systems (2015)
25. Zhang, K., Zhang, Z., Li, Z., Qiao, Y.: Joint face detection and alignment using multitask cascaded convolutional networks. IEEE Sig. Process. Lett. **23**(10), 1499–1503 (2016)

Fighting Detection Based on Analysis of Individual's Motion Trajectory

Jiaying Ren[1,2,3], Yimin Dou[1,2,3], and Jinping Li[1,2,3(✉)]

[1] School of Information Science and Engineering, University of Jinan,
Jinan 250022, China
ise_lijp@ujn.edu.cn
[2] Shandong Provincial Key Laboratory of Network Based Intelligent
Computing, University of Jinan, Jinan 250022, China
[3] Shandong College and University Key Laboratory of Information Processing
and Cognitive Computing in 13th Five-Year, Jinan 250022, China

Abstract. Fighting is a typical malignant event that endangers social security. Video surveillance is a common and effective solution to detect fighting in public places. The conventional method of detecting the fighting events is to analyze the limb movements of each individual in the video. From the theoretical point of view, the conventional approach is more accurate, however, it will be very hard to make it to be practical in a short time. In order to develop a practical system for detecting the fighting events, we put forward an effective method by analyzing the trajectory of each individual instead of analyzing the individual's limb movement. In our proposed method, the key is to find the different laws of trajectories between normal movements and fighting. There are three basic steps in the proposed method: firstly, MobileNets is used as the basic network model of SSD to extract targets to improve the efficiency and accuracy of individual detection; secondly, KCF algorithm is used to achieve real-time tracking of multi-individual in different behavior modes; thirdly, the extracted motion trajectory is preprocessed and the information entropy of the trajectory is calculated to realize the detection of the fighting behavior. The experiment demonstrates that the proposed method is simple and practical, and can efficiently identify the behavior of fighting in real time.

Keywords: Fighting · Object detection · Tracking · Trajectory analysis · Entropy

1 Introduction

Fighting is a typical malignant event that endangers social stability and harmony. Video surveillance is a common and effective solution to detect fights in public places. In recent years, as high-definition cameras have been installed more and more densely,

Foundation item: The National Natural Science Foundation of China (61701192); Shandong Provincial Key Research and Development Project (2017CXGC0810); Shandong Education Science Plan "Special Subject for Scientific Research of Educational Admission Examination" (ZK1337212B008).

Y. Zhao et al. (Eds.): ICIG 2019, LNCS 11903, pp. 654–667, 2019.
https://doi.org/10.1007/978-3-030-34113-8_54

video data collected is also getting more and more massive. Although high-definition cameras have been widely used in public places, due to limited human energy, it is almost impossible to conduct long-term continuous monitoring of massive video resources. Therefore, it is a challenge to precisely detect the fighting behavior in the video.

The conventional method of detecting the fighting events is to analyze the limb movements of each individual in the video sequence. At present, there are many related researches on human behavior recognition based on limb movements, such as motion segmentation, bone modeling (2D modeling and 3D modeling), et al. On this basis, many scholars have carried out research on the detection of abnormal behavior through analyzing the individual's limb movements. For example, Yi et al. proposed a human posture estimation method based on static images of component hybrid model to detect abnormal behavior [1]. However, this method is subject to the accuracy of the character detection. If the individual detection is inaccurate, the method will be invalid, and it is difficult to separate the complete individual when the objects are close to each other. Blank et al., Weinland et al. and Yilmaz et al. express human behavior as a whole and it identify human behavior through the con-tour information of the individual [2–4]. However, such methods cannot capture the internal information of the contour and the background of the video is generally complicated which resulting in low accuracy of human behavior recognition. Cao et al. and Dan et al. combined spatio-temporal information with key points to construct human skeleton model, and making great progress in estimating human behavior in static images, but these algorithms are cumbersome and complex to re-construct human skeleton model [5, 6]. Wang et al. proposed an algorithm to detect the abnormal event via covariance matrix for optical flow features [7], the algorithm proposed a feature descriptor to represent the movement by adopting the covariance matrix coding optical flow and the corresponding partial derivatives of multiple connective frames or the patches of the frames. It solved the problem of difficult contour extraction effectively, but the computational covariance matrix had large computational complexity, so the real-time performance was poor.

So far, research on the detection of fighting behavior has rarely been seen. However, if we use the above methods to detect the fighting behavior, it will inevitably achieve a complex and long development cycle, and the methods are sensitive to changes in lighting and character appearance. The movement of the body is coordinated by various parts, such as running, jumping. These movements require not only leg movement, but also upper limb support to maintain body balance. However, the posture of the characters in the process of fighting is complex and variable, and the degree difficulty in separating and extracting the body information at different angles is different. Therefore, from a quick practical point of view, the existing methods are difficult to extract a relatively complete body structure by analyzing the individual limb movements to detect and recognize abnormal behaviors. Therefore, when used to detect the fighting behaviors, these methods become more complex, especially when used to develop practical detection systems.

In order to realize the practical of the fight behavior detection as soon as possible, we put forward a simple and effective method by analyzing each individual's trajectory instead of analyzing the individual's limb movement to detect the fighting behavior. In our proposed method, the key is to detect and track each individual, get the motion trajectory of the target, and use the different laws of trajectories between different behavior patterns to detect the fight behavior. In 2016, Baotian of our research group used the background subtraction algorithm to detect the foreground targets, developed corresponding rules to detect the fighting behavior and achieved preliminary results based on the calculation of the target centroid speed [8]; this research is to detect the fight behavior under the ideal conditions without obvious illumination changes, it's an improvement compared with the conventional behavior of detecting fighting behavior, but its problems are also obvious. For example, the background subtraction algorithm will inevitably lead to the accuracy of target detection being easily affected by factors such as illumination and complex change scenes, which makes the effect of target segmentation poor.

In recent years, with the development of deep neural networks, the results obtained by deep learning in target detection can be used to improve the effect of character detection and solve the problems of background subtraction methods. Therefore, this paper adopts MobileNets_SSD [9] algorithm for target detection, and improves the rules for detecting the fighting behavior. This method describes the trajectory variation of different behavioral patterns by calculating the variance and entropy of the individual's motion trajectory, and then realize the detection of fighting behavior.

Below we will analyze the feasibility of the method and the specific fighting detection algorithm. The remainder of the paper is organized as follows. In Sect. 2, we discuss the features of fighting behavior. Section 3 introduces our method in details. We experimentally evaluate the proposed model in Sect. 4 and draw conclusions in Sect. 5.

2   The Features of Fighting Behavior

Normal behavior usually has certain stability and order, such as walking, running, jumping. However, abnormal behaviors often have different definitions depending on the different scene. For example, the fights that occur in public places (see Fig. 1) are a typical malignant abnormal behavior that endangers social security. Fighting is a violent behavior takes place between two or more people. The fighters will suddenly appear irregular and violent movements with clustering, suddenness, and disorder for a period of time.

(a)   (b)

Fig. 1. Behaviors in public places (pictures from the Internet)

Our research focus on detecting the fight behavior in the videos taken by surveillance cameras that are fixed in high places in public places. As shown in Fig. 1(a), since the position of the surveillance camera is fixed, the impact of video jitter on the detection is avoided, and the video captured by the surveillance camera is a bird's-eye view, so, there is no long-term large-area occlusion between the individuals in the video, which is beneficial for detecting the tracking target and obtaining an effective motion trajectory. However, for the video of Fig. 1(b), it is obvious that the video is not taken from the surveillance camera but from the handheld camera or mobile phone. In this kind of video, the angle between the target and the camera is a head-up relationship. Therefore, it is difficult to obtain a complete and effective motion trajectory due to a large area of occlusion or overlap between the individuals in the video. The method in this paper is mainly for detecting the fight behavior in the video captured by the surveillance camera shown in Fig. 1(a).

The conventional method to detect fighting is to extract relatively complete limb information through body modeling and then to identify abnormal behaviors by analyzing each individual's limb movements. This method has a good effect in detecting abnormal behaviors when the acquired limb movements are complete. Due to the complexity of algorithms such as body modeling, feature extraction and matching, the method of analyzing limb movements is detected from the perspective of rapid practical application. It is difficult to develop a practical detection system in a short period of time. Therefore, we detect the fight behavior by analyzing the motion trajectory of each individual.

A motion trajectory is a collection of centroid positions arranged by chronological order when a target moves in space, and it is a directed curve. Since the trajectory of the target centroid is difficult to determine, in order to simplify the algorithm, the centroid of the virtual minimum circumscribed rectangle of the target is used instead of the centroid of the character, thereby obtaining each individual's motion trajectory in space. When a person is in a normal movement such as walking or running (see Fig. 2 (a)(b)), the person's centroid change regularly in the horizontal position, when the person is fighting, the position of the person's centroid will show a dramatic change (see Fig. 2(c)(d)). Then we will calculate the direction, speed and other information of the target's motion based on the individual's overall motion trajectory. Statistical analysis shows that when the target moves normally, the trajectory is simple and orderly, the direction of motion is consistent, and the speed change is not obvious. When the target is fighting, the trajectory is complex and disordered, the direction of motion is disordered, and the speed changes significantly. Due to the target has different degrees of chaos in the overall motion trajectory under different behavior modes, the information entropy can reflect the chaos of the system exactly. The entropy of the fighting trajectory of the target is much larger than the normal trajectory. Therefore, the entropy of each individual's motion trajectory can describe the fighting behavior well. Experiments verify the effectiveness and practicability of the proposed algorithm in this paper.

(a)   (b)   (c)   (d)

Fig. 2. Trajectories of normal behavior and fighting

3 Algorithm Design

The method of detecting the fight by analyzing the trajectory information of the target is divided into three steps (see Fig. 3): **step1:** individual detection, that is accurately detecting and segmenting each individual in the original video; **step2:** individual tracking, that is the feature points are initialized in the target area and the overall motion trajectory of the target is obtained by the KCF tracking algorithm; **step3:** fighting detection, that is using the features of the target's overall trajectory entropy and variance to determine the fighting behavior.

Fig. 3. Research steps

3.1 Individual Detection

The accuracy of the fighting detection is closely related to the accuracy of the individual's detection. Background subtraction algorithm [10, 11], frame difference algorithm [12, 13], optical flow algorithm [14] and the like are relatively common object detection algorithms. For example, Suzuki et al. used background modeling algorithm to segment the target region to obtain the motion trajectory of the target [15], trying to understand and identify complex motion trajectories. Mousavi et al. split the video sequence in the space-time body and identify the abnormal behavior by analyzing the statistical information of the acquired trajectory [16]. Shi et al. detected abnormal behavior in video by analyzing dense trajectories extracted from dense optical flow fields [17]. The foreground target obtained by the background subtraction method is prone to ghosting; the frame difference method is easy to generate voids in the moving entity; the optical flow method is complicated to calculate and sensitive to illumination changes. In addition to the shortcomings of noise sensitivity and incomplete foreground objectives, more importantly, these methods cannot accurately determine whether the acquired moving target is a human, thus causing a wrong guidance for further analysis of the trajectory information.

In order to detect the individuals in the video and eliminate the interference caused by other mobile targets, we use the MobileNets_SSD [18] algorithm to detect the actors from the complex background quickly. The basic network with MobileNets as the SSD is to add 8 convolution layers behind the last layer of the MobileNets backbone network and remove the original pooling layer, full connectivity layer, and softmax layer, and extract 6 layers to be used as detection targets. It can effectively reduce network parameters, speed up the calculation and not reduce the accuracy of detection. MobileNets is a lightweight deep network structure for mobile. MobileNets as the basic network structure of SSD can reduce the amount of computation and improve pedestrian recognition speed. The core is to use a depth separable convolution to solve a standard volume integral into a deep convolution and a 1×1 point convolution, and introduce two hyperparameters: width multiplier α and resolution multiplier β to reduce calculated amount.

Assuming that the input channel is a feature map of M, the convolution kernel size is $K \times K$, the output channel is N, then the standard convolution kernel is $K \times K \times M \times N$, the calculation amount of the depth separable convolution is $K \times K \times M \times 1 + 1 \times 1 \times M \times N$, thus, the calculation amount of the depth separable convolution compared to the standard convolution is as follows:

$$\frac{K \times K \times M \times 1 + 1 \times 1 \times M \times N}{K \times K \times M \times N} = \frac{1}{N} + \frac{1}{K^2} \tag{1}$$

At the same time, the width multiplier α can reduce the number of input channels, and becomes αM to make the model thinner, where α has a value range of (0, 1); the resolution mature β can proportionally reduce the resolution of the input picture and reduce the parameters. Therefore, the introduction of deep separable convolution and hyperparameters can effectively reduce the amount of calculation and increase the speed of calculation.

The specific algorithm steps are as follows: **step1:** Create a character data set; **step2:** Build the MobileNets_SSD framework; **step3:** Train and save the model; **step4:** Use the model to detect the individuals in the video and return information about the target's virtual minimum bounding rectangle. The individual detection results (see Fig. 4) are as follows:

Fig. 4. Individual detection map

3.2 Individual Tracking

Individual tracking is a key link in the detection of fighting behavior. Its essence is a more complicated estimation problem, that is determining the corresponding position of the same target in different frames. The kernel correlation filtering (KCF) algorithm [19] is used to estimate the corresponding position of the target in the current frame, and real-time effective tracking of multiple targets is realized. Since the centroid calculation of the target is complicated, the centroid of the target's minimum circumscribed rectangle is used instead of the target centroid, and the centroid motion trajectory of each individual is obtained.

Tracking the target i to get the corresponding position information of the target in the current frame k, $\left\{ \left(x_l^{i,k}, y_l^{i,k} \right), \left(x_r^{i,k}, y_r^{i,k} \right), w^{i,k}, h^{i,k} \right\}$, Where $\left(x_l^{i,k}, y_l^{i,k} \right)$ is the coordinate of the upper left corner of the target virtual minimum circumscribed rectangle, $\left(x_r^{i,k}, y_r^{i,k} \right)$ is the coordinate of the lower right corner of the target, and $w^{i,k}$ and $h^{i,k}$ are the width and height of the minimum circumscribed rectangle, respectively. The centroid coordinate of the target i in the current frame can be obtained by the following formula.

$$\begin{cases} x_c^{i,k} = x_l^{i,k} + \frac{w^{i,k}}{2} \\ y_c^{i,k} = y_l^{i,k} - \frac{h^{i,k}}{2} \end{cases} \tag{2}$$

In order to reduce the influence of the deviation of the position of the track point due to the jitter of the virtual circumscribed rectangle on the experimental result during the tracking process, the track point on the obtained trajectory is evenly sampled every other frame number f to obtain the final motion track T_i as the formula, where f = 3, T_i consists of n track points,

$$T_i = \left\{ \left(x_c^{i,0}, y_c^{i,0} \right), \left(x_c^{i,\Delta t}, y_c^{i,\Delta t} \right), \ldots, \left(x_c^{i,k\Delta t}, y_c^{i,k\Delta t} \right), \ldots, \left(x_c^{i,(n-1)\Delta t}, y_c^{i,(n-1)\Delta t} \right) \right\} \tag{3}$$

Later we will $\left(x_c^{i,k\Delta t}, y_c^{i,k\Delta t} \right)$ abbreviated as $t_c^{i,k} \equiv \left(x_c^{i,k}, y_c^{i,k} \right)$ for the convenience of introduction. The obtained final motion trajectory coordinate sequence is connected in chronological order, that is the trajectory representation of the individual in the space in the surveillance video is obtained. Figure 5(a)(b) are a trajectory diagram and a trajectory representation diagram of normal motion, respectively; Fig. 5(c)(d) are respectively a trajectory map and a trajectory representation diagram of the fight.

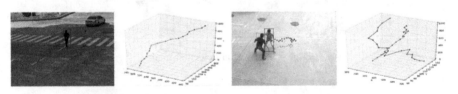

Fig. 5. Trajectory of normal movement and fighting

3.3   Fighting Detection

Actually, the fighting detection is a binary classification problem, that is the classification rules are formulated according to the motion trajectory rules of the individual in different behavior modes, and then detect the fighting behavior in the video. When the targets in fighting, it usually has irregular and violent movements, so the overall movement trajectory is complicated and chaotic. Therefore, the variance and entropy [20] can be used to describe the chaos of the individual's motion trajectory. In the case where the target is knocked down to the ground, the detection algorithm will no longer be applicable. However, in most cases, before the target falls to the ground, the target will have an abnormal trajectory such as chasing and shoving for a period of time. Therefore, the method proposed in this paper can still play an early warning role for such scenarios.

According to the above tracking algorithm, the motion trajectory T_i, $T_i = \{t_c^{i,0}, t_c^{i,1}, \ldots, t_c^{i,n}\}$, where n is the length of the track. Calculate the distance $d_{i,k}$ from the point $t_c^{i,k}$ on the trajectory T_i to the next trajectory point $t_c^{i,k+1}$ by using the following formula.

$$d_{i,k} = \sqrt{\left(x_c^{i,k+1} - x_c^{i,k}\right)^2 + \left(y_c^{i,k+1} - y_c^{i,k}\right)^2} \tag{4}$$

Therefore, define the velocity vector $v = \{v_1^i, v_2^i, \ldots, v_k^i, \ldots, v_n^i\}$, wherein, since the number of spaced frames between adjacent track points is the same after sampling. So, we use $d_{i,k}$ instead of v_k^i as the speed of the track point to reduce the amount of calculation, that is $v_k^i = d_{i,k}$, and the average velocity of the trajectory μ^i can be expressed by the following formula,

$$\mu^i = \frac{1}{n} \sum_{k=1}^{n} v_k^i \tag{5}$$

Then, the variance S_i^2 of the trajectory of the target is calculated by the following formula,

$$S_i^2 = \frac{1}{n} \sum_{k=1}^{n} \left(v_k^i - \mu^i\right)^2 \tag{6}$$

The variance S^2 can reflect the degree of deviation between the speed of the motion trajectory and its expectation μ^i. The larger the variance S^2, the more significant the change in the speed of the target, and thus the greater the possibility of fighting, so the preliminary judgment is made based on the variance of the trajectory. Set the threshold Q. When $S_i^2 < Q$, it is considered that there is no fight in the current video segment. Otherwise, the direction entropy of the trajectory is continuously calculated as a basis for further determining whether it is a fight behavior. Experiments show that when Q is set to 0.35, the accuracy and efficiency of detection are higher.

First, the direction of motion is divided clockwise into 12 sub-intervals with an interval size of $30°$. For any point $t_c^{i,k}$ on the trajectory T_i, the direction of motion θ_k^i is obtained according to the following formula,

$$\theta_k^i = \arctan\left(\frac{y_c^{i,k+1}-y_c^{i,k}}{x_c^{i,k+1}-x_c^{i,k}}\right) k = 1, 2, \ldots, n \tag{7}$$

According to θ_k^i, it is determined which sub-interval the trajectory point falls on, and the distribution of the trajectory points on each interval is counted as $P^i = \{P_1^i, P_2^i, \ldots, P_m^i\}$, where m is the number of intervals, m = 12. And then, calculate the entropy value of each motion trajectory direction in the video segment by the follow formula,

$$E_i = -\sum_{j=1}^{m} P_j^i \log_2 P_j^i \tag{8}$$

The larger the value of E_i, the greater the change in the direction of motion of the target, and the more turbulent the behavior. In order to ensure that E_i changes within the interval [0, 1], the entropy E_i is normalized.

$$E_i' = \frac{E_i}{E_{max}} \tag{9}$$

Where E_i' is the direction entropy value after normalization, and E_{max} is the largest trajectory entropy value of all trajectories, that is $E_{max} = \max\{E_1, E_2, \ldots, E_i, \ldots, E_w\}$, where, w is the number of motion trajectories in the current video segment.

Considering that the fighting behavior is usually continued for a period of time, in order to improve the accuracy of detection and avoid the impact of the error caused by the sudden change of occasional frames on the detection result, thus, for each individual's current trajectory, compare with the average of the direction entropy E_{avg} the previous three-segment trajectory, and make the final detection result as to whether a fight has occurred.

When $E_i' \geq M$, it is considered that there is a fight in the current video segment, and the specific detection process is as follows,

$$\begin{cases} E_i \geq M, & Y \\ E_i < M, & N \end{cases} \tag{10}$$

Among them, Y indicates that there is a fight behavior, N indicates that there is an abnormal behavior, and the threshold M is updated by E_{avg}. A large number of experiments have indicated that when the threshold M is set to 0.5, the accuracy of the fighting detection is higher.

4   Experiment and Discusses

In order to verify the validity and practicability of the algorithm, the intel i7-8550U processor with 8 GB RAM and 1.8 GHz frequency is used to implement the above algorithm in VS2017+OpenCV4.0 environment.

4.1   Experiment Dataset

Since there are few studies specifically for the fight behavior detection, there is no public dataset specifically for the fight behavior, So, we captured simulated videos from different scenes and combined some of the videos related to the fight on the CAVIAR dataset to detect the fight behavior.

The CAVIAR dataset was captured by the inria lab hall in Grenoble, on the corridors of a shopping mall in Lisbon, and on fixed cameras in three scenes across the corridor. Including walking, talking with people, shopping, fighting and other behavior patterns (see Fig. 6). Among them, each video is about 900 frames, the resolution is half of the PAL system (384 × 288 pixels, 25 frames per second) and compressed with MPEG2. In this paper, the experiment is mainly aimed at detecting the fight behavior. In order to ensure the proportion of positive and negative samples in the dataset, only the video of some behavior patterns such as walking, fighting, shopping. in the CAVIAR dataset is used as experimental data, including a total of 9 test videos, where there are 4 fighting videos.

Fig. 6. CAVIAR dataset

The simulation dataset captured in different scenarios used in the experiment is about 1000 frames per video, and the frame size is 856 × 480. Among them, there are 8 videos running, including multiple people running in different directions and at different speeds; there are 5 videos for normal walking, including single or multiple people in different directions, walking at different speeds, etc.; there are 15 videos for fighting, including two or more people fighting (see Fig. 7).

Fig. 7. Simulation dataset

4.2   Evaluation Method

The experiment uses the accuracy *Acc* and the error rate *R* to measure the detection effect. Suppose that there is a fight in a period of time: if the behavior of the fight is detected, called TP, the behavior of the fight is not detected, called FN; Suppose that there is not a fight in a period of time: if the behavior of the fight is detected, called FP, the behavior of the fight is not detected, called TN. *Acc* indicates the probability of correctly detecting the fight and normal behavior, and *R* indicates that the probability of the fight is not detected.

$$Acc = \frac{TP+TN}{TP+FP+TN+FN}, R = \frac{FN}{TP+FN} \tag{11}$$

4.3   Experiment Results

We conducted experiments in the CAVIAR dataset and the simulation dataset, respectively, and the detection results are shown in Fig. 8.

Fig. 8. The results of the fighting detection

The proposed method uses the confusion matrix to calculate the results of the simulation dataset and the CAVIAR dataset. The statistical results are shown in Tables 1 and 2.

Table 1. Statistical behavior results in simulation dataset.

	Fight behavior	Normal behavior	Sum
Fighting behavior	128	17	145
Normal behavior	15	119	134
Sum	143	136	279

Table 1 is the statistical result of the algorithm's detection of the fight behavior on the simulated dataset. Table 2 is the statistical result of the algorithm's detection of the fight behavior on the CAVIAR dataset. When the target suddenly appears to run and jump, it may be considered as a fight; When there is no obvious change in position between the two sides in a short period of time, it may be mistaken for normal behavior. Therefore, it shows that the proposed algorithm has a good detection effect on the chaotic behaviors such as chasing and shoving in public places. Experiments demonstrate that the proposed method can effectively detect the fight behavior, and

Table 2. Statistical behavior results in CAVIAR dataset.

	Fight behavior	Normal behavior	Sum
Fighting behavior	33	7	40
Normal behavior	4	39	43
Sum	37	46	83

achieve 86.94% and 88.58% detection accuracy on the CAVIAR dataset and simulation dataset respectively.

Because there is no public dataset specifically for the fighting detection, there is no contrast experiment. Table 3 shows that the detection effect of this method in the simulation dataset is higher than that on the CAVIAR dataset.

Table 3. Fighting detection rate.

Dataset	Fight behavior	Normal behavior
Simulation dataset	88.59	10.49
CAVIAR dataset	86.94	11.42

According to the analysis and review of the intermediate process, since the resolution of the video in the CAVIAR dataset is low and the target is far from the camera in some videos, there is a large area of occlusion overlap between the individuals, which causes the impact of missed detection. Thus, the obtained motion trajectory is incomplete, which leads to a higher error rate of the fighting detection.

Experiment indicates that the proposed method can effectively detect the fighting behavior in the video captured by the surveillance camera fixed at a high position, and it is simple and has good practical value.

5 Conclusions

The state of human motion is a complicated system with very complex degrees of freedom and uncertainty. It is cumbersome and complicated to separate the complete individuals from the complex background and use the limb movement characteristics to detect the fighting behavior, what's more, it is difficult to develop a practical system in a short period of time. Therefore, we propose a method for detecting the fights based on analyzing each individual's motion trajectory which obtained by the surveillance camera fixed at a high position. Firstly, the target is segmented from the video to obtain the motion trajectory; Then, analyzing the individual's motion trajectory and calculating the entropy and variance of motion trajectory as effective features to describe the fighting behavior; Finally, classifier is designed according to the entropy and variance to detect fighting behavior. The experiment demonstrates that the proposed method is simple and practical, and can efficiently identify the behavior of fighting in short time. A known disadvantage of the proposed method is that the fighting behavior detection performance affected by the individual's trajectory, which should be improved in the future work.

References

1. Yi, Y., Ramanan, D.: Articulated pose estimation with flexible mixtures-of-parts. In: IEEE Conference on Computer Vision and Pattern Recognition. Colorado Spring, USA, pp. 1385–1392 (2011)
2. Blank, M., Gorelick, L., Shechtman, E.: Actions as space-time shapes. IEEE Trans. Pattern Anal. Mach. Intell. **29**(12), 2247–2253 (2007)
3. Weinland, D., Ronfard, R., et al.: Free viewpoint action recognition using motion history volumes. Comput. Vis. Image Underst. **104**(2), 249–257 (2016)
4. Yilmaz, A., Shah, M.: Actions sketch.: a novel action representation. In: IEEE Computer Society Conference on Computer Vision and Pattern Recognition 2005, pp. 984–989 (2005)
5. Cao, Z., Simon, T., Wei, S.E.: Realtime Multi-person 2D pose estimation using part affinity fields. In: IEEE Conference on Computer Vision and Pattern Recognition, pp. 1302–1310 (2017)
6. Dan, X., Yan, Y., Elisa, R., Nicu, S.: Detecting anomalous events in videos by learning deep representations of appearance and motion. In: Computer Vision and Image Understanding, pp. 117–127 (2017)
7. Wang, T., Qiao, M., Zhu, A., Yida, N., et al.: Abnormal event detection via covariance matrix for optical flow based feature. Multimed. Tools Appl. **77**, 17375–17395 (2018). https://doi.org/10.1007/s11042-017-5309-2
8. Baotian, L.: Video-based Fighting Detection System. University of Jinan, Jinan (2016)
9. Howard, A.G., Zhu, M., Chen, B., Kalenichenko, D., et al.: MobileNets: efficient convolutional neural networks for mobile vision applications. arXiv:1704.04861 (2017)
10. Barnich, O., Van Droogenbroeck, M.: ViBe: a universal background subtraction algorithm for video sequences. IEEE Trans. Image Process. **20**(6), 1709–1724 (2011)
11. Kumar, S., Yadav, J.S.: Video object extraction and its tracking using background subtraction in complex environments. Perspect. Sci. **8**(C), 317–322 (2016)
12. Huang, S.C., Cheng, F.C.: Motion detection with pyramid structure of background model for intelligent surveillance systems. Eng. Appl. Artif. Intell. **25**(7), 1338–1348 (2012)
13. Zhu, Q., Song, Z., Xie, Y.: An efficient r-KDE model for the segmentation of dynamic scenes. In: The 21st International Conference on Pattern Recognition, pp. 198–201 (2012)
14. Xiao, J., Zhu, S., et al.: Moving object detection and tracking algorithm based on optical flow method. J. Northeast. Univ. (Natural Sci. Ed.) **37**(6), 770–774 (2016)
15. Suzuki, N., Hirasawa, K., Tanaka, K., et al.: Learning motion patterns and anomaly detection by Human trajectory analysis. In: IEEE International Conference on Systems, pp. 498–503 (2017)
16. Mousavi, H., Nabi, M., Galoogahi, H.K., Perina, A., Murino, V.: Abnormality detection with improved histogram of Oriented tracklets. In: International Conference on Image Analysis and Processing, pp. 722–732 (2015)
17. Shi, Z., Zhu, S., Cheng, Y., Wang, D.: Abnormal behavior detection based on dense tracklets. In: The 36th Chinese Control Conference (2017), pp. 10848–10853 (2017)
18. Liu, W., et al.: SSD: single shot MultiBox detector. In: Leibe, B., Matas, J., Sebe, N., Welling, M. (eds.) ECCV 2016. LNCS, vol. 9905, pp. 21–37. Springer, Cham (2016). https://doi.org/10.1007/978-3-319-46448-0_2

19. Henriques, J.F., Caseiro, R., Martins, P., et al.: High-speed tracking with kernelized correlation filters. IEEE Trans. Pattern Anal. Mach. Intell. **37**(3), 583–596 (2015)
20. Yumei, Y.: K-means dynamic clustering algorithm based on information entropy improvement. J. Chongqing Univ. Posts Telecommun. (Natural Sci. Ed.) **28**(2), 254–259 (2016)

Face Inpainting with Dynamic Structural Information of Facial Action Units

Le Li[1], Zhilei Liu[1(✉)], and Cuicui Zhang[2]

[1] College of Intelligence and Computing, Tianjin University, Tianjin, China
{le_li, zhileiliu}@tju.edu.cn
[2] School of Marine Science and Technology, Tianjin University, Tianjin, China
cuicui.zhang@tju.edu.cn

Abstract. In recent years, the deep learning based face inpainting methods have achieved some promising results, mainly related to the generative adversarial networks (GAN). Based on a large number of training samples, GAN generates a false true from a known training sample, and cannot use the trained parameters to generate image other than training samples. In addition, most of the previous works did not take into account high-level facial structure information, such as the co-existence of facial action units. In order to better to exploit facial structural knowledge, this paper proposes a method that combines prior knowledge based on high-level dynamic structural information of facial action units and GAN to complete face images. We primarily validate the effectiveness of our approach in facial expression restoration during face inpainting on the two datasets of BP4D and DISFA.

Keywords: Face inpainting · Facial action units · GAN

1 Introduction

Face inpainting aims to restore missing facial region, which is catching more and more attentions in the field of facial recognition, especially with the emergence of convolutional neural networks (CNN) [1] and generative adversarial networks (GAN) [2]. Most of previous works contain two branches: conventional methods and deep learning based methods. Conventional methods often calculate the similarity of two facial patches and using most similar facial patch to replace the missing facial patch by searching nearest neighbor [3, 4]. Deep learning based methods usually are end to end models to complete face image, which cannot retain the facial attributes or actions of ground-truth face image in most cases [5, 6]. Though deep learning based methods have achieved a great success, the generated face image often has distortion and fake trace. Some works also use low-level facial structure information to generate the whole face, such as landmarks and face parsing [13, 15], which are captured easily from the contents of face images. But these methods cannot guarantee the facial action comparing to ground-truth. In order to better learn the relation between occluded face region and non-occluded face region, we exploit co-existence of AUs to help complete face image.

© Springer Nature Switzerland AG 2019
Y. Zhao et al. (Eds.): ICIG 2019, LNCS 11903, pp. 668–679, 2019.
https://doi.org/10.1007/978-3-030-34113-8_55

Face inpainting is beneficial to the study of facial emotion analysis, which is easily affected by challenging environment, i.e. low resolution, occlusion, and so on. In the field of facial expression analysis, facial action units (AUs) refer to a unique set of basic facial muscle actions at certain facial locations defined by Facial Action Coding System (FACS) [7], which is one of the most comprehensive and objective systems for describing facial expressions. Considering our facial structure and patterns of facial expression are relatively fixed, it should be beneficial for face inpainting if taking relations of different AUs into consideration under occlusion. However, it is rare to see such face inpainting study by exploring the relations of different facial regions under different facial expressions in previous literature.

In this paper, we propose a novel face inpainting framework by exploiting the correlations of occluded and non-occluded facial region. Based on statistic methods, we can get AUs knowledge. According AUs knowledge, we proposed an AUs discriminator to help the classifier to generate the distribution of AUs in one dataset. The AUs information of coarse face image is connected in refinement network. This weak-supervised design can help generator learn the face image under different distribution of AUs. More accurate AUs results, the generated face image of refinement network will better retain the details corresponding to the ground-truth. The contributions of this paper are three-fold. First, a novel coarse-to-fine face inpainting network is proposed by exploiting the dynamic structure information of facial action units. Second, the weak-supervised design with the help of an AU discriminator is efficient for face inpainting with different facial expressions. Third, AU knowledge is combined into the generative model to recover facial expression information during inpainting, to the best of our knowledge, which has not been done before.

2   Related Work

Our proposed framework is closely related to generative adversarial networks, existing face inpainting methods, and facial action unit detection methods.

2.1   Generative Adversarial Networks

As one of the most popular and significant image generative techniques, GAN [2] achieves promising results by utilizing the mix-max adversarial game to train a generator and a discriminator alternatively. Due to adversarial training, the generator generates realistic face image. Recently, different versions of extended GAN have achieved a great success on face inpainting [5, 8], super-resolution [9, 10], style transfer [11] and face rotation [12]. Motivated by these successful solutions, we develop the face inpainting based on GAN and AUs discriminator.

2.2   Face Inpainting

Human face inpainting is much more challenging than general image inpainting tasks because facial structure is relatively fixed but contain large appearance variations. In addition, face identity information preserving is also very important during face inpainting. Li etc. proposed to complete face with face parsing result [13]. Zhang etc. developed models to complete face images with wavy lines [14]. Both face parsing and facial landmarks were utilized to supervise model learning [15]. However, these low-level geometry information is difficult to recover facial details with semantic relations of different facial regions. To take advantage of the co-existence of different AUs under different facial expressions and to restore the actions of filled region is still an open challenge, which motivate us to complete face image with high-level AU information.

2.3   Facial Action Units Detector

Automatic facial AUs detection plays an important role in describing facial actions. To recognize facial action units under complex environment, many works have been devoted to explore various features and classifier. With the development of deep learning, recent works try to exploit deep representations to recognize AUs, such as [16]. Due to the correction between different AUs, [17] attempts to attention the region centered at facial landmarks, which is efficient for model learning and [18] proposes region layer help learn deep representations. AUs knowledge becomes a possibility that model learning via a weak-supervised way in [19]. These methods achieve good performance for AUs detection, which motivates us to exploit the correlation between occlusion facial region and non-occlusion facial region.

3   Our Method

In our section, the overview of the proposed model is firstly introduce in Sect. 3.1, which exploits prior knowledge of facial action unit to complete face images. Then, the AU knowledge is presented in Sect. 3.2. Lastly, the pre-training of AUs classifier is explained in Sect. 3.3.

3.1   Proposed Method

In this section, the overview structure of our proposed model is introduced from three parts: the first network is the face inpainting generator network; the second network is the discriminator network, which is mainly used to distinguish the real original image and the fake repaired image; the third network is an AUs recognition network. It is worth noting that the discriminator network and the AU recognition network are not used during the time of testing. The overview of our proposed face inpainting framework is shown in Fig. 1.

In the first part, a coarse-to-fine face inpainting generator consisting of a coarse network and a refinement network is proposed. Given a facial image with mask, the coarse network with auto-encode network is used to generate a coarse face image at first. In the refinement network, by taking the facial action unit information of the coarse face image as a condition, refined facial image with corresponding AUs details is generated. The input is a $128 \times 128 \times 3$ face image with a mask and the output is a restored $128 \times 128 \times 3$ face image.

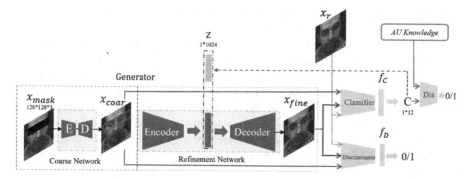

Fig. 1. Overview of the proposed face inpainting framework. E and D represent encoder and decoder networks of coarse network, while Encoder and Decoder combine into refinement network. Pre-trained Classifier is utilized to detect facial action units. The last output 0/1 is to discriminate the detected AU probability from the AU knowledge.

Coarse Network: The structure of the coarse network is shown in Fig. 2(a), in which, four 5×5 convolutional layers with strides 2 are used in the down-sample network, and four deconvolutional of 5×5 are used in the symmetric up-sample network. During the last deconvolutional layer, the *tanh* activation function is utilized in the output layer, and *relu* activation function is utilized in the other layers. To get a better coarse result, pixel-wise loss is adopted to supervise model learning as defined as:

$$L_{pixel\_c} = \|x_r - x_{coar}\|_2^2, \tag{1}$$

in which, x_r is the ground-truth face image without mask, x_{coar} is the output coarse face image.

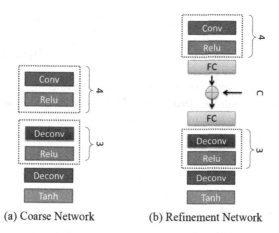

(a) Coarse Network   (b) Refinement Network

Fig. 2. The structure of the coarse network and the refinement network in the generator.

Refinement Network: The structure of the refinement network is shown in Fig. 2(b), in which, four 5×5 convolutional layers with stride 2 are used in the down-sample network, which is followed by a layer of fully convolutional layer. The condition information here is the combination of the output latent feature of the encoder and a one hot vector of the AU classification results. The1024-dimensional concatenate vector is regarded as the bottle-neck of the refinement network, and utilized as the first layer of fully convolutional layer in the up-sample network with the output of an $8 \times 8 \times 512$ dimensional vector. Then the output is reshaped into a tensor of (8, 8, 512). Finally, four 5×5 deconvolutional layers are used in decoder network. Same as the coarse network, the activation of the last layer is *tanh*, and similar pixel-wise loss is defined as:

$$L_{pixel\_f} = \left\| x_r - x_{fine} \right\|_2^2, \tag{2}$$

in which, x_{fine} is the output fine face image of the refinement network.

Due to the fact that the input face image is partially occluded, which will lead to the obvious boundary between the occlusion area and the non-occlusion area in the output. To solve this problem, the total variation (TV) loss are defined in both coarse network and refinement network as following:

$$L_{tv\_c} = \frac{1}{n} \sum_{i,j=1}^{n} \left(\left\| x_{coar_{i,j}} - x_{coar_{i,j-1}} \right\|_2^2 + \left\| x_{coar_{i,j}} - x_{coar_{i-1,j}} \right\|_2^2 \right), \tag{3}$$

$$L_{tv\_f} = \frac{1}{n} \sum_{i,j=1}^{n} \left(\left\| x_{fine_{i,j}} - x_{fine_{i,j-1}} \right\|_2^2 + \left\| x_{fine_{i,j}} - x_{fine_{i-1,j}} \right\|_2^2 \right). \tag{4}$$

Discriminator Network: Discriminator network consists of five 5×5 convolutional layers with stride of 2 and one fully convolutional layer. Following GAN loss is utilized to train the generator network and discriminator network:

$$L_{D\_c} = E_{x_r \sim P_r}[\log D(x_r)] + E_{x_{coar} \sim P_{coar}}[\log(1 - D(x_{coar}))], \tag{5}$$

$$L_{D\_f} = E_{x_r \sim P_r}[\log D(x_r)] + E_{x_{fine} \sim P_{fine}}[\log(1 - D(x_{fine}))], \tag{6}$$

In which, D is the discriminator network utilized to distinguish the restored face image and the ground-truth face image. In order to generate better face image and lead to quick convergence for face inpainting generative model, feature map loss L_{f_D} is defined as following:

$$L_{f\_D} = \frac{1}{2} \left\| f_D(x_r) - f_D(x_{coar}) \right\|_2^2 + \frac{1}{2} \left\| f_D(x_r) - f_D(x_{fine}) \right\|_2^2, \tag{7}$$

f_D is the output of last fully convolutional layer of discriminator network.

AU Classification Network: AU classification network consists of four 5×5 convolutional layers with stride of 2 and one fully convolutional layer. Due to the fact that

AU detection is a multi-label problem, the loss define of AU classifier will be introduce in Sect. 3.3. Here we aim to simplify the loss, we use the AUs knowledge as ground-truth label and the recognized AUs results as generated ones. Only one simple discriminator is utilized to distinguish the generated ones and the ground-truth, the losses are defined as:

$$L_{D_{au\_c}} = E_{l_r \sim P_r}[\log D_{au}(l_r)] + E_{l_{coar} \sim P_{coar}}[\log(1 - D_{au}(l_{coar}))], \quad (8)$$

$$L_{D_{au\_c}} = E_{l_r \sim P_r}[\log D_{au}(l_r)] + E_{l_{fine} \sim P_{fine}}[\log(1 - D_{au}(l_{fine}))], \quad (9)$$

Also, in order to generate better face image and lead to quick convergence for face inpainting framework, the feature map loss is defined as follows:

$$L_{f\_c} = \frac{1}{2}\|f_C(x_r) - f_C(x_{coar})\|_2^2 + \frac{1}{2}\|f_C(x_r) - f_C(x_{fine})\|_2^2, \quad (10)$$

In which, f_C is the output of last fully convolutional layer of AU classification network.

The total loss of our proposed face inpainting network is:

$$\begin{aligned} L_G = {} & l_{pixel_c} + l_{pixel_f} + \lambda_1 L_{tv_c} + \lambda_1 L_{tv_f} + \lambda_2 L_{D_c} + \lambda_2 L_{D_f} \\ & + \lambda_3 L_{f\_D} + \lambda_2 L_{Dau\_c} + \lambda_2 L_{Dau\_f} + \lambda_3 L_{f\_c}, \end{aligned} \quad (11)$$

where λ_1, λ_2 and λ_3 are trade-off parameters.

3.2 AU Knowledge

Due to the fact that facial structure is relatively fixed, the network considering facial high-level structural information should be carefully designed. AU knowledge is statistically obtained from specific dataset. For each AU, the appearance or not is represented by 1 or 0. Assuming that most AUs are located in two facial regions: eye region and mouth region, the status of AUs around eye region could be utilized to predict the status of AUs around mouth region, and vice versa. Due to the co-existence of AUs in whole face image, take the situation of mouth region is masked and eye region is unmasked as an example: Firstly we should observe the accurate AUs around eye region. Supposing there are n AUs which are related to eye region, then there will be 2^n cases for n AUs around eye region. According each case, the conditional probability for each AU around mouth region can calculated in a specific dataset. All these AU conditional distribution cases are regarded as the AUs knowledge here. Mouth region to eye region is same with eye region to mouth region.

3.3 Pre-training of AU Classifier

To get accurate AU information, a pre-trained network on training dataset of each benchmark is utilized as the AU classifier in Fig. 1. AU Classifier is adopted to detect AUs from the whole input face image, coarse generated face image and fine generated face image. AU classifier is used to help generator to learn the facial AU distributions. The loss for training AUs classifier is defined as:

$$L_c = E_{l_r \sim P_r}[\log D_{au}(l_r)] + E_{l_{xr} \sim P_{xr}}[\log(1 - D_{au}(C(x_r)))], \tag{12}$$

where C is the pre-trained AU classifier, which recognizes AUs to predict the AU information in masked region with the help of AU knowledge.

4 Experiment

4.1 Datasets and Settings

Datasets: Our proposed face inpainting network is evaluated in two commonly used datasets for facial expression analysis: BP4D [20] and DISFA [21]. For BP4D, we split the data set into training/test sets based on the subjects. There are 28 subjects in the training set and 13 subjects in the test set. Each group contains 12 AUs whose AU is labeled as appearing or not appearing. A total of 100760 frames are used for training and 45809 frames are used for testing. In BP4D, the differences in color and background of the face image are small. For DISFA, the dataset is processed in the same way as BP4D, with 18 subjects in the training set and 9 subjects in the test set. Each group contains 12 AUs labeled as 0 or 1. A total of 87209 frames are used as the training set and 43605 frames are used for testing. Note that the color and background of the face image are very different in the DISFA data set, which makes it difficult to get good results.

Pre-processing: For each facial image, we perform a similar transformation including rotation, uniform scaling and translation to obtain a $128 \times 128 \times 3$ color face image. This deformation is shape-retaining and does not change the expression. A mask based eye or mouth is added, which is same as the input size, thereby generating an input ill-conditioned face image.

Implementation Details: The AU classifier is pre-trained at first, then the generator is trained at one epoch and the discriminator is trained at every three epochs. For the AU classifier training, we got good indicators, which are slightly lower than the state of art. The settings of the trade-off parameters are $\lambda_1 = 0.0$, $\lambda_2 = 0.05$, and $\lambda_3 = 1.0$. We use Adam for optimization. The learning rate is 0.0001, the batch size is 16. After the tanh layer, Poisson blending method is adopted as a post-process step.

4.2 Quality Results

We aim to use high-level facial AU information during face inpainting. Facial action units represent facial dynamic actions, which is useful for face-related works. To verify the effectiveness of facial action unit information in our face inpainting network, we compare the visual results with baseline and baseline + C. Baseline is a simple autoencoder network to generate face image without any facial AU information and baseline + C is baseline network with AU classifier network to detect AUs. Coarse face images are generated by the coarse network and fine face images are generated by refinement network. The comparison results in BP4D and DISFA datasets are shown in Figs. 3 and 4 respectively. It can be observed that the results of our proposed method are better than others, such as the first row in Fig. 3, our fine result achieves opened eyes which is same as the ground-truth, but baseline achieves closed eyes. In addition, we get good quality of face image in DISFA dataset, which is shown in Fig. 4. More differences can be observed in Figs. 3 and 4.

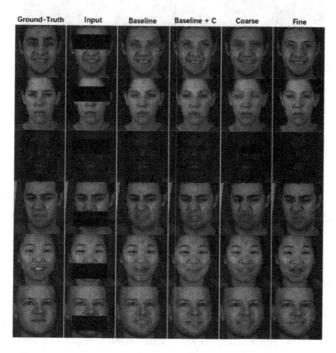

Fig. 3. The results of testing set in BP4D, top three rows show the comparison in eye-masked region and others in mouth-masked region. Zoom in for better view on details.

4.3   Quantity Results

When it comes to face generation task, the scores of structural similarity (SSIM) and Peak Signal to Noise Ratio (PSNR) are usually considered to evaluate image qualities. The quantity results of our proposed method can be observed in Table 1. It can be observed that the fine results achieve the best metrics, which outperforms the baseline about 0.024 and 0.031 for SSIM, about 0.92 and 1.79 for PSNR respectively in BP4D and DISFA dataset. High SSIM and PSNR with high quality of generative face images. These quantity results demonstrate the effectiveness of our proposed method on face inpainting task with dynamic AUs information. Note that there are few improvements in DISFA datasets due to its extreme unbalance distribution.

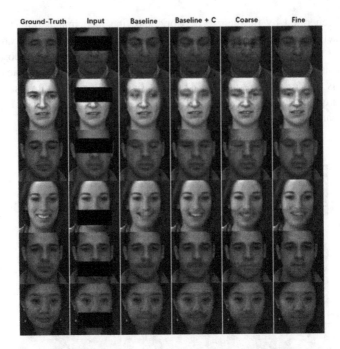

Fig. 4. The results of testing set in DISFA, top three rows show the comparison in eye-masked region and others in mouth-masked region. Zoom in for better view on details.

Table 1. SSIM and PSNR on BP4D and DISFA

Method	BP4D		DISFA	
	SSIM	PSNR	SSIM	PSNR
Baseline	0.896	29.494	0.884	26.108
Baseline + C	0.903	29.862	0.891	26.144
Coarse	0.871	29.460	0.890	27.756
Fine	0.920	30.414	0.915	27.898

Most generative works often generate face images which cannot retain the identity information. The landmarks distance can be used to measure whether the identities are same or not between generated face image and ground-truth. Facial landmarks represents the facial actions and the identity, the comparison of landmarks distance can be observed in Table 2. The fine result achieve 4.131 and 9.694 improvements in BP4D and DISFA respectively, which demonstrated the effectiveness of our proposed method in facial identity preserving.

The AU detection results of the face inpainting results of different methods are shown in Table 3. It can be observed that fine results outperform which of the baseline in BP4D dataset. Fine results bring significant increments of 4.3% and 1.0% respectively for average accuracy of eye-masked and mouth-masked than baseline, and bring

Table 2. Landmarks distance on BP4D and DISFA

Method	BP4D	DISFA
Baseline	85.898	98.255
Baseline + C	85.687	95.459
Coarse	90.259	93.463
Fine	81.767	88.561

increments of 1.4% and 0.9% than baseline + C. For the DISFA dataset, fine results bring significant increments of 4.3% and 3.6% respectively for average accuracy of eye-masked and mouth-masked than baseline, and bring increments of 0.9% and 3.4% than baseline + C. All these results demonstrate the effectiveness of our proposed model in facial expression restoration during face inpainting.

Table 3. AU detection performance of inpainting results on BP4D and DISFA

Method	BP4D		DISFA	
	Eye-masked accuracy	Mouth-masked accuracy	Eye-masked accuracy	Mouth-masked accuracy
GT	0.576	0.576	0.854	0.854
Baseline	0.523	0.536	0.787	0.701
Baseline + C	0.552	0.537	0.821	0.703
Coarse	0.487	0.503	0.767	0.688
Fine	0.566	0.546	0.830	0.737

5 Conclusion

In this paper, we have proposed a novel face inpainting method with dynamic structural information of facial action units like AUs knowledge. The proposed method is beneficial to facial expression analysis under occlusion environments and so on. Extensive qualitative and quantitative evaluations conducted on BP4D and DISFA have demonstrated the effectiveness of our method for face inpainting. The proposed framework is also promising to be applied for other face restoration tasks and other multi-task problems, i.e. face recognition, facial attribute analysis, and so on. Also we can use generator to restore face images, then facial expression analysis for restored face image.

Acknowledgements. This work is supported by the National Natural Science Foundation of China under Grants of 41806116 and 61503277.

References

1. Krizhevsky, A., Sutskever, I., Hinton, G.E.: Imagenet classification with deep convolutional neural networks. In: Advances in Neural Information Processing Systems, pp. 1097–1105 (2012)
2. Goodfellow, I., Pouget-Abadie, J., Mirza, M., et al.: Generative adversarial nets. In: Advances in Neural Information Processing Systems, pp. 2672–2680 (2014)
3. Hays, J., Efros, A.A.: Scene completion using millions of photographs. ACM Trans. Graph. (TOG) **26**(3), 4 (2007)
4. Oliva, A., Torralba, A.: Building the gist of a scene: the role of global image features in recognition. Prog. Brain Res. **155**, 23–36 (2006)
5. Yeh, R.A., Chen, C., Yian Lim, T., et al.: Semantic image inpainting with deep generative models. In: Proceedings of the IEEE Conference on Computer Vision and Pattern Recognition, pp. 5485–5493 (2017)
6. Pathak, D., Krahenbuhl, P., Donahue, J., et al.: Context encoders: feature learning by inpainting. In: Proceedings of the IEEE Conference on Computer Vision and Pattern Recognition, pp. 2536–2544 (2016)
7. Ekman, R.: What the Face Reveals: Basic and Applied Studies of Spontaneous Expression Using the Facial Action Coding System (FACS). Oxford University Press, USA (1997)
8. Yu, J., Lin, Z., Yang, J., et al.: Generative image inpainting with contextual attention. In: Proceedings of the IEEE Conference on Computer Vision and Pattern Recognition, pp. 5505–5514 (2018)
9. Ledig, C., Theis, L., Huszár, F., et al.: Photo-realistic single image super-resolution using a generative adversarial network. In: Proceedings of the IEEE Conference on Computer Vision and Pattern Recognition, pp. 4681–4690 (2017)
10. Chen, Y., Tai, Y., Liu, X., et al.: Fsrnet: end-to-end learning face super-resolution with facial priors. In: Proceedings of the IEEE Conference on Computer Vision and Pattern Recognition, pp. 2492–2501 (2018)
11. Chang, H., Lu, J., Yu, F., et al.: Pairedcyclegan: asymmetric style transfer for applying and removing makeup. In: Proceedings of the IEEE Conference on Computer Vision and Pattern Recognition, pp. 40–48 (2018)
12. Huang, R., Zhang, S., Li, T., et al.: Beyond face rotation: global and local perception GAN for photorealistic and identity preserving frontal view synthesis. In: Proceedings of the IEEE International Conference on Computer Vision, pp. 2439–2448 (2017)
13. Li, Y., Liu, S., Yang, J., et al.: Generative face completion. In: Proceedings of the IEEE Conference on Computer Vision and Pattern Recognition, pp. 3911–3919 (2017)
14. Zhang, S., He, R., Sun, Z., et al.: DeMeshNet: Blind Face Inpainting for Deep MeshFace Verification (2018)
15. Song, L., Cao, J., Song, L., et al.: Geometry-aware face completion and editing. arXiv preprint arXiv:1809.02967 (2018)
16. Han, S., Meng, Z., Khan, A.S., et al.: Incremental boosting convolutional neural network for facial action unit recognition. In: Advances in Neural Information Processing Systems, pp. 109–117 (2016)
17. Li, W., Abtahi, F., Zhu, Z., et al.: Eac-net: deep nets with enhancing and cropping for facial action unit detection. IEEE Trans. Pattern Anal. Mach. Intell. **40**(11), 2583–2596 (2018)
18. Zhao, K., Chu, W.S., Zhang, H.: Deep region and multi-label learning for facial action unit detection. In: Proceedings of the IEEE Conference on Computer Vision and Pattern Recognition, pp. 3391–3399 (2016)

19. Peng, G., Wang, S.: Weakly supervised facial action unit recognition through adversarial training. In: Proceedings of the IEEE Conference on Computer Vision and Pattern Recognition, pp. 2188–2196 (2018)
20. Zhang, X., Yin, L., Cohn, J.F., et al.: A high-resolution spontaneous 3D dynamic facial expression database. In: 2013 10th IEEE International Conference and Workshops on Automatic Face and Gesture Recognition (FG), pp. 1–6. IEEE (2013)
21. Mavadati, S.M., Mahoor, M.H., Bartlett, K., et al.: Disfa: a spontaneous facial action intensity database. IEEE Trans. Affect. Comput. 4(2), 151–160 (2013)

Author Index